ADMINISTRATION OF PUBLIC EDUCATION

ADMINISTRATION OF PUBLIC EDUCATION
Fourth Edition

A Sourcebook for the Leadership and
Management of Educational Institutions

STEPHEN J. KNEZEVICH, Ph.D

Formerly Dean, School of Education,
University of Southern California

HARPER & ROW, PUBLISHERS, New York
Cambridge, Philadelphia, San Francisco,
London, Mexico City, São Paulo, Sydney

1817

Sponsoring Editor: George A. Middendorf/Louise Waller
Project Editor: Pamela Landau
Production Manager: William Lane
Compositor: ComCom Division of Haddon Craftsmen, Inc.
Printer and Binder: R. R. Donnelley & Sons Company
Art Studio: Jay's Publishers Services, Inc.

Administration of Public Education, Fourth Edition

Library of Congress Cataloging in Publication Data

Knezevich, Stephen J.
    Administration of public education.

    Includes bibliographies and index.
    1. School management and organization.   2. Public
schools—United States.   I. Title.
LB2805.K53 1984   379.1'5   83-10724
ISBN 0-06-043737-5

Rededicated
(for the fourth time)
with ever more reasons
to my wonderful wife—

DORIS L. (BOGGS) KNEZEVICH

CONTENTS

PREFACE

Rapidly changing times and the new challenges facing the profession dictated the need for a new edition of *Administration of Public Education.* Enrollment growth patterns that characterized education for more than 20 years came to an end and were replaced by the declines of the 1970s. The new trends and technology have generated a different set of demands in education and its administration.

The first edition of this book appeared 20 years ago. What made it unique then and helped to establish a new text in the field of educational administration was the inclusion of a comprehensive review of the administrative process, leadership concepts, and theory development, together with the more traditional presentation of major educational trends and issues, the implications of current research, and analysis of the typical problems likely to be encountered by the practitioners of the art and science of educational administration. The second edition was the first basic text in educational administration to emphasize systems management, which attempted to bridge the gap between improvements in practice and the emerging emphasis on theory, models, and sys-

tems. The third edition further refined and extended this comprehensive conceptualization of school administration, placing special attention on the importance of the change agent and mediator roles of school administrators caught between conflicting forces confronting education at the local, state, and federal levels.

This fourth edition continues the comprehensive treatment of educational administration and updates the statistics that characterized previous works. The dramatic shifts that saw enrollment declines lead to personnel cutbacks and abandonment of some attendance centers are clarified further. The adjustments to the personnel revolution and civil rights conflicts that started in the 1960s are noted. While school budgets continued to escalate, revenues from local sources failed to keep pace with growing fiscal demands. In short, the 1970s generated even greater pressures on educational administration, which are highlighted in this edition.

The first six chapters are substantially reconceptualized and rewritten. A fresh analysis of the nature and definition of administration is presented to portray its spirit as well as its substance. Single chapters are devoted to a better understanding of the major roles of the educational administrator as a decision maker, leader, planner, and change agent. This places each of these four major administrative processes in a somewhat different context by distilling the essence of the volumes of writing and research on each, translating and applying the concepts to educational institutions, and suggesting the competencies required of practitioners who seek to fulfill these roles. The final chapter of this initial sequence of six chapters focuses on the theories, models, and systems frameworks that provide the scientific bases which undergird the practice of administration. This sourcebook continues to perceive educational administration as a science as well as an art; the former is not neglected but connected to the latter.

Although some sections and chapters found in the previous edition were reduced in size, others were enlarged to express their increased importance. The increased litigation confronting schools, as well as the influence of court orders and mandates on school operations, suggested that a separate chapter on the impact of the judicial branches of government on education was essential for administrators. Issues and information related to crime and violence in schools, the emergence of and conflicts facing the U.S. Department of Education, minimum competency testing, state and national educational policy formulation and implementation, and public attitudes toward public education are expanded or introduced.

There never was a time when public education did not face serious problems. The final chapter outlines past challenges and looks ahead. The decade of the 1980s is viewed as a time of healing within the profession and one during which other conflicts with roots in previous decades will continue unabated.

Neither the interests of practitioners in each of the states nor the contents of introductory courses in educational administration at various institutions of higher learning are precisely the same. This volume provides the flexibility required to tailor courses to individual and regional needs. It is better identified as a sourcebook for practitioners and a basic reference for graduate students in educational administration than as a narrowly oriented text. This fourth edition continues to project the image of educational administration as a field dedicated to the search for and eventual implementation of fresh ways of managing educational institutions to make them more effective and productive in the delivery of essential educational services.

Professors and graduate students influenced the content of this text for more than 20 years. The fourth edition continues to emphasize facts and figures rather than sweeping generalizations. No truly scholarly volume can afford to ignore basic information or fail to provide supporting evidence for generalizations made. Facts and figures relevant to a particular time do not grow obsolete. New information does emerge to support the continuance or a change in trends noted. The sources of the data are noted to help the professor and student procure even more recent data than can be included in a volume printed at a given time.

This sourcebook is addressed to students of educational administration, be they practitioners desiring current information, graduate students considering educational administration as a career, or teachers trying to comprehend the complexity of operating an educational system. It is designed for select uses in in-service as well as preservice programs for prospective and practicing administrators.

No man is an island; many persons have influenced and stimulated my thinking over a professional career now in its fifth decade. I give thanks to my many mentors for their assistance, a list that includes: Dr. Forrest E. Conner, executive secretary emeritus of the American Association of School Administrators, and Dr. Glen G. Eye, the late Dr. John Guy Fowlkes, and the late Dr. Russell T. Gregg, all of the University of Wisconsin-Madison. I also acknowledge the contributions and many professional courtesies received and the debts owed to many professional colleagues who are too numerous to mention. Evident as well in this writing is the impact of productive experiences as a teacher and an administrator in Wisconsin public schools; as an associate secretary at the American Association of School Administrators; and as a professor at such universities as Tulsa University, University of Iowa, Florida State University, University of Wisconsin-Madison, and at the University of Southern California.

The Educational Research Service is a valuable source of current data on public education and its administration. Its publications were consulted frequently in the production of this and previous editions. Their contributions are acknowledged and special recognition and thanks are due to an old and trusted friend, Dr. Glen E. Robinson, president of Educational Research Service, Inc., for the counsel, data pro-

vided, and permission granted for the inclusion of ERS-generated information. The various publications of the National Center for Education Statistics were the basic sources for other data highlighted in this edition. The current data provided by Jeanne Hayes and Quality Education Data, Inc. are worthy of citation as well as my appreciation. Deserving special mention for contributions in the production of the fourth edition are my daughter Mari Knezevich-Notrica and son-in-law Lewis Notrica. Last, but by no means least, I acknowledge gratefully the assistance and understanding of Mrs. S. J. Knezevich for her help during the preparation of the manuscript and the indexes for each of the four editions of this book.

STEPHEN J. KNEZEVICH

PART I

ADMINISTRATION AS AN ART AND A SCIENCE: WAYS OF PERCEIVING THE FUNDAMENTAL PROCESSES, ROLES, AND FUNCTIONS

Administration had its origins when society began to organize to achieve its goals. Although among the ancient arts, its systematic study is a more recent event. Such study and research paralleled the growing complexity of social institutions.

Administration is a means to an end. It is an instrumentality for the fulfillment of the purposes and policies of an organized institution. It can enhance the quality of operations. Administration is perceived as an art and a science.

There are many ways to describe the contributions of an administrator to an organization. Each of the major roles and responsibilities will be probed in the initial grouping of six chapters that follow. The administrator is referred to frequently as a decision maker, leader, planner, and change agent. Separate chapters are devoted to each of these vital roles.

The chapters in Part I break from the traditional mold of viewing administration as a cluster of substantive problems unique to educational institutions. (The discussion of such concerns is delayed until Part IV.) The chapters of this part focus on the general contributions, basic processes, and emerging developments of public school administration. Administrators in all types of organizations are involved in planning, decision making, and communication. Likewise, they are concerned with people and this emphasis places a premium on leadership concepts and competencies for all who would become administrators. Administration is a dynamic field. Recent developments in administrative theory, the use of models, and the implementation of management science techniques are included in one of the longest chapters of this volume. This is testimony to the growing interest and importance of concepts and knowledge that prior to 1950 were rarely found in a general text on educational administration. These suggest that administrators must dedicate themselves to a lifetime of learning. The advent of more powerful technologies, the increasing incidence of conflicts, and the growing demands for innovations in education generate pressures for the acquisition of new management competencies, which are also reviewed in this part.

EDUCATIONAL ADMINISTRATION IN PERSPECTIVE: WHAT IS IT? WHY NECESSARY? WHO IS AN ADMINISTRATOR?

Formal educational services are delivered or made available to specific age groups by special organizations that have been created for such purposes. Individual school centers, local school districts, state education departments, federal education agencies, and many informal units are all parts of this complex delivery system. Each of these demands some type of organizational structure and administrative apparatus to support and sustain the teachers and others who work directly with students and intimately influence the learning process and instructional programs. After the educational objectives are determined, the program of studies is defined, and the scope and sequence of learning specified, there arise the special needs for administrative services to procure the resources to implement whatever educational plans, to organize and coordinate all efforts, to monitor operations, to provide leadership, to facilitate decision making, and so on. Administration is a set of specialized functions within an organization or institution that facilitates realization of objectives and implementation of programs. This book is about educational administration and its contributions to the efficient and effective delivery of educational services primarily at elementary and secondary school levels.

Administration is a complex set of specialized functions within organized institutions that defies complete understanding by a short explanation through one or only a few sentences. It can be argued that study and readings represent only the initial steps, for more complete comprehension demands immersion in the practice of the art. This book represents a beginning in the accumulation of knowledge about educational administration. Often qualifiers, such as *high school, business,* or *personnel,* may precede the word *administration* to further complicate matters. Such modifiers simply specify the context, particular dimension, or given locus for the performance of some responsibilities associated with the art. These qualifiers do not change the fundamental substance of the art, the processes that characterize it, nor the constellation of activities related to administration.

Analysis of the word *administration* through

separation of the prefix *ad* from the root portion *ministration* helps reveal its spirit as well as substance. The prefix simply adds emphasis to what follows. Unfortunately, *ministration* sounds somewhat strange because it is used rarely in education writings and discussions. Webster's *Third International Dictionary* defines *ministration* as the process of caring for someone or some thing. It suggests doing things useful, needful, and helpful. The more common word *administration* can be interpreted as a complex set of interrelated "helping" functions, "serving" activities, "caring" responsibilities, and/or "facilitating" operations. These are far different from the image of administration as being preoccupied with controlling, disciplining, or enforcing. It can contribute more toward successful operations in an organization when its spirit is revealed as *ministration*.

WHAT IS ADMINISTRATION?

A partial answer was provided in preceding paragraphs. It is one of the "helping" professions that focuses on the organization as a whole rather than individuals alone. Thus, the administration "helps" an organization achieve objectives, "serves" the clientele of an organization, "cares" for the material and fiscal resources of an organization, and "facilitates" the performance of personnel employed.

"Getting things done," "following through," and "enforcing the organization's rules and regulations" are among the more common perceptions that tend to obscure the more desirable image of administration as helping, caring, serving, and so on. Administration is concerned with *ministerial,* or *administerial,* functions within an organization.

Administrators are *ministers* in the broad sense than in the narrowly defined religious application. The use of the title "Minister" (e.g., Minister of Education) to identify the executive head of an administrative branch is fairly common in countries of the world other than the United States. "Secretary" is preferred for the head of an executive branch in our country as are "superintendent" and "commissioner" for

executive posts in education at state and local levels. Cultural preference for particular titles does not change the fact that a "minister" is a person duly authorized and/or licensed to conduct certain affairs in behalf of an institution or some branch of government. The ministerial concept places an administrator in a position of trust and can help to project a more humane perception of what management is all about. The implications are that people and the institutions they create benefit from effective administration. Organizations will not run themselves nor are the policies of lay boards self-executing. Administration is the instrumentality for the realization of goals, policies, and dreams a society may have for its social institutions.

The classical writers pictured the administrative dimension as being action oriented. Although recognized as an important art and many great thinkers of antiquity reflected upon it, its formal study (particularly research and scholarly publications devoted to it) is a more recent development. The Cameralists in the 1700s established the beginnings of a scientific orientation to governmental management in the Austrian and German states.[1]

Formal study and research in school administration, in contrast, was a twentieth-century response to the increasing complexity of public education in the United States. It occurred in the more rapidly developing and large urban school districts. Some pioneers such as Henry Barnard wrote about school architecture prior to the Civil War and others published tracts on educational administration during the last half of the nineteenth century. It was not until the 1920s that there evolved a collection of writings of significant size to be recognized as the beginning of a literature for the field.

The recognition of public and private school administration as a professional career that should be based on preservice preparation programs at the graduate university level is a relatively new and distinctly American contribution. It spread slowly elsewhere with grudging acceptance of educational administration as a special field of university study. There are countries in our world where preparation programs for school executives exist in rudimentary form at best. The illusion that anyone with a good general education and without specialized study in education or its administration could become an effective school administrator persisted in Europe and other continents until fairly recently. Education in the United States benefited from the success of American business corporations, with many ascribing such effectiveness to the quality of selection and the executive's professional preparation in these corporations.

There have evolved over time many different types of educational administrators. Local school administrators such as superintendents, directors, and principals constitute the largest body. Intermediate school district administrators are fewer in number. The number and variety of administrators in state departments of education increased significantly during the past 25 years. Federal education agencies, of which the Department of Education is only one of many, generated the need for special types of educational administrators as well. University, college, and community college presidents, chancellors, deans, directors, and so on, can also be classed as educational administrators. Most preparation programs are geared to produce local school and community college administrators.

Within the past few decades new education agencies were created, such as regional education laboratories as well as educational research and development centers that demanded special types of educational administrative staffs. Private industries may employ educational leaders to direct in-house training programs as well as to spearhead the development of educational materials sold to schools. In short, school administrators are more accurately identified as a subset of the expanding field of educational administration.

Administration is a support and facilitating mechanism for complex and multipurpose organizations. Educational administration is influenced to a large degree by the functions and expectations for education in our society. The ends or objectives of education are important in the study of educational administration and have a significant impact on the organizational structure, administrative styles, and operational procedures.

WHY IS IT NECESSARY?

During troubled times, fiscal cutbacks, or just plain political posturing it is asked frequently "Is administration *really* necessary" or simply "Let's cut out the administrative fat because we have too many chiefs and not enough Indians."

Administration appears to many to be quite distant from day-to-day instruction, which may help to account for the fact that the contributions of administration are not readily recognized, much less appreciated. The need for administration was questioned in past years and may continue. Its persistence in face of doubts and criticisms must be explained on some basis other than tradition. It is a relative newcomer to the education scene.

Administration is a constellation of functions that is important to the implementation of policies, coordination of efforts, future planning, efficient use of limited resources, organizing to meet new challenges, and so on. The list of contributions to the welfare of the educational organization is a long one.

Administration emerged as an important function as the complexity, diversity, and challenges facing educational institutions increased. For much of history the home was the cultural institution responsible for coping with the individual's educational development. As long as numbers educated were limited to a few and the educational fare simple and confined to a few programs, this approach appeared to satisfy. But life in a dynamic democracy demanded more than a rudimentary education by unprepared "teachers." Specialized institutions supported by the public were created to expand educational opportunities, make them available to all children and youths, and insure a higher quality of instructional experts. The next step in the evolution of specialized and complex educational institutions was the emergence of administrative specialists to help insure the maintenance and expansion of the relevance, effectiveness, and productivity of complex social mechanisms.

A partial list of specific contributions that helps to establish the need for administrative structures and personnel follows.

The functions and contributions of administration to educational institutions are:

1. To implement the policies and other decisions of the legislative body (usually the board of education or state legislature).
2. To clarify and pursue the predetermined objectives, directions, and priorities of the enterprise.
3. To assemble and insure the prudent use of resources.
4. To help increase the productivity of all employed personnel.
5. To unify and coordinate human efforts and material resource use.
6. To monitor progress toward the realization of objectives.
7. To create a desirable organizational climate and professional working relationships within the organization.
8. To appraise the quality and effectiveness of strategies selected and personnel employed to pursue various objectives.
9. To help project the image of the institution and its personnel as effective, productive, and dynamic entities.
10. To report to the legislative body and to the people on the stewardship of authority and responsibilities.

Administration is important wherever two or more people are involved in the execution of some task. Administrative activities are described in ancient records telling of significant accomplishments of a culture. Constructing the pyramids in Egypt, outfitting Phoenician ships, regulating Babylonian commerce, constructing temples in ancient Israel, operating the city-states of ancient Greece, equipping and sustaining Hannibal's legions, carving roads to the distant reaches of the Roman Empire, propagating and preserving the Christian faith, supervising feudal domains of medieval times, governing colonies in distant hemispheres, and

so on, all demanded some type of administration expertise. The need for management talents has always existed. What is different today is the need to cope with the rapidity of change, the magnitude of the tasks to be performed, and less tolerance for error or dissipation of limited resources. Management today demands more sophisticated procedures, greater talents, and better preparation of executives. As Drucker put it, administrators (managers) are a "basic resource," "the scarcest resource," and perhaps the most precious resource in an enterprise.[2]

Dimensions of Educational Administration

Administration is equally important to educational institutions to propel them efficiently and effectively toward realization of goals, to maintain and sustain productive operations, to steer them through often uncharted problem areas, and to keep them energized and prepared to weather the challenges of fast-changing times. The recognition of the importance of managerial leadership is relatively new, but resistance to it may continue. Again, Drucker perceived administration an essential service that once begotten proves indispensable and is "the organ of society specifically charged with making resources productive."[3]

In chemistry the presence of a unique ingredient called a catalyst stimulates an interaction between components previously indisposed to react even though placed in physical proximity. An administrator can be called an organizational catalyst. Money, quality personnel, and equipment represent potential for excellence. Often another force called administration is needed to translate potential into reality. In short, administrators are needed to make things happen.

In sharp contrast is the admonition to beware of generalizing from the behavior of one or a limited set of administrators. Some administrators find themselves, inadvertently or otherwise, preoccupied with many nonadministrative tasks such as teaching classes, typing reports, assisting in tasks typically performed by custodians, or even taking tickets at a basketball game. This is not intended to deprecate the value of such services. It is just an indication that not everything a given administrator does can be classified as an integral part of educational management as distinct from other functions.

The dimensions and measures of effectiveness of administrative behavior are judged better by objectives and priorities satisfied at some point in time rather than by implied or explicit "absolute standards" of administrative behavior. Existing administrative structures and leadership demands must be modified as new goals and pressures emerge. Thus, the civil rights and personnel revolutions of the prior two decades called for different administrative operating patterns as well as new competencies for effective administrators. Likewise, the accountability movement and fiscal crises of the 1970s demanded the adoption of new administrative operating styles and strategies. The successful administrator is one committed to a lifetime of learning and adjustments.

The systems approach to school administration is one way to perceive the dimensions and contributions of the practice. In the systems point of view the educational organization is pictured as a network of interrelated subsystems, each charged with accomplishment of some of the many tasks involved in converting educational inputs into desired outputs. The organization becomes a unified systematic vehicle for translating resources (such as money, people, facilities, and instructional processes) into outcomes (such as student learning gains, pupil adjustments, or community acceptance of the systems contributions). The systems approach views the primary administrative responsibilities to be clarifying objectives, monitoring progress toward objectives, sensing subtle changes in learner and community needs, and adapting educational strategies to satisfy new demands. The administrator is pictured as the leader and strategist with primary responsibility for allocating scarce resources to the priority and dynamic goals of the system.

Traditionally, educational administration has been defined in terms of the kinds of operational problems encountered in the "running" of a school district or agency. This was reflected in the early introductory textbooks in the field that described "best practices" or recommended procedures for coping with "typical administrative problems" such as employing and motivating professional personnel, financing school operations, preparing budgets, or planning and constructing facilities. Operational problems unique to management of educational institutions will always be important and are analyzed in the chapters that comprise Part IV of this sourcebook. They represent the technical subject matter, but constitute only a single dimension of administration.

There is a process dimension of educational administration as well. Here the emphasis is on the cycle and sequence of activities used in the analysis of and strategies for the resolution of substantive or technical problems. The concern is for how one makes decisions rather than for the specific decision on budgeting or personnel management or with the leadership process whether it is used for motivating professional personnel or gaining community support. Decision making, leadership, planning, and coping with change are illustrations of the major factors in the process dimension of educational administration. The process approach is relatively new in educational administration and represents a more abstract dimension in the study of management. The management processes in education are fairly similar to those in business, industry, or government. They are matters of concern to all institutional managers no matter what the specific organizational setting.

Katz argued that "successful administration appears to rest on three basic skills" called "technical, human, and conceptual."[4] The technical dimension emphasizes effective handling of things and physical resources in the institution. The human aspect stresses the importance of human relationships or working with people in organizations. Conceptual skill is essential as well in enabling the administrator to put it all together, that is, to stand back and see the organization as a whole rather than being lost in the battles of one part.

To these could be added the political, economic, and social dimensions so important to the administration of public institutions such as public education. The exploration of the various dimensions of educational administration separates this volume from the early and pioneering texts in the field as well as from some current ones.

The terms *management* and *administration* are considered synonymous. Management is the term preferred in writings outside education. In recent years educators have come to accept management as a desirable rather than demeaning term.

The kinship that binds managers (administrators or executives) of various types of organizations is rooted in the perception of the practice in terms of the fundamental processes involved. This led some to argue that because "administration is administration," successful managers of one type of institution could perform equally well in any and all other types. This fascinating argument is supported by the fact that it is not unusual for a capable executive of whatever rank in one type of private corporation to move to another with a different product line. For example, some years ago an executive of one of the largest oil companies was selected president of one of the largest fruit companies. Further probing revealed that more than a transfer of training on management processes was involved. The oil company executive had special knowledge and experience with antitrust laws, and antitrust actions were plaguing the fruit company. Its new president brought needed technical knowledge as well as skills in using the administrative processes. The record shows, however, that such transfer of executives from one type of industry to another very different one may not always end with success. Not every great ex-general or ex-admiral proves out as a successful business executive.

Administrative processes are not applied in an organizational vacuum. The executive with experience and understanding of the unique operational challenges facing an institution has an edge over one ignorant of the clientele served and the technical factors involved but with equal competencies in the management processes. This fact makes suspect the argument that the selection of future educational administrators should be open to those without previous experience or knowledge of learning, educational finance, or any other dimension of education. Teaching experience may not be crucial to success as an educational administrator, but it does help. Administrative experience in another field is not an adequate substitute for technical expertise in education or teaching. This does not imply, however, that teaching experience is essential for all types of administrators even though it may be for those who must work closely and professionally with instructional personnel. Public expectations, professional standards, behavior norms, characteristics of the clientele served, societal mores, technology, and traditions influence administrative priorities, styles, and sensitivities. What is demanded today is a new breed of educational administrators with broader preparation and experiences in various facets of the art and science of management, rather than replacement by administrators from other fields without the technical knowledge, professional understandings, and sensitivities to educational institutions.

The "people" dimension of administration deserves recognition along with the others. Organizations are social institutions where the interplay of human factors can make or break the best laid plans. The famous "Hawthorne experiments" of 50 years ago awakened the interest of executives in the human factors in organizational productivity. Administration may also be perceived as the management of a complex network of interpersonal relations within the organization. The science of individual and group psychology can help to illuminate human behavior in organizational settings. Argyris noted that more and more behavorial scientists were developing "a valid systematic theory of human behavior in organizations to go beyond the traditional organizational theory based on such principles as task specialization, chain of command, unity of direction, and span of control."[5] Getzels, as well as others, perceived administration as a social process in which the social system influenced operations.[6] Leadership is the process that places emphasis on human factors, that is, on stimulating or influencing individuals and groups within organizations. This dimension is probed more completely in Chapter 3.

Lastly, there are the more theoretical dimensions of educational administration. The theory movement in educational administration began in earnest in the 1950s. Griffiths considered this "a movement toward a more scientific approach to administration."[7] The various efforts to improve administration beginning with the Cameralists over 250 years ago sought to inculcate more science into the practice. Scientific practices may be based on purely empirical observations or upon more sophisticated models and theories to synthesize empirical observations. Chapter 6, the longest in the book, is devoted to the use of theory and models to improve understandings and practices.

A More Formal and Comprehensive Definition of Educational Administration

The various perspectives, interpretations, and contributions of educational administration provided a background and enhanced readiness for the presentation of a more formal and comprehensive definition. *Educational administration is a specialized set of organizational functions whose primary purposes are to insure the efficient and effective delivery of relevant educational services as well as implementation of legislative policies through planning, decision making, and leadership behavior that keeps the organization focused on predetermined objectives, provides for optimum allocation and most prudent care of resources to insure their most productive uses, stimulates and coordinates professional and other personnel to produce a coherent social system and desirable organizational climate, and facilitates determination of essential changes to satisfy future and emerging needs of students and society.* The definition is complex with many interrelated activities described because that is the nature of the administrative challenge in organizations. It is a summary statement which includes major purposes, processes, and contributions but not all. It reflects what the book is all about for each of these will

be developed more fully in the paragraphs and chapters that follow. The delivery of quality educational services and implementation of legislative policies must undergird whatever is done in the name of administration. Educational administration is a means and cannot be justified as an end in itself. It is concerned with the energy within organizations that is synchronized to produce a unity of operations that facilitates realization of objectives. Administration is judged best, therefore, by its results rather than by its numbers, patterns, or style. The question of what to do precedes the strategies and details of how to do it.

The formal definition borrows from Alexander Hamilton the concept that policymaking and executive activity are separate and distinct organizational concerns with administration focusing on the latter. He stated: "The administration of government, in its largest sense, comprehends all the operations of the body politic, whether legislative, executive, or judicial; but in its most usual, and perhaps its most precise significance, it is limited to executive details, and falls peculiarly within the province of the executive department."[8] The terms *administrator, executive* and *manager* are considered to be synonymous in this book.

Administration—An Art or a Science?

The goal of the scientific approach to administration is the more precise determination and realization of institutional outcomes through reliance on theory, models, sophisticated tools in administrative planning, decision making, and leadership behavior. The resultant administrative behavior would be less intuitive and less dependent on prior experience. The emphasis is on procurement of dependable and accurate data—preferably the most readily quantifiable, mathematical analysis, and use of conceptual frameworks or models of various dimensions of the organization. The systems approach to administration illustrates one effort that seeks to provide the practice with a more scientific base for organizational planning, decision making, leadership, change, and general operations. The systems approach and other such approaches are often criticized for attaching excessive importance to readily available and quantifiable data rather than to other data that could be more relevant to decision making and leadership in education.

In contrast, artistry in administration is based more on the "feel" of the situation, intuition, and experience of the practioner. Those who prefer to picture administration as an art argue that people more than any other factor influence organizational outcomes, and individual or collective personalities defy the more rigid scientific approaches that seek to predict with great certainty what their behaviors will be under what conditions. In other words, it is not possible to identify, quantify, and control all variables that may influence behavior in organizations. Past experience based on interacting with social and political factors is more likely to lead to success. Science has its limitations in dealing with complex human factors and multipurpose social institutions that are service oriented. The truly significant problems of top echelon administrators are too complex and interspersed with too many political, psychological, and sociological intangibles to be resolved via pure science, that is, without the aid of an artistic component.[9] The scientific approaches may assist by improving rather than replacing the intuition and judgment of decision makers. In other words, systems analysis is a way to sharpen the artistic component rather than a substitute for it.

Administration in this book is perceived as an art that can be enhanced through the application of science. This concurs with Drucker's observations that although there are professional and scientific dimensions to management, it is a "practice" (i.e., an art) and "can never be an exact science."[10] The successful administrator has the scientific knowledge and procedures in grasp, and also has the good judgment to know when to use them and what their limitations are in each situation. It is the application of knowledge and systems known that distinguishes the "administrative artist" from the less successful. That is why not everyone with high grades from a university, high scores on objective tests such

as the Graduate Record Examination, and a high level of competency in the technical and scientific dimensions is destined for greatness in educational administration. This argument does not support the reverse because neither ignorance nor incompetence can lead to success in any profession. It does indicate the challenge facing the profession to select persons who have the capability to become outstanding practitioners instead of merely majors in educational administration with high grade-point averages. Administration calls for that intangible "something extra."

There is a third factor that must guide educational administration in addition to science and artistry. It is a social ethic. Mary Parker Follett and others during the 1920s perceived administration as an art, a science, and an ethical practice with criticisms deserved for those who would overstress one dimension to the neglect of others. A similar trinity was evident in ancient Greek philosophy where knowledge, artistry, and goodness of purpose were deemed indispensable to responsible human action.

Analysis of the Nature of Administration

Who the first administrator was is lost in the mists of antiquity. Socrates, Plato, and Aristotle wrote about the importance of the art of administering social institutions, as did Thucydides and, later, Julius Caesar. St. Thomas Aquinas and William of Occam wrote during the Middle Ages on the problems of managing the church and the state. About 300 years later Thomas Hobbes argued for a theory of government based on a "social contract" with individual citizens. The list of philosophers, economists, political scientists, kings and other heads of states, and so on, who had something to say about administration multiplied rapidly thereafter, and the propensity to do so continues unabated today.

In more recent times many writers outside the field of education argued that there were certain basic processes that identified or characterized the nature of the activities called administration. That was not the beginning, however, of the debate as to whether there were universal processes of administration that could be applied to any and all types of organizations. Socrates appeared to support a set of common processes, no matter what the context, that contributed to success in direction or administration. Plato attributes the following to Socrates: ". . . over whatever a man may preside, he will, if he knows what he needs, and is able to provide it, be a good president, whether he have the direction of a chorus, a family, a city, or an army . . . ." as well as ". . . private matters are not managed by one species of men, and public matters by another; for those who conduct a public business make use of men not at all differing in nature from those whom the managers of private affairs employ; and those who know how to employ them, conduct either private or public affairs judiciously, while those who do not know, will err in the management of both."[11] Socrates was among the first to recognize management as a social process and the importance of knowing how to work with people in organizations.

Aristotle disagreed with Socrates and in the first chapter of his *Politics* refuted the concept that there existed a set of universal processes or traits for managers of whatever calling.[12]

Although history is replete with references to the important processes of administration, more modern concepts are about 100 years old and evolved from movements to apply scientific methods and reasoning to management. Henri Fayol's work on industrial management during the very early part of this century abstracted from many substantive problems encountered in management a set of common processes and principles. He identified five basic elements or processes that were common to administration in whatever organizational context as "planning, organization, command, coordination, and control."[13] Other writers in business and industrial management repeated, modified, and extended Fayol's basic processes and continue to do so up to the present.

Such concerns came much later in educational administration, with some continuing the process approach at this point in time. Sears, in 1950, was one of the early writers on educational management to recognize "the school administrative process" and stated "no reason was found for departing significantly from Fayol's classification."[14] After concluding his review of the existing literature, Gregg concluded later in that decade that "only during the present decade (the 1950s) have writers in the field of educational administration dealt specifically with an analysis of the administrative process."[15]

Process Analysis by Raising Key Questions

There are certain key questions that all administrators must confront to satisfy the responsibilities assigned to such positions. These broad queries whose answers may reveal the essence of administrative activity are:

1. "What is to be done?" (In other words what are the objectives or results expected?)
2. "How will the work be divided?" (This is the prelude to organizing by determining the allocation of authority and responsibility.)
3. "How will the work be done?" (This focuses on strategies and methods.)
4. "Who will do the work?" (This leads to the assignment of manpower.)
5. "What will the work be done with?" (Specification of facilities, equipment, money needed, and other resources follows from this.)
6. "When will the work be done?" (This resolves the issues of time schedules and sequence of activities.)
7. "How well should the work be done?" (The focus here is on work standards.)
8. "How well is the work being done?"[16] (The final issue is appraisal and monitoring of work progress toward predetermined objectives.)

Instead of asking key questions, Tead abstracted key statements which were the "elements which together defined the responsibilities of administration as a total process" and included the following:

1. To define and set forth the purposes, aims, objectives, or ends of the organization.
2. To lay down the broad plan for structuring the organization.
3. To recruit and organize the executive staff as defined in the plan.
4. To provide a clear delegation and allocation of authority and responsibility.
5. To direct and oversee the general carrying forward of activities as delegated.
6. To assure that a sufficient definition and standardization of all positions have taken place so that quantity and quality of performance are specifically established and are assuredly being maintained.
7. To make provisions for necessary committees and conferences and for their conduct in order to achieve good coordination among major and lesser functional workers.
8. To assure stimulation and necessary energizing of all personnel.
9. To provide an accurate evaluation of the total outcome in relation to established purposes.
10. To look ahead and forecast the organization's aims as well as ways and means toward realizing them, in order to keep both ends and means adjusted to all kinds of inside and outside influences and requirements.[17]

The similarity between the air force's key questions and Tead's key statements to describe fundamental administrative processes should be evident.

Special Terms That Describe the Basic Administrative Processes

There is considerable agreement among professionals that there exists a set of universal processes that define the nature or basic substance of administration. Somewhat belatedly, professionals in educational administration seem to be accepting that fact as well. The most popular way of expressing the basic and universal elements of the administrative process is through single words rather than through key questions or statements. Some of the sets of descriptive terms used in educational administration as well as other endeavors are presented in Table 1.1. Fayol started it all in 1916 and no one knows when it may end.

Planning

This process is found in all but one of the lists shown. Its omission in that one list is only in the use of the word *planned,* for similar ideas were to be included in what these writers call "programming." This is a special use of the word *planning* for generating one of its products rather than on the process itself. In each case planning is viewed as the activity that generates the organizational goals and objectives, that is, determines the directions to be pursued. It is implied that every executive should be able to respond clearly and definitely to the question "Just what are your goals or purposes in pursuing this course of action within the organization?" Not many have been able to improve upon what Fayol identified or noted almost 70 years ago as the initial concern in all administrative activities.

The systems approach expands upon this and emphasizes the process dimensions of planning as well as the results or orientation demands for the organization.[18] Planning becomes the prime mechanism by which a system adapts to change. The dynamic environment confronting organizations makes the planning function more critical than in other approaches to management. A separate chapter is devoted to the perception of the administrator as an educational planner.

Organizing

This process or function is listed almost as frequently as is planning. Through it the many tasks are subdivided and allocated and then arranged to create a unity of operations. Purposes give direction and, therefore, not only precede but also provide justification for the type of organizational pattern created.

Differences in terminology are noted in some lists prepared by writers in education. Thus, the descriptive word list prepared by the American Association of School Administrators (AASA) Commission employed the term *allocating resources* to include organizing, staffing, bud-

TABLE 1.1

DESCRIPTIVE TERMS USED BY VARIOUS WRITERS TO SUGGEST THE FUNCTIONS OF THE ADMINISTRATOR

Fayol[a] (1916)	Gulick and Urwick[b] (1937)	Newman[c] (1950)	Sears[d] (1950)	AASA[e] (1955)	Gregg[f] (1957)	Campbell et al.[g] (1958)	Newman and Summer[h] (1961)	Johnson et al.[i] (1967)
1. Planning	1. Planning	1. Planning	1. Planning	1. Planning	1. Decision making	1. Decision making	1. Planning	1. Planning
					2. Planning			
2. Organizing	2. Organizing	2. Organizing	2. Organizing		3. Organizing	2. Programming	2. Organizing	2. Organizing
	3. Staffing	3. Assembling resources		2. Allocating resources				
					4. Communicating			3. Communicating
3. Commanding	4. Directing	4. Directing	3. Directing	3. Stimulating	5. Influencing	3. Stimulating	3. Leading	
4. Coordinating	5. Coordinating		4. Coordinating	4. Coordinating	6. Coordinating	4. Coordinating	4. Measuring and controlling	
	6. Reporting							
5. Controlling	7. Budgeting	5. Controlling	5. Controlling	5. Evaluating	7. Evaluating	5. Appraising		4. Controlling

[a]Henri Fayol, "Administration industrielle et générale," in Constance Starrs, *General and Industrial Management*, London: Sir Isaac Pitman, 1949.
[b]Luther Gulick and L. Urwick, eds., *Papers on the Science of Management*, New York: Institute of Public Administration, 1937.
[c]William H. Newman, *Administrative Action*, Englewood Cliffs, N.J.: Prentice-Hall, 1950, pp. 4–5.
[d]Jesse B. Sears, *The Nature of the Administrative Process*, New York: McGraw-Hill, 1950.
[e]American Association of School Administrators, *Staff Relations in School Administration*, 33rd Yearbook, Arlington, Va.: The Association, 1955, pp. 17–22.
[f]Russell T. Gregg, "The Administrative Process," in R. F. Campbell and R. T. Gregg, eds., *Administrative Behavior in Education*, New York: Harper & Row, 1957, p. 274.
[g]R. F. Campbell, J. E. Corbally, Jr., and John A. Ramseyer, *Introduction to Educational Administration*, Boston: Allyn and Bacon, 1958, pp. 179–186.
[h]W. H. Newman and C. E. Sumner, Jr., *The Process of Management*, Englewood Cliffs, N.J.: Prentice-Hall, 1961, pp. 10–11.
[i]R. A. Johnson, F. E. Kast, and J. E. Rosenzweig, *The Theory and Management of Systems*, 2nd ed., New York: McGraw-Hill, 1967, pp. 121–127.

geting, and supply management.[19] Campbell et al. employed a similar but broader term of "programming" for the selection and organization of staff, for housing, for equipment, and for budgeting.[20]

In some lists executive activities related to staffing as well as to gathering and arranging resources were considered separate and distinct from organizing. This is a narrower conceptualization which limits organizing to creating a skeleton, form, or pattern. The structuring is separated from personnel or other resources that must be arranged or patterned to be utilized effectively. The procurement of resources in particular may be separated as noted in Newman's designation of "assembling resources" as a process of "obtaining for the use of the enterprise the executive personnel, capital, facilities, and other things needed to execute plans."[21] Gulick and Urwick's use of the word *staffing* is much narrower and is confined to the "assembling" of a single type of resource.

To Fayol and later writers, to organize was interpreted in a limited framework and meant determination of a general structure or form with specific details indicated. In contrast, a much broader interpretation of the organizing function is presented by the proponents of the systems approach to administration. It is the means for coordinating people and resources into a system, it implies development of interconnections between various subsystems, as well as the design of methods and determination of activities required to achieve the objectives of the institution.[22]

Directing or Stimulating

The planning, organizing, and/or assembling resources set the stage for what is to follow. It is the stimulation to start and keep the institution moving toward its goals. Fayol called it "commanding," others referred to it as "directing," but writers in education preferred "stimulating," "influencing," and "leadership." Whatever the term it is the process that depends upon authority to make decisions (issues directives) as well as to demonstrate the leadership necessary to keep going and on course. More recent writers separate what

Fayol said was commanding into its decision-making and leadership components. Although commanding has a harsh if not dictatorial image today, that was not true during Fayol's time. He considered knowing well all personnel, setting a good personal example for personnel, as well as issuing directives as parts of the comprehensive concept of commanding. Nonetheless, the term is too broad and too authoritarian sounding to be an acceptable description today of the manner in which authority is employed as a means of motivating change in educational institutions.

Coordinating

Where more than one person is involved in completing a project, the need arises for means to unify individual efforts to prevent one person from working at cross purposes to another. Coordination is the process dedicated to the development of teamwork for the realization of objectives in complex, multipurpose organizations. Most include it in the list of basic processes, and no one suggested a different term. Newman excluded it from his list because of its overarching significance. He declared that coordination "should not be regarded as a separate and distinct activity, however, because it is a part of all phases of administration."[23] There is some substance for this argument, because the coordination strategy available will be influenced by the type of organization pattern, communication networks that are operative, the preparation level and in-service programs for various types of personnel, the nature of the supervisory program in place, and the type of sensing and control methods built into the system. Nonetheless, there is a degree of overlap and interaction among all processes and the arguments Newman used for coordination could be applied to others.

Controlling or Appraising

Once again different words suggested similar administrative activities. Fayol used "controlling," Gulick and Urwick, "reporting and budgeting," AASA as well as Gregg, "evaluating," and Campbell et al., "appraising." It may incorporate monitoring progress as well as a determination of how many and how well objectives were realized. It may include both culminating and initiating functions, that is, an appraisal can lead to a modification or a new set of strategies to be implemented that have an even greater probability of achieving the desired results.

Controlling imparted a degree of rigidity and authoritarianism inconsistent with prevailing value orientations. The concept of control was reintroduced by advocates of the systems approach to administration who defined it as "that function of the system which provides direction and conformance to the plan or, in other words, the maintenance of variation from systems objectives within allowable limits."[24] Its function was to keep the organization locked onto targets whose primary concern was prevention of disabling substandard performance. This is far different from the authoritarian interpretation that implies rigid expectations for organizational behavior or punishment for wrongdoing. Control in the system sense becomes one with cybernetics. In cybernetics the control process would include information-feedback-correction to maximize the probability of preventing a system from "going out of control" to waste resources or fail to satisfy the purposes of the mission. Monitoring and appraisal are designed to detect deviations from plan and subsequent corrective actions. Administrators carry the primary responsibility for insuring that the system and operations do not go "out of control."

Decision Making

Decision making was considered part of one or more other processes in the earlier writings. It emerged as a separate function and today is considered one of the most important, with some suggesting it is *the* most important, administrative function. Barnard almost 50 years ago, followed by Simon almost 30 years ago proposed that the decision-making authority determination within an organization was the key to understanding human behavior therein. Barnard wrote: "Acts of decision are characteristic of organization behavior" and that "descriptions of the process of decision are relatively more important to the understanding of organization behavior than in the case of individuals."[25] Simon concurred and added: "Organization behavior is a complex network of decisional processes, all pointed toward their influence upon the behaviors of operatives—those who did the actual physical work of the organization."[26]

Writers in educational administration recognize the importance of decision making but tend to give leadership a higher priority. A special chapter is devoted to this important process.

A DUAL CLASSIFICATION SYSTEM FOR ADMINISTRATIVE PROCESSES

There is a relatively high degree of similarity between administrative processes described through key questions, key statements, or descriptive terms. The various times and the perspectives used may help explain preferences for certain words and the use of more than one word to separate special functions. Less commonly recognized is the fact that the words and the statements selected may have different levels of abstraction. Thus, determining relationships between teachers, building principals, special-subject supervisors, and the assistant superintendent in charge of elementary and/or secondary education may be perceived as the substance of the organizing process. It may also be viewed as planning, that is, deciding in advance what relations there shall prevail among various position incumbents. A process such as organizing may call for not only planning but also decision making, leadership, and appraising. These processes are of a higher order of abstraction than organizing or assembling resources.

A dual classification system has been prepared based on different levels of abstraction of terms used to describe the essence of the administrative process. These are summarized in Table 1.2 and are based on works of earlier writers in business and educational management.

The first-order or higher level abstractions are involved in the discharge of all functions listed with the second-order abstractions. They have overarching significance in the organization and to the administrator. Even within this group there may be a high degree of interrelationship depending upon the interpretation attached to each term. As indicated, special importance is attached herein to planning, decision making, leadership, and to managing change in that separate chapters are devoted to explore each of these in greater depth.

Most terms listed as second-order abstractions were described in previous pages and only the few new ones will be explored further. The term *goal orienting* was slected because it describes more accurately what others called planning. Schools are complex social institutions pursuing multiple objectives with the likelihood of significant shifts in priorities over time. Management-by-objectives-and-results (MBO/R) is a set of strategies that helps to fulfill major dimensions of this process. The term *assembling and allocating resources* implies the twofold tasks of first identifying and procuring resources and then determining their most productive uses. The economics of educational administration focuses on the problem of allocating scarce means to the many purposes of education in an American democracy. Controlling is used in the systems administration context, that is, to monitor and measure operations at critical points to ascertain how well objectives are being pursued and determine what types of corrective actions are needed to keep the institution locked into objectives. Not included in other lists but recognized herein are the ceremonial demands on those in executive positions. Performing ceremonial responsibilities is a time-consuming function, but it may have a significant impact on the public acceptance of the institution as well as on the public image of the administrator.

TABLE 1.2

DUAL CLASSIFICATION OF TERMS THAT DESCRIBE THE ADMINISTRATIVE PROCESS

I. First-Order Abstractions	II. Second-Order Abstractions
A. Planning	1. Goal orienting
B. Decision Making	2. Organizing or Structuring
C. Leadership	3. Assembling and Allocating Resources
D. Executing or Operating	4. Coordinating
E. Managing Change	5. Controlling
F. Appraising	6. Performing Ceremonial Functions

Administrative Roles and Competencies

Administration is a complex set of specialized functions performed within some type of organization. Its facets may be described from many different vantage points, some of which have been outlined. There is one other way to indicate what an educational administrator does or contributes. It is the set of perceptions of the specialized roles performed and competencies demanded of those in such positions. Some major administrative roles and the competencies required to fulfill them would include at least the following:

Major Role	Competencies Desired to Fulfill the Role
1. Direction Setter	a. The competencies are related to those that help orient the organization toward its objectives. This demands the abilities to identify, clarify, and write unambiguous and measurable objectives. It also calls for knowledge and skills in operating in the PPBS and MBO/R modes.

Major Role	Competencies Desired to Fulfill the Role
2. Leader-Catalyst	b. This role demands the competency to motivate, stimulate, and influence human behavior in the organization. Sensitivity to and skills in group dynamics are of value, together with knowledge of the nature of leadership in education.
3. Planner	c. Competencies related to this role will enable the administrator to anticipate future challenges, prepare personnel to cope with new demands, as well as managing whatever changes are required. Special competencies in organizing to facilitate the planning process and skills in the use and interpretation of planning models and techniques as well as computer-based information systems would be desirable.
4. Decision Maker	d. More will be said about this classic set of responsibilities in the next chapter. Competencies in problem solving, the use of decision theories, systems analysis, and so on, contribute to the fulfillment of this role.
5. Organizer	e. The design, modification, and/or creation of new structures demand competencies and understandings of the processes of education as well as the dynamics of organizations and organizational behavior.
6. Change Manager	f. Recognizing what should be changed to enhance the quality of the institution, knowing where to look for valid strategies for change, and sensing a favorable climate for action are as important as competencies in introducing new ideas, professional development of personnel, and evaluation of innovations. Again, there is a special chapter on change.
7. Coordinator	g. There is a degree of overlapping among the competencies desired. Competencies and understandings of human interaction patterns, formal and informal communication networks, desirable supervisory practices, relevant reporting systems, and so on, all contribute to effective performance of the coordinator role.
8. Communicator	h. The more obvious ones are the use of the oral and written language of the profession and the various media available for communication with persons within and outside the organization. Information theory and

Major Role	Competencies Desired to Fulfill the Role
	public relations competencies can be added.
9. Conflict Manager	i. Recognizing the inevitability of conflict and the likely sources of significant conflict must go together with special competencies in bargaining or mediation, and also in the preparation and implementation of conflict resolution, strategies are important for the fulfillment of this role.
10. Problems Manager	j. This is a more generalized statement of the above, for not all problems end up as conflicts. The competencies here are those related to problem diagnosis, problem solving, and setting up problems management teams.
11. Systems Manager	k. Competencies desired would be in systems analysis and related procedures. Understandings in the utilization of models and theories of management are likewise helpful.
12. Instructional Manager	l. Competencies in learning systems, human growth and development, instructional technology, instructional organization alternatives as well as curriculum theory and development are essential in the fulfillment of this role.
13. Personnel Manager	m. Competencies in personnel leadership techniques, negotiations, personnel appraisal, and so on, are demanded in this role.
14. Resource Manager	n. Among the competencies demanded for the execution of this role are school finance, fiscal and material (business) management, facilities construction and maintenance, transportation management, PPBS, and MBO/R.
15. Appraiser	o. Needs assessment, evaluation systems, statistics, and scientific polling procedures are among the competencies useful in the fulfillment of this role.
16. Public Relator	p. Communications skills, image enhancement procedures, group dynamics, interpersonal relations, and information dissemination through the media are often employed in the performance of this role.
17. Ceremonial Head	q. Many of the competencies listed above would be applicable here.

Each role is a part of an interrelated set and hence some degree of overlap is to be expected. What makes administration an art is the ability of the administrator to "put it all together." It is not likely that one person will have a high degree of proficiency in all competencies. An administrative team is needed and the competencies should be represented or distributed among the team members.

The various perceptions, dimensions, and roles performed in the administration of multipurpose organizations testify to its complexity as well as its importance. To summarize here and expand further on many aspects in subsequent chapters: Administrators work with people (who hear different drummers, form social systems, and may generate interpersonal conflicts), with a variety of resources, with ideas (in reports, models, and policies), with values, and with change but always in organizations located within and serving communities (that may be heterogeneous or homogeneous, in harmony or in conflict). Educational administration is a prodigous challenge for these and other reasons.

CULTURAL SETTING FOR EDUCATIONAL ADMINISTRATION

Educational administration does not operate in a vacuum, nor can any social institution be divorced from the mores of the culture where located. Education influences events within the nation and is in turn subject to the forces within the nation. Educational institutions and the culture are inextricably entwined. The culture will determine what administrative styles, standards, and expectations shall be deemed acceptable and when changes shall prevail.

Educational Attainment

Educational attainment of the U.S. population is relatively high and keeps trending upward. In less than one generation, the United States moved from being a nation of eighth grade elementary school graduates to a nation of high school graduates. The median number of years of schooling completed by persons 25 years or older was only 8.1 years in 1910 and increased slowly to only 8.6 years by 1940. More rapid gains were registered in the years that followed so that the median level of schooling hit 12.2 years by 1970 and 12.5 by 1980.[27]

In contrast, illiteracy in the United States declined from 11.3 percent in 1900, to 4.8 percent in 1930, to 2.4 percent in 1960, to 1.2 percent in 1970, and an estimate of less than 1 percent in 1980.[28] This is an impressive accomplishment for our systems of public and private education. No other nation in the world can match the educational attainment of the U.S. population as a whole. The United Kingdom, Japan, and Canada were the closest, but averaged about one year less of educational attainment. Likewise, at a time when illiteracy in the United States was less than 1 percent, an estimated 30 percent of the world population was illiterate. In some parts of certain developing countries illiteracy may be as high as 90 percent. In many countries the female population illiteracy rate exceeds 90 percent. The majority in most African countries continue to be illiterate.

Birthrates for the Nation

The nation's birthrate is one indicator of future trends in school enrollments, the number of professional personnel required, the need for educational facilities, and so on. The decline in the number of live births during the 1930s came to an end during the 1940s. The postwar baby boom started by the late 1940s and the number of live births hit a peak in 1957 with a total of 4.268 million. There was a slight decline to 4.258 million live births in 1960, and then began an accelerated decline to below 4 million, with only 3.731 million live births by 1970. The number of births dropped to its post-World War II low of only 3.144 million in 1975 before beginning some modest increases thereafter.[29] The estimates for 1980 were 3.598 million, which is below that recorded at the beginning of the 1970 decade. The baby boom was followed by a "baby bust" that hit a low point in 1975 with a "mini boomlet" projected for the 1980s. In its 1980 population profile the Bureau of Census noted that "the generally lower birth rates since the mid-1960s caused a drop in population under 15 years of age while the high birth rates of the baby boom era resulted in large increases in the number of persons 25 to 34 years of age during the 1970s."[30] In short, the age structure of the population changed dramatically, for the numbers of those 14 years and younger decreased by 7 million in 1980 compared with the 1970 profile—a drop of 11.5 percent in a decade. This helps to explain why about 6.5 million fewer students were enrolled in elementary schools in 1980 as compared with 1970.[31] There are indications that the worst of the elementary school decline is over, because the under-five age group percentage in 1980 was only about 4.8 percent below that for 1970. In contrast, the percentage of the total population that was in the age of five to nine range in 1980 was 16.4 percent below that for 1970.

There were increases in the birthrate as well as in numbers during the last half of the 1970s in contrast to its first half when this rate was declining. Nonetheless, the 1980 birthrate was 6 percent greater than that in 1976, but was still 25 percent below the 1970 rate, so steep was the decline that was not arrested until 1975. The birthrate (births per 1000 population) was 24.1 in 1950 and 23.7 in 1960 compared with 15.2 in 1978 and 15.7 in 1981. The challenge facing school administrators during the 1950s and the 1960s was a rapidly expanding school system. This changed dramatically during the 1970s when educational systems faced substantial retrenchments.

Rural and Urban Population Changes

Fewer farmers now produce the food and fiber needs for a much larger nation and then some. Our agricultural production capabilities are the envy of the world, but did result in a reduction in the size of the rural farm population. This stimulated, in part, the reorganization of rural school districts and the near disappearance of the one-teacher schoolhouse.

By the same token urban and suburban America grew very rapidly. In 1790 only 5 percent of the people lived in cities; a century later only 35 percent resided in urban communities. The trend accelerated rapidly in this century, for 64 percent of the population was in urban communities in 1950 and almost 70 percent by 1960. The inevitable slowing of the urban population growth rate followed with 73.5 percent of the population settled in urban centers by 1970 and 73.7 percent by 1980.

The shift of the population from rural to urban areas was a significant change in living that made us a nation of urban dwellers. The twentieth century also saw the formation and rapid expansion of metropolitan areas. This trend changed during the 1970s, as the Census Bureau declared in 1980: "Reversing a longtime trend, the population in nonmetropolitan areas grew more rapidly during the 1970s."[32]

The standard metropolitan statistical area (SMSA) is defined as a core city and its surrounding urban and suburban territory as having a population of 50,000 or more. There were 168 SMSAs in 1950, 224 in 1960, 287 in 1970, and 323 in 1980. Almost three-fourths of the population, or almost 170 million, lived in SMSAs in 1980. Most students, teachers, and school plants are in metropolitan areas. Most of the population growth was in metropolitan areas outside their core cities. In the 1920s most of the nation's population increase was in the central cities. The 1960 census was the first to record population losses in 11 of the 12 largest cities and found that almost as many lived outside as within the central city of the SMSA. By 1970 some 54.2 percent of the SMSA population did live outside the core city. In 1980 the majority continued to live outside the central city.

Schools servicing the rural-urban fringe experienced the greatest growth rates. There has been a significant change in the racial composition of large cities in addition to the fact of population out-migration. In 1980, 56 percent of all blacks lived in the core cities of metropolitan areas and 21 percent in the related suburbs. About 83 percent of Hispanics in 1980 were found to live in metropolitan areas.[33] In short, schools served the core cities of metropolitan areas with more students from the minorities than were likely to be enrolled in other school districts.

Metropolitanism is a twentieth-century development made possible by advances in transportation systems. The periodic oil shortages during the 1970s and escalating automobile costs brought the wide separation between the homes of workers and the location of job sites into question. The concept of a single school district embracing all the territory of a metropolitan area, as may be found in a few locations at present, received further encouragement during the 1970s from some court decisions. Population shifts from others areas of the nation to the South and West, the so-called white flight from the core cities, changing age characteristics and aging population profiles, and so on, create special administrative and other problems for all manner of government and social institutions including education.

Economics, Productivity, and Wealth

In 1950 one person could produce as much in 40 hours as three could in 70 hours in 1870. Some projections suggest that further technological developments during the next 100 years would enable one person to accomplish in 7 hours what it now takes 40 hours to do. In 1981 the median family income reached $22,388 in current dollars but only $5926 in 1950 dollars.

The productivity of the work force increased during the post-World War II period, but the gains in output-per-man-hour slowed during the 1970s. By the end of the 1970s and the beginning of the 1980s there were severe adjustments in the work force with unemployment rates growing ominously. The several recessions of the 1970s and the stagnant economy of the early 1980s threatened the continued adequate support of public education. The economics, productivity, and wealth of the nation have a substantial impact on the financing and support for public education.

In addition, education is presently a more potent force in determining initial individual employment capabilities as well as subsequent development for job promotion and personal job satisfactions. It is an integral and important strategy in the design and implementation of the nation's manpower development strategies.

Home, Family, and Education

Formal educational institutions assumed a function that in previous history was primarily a function of the family. Changes in the home and family structures have a significant impact on the education of children and youths in formal institutions. They can reinforce or negate the education of children and youths in schools. Teachers, administrators, and other professional personnel work with the home and have come to expect support from the family of students.

Family size continued a downward trend that started in 1967, but which may have bottomed out in 1975. In 1980 the average family for whites was 3.2 persons, for blacks 3.7, and for Hispanics 3.9. The so-called average woman in 1980 had an average of 1.9 children, which was down about 25 percent from the 2.5 children in 1970 but up about 6 percent from the 1976 figure.[34]

The divorce rate rose 113 percent between 1970 and 1980. The 1980 census revealed that more women are remaining single. There were in 1980 1.6 million unmarried couples living together, over three times the 520,000 that did so in 1970.[35] There were significant declines during the past two decades in the percentage of children living with both parents. In 1960, 88.9 percent of children lived with both parents; in 1970, this fell to 84.7; and in 1980 it dropped further to 75 percent.[36] One child in five in 1980 lived with only one parent, three-fourths lived with two parents, and the remainder lived with relatives or others. The trendline in this home characteristic is down for both white and black families, but the black single parent family for children now constitutes the majority, whereas only about 15 percent of white children live in single parent families. In 1960, 69.2 percent of all black children lived with both parents, but by 1976 only 49.6 percent did.[37] "The sharp rise in the per cent of all children living with the mother only has had an impact on the number of children in families with income below a defined poverty line."[38] The absolute numbers increased even though the percent below the poverty line dropped to 42.6 percent in 1974 from 64.6 percent in 1959. About 15 percent of *all* children live in families whose earnings put them below the poverty line.

The number of working mothers increased substantially during the 1970s. By 1978 over 53 percent of 6- to 17-year-olds were living in a family situation where the mother was a full-time member of the labor force.

SUMMARY

The qualifiers that precede the word *administration* may specify its context, a particular dimension of it, or a given locus for its performance, but do not change its fundamental characteristics. Administration is one of the "helping" professions that focuses on the organization rather than individuals alone. The "ministerial" interpretation of the art places the administrator in a position of trust and helps project the spirit as well as the substance of it.

Although the beginnings of the scientific approach to administration can be traced to the Cameralists of the 1700s, formal study of educational administration is a twentieth-century phenomenon. School administrators are a subset of the expanding field of educational administration. Administration emerged as an important function as the challenges facing educational institutions increased markedly. Administrators perform functions vital to the successful operation of the organization including the implementation of policies, pursuing objectives, making the most productive use of resources, and serving as an organizational catalyst.

Operational problems unique to educational institutions are important, but constitute only one dimension of the complex art. The analysis of educational administration to include the management process is relatively new. The management process is similar in education or business or other types of organizations.

The political, economic, and social dimensions of the art also impact on public institutions such as education. Although the process dimensions are important, they do not operate in a vacuum, thus implying that technical knowledge of the field is of no less significance. What is demanded today is a new breed of administrators with broader preparation and experiences in various facets of the art and science of educational management rather than replacement by executives from other fields without the technical knowledge, professional understandings, and sensitivities to educational organizations.

Organizations are social institutions where the interplay of human factors can make or break the best laid plans. The people dimension of the art is related to leadership. There are also theoretical dimensions to administration that involve the use of models and conceptual frameworks in the improvement of practice.

Educational administration is a set of organization functions that helps insure the effective delivery of educational services as well as the implementation of legislative policies.

Administration is perceived as an art that can be enhanced through the application of science. The successful administrator is one with a firm grasp of the essential knowledge and models and also the good judgment to know when to apply each and the limitations of each. A social ethic as well as science and artistry guide administrative actions.

The argument as to whether there are certain processes common to all administrative activity is an ancient one, with those that take the affirmative stance judged to be the winners at this point in time. The fundamental functions or processes of administration can be phrased as key questions or statements, but are more commonly presented today as descriptive terms. Henri Fayol during the early part of this century provided the basic list of administrative processes that included planning, organizing, commanding, coordinating, and controlling. Others modified and extended these, with writers in educational administration starting to do so during the 1950s. A dual classification system would recognize the different levels of abstraction by the terms used to describe the administrative processes. First-order abstractions would include planning, decision making, leadership, executing, managing change, and appraising. The next or lower level of abstraction would include goal orienting, organizing, assembling and allocating resources, coordinating, controlling, and performing ceremonial functions.

Administration can also be defined in terms of roles and competencies needed to fulfill them. These roles would include direction setter, leader-catalyst, planner, decision maker, organizer, change manager, coordinator, communicator, conflict manager, problems manager, systems manager, instructional manager, personnel manager, resource manager, appraiser, public relator, and ceremonial head. What makes administration an art is the ability "to put it all together," that is, to form a team with talents to make the roles work. Administration is a complex undertaking because administrators must work with people, resources, ideas, value systems, and change.

Educational administration is influenced by the nature of the American culture in which it is located. The educational attainment of the people of the United States is the highest in the world and the illiteracy rate is among the lowest in the world. The nation's birthrate is an indicator of the future challenges confronting educational administration. We went from the baby boom era of some 20 years after World War II to the so-called baby bust of the 1970s when the number of live births hit a low point in 1975. A new uptrend in births is in evidence and can be likened to a "boomlet" for the late 1980s. The age structure of the population changed dramatically during the 1970s, with fewer persons found among the so-called school age population.

The United States is an urban population because 73.7 percent in 1980 lived in urban communities. This appears to be near the peak, for the population growth during the 1970s was greater in nonmetropolitan areas than in metropolitan areas. The core cities saw a net outmigration after 1960s and a higher percent of minority population.

The economics, productivity, and wealth of the nation have a substantial impact on the financing and support for public education. Education is an important part of the nation's manpower development strategies.

Family size continued its downward trend and the divorce rate rose during the previous decade. There was a sharp rise in the number of one parent families with children. The black single parent family for children now constitutes the majority of family units, whereas only about 15 percent of white children live in single parent family units. The number of working mothers increased substantially during the 1970s so that by 1978 over 53 percent of 6- to 17-year-olds were living in a situation where the mother was a full-time member of the nation's labor force.

NOTES

1. Cameralists flourished during the 1700s, but many ideas have been traced to the mid-1500s. See Albert Lepawsky, *Administration: The Art and Science of Organization and Management*, New York: Knopf, 1949.
2. Peter F. Drucker, *The Practice of Management*, New York: Harper & Row, 1954, p. 111.
3. Ibid.
4. Robt. L. Katz, "Skills of an Effective Administrator," in *Skills That Build Executive Success*, Cambridge, Mass.: *Harvard Business Review*, 1964, pp. 21–30.
5. Chris Argyris, "The Individual and Organization: An Empirical Test," *Administrative Science Quarterly*, Vol. 4, No. 2, September 1959, p. 145.
6. Jacob. W. Getzels, "Administration as a Social Process," in *Administrative Theory in Education*, A. W. Halpin, ed., Chicago: Midwest Administration Center, University of Chicago, 1958, pp. 150–165.
7. Daniel E. Griffiths, *Administrative Theory*, Englewood Cliffs, N.J.: Prentice-Hall, 1959, p. 21.
8. Alexander Hamilton, *The Federalist*, No. 72, New York: Packet, March 18, 1788.

9. Gene H. Fisher, "The Role of Cost-Utility Analysis in Program Budgeting," in David Novick, ed., *Program Budgeting*, Washington, D.C.: GPO, 1965, p.39.
10. Drucker, op. cit., p. 9.
11. Plato and Xenophon, *Socratic Discourses*, J. S. Watson, trans., Ernest Rhys, ed., New York: Dutton, 1956, Book 3, chap. 4.
12. See Albert Lepawsky, *Administration*, New York: Knopf, 1955, p. 87.
13. Henri Fayol, "Administration Industrielle et Generale," in Constance Starrs, *General and Industrial Management*, London: Sir Isaac Pitman, 1949.
14. Jesse B. Sears, *The Nature of the Administrative Process*, New York: McGraw-Hill, 1950, p. ix.
15. Russell T. Gregg, "The Administrative Process," in R. F. Campbell and R. T. Gregg, eds., *Administrative Behavior in Education*, New York: Harper & Row, 1957, p. 271.
16. Department of the Air Force, *The Management Process*, Air Force Manual 25-1, Washington, D.C.: GPO, 1954, pp. 3–5.
17. Ordway Tead, *The Art of Administration*, New York: McGraw-Hill, 1951, p. 105.
18. R. A. Johnson et al., *The Theory and Management of Systems*, 2nd ed., New York: McGraw-Hill, 1967, pp. 21–42.
19. American Association of School Administrators, *Staff Relations in School Administration*, 33rd Yearbook, Arlington, Va.: The Association, 1955, p. 19.
20. R. F. Campbell et al., *Introduction to Educational Administration*, Boston: Allyn and Bacon, 1958, p.181.
21. William H. Newman, *Administrative Action*, Englewood Cliffs, N.J.: Prentice-Hall, 1950, p. 4.
22. Johnson et al., op. cit., p. 15.
23. Newman, op. cit., p. 390.
24. Johnson et al., op. cit., p. 72.
25. Chester I. Barnard, *The Functions of the Executive*, Cambridge, Mass.: Harvard University Press, 1938, pp. 186–187.
26. Herbert A. Simon, *Administrative Behavior*, 2nd ed., New York: Macmillan, 1957, p. 220.
27. W. Vance Grant and Leo J. Eiden, *Digest of Education Statistics 1982*, National Center for Education Statistics, Washington, D.C.: GPO, 1982.
28. Ibid., p. 20.
29. U.S. Department of Commerce, Bureau of the Census, *Statistical Abstract of the United States 1980*, Washington, D.C.: GPO, December 1980.
30. U.S. Department of Commerce, Bureau of Census, *Population Profile of the United States: 1980*, Current Population Reports, Series P-20, No. 363, Washington, D.C.: GPO, June 1981.
31. Ibid., p. 1.
32. Ibid.
33. Ibid., p. 2.
34. Ibid., pp. 1 and 13.
35. Ibid., pp. 1 and 14.
36. Ibid.
37. M. A. Gollady, *The Condition of Education*, 1977 edition, Vol. 3, part 1, Washington, D.C.: GPO, 1977, p. 5.
38. Ibid.

CHAPTER REVIEW QUESTIONS

1. What are the "ministerial dimensions" of educational administration?
2. Who were the Cameralists?
3. Why bother to create effective administration for educational institutions?
4. Which two or three of the many administrative functions or contributions are the most important in education? Justify your stand.
5. If "administration is administration," then why wouldn't it help to improve the quality of educational administration by employing as superintendents and principals persons without special knowledge or experience in education?
6. What is the difference between policymaking and executive activity?
7. What are the contributions and limitations in the application of purely scientific procedures in the administration of schools?
8. What is meant by the statement that "administration should be guided by a social ethic"?
9. What are the basic or fundamental administrative processes? (Feel free to select whatever list or approach to describing them.)
10. What factors in the American culture are likely to have the most significant impact on the administration of educational institutions? Justify your stand.

SELECTED REFERENCES

Campbell, R. F. and Gregg, R. T., eds., *Administrative Behavior in Education,* New York: Harper & Row, 1957, chap. 8.

Drucker, Peter F., *The Practice of Management,* New York: Harper & Row, 1954.

Lepawsky, Albert, *Administration,* New York: Knopf, 1955, chaps. 1, 4, 8, 10, 11.

U.S. Department of Commerce, Bureau of Census, *Population Profile of the United States: 1980,* Series P-20, No. 363, Washington, D.C.: GPO, 1981.

2

THE EDUCATIONAL ADMINISTRATOR AS A DECISION MAKER IN AN ORGANIZATION: ANALYSIS OF THE ORGANIZATIONAL STRUCTURE AND PROCESS FOR DECISION MAKING

Most writers on management recognize decision making as one of the most important functions and that success often rests on competencies and judgment in rendering decisions. Decision making is the process that leads to or ends with the final product called a decision. A decision is simply a conscious choice made after rational consideration and from a set of alternatives or possible courses of action. Decision making, therefore, is a choice determination process. As another group of writers put it, decision making is ". . . a process whereby management, when confronted with a problem, selects a specific course of action, or 'solution,' from a set of possible courses of action."[1]

Educational administrators are decision makers, but the process is not limited to them or to business executives, government officials, or military commanders. All kinds of people make choices daily as to what direction to follow, when to cross a street, or whether to greet a passerby. A teacher makes decisions about what will be taught that day, how the class time will be used, and upon whom to call. In short, rendering choices or making decisions is a characteristic of life and falls upon all in society.

What imparts a degree of uniqueness as well as importance to educational administrative decision making is that it occurs in and influences the welfare of the educational organization. The choices made from the alternatives available may influence the behavior of students and personnel, determine the directions to be pursued and programs to be offered, impact on what and how resources are used, and, in general, influence the welfare and effectiveness of the organization. This is why this chapter is devoted to organization as well as to decision making. The first step is to examine organizing and the nature of organizations and then the process of decision making therein.

ORGANIZATION OF INSTITUTIONS

An organization is a social unit with a purpose as well as with formal linkages among those who are a part of it. Organization members seek to achieve a set of goals through coordinated efforts. The need for the creation of such mechanisms stems from the fact that the multiplicity or complexity of objectives necessitates collective, coordinated, and productive efforts.[2] The whole, or organized institution, becomes more than the sum of its part because "the component units stand in some relation to one another."[3] There are official rules regulating organizational behavior, a social structure that defines the formal hierarchy of authority as well as shared commitments to goals achievement.

Through the organizing process a previously unrelated group of people may be patterned into a unified social group to enhance the productive capacity of the institution. Blau and Scott emphasized that a "network of social relations transforms an aggregate of individuals into a group" making it "more than the sum of individuals composing it since the structure of social relations is an emergent element that influences the conduct of individuals."[4] The acceptance of shared goal orientations and organizational expectations may influence a person's conduct within the institution but not necessarily away from it.

Transmission of the cultural heritage, intellectual and related development of children and youths, and other educational objectives demand for their achievement collective and unified efforts as well as complex organizational arrangements. Educational organizations, more commonly referred to as "systems," such as local school districts, state education authorities, and federal education agencies are illustrations of formal and special-purpose social organizations.

The end product of the organizing process is a formal and systematic means for differentiating functions, distributing decision-making authority, structuring work patterns, coordinating resources (both human and material), designing machinery to sustain operations, and clarifying objectives. Specialized divisions or bureaus may be created to take advantage of special talents or to complete unique tasks. The bureaucracy is generated to maximize the potential inherent in human diversity as well as the resolution of task complexity.

Weber[5] gave the concept of bureaucracy its most respected and objective meaning. After a study of what went on in organizations, he generated the theory of bureaucracy as a rational and efficient model for the administration of an institution. Weber's theory of bureaucracy perceived the organization in terms of its formal structure and the following additional characteristics:[6]

1. Division of labor based on specialization of talents.
2. Well-defined hierarchy of authority with superior–subordinate relations clearly and formally indicated.
3. A system of rules and regulations which clarify the rights and duties of all position incumbents.
4. A statement covering work to be performed.
5. Impersonality prevailing in interpersonal relations, that is, no favoritism to friends or those with special social status, and special emphasis on maintaining "social distance" between persons employed in positions at different levels in the organizational hierarchy.
6. A commitment to merit, objectively determined, in the selection and assignment of persons to various positions. Technical qualifications and past performances or experiences rather than political, social, family, or other connections were to be used in position determination for persons employed.

Weber sought an organizational arrangement that would enhance rationally based decision making. This he felt could be achieved best through bureaucracy that he perceived to be "the most efficient form of administrative organization, because experts with much experience are best qualified to make technically correct decisions, and because disciplined performance governed by abstract rules and coordinated by the authority hierarchy fosters a rational and consistent pursuit of organizational objectives."[7]

Although Weber is recognized for the development of one of the clearest statements on formal organizations, he is criticized by some for his idealized conception of bureaucracy, his insensitivity to the informal dimensions of formal organizations, and his failure to recognize the potential conflict in organizations that arise when expert judgment based on technical specialization disagrees with the disciplined compliance with directives of a superior.[8]

In popular usage, bureaucracy implies a morass of red tape faced by people who must deal with it, as well as rigid application of organizational rules and regulations. These undesirable connotations of "rule-encumbered inefficiency" or rigid interpretation of overelaborated guidelines are in stark contrast to what Weber had hoped to project.

Weber's model for a formal organization was designed to facilitate rational decision making and was less concerned with human relationships and leadership. Actually, the model sought to minimize human capriciousness by institutionalizing authority and insisting upon all following carefully prescribed procedures of operation. Underlying the theory is the belief that human beings are unpredictable in behavior, given to more emotional than rational responses, are disorganized in tackling serious problems, and possessed with other predispositions that could interfere with achieving maximum efficiency in organizations. Weber conceptualized an organizational form to overcome the limitations of human resources working within it. It may have suggested a resolution for one set of organizational problems at the price of creating a different set, namely, human relations conflicts. Nonetheless, Weber had a profound impact on formal organizations. One evidence of this is that the so-called formal charts of organization are diagrammatic translations of Weber's bureaucratic model for a specific institution.

Weber was not, however, the only one of his times to be insensitive to human factors and informal organizational patterns. Frederick W. Taylor, credited as the founder of scientific management (not to be confused with the more recent "management science" movement), was also criticized for stressing mechanical procedures and failing to understand the full impact of human factors on productivity. Henri Fayol, another contemporary, likewise paid little heed to the human or psychological elements within the productive enterprise. Many find it difficult

to avoid castigating the pioneers who were creatures of their times but who nonetheless contributed much to increased productivity and reduced chaos in the emerging complex institutions of the period.

Blau and Scott[9] noted that the colloquial connotation *bureaucracy* as "rigid enforcement of the minutiae of extensive official procedures" is inconsistent with the more neutral interpretation of the term in sociology as referring to the "administrative aspects of organizations" or to the "amount of effort devoted to maintaining the organization rather than to directly achieving its objectives." Preoccupation with "administrivia" or with undue emphasis on preserving and protecting organizational support mechanisms at the expense of important educational outcomes to be achieved is a serious defect that can lead to the demise of the chief executive of any institution.

Simon pictured the organization as a decision-making mechanism that limits the scope of decision authority for individuals in various positions.[10] The structure or pattern that is created serves to enhance the rationality of decisions by setting up the formal rules, the flow of information through channels, and the personnel training programs that can help frame the alternatives essential to formal decision making. Through organizing, departments are created with objectives defined and decision-making authority of each unit limited to responsibilities allocated. By allowing each unit to focus on a limited range of decisions, the choice-rendering process can attain a higher degree of rationality. In short, the measure of the effectiveness of the organization pattern created is the quality and rationality of decisions rendered therein.

Designing the Organizational Structure

All organizations design some type of structure that facilitates the division of tasks or operations related to the achievement of objectives, establishes a hierarchy of authority or command, determines the degree of delegation or decentralization, and so on.

Creating Operating Work Units or Departmentation. The structuring of tasks or operational responsibilities into specific assignments, work stations, departments, attendance centers, divisions, and so on, is referred to as "departmentation" by some writers in business management.[11] *Departmentation* is not a commonly used term in education, but it is helpful in determining on what bases to create operating units. The more common bases for departmentation are:

1. *Products or Services.* Creation of work units on the basis of delivery of services such as instruction, counseling, health, and business affairs is a fairly common practice in education.
2. *Location.* The grouping of functions on the basis of location is a common organizing practice in education. Area superintendents, as the name implies, are established in the very large and complex school districts. School attendance units are designed to serve a geographic area of a district.
3. *Time.* The organization of some educational operations as night schools or day schools, and also summer and regular terms is a widely used practice.
4. *Clients Served.* School district operations are commonly organized according to the age level of learners, that is, elementary, secondary, and adult education centers. There may be further divisions for clients served to include nursery, kindergarten, middle school, and so on, units.
5. *Processes.* Teaching is the dominant process in education and perhaps is much too broad a designation around which to organize other than to separate it from other specialized activities such as administration and counseling.
6. *Functions.* This is a more detailed set of activities than the more general processes mentioned above. Functional departmentation in education is increasing, although a precise definition of this does not exist. Public relations, research, testing, and building maintenance are illustrations of grouping of tasks by specialized functions in education.
7. *Subject Matter.* This is a very commonly used basis for subdividing responsibilities in education. Subject matter departments are more often found in secondary schools than at the elementary school level.

There is a degree of overlap among the various criteria or bases around which to organize the complex and diverse work responsibilities in education as in other organizations.

Establishing the Hierarchy of Authority or Command. The hierarchical division of authority among persons and positions gives the vertical dimension to the organization. The concept that every organization, starting with the top administrative post and concluding with those who provide the direct services or the completed product, is referred to as the "scalar principle."[12] The number of authority levels, or decision points, created is influenced by the size and/or complexity of the institution. "Chain of command" may be used to describe how decision making and other authority is to be distributed. In education, people acting through representatives in the legislature and on school boards are the source of legitimate authority in public education. The chief executive officers and other administrators derive decision-making powers from boards or legislatures.

The organizational pyramid used to depict the scalar principle in business and industry is structured around four major levels: top management (boards of directors and the chief executive officer), middle management (senior level executives, department or division heads, and superintendents of major operations), supervisory management (general foreman and first-line supervisors or line foreman), and the operatives or workers. An adaptation of this can be made for the organizational pyramid of decision-making authority for educational institutions. The term *general administration* to include the board of education, general superintendent, and deputy superintendent is preferred to designate the top of the pyramid. The next level is the central office administration consisting of associate and/or assistant and/or area superintendents, directors, consultants, and supervisors. This includes the middle management group of business and industry and some at the next lower level. The next part of the organizational pyramid in education is site or building or attendance center administration. It includes the principals, assistant principals, and project directors at this level. A fourth administrative level, which may be considered as quasi-administrative because teaching responsibilities are often included, is classroom administration and consists of building level department heads and some teachers. It is the farthest removed from general administration and has the most limited field of administrative decision making. It is closest to the instructional functions and may be considered as the gray area in which personnel activities move from administrative to nonadministrative functions without any change of title or location. Teachers perform nonteaching activities which are essential to the administration of schools, but department chairpersons and others do more of the administrative functions at this level.

Unity of Authority, Decision, or Command. This organizing principle holds that one chief executive in the organization must possess the final decision-making authority to delegate decision making and responsibilities to other persons and positions. Such unity of authority or command is granted to the chief executive or administrator by the policymaking body, namely, the board of education and/or legislature. Unity of command also means that only one person reports directly to the policymaking authority, all others do so through the chief executive. Each individual, in turn, at whatever other levels in the hierarchy reports primarily to one executive or superior no matter how many other superordinate positions there may be in the organization.

Some modifications of the unity of authority concept may be necessary at lower echelons. The concept of dual supervision may come to play when both the subject matter supervisor and the site administrator (principal) assume a measure of responsibility for the effective performance of the teacher. This need not be confusing, because teachers expect to receive something different from each. The subject matter supervisor or consultant provides technical guidance and support in a specific teaching field or limited range of subjects. The principal has more general operational responsibilities and works with teachers on a more frequent basis as well. An analogous situation may be found in the army post hospital that is under the direction of the post commander but also a part of the technical supervision of the surgeon general.

Dual supervision, as an exception to the unity of command principle, does work in practice despite the tradition that no person can serve two masters.[13] There are few, if any, absolute rules for organizational behavior. Concepts and principles are true only within certain limits. Greater specialization and more highly sophisticated approaches within educational institutions will bring problems of possible conflict between unity of command and dual supervision practices into sharper focus in the years ahead.

The larger and more complex the school system, the greater the series of delegations and redelegations before the actual task or duty is executed. Nonetheless, it must be recognized that accountability for the effective performance of the delegated task rests with the administrator who delegated the responsibility as well as the person who accepted and performed it. Delegation is not a means for escaping accountability, thus pointing to the need for a system of monitoring and reporting to ascertain how well the task is performed.

Authority and Power in Organizations. Power and authority may be confused with one equated with the other. The differentiation between the two begins with a more detailed analysis of the nature of authority. Simon defined authority as "the power to make decisions which guide the actions of others."[14] It determines the relationship that exists between individuals occupying different positions within the organization. Barnard declared "authority is another name for the willingness and capacity of individuals to submit to the necessities of cooperative systems."[15]

There is authority that emanates from a position in the hierarchy as well as the kind related to an individual in possession of special expertise. The latter is called technical authority which goes with the person rather than the position. It is demonstrated by performance and reputation rather than by title. Unlike titular authority, technical authority cannot be delegated by fiat to an individual not recognized by others in the organization as possessing the necessary knowledge or expertise. Technical authority moves with the person and has to be earned by newcomers moving into the former position.

Max Weber recognized the subtle differences as well as the importance of both authority and power as a means of establishing social control. Authority is established through legitimacy to stimulate action or compliance to commands, because the persons subject to the authority recognize and accept the condition willingly and voluntarily. As Blau and Scott put it, "authority exists only when a common value orientation in a collectivity legitimates the exercise of control as appropriate and proper."[16] Persons influenced by authority must accept the commands willingly and voluntarily because they see them emanating from an individual and/or system that has legitimacy that goes beyond control over rewards and/or recognition sought or punishments and losses to be prevented. Group norms are the primary force for achieving social control through the exercise of authority.

To Weber power was a raw form of energy that influences social control against the will or protestations of those being subjected to the social control. Power begets compliance involuntarily, with resistance evident but overcome through threats or actual use of physical, economic, or social force. Power accrues to a person without regard to legitimacy of its exercise because *the power person holds access to or actually possesses resources—physical, personal, economic, social, or psychological—that someone else desires.* In a power play situation, subordinates comply to procure rewards sought or to prevent suffering some kind of deprivation. In a negative sense, power that forces compliance to command may be related to control over the execution of punishment (or other negative reward) that people seek to avoid. Power to demand involuntary acceptance is lost when the person with the power loses control over the rewards desired or punishments to be avoided.

Persuasion is yet another way to procure compliance. It is similar to technical authority in that the compliance is voluntary except that the persuasive person has no formal or legitimate position in the organizational hierarchy. One goes along, that is, is persuaded to do something, because of the cogency of the arguments or faith in the persuader. It is compliance without consideration of personal wants (such as in power) or the person in a legitimate position (such as in authority).

The similarities, differences, and relationships among power, authority, and persuasion as a means of social control or organizational action are summarized and diagrammed in Figure 2.1.

Span of Supervision, Structural Patterns, and Layering. The act of organizing considers objectives, determines where decisions are to be made, how the tasks shall be subdivided and grouped, and what the hierarchy or distribution of authority shall be. It can also influence the span of supervision for each administrator and the shape of the organization structure.

The span of supervision, or span of control, defines the numbers reporting to a given executive at a specific level in the hierarchy. There are limits, because the larger the number, the less effective is the monitoring of performances and coordination of efforts. The optimum number for this span is determined by such factors as time available for supervision given the other functions assigned to the executive; complexity of tasks, interrelationships, or other dimensions of the situation being supervised; the supervisor's mental capacity, preparation, experiences, and other personal or professional

FIGURE 2.1

Relations and differences among power, authority, and persuasion.

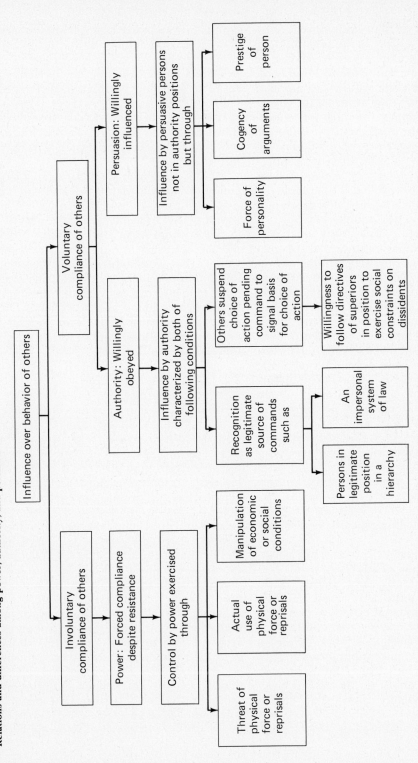

Source: Based on Max Weber's theoretical analysis as presented in P. M. Blau and W. R. Scott, *Formal Organizations*, San Francisco: Chandler, 1962, pp. 27–32.

characteristics; and stability of operations and/or personnel turnover rate in the organization.

There is no single number per supervisor or optimum span of supervision for all administrators in all types of organizations. As implied above, the greater the time available for supervision, the less complex the situation supervised, the greater the competencies of the supervisor, and the greater the stability of operations, the larger may be the span of supervision. There are limits with executive burnout likely when these are exceeded. The complexity of human relationships within an organization multiplies rapidly as the number of persons that are being supervised increases.

The size of the supervision or control span allowed will determine the shape of the organizational structure. Where the span is large, meaning a sizable number report to a single executive, a relatively flat structure will result. "Flat" should be interpreted to mean "relatively flatter than other patterns." Flat organizational pyramids are characterized by relatively few administrative levels between the lowest and the highest echelons in the hierarchy. This should not imply that contact among persons at various levels will be increased, that is, that there is easier access to persons at higher levels in the hierarchy. Flat organizational structures may result in overburdening top level administrators if the span of supervision is of unusually large size. The flatter pattern may work better where the quality of personnel is higher, turnover lower, tasks simpler, and competencies of the supervisors greater.

In contrast, a relatively tall framework is produced where the span of supervision involves fewer numbers and, therefore, there will be relatively many administrative levels between the highest and the lowest executive positions in the hierarchy. This may be more necessary in more complex organizations where there is rapid growth and/or more rapid technological change. The many hierarchical levels in such organizational pyramids do not necessarily compound the problems of access to higher level administrators.

Increased numbers of echelons characteristic of tall pyramids may compound problems of communication among the various layers, particularly if there is insistence that "proper channels" be followed and the "chain of command" respected. *Layering* is the term used to describe communications getting delayed, if not lost, as they flow up one branch of the system and then down another to allow those at lower levels but different branches of the system to exchange information.

It is not unusual to find informal responses to communication hangups because of layering that may be more severe in relatively tall organizations. A "transhierarchical bridge" may evolve without formal recognition but which may be necessary to facilitate faster communication between administrators at the same level but in different divisions of the same organization. This informal network of communication between coordinate levels is useful, but may generate problems if those in superordinate position are kept ignorant of what transpires in their respective divisions.

Differentiation in Organizing Based on Staff and Line Positions. All organizing is based on some type of differentiation whether it be based on gradations of decision-making authority, the degree or type of specialization of work performed, or the various groupings of tasks. Differentiation may also occur among those recognized as occupying line positions as opposed to staff positions. These may be described in terms of the vertical and horizontal components of the organization that reflect the varied functions and authority distributions. The line position carries responsibility for direct operational functions, is part of the established hierarchy of authority, and gives the vertical dimension to the organization. Line positions emerge through departmentation that results in grouping tasks, sections, and divisions. Authority should be delegated commensurate with responsibilities assigned line officers by the general superintendent of schools who defines all duties and the scope of authority for position incumbents. The authority of a line executive is not inherent in the position or person, but is derived from the chief executive officer whose delegations may change.

A staff position is a support rather than a direct operations post, carries no authority over any line officer, and is part of the horizontal dimension of the organizational structure. There can be no staff position without first establishing a line position. A person in a staff role serves the line officer, that is, the nature of the position or duties is defined by the line administrator to whom the person is attached. A staff official supplements what a line officer would perform if the latter had the time and the specialized knowledge to do it. The staff position is an extension of a line post and can be related to an executive at any level. Staff functions are primarily advisory and consultative to the line executive. Such posts do not usually have authority to direct the activities of operatives.

The staff-and-line position arrangements were developed to a high degree of organizational proficiency by the Prussian Army just prior to the turn of the twentieth century, and for that reason the concepts may be equated with the military. The staff-and-line relationships may be applied to any type of organization without also accepting the rigid discipline or authoritarian posture characteristic of the military.

Increased enrollments may call for more line administrative positions but not necessarily staff positions as well. It is the complexity of operations more than any other factor such as system size, increased specialization, or rapidity of growth alone that stimulates the need for the formation of a staff component to line administrators. The growing need for technical experts in educational organizations, as well as the need for monitoring and improving personnel performances, generated the formation of larger staff complements in educational organizations. The typical staff person has functional responsibilities and can recommend the pursuit of a specific course of action only within a narrowly defined or specialized dimension in education or its administration. Any directions issued from a staff office must be submitted in the name of or the authority vested within a line executive to whom attached.

Special subject or grade level supervisors are among the more common staff posts in education. Such staff personnel must depend primarily upon technical or personal authority, that is, the authority given to a person willingly because of being a recognized specialist. This authority through reputation adheres to a particular person, moves with the person, and cannot be transferred arbitrarily to another. If professional persuasiveness fails, then the supervisor must turn to the general or some associate superintendent such as line officers for support to compel compliance with recommendations.

There is always the danger of rigid interpretation of the staff-and-line concepts. Duties assigned usually to a person in a staff position by the line officer may include the following: assembling, summarizing, and interpreting information related to a particular dimension or operation in the institution; recommending a set of alternatives to resolve a situation; reviewing information and plans with others to procure their reactions and recommendations; preparing a set of written orders for the line officer that are needed to activate a plan; developing explanations or interpretations for directives issued by a line administrator; monitoring or appraising the impact of operational plans; and scheduling ceremonial and professional activities of a line official.

Intraorganizational conflicts between staff specialists and line executives to whom they are not attached or to whom they are not responsible directly are not uncommon. Obviously, staff persons are at a serious disadvantage in any conflict with the line officer to whom they report and at whose inclination they serve. The larger the staff component attached to various line officers in the hierarchy, the greater are the likelihood and incidence of conflict between staff persons serving a line officer at one level with line administrators at a coordinate or lower level. The depth of knowledge and special concern for a limited dimension of the organization results in perceptions of operational problems quite different from those with broader responsibilities who seek to establish a balance among the various dimensions. The larger the staff component, the higher are the operating costs. It is not unusual during periods of fiscal retrenchment for position cutbacks to occur first among staff personnel.

Charts that depict staff-and-line position relationships are idealized versions of operations. Education is unique in that direct and often personal contact between a teacher and the general superintendent is more common even in the very large school districts than is typical between a worker and a chief executive of an industry of lesser size. One reason is that teachers and administrators are members of the same profession. Another is that school superintendents are actively and personally involved in the selection and employment of teachers. Obviously, the larger the school district, the less the frequency of contact between administrators at top levels and teachers.

Concepts such as unity of command, hierarchy of authority, and line-and-staff continue to experience modification as the objectives of the organization and qualifications of people to fill positions change. The traditional interpretation of line-and-staff assumed that a person at any level can be replaced by another of similar rank, preparation, or experience. This has changed in the military as well as elsewhere. An air force captain who can pilot a jet fighter no longer has the expertise to replace another captain with expertise in engineering, electronics, or missiles. We live in an age of specialization that has made persons of equal rank unlike. Similarly in teaching, certification laws and accreditation do not permit one type of teacher to be replaced by another with a very different specialization.

Specializations in administration compound problems of interpreting the relative hierarchical status of persons in the organization. Creating new central office administrative specializations such as in computer operations, research, or legislative analysis often raises questions of who is superordinate or subordinate to whom?

The term *superordinate* is preferred to superior to designate a position of higher rank in the hierarchy, greater decision-making authority, or more prestige than one or more other persons. Coordinate positions are those of relatively similar rank, authority, or assumed prestige but in different branches. Such differences are relative and apply only to relations in the organization, even though some may equate them with similar social standing in personal relations outside and unrelated to the organization. Differences in administrative salaries may compound problems where supply and demand may dictate that an administrator of lower rank in the organization be paid a higher salary than that allocated to those of higher administrative rank.

Most accept that in terms of standing in the hierarchy, a high school principal position is subordinate to the assistant superintendent-in-charge-of-secondary-education position. It is less clear whether the elementary school principal is coordinate with the junior and senior high school principal if there is an assistant superintendent for elementary education position but no assistant superintendency for secondary education. Likewise, where there is an assistant superintendent for curriculum but none for elementary or secondary education, are the elementary and secondary school principals subordinate, coordinate, or superordinate to the assistant superintendent for curriculum?

One resolution to the dilemma is to ignore the implied designations of rank and authority (or assumed prestige) by suggesting that each has a job to do and is important to the system. This may not preclude informal understandings, social status in a lay community impressed more with titles attached to positions than performances, or debates from arising elsewhere. Another is to establish a standard for awarding titles for administrative positions based on hierarchical distance of each position from a focal point in the organization such as the general superintendency or board of education. Positions once removed from the general superintendent would be judged superordinate to all others that are twice or more times distant regardless of location in various branches of the organization. Likewise, those once removed would be called associate superintendents, twice removed, assistant superintendents, and so on. This, unfortunately, does not resolve all problems of status in the system, for emotional predispositions may overcome rational analysis. Perhaps it is because no true professional really cares about such subtle differences in rank or placement in the hierarchy that few have addressed such problems or had the discipline to resolve them.

An Organization Chart for Education. Every institution seems at least to make an attempt to create an organization chart (to be abbreviated as org chart hereafter) with its familiar pattern of solid or dotted lines and boxes. These charts project the image that the position with the greatest responsibilities and authority is placed at the apex. For schools, the school board is placed in such a position and immediately underneath them is the general superintendent.

Org charts present some serious problems. They seldom take into account informal relations established over the years within an organization. They frequently become obsolete in relatively short periods of time, particularly in more dynamic districts. Frequently overlooked is the fact that people with all their emotions and political alliances are being reorganized rather than simple lines and boxes on a chart. Often personalities of people within stated positions, rather than the best thought on administration, dictate who reports to whom or who has the greatest measure of authority. Some say that the architect of an org chart that satisfies all is either a mediation expert or a great fiction writer.

Nonetheless, few can resist the urge to pattern boxes and lines to illustrate how a system works. The typical org chart focuses primarily upon the operational dimensions of the school system; few attempt to show how change takes place or professional development is accomplished. An illustration of an org chart showing various and major functions in educational administration is presented in Figure 2.2.

The major organizational divisions in the org chart shown are Operations—with primary concerns for the efficient and effective delivery of educational services to all age groups; Innovation and Development—whose primary thrusts are to develop new practices, introduce

and manage changes in cooperation with the Operations Division, professional staff growth and development, and program appraisal; Internal Relations—which seeks to emphasize special services for pupils (counseling, medical, attendance, discipline, etc.), personnel services, and negotiations; Environmental Relations—which assumes responsibilities for federal, state, and community relations as well as relations with accrediting bodies and professional associations; Administrative Affairs—with concerns for educational planning, enhancement of administrative effectiveness, school board relations, and information (computerized) services; and Logistical Support Services—which protects the resources and security of the system as well as handling transportation, food management, and fiscal operations.

The functions of most of the organizational divisions identified in Figure 2.2 are reviewed in greater detail in chapters that follow. The org chart shown outlines the significance of operations, maintainance, and further development of the educational institution. There is nothing sacred about any org chart; it can and should be changed as new demands emerge.

The School as an Organization—a Brief Overview. All formal organizations, and school systems are no exception, possess the following characteristics: a statement of goals or directions; a formal structure; a social system of people operating within; a pattern for the distribution of authority to make decisions; communication networks that are both formal and informal; a set of resources made available to it; cultural and environmental constraints; means for establishing a measure of social control over people and procedures; service functions; and a dynamic life cycle.

The Informal Organization

Formal organizations are created to establish a coherent system of relationships that could facilitate cooperation and coordination of its sub-

FIGURE 2.2

Functional administrative organization.

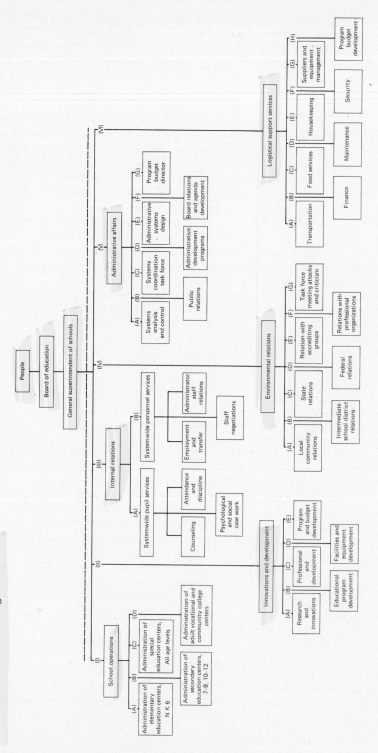

divisions or positions and their incumbents to achieve complex and varied objectives. The positions created are staffed by persons with diverse values, interests, motivations, and talents. People bring their positive and negative characteristics to the organization. The human factors may generate communications and/or actions not contemplated in the formal structure.

The informal organization within the formally defined one grows out of interpersonal interactions. These interactions may in turn generate special loyalties among various groups of people, a set of behavioral norms or values that influences the actions of workers without regard to what the formal organization may demand, and/or communication networks neither planned nor completely understood by administrators at the top levels.

According to Simon, "the term informal organization refers to interpersonal relationships in the organization that affect decisions within it but either are omitted from the formal scheme or are not consistent with that scheme."[17]

Not every gathering of or communication between employees outside of or inconsistent with the formally defined organizational pattern can be called an informal organization. The potential for creating an informal organization is present in such incidental contacts as the following:

1. Teachers with the same "planning" (or nonteaching) period during the school day may meet regularly in the teachers' lounge and as a consequence of what may appear to be "socializing" develop a personal and professional rapport that over time may influence their thinking and decisions.
2. Administrators with offices in close proximity may enjoy a "coffee break" at about the same time and place to find that this is perceived by some as the gathering of an inner circle.
3. Principals from various schools may gather to play golf together on frequent occasions with the incidental conversations during the game providing special information that may influence decisions.

In addition to social or other informal relations that are not part of the recognized roles of the position, there must be activity or communications that may influence professional decisions or other actions in a manner not consistent with the recognized chart of operations. The fact that a rather consistent pattern of "shop talk" during social and other nonformal relationships influences decisions formalized during regular professional meetings is recognized rather readily by persons who have been a part of the organization for some time and are astute observers of what is happening.

Not all informal organization has its roots in socially based or out-of-school interactions. Thus, a group of administrators with common interests may gather in one office during the regular school day to deliberate on a set of problems only to probe others not assigned and develop decisions on strategies to be pursued in resolving them. Likewise, an individual may enjoy a reputation as an authority on an aspect of educational operations that had never been assigned to him/her nor so stipulated in the org chart, but, nonetheless, other administrators (or school board members) may consult with that person and be influenced by the analysis or recommendations made.

In most complex organizations there are many clusters of informal influence groups. The more heterogeneous the professional preparation, age levels, experiences, professional schools attended, or philosophies of the people within an organization, the greater is the likelihood that a number of different informal influence groups will be formed. Complexity and rapid changes tend to stimulate formation of such groupings.

The informal organization may be a positive or a negative force. It may be useful in the introduction of change in the formal pattern of operation. The so-called grapevine may help speed the interpretation as well as the dissemination of essential professional information. It may serve as a means of disseminating feelings or information of a very sensitive nature that would be difficult or even somewhat embarrassing to present through formal communication channels.

On the other hand, informal groupings can generate morale problems when competing influence groups degenerate into warring cliques or opposing "invisible governments" that ignore formally recognized channels of decision making. The existence of extensive and competing informal organizations may compound problems for the unsuspecting new chief school executive who is unaware of the informal and undefined roles played by a predecessor. "Knowing the power structure" in a community or school system often implies a sensitivity to and knowledge of how best to work with the informal as well as the formal organization. This is why it takes a while for a stranger to the system to get to "know the ropes."

DECISION MAKING

The objectives and the formal structure of the organization have a significant impact on administrative decision making. There exists a process of decision making that can be abstracted from the various types of decision problems and various settings for the decision acts. This process has attracted the interests of scholars and practitioners from many disciplines such as economics, political science, statistics, psychology, operations research, systems analysis, and many other behavioral sciences. Each brought a unique perception and often special techniques for approaching decision problems. Thus, the economist focused on how consumers make choices and how economic organizations determine the optimum course of action to maximize certain conditions. Economists viewed decision making as occurring under conditions of certainty, risk, and uncertainty. In the first case, the decision maker (under certainty) knows all relevant alternatives, the specific consequences of each, and chooses accordingly. The concept "economic man" is applied to the person in possession of all pertinent data and who always acts rationally! Decision making under risk is similar to the conditions surrounding certainty with the exception that a given alternative does not always or invariably lead to specific outcomes.

The end result of pursuing a given course of action can be computed as a probability rather than a certainty. The situation under uncertainty is even more difficult because the probabilities of a given outcome occurring from a specific strategy are so complex that it is beyond the means of computation available at this point in time.

The behavioral scientists, operations researchers, and systems analysts are relative newcomers to the study of organizational decision making. The operations researchers and systems analysts brought a mathematical orientation and preference for the construction of models as ways to sharpen the decision-making skills of administrators.

Most of what follows is derived from writings in business management, operations research, economics, and the behavioral sciences. Interest in the special study of decision making in educational organization is very recent. It had to await the readiness of those in the profession to find new ways of perceiving the nature of educational administration. When the focus moved from almost complete reliance on the operational and concrete problems of administering a set of schools, such as personnel employment and plant construction, to include an analysis of fundamental processes and some theoretical bases undergirding educational administration, then decision making emerged along with communications as areas of special significance and study. For the moment educational administration must borrow and adapt from other disciplines the concepts, models, and special approaches to the understanding and the improvement of decision making in organizational settings.

There exist in the literature different conceptualizations as well as emphases on the nature and substance of the decision-making process. Simon viewed decision making "as though it were synonymous with managing,"[18] that is, it was what the art of management was all about. Dorsey considered the decision process as an extension of or a series of interrelated communication events.[19] Newman and Warren related planning and decision making so closely it was difficult to distinguish the two as evidenced by their Part III that is devoted to decision making and entitled "Planning: Decision Making in an Enterprise."[20]

Decision making was defined earlier as a conscious choice made after rational consideration of a set of alternatives. An organizational decision made by a school administrator commits the school system, for better or for worse, to a given course of action. Therein lies its importance and which helps to explain why Simon among others perceived rational decision making as being the substance of administration.

The outcomes of the decisional process may be the statements of organizational policies, institutional rules to guide subsequent behavior of all personnel, development of long-range plans, or the commitment of resources to various programs and projects. As indicated earlier, one reason for creating a formal organization—as stated by Simon and Barnard—is to improve the rationality and quality of complex decisions as well as to insure that they are made at the right point in the decision structure. The organization sets the goals, establishes the information channels, creates the conditions which give rise to the need for decisions, distributes the authority to render certain types of decisions at various points in the formal structure, and so on.

Decision making may be considered a culminating activity or it may include as well all prior activities that led to the choice. When Simon pictured the decision-making process as being synonymous with managing, he referred to the entire process to include finding occasions for making decisions, procuring data, identifying possible courses of actions, and finally selecting one course of action.[21]

Some political scientists define politics, in the best sense of that word, as making and executing authoritative decisions for society. In that sense, decision making may be considered to be synonymous with politics as well as management.

On the other hand, Dorsey emphasized that because the decision rests upon receipt of some kind of communication and can be effectuated only through communication to others, communication was judged to be the more important of the two.[22] Pfiffner and Sherwood tended to support this point of view by stating that although in practice decision making and communication were almost inseparable they were not identical.[23]

The systems management approach views the organization as an integrated decision system.[24] This perception tends to blend together communication and decision making to refer to the new unity as an "information–decision system."

Decision making is action oriented. The late John F. Kennedy at the time of his presidency made the following statement in his 1961 State of the Union message to Congress: "Capacity to act decisively at the exact time needed has been too often muffled in the morass of committees, timidities, and fictitious theories which have created a growing gap between decision and execution." This decision gap continues to be a matter of concern to administrators of all types of institutions. Some suggest that inflexible adherence to channels of communication and lines of authority be relaxed on occasion to permit the top level executive direct interchange with lower level executives to facilitate the information flow and responses essential to more timely decision making and decision execution.

Elements of the Decision-Making Process

The process leading to some kind of a choice may appear to be simple. What makes it complex is determining in advance that one course of action over all other available courses will produce what was anticipated. It is the prediction of likely consequences plus recognition that accountability will be the decision makers no matter what the intentions or circumstances surrounding the choice determination that makes it an awesome responsibility.

The lack of agreement on what is involved was well put by one set of writers who declared: "Ask 25 managers, consultants, and professors of management to list the steps in the decision process and you will probably get 25 different lists."[25] These would contain elements in common and at variance as well as in differing sequences.

Taylor declared that problem solving, decision making, and creativity were essentially the same processes.[26] Each was perceived to be a variety of thinking and he suggested there was a need for a general theory of thinking. Taylor differentiated each intellectual process by results rather than processes employed. Thus, creativity is thinking that produces ideas, decision making a choice among alternative courses of action, and problem solving a solution to a dilemma.

John Dewey's classic work *How We Think* is aptly titled and preceded by at least a generation the more current writings on the sequential process and activities called thinking. Dewey's steps in thinking called for:[27]

1. Stimulation to begin the process of thinking through experiencing a "felt need" for it.
2. Location and clarification of the nature of the problem.
3. Suggestions of possible solutions.
4. Hypothesis formation, that is, development of a vehicle which can initiate and guide observation as well as the gathering of facts and ideas.
5. Mental elaboration, or reasoning to determine the consequences of the suggested hypothesis or solution.
6. Experimental corroboration of the hypothesis selected by overt or imaginative action.

Writers mindful and unmindful of Dewey's seminal work have used other words and perhaps expanded a bit on what Dewey first developed. The steps in thinking and decision making in new terminology stress the following:

1. There must exist first of all a situation that calls for a decision.
2. It is imperative to define and diagnose the nature of the decision problem.
3. Data pertinent to the analysis of the decision problem are gathered.
4. Alternative courses of possible action are generated followed by formulation of preferred solutions.

5. Each alternative is analyzed and appraised preferably through the development of a model that portrays the essential elements of phenomena under investigation.
6. The consequences of each possible choice are analyzed employing techniques such as cost–benefit analysis or at least informal approaches such as what may happen after a given choice is pursued.
7. There should be an evaluation of the impact of the decision made at some time after the fact.

Simon identified the initial phase of the decision-making process as "intelligence activity" or the survey of the environment to determine what conditions therein called for new actions.[28] This is what Dewey called "felt need" and others "sensing the need for a decision." Simon's second phase was called "choice activity" that encompassed much of what is detailed in the steps above. He believed that good decision makers were made, not born, because the skills or competencies required for effective performance could be learned.[29]

Newman and Kirby saw the four basic elements of a "rational decision-making model" as "diagnosis, search, projection, and choice."[30] Diagnosis is essential to prevent false starts, clarify the major dimensions of the problem, and to find root causes. A degree of judgment is involved. They warned: "The love of quick action—and perhaps an illusion of omniscience—makes some administrators impatient with careful diagnosis and detailed planning."[31] Diagnosis sets the stage for the search.

The search for alternatives is the more creative element in the decision-making process. Recognizing that no two minds work alike, Newman and Kirby described the following as phases in the creative process:[32]

1. *Saturation.* Immersing oneself in the problem situation to understand it from all angles.
2. *Deliberation.* Following immersion comes analyzing, reviewing, rearranging, and rethinking in a more formal and serious fashion to identify what previously may have been obscure relationships.

3. *Incubation.* Relaxing and doing other things for a while to allow ample time for fresh ideas to gel.
4. *Illumination.* This is the "Aha!" phase, the coming of the sudden great idea, the "closing of the gap," or the emergence of solutions.
5. *Accommodation.* This is further development and refinement of the proposed resolution by reframing and modifying it as necessary on the basis of the reactions of others or further contemplation.

Individual creativity in seeking new alternatives in decision making can be facilitated by overcoming the kinds of attitudes or habits that may generate psychological barriers to creativity, by searching for fresh viewpoints to the problem under study, and by serendipity (the gift of discovering the unexpected).

There are occasions when groups of people can meet to exchange ideas that could lead to creative approaches in generating decision alternatives. Creative group interactions, such as brainstorming, work best if the decision problem is simple, specific, and within the competencies represented by the group. Brainstorming as a process is most likely to be productive when (1) the group refrains from criticizing or evaluating any ideas that may be thrown out for consideration; (2) even wild ideas are encouraged from any and all members of the group; (3) large numbers of different ideas are produced; and (4) "hitchhiking" on another's ideas occurs, such as when various notions are combined and expanded. A permissive atmosphere free of any subsequent recriminations for what was offered and the willingness to adapt and build on ideas from others enhance the relevance of the process.

By projection Newman and Warren meant "projecting the probable consequences of each alternative . . . in a way that helps us compare these possible courses of action."[33] Analyzing and comparing is a kind of a reduction process (reducing the many to the one selected) and is often regarded as the fundamental substance of decision making. Here is where analysis based on the use of models, interdisciplinary teams, and quantitatively oriented tools or procedures (often stressed in operations research) can contribute much to the decision-making process. Cost-effectiveness of each alternative may be useful at this point as well. Obviously, personal value judgments come into play when attempting to forecast the likely consequences of pursuing a given alternative. This is what makes decision making exciting and at the same time worrisome. Those who have the advantage of hindsight are seldom kind to decision makers who must determine the course of action before all facts or likely reactions are known.

The final step is determining the choice of action. Others may assist in clarifying the issues surrounding a decision to be made, suggesting alternatives, and analyzing the consequences likely, but the final choice is the decision maker's. The decision maker may accept the counsel of others, but the ultimate accountability is his/hers. What most consider to be decision making is simply the culminating activity or the final act that determines what will be done. The key to effective decision making lies in the procedures, techniques, data, and judgments that were available before the final choice was made. Improvements in decision making are most likely to come from a review of the phases leading to the final choice.

Decision making, as implied in the paragraphs above, is not a fragmented or isolated activity unrelated to the many and varied functions pursued in the organization as a whole. It is a sequential and continuous process that often involves many, including the so-called decision maker. This is as it should be, for the decision is evaluated best in terms of its value and impact on individuals and the organizations. Rational or logical processes facilitate effective decision making, but very often the subjective personal, political, or social factors have an even greater impact on the final choice rendered.

The relationships between decision making and other rational activities are summarized in Table 2.1. Here again Table 2.1 presents data with obvious similarities to support the contention that operational analysis of rational processes such as decision making reveals a common base in the thinking process. Differentiation between planning and thinking can be made on the basis that the former is the preparatory phase and the latter the culminating phase of reflective thinking.

Types of Decisions

Simon prepared a taxonomy based on programmed and nonprogrammed decisions in an organization.[34] The choices that must be rendered to govern or to resolve what can be called basically repetitive and/or fairly routine activities within an organization were labeled as "programmed decisions." A unique response is not necessary for the frequently recurring situations or problems. Such matters may be resolved by applying the "standard operating procedures" that were designed to cope with them.

The novel and previously unstructured issues, which cannot be resolved through the application of standard operating procedures or existing policies, are called "nonprogrammed decisions." Nonprogrammed decisions rely on creative, adaptive, or problem-solving behavior instead of mere application of previously determined procedures.

Simon argued that programmed and nonprogrammed decision making within an organization are based on different techniques and procedures for their resolution. Improvement in programmed decision making may occur through development of better standard operating procedures, more precise and relevant policies, and more careful allocation of such decision-making responsibilities among certain administrators who comprise the hierarchy. In contrast, enhancement of nonprogrammed decision making will be more likely to result

---

TABLE 2.1

STEPS IN PLANNING, DECISION MAKING, PROBLEM SOLVING, AND THINKING

1. Analytical planning[a]	**3. Problem solving**[c]
Clarify the problem	Become aware of the problem
Determine the alternatives	Collect and analyze information
Get the facts	Assemble and organize information
Analyze the facts	Set forth possible solutions or hypotheses
Decide on action	Eliminate weak hypotheses
	Apply solution to the situation
2. Decision making[b]	**4. Thinking**[d]
Recognize, define, and limit the problem	Stimulate through "felt need"
Analyze and evaluate the problem	Locate and clarify problems
Establish criteria or standards	Suggest possible solutions
Collect data	Hypothesize, to initiate and guide observation, and gather facts and ideas
Formulate and select preferred solutions (test them in advance)	Mentally elaborate; reason to determine consequences of the suggested hypotheses of solutions
Put into effect preferred solutions	Experimentally corroborate hypotheses selected by overt or imaginative action

---

[a]William H. Newman, *Administrative Action*, Englewood Cliffs, N.J.: Prentice-Hall, 1950, pp. 88–89.
[b]Daniel E. Griffiths, *Administrative Theory*, New York: Appleton-Century-Crofts, 1959, p. 94.
[c]J. G. Umstattd, *Secondary School Teaching*, Boston: Ginn, 1953, pp. 155–156.
[d]John Dewey, *How We Think*, Boston: Heath, 1933, rev. ed., pp. 106–116.

through special training in the more scientific approaches to decision making such as operations research, quantitative analysis, and/or information management.

The problems of effective decision making are compounded not only from limited competencies in clarifying issues, procuring the essential data, generating relevant alternatives, and utilizing more sophisticated procedures for the comparison and analysis of alternative, but also from the variety of constraints faced by administrators and/or the organization. Such constraints as time limits for task completion or limited budgetary resources, whether measured by money or personnel available, may reduce the optimization of the decision process. Likewise, nonavailability, or the availability of only incomplete, information may reduce the number of alternatives that could be generated as well as their careful analysis and comparison.

Special Mechanisms and Procedures to Facilitate Decision Making

Traditional interpretations of the decision process emphasize the importance of experience to habituate the administrator to kinds of problems likely to be encountered or expected and some standard responses to them. Experience and knowledge of the technical dimensions of education and of its administration are very useful in the decision process but are not the only important factors. Experience has its limitations if limited growth in decision-making competencies occurs as well as its values.

As one set of writers in business management put it, "Decisions about matters of which we are ignorant can only work out well by lucky accident."[35] Many professionals in education question the soundness and relevancy of a set of alternatives prepared by persons lacking special expertise in learning, human growth and development, the instructional process, professional standards in education, curriculum, educational finance constraints, and so on. Effective decisions in an educational enterprise will always demand special sensitivities and knowledge about all that goes on in the enterprise

and how it relates to the clientele and community served.

The conflict lies in part in comprehending the complexity of services, procedures, and personnel within the institutional context for decision making and in part in comprehending the intricacies of the decision process itself. To illustrate, the same writers who argued that only by knowing the phenomena involved can there be wise decision also insisted that more complete understanding is based on having and using models of the situation requiring some decision action. They added "Two decision makers will often come to different conclusions because they are using different models."[31] The nature and use of models are developed more completely in Chapter 6. Suffice it to say at this point that models are a representation of reality that includes only the relevant and dynamic dimensions of the situation being "modeled." The model becomes a device useful to the enhancement of decision making because it reduces the tremendous complexity of reality to the fewer important factors which in turn makes it easier for the decision maker to manipulate or compare the possible alternatives and consequences of each.

A number of tools and procedures are derived from operations research and systems concepts that can help the decision maker to cope and determine with a higher degree of probability the future consequences of selected courses of action. The operation researchers were among the first to introduce the concept of model construction as a means of improving decision making in complex situations. A special and new model is constructed for each type of decision problem. This is followed by developing or discovering the mathematical relationships between the key variables of the model of the decision situation, collecting the key data on each variable, and then completing the statistical analysis of the data to produce hard data essential to rational decision making. The quantitative analysis techniques such as linear programming, statistical decision theory, and Monte Carlo techniques are described in greater detail in Chapter 6.

Where the decision follows a sequence of steps such that the second rests on the first, and so on, and there is a degree of uncertainty at each step, a "decision tree" can be modeled to clarify to some extent the decision situation. It is "a graphic tool for describing the actions available to the decision maker, the events that can occur, and the relationship between these actions and events."[36] The decision tree is a picture or diagram of decision alternatives, events, and consequences. It is useful in decision making under uncertainty and therefore relies on statistical probabilities in analysis of the consequences of each alternative. Even the simpler of the mathematical or quantitative approaches to the improvement of decision making are relatively uncommon in educational administration. There continues to be an overreliance on the subjective opinions and raw judgments of educational decision makers even in situations where the data and quantitative analysis techniques are available and have much to offer.

Game theory is decision making in conflict situations and reveals the dynamic qualities of decision situations where for every action there may be reactions that may necessitate the formulation of new choices of action. The program evaluation and review technique (PERT), also discussed further in Chapter 6, is one of the more sophisticated decision tools dealing with scheduling and allocation of resources to various tasks that has been employed to some extent in the construction of educational facilities. In contrast, cost-effectiveness is talked about more than used as a tool in decision making in educational administration. In this approach every alternative is assumed to require a given set of resources (costs) to achieve the goal in mind. These costs are weighed against the degree of effectiveness likely to be achieved, which implies an analysis of the mathematical relationships between the two. The major problem in applying the technique to educational decisions is that although costs can be measured with well-defined units and expressed in terms of dollars, it is far more difficult to measure effectiveness and to translate such a measure into dollar units.

Developments in the perceptions of and procedures employed in decision making have changed over time and doubtless will continue to do so. The four stages in the development of decision making, according to one group of writers, are:[37]

1. *Instinctive Approaches to Decision Making.* This is perhaps the oldest phase and is closely related to the preprogrammed or instinctive behavior of animals. The choices of action are made by instinctive responses without conscious or rational thought processes. It can be called "shooting from the hip," a common reaction when threatened.
2. *Traditional Approaches to Decision Making.* This is decision rendering rooted in prior actions of successful administrators (who may have experienced different contexts for decisions). It is making choices by emulating practices and procedures passed down from one set of administrators to another. The decision is reached in a particular way "because that's the way it has always been done."
3. *Common Sense Approaches to Decision Making.* As the name implies there may be a break with past traditions if "common sense" warrants it. It also suggests conscious thought so it can be separated from the instinctive reactions. It is relatively unsophisticated and rooted in the experience and judgment of the decision maker.
4. *Scientific Method Utilization in Decision Making.* This is decision making based on understanding the process, knowing the context for it, generating models for each situation under decision, identifying and clarifying alternatives, employing quantitative analysis techniques, and so on. It is the rational approach based on hard data with subsequent modifications to consider the impact of good judgment or political, social, and other factors not readily quantifiable.

Phases 1, 2, and 3 above are more commonly found in educational administration at this point in time. The scientific method may make a greater contribution to the process before the end of the present century, sooner perhaps if the necessary competencies are available among practioners of the art in education.

DECISION LEVELS AND COMPETENCIES IN EDUCATIONAL ADMINISTRATION

The decision process is applied in some context. The school system is a unique context and may be conceptualized as a decision-making organization where specific kinds of decisions are allocated to administrators in various positions in the hierarchy. These decision points must be interrelated to maximize the potential within the organization to fulfill predetermined objectives. Decisions on the exceptional or unusual educational or management problems as well as those that have system-wide implications or which represent a significant departure from past practices are usually responsibilities of the chief school executive or superintendent. The superintendency represents the top level decision point that focuses on the strategic, the coordinating, and the unusual problems of the system. Decisions related to the day-by-day operational problems of a school building or attendance center are delegated to site level administrators. In very large districts the area superintendents may be involved in some of these operational decisions without reducing the effectiveness of site level administrators. The emphases at the general superintendency level and those immediately below it are on the system-wide planning and strategic decisions.

The decision points at the middle level of the hierarchy focus upon the decision needed to further implement the general educational and administrative strategies adopted for the system as a whole. These decision points have more specific and narrower responsibilities such as the curriculum for learners of a certain age group, health services, personnel employment and relations, and business affairs (logistical support services).

The largest number of employees are found at the classroom, department, or special support service activities. The basic choices on teaching procedures used from one day to the next or how a given support activity will be discharged on a daily basis are made at these decision points. The authority to make these necessary decisions at this level is delegated from the site-level and middle-level administrative personnel. Teachers are involved in the decision-making process, which is usually confined to their day-by-day professional responsibilities. Through professional negotiations teacher organizations have sought to increase teacher involvement in the broader and more strategic decisions as well. Collective bargaining is an agreement-making process. The process of decision making also includes many elements of bargaining as an agreement-making process.

What differentiates decision making at the top level of the organization from others is the scope, strategic nature, and/or unusual nature, or exceptionality, of the choices that must be made. Administration by exception is sometimes used to describe the practice whereby administrators at top echelons are consulted or involved only when the unusual situation not covered by existing policies is encountered at operational levels. Educational administration has been slow in recognizing the unique decision responsibilities at various decision points in the hierarchy. This has led some top level administrators to interefere with and thereby reduce the effectiveness of administrators at other levels in the hierarchy.

Barnard observed that one choice is that no decision is made. He stated: "The fine art of executive decision making consists in not deciding questions that are not pertinent, in not deciding prematurely, in not making decisions that cannot be effective, and in not making decisions that others should make."[38] This very significant summary points to the importance of good judgment in decision making and that it is an art that can be enhanced but never replaced by scientific approaches. The chief school executive must know what decisions are better made by administrators other than the general superintendent and what belongs at the top level.

Recognition of what Barnard described as

"the fine art of decision making" may be the initial step in the improvement of such practices in educational administration. What are other ways of enhancing competencies in this very important dimension of executive activity? What was implied or referred to earlier can be summarized as follows:

1. Creation of the kind of organization structure conducive to more effective decision making is important. During the organizing process it should be made clear (a) who has what kinds of decision-making authority and responsibilities; (b) what types of decisions will be made by the school board, the chief executive officer (general superintendent), central office administrators, principals, department chairpersons, and so on; (c) what limitations for decision making prevail; and (d) what time frames will be followed in designing the hierarchy.
2. Wise choices demand accurate data and other essential support services within the organization. These support services should insure that the data base essential to prudent decision making is accessible, that all are schooled in the utilization of the computer-based information system, and that special data consultants or other personnel are available to assist decision makers.
3. Decision makers are made and not born. Competencies necessary to utilize the scientifically oriented procedures that may enhance the quality of decisions such as operations research, decision trees, and nonquantitative approaches should be developed by the administrators of the systems through training programs and through cooperative associations with experts in these areas available as part of the permanent staff or through consulting relationships.
4. Competencies needed to lead groups in brainstorming the generation of alternatives as well as to discriminate between the conditions that may enhance or limit group decision-making activities are needed by educational administrators. These may be learned through attendance at in-house or external seminars designed for such purposes.
5. Decision making can be improved through sensing and identifying the political, social, psychological, or other similar factors that may be involved in the decision situation facing the organization.
6. Decision-making capabilities can be improved over time only if there are frequent reviews, analyses, and evaluations of the consequences of previous actions. This implies a willingness to admit, at least to oneself (it does not have to be a public declaration), that prior decisions were not the best and could be improved upon. It takes courage to do so. More important than the person making the choice is what procedures, data, and mechanisms were used in arriving at the decision with special concern as to how each could be improved to lead to more effective decisions.

SUMMARY

Decision making is a choice-rendering process that is common in all walks of life. What imparts uniqueness as well as importance to educational administrative decision making is that it occurs in and influences the educational organization as a whole. The process of organizing and the nature of the organization have an impact on decision making.

Through the organizing process a previously unrelated group of people may be patterned into a unified social group to enhance the productive capacity of the organization and insure realization of its goals. The end product includes a formal and systematic means for differentiating functions, distributing decision-making authority, structuring work patterns, coordinating resource use, and clarifying objectives.

Weber developed the theory of bureaucracy with the following characteristics: a division of labor, a well-defined hierarchy of authority, a system of rules and regulations, a statement covering work to be performed, impersonality in working relationships, and a commitment to merit. Some popular and undesirable images of bureaucracy see it as "rule-encumbered inefficiency" and rigid interpretation of overelaborated guidelines. This is at odds with Weber's conceptualization that promoted the creation of an organization with a bureaucracy to facilitate rational decision making.

Simon pictured the organization as a decision-making mechanism that limits the scope of decision authority for individuals in various positions.

The organizational design seeks to fulfill objectives through departmentation (patterning work subdivisions), establishing the hierarchy of authority, the span of supervision, and differentiation based on staff-and-line positions. "Chain of command" is another term that describes how decision making and other authority are distributed through the organization. Unity of authority means that only one person reports to the policymaking body and delegates responsibilities to others. Some modification of this principle may be necessary at lower echelons. Dual supervision is the exception to the unity of command concept and seems to work at a time of increasing specialization of functions in organizations.

Authority can be differentiated from other concepts such as power or persuasion. Persons influenced by authority accept commands from a source willingly and voluntarily because they perceive the commands as emanating from a person or system with legitimate rights to do so. Power is obeyed involuntarily, without regard to legitimacy because the power person controls resources the individual covets or controls punishments (negative rewards) the individual seeks to avoid. Persuasion leads to voluntary compliance even though the persuader has no formal or legitimate position in the organization. It is faith in or acceptance of the cogency of arguments that persuades one to comply.

Span of supervision defines the numbers of employees in a unit of operation reporting to a given executive. There is no absolute number for a span of the most effective size. The optimum span is influenced by time available for supervision, complexity of the situation, stability of operations, and competencies of the supervisor. Where the span of control is large, a relatively flat organization structure will result. Relatively tall organizational structures mean a limited span of supervision but many executive positions between the lowest and the highest in the hierarchy.

The transhierarchical bridge is an informal creation to facilitate faster communication between administrators at the same level but in different branches of the organization.

The staff-and-line concept, in its idealized version, is illustrated in the diagram called the "formal chart of organization." Line officers have decision-making authority over direct operations related to achievement of the goals of an institution. Staff personnel are advisors, consultants, or assistants to those in line positions. The duties of staff personnel are defined by the line administrator to whom such personnel report. There can be no staff position without first creating a line post. There is always the danger of rigid interpretation of the staff-and-line concept and intraorganizational conflicts between some staff specialists and line executives to whom the staff is not attached.

The formal org chart of educational institutions focuses primarily on day-by-day operations at the expense of system change and development. Most org charts do not show the existence and operation of the informal groupings of personnel without legitimate authority who have a significant impact on operations. The more heterogeneous the preparation, age levels, experience, and philosophies of persons, the greater are the number of different influence groups that will make up the informal organization of the school system.

Many different disciplines have demonstrated an interest in the decision-making process. Its special study in educational administration is very recent. There exist many different conceptualizations of the nature and substance of decision making. It may be considered only in terms of the culminating act of deciding or it may include all prior activity leading to the choice. There is also a lack of consensus on the number and sequence of elements in the decision process. John Dewey's analysis of thinking is often the base used for identifying the steps in rational decision making. Most analyses include a situation calling for decision; diagnosis of the problem; collecting data about it; generating alternatives; analysis of each alternative; determining the consequences of each alternative; and evaluation after the fact. The search for alternatives is the creative element in decision making.

Decisions may be classified as programmed (routine and recurring) and nonprogrammed (new and unique) with different approaches for improvement in each. It is important to have the technical knowledge about the situation or problem as well as the process of decision making. Decision makers may often act in the face of serious constraints such a limited time, absence of key information, or scarce resources. Improvements in the quality of decisions can be developed through the use of the scientifically oriented tools and procedures such as operations research and decision trees.

A school system may be conceptualizatized as a cluster of decision points. What differentiates decision making at the top level from other levels is the scope, strategic nature, and exceptionality of the choices that must be made. Barnard noted that the "fine art of decision making" may include not making a decision that others should or deciding upon questions that are not pertinent.

Competencies of administrative decision makers may be enhanced by designing structures that clarify decision responsibilities, providing access to data and other support services, training personnel in the art and science of decision making, developing skills in group decision-making activities such as having brainstorms, developing sensitivity to political and other similar factors in the process, and frequent evaluation of the consequences of previous decisions.

NOTES

1. Harold Bierman, Jr. et al., *Quantitative Analysis for Business Decisions,* 5th ed., Homewood, Ill.: Irwin, 1977, p. 3.
2. See Peter M. Blau and W. Richard Scott, *Formal Organizations,* San Francisco: Chandler, 1962, pp. 1–26.
3. Ibid., p. 3.
4. Ibid., p. 2.
5. Max Weber, *The Theory of Social and Economic Organization,* A. M. Henderson and Talcott Parsons, trans., and Talcott Parsons, ed., Glencoe, Ill.: Free Press and Falcon's Wing Press, 1947.
6. Adapted from R. H. Hall, "Concept of Bureaucracy: An Empirical Assessment," *American Journal of Sociology,* July 1969, p. 33.
7. Blau and Scott, op. cit., p. 33.
8. Ibid., pp. 34–35.
9. Ibid., p. 8.
10. Herbert A. Simon, *Administrative Behavior,* 2nd ed., New York: Macmillan, 1957, pp. 1–11.
11. W. H. Newman and E. K. Warren, *The Process of Management,* 4th ed., Englewood Cliffs, N.J.: Prentice-Hall, 1977, p. 20.
12. D. E. McFarland, *Management Principles and Practices,* New York: Macmillan, 1958, p. 165.
13. Albert Lepawsky, *Administration,* New York: Knopf, 1955, p. 333.
14. Simon, op. cit., p. 125.
15. Chester I. Barnard, *The Functions of the Executive,* Cambridge, Mass: Harvard University Press, 1938, p. 184.
16. Blau and Scott, op. cit., p. 30.
17. Simon, op. cit., p. 148.
18. Herbert A. Simon, *The New Science of Management Decision,* New York: Harper & Row, 1960, p. 1.
19. J. T. Dorsey, Jr., "A Communication Model for Administration," *Administrative Science Quarterly,* December 1957, p. 309.
20. W. H. Newman and E. K. Warren, op. cit., pp. 225–432.
21. Simon, op. cit.
22. Dorsey, op. cit.
23. M. Pfiffner and F. P. Sherwood, *Administrative Organization,* Englewood Cliffs, N.J.: Prentice-Hall, 1960, p. 309.
24. R. A. Johnson et al., *The Theory and Management of Systems,* 2nd ed., New York: McGraw-Hill, 1967, p. 281.
25. A. R. Oxenfeldt et al., *A Basic Approach to Executive Decision Making,* New York: AMACON (American Management Association), 1978, p. 2.
26. D. W. Taylor, "Decision Making and Problem Solving," in J. G. March, ed., *Handbook of Organizations,* Chicago: Rand McNally, 1965, pp. 48–86.

27. John Dewey, *How We Think,* Boston: Heath, 1933, rev. ed., pp. 106–116. (Originally published in 1910.)
28. Herbert A. Simon, op. cit., pp. 2–4.
29. Ibid.
30. Newman and Kirby, op. cit., p. 347.
31. Ibid., p. 230.
32. Ibid., pp. 249–253.

33. Newman and Warren, op. cit., p. 266.
34. Simon, op. cit., pp. 5–26.
35. Oxenfeldt et al., op. cit., p. 31.
31. Ibid., p. 56.
36. Harold Bierman, Jr. et al., op. cit., p. 74.
37. Oxenfeldt et al., op. cit., p. 2.
38. Chester I. Barnard, op. cit., p. 194.

CHAPTER REVIEW QUESTIONS

1. What is an organization?
2. Why did Weber develop his theory of bureaucracy?
3. What were the essential elements of a bureaucratic organization from Weber's point of view?
4. What were the major criticisms of Weber's organizational theory?
5. Differentiate between each of the following concepts: authority, power, and persuasion.
6. Why is there no absolute and optimum number of persons who can be supervised effectively by an administrator?
7. What are the sources of conflict that can arise between staff personnel and line administrators? How can they be avoided or minimized?
8. What is meant by informal organization? Can it exist in school systems? Justify your position.
9. What are the essential elements in the decision-making process?
10. How do programmed decisions differ from nonprogrammed ones?
11. In what ways are creativity, problem solving, and thinking related to decision making? How can these processes be differentiated?
12. Why is decision making an art?
13. What are the contributions of operations research to the improvement of decision making?
14. What are the limitations of the scientifically oriented approaches to decision making?
15. How can decision making in educational administration be improved?

SELECTED REFERENCES

Bierman, Harold, Jr., Bonini, Charles P., and Hausman, Warren H., *Quantitative Analysis for Business Decisions,* Homewood, Ill: Irwin, 1977, chap. 1.
Blau, Peter M., and Scott, W. Richard, *Formal Organizations,* San Francisco: Chandler, 1962, chaps. 1–4.
Newman, William H., and Warren, E. Kirby, *The Process of Management,* 4th ed., Englewood Cliffs, N.J.: Prentice-Hall, 1977, chaps. 1–6; 11–14.
Oxenfeldt, Alfred R., Miller, David W., and Dickinson, Roger A., *A Basic Approach to Executive Decision Making,* New York: AMACON, 1978, 229 pp.
Taylor, D. W., "Decision Making and Problem Solving," in J. G. March, ed., *Handbook of Organizations,* Chicago: Rand McNally, 1965, pp. 48–86.

3

LEADERSHIP DIMENSIONS OF EDUCATIONAL ADMINISTRATION: A REVIEW OF HUMAN BEHAVIOR, COMMUNICATIONS, AND CONFLICT IN ORGANIZATIONS

The previous chapter introduced the basic concepts of formal organizations and then analyzed the nature of the decision-making process in the organizational context. There are many perceptions of management as well as organizations. Those in business management place a high priority on the decision process and only belatedly have come to appreciate fully the importance of social processes related to human factors within an organization. Those in educational management granted a higher priority to the understanding of the leadership processes because they are so important to the comprehension and motivation of the human factors in organizations and very belatedly demonstrated concern for the improvement of the decision-making process in educational institutions.

The holistic approach to the study of educational administration dominates the writing of this book and therefore no effort will be made to suggest that one administrative process is *the* most important. The holistic management position is that all processes are important and effectiveness in educational administration can-

not be attained by emphasizing one above all others. Educational administration is an art that demands the judicious blending of each of the fundamental processes, at the appropriate time and situation, to make the most productive use of resources essential to the realization of organization objectives.

The organization may be perceived as a structured social system as well as a structured decision-making mechanism noted earlier. To declare that a social system prevails within an organization means that there are complex sets of human interactions within it that were determined, in some measure, by the act of organizing and, vice versa, influenced, albeit unintentionally, human behavior patterns not contemplated when the initial organizational structure was designed. The latter suggests the complex nature as well as the unpredictability of human behavior in organizations. In addition, the concept of a social system implies that there are psychological and sociological factors operative within the organization as well as the structural and economic factors.

There is a symbiotic relationship between

people and organizations, that is, organizations need people even though the most sophisticated technology may be available and people need organizations to fulfill their aspirations. Sometimes this becomes a love–hate relationship, but the mutuality of interests and/or needs is a fact of life.

This chapter focuses on human factors, their characteristics and behaviors in the organization. Leadership is a people phenonemon by and large. It is a set of behaviors that challenges administrative performance as few others can. How well an administrator understands and is able to work with the human side of the organization will determine to a large degree success in reaching goals, delivering essential services in an efficient manner, and gaining community acceptance.

EMERGENCE OF THE RECOGNITION OF HUMAN FACTORS IN ORGANIZATIONS

Profit-making corporations at first tended to view persons employed as a means or as specialized resources. Weber designed the bureaucratic structure to overcome the shortcomings of human factors. Frederick W. Taylor, the father of "scientific management," during the early 1900s recognized the importance of people in industries.[1] In fairness to his critics it was not a holistic view of humankind but rather a desire to increase the productive potential of employees, that is, the perception of people as efficient and productive resources.

An early reaction to the seemingly mechanistic interpretation of organizations by Weber and the impersonal perceptions of the human factors therein by Fayol and Taylor came from Mary Parker Follett. She was among the first to speak out on the dignity and value of satisfied workers which helped lay the groundwork for organizational behavior as an interdisciplinary science.[2] Her influence and contributions, which some consider to be on a par with those of Florence Nightingale and Marie Curie, were publicized through a series of speeches on the growing professionalization of business management and the significance of human factors therein.

The Hawthorne Experiments and Organizational Behavior

The term *behavioral science* is often used to describe social science concerns for understanding and projecting why people behave the way they do. As Davis indicated, "It has been said that the formal organization view sees 'organizations without people' while behaviorists speak of 'people without organizations.' "[3] But no organization can be created or exist without persons and it is very difficult, if not impossible, for people to pursue complex and varied objectives without an organization of some sort. "Organizational behavior is the study and application of knowledge about how people act in organizations."[4] At one time the term *human relations* was preferred, but today organizational behavior is more commonly used to merge organizational theory together with human behavorial and/or social theories.

The works of Mayo and Roethlisberger during the 1920s and 1930s sparked the early interests in organizational behavior. It all began with the productivity studies at the Western Electric Company's Hawthorne plant located in Chicago. They were not designed to ascertain the impact of human relationships. They followed the traditions of the World War I research on productivity that focused usually on the impact of physiological fatigue and other physical conditions of work on worker productivity. As a consequence, research designs were based on manipulation of various environmental elements to ascertain their impacts on human productivity. To illustrate, they anticipated that as light levels were improved in the work area, productivity would increase accordingly. This occurred as assumed.

What surprised researchers was that as illumination levels were reduced, subsequently high production levels continued even when there was only the equivalent of bright moonlight on the work surfaces! The explanations for the productivity pehnomenon had to be in something other than environmental conditions in the work area or the physical conditions of the work force. This prompted some to speculate about social and psychological interactions among human resources.

There was a series of Western Electric studies. Some concentrated upon the relationship between economic incentives and productivity. One such research effort involved six women assembling electrical relays. They were asked to work at a comfortable pace rather than to race. Here again there were results that were expected but also some unanticipated.

The unexpected results prompted researchers to probe more completely the social and psychological factors that could impact upon human productivity. The six women, it was reasoned, may have been influenced by the special recognition resulting from selection as participants in an experiment. This special status could have elevated morale or positive job satisfactions that in turn increased productivity.

This led to the discovery of the existence of an informal work group or minisociety in a large corporation. The interactions among the work group members resulted in the formulation of unique value systems and special personal work rules unrelated to those prescribed by the formal organization. These mutually agreed-upon and informal work procedures or standards had a positive impact upon work performance and productivity.

To learn more about the psychological forces in the work place, Western Electric in 1927 turned to Harvard professors Elton Mayo, an industrial psychologist, and F. J. Roethlisberger, a sociologist. They designed additional research projects to measure the impact of rest pauses, lunch breaks, and length of the work day and work week upon productivity. The locale was the bank wiring room where workers attached and soldered wires in rows (or "banks") to a telephone switchboard component. These new studies lasted more than five years and the summation of results and conclusions were not published until 1939.[5]

In the bank wiring room experiments physical conditions were varied and another variable consisting of a series of wage incentives was added. About the time wage incentives were added the nation moved into the Great Depression of the 1930s. It was assumed that employees would work harder if wage incentives were available. In the value system of the workers a primary concern during the early years of this depression was job security. This was translated into worker behavior that maintained rather than increased production levels in the face of whatever wage incentives management had to offer.

The informal social system that restricted output in the face of positive changes in work conditions and wage incentives demonstrated anew the strength of worker group-value systems not consistent with the formal organization's plans and designs. It reconfirmed that persons in continuous and close contact create informal social structures that may influence their productive behavior more than management incentives or working conditions alone.[6]

The Western Electric Company experiments stimulated further investigations of human behavior in formal organizations. They helped generate a new perception of management as a social process of influencing human behavior in organizations rather than a mechanical process of manipulating impersonal production factors. These experiments may be classic illustrations of serendipity, that is, where the search starts for one thing only to discover another.

The experiments gave birth to the term *Hawthorne effect*, which implies changes resulting from the special attention or recognition given to those involved rather than from modification or introduction of other factors in the experiment.

Barnard and the Cooperative System

During the late 1930s, Chester I. Barnard viewed the organization as a system composed of human beings working cooperatively to reach goals, rather than as a formally structured impersonal mechanism.[7] The system was held together and activities coordinated by the commitment of people desirous of making a contribution toward the attainment of goals. He was among the first to recognize that within every complex organization there were smaller operating groups in interaction that often led to the creation of informal working relationships and standards within the formal organization. The informal groups were basically unpredictable, unanticipated from management designs, and less structured than the formal organization.

Barnard placed great stress on the importance of leadership in management of institutions and saw cooperation as the basis for creative activities within the organization. He recognized leadership as being influenced by such variables as the individual, social groupings, and conditions surrounding the organization.

HUMAN NATURE, NEEDS, VALUES, AND MOTIVATION

The perceptions of the basic nature of man vary with the experiences of those addressing this controversial topic. Novels have been written about the best and the worst of human qualities. Machiavelli in *The Prince* (1515) based his recommendations on how to govern on the fundamental qualities of human behavior. He pictured man as rebellious, selfish, greedy, and uncooperative who therefore had to be controlled by whatever means by those seeking power or responsible for maintaining order in a society. The philosopher Herbert Spencer adapted Darwin's law of natural selection and declared that even among humans the fittest survive. The fittest were characterized by aggressiveness, the urge to dominate, and a drive to acquire material possessions; all of which makes conflict within organizations unavoidable. There is an old viewpoint that holds that people will prey upon others for personal gain and such predatory urges must be restrained by social mandates. Something more than an appeal to self-control or the application of fairness and rationality is needed to develop effective and productive working relationships within an organization. This is the conception of man as governed primarily by strong emotions and selfish appetites rather than by reason

and social concerns. It is an adaptation of the original sin and innate depravity of mankind.

It was indicated in the previous chapter that Weber conceptualized the bureaucratic form of organization to overcome human limitations such as the propensity toward capriciousness, unpredictability, and disorganization. The more recently developed organization theories are based on exceptions to this pessimistic view of human behavior. They start with the premise that it is natural for human beings to be self-motivated and self-controlled, although these qualities may be compromised if the situation prevents their full expression. In short, a person's behavioral reactions are influenced by the treatment received from others.

McGregor went a step further and argued that how an administrator perceives and interacts with organizational personnel relates closely to assumptions about the fundamental nature of humankind. The two contradictory views of human behavioral propensities were catagorized in a Theory X and a Theory Y.[8] Theory X assumes that people dislike and will avoid work, shirk responsibilities whenever they can, are innately lazy, lack creativity, are unreliable, treasure security above all else, are inclined to be ruthless, are ungrateful, and yearn for external direction. This is consistent with Calvin's position on the innate depravity of man. The management orientation of the executive who implicitly or openly embraces the worst interpretations of human behavioral propensities is in careful control over the work force based on rigid structuring of all operations, operating "by the book," and emphasis on respect for authority. There would be frequent supervision as a control mechanism, publishing of demands for adherence to detailed rules and regulations, rigid compliance with standard operating procedures, and frequent threats of firing or demotion to motivate the recalcitrant. The Theory X-oriented administrator may disavow complete acceptance but would "have to admit that Machiavelli had some good ideas." Institutionalized authority of the Weberian bureaucracy would be the preferred and trusted organizational model.

In contrast, Theory Y starts with basic assumptions that people find work as natural as play; prefer constructive work experiences to doing nothing (not inherently lazy); prefer and seek to establish cooperative social relationships; are capable of self-direction; exhibit self-control; are naturally creative; and strive for excellence. Under proper conditions, it is argued, most seek greater responsibility and new challenges as well as situations where their imagination, ingenuity, and creativity can come into play to attack organizational problems. The Theory Y administrator designs a formal structure and uses a leadership style that allows individuals greater freedom to act or to express themselves, places less emphasis on external supervision or controls, and motivates through encouragement and recognition for achievement rather than through threats and punishment.

In short, the Theory X set of assumptions leads to or justifies an autocratic approach to management, whereas Theory Y leads to a humanistic or democratic approach. "McGregor's argument was that management had been . . . following an outmoded set of assumptions about people because it adhered to Theory X when the facts are that most people are closer to the Theory Y set of assumptions."[9] It may be that traditional bureaucratic assumptions and administrative styles rather than the basic nature or behavioral propensities of people in organizations trigger lazy, indifferent, and intransigent reactions from employees.

Theory X and Theory Y may be based on extreme assumptions about characteristic human behavior in that an individual may not always be viewed as behaving at one extreme or another. A more realistic set of assumptions would be that not all people can be described under either Theory X or Theory Y. Even the most autocratic administrator laboring under the behavior assumptions of Theory X might have to admit, albeit grudgingly, that in the real world some personnel give evidence on occasion of a measure of reliability and internal motivation. Likewise, those who subscribe to the behavior assumptions that make up Theory Y would have to admit reluctantly that in the real world some people, during at least short periods of time, were known to display laziness or a loss of self-control. Therefore, administrative authority and control can be justified under Theory Y as well as Theory X to cope with unique personnel situations. It is frequency of use of external controls when working with people over an extended period of time that indicates whether the administrator is more likely to accept the assumptions in Theory X as opposed to those in Y. Some have suggested a middle ground set of assumptions about human behavior in organizations such as a Theory M (for middle) or Theory Z (to complete the alphabet).

Maslow provided another approach to understanding human behavior by recognizing human needs and priorities attached to fulfilling the hierarchy of needs. It starts with the implied assumption that there is a cause or reason behind human interactions. Behavior is influenced by a hierarchy of human needs ranging from the need to satisfy basic physiological urges, such as hunger and thirst, through self-actualization.[10]

Maslow postulated a human needs hierarchy based on five levels: basic physiological needs; safety and security demands; social affection and belonging desires; esteem and status striving; and self-actualization hopes. Satisfaction of physical needs is related to survival and may dominate behavior patterns under conditions of extreme hunger or prolonged periods of working without sleep. It is our good fortune to live in an affluent society and that most survival needs are satisfied at a relatively high level. The lowest level of needs in the hierarchy sets limits on human endurance or on the span of attention. Once physiological demands have been satisfied, then the second level of needs (safety and security) begins to assume dominance over behavior patterns. There are physical, economic, and psychological security demand dimensions. There are individual differences in the amount of protection required to eliminate concern from these factors to move to the next higher level of need satisfaction. Personnel worried about job security or economic survival may be less status conscious or concerned about self-expression. More subtle are the feelings of psychological security that may be related to an individual's confidence in coping with personal, social, and organizational challenges.

Although satisfaction of social needs and the feeling of belonging may occur primarily outside the work environment, affiliation with a particular organization may contribute to or facilitate their achievement as well. The fourth level in the hierarchy is related closely to the previous one. The desire for self-esteem and status is essential and the organization and work environment may have more to contribute here. No matter how low one's position in the organizational hierarchy, respect from others is important to morale and can influence productivity. People have been known to value titles and the status that goes with them over added pecuniary rewards. The highest level is the striving for self-actualization, self-expression, or personal fulfillment. This is the desire for a sense of personal accomplishment, a feeling of growth or "going somewhere," and a sense of independence or control over one's destiny.

As Davis indicated, "Although physiological needs can be oversupplied, the needs at the third, fourth, and fifth levels are substantially infinite."[11] According to Maslow, a satisfied need no longer motivates. Although there is just so much food one can eat or shelter one can enjoy, the threat or possibility of losing basic comforts may trigger behaviors inconsistent with professional standing. Thus, collective bargaining behavior or actions of professional educators during a strike may be more aggressive and unusual, particularly if economic deprivation or threats to job security are perceived by such persons. Threats, real or imagined, can unleash the worst even among persons with a previous history of exemplary professional conduct during other types of stress. This may be a warning as to the type of behavior that may be manifested when faculty position cutbacks become an economic necessity for the educational system.

Individual behavior in formal organizations is complex and defies precise description. Psychologists, psychiatrists, and other behavioral scientists have contributed much to increase our understanding of why people behave as they do. Such studies are characterized by vast unknowns and great unpredictability as to behavior patterns that may emerge. Every educator is prepared professionally to recognize and accept the fact of individual differences. Administrators must base their human relations strategies on the reality of individual differences within organizations; not everyone hears the same drummer. Each person's valuation of oneself transcends the economic or professional valuation of the person by the organization. Respect for human dignity should be a cornerstone of leadership styles adopted. Motivation strategies to be effective must be based on understanding individual differences, human dignity, recognition of the hierarchy of human needs, and that human behavior is caused whether or not what triggers particular behavior patterns is or is not known.

Motivation

How to motivate teachers and other personnel toward excellence in performance, acceptance of the educational objectives, and further professional growth and development is perhaps one of the most important leadership challenges facing an administrator. As indicated in prior paragraphs the motivation strategies preferred by an executive will be influenced by the perceptions of human nature and organizational behavior. The choice of rewards, recognition, reprimands, or punishments to motivate personnel help to project the leadership style of the administrator.

Given the fact of individual differences, not all personnel will be stimulated by a single strategy and not all will perceive the school situation the same way. The common perception that the power of economic rewards to motivate, in education, revolves around the use of "merit pay" to stimulate superior performance fails to recognize the power of the higher-order human needs. The work ethic that perceives work as something satisfying and essential was an important motivational force in the United States, but its influence over the work force "has been declining gradually since the

1930s."[12] The so-called pride of profession or pride of craftsmanship has lost much of its potency to competing value orientations, such as enjoyment of leisure, that grew out of the social changes in the years following World War II. Sensitivity to the newer work values within the culture, or perceptions of their employment situation as well as their life-style, is a key to the development of more effective motivational strategies.

Davis identified the four significant "motivational patterns" as "achievement," "affiliation," "competence," and "power" motivations.[13] The "achievement-motivated" are not likely to be "money hungry" and express a preference for situations or challenges that lead to personal growth or professional development. The 10 percent said to be achievement-motivated "work because of their desire for challenge, accomplishment, and service."[14]

The "affiliation-motivated" want to belong and be accepted by others and by the organization. Feelings others have about them are important and provide the drive or urge to relate effectively and frequently with other people. They are more likely to be motivated and tend to work harder when praised for cooperative spirit, positive attitudes, and concern for others. "Competence-motivated" employees seek job mastery and professional growth even to the point of slighting interpersonal relations on the job.[15] Excellence in the performance of professional responsibilities is expected from co-workers as well as themselves. As the term implies, the "power-motivated" seek influence or control status over persons and their work situation.

Maslow's model focused on a hierarchy of individual needs which motivates behavior as long as the need remains unfulfilled. Herzberg developed a model of motivational factors that also recognized the importance of human needs but in relationship to the work situation.[16] The Herzberg model was confined to two major elements: maintenance factors (or hygiene factors) and motivational factors. His approach to the study of motivation was to ask what conditions or events made a person feel good or bad about a job. There were factors within the work context that if not present precipitated feelings of dissatisfaction. These, according to Herzberg, had to be recognized and maintained (hence, the term *maintenance factors*) to reduce the probability of dissatisfaction even though they were not potent stimulators of desirable performance. Thus, if the work environment failed to reflect the value orientations important to workers or if personnel policies on promotions or fringe benefits were perceived negatively, it would be difficult to realize personnel satisfactions even in the face of other motivational efforts. The presence, as opposed to the absence of certain conditions noted above, of other conditions that actually build motivation or satisfaction were called "motivational factors" by Herzberg. These were the more usual or commonly recognized factors of achievement, status, opportunities for advancement, and so on. They are related to the higher level of needs in the Maslow hierarchy. Herzberg's "two-factor model is both supported and rejected by other analysts of motivation" with some stating it "is based on one factor along a continuum, rather than two factors."[17]

Another is the "expectancy model" of motivation developed by Vroom.[18] It is strongly individual-psychology-oriented and stresses intrinsic or internal drives as mainsprings of motivation. It views motivation as the product of how strongly one desires something and one's perception of the probability that certain strategies or instrumentalities are likely to fulfill those desires. The intensity of the personal desire was called "valence" by Vroom, and the achievement probability by pursuing a given vehicle or strategy was identified as the "expectancy." This model implies that motivation works best when based on internal drives or desires of persons and when it enhances the "expectancy," or likely outcome, of pursuing a given course of action. To illustrate, a professional's desire for promotion to an administrative or supervisory position (valence) may be increased further by a superior's encouragement to file an application for consideration for such a position. The use of rewards to make possible the completion of a preparation program is further enhancement of the "expect-ancy" side of the motivation equation. Self-appraisal of abilities may temper or intensify the desire. All motivation has a measure of in-tensity or desire that may be satisfied through pursuit of a given strategy or direction. Motiva-tion seeks to arouse and to channel productive efforts within an organization.

Management - by - objectives - and - results (MBO/R) may be a part of a personal motiva-tion strategy as well. A basic assumption is that teachers and administrators may be motivated through an opportunity to work together to-ward professional goals defined jointly and mu-tually agreed upon. Its appeal will be primarily to the achievement-motivated personnel and will work best in situations where the higher order of human needs satisfactions is the great-est.

In education, motivation is readily recog-nized as a most important element in instruc-tional strategies at the classroom level. Its im-portance in educational administration is only beginning to be understood and applied to pro-fessional and other adult employees. Teachers motivate learners through a variety of strate-gies based on understanding of a learner's growth and development pattern, individual ability differences, and of internal and external factors that may arouse and sustain the desire to learn more. These general principles may be adapted to adult motivational strategies of the administrator working with teachers, supervi-sors, other administrators, and other adult workers. Recognition of the motivational value of intrinsic factors such as desire for achieve-ment or self-fulfillment is needed to balance what has been an overreliance on extrinsic motivators or factors external to the person and job satisfaction. What some call the "behavior modification" approach to motivation domi-nated the practices of administrators. It as-sumes that behavior finally adopted will be de-pendent upon the consequences experienced by the individual. Positive reinforcement from some external source encourages continuation of the behavior pattern. Negative reinforce-ment results in discontinuance and eventual ex-tinction of the undesirable behavior. Organiza-tional behavior modification is mechanistic in its orientation, often results in the use of auto-cratic management styles, and can be criticized for its overreliance on force to change behavior and for its manipulation of people. The condi-tioning approach to human learning in class-rooms evokes a similar negative appraisal.

LEADERSHIP IN EDUCATIONAL ADMINISTRATION

Leadership is a process of stimulating, develop-ing, and working with people within an organi-zation. It is a human-oriented process and focuses upon personnel motivation, human re-lationships or social interactions, interpersonal communications, organizational climate, inter-personal conflicts, personal growth and devel-opment, and enhancement of the productivity of human factors in general. Leadership takes place in an organizational context and, there-fore, must be concerned with the realization of objectives, determining new directions, deliv-ering quality educational services, implement-ing essential change, and so on, as well as the satisfactions and dissatisfactions of personnel and related human activities.

Educational leadership is a highly praised and sought after status. Some consider educa-tional leadership and administration as synony-mous, that is, one and the same thing. The ho-listic approach to administration taken in this volume recognizes the tremendous importance and impact of leadership, but it is only one of many such important processes in the adminis-tration of social organizations.

Unfortunately, there exists no general agree-ment as to what the term means, how leader-ship is best demonstrated, how one is prepared best to become a leader, or what special compe-tencies are demanded of those who would be leaders in educational institutions. Some per-ceive the leader as a direction setter, that is, "one who knows where he/she is going" or, better, is able to get an organization moving productively once again toward relevant goals and objectives. Unfortunately, not all goal-oriented executives exhibit the full range of talents to deserve recognition as leaders. Equating leadership with direction setting may result in preoccupation with the ability to articulate or pursue goals at the expense of understanding, motivating, and working with people. It is only one of many competencies required for leadership stature.

Closely related is the perception of the leader as the "great organizer." Another is the picture of the leader as one "who gets things done." Finally, the leader may be defined as the person who knows what needs to be changed and does it. The change agent role of the administrator is reviewed more completely in another chapter.

The point being made is that leadership is complex and multidimensional. There are many other unidimensional definitions of leadership that may produce misperceptions of the nature of the process and competencies demanded. Leadership is first of all a process that focuses on people and can be measured by its impact on organizational behavior. It includes helping people within an organization gain a new sense of direction where this is lacking or unrealistic, creating the kinds of structural patterns that will enhance the productivity of personnel, motivating people to higher performance levels, and so on.

Separating research and facts from the romance and rhetoric that surround leadership as a concept is a difficult task. It has been perceived by various writers as (1) a set of personality traits (symbolic leadership); (2) a status, title, or position recognized in the formal org chart (formal or titular leadership); and (3) a function or role performed in an organized group or setting (functional leadership). These will be examined before the analysis of leadership theories, styles, and measures of effectiveness.

Symbolic Leadership Perceptions

Among the oldest and more persistent perceptions is the highly romanticized view of the leader as one with well-developed and critical "leadership personality traits." It is reinforced by clichés such as "leaders are born, not made." Leadership attributes are assumed to include a commanding voice and personal appearance, resolute and/or "attractive" personality, warm and sincere demeanor, and so on. Honesty, integrity, and perseverance are included as well. This perception is sometimes called "charismatic leadership" for its emphasis upon the charisma alleged to emanate from the person. It grew out of trait psychology that sought to define the gifts or special endowments of leaders. The special or related leadership traits such as dependability, enthusiasm, and forcefulness were seldom well defined or capable of precise measurement.

Impressive physical size is often confused with leadership. Thus, a tall and muscular stature was often considered to be important in the selection of someone for an educational leadership position such as the principalship of the secondary school. There is no evidence to support the contention that height, girth, or any other physical dimension have anything to do with leadership capabilities. Someone of relatively short stature such as Napoleon and someone fairly tall such as Lincoln succeeded in gaining leadership image in history.

Another myth is based on gender that made leadership a predominately male preserve. Women in administrative and other positions have demonstrated effective leadership behavior to match the best of male counterparts in similar organizations.

The educational leadership search, according to the symbolic or charismatic point of view, places the focus on those with desirable physical and personality traits. More than 50 years of research refute the contention that leadership is primarily a matter of physical characteristics, personal appearance, or personality qualities. A review of the findings in over 100 studies leads to the generalization that only about 5 percent of human traits reported to be related in some way to leadership were commonly reported in four or more of these studies.

Some argue that the romantic concept of the leader as a person endowed with almost magical attributes can be traced to a longing for security.[19] The leader is idealized as a prestige figure with unusual powers or abilities and with none of the faults or shortcomings found in ordinary people. The leader becomes kind of a "knight on a white horse" and is depicted as being larger in physical size, with great strength and endurance, more intelligent, more mature, and, in general, more impressive than you or I or any followers. The leader in fact becomes a symbol of strength and security.

Charismatic conceptions of leadership are more likely to emerge where actual day-by-day interactions between "followers" and the symbolic leader are few and far between. Personal interaction is limited or discussions of vital issues infrequent because the distance, in a physical and functional sense, between the people and the leader is very great. For example, the president of a large nation or a king seldom, if ever, can find time for close personal or frequent direct contact with people of the nation. The media seeks to bridge the gap, but its success is limited by the availability of the person as well. The distant, but necessary, leader becomes more symbolic than reality, particularly where information surrounding the person and office is controlled carefully. There are case histories where the image of the leader as one endowed with unsual and vital characteristics, if not infallibility, was developed and perpetuated by revealing to the public only those qualities of the symbolic leader that would reinforce the image.

The myth of the great qualities of the distant or inaccessible leader can be exploded or at least threatened by increasing intimate contacts or not processing information released about such a leader. The image makers whose job it is to communicate only the best attributes endeavor to prevent that situation, but are not always successful when faced with persistent investigative reporters.

The superintendent in a very large school district may find it difficult, if not impossible, to have a close and continuing personal contact with large numbers of teachers, principals, parents, or the community as a whole. It may be necessary to project the image and capabilities desired through a coordinated program of television appearances, other media releases, and special speeches before professional groups of teachers and administrators. The image of an educational leader may be created and projected with the assistance of the "image makers" and the media. This has always been easier to speculate about than to achieve.

Formal or Titular Leadership Perceptions

Leadership may be related to a position in the hierarchy whence it is assumed to emanate. The person and position are confused as one and the same. *Formal, titular, status,* or *hierarchical* leader are interchangeable terms. The authority or influence of the person may be lost or at least compromised when the title, position, or office is abdicated. The replacement then assumes the mantle of leadership.

There are many administrative positions in the hierarchy, including the superintendency and the principalships, which are recognized as educational leadership posts. Occupancy is no guarantee that the incumbent will prove to be a functional leader. Nonetheless, the leadership potential of the person occupying legitimately such recognized positions is far greater than for persons not holding such positions. In other words, there is value to such organizing if special platforms are created that can facilitate the performance of leadership responsibilities. Teachers join professional associations and seek election to their offices to acquire a platform from which to project leadership capabilities or to influence the formulation of plans and programs.

Although there is some justification for structuring educational organizations with potential leadership platforms, there exists the danger that highly directive behavior from such positions could stifle the emergence of true leadership talents elsewhere in the system.

Functional Leadership Perceptions

Leadership, according to the functional interpretation of it, emerges in a group context and is a set of functions essential to the operation and productivity of organized groups. Stogdill defined leadership "as a process of influencing the activities of an organized group in the tasks of goal setting and goal achieving."[20] Others add group maintenance as a third responsibility. House perceived leadership as a function that generates a greater desire for goal attainment and also clarifies the strategies or "paths" most likely to lead to goal realization.[21] The "path-goal model of leadership" is consistent with Stogdill's interpretation but adds a motivation dimension, that is, places a special responsibility upon the leader to connect organizational rewards with the production of the goals and paths generated to attain them. It bears a kinship as well to Vroom's "expectancy model" discussed previously under motivation.

Fiedler went further and related leader effectiveness with changing demands and performance levels of groups. In other words, appraisal of a leader is based not upon what personality attributes are present or missing, but rather upon how one functions and contributes to the various needs of a group. Fiedler's Contingency Theory of Leadership Effectiveness, or the Contingency Model of Leadership, focuses upon leader–group relations and the situation facing the group.[22] The situation confronting the leader and the group defines the leader's contributions as well as the leadership style as most likely to maximize group performance and achievements. The leadership style could be relationship-oriented, where maintaining good interpersonal relations with group members was deemed most important. It could also be task-oriented, where the emphasis is placed upon successful task completion rather than on smooth personal relationships. Whether a relationship-oriented or a task-oriented leader was effective was contingent upon the work situation. As situations change so too must the orientations change if leader effectiveness is to be maintained. This helps to explain why there is no one leadership approach that is effective in any and all situations. The Contingency Theory postulates dynamic interaction among leadership style, group task situations, and group productivity.

In addition to leader–member relations and how well or how poorly group tasks are defined in terms of outcomes expected and strategies to be utilized, the leader's power to influence from the position may also impact upon effectiveness. Thus, a leader with little personal influence with group members or limited, or no, support from the organization's infrastructure (other administrative or policy positions) would be at a disadvantage in fulfilling objectives when compared with another leader with considerable group influence and stronger support. The major concepts of leader–group member relations, task structure, and leader position power are conceptually and dynamically interrelated in the realization of group or organization objectives as well as their productivity.

The prevailing view today within the behavioral sciences is that leadership is a function or role within a social system and is heavily influenced by a system of interpersonal relations. To better comprehend functional or operational leadership, it is essential to analyze the nature and functioning of the organized group with its members, role differentiations, and changing needs. In other words, leadership is better understood when analyzed in terms of human social behavior in organized settings.

The functional concept assumes that leader roles and effective behavior can be learned. That which is to be learned by superintendents and principals seeking to develop leadership competencies is the dynamics of human social behavior sometimes called "group dynamics." Educational administrators interact with a variety of groups. The board of education is one, the PTA another. There are professional as well as lay groups. The more complex the school community, the more varied and more demanding are the group leadership roles. It is through a better understanding of the nature and functions of groups such as group member behaviors, the variety of roles within a group, and the dynamics of group interchanges that one can better understand the nature of the leadership process and competencies required to perform effectively as a leader.

The Nature of Groups

The meeting or conference occupies much of an administrator's time schedule. Bringing together those likely to be affected by the implementation of a plan, a decision, or a series of special problems is a basic strategy for an administrator who must with and through others realize the objectives of the organization. Sociologists and social psychologists (or behavioral scientists) have devoted considerable study to group creation, group behaviors, group productivity, and, in general, the dynamic interplay of social forces within groups. The meeting or conference may be perceived as special purpose or general and continuing small group situations. The effectiveness or success of an educational administrator may be influenced to a considerable degree by how well or poorly the meetings (small group situations) are planned and whether they are productive or a waste of everyone's time.

A group is a cluster of any two or more persons in social interaction and who share a common purpose or commitment. It may emerge formally through a legislative act or by request of another legitimate authority to bring together a group as well as through informal means. Through the face-to-face interactions, or group dynamics, the group members may arrive at commonly defined goals and decide to act in a unified manner toward a specific situation or toward the environment in general. A group is more than a collection of individuals in physical proximity. Witness the so-called elevator behavior of people being conveyed to different floors. The crowded elevator demands that all be in very close physical proximity, but few if any look at each other, speak, or do any more than stare at the floor arrival indicators. Unless there was interaction prior to entering there is not likely to be social interaction in the elevator. Likewise, a mass in a crowded air terminal does not become a group until its members perceive common interests and begin to interact. Groups have special personalities and unique properties that can be measured. Hemphill described ten characteristics of a group as (1) size; (2) viscidity (the degree to which group functions as a unit); (3) homogeneity

(similarities in age, sex, preparation, etc.); (4) flexibility (how rigidly group rules are enforced); (5) stability; (6) permeability (how easy or difficult it is to accept new members); (7) polarization (the degree to which a group is able to focus on a single goal); (8) autonomy (the degree to which the group is independent in its action from other and larger groups); (9) intimacy (how well group members know one another); and (10) control (the degree to which the group restricts the freedom of member behavior).[23]

Cartwright and Lippitt observed that groups are the inevitable result of human propensities, are ubiquitous, "mobilize powerful forces which produce effects of utmost importance to individuals," "produce both good and bad consequences," can be understood better through knowledge of group dynamics, and may generate subgroups.[24]

Group Roles and Behaviors

Once created, groups tend to organize and a differentiation of member roles based on functions or other needs begins to emerge. It is incumbent upon educational administrators to sharpen their observational skills and special sensitivities to note the various roles played by group members while attacking group tasks in committee, conference, or other meetings. Persons, knowingly or otherwise, may play any one or more of the following roles that may facilitate or impede group progress:[25]

1. "Group Task Roles"—(a) initiator–contributor; (b) information seeker; (c) opinion seeker (seeks value rather than facts clarification); (d) information giver; (e) opinion giver; (f) elaborator; (g) coordinator; (h) orientor (defines or questions group's directions); (i) energizer; (j) evaluator–critic; (k) procedural technician (expedites procedures and activities); (l) recorder.
2. "Group Building and Maintenance Roles"— (a) encourager; (b) harmonizer; (c) compromiser; (d) gatekeeper and expediter (keeps communication channels open and people talking); (e) standard setter or ego ideal (proposes standards for group achieve-

ments); (f) group observer and commentator (expresses and evaluates group functioning); (g) follower (follows others passively).

3. "Individual Roles"—(a) aggressor; (b) blocker; (c) recognition seeker; (d) self-confessor (uses group to express personal nongroup-created feelings); (e) playboy (shows off lack of group involvement); (f) denominator; (g) help seeker (seeks sympathy response from group); (h) special interest pleader.

The following were identified as characteristics of group process development and indications of group maturity and increased productivity:

1. Special training in human relations techniques to help make leaders and others more sensitive to individual and group needs.
2. The group becomes more sensitive to needs of individuals.
3. The individual begins to share in setting group goals, which in turn impacts on his/her own development.
4. Expressions of individual differences begin to increase in permissive environments rather than in those characterized as autocratic or where manipulation of persons is countenanced.
5. Individual significance is enhanced where decision making by consensus is practiced.
6. In mature groups the individual is delegated responsibility and authority which enhance individual feelings of independence, growth, and improvement.
7. Individual contributions to group operations increase in range and frequency.
8. Individual action and responsibility are stimulated through shared decision making in group situations.
9. Where leadership skills are perceived by group members to be acquired rather than inherited.[26]

Groups (be they committees, cabinets, small conferences, or other types of small meetings) vary in maturity and productivity. A not infrequent complaint is the time spent in various meetings (group situations) could be better ap-

plied elsewhere, that "committees keep minutes and waste hours," or that little of relevance and value seems to come out of committee deliberations. These and other complaints are indicators that point to a need to study group dynamics and the design of more productive procedures or operations for such groups. Group dynamics skills can be acquired to increase effectiveness of groups, and techniques are available to resolve various types of group problems. A group fails to function effectively without something relevant to accomplish, without clarification of expectations from group deliberations, without resources to attack responsibilities, and without some assurance that recommendations that may be submitted will make some difference. The three most common group operational and image problems are (1) conflict within or with external sources (brought about by frustrations from assignment of impossible tasks, conflicting interests, the use of the group by some to acquire status, etc.); (2) apathy (fostered by preoccupation with unimportant issues, inadequate procedures, a feeling of powerlessness, etc.); and (3) inadequate decision-making procedures and/or authority.[27] Group problems may be reduced or resolved through objective diagnosis, feedback of the diagnosis to its members, special group dynamics training sessions where necessary, and other strategies. Special competencies in forming effective working or social groups, interacting with groups, sensing the level of group productivity, and diagnosing and resolving group operations problems are essential for educational administrators.

The Leader, the Group, and the Situation

The leader may serve as the focal point for the creation of an organized group. To illustrate, new religious groups emerge (which some may label as cults in the early group formation phase) through a commitment to someone recognized as a prophet or of higher religious leader status, as well as through acceptance of a unique doctrine or special ways of religious worship. Also, new political parties may be created by clusters of people rallying around a well-known or powerful personality, as well as by endorsing policies and programs not embraced, or granted a lower priority, by established parties. Individual members will continue to accept leader- (or group-) determined constraints on activities and embrace significant changes in personal life-styles as long as the leader's behavior, programs, and promises are perceived (with or without hard evidence to support such perceptions) as means for enhancing the individual's needs and personal priorities of the moment. Likewise, the leader and the group may be abandoned when it is perceived that neither offer any further hope of satisfying an existing priority of real or imagined personal needs. Where the leader and group demands include a heavy emotional commitment, individual severance of such leader and group ties can be a wrenching experience.

Leadership is a group phenomenon. It is a unique role of special importance to the formal and informal organization and operation of groups. To illustrate, even the simple task of ordered group discussions demands recognition of someone with legitimate authority to play the role of determining who shall speak first and the order of other speakers in situations where many desire to contribute ideas. Likewise, actions agreed upon by a group are not self-executing and usually demand that someone assume leadership for the execution of group decisions. There are other specialized functions that a leader may be asked to perform in behalf of the group.

A person is selected to perform the leadership role because of possessing the set of sensitivities, insights, or personal qualities the group may require for realization of group objectives and decisions. At one time it may be special knowledge about school finance, at another it may be sensitivity to and skills in intergroup (race or religous) relations, and still another it may be the intellectual or professional qualities related to curriculum and learning that the group determines is essential for the success of the system. The leader is selected and followed because of being capable to achieve what the followers need or want. A leader successful in one community with a unique set of educational needs may not experience similar success when moved to another with a markedly different set of educational problems, personnel, and value orientations. Changing the situation, or group's nature and purposes, results in a significant variation in leader characteristics desired that upsets all but the broadest interpretations of personal attributes.

The most effective leader (and, similarly, the most effective teacher) is one who knows and works best in the group situation. This has caused some to wonder if the leader is someone who seeing the group moving in a given direction hastens to get out in front. This is probably an oversimplification of the process, for as the path–goal leadership model suggests, a leader may be the person in the group who helps to identify and clarify goals as well as motivating group actions for realizing them.

Leadership Styles and Behavior

The preferred, and therefore frequent, patterns of behaviors, actions, and/or strategies define the leadership style. The style, or preferred way of "getting things done," adopted is influenced by many factors, with some reflecting the culture and the times, others the formal preparation and experiences of the leader, and still others perceptions and estimations of the priority and expectations within the leadership situation. A leadership position is one with some measure of power and authority to direct the most productive use of resources within an organization toward objectives. When, how, and to what degree what type of leadership force or persuasion is employed also reflect the basic style of the leader. Leadership behavior patterns may vary with the problems addressed, persons involved, and other dimensions of the situation. Styles may change, but there usually tends to be a dominant behavior pattern for individuals playing the leadership role.

Three common descriptors of leadership style are autocratic, democratic, and laissez faire, with "anarchic" preferred for the third one for the sake of semantic consistency.[28] A variant of these basic three is a fourth style called "manipulative leadership." Davis preferred the terms *autocratic, participative,* and *free-rein* to describe the three well-known leadership styles.[29]

In the *autocratic* style, the behavior of the person in the leadership role is characterized by a decided preference for centralized decision-making power in the leader and a reluctance to share position power and/or authority with others. Tasks are assigned without consultation (arbitrarily), and the leader expects acceptance without questioning. The leader is personal in praise and criticisms. There are few if any group-inspired actions. Threat and punishment are part of the negative orientation of the style, with the more benevolent autocrats granting rewards to those who followed orders well.

Adolf Hitler provided the rationale for the autocratic style in the following excerpt: "Nothing is possible unless one will commands, a will which has to be obeyed by others, beginning at the top and ending only at the very bottom." In his authoritarian state he believed that "everyone is proud to obey, because he knows: I will likewise be obeyed when I must take command."[30]

The *democratic* leadership style is a participative approach, meaning there is group as well as leader involvement in key policies and decision determination. Authority and power are shared and not confined to the top echelons. The leader is objective in praise and criticisms. Group activities are encouraged with the leader and group often working in concert and as a social unit. Those who are part of the organization are encouraged to submit ideas and "participate" in the pursuit of mutually agreed upon objectives. This is a style encouraged in most writings in educational administration, but it is not always clear how the style is best implemented.

The *anarchic* (laissez faire) or free-rein leadership style grants complete freedom of action to groups or individuals without leader participation or direction. The primary leadership role is to provide support services, such as materials and supplies, and to participate only when requested by the group. Leader comments on group activity are infrequent as further evidence of the minor or limited role played. Anarchy implies a "leaderless" social situation where groups are assumed to have the competencies and self-motivation to realize objectives. As Davis put it, "Free-rein leadership ignores the leader's contribution approximately in the same way that autocratic leadership ignores the group."[31]

Leader position power is not the same in all organizations or school communities. In some cases it may include substantial authority to control appointments, expend resources, and dispense whatever rewards and punishments are part of the organization. In others the leader must first seek approval for the use of authority before it is exercised in specific situations. A leader may use any of the four approaches to direct or influence group productivity depending upon organizational policies and cultural mores: (1) force or demands which can be backed up by control over resources and rewards sought by group members; (2) paternalism with appeals to group member loyalty to the organization and the leader; (3) bargaining; and (4) mutual means.[32]

In the *manipulative* or *pseudodemocratic* leadership style, leader desires are made known in advance and then a committee appointed, ostensibly to deliberate but primarily to approve what the leader wanted. Group members go through the motions consistent with participative management, but the end product is preordained and automatic endorsement expected. Obviously, this style is tolerated where the magnitude of leader position power is substantial and group experiences very limited. It may be particularly repugnant to many because in the manipulative leadership style "the group members not only follow orders but take full responsibility for creating the orders as well."[33]

Another approach to classifying leadership styles is based on conceptualization of administration as a social process that includes a structured hierarchy which defines subordinate and superordinate relationships (nomothetic dimension) and a set of individuals with unique personalities and need-dispositions (idiographic dimension).[34] The leader's propensity to emphasize the institutional or system demands would identify such behavior as a *nomothetic* leadership style. It is a system-oriented pattern of behavior that tends to stress acceptance of the authority of those in the administrative hierarchy, operating within published rules and regulations, preserving the integrity of the organization, and pursuing objectives. Sanctions may be imposed upon group members to insure compliance with leader directives and organizational goals. The nomothetic leadership style is task-oriented, by and large, and places institutional operating integrity above the necessity for establishing pleasant working relationships and leader acceptance by members of the social system.

The *idiographic* leadership style, on the other hand, is more relationship-oriented, or person-oriented, with high priority in the leadership behavior pattern given to enhancing morale, human needs satisfactions, and individual development. This type of leadership behavior emphasizes opportunities within the organization for individual expression and self-fulfillment. Institutional demands do not overshadow or dominate human concerns. This orientation challenges organizational demands that are not congruent, or are inconsistent, with the value systems, needs, and predispositions of individuals and/or leader. One problem likely to be encountered is the possibility of idiographic role conflicts, that is, where individual or group need-dispositions are at variance or cross purposes with those of other persons and groups in the system. The greater the heterogeneity of personalities in the social system, the greater is the probability of personal conflicts and frustration level increase for the leader using this style.

The *transactional* leadership style represents a compromise between the extremes of the nomothetic and the idiographic. Productivity and maintaining the integrity of the system are important, but it is not always necessary to allow these institutional demands to ignore or distort individual personalities and feelings while pursuing efficiently the realization of goals. This leadership style would facilitate personal self-fulfillment of organization members through their acceptance of the challenge to increase productivity and recognition for contributions to the goal achievements. Some using this style may alternately stress the system demands at one time followed by personality concerns at another. A better resolution would be integration of personal needs and organizational demands.

Democratic School Administration or Leadership

Democratic school administration is a term preferred in education, whereas the field of business management uses the term *participative management*. Whether called democratic leadership or participative management, the style is based upon specific value orientations that emphasize group as well as leader participation in the formulation of operational policies and procedures for the organization.[35] The "climate of beliefs," or value orientations, which characterize democratic administrative behavior includes the following:[36]

1. Full, free, and open communication unfettered by hierarchical rank or authority.
2. Consensus seeking rather than coercion or compromise to cope with conflict.
3. Influence is based on special competence or knowledge rather than position, authority, or other status indicator.
4. Uninhibited expression of feelings by group members without fear of punishment for personal reactions or task-oriented responsibilities.
5. Biases in favor of people with acceptance of the belief that human conflict will occur in organizations and can be mediated.

The democratic leader accepts without ego involvement or personal distress the criticisms that may emanate from open and free group expressions. The reason: Criticism may be one means by which the organization can identify what must be changed if there is to be continued growth.

Policy formulation under democratic leadership includes all likely to be affected by it. This implies that teachers and other personnel deliberate with administrators to develop operational educational policies. There is a degree of similarity with collective bargaining concepts, but it is the administrative style rather than legal or collective demands from teacher associations that includes all professional personnel in certain kinds of decision making.

One misconception may be that this style precludes those in administrative positions from participating in the policy process. This is more characteristic of the anarchic or free-rein leadership style which limits superintendents and principals to support functions for the group that determines policies without them. Likewise, democratic leaders are neither silent nor indecisive until all votes are counted in the policy formulation process. Their special insights and information may contribute to the enhancement of policy determinations. The group interacts with but does not replace the administrative expert.

Long before the advent of educational collective bargaining that emerged during the 1960s teachers expressed the desire to be a part of the operational policymaking process, particularly in policies related to curriculum, discipline, salary schedules, and working conditions.[37] Studies made prior to the popularity of collective bargaining (i.e., during the 1940s and 1950s) reported that teachers with greater opportunity to participate actively and regularly in the operating policymaking process were more likely to be enthusiastic about their school organization than those with limited opportunity to participate. Through the democratic leadership style the talents of teachers and other personnel may be tapped. This leads some to describe this as the *creative* leadership style.

Benne summarized some benefits of democratic leadership as follows:[38] It promotes or enhances group productivity; it may forestall crises in group life and interactions; and group member personalities shaped by democratic participation in vital issues are more mature, more capable of objectivity, and less aggressive.

It is not easy to abandon an autocratic leadership style of long standing, for this demands a dramatic change in value orientations and long entrenched behavior patterns. The authoritarian person may have been driven to autocratic behavior to achieve security (personal) or because of a lack of confidence in the organization's personnel. The authority and title of office serve as a shield behind which may be hidden real or imagined personal shortcomings that might be revealed in open discussions. Some autocratic administrators are arrogant and domineering with subordinates, but exhibit meek and submissive behavior with board members, community leaders, and others perceived as superiors. The autocratic leader views the world as essentially friendless and therefore strives for more power and greater toughness while becoming more rigid in personal relationships (a Theory X adherent). There is a reluctance to delegate authority lest it be abused or used against the leader. Thus, anyone envisioning the world as populated with scheming incompetents would find it uncomfortable to play the role of a democratic leader.

In contrast, democratic behavior rests on the beliefs that professional personnel at all levels are competent, by and large; desire to improve the quality of the educational system; and know enough to do the right thing. Better professional preparation programs for teachers and administrators have made the democratic style more attractive as an alternative and more likely to meet with success.

Some teachers who have spent most of a professional career in which the autocratic or manipulative style predominated may question whether the democratic style can work. It takes time to develop maturity in group-oriented environments and to acquire the skills necessary to be a contributing group member. To compound matters, autocrats in the classroom claim to "understand" the similar behavior or style in administration and "enjoy" being told what to do or are spared "the waste of time" in committee deliberations. There is a tendency for those relatively inexperienced in committee work to legislate rather than deliberate on alternatives. The easy way to resolve a dilemma is "to make a rule." Decisions reached without adequate understanding of the many dimensions of a complex problem are questionable whether issued by an uninformed group or an uninformed autocrat.

Democratic leadership encourages group involvement in policy formulation. Execution or implementation of policies is another matter. Confusion may result unless a single person with the time and the resources necessary for the implementation is assigned such responsibilities. The status and titular leaders perform an essential organizational function when it comes time to execute policies arrived at through group interactions during democratic deliberations. Democratic school leadership does not imply, nor should it encourage, attempted execution or implementation of policies by all group members.

INDIVIDUAL BEHAVIOR, ORGANIZATIONAL BEHAVIOR, AND CONFLICT MANAGEMENT

People may behave as individuals, as members of a group interacting with others, or as persons with roles structured within a formal organization. The emphasis here is on the organizational behavior of individuals, which implies the performance of defined roles essential to the realization of organizational objectives. There are terms developed by sociologists and social psychologists that may facilitate the understanding of human behavior in an organizational or structured setting. The most frequently used and basic terms are:

1. *Position.* This means the location of a person (sometimes called an actor) within the structured or organized system of social relations. It is less a set of functions per se and more a placement in an organization or hierarchy.
2. *Expectation.* An evaluative standard applied to a position incumbent; a responsibility or obligation to perform placed upon a person in a given position in the organization. It is anticipatory in nature, that is, it is behavior that is "expected."

3. *Role.* A series of somewhat unified expectations applied to a position incumbent. An actor's role in a social system includes the obligations to perform attached to the position. The role places the actor in organizational perspective and with other role players in the social system.
4. *Incumbent.* A person or actor actually in a position at a given time.
5. *Alter Group.* A group of actors who, because of certain status or relationships, may define legitimately the role another actor is to play in the formal structure. This group may also be identified as "counterposition" or referent group.[39]

An organization as a social system defines the roles (sets of expectations) for all who hold positions. The formal interactions that follow are influenced by the configuration of positions and the expectations from those assigned to them.

A supervisor of instruction may perceive his/her professional roles in the school district as a social system. Teachers compose an alter group to the supervisor, are in frequent contact with the supervisor, and have their own perception of what the supervisor's roles should be. The general superintendent and the assistant superintendent for instruction probably helped draft the expectations for the position incumbent, but can be identified as yet another alter group for the supervisor. Principals interact with the supervisor and comprise a third referent group. Usually there are many referent groups for a given position incumbent with differing expectations (or interpretations) of roles to be played. For that and many other reasons there would be different appraisals of the supervisor's effectiveness.

Role occupancy makes individual behavior demands related to personal need-dispositions as well as to satisfaction of organizational objectives. Institutional obligations are labeled the nomothetic dimension and personal needs satisfactions labeled the idiographic dimension. These dimensions of human behavior in organizations enable the differentiation between effectiveness and efficiency.[40] Organizational behavior is deemed effective when it contributes to institutional goal attainment. Effectiveness is related to the institutional or nomothetic dimension. An effective actor, or person, may be productive but only at the expense of considerable stress and strain within the personality. Such behavior is judged inefficient, although effective, because of the personal or professional problems generated to fulfill institutional demands. Individual behavior within an organization is efficient if consistent with the need-dispositions of the position incumbent.

These concepts can contribute to a better explanation and understanding of morale and job satisfactions. It may be illustrated by a study by Bidwell of teacher conflicts and job satisfactions.[41] Dissatisfied teachers claimed they could not predict how their principal would react in a given situation, the administrator modified working procedures from day to day, and the principal held conflicting expectations of the teacher's role, particularly on what and how to teach. As a result the teachers were tense about relations with the administrator, and were confused as to what would be appropriate interactions with the principal. These feelings of tension and insecurity were generalized into dissatisfaction with their jobs and the school system in general, as well as with fellow teachers, pupils, and school patrons.

In contrast, satisfied teachers reported pleasant and secure relations with their principal. There was no difficulty in knowing what the expectations were for them nor in predicting how the principal would react to their teaching behavior. The superintendent and/or principal was perceived as behaving in a consistent fashion and in a manner that gave them advanced warning of impending changes that might affect teachers. They gave no evidence of tension related to job factors. Instead the feelings of security were generalized into satisfactions with the operation of the entire school system and their role in it.

A startling revelation in the study was that one administrator worked with both satisfied and dissatisfied teachers. The same administrative behavior precipitated feelings of security

and of tension, respectively, in two different groups of teachers in the same school. The conflicting role interpretations were related to contrary feelings related in some way to the same set of administrative behaviors. Bidwell concluded: "There is no doubt that a teacher's feeling of security or tension regarding his own behavior is very closely related to his view of proper behavior on part of the administrator."[42]

Organizational behavior is influenced by personal predispositions as well as by institutional expectations defined by the person or by the many alter groups. Levinson observed that "if the two sets of needs do not mesh, then a man has to fight himself and his organization, in addition to the work that must be done."[43]

Sources of Conflict

Where there are people, particularly from heterogeneous backgrounds and within complex or socially sensitive organizations, there will be conflict. It is the sign of the times and a test of the competencies of an educational administrator. The emphasis here will be on intraorganizational conflict rather the personal conflicts an individual must face in life situations outside of working responsibilities.

Knowing where intraorganizational conflicts are likely to occur should be among the early concerns in conflict management approaches. Conflicts have their roots in competing interests, differing perceptions, and unfulfilled desires. In general, they are more noticeable during times of rapid change in significant social values and in patterns of operation.

Newman and Warren identified "five typical sources" of conflict as:[44]

1. "Competition for Scarce Resources." Resources are essential to the fulfillment of responsibilities and achievement of goals. The probabilities of conflicts arising among workers or departments increases during periods of retrenchment or when new services are demanded without a corresponding increase in resources available to the organization.

2. "Built-in Conflicts." Organizations with many staff positions have a "built-in" conflict situation with line or operating personnel. Likewise, operational control may be designed to enhance product or service quality, but such organization features may also generate internal conflicts.

3. "Differences in Work Characteristics." Not all personnel have the same perception of what a system of education is all about or what the priorities should be. The differences in technology available and used may be one basis for increasing friction among divisions in a complex organization.

4. "Divergent Personal Values and Aims." Not all hear the same drummer or are motivated by the same needs satisfactions. Divergent views about where the organization should be going generate some of the more long-standing conflicts.

5. "Ambiguous Organization." Jurisdictional disputes take their rise in the lack of definition or clarity as to who should do what.

Getzels, Lipham, and Campbell focused more sharply on conflict in educational settings which were framed in their "administration as a social process context." They classified the sources of conflict as follows:[45]

1. "Conflict Between Cultural Values and Institutional Expectations." This goes beyond intraorganizational conflict noted earlier. It may be phrased as school-community disputes when the expectations for the school system appear to be inconsistent to some degree with the values held by some or all in the community or culture served. A school system may be caught in the middle of an intracommunity battle on sensitive social issues such as student busing to enhance integration.

2. "Conflict Between Role Expectations and Personality Dispositions." The teacher whose personality suggests an authoritarian approach to instructional procedures and student discipline may encounter conflict in significantly different school climates based on "more permissive" approaches to instruction and discipline or where team teaching and small and large group instructional organizational patterns prevail.

3. "Conflict Between Roles and Within Roles." This is likely to occur "when a role incumbent has to conform simultaneously to a number of expectations which are mutually exclusive, contradictory, or inconsistent so that the performance of one set of duties makes performance of another set impossible, or at least difficult."[46]

4. "Conflict Deriving from Personality Disorders." Such conflicts take their rise from within the individual personality rather than from other types of dislocations.

5. "Conflict in the Perception of Role Expectations." This is the classic situation where alter groups may have diverse perceptions with some or none concurring with those of the position incumbent.

The educational institution has unique public functions and relates to government agencies outside the community. Conflicts may arise between a school system and state or federal educational agencies. In addition, there are some unusual relationships between the school and persons in the community that can lead to misunderstandings or disputes. The teacher–parent conflict is not uncommon. There may be intraschool board disputes that likewise have ramifications among educational administrators.

Conflict Management

For much of history educational administrators hesitated to admit the existence of organizational conflicts, and internal discussions of such possibilities were discouraged if not forbidden. It was assumed falsely that recognition of the existence of conflicts within the educational enterprise was tantamount to admission of administrative or leadership failure or ineptness. The strategy was to ignore or cover up as long as possible. Such approaches are no longer feasible administrative strategies, for conflict is a signature of the times. Recognition of the inevitability of conflict in educational systems and identifying the potential sources of disruptive discord represent the foundations of newer approaches to educational conflict management.

Not all conflicts are destructive to the purposes of the organization. Constructive conflict, like constructive criticisms, may be beneficial and even provide motivation for productive change. Obviously, the prevention of destructive conflicts that may paralyze a system and exact a harmful emotional toll on individuals therein is what conflict management is all about.

Conflict management begins with the search for and expectation of conflict wherever there is collaboration or close working personnel relationships; there may be divergence of views as to the roles various educational specialists play; there may be power struggles among individuals at various levels in the hierarchy; there are social upheavals in the community; there are external sources of criticisms of the school system; there are implementations of significant changes in organizational structure and operations; and so on. Simple conflicts ignored or uncovered may lead eventually to more serious disruptions as well as to the creation of informal mechanisms, or "underground" activity, to deal with or resolve matters that should have included the formal leadership of the system but does not.

Berelson and Steiner noted that "within an organization, conflict between leader and subordinates tends to increase the number and concreteness of the organization's regulations, and vice versa—i.e., regulations go along with conflict."[47] This observation can be confirmed by experiences in education which point to shorter tenure for educational administrators as well as to acceptance of the questionable procedure of attempting to resolve conflicts "by making a rule," that is, by piling on regulations that may or may not go to the root of the conflict.

Terry identified a "well-defined pattern" followed during the course of a conflict as:[47] "First, a crisis emerges" evidenced by disagreements which pose a threat to effective operations; "Second, escalation of the disagreement takes place" which captures the attention of the administration if not already involved; "Third,

confrontation occupies the center of attention"; and "Fourth, further crisis is resorted to" because efforts used to resolve it are not accepted by the parties involved. This may continue until the adjustments or other changes made are accepted and implemented. This is the point of view that suggests that "things have to get worse before they get better."

Much blame, finger pointing, posturing, threats, and a variety of emotional outbursts may occur during the "panic time" or peak period in a crisis. These compound the challenges of conflict management, but are to be recognized as an almost inevitable accompaniment of the process. When others lose their objectivity or problem focus, it is essential for the conflict managers not to do so. The more serious the disputes among personalities, between teachers and parents, or over resource allocations and use, the more likely the complex conflicts will come to the top administrative echelons for mediation or resolution. The nasty problems not capable of resolution at other levels should be expected by principals and superintendents as a test of their conflict management competencies.

Conflict management is problem solving under great stress and strain, in the face of intensely emotional environments, and under serious constraints such as limited time or resources to cope with the crisis. These include techniques cited in the previous chapter such as gathering all possible data related to the situation; formulating hypotheses on the nature of the problem; generating relevant alternatives; and so on. The emotional or nonrational elements as well as the political factors compound the conflict resolution efforts.

The creation of a series of crisis management teams with personnel with special expertise or talents as well as their capability for rapid deployment to problem areas should be an integral part of the conflict management plan. These can and should include community members to act on school-community conflicts or criticisms as well as special consultants on call. The other side of the coin is conflict prevention through better communication, quicker identification of potential trouble spots, and special preparation of administrators and key leaders in conflict management. Some progress in education has been observed in coping with conflicts generated as the result of breakdowns in collective bargaining. School districts prepare operational plans for strike situations to lessen the impact of such disruptions.

Although the turbulence of the past two decades helped sensitize educational administrators to the importance of conflict management, the state of the art is labeled as being rudimentary at best in most school systems. Most seem to muddle through and hope for the best, with the frequent result that such crises tend to intensify and multiply.

There are limits to the conflict resolution capabilities of educational leadership, particularly where great social change is compressed in a relatively short period of time and where factors triggering upheavals lie outside the educational system. Many of the great social problems of our times have been brought to the schoolhouse door. The school has been asked to resolve racial integration issues, economic issues related to overcoming the harsh cycle of poverty in which some are entrenched, costly but necessary educational services for the severely handicapped, and so on. Communities splintered into warring factions for reasons other than education may vie for control of the educational system by electing their representatives to the board of education. A school board divided into factions compounds the problems of conflict management. Often those in educational positions lack the additional resources as well as the political or legal clout demanded for effective crisis resolution.

These severe limitations should not be interpreted as reasons for ignoring the development of conflict management competencies or the design and creation of crisis management teams.

ORGANIZATIONAL COMMUNICATION

Communication is the vital link and dynamic connection between all persons, parts, and activities. It is a part of and influences all administrative processes. Without the establishment of formal and informal communication networks, information essential to the decision process as well as the dissemination of directions and activities related to the choice determined would not be transmitted. Communication is concerned with transmission and reception of feelings as well as facts, ideas as well as information, and values as well as directions.

Many writers argue that an organization cannot exist, or survive for long after its creation, without a means for interchanging messages essential to coordination, motivation, and cooperation. Some conceptualize the organization as an elaborate system of communication where positions are sending and receiving stations. Even the network of relations among organizational personnel is a function of the formal and informal communication systems. In stressing the importance of communication, Davis depicted it as a "bottleneck" through which "all management acts must pass," for without communication "employees cannot know what their associates are doing, management cannot receive information inputs, and management cannot give instructions."[49]

Perceptions and Conceptions of the Communications Process

To some the term *communication* suggests the media for mass communication such as radio, television, newspapers, and magazines. It may also be considered synonymous with public relations. Thus, the failure of a superintendent "to communicate effectively" with school patrons or the public in general is primarily a public relations problem, according to some. There are specific courses identified with the term. To illustrate, English courses that stress writing skills may be called "communications skills development courses." This is reinforced when emphasis is placed on semantics, the science of meanings of words and nonverbal expressions.

The many definitions of communication consider it (1) imparting or exchanging attitudes, ideas, and information through the use of human abilities or technology; (2) transmission and reception of ideas; (3) the broad field of interchange of thoughts and opinions among humans; or (4) a process of giving and receiving facts, feelings, and ideas. There is a degree of similarity among all.

Another approach is necessary to conceptualize the process from an operational point of view that could facilitate analysis of its operational dimensions and point to ways of improving upon it. The process demands at least two persons with different roles to play. One person sending a message must have means to transmit the message as well. The person sending is identified by the term *communicator*. The second receives the message and is called the *communicatee*. A fairly simple operational definition of communication would be: *Communication is the process in which a communicator attempts to convey a message, or image, to a communicatee.* The definition does not indicate the means of transmission, whether the communicatee actually received the message or was made aware that someone was trying to communicate, or what the interpretation or impact of the message reception was.

The message or image is a representation of the communicator's intent or purpose. It may be an idea, a signal, a statement, a picture, a diagram, a bit of information, an attitude, or an emotion. The act need not be confined to oral or written language; there are nonverbal expressions such as "body language" or voice tone.

The conveyance of the message or image can be divided into two parts, namely, the instrument and the channel. The instrument which encodes the message could be a pen or a typewriter. It is then sent or actually transmitted through some channel: the mails, by radio, by TV, by computer, and so on.

The receipt of the message in its precise or distorted form is determined on the communicatee's side of the equation.

The operational dimensions of the communication process may be outlined as follows: communicator→image (message or information)→instrument (transmitter such as voice or writing)→channel (the medium of transmission)→communicatee (receiver)→impact. The above diagram does not show whether any noise (such as static or other interference or distractions) cluttered the communication process. What was encoded as a set of ideas prior to transmission through some channel by the communicator may not be what was decoded and interpreted after reception by the communicatee.

The many dimensions of complex communications activities may be analyzed further and in greater detail by examining: the organization's structural factors (how parts or positions are linked in the communication network); organizational functions and goals; the contents of communications moving through the organization; the psychological concomitants of the communication process; and other properties of communication activities.

Perceived and Unperceived Communications

Communication is a word derived from the Latin word "communis" meaning common, or to hold in common. The communication process is a means of establishing a commonality of purposes, information, direction, and so on.

There is no guarantee that attempted communications will result in commonality within the organization or that any image transmitted through established channels will be received and interpreted precisely by those intended as recipients. If the image is actually received, in whole or in part, the event is called a "perceived communication." The attempt to convey something may result in what is called an "unperceived communication" if there is no measurable degree of knowledge or awareness by the intended communicatee of the message. "Two-way communication" may be a goal unrealized because of unexpected malfunctions within complex organizations or ineptness of those involved in communication activities.

The following illustration is only one of several possible breakdowns that could occur. If a principal loses a memo sent by the superintendent, or fails to read it at all or "in time," the two-way communication loop is broken, and there is only an unperceived communication despite the best intentions of the superintendent.

There can be a communication breakdown if the communication was perceived (by being received) by the principal, but there was a lack of congruence between what the principal thought was said (the decoding at the principal level) and what the superintendent desired to communicate (the encoding at the superintendent level). The reasons are many, including different interpretations of the same words, unclear phrasing by the sender, inaccurate reading by the receiver, or distortions in the transmission process. There may be barriers within the organization that make difficult the clear transmission of messages among its persons or its parts. There are personal barriers to communication related to human emotions or poor listening. The physical barriers are best typified by oral communication made difficult by the competing volume of sound from other sources. The semantic barriers stem from cultural and professional preparation differences that result in attaching different meanings to the same words or variations in the "slanguage" used.[50]

Organizational Structure and Other Factors Influencing Communication

The communication process is concerned with who says what through what channels to whom and with what impact. It is influenced by how the institution is organized, because through the organizing process channels or pathways are created through which messages travel as well as by the various position relationships from or to which the messages move. Operating policies may decree that all formal communications shall respect the chain of command. This could create an "organizational" barrier because of the increase in travel time span for communications among administrators of coordinate rank but in different divisions. As indicated elsewhere the creation of the informal mechanism called the "trans-hierarchical bridge" could resolve one part of this problem to create another, namely, superi-

ors with incomplete information on what is happening within their divisions. The use of monthly "principals' meetings" where those at elementary, junior high, and senior high school levels attend could be the communication channel to reduce the informal exchanges across rather than up and through the hierarchy.

Telephone communications have many advantages in rapidity of transmissions and a relatively greater degree of informality. They fail to resolve problems inherent in most oral communications, that is, the difficulty in precise interpretation of oral messages and the lack of hard evidence of message transmittal and receipt. That latter may be an advantage even though some insist that anything worth saying is worth putting in writing. The follow-up written memo could answer most of the criticisms.

One justification for modifying an existing structure is to create a new design that had the potential, at least, of enhancing the frequency and quality of communication among certain administrative personnel. Communication events, when repeated over time, tend to take on a characteristic form as noted by their form, purposes, content, style, and psychological concomitants. One way to analyze the working relationships between individual administrators or administrators and teachers is to examine the communication patterns and style over a stated period of time.

One indication that an organization is "too big," or better, overcentralized, is the number of inordinate delays in vital information exchanges among administrative personnel responsible for policy development and operations. Overloading formal information channels may stimulate the creation of informal communication networks, including the so-called rumor mills. Organizational effectiveness can be impaired, if not more seriously damaged, where difficulties in the exchange of messages vital to various points in the hierarchy are not resolved. One advantage of the relatively small school systems is the high degree of direct face-to-face communications.

One writer likened the administrator in a complex organization to a person driving a car with another sitting alongside. If the driver (the educational administrator) were blindfolded or not able (because of complexity and many demands on the time available) to view the road and surrounding environment directly and forced to depend on communications from the nonblindfolded passenger, then precise and prompt reporting of road events and recommended maneuvers is absolutely essential to the safety of the driver, the passenger, as well as persons and other objects in the surrounding environment. Administrators of large and complex organizations cannot be involved personally in each and every educational activity and do not "see" first hand what is going on. An administrator becomes dependent upon others who report what is going on and from such communications ascertain what corrections and adaptations should be made to the system to insure reaching objectives. Like the blindfolded driver of the car, a breakdown in communications to top level administrators can prove disastrous.

The administrative problem may be complicated further if the information processed and submitted about the school contains more history of past events because of the lateness of reports rather than current data. The analogy of the blindfolded driver can be made even more frightening if the passenger communicates to the driver events observed through the rear window of the car, that is, what happened during the last block of travel. Communications sharpen the "eyes and ears" of administrators, who, because of the nature of the positions, are unable to be every place to see and hear everything first hand. Up to this point in time the design and operation of effective communication systems are the least understood dimensions of educational institutions.

The nature and timing of information necessary to describe the quality of operations, to detect potential sources of conflicts, as well as to monitor progress toward objectives is one of the crucial but unresolved problems in educational administration. Calling for voluminous reports in the hope that somewhere in that mass is a clue as to what to do or change in the system merely intensifies communication problems. It is possible for an administrator to be overwhelmed by what some call "systematically organized ignorance" and "information overload." The careful determination of what is needed by whom, when, and in what format is the first step toward unraveling the communication gaps as well as to prevent information overloads. The simple question "What do I need to know about each dimension of the school system to sense accurately what is going on, where the problems are, and what changes should be made?" remains very difficult to answer precisely.

The propensity of the educational leader to project ideas through face-to-face contacts, via telephone, through written memos, via frequently called meetings, via in-house publications, through directives, and so on, helps to describe or classify the communications preference style. Some organize "information trees," a formally organized system of spreading information throughout a complex system by assigning each person a fixed number of others to contact, who in turn call another number and so on. This facilitates rapid dissemination of relatively simple announcements. This formalization and recognition of what may be an informal communications channel elsewhere are valuable within certain limited parameters.

Published bulletins (which may become outdated in a rapidly changing system), manuals, and newsletters are fairly common in educational systems as in-house communication vehicles. The quality of production, relevance of information, and degree of acceptance vary from one place to another. Meetings are perhaps the most common, but are not always the most effective communication vehicles in education. When called for a relevant purpose, carefully planned, and scheduled for the briefest period possible, meetings can be productive.

Communication down the hierarchy is more frequent than the upward flow, yet the two-way flow is recommended strongly. Davis stated that "Downward communication is used more by Theory X managers than by Theory Y managers" and "tends to dominate in mechanistic organizations."[51] The propensity to make predominate use of downward flowing communications does not imply that either the effectiveness or the relevance of the communication is greater. Without a plan and without the trust with whom one communicates, communication breakdowns will occur. Upward communication is something that takes time to build. It is more likely where there is an open-door policy by administrators and where participative management styles prevail. Those at lower levels of the hierarchy need considerable confidence and feelings of security to communicate openly and frequently with others in superordinate positions.

The fine art of listening is essential for educational administrators if upward communication is to be established or to have value as well as if others are to come to those in superordinate positions for counsel. Not all who complain that "the administrators simply don't listen" can document such complaints with specific instances. Frequently, the complainant is heard but not given the satisfaction requested with the accusation that "they just don't listen." Davis reported that "training can increase listening comprehension 25 percent or more" and offered suggestions for improvement of listening competencies, or for removal of "listening earmuffs."[52] He suggested that to improve listening managers should "stop talking" if you want to listen, "put the talker at ease," "remove distractions" to listening (don't doodle when others talk), "empathize," "hold your temper," hold back on criticisms that could put people on the defensive, "ask questions," and so on.

It is never pleasant when communication channels become clogged with the so-called memo wars between administrators. Those in superordinate positions usually must step in to end the squabbling.

Lane, Corwin, and Monahan stressed that the internal and external communication system that permeates an organization has a profound effect on goal-attainment effectiveness.[53] They called for practicing administrators to recognize that communication problems in education "are not solved merely by increasing the flow of information," that "people may hear but not always listen," that "a message may reach a person's desk but not his mind," and that "people may become almost immune to much of the enormous volume of messages that reach them daily."[54] Sociopsychological forces add to the complexity of the process and simply a few words in a message or switching to a new channel or medium may not be enough to overcome the barriers to communication. Predispositions, or individual personality factors, have a great influence on what is read or heard by the person, on individual perceptions of a communication event, and what is or is not believed in a message. This so-called selected perceptions confounds even the most precise communicator.

Research on Communication

Berelson and Steiner presented the following summary of some significant research and points of view on communication:[55]

1. People are likely to seek out congenial communications, those favorable to their predispositions, when confronted with controversial matters and just after coming to a decision on the matter. The communications sought are those that reinforce existing attitudes which may be why some declare "I only read things that interest me."
2. Rumors spread in direct proportion to the receptivity of the audience.
3. If the substance of the rumor is congenial to the persons hearing it, it will be passed on to others and/or modified to reflect more personally satisfying versions.
4. Objective information on the subject not tied to the substance of the rumor is the best counterattack to deflate the rumor.
5. Misperception and misinterpretation of a communication follow one's psychological propensities to evade or distort a message.
6. The impact of and propensity to use the printed word in communication vary with the level of education; the higher the education level, the greater reliance placed on what was transmitted in print, and the lower the education level, the greater the preference for oral and visual presentations.
7. People seek out and respond to persuasive communications consistent with their predispositions to agree with the substance of an issue.

8. Facts are not always effective in changing audience opinion where the audience predispositions run in a contrary direction; the stronger the emotional or psychological factors, the less the impact of the communication of information which fails to support the prevailing attitudes. In short, facts alone don't win many converts on emotional and controversial issues.

9. The higher one's intelligence level, the more likely it is that information will be gained and used from the mass media.

DEVELOPING LEADERSHIP AND COMMUNICATION COMPETENCIES—A SYNOPSIS

The key point and basis for hope lie in the fact that leaders are made and not born fully endowed with the competencies essential for effective performance. Leadership is something that must be earned through special study and the acquisition of special sensitivities. It demands an understanding of organizations as expressions of large and complex, formal and informal, human interactions or social systems; leadership as a complex, human-oriented process in which the challenges of the situation outweigh the importance of any fixed set of personal traits; motivation based on satisfaction of a hierarchy of human needs; organizational climate which gives the subjective tone and feel to the working environment; conflict management within organizations; and of communication systems and their contributions to the coordination and unification of human and other factors toward realization of goals.

Leadership is an art demonstrated, tested, and refined during the practice of educational administration. Preparation increases readiness, but the proof of the pudding lies in the real world of motivating the recalcitrant, resolving the emotionally tinged conflicts, creating the productive and personally satisfying organizational climate, and designing the effective communication systems while pursuing and achieving the goals of the system. The ability to project a positive leadership image is important in small as well as very large educational institutions. Charisma has its advantages, but not as a substitute for developing competencies in group dynamics, motivation, conflict resolution, communications, and so on. Likewise, other personal qualities such as persuasiveness, a high degree of intelligence, and ability to articulate one's thoughts clearly and precisely should complement rather than replace situational thinking and human relations orientations.

The leadership/administration dichotomy is rejected herein, for in the holistic approach, leadership is a single, albeit a very important, dimension of educational administration. Likewise, the task-oriented and the relationship-oriented leadership styles are not viewed as mutually exclusive categories forcing a choice of one or the other. They can be balanced with focus on one without ignoring the other. As Fiedler indicated in the Contingency Theory, there is no single leadership style that is effective in any and all situations.

A key set of competencies is related to the understanding of and working with people in group activities. The dynamics of social interactions in group situations can be studied and learned. Group roles are interpreted from different vantage points called "alter groups." Foremost among these is sensing why, how, and when the leadership role emerges in group situations.

Lipham concluded the following after surveying recent research on educational leadership behavior:

1. The leadership behavior of administrators is a powerful factor which influences the adoption and institutionalization of educational change . . . moreover, different styles of leadership may be necessary at different stages of the change process.

2. The nature and quality of leadership provided by administrators and supervisors is directly and positively related to the following outcomes of the school: perceived effectiveness of the decision-making process; perceived effectiveness of instruction; and staff satisfaction and morale.[56]

The competencies to analyze communication acts through each of the major elements involved, to design effective communication networks, and to resolve communication breakdowns represent an additional set of abilities demanded for effective educational administration.

SUMMARY

The holistic management position is that all processes are important and effectiveness in educational administration cannot be attained by focusing on one at the expense of others. The organization may be perceived as a structured social system as well as a structured decision-making mechanism. There are complex sets of human interactions which exert a significant influence upon the operations and productivity of formal organizations.

Mary Parker Follett was among the first to speak on the dignity and value of satisfied workers. Her writings sparked interest in the significance of human factors in organizations. Today the term *organizational behavior,* rather than human relations, is used to describe human and social behavior in organizations.

The Hawthorne studies led to the examination of social and psychological factors that impact on human productivity, the revelation of the existence of the informal organizations, and the existence of the "Hawthorne effect" in research studies. Barnard also reacted against the mechanistic conceptualizations of the organization and viewed it instead as a system of human beings working cooperatively to attain goals.

McGregor argued that how an administrator interacts with personnel is related to assumptions about the fundamental nature of humankind. He postulated Theory X and Theory Y sets of assumptions which were contradictory interpretations of basic human characteristics and motivational approaches. Maslow postulated a hierarchy of human needs ranging from satisfaction of basic physiological needs to self-actualization as the basis for understanding human behavior as well as motivation. According to Maslow a satisfied need no longer motivates.

Not all personnel will be stimulated toward greater productivity with the same motivational strategy. The so-called work ethic that viewed work as satisfying and essential to people is changing as new perceptions of employment situations and life-styles began to emerge since about 1945. Herzberg's two-factor motivational model includes maintenance (or hygiene) factors and motivational factors that were related to what made a person feel good or bad about a job. Vroom's expectancy model of motivation is based upon the intensity of the desire (called valence) and the probability of satisfying the desire (called expectancy). Motivation is a means to arouse and to channel productive efforts within an organization. Management-by-objectives-and-results (MBO/R) may be used as part of a motivational strategy as well.

Leadership is a human-oriented process concerned with motivation, social interactions, interpersonal communications, organizational climate, conflicts, and personal growth of human factors as well as with the direction of organizational efforts and the attainment of objectives. There are varying interpretations of it, with most recognizing its importance in organizations. The various major classifications of leadership are symbolic or charismatic, formal or titular, and functional or operational leadership. The symbolic interpretation is based on personal traits, with the leader possessing those necessary for success. It is most likely to flourish when the distances from, and opportunities for interaction with, followers are remote. In the second, leadership is related to a position in the hierarchy. Positions with leadership potential are essential, but overemphasis on this dimension could stifle emergence of leadership talents from elsewhere. Far more likely to be accepted by organizational scientists is the conception of leadership as a set of functions essential to the operation and productivity of organized groups. The functional concept assumes that leadership roles can be learned.

House developed the "path-goal model" of leadership that related it more closely than most to motivation. Fiedler emphasized the group orientation of leadership. He offered the Contingency Theory of Leadership Effectiveness that related leader effectiveness to the situation or that was influenced by changing demands and performance level of groups. The prevailing view is that to better comprehend functional leadership, it is essential to understand the nature and functioning of organized groups or human behavior in organized settings.

A group is a cluster of two or more persons in social interaction and who share a common purpose. Once created, groups tend to organize by differentiating roles for members. Committees, cabinets, small conferences, and other small meetings of persons are illustrations of groups that vary in maturity of social interactions and productivity. The more common problems experienced by groups are internal or external conflict, apathy, and inadequate decision-making procedures. Special competencies in forming working groups, interacting with groups, sensing the level of group productivity, and diagnosing group problems are essential for educational administrators.

Leadership style is the preferred mode of behavior for "getting things done" or relating to group members. The three most common descriptors of leadership style are autocratic, democratic, and anarchic. A fourth could be manipulative leadership. Others have used terms such as *nomothetic, idiographic,* and *transactional* leadership styles. Styles may be differentiated on the basis of who is involved in the formulation of policies, motivational strategies, and leader–group interactions. Another basis is whether the leader is task-oriented or relationship-oriented. Still another is whether the emphasis of the leader is on satisfying institutional demands or personal needs. Policy formulation under democratic leadership, or the participative management style, involves all likely to be impacted by the policy. To abandon an autocratic style it is necessary to change value orientations as well as entrenched behavior patterns.

Bidwell concluded that a teacher's feeling of security or tension is dependent upon the teacher's view of appropriate administrative behavior. It is possible for the same administrative behavior to bring about feelings of security or tension if the different groups of teachers perceive the principal's role to be at variance with each other.

Conflict is inevitable in most complex organizations and conflict strategies can be developed to cope with them. Constructive conflict, like constructive criticisms, may be beneficial. Conflict management is problem solving under great stress and strain, in an intensely emotional environment, and under severe constraints. The creation of crisis management teams with rapid deployment capability may be one way to prepare for and deal with disabling conflicts.

Communication is vital to the organization as well. An operational definition of communication is: Communication is the process in which a communicator attempts to convey a message, or image, to a communicatee. The receipt of the message is not guaranteed and its impact is measured on the communicatee side of the equation. There are many barriers to communication; one indication of an organization becoming too big for its prevailing organization pattern are inordinate delays in the processing or transmittal of vital information. Communication down the hierarchy is more common and easier to develop than upward communication. The fine art of listening is a communication skill as well as sending clear messages through appropriate channels.

Leadership is an art demonstrated, tested, and refined during the practice of educational administration. Charisma and other personal qualities have their advantages but not as substitutes for developing competencies in group dynamics, motivation, conflict resolution, communication, and so on.

NOTES

1. Keith Davis, *Human Behavior at Work/Organizational Behavior,* New York: McGraw-Hill, 1981, p. 6.
2. H. C. Metcalf and L. Urwick, eds., *Dynamic Administration: The Collected Papers of Mary Parker Follett,* New York: Harper & Row, 1942.
3. Davis, op. cit., p. 15.

4. Ibid., p. 17.

5. F. J. Roethlisberger and W. J. Dixon, *Management and the Worker*, Cambridge, Mass.: Harvard University Press, 1939.

6. M. S. Olmsted, *The Small Group*, New York: Random House, 1959, pp. 30–31.

7. Chester I. Barnard, *Functions of the Executive*, Cambridge, Mass.: Harvard University Press, 1938.

8. Douglas McGregor, *The Human Side of Enterprise*, New York: McGraw-Hill, 1960.

9. Davis, op. cit., p. 10.

10. A. H. Maslow, *Motivation and Personality*, New York: Harper & Row, 1954.

11. Davis, op. cit., p. 48.

12. Ibid., p. 27.

13. Ibid., pp. 28–29.

14. Ibid.

15. Ibid., p. 29.

16. Frederick Herzberg, *Work and the Nature of Man*, Cleveland: World, 1966.

17. Davis, op. cit., p. 59.

18. Victor H. Vroom, *Work and Motivation*, New York: Wiley, 1964.

19. Irving Knickerbocker, "The Analysis of Leadership," in C. G. Browne and T. S. Cohn, eds., *The Study of Leadership*, Danville, Ill.: Interstate Printers and Publishers, 1958, pp. 3–4.

20. Ralph M. Stogdill, "Leadership, Membership, and Organization," in Browne and Cohn, eds., op. cit., p. 38.

21. Robert J. House, "A Path Goal Theory of Leadership Effectiveness," *Administrative Science Quarterly*, September 1971, pp. 321–338.

22. See Fred E. Fiedler, *A Theory of Leadership Effectiveness*, New York: McGraw-Hill, 1967, and also F. E. Fiedler, M. M. Chemers, and L. Mahar, *Improving Leadership Effectiveness: The Leader Match Concept*, New York: Wiley, 1976.

23. John K. Hemphill, "The Leader and His Group," in Browne and Cohn, eds., op. cit., p. 369.

24. D. P. Cartwright and R. Lippitt, "Group Dynamics and the Individual," *Group Development*, Washington, D.C.: National Training Laboratories, 1961, pp. 11–24.

25. K. D. Benne and P. Sheats, "Functional Roles of Group Members," in *Group Development*, Washington, D.C.: National Training Laboratories, 1961, pp. 51–59.

26. See L. P. Bradford and G. L. Lippitt, "The Individual Counts . . . in Effective Group Relations," in *Group Development*, op. cit., pp. 25–32.

27. L. P. Bradford et al., "How to Diagnose Group Problems," in *Group Development*, op. cit., pp. 37–50.

28. C. G. Browne, " 'Laissez Faire' or 'Anarchy' in Leadership?", in Browne and Cohn, eds., op. cit., pp. 305–309.

29. Davis, op. cit., pp. 135–137.

30. See Clyde M. Campbell, ed., *Practical Applications of Democratic Administration*, New York: Harper & Row, 1952, p. 29.

31. Davis, op. cit., p. 137.

32. Irving Knickerbocker, "Leadership: A Conception and Some Implications," in *Leadership in Action*, Washington, D.C.: National Training Laboratories, 1961, p. 81.

33. Ibid., pp. 36–37.

34. Classification based on nomothetic, idiographic, and transactional leadership styles was taken from original concepts and models introduced and developed by J. W. Getzels and E. G. Guba. The adaptations, or special liberties taken, of these terms are the writer's with any faults ascribed thereto rather than to Getzels and Guba. See J. W. Getzels and E. G. Guba, "Social Behavior and the Administrative Process," *School Review*, December 1957, pp. 423–441.

35. Browne, op. cit., p. 304.

36. Warren G. Bennis and Philip E. Slater, "Democracy Is Inevitable," *Harvard Business Review*, Vol. XLII, March–April 1964.

37. "The Teacher and Policy Making," *Administrator's Notebook*, Vol. 1, No. 1, May 1952, Chicago: Midwest Administration Center, University of Chicago.

38. K. D. Benne, "Leaders Are Made Not Born," in *Leadership in Action*, op. cit., p. 19.

39. Adapted from Neal Gross et al., *Explorations in Role Analysis*, New York: Wiley, 1958, p. 67.

40. J. W. Getzels, "Administrations as a Social Process," in A. W. Halpin, ed., *Administrative Theory in Education*, Chicago: Midwest Administration Center, University of Chicago, 1958, pp. 150–165.

41. Charles E. Bidwell, "Some Causes of Conflicts and Tensions Among Teachers," *Administrators Notebook*, Vol. 4, No. 7, March 1956, Chicago: Midwest Administration Center, University of Chicago.

42. Ibid.

43. I. P. Levinson, "Management by Whose Objectives?", *Harvard Business Review*, July–August 1970, pp. 125–134.

44. William H. Newman and E. Kirby Warren, *The*

Process of Management, 4th ed., Englewood Cliffs, N.J.: Prentice-Hall, 1977, pp. 175–179.

45. Jacob W. Getzels, James W. Lipham, and Roald F. Campbell, *Educational Administration as a Social Process,* New York: Harper & Row, 1968, pp. 108–119.
46. Ibid., p. 113.
47. Bernard Berelson and Gary A. Steiner, *Human Behavior: An Inventory of Scientific Findings,* New York: Harcourt Brace Jovanovich, 1964, p. 377.
48. George R. Terry, *Principles of Management,* 7th ed., Homewood, Ill: Irwin, 1977, p. 84.
49. Davis, op cit., pp. 399–400.
50. See Davis, op. cit., pp. 404–406.

51. Ibid., p. 422.
52. Ibid., pp. 134–141.
53. W. R. Lane, R. G. Corwin, and W. G. Monahan, *Foundations of Educational Administration: A Behaviorial Analysis,* New York: Macmillan, 1967, chaps. 3 and 4.
54. Ibid.
55. B. Berelson and G. A. Steiner, op. cit., pp. 527–554.
56. James M. Lipham, *Review and Discussion of the Research of Educational Practices: Administrative and Supervisory Personnel,* a paper prepared for the state of Georgia's Department of Education, Atlanta: Georgia Department of Education, 1979, p. 25.

CHAPTER REVIEW QUESTIONS

1. What is the holistic approach to the study and practice of management?
2. What was the significance of the Hawthorne research studies to the development of formal organizations?
3. Compare the similarities and the differences of the conceptions of human nature and motivation developed by McGregor, Maslow, Herzberg, and Vroom.
4. How does symbolic leadership differ from functional leadership?
5. Why is it necessary for a leader to have a position in the hierarchy with authority and control over certain resources?
6. Describe the essential characteristics of the following leadership styles: (a) nomothetic; (b) relationship-oriented; (c) democratic; (d) autocratic.
7. What are the essential elements of the Contingency Theory of Leadership Effectiveness?

8. Why is a knowledge of and special competencies for working with groups essential to educational leadership performance?
9. What is an "alter group"? How does it function in organizations?
10. What are the various sources of potential conflict in organizations?
11. In what ways are conflict management and problem solving similar? Different?
12. Why is an effective communications system vital to an organization?
13. What is the difference between a perceived and an unperceived communication?
14. What are the factors that help to define the communication style of an administrator?
15. What are the barriers to effective communication in an organization? How can they be minimized or overcome?

SELECTED REFERENCES

Browne, C. G. and Cohn, T. S., eds., *The Study of Leadership,* Danville, Ill.: Interstate Printers and Publishers, 1958.

Davis, Keith, *Human Behavior at Work/Organizational Behavior,* 6th ed., New York: McGraw-Hill, 1981, chaps. 1–4, 7, and 9.

Fiedler, F. E., Chemers, M. M., and Mahar, L., *Improving Leadership Effectiveness: The Match Concept,* New York: Wiley, 1976.

French, Wendell, *The Personnel Management Process,* 3rd ed., Boston: Houghton Mifflin, 1974, chaps. 6 and 7.

Getzels, J. W., Lipham, J. W., and Campbell, R. F., *Educational Administration as a Social Process,* New York: Harper & Row, 1968.

Leadership in Action, Selected Reading Series Two, Washington, D.C.: National Training Laboratories, 1961.

Schmuck, R. A. et al., *Handbook of Organizational Development in Schools,* prepared at CASEA, Eugene, Ore., Palo Alto, Calif.: National Press Books, 1972.

Stogdill, Ralph M., *Handbook of Leadership: A Survey of Theory and Research,* New York: Free Press, 1974.

4

EDUCATIONAL PLANNING AS AN ADMINISTRATIVE PROCESS: ANALYSIS OF THE OPERATIONAL AND STRATEGIC DIMENSIONS

Rhetoric accords planning an exalted status. Few can resist declaring with great conviction that "the future will come whether we are ready for it or not" or "the future is where we shall spend the rest of our professional careers." There is the implication that through planning one can anticipate and get ready for whatever the future has in store. It is not unusual to find education writers inserting planning in a title even though the body of the article gives but passing reference to it. The propensity toward rhetorical excesses or primarily ideological discourses on the importance of planning that characterized much education writing prior to 1960 compounded problems of building an understanding of planning as an administrative process.

Webster's International Dictionary (1981), in stark contrast, is almost brutal in the brevity of its treatment of planning. It is defined therein simply as the "act or process of making or carrying out plans." This dictionary devotes more space to the plan or the outcome of the process. A plan is conceptualized as a predetermined strategy, detailed scheme, or program of action related to the accomplishment of an objective.

It implies mental activity during the course of analyzing or laying out a method for achieving something.

How the plan that can lead to more effective administration, operations, or performances is generated is neglected in the rhetoric, the ideological discourses, and dictionaries. Over the past 20 years there have emerged in the education literature and in other fields discussions and descriptions of models, special tools, data, and other resources useful in planning as a process. This chapter focuses upon these and bases much of the effort to build a better understanding of planning as a concept and as a means. The emphasis shall be on the why, what, and how of planning as a means for enhancing effectiveness in educational administration in general and decision making and operations in particular.

PERCEPTIONS OF PLANNING

The definitions, perceptions, and interpretations of planning are as many and varied as there are writers and speakers on this topic. What follows is a summary or distillation of the more common perceptions of purposes or activities that characterize planning. Planning may be perceived as the following:

Futures Determination or Uncertainty Reduction. Planning, from this point of view, has as its primary thrust describing, defining, or determining events, conditions, and/or needs at some future point in time that may confront an organization, personnel, or a profession. By anticipating what might be, the level of uncertainty is reduced. The basic tools or approaches are forecasting or projections of important factors in education such as numbers and types of students, fiscal and material resources, or new program requirements. Others base future expectations on the so-called Delphi technique (named after the famed oracle in Greek legend) or scenarios generated by select specialists at the cutting edge of various dimensions of the field.

Futures Preparation or Readiness Enhancement. This is related to the above but does not stop at description of what is likely to be. It is interpretation of futures data and translation into competencies or operational capabilities demanded to maintain or extend effectiveness under the conditions anticipated. The end product is a set of training programs for personnel and other modifications in the organization. The preparation to meet anticipated challenges is rooted in the basic data collected in the preceding paragraph.

Direction Determination. This is a relatively common perception of planning as a means of generating relevant present or future goals and objectives for the organization. To illustrate, "planning" in the well-known PPBS is concerned less with the process per se and more with its product, that is, the identification and clarification of outcomes to be pursued by the organization.

A Decision Precursor or Decision Making. Some writers relate planning and decision making so closely that differentiation between these two administrative processes is blurred at best. The so-called steps in rational decision making and analytical planning are very similar. Others acknowledge the interrelationship but perceive as planning those activities performed to support or help determine the actual choice or decision. Planning in this sense is the preparation phase or a precursor in the decision-making process. In short, the purpose of the planning is to help determine the optimal decision or choice rendered.

Innovation Preparation. Planning may be related to other administrative processes such as the management of change. It may be perceived as a special case of the paragraph above whereby the purpose of the planning is to help insure the readiness of an organization to implement and assimilate a significant modification in operations or purposes with a minimum of dysfunction and cost as well as a relatively low probability of subsequent discontinuance or lapsing into any previous ineffective behavior modes.

Operations Optimization or Performance Improvement. This perception is focused more on the here and now rather than the long-range time frame. It is planning for the enhancement of existing conditions rather than those in the uncertain future. The emphasis is on planning that results in the production of the so-called standard operating procedures, operations manuals, administrative guidelines, or system "policies" in the belief that the application of these can result in improved performance. The end product is a set of plans to guide the actions of operatives.

Contingency Anticipation or Problems Prevention. This may be a special case of one or more of the above. A "plan of action" may be developed that could minimize the magnitude of an educational problem likely to be encountered at some future point in time or that would spell out the procedures to be followed should certain "crises" or contingencies arise within the organization. A "campus security plan," plan for weather emergencies, plan for operations during a strike by personnel, and so on. have become fairly common in most school systems at the present time.

A Mechanism, Model, or Tool. It is not unusual to find planning equated with one of the more common procedures or tools utilized in the process. Thus, planning implied PERT or CPM during the heyday of applying these procedures during the design and construction of educational facilities. "Needs assessment" may be confused by others as planning. Forecasting, PPBS, or the so-called Delphi technique have been at various times equated by some writers with the sum and substance of planning.

Complexity Resolution, Coordination, and Control. The very large, complex projects that occur every now and then are recognized as those demanding a predetermined strategy for their realization. Planning is interpreted as a means of coping with complexity or coordinating the various facets of a "once through" project of considerable magnitude.

The above summary is not exhaustive but does convey the many ways of perceiving the nature of planning and what it might contribute toward the attainment of greater effectiveness. Not everyone writing or talking about planning has the same reference points or perceptions of the nature and purposes of the process.

PLANNING ISSUES AND ORIENTATIONS

Problems in understanding planning as an administrative process are compounded further by the time frames and institutional contexts in which it may be found. These issues may be summarized as follows:

Strategic vs. Operational Planning Time Frames. Assuming that it is obvious that planning may cover a variety of time frames, most writers do not take the time to clarify the advantages and limitations of a given planning approach or mechanism over various time periods. Long range or strategic planning is relatively uncommon in education at this point in history. Most efforts to date focus upon the short run (five years or less) and operational plans. The so-called educational futures are more speculative than definitive of likely future courses of action in educational organizations.

Institutional vs. Unit Planning Orientations. With the exception of some institutional wide planning efforts, such as the budget or fiscal plan for a forthcoming year, most educational planning thrusts have been oriented toward specific projects at the unit level. Centralized planning thrusts are not common in education as yet. One of the issues involved in increasing effectiveness through planning is whether centralized and team specialist planning activities will be organized to support decentralized and individual unit efforts.

Formal vs. Informal Planning Orientations. Planning can occur in the well-organized head of administrator as well as through formal mechanisms such as planning councils, committees, or departments. This may be viewed as a variation of the preceding paragraph with a debate generated as to the desirability of creating a formal planning infrastructure as opposed to the more common practice of wider diffusion of planning responsibilities to all levels.

Planning Process vs. Product Emphasis. The primary focus is placed on the "how" of planning in the former and on its outcomes in the latter. Most education literature has a product emphasis with the implication that the process is of little consequence or that any set of activities will generate the effective plan.

Planning Rhetoric vs. Competencies Orientation. There are those in education who sense the public relations value of declaring the organization's commitment to planning while at the same time hesitating to allocate the resources essential to the development of special planning competencies.

Planning vs. Other Administrative Processes. Many writers in management prefer to champion the cause of one administrative process over all others. It is argued that the "essence" of management or administration can be found in leadership or decision making. Most education writers opt for the supremacy of leadership, but none to date would grant such status to planning. That is less true in other fields. To illustrate, Pfiffner and Presthes writing in the field of business management declared "planning, in a word, is management" because "planning touches upon every aspect of management, including decision making, budgeting, coordination, communications, and problems of structure."[1] Newman and Warren writing in the same field recognized the overarching significance of planning, as did Pfiffner and Presthes, by acknowledging that "Planning is a basic management task, one that had a major place in our overall division of management functions along with organizing, controlling, and activating."[2] These writers went further to relate planning and decision making so closely that distinctions between the two were blurred at best. Thus, they stated that "the process of planning can best be understood if we first examine the basic stages in making a decision rationally . . ."[3] Part III of their volume was organized around the theme of "Planning: Elements of Rational Decision Making" and Part IV around "Planning: Decision-Making in an Enterprise."[4] Yet another group of writers in business management related planning more closely to the change process by defining planning as "the process by which the system adapts its resources to changing environmental and internal forces" and as the "vehicle for system change" but at the same time admitting it provides a "solid foundation for the remaining managerial activities."[5] It is unfortunate that planning is more likely to be neglected or given a lower priority in the preparation of educational administrators.

It is difficult to distinguish and separate planning from other administrative functions. It is a process utilized at times by the educational administrator while performing the role of leader, decision maker, change agent, and so on. Planning, somewhat like thinking, represents a higher level of abstraction than other processes such as decision making and leadership. Planning is a means of achieving higher levels of effectiveness in other management functions rather than a substitute for any. The uniqueness of planning may be related to its future orientation or anticipation mode, but even that does not always hold true.

Planning Defined

The outlining of perceptions and issues facilitates the development of an operational definition of planning. Dror noted that "we are faced with a wealth of definitions" but added "some authors get weary of the whole business and despair of any attempt at formulating a generally valid definition of planning."[6] He developed his own nonetheless, namely, "Planning is the process of preparing a set of decisions for action in the future directed at achieving goals by optimal means."[7] It is one of the better ones and relates planning to decision making. This writer acknowledges the influence of Dror's writing on this chapter.

The following is yet another definition of planning and represents this writer's efforts to distill its purposes and/or hoped for results: *Planning is any set of formal and rational activities that seeks to anticipate conditions, directions, and challenges at some future point in time for the purposes of enhancing the readiness of personnel and the organization to perform more effectively and to attain relevant objectives by optimal means.* This definition would recognize as planning those activities that would satisfy most or all of the following conditions or criteria: (1) future-oriented, (2) goal-oriented, (3) based on rational and verifiable procedures and data, and (4) related to performance enhancement and goal achievement by optimal means.

Stated in negative terms there would be a rejection, by definition, of "planning for the sake of planning" or where planning was an end rather than a means; nonrational or occult approaches that depend upon the subjective interpretations of so-called signs of the future; idle speculation, wishful thinking, or simply unsupported, but "sincere hopes to do the best job possible"; and unfocused activities of dedicated persons without the special knowledge and competencies to engage in rational planning.

The end product of the process may be a plan of operations, an awareness of future conditions likely to be encountered, a design and/or a schedule for the construction of a needed facility, a new program to be implemented, a fiscal plan for one or more ensuing years, an approach for the resolution of persistent problems, a new in-service training program, and so on. Whatever the end product, it is only as good as the procedures employed, the data available and interpreted, and competencies of the personnel involved.

PRACTICES AND TRENDS IN EDUCATIONAL PLANNING

Dror referred to specific applications such as economic planning and regional planning as illustrations of a "limited area of planning."[8] Perhaps terms such as *sharply focused, specific dimension,* or *targeted* planning may be preferred, because the word *limited* could be misconstrued to imply something less than comprehensive. Most planning in education is targeted or focused on a specific dimension of the system. It has been assumed that the prime requirement is possession of substantive knowledge or expertise in a given specialization within education with little attention to planning as a process that could be adapted and applied to any dimension.

Planning is not a strange or seldom used function in education, if the context is targeted planning or what Dror called "limited areas of planning." Fiscal planning started over 60 years ago in the very large school systems and was mandated by law in others about 25 years later. Curriculum planning, although a less precise term than fiscal planning, has been an ongoing activity almost from the inception of formal systems of education. Educational facilities planning is likewise relatively old and reached a high level of sophistication during the 1950s

and 1960s. Most so-called Planning Departments organized in State Departments of Education focused on various dimensions of facilities planning and construction that demanded objective approaches to student enrollment projections as well as school plant designs and construction scheduling. Perhaps the most common activities were the preparation of daily lesson plans by teachers and semester or yearly class schedules by principals.

A long tradition of planning in education has sought to enhance instructional effectiveness and more prudent utilization of limited resources. It can be characterized, however, as primarily operational in scope, limited in time frame, relatively uncoordinated with specialists in various dimensions operating independently and without much knowledge of what others were doing, and based on relatively unsophisticated procedures and mechanisms for implementing planning as a process. Planning has been and continues to be a relatively old, respected, and frequently employed process in education that can be refined and extended by recognizing existing limitations in the manner in which it is implemented, as well as by recognizing the potential inherent in the newer and more sophisticated models, tools, and approaches. The typical planning time frame in education is limited to getting ready for what is to transpire the next day, week, or at most the next semester. With few exceptions, the next school or calendar year was the longest time horizon.

The pressures on educational administrators to enhance the quality of educational planning and to develop more sophisticated planning competencies intensified over the past 20 years or so. Some factors responsible for this, and which promise to continue to exert such pressures in the future, are:

1. A dynamic environment with rapidly advancing technologies demands modifications in existing behavior, social relationships, and operations patterns, which in turn generate uncertainties. Planning pressures increase as uncertainties in the environment multiply.

2. Value patterns once rooted in stability have been modified to the point where change, as a value orientation, is no longer resisted but rather encouraged. We live in a culture where adaptation and innovation are "sought rather than fought." Dislocations resulting from change can be reduced through more effective planning.

3. Educational systems are larger and more complex than ever before in history. Total school enrollment almost doubled in the 45-year period after 1930, whereas about 87 percent of the local school districts and 67 percent of the public school attendance locations were eliminated during the same period. In addition, educational programs multiplied and a greater diversity of educational services was made available. Larger and more complex school operations demand more effective planning.

4. The expectations from educational systems have increased materially.

5. Educational resources are scarcer and resistances to education tax increases are greater than in previous years. Educational planning is one way of discovering alternative approaches to doing more with less.

6. Time frames to meet social and educational goals have grown shorter. Trying to get the most out of a shorter time period stimulates more planning activity.

7. The public seeks to reduce the magnitude of risks related to any future uncertainty about the quality or availability of educational opportunities.

Stated in contrary terms, educational planning is less important or demanding during periods of relative stability, when operating units are of smaller size, when tasks confronting an institution are less complex, when expectations are lower, with greater availability of resources, and when higher degrees of certainty prevail.

What is demanded in the newer approaches to educational planning as an administrative process, or what can be called departures from previously existing modes, can be summarized as follows:

1. Greater emphasis on the strategic or long-range time frames.

2. Utilization of more sophisticated educational planning models and procedures.

3. Creation of centralized and relatively permanent educational planning units, support systems, or infrastructures to assist and extend the planning capabilities at all levels in the system.

4. Better comprehension of the theories and concepts that undergird educational planning as a process.

5. Increasing involvement with greater time commitments from high level administrators in the educational planning process.

6. Allocation of more resources (time, personnel, and money) to educational planning functions.

Educational Planning and Other Administrative Functions

Terry declared: "Planning is vital in management because it is basic to the other fundamental management functions" and it "must be done at all management levels."[9]

The decision-making process initiates planning functions within an organization. The other side of the coin is that subsequent decision activity is influenced by planning outcomes. The flow, once a choice triggers planning, is Planning→Decision→Action (Implementation)→Evaluation→Improvements in Planning, and so on. Planning is the preparation phase, an aid, in the decision process; but planners do not make decisions. Planners provide the data, alternatives, and interpretations to enhance the quality of decisions in the organization. Related to this, Steiner pointed out "Planning is not making future decisions" but it is "concerned with making current decisions in the light of their futurity."[10]

The relationship between planning and the change process was noted as well. Here again, planners are not change agents but provide the data and other support services to facilitate the process by helping to remove to some degree the level of uncertainty that accompanies significant shifts in established practices. Again,

Steiner noted that "Planning is not forecasting," but "Forecasts are essential in planning."[11]

The Plan and the Planning Process

In education, as well as in many other endeavors, the focus is on the plan. The plan can be no better than what the process was capable of generating. Some plans simply reflect the unrealistic expectations or emotional expressions of "hopes for the best." Documents based on wild guesses or feelings rather than facts may do more harm, and reduce credibility, than no plan at all. Likewise, plans based on inadequate data, invalid interpretations, or questionable procedures do not represent much improvement over those rooted in emotions or unrealistic hopes. The improvement of operational or strategic plans lies in improving the quality of the process that produced them.

The relevance and the potential effectiveness of a plan may be appraised prior to implementations by analyzing the validity of assumptions, relevance of data used, quality of procedures employed, soundness of interpretations, degree of expertise among personnel employed, and so on. The well-known GIGO acronym applies: "garbage in, garbage out."

The best tests of plan quality, of course, are what happens during implementation and the results. Things may not "go according to plan" for a variety of reasons only one of which may be the quality of the planning process. To illustrate, unexpected or rogue events may intervene, plan implementation strategies may have been ill conceived, inadequate resources were made available for plan implementation, and so on. Postplan assessment may contribute to the improvement of the process as well as the implementation approaches.

A common misconception is that once adopted a plan must never be modified. The so-called midcourse corrections should be anticipated, because uncertainty may be reduced but never eliminated completely. Early in this century Fayol recognized the importance of flexibility in planning and the necessity for plan modifications during the course of implementation. Fayol's four major characteristics of an effective plan were:

1. *Unity.* No more than one plan for any single dimension should be approved and implemented at any one time.
2. *Continuity.* The planning process is continuous with the preparation of other plans in readiness to follow the completion of the first.
3. *Flexibility.* Allowing for modifications as circumstances may demand.
4. *Precision.* Vague, ill-defined, imprecise, and so on, dimensions of a plan must not be tolerated. Accuracy and clarity of all elements and strategies should be demanded.[12]

In short, peering into the future is an imprecise art at best. Plans are made, and can and should be modified as subsequent hard data and/or experiences suggest, and may be discarded when something better comes along. This is not meant to infer the opposite extreme to inflexibility, that is, that the plan is modified so often that it has little impact on operations.

Types of Plans

Planning expectations and outputs are many and diverse but are related to one or more purposes of the organization. A strategic plan probes where the organization should be going over the long run as well as the short run, what programs and services should be characteristic of the institution, or what major changes may be necessary in the organization as a whole to meet future challenges. The time frame is medium to long range and therefore the level of uncertainty in strategic planning is greater. It is the prime responsibility of top level management that Steiner called "strategic management" because it is the locus for strategic planning.

Tactical or operational plans grow out of, support, and focus on the major tasks required to achieve the strategic plans and objectives. As Steiner put it, "Just as strategic management is concerned with operational management, so strategic planning is interrelated with operational planning."[13] Most of what goes on in a school system is operational planning characterized by the teacher's daily lesson plans, a principal's schedule of classes for a semester, or the superintendent's budget plan for the year. Operational plans are more specific and detailed, focus on a dimension of operations, have a shorter duration or time period, encounter less uncertainty than that characteristic of strategic plans, and involve administrators at all levels but primarily those at the lower echelons. Tactical or operational plans assume the existence of a set of consistent strategic plans, an assumption that is suspect in most educational institutions. Terry said it well: "For tactical planning to exist, it must have the directions given by strategic planning."[14] The strategic plan clarifies objectives, gives direction, and spells out the general operating policies. The specific operational plans at all levels should be consistent with and contribute to the realization of the strategic plan for the organization. Tactical plans spell out how to reach strategic objectives.

The following is a summary of the types of plans of action that may be generated within an educational organization:

1. Strategic plans focus on the system as a whole, emphasize goals to be attained, and give general directions to all other efforts.
2. Organization structuring plans stipulate authority, responsibilities, and relationships among position incumbents, clarify such patterns, or modify what existed previously.
3. Educational programs and/or services plans are more detailed and fairly common in the system.
4. Standard operating rules and procedures plans apply to teachers, administrators, and other personnel.
5. Conflict and crisis management plans.
6. Innovations, identification, adoption, and management plans.
7. Ad hoc or special-purpose plans to deal with the endless variety of operational challenges within a school system.

The above classification can be made more general to identify at which hierarchical level primary planning responsibility is placed:

1. Goals identification, clarification, and orientation plans are usually the primary responsibility of top level management although others are involved.
2. Operational policy plans that guide the actions of administrators at all levels are assigned to administrators close to the top level even though many others are involved in the plan development.
3. Procedures-determination plans are usually the responsibility of operating level administrators.
4. Standard operating rules and procedures plans are likewise developed and implemented at the lower or operational administrative levels.

The final written document, or formal plan, should include at least the following:[15]

1. Descriptive title and date of plan submission.
2. Names and titles of those authorizing the plan development accompanied by careful documentation of the authorization by letters, minutes, and so on.
3. Names and titles of planning commission or committee members.
4. Names of official agencies or executives reviewing and adopting the finished plan.
5. Plan objectives and purposes, with stipulation of scope and limitations.
6. Definition of specific problems addressed in the plan.
7. Assumptions, data used and sources indicated, future conditions anticipated, and so on, that influenced plan preparation and recommendations.
8. Consultants or special resources employed in plan development or writing.
9. Alternatives identified and pursued.
10. Recommendations for action.
11. Expected results with time lines indicated.
12. Major plan assessment or "review points" to allow midplan corrections.

13. Plan implementation cost estimates and resources required.
14. Dates for starting, adjusting, and/or ter-
minating the plan.
15. Supporting evidence or justifications for
recommendations.

Planning Process Essentials

The educational planning process is neither automatic nor self-executing. It is stimulated in
some way, resources to support it must be gathered, strategies and tools identified, and operating time lines established. In short, there is a
need for a "plan to plan."

Commitments for planning usually come
from top administrative levels, although for tactical plans it may come from other administrative levels. Commitment is evidenced by follow
through and dedication of resources required
to pursue the planning.

Steiner identified the four approaches to
formal planning as the "top-down approach,"
"bottom-up approach," "combination of top-
down and bottom-up approaches," and "team
planning."[16] Note that these are divisions of
the formal or systematic approach as opposed
to the informal or "intuitive-anticipatory" approach to planning. In the "top-down" pattern, superordinates submit guidelines to
subordinates and all planning is centralized at
the top echelon level. In the "bottom-up"
style, the subordinates are given no guidelines, but are asked to submit guidelines for
planning.

The quality of planning is influenced to a
considerable degree by the relevance and accuracy of data available, ease of access to needed
information, authority to release data to the
public, ease of processing data, validity of interpretations of treated data, and so on. Information gathered, processed, and interpreted is
basic to the construction of all plans.

The creation of a data base and an information system precedes and defines the degree of
readiness to pursue formal and objective planning. It requires access to a computer and assistance from data management specialists to
support activities of those engaged in planning.

The problems may be compounded by the
rights to privacy legislation which may restrict
procurement and release of certain types of information involving individuals.

Planning Mechanisms and Structures

Planning is an attitude, a frame of mind, but it
requires some kind of structure, definitive
procedures, and special mechanisms to fulfill
its potential. Uniquely designed systems to facilitate the planning process within the organization vary in their composition, functions, authority, resources available, and position in the
hierarchy.

Planning mechanisms may be created or designed for varying periods of duration. Ad hoc
or special-purpose planning units (committees
or projects) may exist for a period as brief as a
week to as long as several years. In contrast, a
system-wide formal planning mechanism may
be designed to function as an integral part of
the organization for an indefinite period.

Although informal planning bodies may arise
almost spontaneously to satisfy the needs of an
informal group, formal planning units come
into being only through an executive act that
cloaks the planning activity with legitimacy,
special charges, and resources. Formal recognition and determination of reasons for being are
particularly important to ad hoc planning units
which without status could get bogged down in
internal disputes and an identity loss that could
cause them to flounder or fail.

Mechanisms assigned very sensitive and vital
planning assignments may precipitate a need for
some restructuring of organizational monitoring of planning progress and activities. This may
be more necessary where public hearings are employed to gather or present data on socially sensitive dimensions of educational operations.

Where there are many special-purpose planning mechanisms including a variety of administrators representing various levels of the
hierarchy, coordination becomes necessary to
cope with the complexity of interrelationships.
This may require creating a system-wide "planning council," not to engage in or substitute for

other planning activities in the system but to stimulate, coordinate, monitor, and assist other ad hoc units engaged in the process.

In addition, a "planning infrastructure," that is, a planning support system that facilitates planning by other mechanisms, is desirable in large and complex educational organizations. Its functions may include generating or processing data essential to rational planning, programming, and other computer services, and providing specialized consultants with competencies in the application of planning models and special techniques to particular planning challenges. The term *planning infrastructure* includes the institutional commitment to planning (acceptance of the importance of planning) as well as the essential support services to fulfill planning needs.

There are a variety of techniques that can enhance the quality of the planning activities that range from the "general estimate of the situation" to specific forecasting tools. The military commander's situation estimate follows the steps in rational thinking or problem solving. It includes such matters as understanding the purpose and nature of the task assigned; gathering data on all dimensions of the planning problem; identifying the significant difficulties to the realization of the mission; determining the feasible alternative courses of action that are available; analyzing each course of action in terms of its advantages and disadvantages; selecting the most promising course of action; and translating the decision into a detailed plan of action showing who, what, where, how, and why each is involved. The general planning model is very similar to other general models of rational decision making, and so on.

The more specific techniques such as PERT or CPM for scheduling, PPBS for budgeting planning and decisions, operations research emphasis on the use of model and quantitative analysis techniques, and management information systems are reviewed more fully in other chapters and will not be repeated at this point.[17]

The degree of sophistication in forecasting ranges from "seat of the pants forecasts" prepared by experienced and knowledgeable professionals to reflect subjective opinions, to simple extrapolation of trends established over previous years, to fitting of curves by visual means, to the use of regression analysis that seeks mathematically to establish relationships between a key factor to external factors that are thought to have a significant impact on the key variable. Regression analysis is more sophisticated than other less scientifically oriented forecasts such as those based primarily on the prior experiences of professions or simple extrapolation. Its use has increased with the greater availability and accessibility to computers that take the work out of the mathematical computations.[18]

Chambers et al. identified 18 different forecasting techniques that emphasized qualitative methods, time series analysis and projection, and causal methods.[19] They claimed "it is not too difficult to forecast the immediate future, since long-term trends do not change overnight" and added that the forecasting need "is not for better forecasting methods, but for better application of the techniques at hand."[20]

Expectations from the Process

Needs assessment is a popular term in education and is recognized as the beginning or foundation for the planning process. A need is related to an unfulfilled and realistic objective. It is the gap between what actually exists in an organization and the realistic condition or production desired. The need represents a discrepancy between what is and what is desired.

A "needs assessment" determination helps define the magnitude of the operational and detailed planning that follows. The assessment itself stops after definition of needs, that is, does not go on to a definition of the alternative strategies available to reduce the gap disclosed or to a decision as to which alternative should be selected.

Other educational planning outcomes are reviewed in greater detail in the remainder of this volume. These are specific and focused on a particular dimension of administration such as personnel, fiscal, facilities, instructional, and curriculum administration. There is a general process model that applies to all such situations, which is diagrammed here.

→Definition of the organization's planning needs through

→Needs Assessment

→Specification of Expectations

↓

Assignment of planning responsibilities—creating special units

↓

Provision of resources to facilitate planning

↓

Execution of the planning process to fulfill expectations

↓

Production of the educational plan

↓

Implementation of the plan

↓

Midplan appraisals and appropriate corrections

↓

Evaluation of the plan and planning process

↓

Feedback loop: Assimilation of new information for planning improvement

FUTURES

Fascination with the future has characterized humankind throughout history and may never cease. The early tools of long-range prediction were crude and relied heavily upon the occult arts. The future, it was argued thousands of years ago, was preordained but could be revealed through selected signs which could be interpreted by the gifted seers and oracles. Futures prediction by interpreting signs found in the entrails of a freshly killed chicken is no longer accepted as valid today even though some of the most prestigious generals and other leaders in ancient Rome staked their lives or careers upon such predictions. In contrast, the casting of horoscopes, palm reading, gazing into crystal balls, and interpretation of special types of cards have continued for more than 2000 years, right up to the present, as valid means of ascertaining the future, according to the modern devotees of such occult arts. Witness the publication of daily horoscopes for persons born under various signs in just about every newspaper of any significance in our nation. Implicit in these questionable approaches is that the future destiny of anyone or any organization was to be found "in the stars" and beyond the control of mere mortals. There was

little point, therefore, in trying to prepare for a future destiny that is preordained.

Futurism today abandons both the reliance on occult arts and their highly subjective interpretations of alleged signs to foretell the future as well as the concept of preordination. Reliance instead is placed on objective data of past trends and disciplined analysis of such data through the use of models and scientific, if not quantitative, methods. The objectives are to prepare for the inevitability of changes that will create the new conditions or environments of the future, to shape to some degree the future that may face the organization, and to enhance the probability of effective performance of all personnel in the future. The present-day emphasis is on generating alternative futures that may confront an institution.

The field of study called "futures," or futurism, took its rise in the 1960s and began to be applied as "educational futures" in the 1970s. It is an extension of planning efforts to further reduce uncertainty of subsequent events beyond relatively short time frames or more immediate operational concerns. Steiner wrote in 1979 that "Futures research has escalated much more rapidly in universities, service organizations, and government than in business, but it is being adopted increasingly by business."[21]

Terms such as *alternative futures* and *future*

scenarios have gained much popularity during the past decade. These start with a unique set of assumptions based on extrapolation of trend lines. Such extrapolations are only as valid as the assumptions upon which based and the extent of the knowledge base of the person performing the long-range future projections. Alternative futures have been talked about in the education literature more than they have been applied to influence decision making by educational administrators.

The fanciful speculations of the uniformed, or those with only limited insights into research and development in a given discipline, were not accepted. The emphasis was on those with special expertise or at the cutting edge in a given field to perform the more disciplined analysis of data and to interpret the future significance of such information.

Special devices such as the Delphi technique, named after the famed oracle in Greek legend, were designed to procure opinions from groups of experts in a given dimension of a discipline. The Delphi approach is a refinement of the older "panel of experts" forecasting method and uses more precise sampling and more disciplined selection of experts who are to submit opinions as to future environments or developments. The panel of experts responds to a series of written interrogations on an individual and isolated basis, that is, there are no face-to-face confrontation, debates, or discussions among experts. A series of questionnaires is used with responses on one questionnaire used to prepare subsequent ones. The responses are consolidated to procure the consensus of expert opinion on what the future has in store. In short, the Delphi technique can be called a sophisticated questionnaires approach for divining the future by consulting a panel of qualified experts who respond separately to the series of inquiries submitted to them. It has been abused and misused by assuming that it is possible to prepare relevant futures scenarios by polling groups without special insights or persons not at the cutting edge in a field, using a single questionnaire of questionable design and failing to process the data procured with the skill necessary. It is the

use of recognized experts (modern-day "oracles") rather than the questionnaire that is most likely to produce the scenarios desired. Chambers et al. rated the accuracy of the Delphi method as "fair to very good" over the short term and long term (two years or more).[22] The Delphi, or more precisely "oracular," approach is a significant advance over the visionary forecasts or prophecies based on personal judgments or revelations as well as the panel consensus method, assuming that the experts used are legitimate and the series of questionnaires is designed precisely.

"Readiness" is what peering into the future is all about. The value of futurism lies in its ability to help administrators to reduce the level of uncertainty about future conditions and to define future environments with sufficient detail that the necessary adaptations or new competencies needed to maintain effectiveness can be known in advance. At this point in time the generation of alternative educational futures with relatively high levels of credibility has not been developed to where it can enhance educational decision making. There could be some improvements in long-range forecasting techniques for education during the 1980s, but the 1990s seems to be a more realistic time frame for such developments, thus improving the readiness and quality of educational administration.

Failures and Successes in Planning

Planning has potential for helping an organization to cope with the uncertainties of the immediate, medium, and long-range future. There are no guarantees, for the process quality is influenced by:

1. Time dedicated to it; hurried planning is less effective.
2. Resources available; "from nothing comes nothing" applies to planning.
3. Competencies available; planning does not come naturally, that is, without special preparation.
4. Infrastructure in place; without specialists in

data analysis, computers, planning models, and so on, more problems emerge and the quality may be reduced.

5. Experience in planning; first efforts are not always the best.
6. Attitudes; resistance to planning compounds the problems.
7. Past impact of plans; plans developed and then ignored create an undesirable precedent.
8. Leadership; stimulation from leadership positions always helps.
9. Unrealistic expectations; ask more than is possible and you will receive even less from the planning activities.

Terry cited major reasons "why plans go wrong" that were consistent with the above. They included "having unrealistic and too many goals"; "failing to develop up-to-date strategic and tactical plans"; "ignoring the use of plans in everyday activities"; "forgetting about creativity in developing plans"; "utilizing a standardized plan for individual needs"; and "concentrating on immediate short-range problems" (or planning to put out fires only).[23]

A common shortcoming in educational planning is the lack of production and emphasis upon strategic dimensions. Steiner listed the ten major mistakes or pitfalls in strategic planning in business which could be avoided if and when educational administrators accept the importance of strategic planning. These pitfalls to be avoided are:[24]

1. Top management believes it can delegate strategic planning to planners. (Strategic planning must be a top management responsibility for development and execution.)
2. Top management becomes too involved in operational problems at the expense of strategic planning (which is neglected).
3. Major line personnel are not involved in strategic planning.
4. Strategic plans are not used as standards for measuring managerial performance.
5. Climate is not congenial to strategic planning.

6. Assuming falsely that strategic planning is separate from management in general.
7. The approach used is too formal, with a consequent loss of flexibility and creativity in strategic planning development.
8. There is a failure to review strategic plans of divisional and department heads.
9. There is a failure to develop goals and objectives to guide other long-range planning.
10. There may be too much emphasis on intuitive approaches (rather than formal) to planning.

Administrators must be planners as well as decision makers, leaders, change agents, and so on. The higher one moves up the administrative hierarchy, the more emphasis and the higher priority are granted in the administrator's time schedule to planning. This points to the need for the development and sharpening of planning competencies with experience as an administrator.

The administrators at top levels should know enough about the planning process to be able to differentiate between the well done and the poor plans.

SUMMARY

Perceptions of planning vary, with most recognizing its futures orientation, readiness, and direction-setting and decision-making contributions. At times it is difficult to distinguish planning from other administrative functions, for it has something to contribute to each.

Planning is defined as any set of formal and rational activities that seek to anticipate conditions, directions, and challenges at some future point in time for the purposes of enhancing the readiness of personnel and the organization to perform more effectively and to attain relevant objectives by optimal means.

The process when conceived as targeted or operational planning has a long history in education. Curriculum, facilities, and fiscal planning are fairly common in education. A dynamic environment and more complex educational institutions served to intensify the need for more effective educational planning.

The decision process initiates planning and is in turn influenced by the process. The best measure of the quality of a plan is found during its implementation phase and when the results of the plan are evident. Planning is seldom perfect and modifications of plans as new information or unanticipated situations occur should be the rule rather than the exception.

Strategic planning probes where an institution is going, long-range objectives, what future programs and services should be, and so on. Tactical plans grow out of and support the major tasks required to achieve the strategic plan. Most of what goes on in a school system is operational or tactical planning.

Planning is an attitude or frame of mind, but it requires some kind of structure and procedures to realize its potential. A "planning infrastructure" or support system is necessary to facilitate the implementation of the functions. A variety of techniques can enhance the planning quality, ranging from the general estimate of the situation to mathematical forecasting tools. The degree of sophistication in forecasting can range from subjective opinions to objective and mathematical analysis of trends and factors influencing a series of events.

Needs assessments seek to define the magnitude of the gap between what is and what is desired. It sets the stage and gives direction to the planning activities that follow.

Fascination with the future is as old as history. The futurists of today analyze hard data rather than the movement of the stars for portents of things to come. Educational futures had its serious beginnings during the 1970s. The Delphi technique can be called a sophisticated questionnaires approach for divining the future through use of a panel of qualified experts who respond separately to a series of inquiries. It has been distorted by some to describe the use of any questionnaire to anyone to procure whatever type of data.

Planning represents potential and carries no guarantees. Without adequate time devoted to it, resources, special competencies, and so on, it is not likely to be effective. The higher one moves up the administrative hierarchy, the more important planning competencies as well as time to plan become.

NOTES

1. J. M. Pfiffner and R. V. Presthes, *Public Administration,* Englewood Cliffs, N.J.: Prentice-Hall, 1953, p. 83.
2. W. H. Newman and E. K. Warren, *The Process of Management,* Englewood Cliffs, N.J.: Prentice-Hall, 4th ed., 1977, p. 225.
3. Ibid., p. 12.
4. Ibid., pp. 225 and 328.
5. R. A. Johnston, F. E. Kast, and J. E. Rosenzweig, *The Theory and Management of Systems,* New York: McGraw Hill, 2nd ed., 1967, p. 21.
6. Y. Dror, "The Planning Process: A Facet Design," in F. J. Lyden and E. G. Miller, eds., *Planning-Programming-Budgeting: A Systems Approach to Management,* Chicago: Markham, 1967, pp. 93–116.
7. Ibid., pp. 99–100.
8. Ibid., p. 96.
9. George R. Terry, *Principles of Management,* 7th ed., Homewood, Ill.: Irwin, 1977, p. 173.
10. George A. Steiner, *Top Management Planning,* London: Macmillan, 1969, p. 18.
11. Ibid., p. 17.
12. Henri Fayol, "Planning," in *Readings in Management,* Harold Koontz and Cyril O'Donnell, eds., New York: McGraw-Hill, 1959.
13. George A. Steiner, *Strategic Planning,* New York: Free Press, 1979, p. 11.
14. Terry, op. cit., p. 188.
15. Based on ideas presented by Preston P. Le Breton and Dale A. Henning, *Planning Theory,* Englewood Cliffs, N.J.: Prentice-Hall, 1961.
16. Steiner, *Strategic Planning,* op. cit., pp. 63–65.
17. For a specific education application, see Daryush M. Nowrasteh, *Planning and Management Systems for State Programs of Vocational and Technical Education: An Application of Research,* Columbus, Ohio: Center for Vocational and Technical Education, November 1971.
18. G. G. V. Parker and E. L. Segura, "How to Get

a Better Forecast," *Harvard Business Review*, March–April 1971, pp. 99–109.

19. John C. Chambers, S. K. Mullick, and D. D. Smith, "How to Choose the Right Forecasting Techniques," *Harvard Business Review*, July–August 1971, pp. 45–74.

20. Ibid., pp. 73–74.
21. Steiner, *Strategic Planning*, op. cit., p. 243.
22. Chambers et al., op. cit., p. 55.
23. Terry, op. cit., p. 211.
24. Steiner, op. cit., p. 294.

CHAPTER REVIEW QUESTIONS

1. Why did educational planning become more important during the 1980s than ever before in history?
2. How is operational or tactical planning related to strategic planning?
3. Should deviations from a carefully developed, well documented plan be tolerated during its period of implementation? Justify your stand.
4. How is planning related to the other administrative processes?
5. What are three of the newer and more sophisticated approaches used in educational planning?
6. What is meant by the term *planning infrastructure*?
7. What is the Delphi technique? Indicate its value and limitations.
8. What are the advantages and disadvantages of creating a central planning agency in a school system?
9. Why should educational planning become more important and more time consuming the higher one moves up the administrative hierarchy?
10. Why do the best hopes and efforts in planning sometimes fail?

SELECTED REFERENCES

Chambers, John C., Mullick, Satinder K., and Smith, Donald D., "How to Choose the Right Forecasting Technique," *Harvard Business Review*, July–August, 1971, pp. 45–74.

Educational Research Quarterly, "Futures in Education," R. A. Weaver, special issue editor, Vol. 1, No. 4, Winter 1977, 100 pp.

Dror, Yehezkel, "The Planning Process: A Facet Design," in Fremont J. Lyden and Ernest G. Miller, eds., *Planning-Programming-Budgeting: A Systems Approach to Management*, Chicago: Markham, 1967.

Hack, W. G. et al., *Educational Futurism 1985: Challenges for Schools and Their Administrators*, Berkeley, Calif.: McCutchan, 1971.

Steiner, George A., *Strategic Planning*, New York: Free Press, 1979.

Terry, George R., *Principles of Management*, 7th ed., Homewood, Ill: Irwin, 1977. chaps. 9–12.

5

EDUCATIONAL CHANGE MANAGEMENT: THE FACILITATION OF ORGANIZATIONAL GROWTH, RETRENCHMENT, AND/OR IMPROVEMENT

Maintaining the status quo, in an efficient manner, was accepted as the prime responsibility of administrators during much of past history. This was a reflection of the times and cultural values that revered ancient virtues and preferred stability. To illustrate, in ancient Greece the philosopher Xenophon attacked the Sophists of his day as innovators leading youths away from the established and unchanging virtues. Socrates, a great teacher as well as philosopher, was judged guilty of corrupting the youths of Athens by stimulating them to think rationally and objectively about purposes, values, and ways of living not in harmony with his contemporaries or other approaches to education. The price for advocating change in educational approaches at that time was to drink the poisoned hemlock. Proponents of change were not treated well during much of history, which may help to explain, to some degree, why those who had something to lose if they were on the wrong side of the change-no-change debate hesitated to declare themselves on such sensitive issues.

Weber's bureaucratic model reflected the needs of a society for order and efficiency where chaos and waste prevailed previously in organizations that were growing in complexity. This model may be judged harshly now by many insensitive to the needs of its times because it was a design for preserving and perpetuating efficiently the status quo and offered little by way of facilitating the management of organizational change.

The last half of the twentieth century saw the intensification of tensions in society that in turn stimulated the need for more rapid and more frequent changes in social institutions including systems for education. The concept of a school system as basically a relatively stable social institution was torn asunder by the variety of forces that emerged in the years following World War II. These social forces were not confined to advances in technology but included fundamental value reorientations in the way persons of various races, employees and employers, and people at various economic levels were to interact and the new human relationship patterns that were to prevail.

Change as a social value was placed in a new perspective. Change was something "to be

101

sought rather than fought." The management of educational change, along with the efficient management of ongoing operations, was accorded recognition as an important competency in educational administration that deserved a higher priority in the administrator's time schedule as well. If the educational organization seeks to grow in complexity, strive for excellence, or cope with retrenchment (a negative change), then those responsible for its efficient and effective administration must facilitate whatever relevant transitions are necessary to insure its relevance in future as well as in present environments. Drucker, as well as many others in business management, called for a fundamental shift in administrative posture toward building and managing innovative systems.[1]

It should not be assumed that no school systems changed to any degree prior to 1945. School systems of today are not exact replicas of their counterparts of 100 or 200 years ago. Far from it; they neither look, act, nor feel like their historical counterparts. The professional behaviors of teachers, comprehensiveness of educational opportunities made available through formal schooling, methods of instruction, design of facilities, systems of financing education, and so on, are very different now from what they were a generation ago, much less a century ago.

By way of some specific illustrations, by 1870 the graded school instructional organization pattern—then an innovation—was implemented in practically all city school districts. In moving from the less learning efficient, relatively cumbersome nongraded approach, many went to the opposite extreme of rigidly implemented grade classifications for elementary schools. There followed a reaction that led to a passing parade of other instructional improvement plans that modified the rigid age-grade classifications. Many were named after cities, such as Pueblo, Gary, Dalton, and Winnetka, where the innovations originated. Efforts to improve upon the school's curriculum and instruction have seldom ceased since then.

There came into being a wave of revisions, called "innovations," of the subject matter content of high school science and mathematics courses during the 1960s and 1970s, such as BSCS (biology), PSSC (physics), CHEM (chemistry); and SMSG (mathematics). Most were led by persons outside of professional education and the costs were borne by federal and foundations grants rather than by state or local school district funds. This so-called curriculum revolution is better called an "evolution of subject matter content of disciplines" taught in secondary schools and is a conservative curriculum reform. It did not approach the zeal of the so-called progressive education movement that sought a generation earlier to significantly restructure the secondary school curriculum and to replace the emphasis on the traditional disciplines or subject matter curriculum. The more drastic curriculum reform efforts based on formats such as the core, broad fields, and "experience" curriculums were rejected with some degree of finality by 1940.

Those who championed the more recent curriculum and instruction "innovations" were not of a single philosophic, psychologic, or other pedagogic persuasion. Eclecticism prevails. No one emerged during the recent educational reform efforts to exert an influence equal to, much less surpassing, John Dewey and E. L. Thorndike.

Educational administrators of prior years had to deal with some change; but it was not of the rapid pace, scope, or range evident in more recent years that promises to continue for at least the rest of this century.

INNOVATION DEFINED AND ANALYZED

Miles defined innovation as change that is thought to be more efficacious in accomplishing the goals of the system.[2] This general concept defines change in terms of its purposes and does not limit it to a single dimension of education such as curriculum and instruction. Thompson viewed innovation as "the generation, acceptance, and implementation of new ideas, processes, products, or services."[3] This is more specific and describes its major dimensions. Paul Mort and his students preferred the term *adaptation,* to innovation, which was defined as the capacity of the institution to respond to its role in society.[4] These studies which began during the late 1930s sought to identify factors that enable some school systems to be more highly oriented toward "adaptation" than others. They were concerned more with triggering mechanisms than with the process of innovation per se, but stopped short of identifying administrative competencies related to educational change management. Most writers focus on change models, theories, or processes rather than their implications for administrative behavior and change management.

The common dictionary definitions of innovation view it as dealing with change in something established; hence, a novelty. An innovation, then, focuses on something established that should be changed but which must await the discovery or development of the novel (something different) before the switch or replacement can take place. The verb form "to innovate" means "to introduce new ideas or things," that is, focuses more on the implementation phase or process.

Change may or may not beget improvement. It is possible to regress, that is, change for the worse rather than better. That is why innovation may create the illusion of progress, but when the final results are in there may be none.

Disillusion sets in when a highly touted innovation fails to live up to expectations, and this is followed soon after with discontinuance or reversion to prior behavior modes or structural patterns. One of the more perplexing problems in change management is determining when a change to a new mode has become institutionalized, that is, become an integral and permanent part of the system.

OPERATIONAL DIMENSIONS OF CHANGE: INVENTION, IDENTIFICATION, INNOVATION, AND IMPROVEMENT

The change process in an organizational setting is far more complex than the simple act of decreeing that a new approach will be adopted by all in the system. From an operational and management point of view it helps to perceive of change in terms of four separate but interrelated components: invention, search and/or identification, innovation, and improvement.

There can be no change unless there is something in existence to change to. The invention or creation of a new instructional strategy, a more promising instructional organization pattern, a new teaching machine or device, a more relevant curriculum, and so on, must exist if change from prevailing operations is to be triggered. An invention of significance to education is the product of a creative mind somewhere in a school system, in an educational research and development center, in a university, or in some other discipline. Originality need not be confined to gadgets or machines. It may be expressed in social (as opposed to physical) inventions that stress procedures and relationships. Grading of pupils, ability grouping, and team teaching are illustrations of social inventions. Intellectual, scholarly, and creative abilities operating in an environment where there is time to think and resources to develop ideas into operational reality are essential for creating new models of instruction, administration, and so on. One of the problems in educational change management, in contrast to medicine and agriculture, is the dearth of investments in the production of new products, treatments, or systems. What is generated is not tested in field situations as rigorously as is noted in fields outside of education. Educational change management would be able to proceed more vigorously if there existed a greater number of more promising things and systems to change to (and that are within the fiscal ability to procure).

Most school systems have barely enough resources to operate effectively at present levels much less to invest heavily in research, generation, and development of new physical and social inventions. By tradition our society has opted not to allocate or even consider seriously making R & D (research and development) investments in educational organizations to rival the dollar value found in business and industry or medicine or agriculture. Local school systems must go out to search and identify promising practices or technology generated elsewhere. The starting point in educational change management is the development of a formal, systematic, and continuing pattern of searching for and identifying that which may help the organization to perform more effectively, make more productive use of limited resources, or, in general, insure the relevancy and greater likelihood of realizing the goals and objectives. The search process may include the reading of professional journals, attendance at professional convocations, or visiting R&D centers or wherever there may be created or tested the promising new approaches and mechanisms.

What is commonly called innovation has a restricted meaning herein and applies primarily to implementation and diffusion of the promising practice or mechanism uncovered during the successful search phase. It implies that that part of the educational operation that needs changing in order to resolve a problem or to produce greater progress is known as well. This is change for a purpose rather than by accident of running into an interesting idea. Qualities of mind, personality, or position essential for generating the new are not necessarily the same as those required for effective dissemination or implementation of the invention. The inventor of the novel does not have to perform all strategic or operational roles demanded in change management. It is important for those responsible for implementation and diffusion of a promising practice to hold a position in the hierarchy with decision-making authority that includes a measure of control over a set of resources. Innovation, as perceived herein, is field- or practice-oriented rather than a laboratory or university activity. State education agencies and local school systems have significant roles in the innovation (or dissemination and implementation phase) process, but may or may not be generators of new approaches or mechanisms.

Special criteria, often applied or interpreted by external auditors, are needed to judge whether a change from previous modes is good, bad, or indifferent. This is the normative aspect of change management. The goal is improvement in the organization, either in the quality of stimulated learning or in the degree of productivity in resource use, rather than change for the sake of change. Change is the means and represents potential for improvement. This is a difficult and sensitive task because many prefer to avoid knowing how much learning was improved, how much better educational resources are being utilized, or how much community relations were enhanced as a result of implementing the new and abandoning the old ways. Educational administrators are beginning to establish preconditions for innovation based on hard data or other objective evidence that demonstrate a new approach was adequately tested and found to result in improvements in field applications. The special emphasis on evidence to support the possibilities of improvement tends to minimize the probability of being trapped by the appeal of gadgetry or the rhetoric that often surrounds change, as Eye, Netzer, and Krey warned:

> . . . the gadgetry of any profession seems to be the rallying point for the quacks of the profession. . . . There have been, there are, and probably will continue to be "operators" in the educational profession who are willing to single out any vehicle of change and deal with it as though it satisfied all of the professional program needs.[5]

THE RESEARCH ON SOCIAL CHANGE AND ITS CONTRIBUTIONS TO UNDERSTANDING INNOVATION IN EDUCATION

The management of educational change often requires determination of what strategies for the implementation of the novel are most likely to be effective in particular school and community settings. The modification of previously crystallized professional behaviors in education may be viewed as a special case of social change and profit from the research in that area.

Much of what follows is an adaptation to educational change management from the summary of conclusions of significant research on social change prepared by Berelson and Steiner.[6] It is possible for large and complex social change (e.g., changing professional behavior patterns of teachers to accept teaching with other instructors as a member of a social group or team rather than as the only professional in the classroom) to be assimilated with a minimum of social disruption if the behavior modifications are desired by the persons affected. The reverse is also true, namely, that even a small social change not desired will be resisted and be achieved only at considerable social and personal costs. If teachers are not consulted about a minor modification in existing instructional styles, major implementation problems are likely to be encountered. Likewise, changes imposed on a school unilaterally by groups external to the system (i.e., an undesirable approach to teacher evaluation mandated by the legislature) are not likely to be accepted without considerable resistance, struggle, and expenditure of resources. Reliance on pure pressure upon teachers or others to modify school behaviors may result in false or surface compliance while covert resistance continues.

The more a proposed change appears to threaten traditional values of the group involved, the greater the resistance is likely to be encountered. Modification of behaviors in spite of resistance will result in considerable cost in social and personal disorganization. As Davis reported, "In some cases the psychic costs of change can be so severe that they affect even the physical health of employees."[7] Resistance can be "logical" (based on good or rational reasons), "psychological" (a reflection of the attitudes and feelings of individuals), or "sociological" (based on the values and interests of peers or groups).[8]

The slower the social change rate, the greater is the commitment to discussions by those affected by it. The more new proposals introduced through existing and familiar institutions or channels, the less likely the change will be considered a serious disruption of a prevailing way of life. Allowing more time and exerting less pressure for immediate adjustment permit greater opportunity for rationalizing the change with existing practices.

Social change is more likely to be stimulated in heterogeneous rather than homogeneous societies. Innovation in systems where most of the professional personnel have completed professional preparation at the same or similar schools, are of the same age group, have similar experience profiles, and so on, the more likely they are to encounter implementation problems than in systems where a pattern of heterogeneity prevails.

Social change is more likely and more readily accepted in material aspects of the culture, such as in technology, than in the nonmaterial dimensions, such as value patterns or educational aims. Thus, a teaching machine may be more readily accepted by those who consider mastery of subject content to be of great importance and whose psychology of learning is consistent with the one upon which the machine is based. Furthermore, innovations are more readily accepted in less emotionally charged, less sacred, and in more technical sectors of a practice (such as new tools or tactics); in the simple rather than the complex dimensions of a profession; in the nonsymbolic as opposed to the symbolic facets; in the form rather than in the substance of a practice; in elements congenial rather than strange to the profession; and during periods of pressure, crisis, and stress rather than normal times. Modifications of teacher and administrator behaviors are more likely to occur when the school system is subject to criticisms or when a respected leader expresses dissatisfaction with results while others appear to be satisfied.

There is a tendency to move toward stability following drastic social change. Reorganizations follow disruptions and reestablish a new security base for stability. Within any profession major changes are not likely to be stimulated by those in the lowest social stratum. Major changes in professional practices are not likely to be led by those not traditionally or legitimately in control. Change agents are more apt to be members of the deviant or disaffected groups, but must have some status (or at least visibility) to stimulate change. Those without power in an organization to introduce change must depend upon media attention to gain visibility, and informal or unusual tactics to stimulate movement toward their objectives. Studies show innovators to be younger than those inclined to resist change and also more oriented toward the outside world. They also have a tendency to embrace new ideas and practices in less time and are less likely to discontinue the new after adoption.

A social conflict is likely to intensify when the goals of disputants are held onto rather rigidly; contact or openness between parties is limited; each of the opposing groups is closely knit; the participants on each side of the conflict are committed to a cause; and where the rules for resolving conflict are poorly defined or unstable. A sharpening of the conflict will stimulate participants in opposing camps to associate primarily with those who believe as they do. This may deepen the strife through polarization of participants and hardening of antagonistic positions. Cliques come into being and are more easily identified in school systems experiencing conflict.

Elimination of the original source of the dispute may not resolve the interpersonal conflicts. As persons other than the original disputants become involved, settlement based on purely rational means becomes more difficult. An external threat may result in subordination of internal group conflicts to achieve victory over the common or outside attackers. Removal of the external threat, however, usually causes resumption of internal disputes once again.

During polarization around controversial issues a succession of leaders may result in a new one usually assuming a more extreme position on the issues than the predecessors; word of mouth communications are used more because this medium is more adaptable to partisan purposes than the mass media of communication; and arguments will tend to move from specific to more general issues, from the original issue of contention to issues not previously contemplated, and from a simple divergence on controversial issues to personal antagonisms.

The impact of a social upheaval or crisis upon social and professional relations depends upon preexisting conditions in the community as a whole or the school community in particular.

The crisis will tend to deepen the chasm that separates opposing groups if the community is heterogeneous.

The introduction of social inventions in educational institutions may trigger internal professional conflicts if the process is poorly implemented. Effective change management is related to sensitivities to the value orientations and dominant professional qualities of the professional staff affected by the change process.

Other studies that focused on change within the educational institution reported that resistance to innovation is not always based upon stubbornness of some professional groups. Inadequate field testing of the new practice, overloaded personnel, unrealistic implementation goals, lack of special skills to introduce or promote innovations, and alienation from the surrounding environment can work against the facilitation of change in an organization. One source indicated that the rejection of change in an elementary school setting was related to such factors as ignorance of the potential within an invention, default (lack of interest), preference for maintaining the status quo, societal mores, interpersonal conflicts, erroneous logic, and so on.[9] Carlson identified three barriers that are partially responsible for the slow rate of change in schools as absence of a change agent, a weak knowledge base, and "domestication" of the public schools.[10] These suggest that the promotion of change is related to incentives and motivation, that is, whether financial, political, professional, or personal incentives are most likely to promote the realization of objectives in the educational organization.

Social change is facilitated when pressures from various forces demand a response. Figure 5.1 presents an idealized version of the flow of forces from pressure to response. The time factor is absent. Of course, not all ideas define issues and give birth to social movements.

Education innovation may result by (1) plain drift (seemingly aimless and uncertain activities over a period of time); (2) accident (primarily unplanned or fortuitous occurrences); (3) revolution (violent social protests and upheavals that follow); and (4) purposeful and rational planning. Revolutions in education are bloodless. They may be evidenced by actions such as mass resignation of school board members, administrators, and/or teachers to demonstrate opposition to some event or unwelcome restrictions or modifications on existing practices.

THE MANAGEMENT OF PURPOSEFUL AND RATIONAL CHANGE IN EDUCATION

The purposeful and rational approach to change is based upon answers to such queries as Why change?; What should be changed?; What to change to?; How, where, and when to introduce the new?; How best to support and monitor acceptance of the new?; and How well are the new and the novel satisfying expectations or initial objectives?

Strategic change management should begin with a probe of problems and pressures facing the organization that generate criticisms of the institution, in general or in specifics. It may result in the formulation of a policy on change for the organization as a whole, its major divi-

sions, and for its educational leaders at all levels in the hierarchy. The responses to Why change? provide the rationale or justification for educational change management strategies and related activities.

The next is a more detailed specification of the initial phase described in the previous paragraph. In operational terms it is diagnostic in thrust and concerned with setting priorities as to what dimensions of the organization should be changed first or what fundamental shifts are needed to facilitate changes in other dimensions. The question What to change to? calls for specific diagnosis, or needs assessments, of all parts and services of the educational organization. There is examination of that which is criticized and that which has escaped negative reactions for the moment. It includes at least gross analysis of vital dimensions such as the curriculum, instruction, services for special types learners, the administrative organization, resource management practices, community relations, and so on.

The answer to the query What to change to? reveals initialing what needs changing and ends with identifying the new or the novel generated

FIGURE 5.1

Flow of forces from pressure to response in the accomplishment of social change.

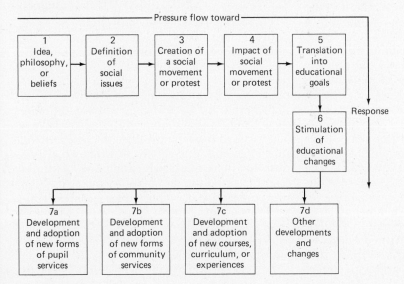

either within or outside the system. A change agent must know where to search and to judge the potential of that which is new. Education would do well to impose the discipline demanded in other fields when a new and highly touted product or remedy comes upon the scene. The medical profession, for example, refuses to tolerate extravagant or premature claims of cures; it insists on hard evidence that goes beyond testimonials of so-called cured patients or some practioners of the art. To report "cures" that cannot be verified may lead to disciplinary action from the profession. In addition, there are federal agencies that monitor any undesirable side effects of drugs that may cure specific conditions in humans. Undesirable side effects can occur in social inventions as well. What is gained if a pupil "learns" more math and science only to develop a lifelong hatred and subsequent avoidance of both? The lot of the educational change manager would be a happier one if more disciplined appraisals based on hard evidence of the improvements and possible side effects were in evidence in education.

The above assumes that each school system pursues a search for innovations to meet its unique needs for change leading to improvement. This is consistent with Goodlad's thesis that "an effective change strategy is one through which the alternative best suited to the needs of a given institution come to the attention of those in it and are used in a continuous process of improvement."[11] It limits the role of external agencies to research and the production of possible new approaches or mechanisms for the consideration of educational institutions. Goodlad noted that the "educational reform movement of the 1960s" was strongly impacted by the "research, development, diffusion (R,D,&D) model" which assumed that federally funded agencies external to local school systems would stimulate change that was consistent with a federal educational policy on change in schools. Goodlad added that much of what these federally supported external agencies "developed and diffused turned out to be answers in search of problems" and also that "practitioners perceived their problems differ-

ently and, frequently, did not see these answers, however elegantly packaged, as relevant."[12]

When the new and the novel are not supported by research or able to demonstrate practicability through adequate field testing, its prime advocates may use testimonials, unverified data, or rudely dismiss the call for supporting evidence as the "last refuge of the antiinnovation-minded establishment." Resistance to some highly proclaimed "promising practices" can come from many sources. It may stem from those among the first to note that the so-called innovations were inadequately conceptualized and/or tested. The dashed hopes of some early adopters who implemented the questionable new practices is a lesson that is not lost on those responsible for effective educational change management.

Assuming there exists something new with high potential for stimulating improvement in a given educational setting, the next phase in educational change management focuses on how to introduce change, where in the system does one begin the change, and when is the most opportune time or what is the best schedule for implementation. Many may assume that these are the real issues in educational innovation and may slight the strategic change plan and policy, the diagnosis of what needs changing, as well as the careful and critical search.

There can be no real innovation, or likely improvement therefrom, until the new or the novel reaches the operating level whether it be the classroom, decision-making behavior of administrators, or existing program modifications. Most strategies are based on the belief that there must be a change in people before there can be a shift in procedures and practices. The issue of how to introduce the new and the novel becomes one of how to create an awareness that there exists something worthy of professional attention; how to move next from simple awareness to continuing interest that prompts action; how to motivate professionals to acquire the competencies necessary to better understand and be able to implement the new and the novel, and so on.

In short, personnel that will be influenced by

the new and the novel need time and training to develop understandings and new skills related to the change. There may be printed articles, special conferences, special visits to places where the new and the novel have been implemented, and so on, to attract attention and to stimulate interest. The more difficult, more costly, and more time-consuming dimensions are the professional development seminars that focus on new competency development. Personnel responsible for the implementation and diffusion of new practices and mechanisms must sense what combination of motives and experiences is likely to prompt teachers, administrators, or other personnel to abandon or modify previously established modes of behavior in favor of behaviors consistent with the new and the novel. This is a real challenge, for it is not uncommon for professional personnel to negate the impact of an innovation by seeming to embrace it as a description of what is desired and then continuing to behave or perform as always. This prompted one researcher concerned with the implementation of BSCS biology to declare:

> The data would suggest that there really is no such thing as BSCS curriculum presentation in the schools. . . . Each teacher filters the materials through his own perceptions. . . .[13]

The discrepancy between promise and actual practice is the bane of those responsible for educational change management as well as for the original researchers and developers. The impact of personnel at the operating level, where the services are delivered, on the "quality assurance factor" must be recognized. Again, Gallagher noted on another occasion that curriculum developers could not rest after "packaging" a "cognitively valid and consistent set of materials," but must be concerned with "how these materials are operationally introduced in the classroom environment" lest they "be left with certain unqualified assumptions as to how their package is unwrapped in the classroom."[14]

Where in the system a pilot project or full implementation shall take place is a part of the strategy that must be determined before the serious efforts at personnel development begin. This is the horizontal dimension of the educational change plan and ascertains whether the new and the novel are to be system-wide, confined to a few positions, limited to a few classrooms, confined to a single building or office, and so on. Likewise, if substantive changes in the curriculum are contemplated, there arise the strategy issues of whether the entire shift is to be attempted within a short period of time or whether it will be phased in over a longer period on a piece-by-piece basis. This deals with the rate of innovation and reveals attitudes as to how quickly the system can assimilate part or all of a substantial modification in existing practices. Distortions in social inventions are more likely to occur when its precepts and concepts are diffused more rapidly than personnel or the system can assimilate them.

A leader may be defined as one who purposely sows dissatisfaction with existing approaches. This is done to highlight present shortcomings to set the stage for subsequent purposeful and rational change. There is the risk of gaining considerable unpopularity when doing so. Timing is a factor in successful educational change management as it is in other endeavors. The usual strategy is to identify those in the system most likely to accept the new and the novel. In a certain sense it is identifying the specific environment most conducive to accept or to tolerate change with the least amount of dissension or disruption. "Saving the worst for the last" may facilitate initial success, but could haunt one in the long run with its many areas of serious resistance to change.

There are problems to be faced during the course of a major modification in personnel behavior. The introduction may meet with immediate success only to raise doubts as ongoing difficulties are encountered. These should be anticipated, sought out during the monitoring of progress, and special strategies developed to support and sustain those facing new experiences.

Evaluation is the most important but, more often than not, the most neglected phase of educational change management. Perhaps it is the assumption that all changes will work out and produce desired results. Such unrealistic assumptions can hide serious defects in the world of reality until pressures bottled up or ignored are so great that an explosion occurs that can no longer be ignored. When the novelty wears off, there is the danger of reversion to previous modes of less effective behavior and the innovation is then blamed for lack of productivity. Miles noted many years back that "Educational innovations are almost never evaluated on a systematic basis."[15] Evaluation may seem superfluous to creators with vested interests and the enthusiastic early implementers. Such attitudes are unfortunate and preclude the further refinement and applicability of the new and the novel.

A model of the innovation process presented in Figure 5.2 summarizes much of what was described above. It bears a kinship to Dewey's model of thinking process.

The condition of "disequilibrium," that is, dissatisfaction with the current "equilibrium," is required to start the process. The trigger for the disequilibrium may be the result of either internal or external forces. Goodlad observed that during what he called the "schooling decade" of 1957 to 1967, "Curriculum reform came almost exclusively from outside what has sometimes been described as the interlocking

educational establishment" whereas the "Attack on the locked-in structures of schooling and on the regularities of how pupils are classified and advanced through the grades and how teaching resources are distributed came more from within and especially from teachers of teachers."[16]

Conceptualization of the problem may lead to generating a social invention or the search and eventual identification of a promising practice. Experimentation is then possible to ascertain its effectiveness. Evaluation is concerned with what improvements, if any, can be traced to the novel and the new.

The first five steps of the model deal with facets of the change process prior to actual implementation in a school setting. The laboratory stage of experimentation is a controlled environment where variables can be manipulated more easily.

Pilot programs, or small-scale field tests, provide environments for further refinement of the new and the novel. Many new practices fail in the real world because of human shortcomings or unanticipated events even though based on conceptually sound and experimentally valid premises. Pilot programs make it easier to work out the "bugs" in an invention prior to more widespread dissemination.

Diffusion follows the development of the "debugged" new social invention. A well-designed program of introduction leads to successful installation and the generation of new equilibrium for a given period of time. As Goodlad put it, "Today's innovations become tomorrow's regularities."[17]

There are many other such models. The Guba–Clark model of educational change has four stages (research, development, diffusion, and adoption) plus eight subcomponents (invention—formulating new solutions, design—engineering and packaging of the invention, dissemination—informing or creating widespread awareness, demonstration—presenting the invention, trial—tryout or test in a given context, installation—operationalizing within an institution, and institutionalization or complete assimilation to reduce eventually its status to a "noninnovation").[18]

FIGURE 5.2

Model of the innovation process.

1. Disequilibrium
   ↓
2. Conceptualization
   ↓
3. Identification or design for invention
   ↓
4. Experimentation
   ↓
5. Evaluation (return to step 2 if necessary)
   ↓
6. Pilot programs
   ↓
7. Diffusion
   ↓
8. Successful installations
   ↓
9. New balance or equilibrium

Administrative Roles and Responsibilities

Purposeful and rational change in educational institutions requires a plan of action, specially prepared personnel, and a system of organizational values, commitments, and resources to facilitate the process. Commitment to change at the local school district level must be supported by similar orientations within related educational agencies in the state and nation. This includes the state education department, institutions of higher education that prepare professional personnel, intermediate units of education that support local educational activities, laboratory schools, and federal agencies.

Administrators and supervisors are released from daily classroom activities to give them time to diagnose education problems as well as to search the new and the novel that might result in further improvements in professional practices and services. If the administrative and supervisory personnel are preoccupied with preserving the status quo because of work overloads, lack of vision, or other reasons, the probability of much significant progress toward meaningful educational change will be relatively low.

People, teachers, and administrative personnel represent one facet of the educational change equation, the creation of promising social inventions another, and the work situation is the third. The organizational structure may facilitate or impede the change process. Thompson examined the structural characteristics of the innovative organization and reported that most included the following:[19]

1. Special resources were allocated to foster innovation such as uncommitted money, time, skills and goodwill.
2. A climate was created to facilitate the generation of new ideas.
3. Recognition was granted for search for creative ideas and innovation in addition to the usual extrinsic organizational rewards of income, power, and status (esteem-striving replaces status-striving).
4. Construction of a creative atmosphere free from external pressures that develops successful inventions in relatively short periods of time.
5. There is designed a greater structural looseness, less stratification, and less emphasis on preventing overlapping duties and responsibilities.
6. Group processes are used more with freer communications and less emphasis upon authority in working relationships.
7. There is more thinking in terms of innovative areas than upon the form of research and development departments.

FACTORS INFLUENCING THE DEVELOPMENT AND SPREAD OF INNOVATIONS IN EDUCATION

If an innovation is defined as any new practice implemented for any period of time by whatever size group in the system, then it can be said that school systems have and continue to change. If the standard used to determine change is that it is system-wide in scope or that the practice is assimilated by and still in operation two or more years after its inception, then the record of recent educational changes would be much less impressive. There are problems in interpreting the claims that public school systems are laggards or are dynamic because the criteria for arriving at such conclusions are ill-defined and seldom applied with complete knowledge of the facts. To compound matters further the disputants may be generalizing from a totally different sample of systems.

Most beginnings are characterized by the actions of a small group of change proponents, approximately 2 or 3 percent of the total in the system, who makes the earliest commitment to implement the new.[20] This group exhibits a high degree of awareness of new developments in the field, consults usually with experts away from the local area, enjoys a high level of education, demonstrates leadership capabilities recognized by others, and shows relatively little concern for what others may think about worthwhile changes.

The "early adopters" wait a little longer than the initial group of trail blazers. They constitute a relatively small group as well (no more than one-eighth of the total population), tend to be of a younger age, read special bulletins, are well educated, and are considered leaders as well. They in turn are followed by the "early majority, the majority, and then the laggards."

The North Central Association Study of Innovations

A national inventory of instructional innovations implemented during the early 1960s in a large number of regionally accredited secondary schools was prepared by the North Central Association.[21] These were classified on the basis of fully implemented and operating, tried on a limited basis, the timing of the start of a new innovation, the definiteness of plans to adopt something new in the following year, tried the new and abandoned later, and whether any new practice was not implemented to any degree. An innovation was considered to be implemented if found operating in at least one class.

The 12 most commonly implemented secondary school innovations of the early 1960s were SMSG mathematics (in over 36 percent of the schools), PSSC physics (in 43 percent), CHEM or CBA chemistry (in almost 50 percent), programmed instruction (in use in 29 percent but abandoned by 5 percent), language laboratory (in 75 percent), electronic data processing (in 28.3 percent), team teaching (in 41 percent), and teachers' aides (in 20 percent). The larger the school enrollment and the greater the pupil expenditures, the larger are the number of innovations implemented in these schools.

In contrast, relatively few schools reported implementing the nongraded instructional organization, school-within-a school concept, and extended school year operations. These schools appeared to be implementing innovations at a faster rate than in previous years.

Relatively high abandonment rates (3 to 6 percent) were reported for the newly designed science and math courses, programmed instruction, team teaching, and honor system study halls. Teacher resistance, high teacher

turnover rates, and inadequate facilities were among the common reasons given for abandoning the new practices. The North Central study documents the fact that many secondary schools were implementing the new and the novel by the mid-1960s, that some social inventions were accepted more readily than others, and also that discontinuance can follow the implementation of innovations.

Other Reports on the Fate of Educational Changes

Goodlad classified the "schooling" reforms during 1957 to 1967 as those related to curriculum (a "discipline-centered curriculum reform"), school and classroom organization (such as student promotion and nongrading), and instruction (such as self-directed instruction related to teaching machines and computerized instruction).[22] In addition there were the "changing expectations for schools" where they "were to do almost everything: prepare well for further schooling, provide for work experience, fight prejudice, mitigate the ravishes of inequity, improve the qualities of urban life, relieve joblessness and poverty, and even bring about peace—all the things the larger society apparently could not do for itself."[23] He recognized that much good could be found in many new practices, but they "suffered from unrealistic expectations and inflated press notices." What he called "the schooling decade" (1957–1967) "was an extraordinarily innovative period in American education" but concluded "that it ended in considerable disillusionment regarding the potency of schools was in large part the result of unreasonable expectations."[24] Many other writers and observers of educational change during that and subsequent periods also decried the excessive rhetoric surrounding innovations as well as the propensity to promise more than could be delivered. One of the challenges facing educational change management is to harness the energy of the enthusiastic innovators to the task of educational improvement and withholding press releases until the objective facts or results can support success claims.

Based on his extensive experiences, Goodlad proposed eight postulates for school improvement. These included that "the optimal unit for educational change is the single school with its pupils, teachers, principal—those who live there every day—as primary participants" and "if change within the school is going to be significant and, therefore, probably to deviate from the established expectations and procedures of the system, the school will require a supportive peer reference group."[25] His educational change strategy and management included a strong recommendation for the creation of a "League of Cooperating Schools" as the "supportive peer reference group."

The *Kappan* published a series entitled "What Ever Happened to. . . ." during late 1981 and early 1982. They included administrative changes such as the Kalamazoo "merit/demerit pay plan"[26] which "quietly faded away" after less than ten years of trying, and the ungraded Melbourne High School, started by B. Frank Brown,[27] which continues to function after some 20 years but without the once great publicity it once had.

Educational change management usually assumes that the challenges are related to coping with growth or, more often, introducing the new and the novel. The 1970s witnessed a new dimension, namely, coping with the change brought on by retrenchment. Retrenchment is a change no less painful than accommodations to growth or modification of practices. Emotions run high within the community as well as the school staff when a neighborhood attendance center is closed for valid reasons and pupils transferred to another. Criticisms of educational administrators who must implement what is an economic and educational necessity may be even more severe than those related to changing the curriculum or the dislocations of operating with double sessions.

The Impact of Technology on Changes in Instruction

Technology is on everyone's list of forces generating the necessity for change in teaching and learning. It focuses on application and the practical uses of knowledge. There are physical inventions such as television and the computer that have been adapted to the purposes of education, and there are social inventions such as programmed instruction and the systems approach to administration.

Education has benefited from advances in technology throughout history. The development of the alphabet and the writing instruments influenced greatly ancient systems of learning and instruction. The invention of paper further enhanced the utility of the alphabet and writing which, in turn, facilitated the transmission and extension of knowledge during thousands of years.

Gutenberg's invention of the movable type and printing in the West (there is evidence of earlier breakthroughs in printing in the Orient) represented another technological advance which had profound implications for educational institutions. When it ceased being a novelty, it became apparent that the quality of ideas was neither increased nor diminished by appearing in print form. This obvious fact had to be relearned when modern-day technology that made television and computers was adapted to educational purposes. The accuracy, relevance, and strategies for learning concepts and facts remain important no matter how new or advanced the technology for processing or presenting them. Throughout history there has been the ever-present danger that, at least in the short run, the glamor of a new gadget may obscure the shabbiness or limitations of ideas being disseminated through it.

The alphabet, paper, movable type, chalkboards, globes, and so on, were yesterday's exciting technological developments that had an impact on the education process. The more recent technologies of significance to the instructional dimensions of education are outlined in the following paragraphs.

Photography. It was the sound film (first 16 mm. and then 8 mm.) that gave rise to the enthusiasm related to what was at first called audiovisual instruction, but is today a part of a broader concept of educational technology. Along with slides and filmstrips, the use of sound films serves as an illustration of an "institutionalized" innovation, that is, it is so completely integrated with ongoing instruction in most schools that few consider audiovisual instruction a modern-day technology or innovation. Instant photography has not had a similar impact as yet. The emphasis today is on the development of specific materials to stimulate particular kinds of learning outcomes for this relatively "mature" educational technology.

Recording, reproduction, and transmission of sound. Edison's pioneering efforts to record and reproduce sound on cylindrical and flat recording surfaces were reflections of a mechanical approach that had limited and curiosity value in education. The advent of further technological developments based on electronic sound recording was necessary for this to have an impact in education. First came the discs, then magnetic wire, and finally, the more convenient recording tape gave rise to the ubiquitous tape recorder in most schools. This technology has likewise achieved substantial assimilation. Foreign language laboratories and commercial education laboratories are additional applications of this technology related to sound.

The transmission of sound over long distances through first the AM and then the FM radio was accepted in education, particularly in rural and less densely populated areas. It is being replaced by TV and the video-recording devices that project a visual as well as sound image. The technological improvements in high fidelity and stereo sound have not enjoyed the impact in education that variations of sound recording and reproduction devices have.

Educational Television. Educational television (ETV) has been praised and damned. It may be one of the technologies that never lived up to assumed potential. Millions were poured into the development and dissemination of ETV by the federal government, foundations, and business and industry. In 1966 Mitchell testified that television "stands today (1966) as perhaps the most expensive and disastrous single failure

in the history of educational technology."[28] This is a reflection of the early problems in TV signal transmission, lack of extensive programming, and wildly unrealistic expectations of TV as an instructional device.

Educational television makes possible wider dissemination of outstanding teaching, but limits the presentation to the lecture mode or where learners are passive recipients in the process. The teaching appearing on the TV screen is only as good as that presented before the TV camera. Its successes come from use as a supplement or a special instructional device rather than as a replacement for the live classroom teachers that some of the more enthusiastic proponents of ETV expected. It has served well as an independent study aid in reaching adults through special programs and, in some cases, during strike emergencies.

Educational television has not been assimilated as completely as other audiovisual instructions devices such as the sound film, slides, filmstrips, tape recorders, microfilms, and microfiche, but since it has been around for more than a generation it is not considered new. Further refinements in the technology with videotape recorders and players as well as cable and satellite transmissions of TV signals are relatively new. Videotapes give greater flexibility to adapting instructional materials to individual school class schedules and may compete directly with sound films and their projectors.

To summarize, ETV has had an impact on the process of instruction in schools and will have even more in the years ahead with the advent of videotape cassette and improvements in the distribution of TV signals. The criticisms stem from the unrealistic expectations of some early devotees and the production costs for the "software" or programs.

Using Computers and Microprocessors to Promote Learning. The computer is an electronic device for the manipulation, storage, and retrieval of information. Some consider it to be the greatest invention since the wheel, for it multiplies human intellectual powers and enables completion of tasks in a shorter period of time, and that could be done no other way. It was designed originally for tasks other than those related to the improvement of instruction in education. It took time and money, therefore, to adapt computer technology to the purposes of education. It necessitated the design of new ways of presenting learning sequences, new roles for teachers, and new ways of organizing for instruction. Computer-assisted instruction (CAI), computer-assisted learning (CAL), and computer-managed instruction (CMI) are blends of computer technology and programmed learning. CAI and CAL are similar and focus on the direct use of the electronic computer in the instructional process. CMI, as the name implies, is a teacher and an administrator tool for more effective management of tasks related to instruction such as the posting of student grades on report cards, class scheduling, and other instructional information storage and rapid retrieval.

CAI captured the imagination of many educators, as well as much attention in the press, when it appeared in the early 1960s. It also became controversial because of the grossly underestimated costs of operation, the early focus on the more mundane aspects of education such as drill and practice, and the lack of educationally relevant programs or software. CAI was referred to popularly as "teaching machines" and the overly enthusiastic proponents felt that these machines would replace the need for teachers to repeat the same mistake of earlier innovators who said the same thing about films and ETV. In testimony before a congressional panel in 1966, Arnstein declared: "There is not now in existence anywhere in the United States, a tested, validated, usable computer-assisted teaching program which is economically competitive with 'live' teachers."[29] This was equally true during the 1970s although there was room for hope as the very high computer operating costs began to decline and new technology based on the "computer chip" led to microprocessors or microcomputers.

The economics of change is a matter of concern to educational change management. Computers for instructional purposes did not begin to attract serious and widespread attention until the microprocessors or microcomputers enabled substantial reductions in costs, about one-fifth of the early "large frame" classroom computer systems. This occurred in the early 1980s. In July 1981, *Business Week* reported "More computers have been installed in classrooms during the past 18 months than in the entire preceding decade"; about 70,000 units worth $102 million in 1981, with annual growth rate of 31 percent to a predicted 270,000 units annually worth $350 million by 1985.[30] It took about 25 years and billions of dollars to further improve upon the computer to satisfy educational needs within the limited resources of school systems. The 1980s will finally be the decade that computers are assimilated to a considerable degree in education. It took more than continuing advancement in "hardware," as important as this was to bring computers into common use in schools. The new developments in the reducing size, speed, and cost came very rapidly during the 1970s; some computer models became obsolete in only a few years. In the late 1960s this writer literally "walked through" the banks of vacuum tubes that made up the "insides" of a large, complex, and fast computer. The desk top models of today exceed the power of many large computer main frames of the 1960s.

Of no less consequence is the tremendous development of instructional computer "software," often called "courseware." The computer can only do what it is programmed to do. It takes time and special talents to program a computer to satisfy instructional objectives. Publishers of printed materials have joined hardware manufacturers to produce computer-based instructional materials. In addition, the mystery and fear that surrounded the computer have been pretty well dispelled with a new generation of learners, as well as their parents, seeking to achieve what is called computer literacy. There exist special schools and summer camps for children and youths interested in developing special operational talents for the computer. The video game craze also helped make students at ease at the computer keyboard. The home computer market also facilitated the greater use of computers in schools.

Although it may seem that 25 years is a long time for an instructional innovation to be assimilated into educational systems, it must be remembered that the instrument in question was not designed originally for school use, there was a dearth of educational computer software, and the initial purchase and operating costs were beyond the limited fiscal resources of most school districts. Computer-related instruction will continue to expand throughout the remainder of this century with a host of electronic teaching aids. Their wise use will continue to be dependent upon the professionally prepared educator in the classroom; the computer will not replace but only redirect the talents of teachers.

Programmed Instruction. Without the social invention of programmed instruction, the assimilation of computer-assisted instruction would have taken even longer. According to Lange, there were three major phases in its development.[31] The initial phase was characterized by a false sense of development engendered by little more than enthusiasm for and the overselling of the early program designs. The secondary phase was disillusionment with the primitive early applications. During the 1960s many schools implemented programmed instructional approaches in selected areas only to drop it subsequently as it failed to meet the learning gains and cost savings anticipated. The third phase was signaled by further improvement in the new technology stimulated by the remaining disciplined, dedicated, and imaginative developers. This in turn helped with the revival of interest. Less was heard about it, in a form separate from CAI, during the 1970s and 1980s.

Whether this is the reincarnation of an ancient approach or a relatively recent development depends upon one's interpretation of the history of pedagogical systems. Systematic arrangements of materials to be learned, and step-by-step introduction of concepts, can be traced back to Socrates' style of questioning,

catechetical instruction in the early Christian Church, and the early nineteenth-century interests in the psychology of learning. Programmed instruction is based on a sequence of concepts or experiences that follow a preset order that facilitates evaluation of that which is learned. Each subsequent learning set is built on the preceding one so that one learns by following the preordained sequence. Closely related to it is teaching calling for a breakdown of all that is to be learned by the students into a series of "behavioral objectives"; when a single objective is satisfied, it is followed by another and related challenge. Some argue that this is "neo-Skinnerian" learning direction by teachers or by a "self-instruction" or "self-pacing" set of learning materials.

CAI is another offshoot of programmed learning where the computer displays the sequence of questions or instructional materials and responses to indicate to the pupil a successful response, or to "try again," on a TV tube (cathode-ray tube) or presents the learning materials and responses through the typewriter activated by the computer (much slower approach). Programmed instructional material can be presented in written or printed form in the so-called programmed texts which appear to be out of favor at present.

Programmed instruction's assimilation in schools appears to be related directly to the success of CAI rather than to other modes.

Some Possible Future Technology that May Impact upon Instruction. Corey defined instruction operationally as "the process whereby the environment of an individual is deliberately manipulated to enable him to learn to emit or engage in specified behaviors, under specified conditions, or as responses to specified conditions."[32]

Many issues surround the impact of future technology on the instructional processes in a school setting. Among these are the following: Is it possible to design human learning to be a completed automated process? Can human learning proceed effectively without any human and professional intervention?

At this writing the concept of a completely automated instructional system, that is, primarily an electronically controlled system, appears to be unlikely during this century. Such a system, if and when it does occur, need not exclude all people. Human intervention with the learner and in the process is likely to remain a necessary and positive factor to enhance the quality of learning. New technology of the future is more likely to be means to enhance the effectiveness of professional personnel rather than systems to replace human factors in learning.

Educational strategies during the remainder of this decade and century will continue to change thanks in large part to microcomputers, lasers, and hollography. What is less likely to be tried, much less assimilated, is the technology related to direct stimulation of the human mind by electrophysiological techniques as a means of promoting or improving learning. The "electrical thinking cap" is not likely to be donned by students upon entering classrooms during the remainder of the twentieth century. "Chemically assisted" instruction, based on the technology related to pharmacology with the potential to produce a substance to enhance the learning capability of students, is not likely to develop until sometime during the twenty-first century. Given the prevailing problems with drug abuse on school campuses, there would be considerable resistance to the use of any newly developed "get smart" pills for students in schools.

The projections made in the above should not be interpreted as an indication of little change in instructional approaches. The emphasis will continue to be on social inventions as a means of stimulating learning improvement rather than physical inventions alone.

The Impact of Technology on Changes in Educational Administration

The invention of the automobile during the early part of this century brought about a subsequent revolution in the organization and administration of public education. Developments in transportation technology made it feasible to eliminate over 87 percent of all school districts and to form larger and more efficient administrative units. There were advancements in the technology of construction of physical facilities that helped to bring about the "golden age" of educational facilities planning and construction following World War II. The focus of what follows will be on the technologies related to the computer and the systems approach to administration.

Computers and the Enhancement of Administration. Computers were utilized in school administration at a later date and introduced at a slower rate than in industry or the federal government. The initial uses were in electronic data processing (EDP) applied to school business management rather than instruction. As late as 1961 less than 5 percent of the nation's public school districts employed computer-based EDP.[33] Computer technology applied to education was a "solution searching for some problems." Progress was limited until professional educators acquired more sophisticated insights into the technology which then enabled them to determine what administrative problems could be facilitated through the application of computers. It was also necessary to delay further until costs of leasing or purchasing were reduced, more and better prepared computer technicians were available to operate the new systems, and there were further refinements in the technology.

Frustration was common during the 1960s because early adaptations to educational purposes encountered unanticipated problems as well as operating costs that skyrocketed beyond preliminary estimates. This is typical of most new technologies and explains, in part, why time is an important factor in the assimilation of change. Computer technologies advanced rapidly as new circuitry was developed to enhance the computer's internal memory, retrieval of data and computations were accomplished in shorter time periods, computer programming was simplified, and the bulk or size of computer equipment was reduced initially through the use of transistors and then with silicon chips. Early generations of computers reached obsolescence in only a few years.

The introduction of computers to the various tasks of educational administration increased rapidly during the 1970s. By 1980 it was the unusual school system that did not have access to or did not own and operate electronic data processing equipment. The introduction of the microprocessors in the late 1970s and early 1980s provided further impetus to the assimilation of this technology in education as well as the personal or home computer market. This is not to imply that the computer technology reached its full potential and complete assimilation within a period of about 20 years. It has lost some of the early glamour and some may feel it is no longer a new technology. The remainder of this century will witness further utilization of computers to challenge those responsible for educational change management.

The educational administrator is challenged by the tremendous potential of the advanced state of the computer art as well as the wise use of this resource in all dimensions of the organization. What is called "computer literacy" is an essential competency for educational administrators at all levels of the hierarchy. This implies knowledge of: what it takes to operate a computer system, the various kinds of computer hardware and software that are available or may soon be, the cost-effectiveness and other characteristics of competing systems, how rapidly further changes in computer utilization in the schools can be accomplished, as well as the limitations and advantages of various computer configurations.

All computers, large frame or microprocessors, are characterized by four basic operations: (1) input—the introduction of information into the computer in a form acceptable and comprehended by the machine; (2) storage—a device that holds some or all items in abeyance until commands retrieve them; (3) processing—manipulating the data in accordance to directions included in a computer program; and (4) output—procuring the results of the processed information from the computer with commands to have it appear on a TV screen, typed copy, magnetic tape, and so on. The main frame, or heart, of the computer is the central processing unit (CPU) which operates from a program of instructions (called the "software" or "program"). The computer does only what it is told to do (via the program of instructions); it lacks imagination, initiative, and creativity but "knows" how to follow directions with great speed and accuracy. There are different programming languages; those designed for one brand of computers or a given generation of the same brand may not work on another. A task that may take only a few seconds of computer time may require weeks or months of program-writing time. Programming, or availability of previously prepared programs for a given type of computer, is very important and a cost over and above that of the purchase price for the hardware (the CPU and the so-called peripherals for input, storage, and output).

An AASA report on EDP well over a decade ago made a point that is equally valid today: "It takes more than a machine to produce a technological revolution."[34] It takes people, other resources, and the careful planning for change. Many computer-related specialists such as a director of computer operations, programmers, computer technicians, key punch operators (who may not be necessary for very long) or other data input personnel, and information-systems analysts must be employed to keep the system relevant and operating at efficient levels. Small school systems may "buy" computer services or gain access to the computer hardware available at a regional educational service agency, a local bank, or some local computer service agency. One of the serious problems encountered during the early years of computer technology was the identification of computer information-systems analysts to whom were delegated responsibilities for making the computer system work efficiently and effectively. More than one chief school executive faced embarrassment during the early years when the slick-talking alleged computer specialist failed to deliver on promises. As in so many things in administration the failure to execute effectively according to plan may negate almost completely the great potential inherent in some new technology.

By the mid-1960s computers were harnessed to execute such tasks related to educational administration as maintaining the school census files and preparing related reports, recording and reporting school attendance, financial accounting, recording and reporting student grades and report cards, scheduling classes, preparing and managing the weekly or monthly payrolls, controlling inventory of physical property, and maintaining personnel records. There were refinements in these practices and more were added during the 1970s. The use of electronic typewriters and word processing equipment became more common during the 1970s to increase the productivity of the secretarial staff in administrative offices. The concept and the implementation of the electronic work station for administrators may begin to appear in education during the late 1980s. There must be the competence to address a computer terminal in an administrator's office, an attitude of acceptance of this approach to calling for and reading data essential to prudent decision making, as well as an understanding of models and theory.

The computer technology has been assimilated to some degree in educational administration at this point in time. It has affected the organizational hierarchy and new specializations have been added to the administrative staff. The school business officer was among the first to recognize the contributions of the computer and this led many to assign computer operations at this level. It is presently a technology that has an impact upon all dimensions of the educational system and for that reason should be directed out of the chief executive's office.

The Technology of Operations Research or Systems Management. Just as CAI demanded refinements related to programmed instruction as well as the computer so too must "computer-assisted management" (CAM) call upon the social invention of operations research or systems management to reach the full potential of the computer. An understanding of and competencies in the use of theories and models of the practice of educational administration are necessary in CAM. It is no accident that disciplines that traditionally place greater reliance on the use of theories and models have moved most rapidly toward more sophisticated utilization of computer systems. More about specific theories and models in educational administration will be found in the chapter that follows as well as others. It is important at this point simply to point out the close relationship between systems management as a social invention and the computer as part of the "electronic work station" for educational administrators.

INNOVATION, RISK, AND THE SURVIVAL OF ORGANIZATIONS

It may appear to some to be simpler in the short run to administer an institution along the more comfortable and well-established patterns than to face the turmoil and possible risks to survival that often accompany the introduction and assimilation of change. This is an illusion because no organization can survive for long in a dynamic world without recognizing the need and implementing the essential changes. Charting a new course requires knowledge of the most effective way of reaching the goal of continuing improvement.

There is considerable risk in innovation. Not everything tried will prove effective, and when a change fails to meet expectations, the innovator must expect to be criticized for many things including the squandering of precious resources. Nevertheless, clinging to the traditional ways is as futile as compulsive innovation.

The issue in educational change management is not whether schools should or should not change. Education continues to evolve as evidenced by the many technologies assimilated in various degrees over the past three or four decades. To repeat, the educational change management challenges are deciding what needs changing, what to change to, and sensing the organization's readiness and most appropriate strategies for change. The late Dag

Hammarskjold's, former U.N. General Secretary, advice on mountain climbing is relevant to the educational change manager, namely, "Don't move without knowing where to put your foot next, and don't move without having sufficient stability to enable you to achieve exactly what should be the next step. One who is really serious in his determination to reach the top does not gamble by impatiently accepting bad footholds and poor grips." It could be added that it is equally bad to "freeze" in the same position and not move at all because not everything is perfect.

Education cannot be classified as a "high technology" industry that either generates or readily implements the latest advances in the state of the art. Nonetheless, it does recognize the potential in various technologies that can be implemented and are cost-effective.

In the late 1960s Kahn and Wiener prepared a list of what they called "One hundred technical innovations very likely by the last third of the twentieth century."[35] Many had important implications for educational institutions and provide further evidence of the continuing necessity of educational change management as an important set of responsibilities for educational administrators in the years ahead. A few of these innovations yet to come are "multiple application of lasers and masers," "major reduction in hereditary and congenital defects," "three-dimensional photography," "direct electronic communication with and stimulation of the brain," "chemical methods for improving memory and learning," and "personal electronic equipment for communication, computing, and data processing."[36] They generated a list of "Ten Far-out Possibilities" such as life expectancy of 150 years, interstellar travel, use of extrasensory phenomenon, and lifelong immunization against diseases which may have implications for education after the year 2000.[37]

SUMMARY

Historically the administrator's prime responsibility was to maintain the status quo in an efficient manner. Stability was prized more than change. There was a dramatic shift during the last half of the twentieth century with change becoming something "to be sought rather than fought."

School systems have changed during most of their history as witnessed by the adoption of graded instructional organizations. The more recent periods differ primarily by the rapidity and extensiveness of changes in education. No one has emerged during the recent instructional reforms with influence equal to that of a John Dewey. Much of what prevails as innovation in instruction can be called eclecticism.

Change may or may not beget improvement, for it is possible to change for the worse as well as for the better. There can be no change unless there is something to change to. Most school systems have barely enough resources to keep operating at present levels of effectiveness much less to consider substantial investments in the generation and development of physical and/or social inventions. The starting point for most educational change is the search for the new and the novel rather than its generation. What is commonly called innovation has a restricted meaning herein and applies primarily to the implementation of the promising practice uncovered during the search process.

The stimulation of change in education may be perceived as a special case of the broader concern for social change. The research in social change indicates that complex social change can be assimilated with a minimum of disruption if the change is desired by the persons affected, that changes that threaten traditional values are more likely to be resisted, and that change is more likely to be stimulated successfully in heterogeneous societies than homogeneous ones. There is a tendency to move toward stability following drastic social change.

Purposeful and rational educational change is more likely to result in organizational improvements. Such change searches for answers to the following questions: Why change?; What should be changed?; What to change to?; How, when, and where to introduce the new?; How best to monitor and support acceptance of the new?; and How well is the new satisfying the initial objectives?.

Personnel that will be influenced by the new and the novel need time and training to develop understandings and new skills related to the change. The discrepancy between the inherent promise and results from actual practice is the bane of those responsible for educational change management as well as the original researchers and developers. A leader may be defined as one who purposely sows dissatisfaction with existing approaches in the hopes of stimulating interest in necessary changes. Evaluation is an important but often the most neglected phase of educational change management.

Most educational change models start with the creation of a disequilibrium condition, include the introduction of the new, and conclude with creating a new or improved equilibrium.

Administrators and supervisors are key personnel in the introduction and management of educational change. People represent one facet of educational change equation, the existence of promising inventions another, and the work situation the third. Usually a very small group (2 to 3 percent) begins the change process followed by the early adopters, the early majority, the majority, and finally the laggards.

A North Central Association inventory of instructional innovations during the 1960s showed that schools did assimilate many new practices in curriculum, instructional reorganization, and new technologies. The "schooling decade" from 1957 to 1967 was a time of considerable innovation in education. Goodlad felt that the optimal unit for educational change was the single school with its personnel, pupils, and community. He emphasized the need for "a supportive peer reference group" to help sustain the innovators during difficult periods.

Many technologies in the past and present have had an impact on instruction. The invention of the alphabet, paper, and movable type were the early technologies influencing instruction over history. Photography, recording and transmitting sound, educational television, the computer, and programmed instruction have had more recent impact on instruction. Most of these recent developments have been assimilated in the schools in varying degrees. CAI had to await further advancement in computer technology that led to the relatively inexpensive and smaller-sized microcomputers or microprocessors.

Many technologies related to transportation and construction greatly changed the administration of public education in prior years. The computer moved into educational administration relatively slowly, but within a 20-year period a number of administrative tasks were reported, processed, and recorded with the help of the computer. Frustration was common in the early years of adapting the computer to educational uses. All computers demand four basic operations: input, storage, processing, and output. The central processing unit (CPU) is the heart of the computer. The computer does only what is told to do via a program of instructions; it lacks imagination, initiative, and creativity but "knows" how to follow directions with great speed and accuracy. It takes people as well as machines to produce a technological revolution.

Computer literacy is one of the most important competencies for educational administrators at all levels of the hierarchy. Just as the CAI demanded refinements related to programmed instruction as well as the computer, so too must "computer-assisted management" (CAM) call upon operations research or the systems management techniques to reach the full potential inherent within the computer. Electronic typewriters and word processors were being adopted in education during the 1970s. The creation and effective use of electronic work stations for administrators remains a challenge for the 1980s.

There is considerable risk involved in the innovation process. The major educational change management challenges are what needs changing, what to change to, and how to introduce change. Kahn and Wiener helped to define the dynamic environment facing education and other institutions during the remainder of the twentieth century by indicating the 100 most likely innovations to come and "ten far-out possibilities."

NOTES

1. Peter F. Drucker, *The Age of Discontinuity,* London: Wm. Heineman, 1968, p. 51.
2. Matthew B. Miles, ed., *Innovation in Education,* New York: Teachers College, Columbia University, 1964, pp. 13–18.
3. Victor A. Thompson, "Bureaucracy and Innovation," *Administrative Science Quarterly,* Vol. 10, No. 1, June 1965, pp. 1–20.
4. Paul R. Mort, "Studies in Educational Innovation from the Institute of Administrative Research," *IRA Research Bulletin,* Vol. 3, No. 1, October 1962, pp. 1–8.
5. G. G. Eye, L. A. Netzer, and R. D. Krey, *Supervision of Instruction,* 2nd ed., New York: Harper & Row, 1971, p. 73.
6. See Bernard Berelson and G. A. Steiner, *Human Behavior,* New York: Harcourt Brace Jovanovich, 1964, pp. 613–623.
7. Keith Davis, *Human Behavior at Work/Organizational Behavior,* New York: McGraw-Hill, 1981, p. 204.
8. Ibid., pp. 207–208.
9. G. Eichholz and E. M. Rogers, "Resistance to the Adoption of Audiovisual Aids by Elementary School Teachers," in Miles, ed., op. cit., chap. 12.
10. R. O. Carlson, "Barriers to Change in the Public Schools," R. O. Carlson et al., *Change Process in the Public Schools,* Eugene, Ore: Center for the Study of Educational Administration, University of Oregon, 1965, pp. 3–8.
11. John I. Goodlad, *The Dynamics of Educational Change: Toward Responsive Schools.* A Charles F. Kettering Foundation Program, New York: McGraw-Hill, 1975, p. 19.
12. Ibid., pp. 15–16.
13. J. J. Gallagher, *Teacher Variation and Concept Presentation in BSCS Curriculum Programs,* Urbana, Ill.: Institutions for Research on Exceptional Children, University of Illinois, 1966, p. 33.
14. J. J. Gallagher, *Analysis of Classroom Strategies Associated with Student Cognitive and Affective Performance,* Cooperative Research Project No. 3325, Urbana, Ill.: University of Illinois, 1968, p. 43.
15. Miles, op. cit., p. 657.
16. Goodlad, op. cit., p. 32.
17. Ibid., p. 13.
18. Egon G. Guba, "Methodological Strategies for Educational Change," a position paper for the conference on Strategies for Educational Change, Washington, D. C.: November 8–10, 1965.
19. Thompson, op. cit.
20. E. M. Rogers, "What Are Innovators Like?", in R. O. Carlson et al., op. cit., pp. 55–61.
21. Gordon Cawelti, "Innovative Practices in High Schools: Who Does What and Why and How," *Nation's Schools,* April 1967.
22. Goodlad, op. cit., pp. 28–39.
23. Ibid., p. 43.
24. Ibid., p. 45.
25. Ibid., pp. 175–180.
26. Richard R. Doremus, "What Ever Happened to . . . Kalamazoo's Merit Pay Plan?", *Kappan,* February 1982, pp. 409–410.
27. Richard R. Doremus, "What Ever Happened to . . . Melbourne High School?", *Kappan,* March 1982, pp. 480–482.
28. Statement of Maurice B. Mitchell, *Technology in Education,* Hearings before the Subcommittee on Economic Progress, 89th Congress, 2nd Session, Washington, D.C.: GPO, p. 12.
29. George G. Arnstein, *Technology in Education,* op. cit., p. 110.
30. "School Computers Score at Last," *Business Week,* July 27, 1981, p. 66.
31. B. C. Lange, "Future Developments," in B. C. Lange, ed., *Programed Instruction,* Chicago: University of Chicago Press, 1967, pp. 286–287.
32. S. M. Corey, "The Nature of Instruction," in B. C. Lange, ed., op. cit., p. 6.
33. American Association of School Administrators, *EDP and the School Administrator,* Washington, D.C.: The Association, 1967, p. 4.
34. Ibid.
35. Herman Kahn and A. J. Wiener, *The Year 2000,* New York: Macmillan, 1967, pp. 51–55.
36. Ibid.
37. Ibid.

CHAPTER REVIEW QUESTIONS

1. Why has educational change become something "to be sought rather than fought"?
2. Why were the revisions of the subject matter content of the secondary school curriculum of the 1950s and 1960s judged to be a conservative approach to curriculum reform compared with earlier such reform movements?
3. What research findings tend to support that

teachers and others likely to be affected by a change should be involved in the change process?

4. Why is it desirable to determine what needs changing before developing an educational change management plan?

5. What are the strengths and weaknesses of the research, development, and diffusion (R,D,&D) model for promoting educational change?

6. What is the significance of the statement that "there can be no real change until there is first a change in people"?

7. What organizational factors are most likely to encourage the implementation of change with a minimum amount of disruption?

8. What kinds of educational reform came into education primarily from sources outside the so-called educational establishment and which of the more recent reforms were stimulated from within the education profession?

9. Why are administrators and supervisors consid-

ered to be key personnel in the educational change process?

10. What were the most commonly implemented secondary school innovations during the so-called schooling decade?

11. Which of the recent (since 1945) technologies have been assimilated to some degree in instructional practices and educational administration?

12. What factors helped the greater assimilation of CAI and other computer-related educational approaches during the early 1980s?

13. What innovations that are projected to be perfected during the last few decades of the twentieth century are likely to bring further modifications of educational practices?

14. Why is the technology related to operations research or systems management necessary for the realization of the full potential of computers in educational administration?

15. What are the four basic components in all computer operations?

SELECTED REFERENCES

Doremus, Richard R., "What Ever Happened to . . . Kalamazoo's Merit Pay Plan?," *Kappan,* February 1982, pp. 409–410. (See other *Kappan* articles in this series both earlier and later than the above.)

Goodlad, John I., *The Dynamics of Educational Change: Toward Responsive Schools,* New York: McGraw-Hill, 1975.

Hack, Walter G. et al., *Educational Futurism,* Berkeley, Calif.: McCutchan, 1971.

Hechinger, Fred M., "Where Have All the Innovations Gone?," *Today's Education,* September–October 1976, pp. 81–83, 125.

Kahn, Herman, and Wiener, H. J., *The Year 2000,* New York: Macmillan, 1967.

"School Computers Score at Last," *Business Week,* July 27, 1981, pp. 66–68.

Toffler, Alan, *Future Shock,* New York: Bantam Books, 1970.

6

EDUCATIONAL ADMINISTRATION AS A SCIENCE: THEORIES, MODELS, AND MANAGEMENT SCIENCE CONCEPTS UNDERGIRDING THE PRACTICE

As the proof of the pudding is in the eating, so too is the fundamental value of administration revealed in the performing. Educational administration as a profession is practice oriented, and the quality of a particular administrator will continue to be measured best by performances while under pressure in the uncontrolled environments that characterize educational organizations. For this and other reasons preparation for successful performance was predicated on the reflections of the experienced practioner and the transmission of the "bag of tricks" that worked for others even though no one was quite sure why they did. The acquisition of the unique set of understandings and operational skills related to the primary responsibilities facing an educational administrator such as budget making, class scheduling, public relations, and personnel relations shall always be important. These and other challenges characteristic of administration of educational institutions are contained in the chapters that follow.

The issue is not whether the practical and operational knowledge and competencies related to administration are or are not important; they are essential to success. Rather the issue is whether to limit the understandings by failing to probe why a given approach works under one set of conditions but not another. During the last half of the twentieth century efforts were aimed at moving an ancient art away from pure empiricism and give it a basis in science as well.

Educational management was not alone in its recent striving to provide theoretical underpinnings to the practice. Massie, writing on management in general during the mid-1960s, noted that much of the literature on management during its early years consisted of "reflections of practitioners in business and academicians specializing in education for business and public administration" and these "classical writings" were not "based on formal empirical research but on judgment supported by personal experience and thoughts of the writers."[1]

Educational administration, as well as management in general, is complex and differing

125

degrees of abstraction are employed in the perceptions of it. Early perceptions of most fields tend to emphasize the concrete and operational rather than the abstract and the theoretical. The movement in the study of educational administration from the more concrete to the more abstract levels can be summarized as follows:

Level I: *Awareness of the need for administrative functions and their separation from other functions in the educational institution.*

Administration is perceived initially as a set of discrete functions separate from but essential to the support of teaching and other educational functions. This is the most rudimentary level of perception expressed in very concrete terms and which related administration to operational concerns by and large.

Level II: *Identification of the special skills, practical knowledge, personal qualities, and relevant experience base for full or part-time administrators.*

This demands precise and detailed delineation of administrative functions. A special literature begins to emerge at this level, but its focus is on practical problems; reflections of practitioners dominate the writing. Educational administration is defined in a concrete way as being related to the substantive problems encountered by practitioners of the art.

Level III: *Perceptions of administration as a set of processes distilled from the similarities noted in the management challenges found in various types of institutions.*

This is a higher level of abstraction than noted earlier. The general processes of decision making, leadership, planning, and change management were described in earlier chapters. Massie referred to the process emphasis as "early conceptual frameworks" and "classical management theory."[2] In this volume this level of abstraction is considered to be at the "pre-theoretical" level, but recognizes its attempts to rise above the morass of detailed management activities to find the essence of management.

Level IV: *Greater emphasis on the generation, use, and testing of theories and models of various aspects of administration as a means of enhancing knowledge of and improvements in the management of organizations.*

The perception of the practice of administration as being undergirded and guided by theories and models represents the highest level of abstraction. As in the process orientations the emphasis is upon the key variables, and the interrelationships among them, in the kinds of situations confronting the administrator. It includes what is often referred to as the management science, operations research, and the quantitatively oriented management systems. It includes but does not stop at the empirical observation levels. It is heavily influenced by science rather than practical experiences alone.

EMPIRICISM AND SCIENCE

Empiricism refers to approaches to learning characterized by reliance on direct observation of events as a way of knowing something but without the aid of theory or models to help organize and interpret such directly observed events or activities. It is not a complimentary term in medicine where it is defined as the "practice of medicine founded on mere experience without aid of science." Present-day recommendations calling for the development of theories and models in educational administration are likewise efforts to integrate empirical observations with science.

Science is concerned with observation, description, explanation, and prediction. Its purpose is to discover general laws and relations. Kerlinger said that "the basic aim of science is theory," and theory was a mechanism to help understand and explain natural events.[3]

In the philosophies of realism and pragmatism, science is a way of investigating phenomena and reasoning that supplements formal (Aristotelian) logic expressed in the form of the syllogism. Science is a means of investigating the nature and facts of reality through the techniques of objective observation and description, and these objectively determined facts generate the major premise which is the starting point in deductive inference.

The syllogism is a form of logic, that is, a form for examining the validity of thinking. In the syllogism one specific proposition (the so-called minor premise) is related to a general proposition. (the so-called major premise) to arrive, if possible, at a logically consistent conclusion (a conclusion possible only if the specific proposition is included within a class of subjects within the major proposition). The syllogism is the logical form of deductive reasoning, that is, reasoning from something general to something particular. Through the valid application of the deductive process, a conclusion may be drawn from something known or assumed to be true.

The scientific approach or method is essentially an inductive form of reasoning. Inductive inferences lead to generalizations only after accumulating a series of discrete, verifiable observations that justify doing so. Induction as a form of valid thinking or reasoning has value in the experimental method which focuses on individual cases. A comparison between steps in the syllogism and the scientific method is presented in Table 6.1.

The first two steps of the scientific method are primarily sensory and concerned with disciplined observation. The third is rooted in experience as well, but moves or advances to the "preconceptual" level. Conceptual frameworks facilitate the gathering and organizing of facts derived from observations. The present-day concern for theories, or conceptual frameworks, in educational administration stems in part from the need for valid mechanisms to direct the search for objective evidence to organize such data, to explain the significance of the data collected, as well as to eventually predict the occurrence of certain events.

THE DEVELOPMENT OF A SCIENTIFIC BASE FOR ADMINISTRATION

The beginnings of efforts to provide a scientific base for management can be traced to the Cameralists in the seventeenth century. Cameralism as an administrative technology in the small German states was cited in the first chapter. The work of Max Weber and the development of his bureaucratic model contributed to the application of the scientific method to the study of organizations and their management. A more complete review of Weber's contributions is found in Chapter 2. Likewise, the classical writers in management that emerged early in this century and outlined the fundamental processes and dimensions of administration were oriented toward science in the practice of the art. In short, in management in general that applies to business, industry, and government the efforts to provide a scientific base to the

TABLE 6.1

SYLLOGISM VERSUS THE SCIENTIFIC METHOD

Syllogism	Scientific method
Major premise or proposition	Define the problem to be solved or the event to be explained.
Minor premise or proposition	Observe all factors relating to the problem or event
Conclusion (if possible)	Describe or classify the observable phenomena.
	Formulate a hypothesis or hypotheses which may meet all conditions and, thus, explain the observation.
	Test hypotheses by putting them to work in controlled situations in which the event or problem is the only variable factor.
	Predict events explained by tested and verified hypotheses.

study and practice of management occupied all of this century and had its roots in earlier centuries as well.

The more science-oriented approaches to educational administration have a shorter history and were twentieth-century developments by and large. These early efforts included at least what follows.

The School Survey Movement

Although the school survey approach to the analysis of problems confronting educational institutions may be traced as far back as the Lutheran reformation when studies were made of the condition of Latin schools and universities that suffered from the violence of religious and other changes of the times;[4] it was not employed extensively in American public education until about 1920. Although relatively unconcerned with a sophisticated conceptual framework to guide their data gathering, the observations and descriptions of administrative and other educational practices of the twentieth-century school surveyors did lay the foundation for further scientific study and investigation of school administration. School surveys lost popularity for a period and then became very common during the rapid enrollment growth period for the public schools that followed World War II only to decline again during the retrenchment periods following the 1970s. The school survey approaches fell short of generating fertile hypotheses capable of revealing the essential nature of educational administration as a whole or in any of its major dimensions. It was not the precursor to the theory movement in educational administration, for it failed to develop the types of explanations and predictions from which theories and models might flow. It remained the application of the scientific method, but primarily at the sensory or objective data-gathering level.

Taxonomies

It is possible to feel overwhelmed by large volumes of collected data unless there is some means to organize and classify them. As more study was devoted to understanding the nature of what is involved and demanded in educational administration, various classification schemes or taxonomies were created to group the behaviors or competencies. There were several tridimensional classification schemes for administrative behaviors and competencies based on elements such as "the job, know-how, and theory" (where what was called theory was more akin to a philosophy of life than what is defined herein) or "the job, the office holder, and the situation."

Taxonomies are valuable in handling large amounts of data, but contribute little to the production of new knowledge, models, or theory. Halpin argued that the limits on classification schemes possible are related to the limits on one's vocabulary, and that there was always the danger of inappropriate mixing of different factors in the same classification. He warned that it was naïve to assume "that placing two taxonomic schemes side by side will somehow produce a theory."[5]

The further development of a scientific base may be enhanced by creating relevant and precise taxonomic schemata. However, there are severe limitations to such assistance. Approaches to classifying data or the nature of discipline should not be confused with their being theories of the same.

THE DEVELOPMENT OF THEORIES AND MODELS IN EDUCATIONAL ADMINISTRATION

The generation and use of theories and models to guide practice, research, and thinking about educational administration represent the real test of the scientific maturity of field or profession. The more serious efforts to provide a theoretical underpinning to educational administration can be traced to 1954, but some argue that it all began some 40 years earlier than that. The earlier date can be questioned, for although the word *theory* is not unfamiliar in the field, the interpretations and definitions of theory in the early half of this century were quite different from what they were after 1954.

Dissatisfaction with the overemphasis on only the acquisition of techniques and skills eventually helped to stimulate an interest in the development of theory in educational administration. Being a latecomer on the scene, the theory movement in educational administration borrowed and adapted theoretical frameworks from other disciplines. Although about 30 years have passed (by this writing), the concern for theory appears to rest among professors of educational administration, with the majority of practicing school administrators viewing what exists as theory as an intellectual exercise with little to offer as solutions to persistent problems faced in the field.

Definitions of Theory

A theory (or model) may be defined as a cluster of interactive and interlocking concepts systematized into an abstracted intellectual framework capable of interpreting and predicting generalizable trends and interrelationships within a set of varied facts within the real world. A theory may be perceived as being (1) an abstraction from reality; (2) based on concepts that are interrelated; (3) a conceptual or intellectual framework based on concepts; and (4) a mechanism useful in interpreting and predicting trends and relationships in the real world.

This demands a definition of a concept. A "concept" is an intellectual interpretation, or image, of a process, event, or thing. It is a mental image that is: generated through exercising imagination, recalled by retrieving it from memory, or developed from a set of sensory experiences. However generated there is subsequent intellectual processing, organizing, or abstracting. In short, the concept is the product of intellectual distillation. Concepts become starting points, essential elements, or building blocks in the creation, comprehension, and utilization of theories. Theory building begins with a seriousness when a collection of concepts is interrelated to produce a system of connected ideas or unified thought patterns that help to explain, understand, or predict some

portion of reality. This is a more restricted meaning of concept than when defined generally as any term with an accepted meaning; the general interpretation would imply that all words in the dictionary are concepts.

Other interpretations and definitions of theory are consistent with the above as well as with others that are not. Kerlinger's conception is very similar to what has been submitted above. He saw a theory as "a set of interrelated constructs, definitions, and propositions that presents a systematic view of phenomena by specifying relations among variables, with the purposes of explaining and predicting the phenomena."[6] Perhaps the most frequently used definition of theory employed in educational administration writings during the last few decades was the one offered by Feigl: A theory is "a set of assumptions from which can be derived by purely logico-mathematical procedures a larger set of empirical laws."[7] According to Feigl, the formulation of a theory begins with empirical observations, which in turn stimulate further contemplation or intellectual speculation to produce a pattern or system from which hypotheses can be drawn. A "hypothesis" is a proposition, or condition, that is assumed in order to consider its logical consequences or to test subsequently the assumed relationship between two or more variables. The fact that evidence is lacking is not crucial, for assumptions in the hypothesis are conceded for the moment just to start action and to test the validity of the conjectures made. In this sense, a hypothesis is a provisional conjecture about relationships among specified phenomena. A legitimate hypothesis, in a scientific sense, includes two or more measurable variables plus a statement on what relations exist among the variables. The theory may be tested by deducing hypotheses from it, measuring the variables considered to be important to the hypothesis, and then determining whether the assumed relationships among the variables were or were not valid in the world of reality. Thus, Kerlinger declared "hypotheses are important bridges between theory and empirical inquiry" and a hypothesis can be "a powerful tool for the advancement of knowledge."[8]

Feigl's emphasis was on theory construction as a means of giving direction to research or gaining new knowledge by describing and classifying a set of experiences, creating and testing hypotheses related to such experiences, applying logico-mathematical procedures when doing the testing, and subsequently determining empirically whether the conclusions derived from the deductive inferences had any basis in fact or correspond with what exists in the real world. A theory is evaluated not only in terms of its contribution to the generation of new ideas, but also in terms of its usefulness in explaining and predicting certain conditions or phenomena in the real world. It is the latter that was stressed in the first two definitions of theory and the former in Feigl's conceptualization.

The are other definitions of theory that are not related closely to the above three. These include one or more of the following: a style or jargon for recording descriptions; a taxonomy or scheme for classification or inventory of data; a bold guess; a program of research; or arguments by analogy. These are not supported herein. Nor should theory be confused with philosophy.

An Illustration of Theory Construction

Greenwood's outline of Durkheim's work on suicide can illustrate how one social scientist moved from a set of discrete facts collected in the real world to the construction of a theory.[9] Durkheim collected the following data on the societal causes of suicide:

1. Predominantly Protestant countries had higher suicide rates than those predominantly Catholic.
2. There were higher suicide rates among Christians than among Jews.
3. Countries with higher literacy rates had higher suicide rates than those with lower literacy.
4. Persons in white-collar liberal professions, as a group, had higher suicide rates than those engaged in manual occupations.

5. The unmarried had higher suicide rates than the married.
6. The divorced had a higher suicide rate than the married.
7. The childless married had a higher suicide rate than the married with children.
8. The average family size is inversely related to the suicide rate.

Durkheim pondered what it was that Protestant countries, white-collar professions, unmarried, divorced, and childless married had in common to explain higher suicide rates. He reasoned that it could be because the more suicide prone were not as closely related to others, that is, had fewer common bonds, as compared to those who were less inclined toward self-elimination. This then led to the idea that closely knit groups controlled their members with strong bonds of attachment and had similar value orientations that helped to minimize the probability of evading social obligations by self-elimination. Such ties were the key because they provided the added support necessary during times of acute stress as well. Durkheim's theory was that suicide was a function of the degree of group integration that existed and that provided the psychic support to a group member during a time of acute personal stress.

This is one illustration of the steps that move from empirical observations (gathering of facts) to empirical generalizations to the intellectual processing that resulted in the creation of a model or theory. With a theory the social scientist was able to explain what were previously unconnected phenomona by going beyond the limitations of empiricism.

The Usefulness of Theory and Models

Theory suffers from an image problem, that is, it is equated with impracticality, something "that sounds good but doesn't work," or something "too complicated to make any sense." The "antitheory" attitude that prevails among practitioners limits rather than expands the potential within the art. John Dewey contended that theory is perhaps "the most practical of all things" that widened and expanded the human potential to deal with a larger range of conditions.[10]

Einstein portrayed the usefulness of theory with the "closed watch" analogy, that is, when we try to understand reality we are "somewhat like a man trying to understand the mechanism of a closed watch."[11] What is apparent is a set of hands that can be seen moving and ticking that can be heard, but there is no way that the watch can be opened to understand completely what can be seen and heard. The more creative persons try to form a creative picture that explains it all, "but he may never be quite sure his picture is the only one which could explain his observations."[12] There may be many explanations of observable phenomena in this complex world that are right or good as judged by their capability to describe accurately conditions or to predict events.

The well-conceived theory, through its capability to portray a meaningful mental picture of how an organization works, can be an immensely productive means of generating better practices and thereby to enhance the effectiveness of administration. A theory may serve as a means of focusing on relevant variables, of perceiving specified operations, of interpreting facts gathered within the organization, of explaining complex events, and of predicting the future consequences of present actions.

A set of theories about various dimensions of educational administration could enhance the quality and range of insights gained through experience. Thompson suggested that a theory is useful in "deriving answers or approaches to specific situations," in conditioning the administrator "to think of the administrative process as a complex of simultaneously variable factors rather than a set of specific techniques," and in allowing the administrator to turn to knowledge and procedures of other disciplines to enhance the gathering of "significant facts relevant to administration."[13]

Use is often made of concepts, conceptual schemes, or theory even by those who are most vociferous in their attacks on unfamiliar concepts as a violation of the so-called common sense, for "Common sense itself is a loose collection of conceptual schemas, and is the end product of cultural accretions, of folk wisdom, habitual modes of thought and hidden assumptions about human nature, and the social arrangements of man."[14]

There are limitations to theoretical models, for "all abstractions deal with restricted aspects of the phenomena they seek to codify just as all maps deal with restricted aspects of the terrain they seek to describe."[15] There is the quality factor in theory development and a danger that they can be applied in situations for which they are not designed. A theory seeks to explain a unique set of relationships that exists in the complex world of reality. It is an abstraction. The theorist's full meanings attached to concepts and interrelationships must be comprehended if appropriate use and value are to be derived from the intellectual contribution.

Theory Construction in Educational Administration

This chapter seeks to examine the nature of theory and its contributions to the extension of the scientific method in educational administration. It is not a chapter in which is presented all theories of possible relevance to educational administration. There are many such creations and separate volumes have been devoted to some or all. Theories and models dealing with specific dimensions of administration in general or school administration in particular were outlined in earlier chapters. Thus, Weber's theory of bureaucracy was presented in Chapter 2, as were the decision-making models and interpretations of Barnard and Simon. Likewise, McGregor's Theory X and Y, Maslow's Hierarchy of Human Needs, Vroom's Expectancy Model, Fiedler's Contingency Theory, and others related to leadership, organizational behavior, and human motivation were reviewed in Chapter 3. The various theories were analyzed in the context of the part of management to which they could be applied. As pointed out then, most theories on organization or human behavior were developed outside the field of educational administration; attempts to relate them to education are relatively recent.

The literature that sought to establish a theory base for educational administration was relatively sparse and had a narrow scope during the 1950s and 1960s. Specific applications of particular theories to school administration were limited in number. Most were confined to a social science orientation and reflected thinking in a few disciplines such as sociology, social psychology, and the behavioral sciences. Economic theory, systems theory (other than general systems concepts) that related to operations research, decision theories, and other more quantitatively oriented conceptual frameworks were given scant attention by the early proponents of "theory in educational administration." Educational theory courses at the graduate level reflect this social science bias. The volume of literature on the theoretical underpinnings for the field increased somewhat during the 1970s as more professors of educational administration came to accept the potential inherent in such developments. There was no substantial shift in the posture of practitioners in the field, with theory having only slight impact on decision making, leadership, planning, and so on. There was relatively little advancement in the application of economic theory or quantitatively based systems theory to educational administration during the 1970s or early 1980s.

The bias of this volume is that before this century comes to a close the commitment and development of theory in educational administration will have matured to the point where there will be no separate course "in theory," but there will be included a theory component in the study of the many specializations within educational administration.

The emphasis on a single or global theory of educational administration has not had, unfortunately, the desired effect of generating as much interest in theory as hoped for. A more fruitful approach would be to encourage the generation and application of theory to describe, explain, and predict each of the many dimensions of the complexity of educational administration. This would include theories that focus on educational finance, resource management, scheduling, transportation, as well as other dimensions such as the social interactions that presently dominate the more universal models. Dynamic development will be delayed until theory is focused on the specific operational problems that are meaningful and that confront educational administrators in the field. This could lead to creating conflicting conceptualizations as exists presently in the natural sciences where there are different explanations of the same phenomena. Such conflict and debate could be healthy by leading to the discovery of new knowledge and better ways of doing things.

What follows is a further review of the theory of educational administration as a social process, an analysis of models, and a look at some specific theories and models related to the quantitative orientations of systems management.

The Social Process Theory of Administration

As indicated in previous chapters a variety of theoretical frameworks could be applied to educational administration. Doubtless many practitioners may have formulated, but not verbalized, what the key variables were in an administrative situation and how these variables were interrelated. These informal, nonverbalized conceptual frameworks often influence behaviors and actions of administrators.

What is less common is the existence of many formal theories designed or announced specifically for educational administration. By far the most frequently quoted is perhaps the oldest formal theory (since about 1954), namely, the theory of educational administration as a social process. Developed initially by Getzels and Guba,[16] it was expanded further in a subsequent publication by Getzels, Lipham, and Campbell.[17] These writers acknowledged that the social process conceptual framework was "influenced by *parts* of (Talcott) Parson's formulations where these parts seem fruitful, without thereby necessarily accepting the entire structure of the *general* theory."[18]

The educational organization was depicted as a unique social system wherein administration "functions within a network of interpersonal or, more broadly, social relationships" and this network of social interactions was construed to be "a crucial factor in the administrative process."[19] Behavior within this social system was said to be shaped by two major factors: psychological factors that grow out of the nature of the individual as expressed in a set of personal needs or desires that must be satisfied to some degree, and sociological factors that are related more closely to the nature of the organization or institution that bestows some type of identity and status upon each member of the organized social group and also places certain constraints and demands upon position holders. The resultant organizational behavior was a product of or transaction between the personal and institutional forces.

The organization as a "social system" was postulated to possess three characteristics: "the interdependence of the parts, their organization into some sort of whole, and the intrinsic presence of both individuals and institutions."[20] The two "conceptually independent" components of the social system were identified as (1) what was called the nomothetic or normative dimension and (2) what was called the idiographic or personal dimension.

The equation $B = f(RP)$ expresses the interaction between the nomothetic and the idiographic dimensions to influence the observed behavior. In other words, the observed behavior (B) is a function (f) of the institutional, or nomothetic, role (R), as defined by the expectations attached to it, and the personality (P), a part of the idiographic component, of the role

incumbent as defined by the person's need-dispositions. The well-known model of administration as a social process is presented in Figure 6.1.

The upper or "normative axis" of the social system "is defined by its institutions, each institution by its constituent roles, and each role by the expectations attaching to it."[21] The lower or "personality axis" of the social system reflects the individual personality as each personality is defined further by personal need-dispositions. The upper portion of the diagram reflects the institutional goal-seeking behavior element of the position incumbent performing according to role expectations. The lower part reflects the impact of each individual personality upon institutional role performance, that is, the influence of personal needs and goals on organizational demands.

There were subsequent efforts to further refine this model of administration as a social process by adding the impact of the culture and values on behaviors within a social system. This reflected the special milieu that surrounds and influences both model components.

Critique of the Status of Theory Applied to Management

The social process model stimulated much research in educational administration, but to date has had very limited impact upon practice in the field. It is obviously restricted, as are all theories and models, to organizational behav-

---

FIGURE 6.1

Model of administration as a social process.

SOCIOLOGICAL COMPONENT
Nomothetic, Normative, Institutional, or Formal Dimension

Idiographic, Personal, or Informal Dimension
PSYCHOLOGICAL COMPONENT

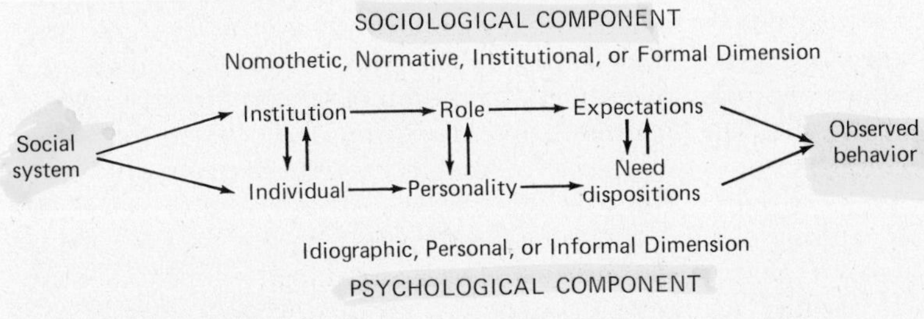

Source: Adapted from Getzels, Lipham, and Campbell, p. 80.

ior. The authors and proponents readily admit to limitations of all attempts at abstraction. It may contribute to a better understanding of the sources of conflict within organizations as well as to motivations and other human or social interactions. Its applications to planning, decision making, and other administrative processes are more limited. It has nothing to offer for the better management of fiscal or material resources, curriculum development, and so on. In short, the social systems model deserves special recognition for stimulating greater interest in the generation and utilization of theoretical frameworks in the study and practice of educational administration. Its greatest contribution may well be that it motivated others to generate further refinements on what existed during the early periods as well as to produce new ways of perceiving the nature and substance of educational administration.

The criticism of theory because it is divorced from reality and fails to provide sufficient guidance for the improvement of practice is not confined to educational administration. This was noted in the literature for business management during the 1970s. To illustrate, Lee[22] reviewed what he called the "modern human resource management theories" related to the writings of behavioral theorists such as McGregor, Herzberg, Argyris, Likert, Blake and Mouton, and Maslow. Most theorists were professors who generated their conceptual frameworks through observation rather than involvement in direct management of an organization. This, according to Lee, might explain resistance to the application of such concepts to practice. McGregor, who was first a theorist and then a president of Antioch, later in life noted the limitations of the insights of the detached observer. He claimed that he thought he knew how top executives "felt about their responsibilities and what led them to behave as they did," but he admitted to being wrong, for "it took the direct experience of becoming a line executive and meeting personally the problems involved" to teach him "what no amount of obsevation of other people could have taught . . ."[23] Some studies indicated, according to Lee, that human relations training programs

that included role playing, group dynamics, and so on, had limited or no measurable impact on subsequent on-the-job behavior.

Mockler declared a few years earlier that although "Business executives have often criticized management theory" that because these theories are more affected by the conditions of practice there is the "hope that a more unified and practical body of management theory will be developed in the 1970s and 1980s."[24]

The criticisms of a lack of ability to utilize theory in educational administration are indications of both the slowness to harness the potential inherent in this dimension of the field as well as the relatively low level of maturity in implementing a more sophisticated scientific base. The emphasis should be more on stimulating those in the field to generate more relevant conceptual frameworks of more dimensions of educational administration rather than sterile reviews of the limited numbers of theories that prevail at this point in time. The systems management theorists with their broader than social or behavioral science orientations offer considerable hope in bridging the gap between intellectual activity leading to the generation of conceptual frameworks and the practical responsibilities of educational executives whose survival as professionals is dependent upon performance. A closer look at models as a way to enhance the application of conceptual frameworks follows.

FROM THEORY TO MODELS

Models are a bridge between the purely abstract intellectual activity and practical performance. The synthesis of theory and practice is more likely to occur when the focus is upon the generation of models of specific dimensions of educational administration. Model building is one means of spanning the chasm that separates the theoretically oriented professors from the practice-oriented school administrator.

Model building starts as does theory in the gathering of concepts and facts considered significant to understanding the situation and concludes when a pattern of interrelated ideas is generated that is useful in explaining or understanding better the situation. A model, therefore, is defined as an abstracted intellectual configuration of interlocking and interactive concepts capable of interpreting, explaining, or predicting trends and interrelations that prevail within the real world or some dimension thereof.

A model is a representation of reality; that is, as a simplified version of part or all of the real world it contains only those variables and/or concepts that are considered important to better understanding, control, or prediction. It is a symbolic approximation of the real thing under scrutiny. It is more akin to an image or an analogy than to an aerial photograph or precise miniaturization of the real situation as suggested by the dictionary definition of the term.

By definition, the model is an incomplete abstraction and not a perfect facsimile. This is not meant to imply that other variables in the real world that were left out of the model are ignored forever; they could be introduced at a later time to ascertain their effects. As Baumol put it, "The model should be a sufficiently simple version of the facts to permit systematic manipulation and analysis."[25] He emphasized further the more "realistic model," one that includes more variables from the real world, often is the poorer model for intellectual inquiry because of the increased complications resulting from the excessive number of variables that must be manipulated. It is likely that a model "appropriate for the examination of one problem arising out of a given set of circumstances may be totally useless and even misleading for the investigation of another problem arising out of these same circumstances."[26]

There is always the danger of going to the opposite extreme. To be functional, and that is the reason for such intellectual abstraction, a model must be a sufficiently close approximation of the relevant facts in the real situation. The quality of the model is determined by factors that are included and omitted as well as by its ease of manipulation and internal consistency. If the model, as a system of internally consistent propositions, fails to describe or predict accurately conditions affecting events in the real world, it is the model and not the world that must be abandoned. Scientific inquiry has a built-in self-correcting character and never loses sight of the world of reality.

Educational administration may never attain the tightly structured theories characteristic of the "hard" sciences such as physics; human behavior may be clouded by emotions and is influenced by far more antecedents and stimuli than the behavior of electrons or other inanimate objects. Nonetheless, it is possible to establish on at least a probabilistic basis a set of functional relations between antecedents and consequences in human behavior in organizations or elsewhere. This approach enables a reduction in, even if it does not eliminate, the margin of error in administrative decisions.

Bross classified models into physical, verbal, symbolic, and mathematical types.[27] Thus, the physical model, as the name implies, is a concrete representation of certain relationships. Being much smaller than say a building or an airplane that it represents, the rather commonplace physical model is easier to manipulate or to help explain certain features of its counterpart in the real world. Its purpose will determine what is left in. Thus, if the purpose is to better understand flight characteristics, then the shape of the wings, tail, and body would be important model characteristics, but interior color schemes and seating arrangements would not. Physical models are used infrequently by physical and social scientists and then primarily for instructional purposes.

The verbal model, as the name implies, is based on words employed to describe or explain relations, key factors, or other dimensions. Unfortunately, the same word projects different interpretations to persons from different cultures or with varying experiences. Confusion may result from imprecise use of words to describe or predict complex events.

The symbolic model is based on a verbal model, but specially designated symbols are substituted for complex words and phrases. It results in a higher degree of abstraction, but the symbolic model has the advantage of more precise presentation and easier manipulation.

The mathematical model is derived from the symbolic model as quantitative relationships are introduced. The mathematical model is, therefore, a special type of symbolic model. Many writers believe that the most sophisticated and most powerful models are sets of mathematical equations. The economist describes complex business phenomena as mathematical relationships or equations as well as through graphic presentations. There are quantitatively oriented decision-making models.

Other classification schemes such as one based on terminology are iconic, analog, function, quantitative, and qualitative models. The "iconic model" is a scaled down or diagrammatic representation of a thing or system; it corresponds in part to what Bross called a physical model. The globe representing the earth, the "model" plane, the building blueprint, the map, and the timetable for train departures are all types of iconic models. This type of model projects a static view of some events or relationships in the real world.

The "analog model," as the name implies, is based on substituting something similar, that is, it utilizes something with sufficiently similar characteristics for the part of reality studied. The wind tunnel used to test the flow of fluids around a submarine or airplane shape is an analog model. The same can be said for animal analogs for certain human organ functioning or replacements.

The "function model" is simply a grouping of models by similarity of functions or purposes performed.

The "quantitative model" is designed to facilitate measurement. The qualitative model focuses on the subject content or characteristics that reveal the essential qualities of something or some area. Education models, social models, business models, and so on, are illustrations of the qualitative models.

Deutsch classified various kinds of models around four major functions: organizing, heuristic, predictive, and measuring (better, mensurative) functions.[28] The organizing function of a model is its ability to order and relate disjointed data and to help illuminate any similarities or connections that without it had remained unperceived. Some call this the facilitation of the "aha!" experience based on new ways of looking at the facts. It is somewhat naive to assume that "facts speak for themselves." In reality, facts are interpreted within an implied or explicit framework of varying degrees of validity. Baumol argued that a theory was necessary "because facts unfortunately do not speak for themselves" and that there are occasions when people "reject conclusions which appear to be implied by the facts because these conclusions conflict with the rudimentary theoretical structures which we implicity accept."[29]

As a heuristic device, a model may point the way to the discovery of new facts, concepts, or relationships. That which is heuristic, by definition, is discovery-oriented. The prediction function of a model is, as the name implies, concerned with prophecies of things to be. The model may also propose standards or criteria essential to measurement and evaluation.

A Classification Scheme for Various Types of Educational Administration Models

In essence, models serve to strip away the minutiae and less important variables to bring one to focus on the crucial determinants of a condition or relationship. Useful and precise models of the various aspects of educational administration will take many years to evolve as more effort is dedicated to such purposes and as the imperfect model generated is refined or merged with others focusing on the same dimension. As Bross put it, "Few scientists are so fortunate or clever as to devise a useful model on the first attempt."[30] This is important to those fearful of even trying to reason analytically by generating models to facilitate the process because such efforts might be condemned as poor or inaccurate. Poor and inaccurate models are better than none, for a field that avoids or lacks models is relatively immature as a science because of an overreliance on disconnected and purely empirical observations. Improvement comes with practice rather than from not trying.

A variety of function models that could be useful in the furtherance of a scientific base for research and practice in educational administration are grouped under two broad categories in the paragraphs that follow. Category one grouping is entitled "Organization-Oriented," or OO, models. The next grouping is labeled "Administrator-Oriented," or AO, models because the emphasis is more on the administrator as an actor rather than upon the organization per se. Although there is a degree of overlap in the groupings, the perspective is different.

1. Organization-Oriented Models

a. *Social-system models.* Models of this type picture the organization as a social system in which human organizational behavior is a function of many forces interacting within the system, which in turn determines the productivity of the system. The Getzels–Guba model, reviewed in greater detail earlier, would be classified here. There are others which focus more on the formation and activities of coalitions, on collective bargaining, and so on. Models of this type may lead to a better comprehension of organizational behavior, coalitions, conflict resolution, and motivation within the school system.

b. *Economic models.* These models tend to view the organization as a converter of limited resources into the products and services desired. Economics may be defined as the study of how a society, or part of it, allocates scarce resources among competing ends. Specific examples of these are the educational finance models (which focus upon the effective and efficient means of procuring and distributing local, state, and/or federal funds for the support of educational objectives) and the logistical support models (which focus more on allocating, protecting, and making the most productive use of the re-

sources procured through the finance system). Each of these may be subdivided further. For example, the logistical support models would include budgeting and accounting models, personnel allocation models or manpower-utilization models, transportation models, and educational facilities models. The productivity models would be a part of this grouping as well.

c. *Decision-rendering, power, or political models.* The educational organization may also be viewed from the perspective of the locus, flow, and impact of decision-making authority. This is a unique power flow analysis that impacts on policy and operational dimensions of administration. They may be called political models, in the broad sense of the word *politics,* to differentiate them from the social and economic models reviewed above. It can be argued that decision-rendering models should be kept distinct from power and authority ones; nonetheless, grouping them together has merit, for the true impact of power and authority is measured best in the decisional process.

d. *Communication models.* Here the organization is depicted as a giant processor, distributor, and/or network of information received or transmitted by various positions in the hierarchy or system. The emphasis is upon how information is secured, what channels are used, what distortion or delays occur, what is done with data, and so on.

e. *Service models.* The organization is conceptualized in terms of its educational, instructional, counseling, and related functions in the so-called service models. These are the traditional perceptions of educational organizations. The various subtypes in this classification would include models of teaching, learning, counseling, student welfare (health, food services, social services, etc.), student-body activities (clubs, athletics, special programs, etc.), and curriculum and instructional programs.

f. *Organizational structure models.* These models focus upon structured relationships of line-and-staff positions, shape (whether "tall" or "flat"), span of control, departmentation, and allocation of responsibilities within the hierarchy.

g. *Dynamic or change models.* These models seek to explain or predict how the organization maintains equilibrium, factors causing disequilibrium, implementation of innovations, or, in general, how the organization confronts change and adapts to new challenges. These models may reflect or apply the biological models relating to adaptation of species.

2. Administrator-Oriented Models

a. *Leader models.* There exist many models that describe leadership behavior, contributions of the leader role to group operations and productivity, and the interrelationships between the leader and the problem situation.

b. *Innovator or change-agent models.* Such models focus on the specific change-agent role of the administrator. Some prefer to include this as a special case within the more general leader models.

c. *Policy-scientist models.* The administrator is conceptualized in these models as the architect or influencer of major educational and administrative policies, that is, assisting the board of education to formulate policies and then assuming responsibilities for their effective implementation.

d. *Mediator or conflict resolver models.* With increase in the incidence of conflicts, confrontations, and bargaining, such role models have been accorded greater relevance and emphasis.

e. *Technician-expert models.* These again emphasize the more traditional perceptions of the administrator as one with special competence in school finance, business management, personnel employment, and so on. The focus is on the technical skills related to operational problems.

f. *"Organization-man" models.* These models focus upon the administrator as one committed to the organization, with special emphasis upon such qualities as loyalty, establishing harmonious relations, and "getting the job done" or dedication to tasks.

g. *Decision-maker, or influence, models.* The prime roles of the administrator in such models are generating alternatives and determining the course of action to be pursued by the organization. They may include the use of models of decision making by the decision-maker.

h. *Educational planner models.* The emphasis in these models is upon the educational planning role or functions of the administrator.

Synthesizing Models, Research, and Practice

The recurring theme in this chapter is that theory and models can be powerful forces for the improvement of both practice and research in educational administration. The complexity of the field is such that no single global theory or model is likely to suffice. The most productive approach is to involve many in the generation and subsequent testing of theories or models of various dimensions of educational administration.

Educational administrators will begin to recognize, if they have not already done so, the value or contributions of theories and models for the further enhancement of practice relevance and quality, if for no other reason than the failure of the traditional empirical approaches (i.e., the lack of a theoretical base) to cope with the many challenges confronting educational organizations. It is argued that theory and practice are not polarized entities, but can and should be complementary activities.

The classification scheme for the various types of models of particular dimensions of educational administration was included for illustrative purposes and to stimulate further discussions along these lines. There doubtless will emerge better schemes for grouping or identifying various types of models as the field gathers more experience and gains greater maturity in the generation, testing, and utilization of models in practice and research.

Research in educational administration has not had any great impact upon the improvement of practice. There are many reasons, not the least of which is that the quality and focus have not been of the level necessary to attract attention or stimulate modification of practice. The absence of a theoretical orientation and overemphasis on the gathering and reporting of isolated or poorly connected facts are contributing factors as well. If subsequent research in educational administration, or related fields, is to influence practice in the future, then it must move beyond the collection of "interesting data" to the more scientific and creative level of developing mechanisms that better explain and interpret facts, or better yet, employ the data to test hypotheses that may generate a new theory or determine the validity of an existing one. One writer questioned how much can be gained by simply "accumulating empirical facts without hypotheses or anticipation of nature," for without some kind of guidelines it is hard to determine what facts to gather; that is, "without something to prove, we cannot determine what is relevant and what is irrelevant."[31] The initial (but certainly not the only) step in determining the relevance and worthiness of a proposed doctoral or other research proposal is whether or not it is undergirded by a meaningful theory or model.

The professor of educational administration can be conceptualized as an administrator–scientist, rather than a former successful practitioner alone, who has a special sensitivity for the practice and has the competencies and creativity needed to generate and test models of various dimensions of the discipline. The instructional or "training" responsibilities remain relevant and focused on current and future challenges of the profession when new concepts, perceptions, and theories of the practice are interwoven with established facts and techniques. Practitioners in the field bear the same relationship to professors of educational administration as do medical practitioners to professors of medicine. The practitioner brings to the professor the more difficult problems

that have defied solutions with known approaches. The two may blend talents and special information to generate new conceptual frameworks that hold promise of resulting in new breakthroughs on the more persistent problems in the field.

MANAGEMENT SCIENCE AND THE SYSTEMS APPROACH TO EDUCATIONAL ADMINISTRATION

Management science, sometimes called operations research or systems management, is an approach that seeks to harness the potential inherent in theory and models for the enhancement of administrator performance and effectiveness in realizing the objectives of the organization. It emphasizes the scientific method in confronting organizational or administrative problems. It perceives the organization as something greater than the sum of its parts, and that all units or pieces must fit into a unified system pursuing mutually agreed-upon goals. It accepts the perceptions of those who consider management to be concerned primarily with how executives make decisions, formal and informal social or cooperative systems, processing and establishing communication networks, stimulating and managing necessary change, and so on. Being holistic by nature, management science recognizes the limitations of fragmented interpretations of the complex process of administering dynamic institutions, but embraces the special contributions that each interpretation can make to a better understanding and improved performances.

There may be some confusion in terminology between the scientific management movement stimulated by Frederick Winslow Taylor during the early part of this century and management science that began in the early 1940s, grew more rapidly during the 1960s and 1970s, and had some name changes during the interim. Scientific management was the contribution of production engineers who focused on improving the productivity of workers engaged in specific tasks. It did not move much beyond the level of the shop-room or the basic production tasks of workers. Scientific management used such techniques as time-and-motion studies and selecting the best set of tools for the particular job. The piece-work approach to determining wage rates for workers was developed. The important part here is that it never moved far beyond the management of the work force at the shoproom level. Management science, in contrast, focuses on all levels of management, does not promote time-and-motion studies or piece-work pay incentive systems, and emphasizes more sophisticated scientific and quantitatively oriented systems of problem analysis.

At one time or another and by one group of writers or another, what is called management science herein was identified as operations research, the systems approach to management, or systems analysis. These terms are not precisely similar, that is, were not all titles for precisely the same set of procedures or techniques. There is a high degree of similarity. The preferred terms in this volume will be *management science* and *systems management*. On occasion reference will be made to *operations research* (OR), which was the earliest term employed. To illustrate, Churchman et al. defined operations research that grew out of the World War II applications of this approach as "the application of scientific methods, techniques, and tools to problems involving the operations of a system so as to provide control of the system with optimum solutions to the problems."[32]

Operations research utilized a multidisciplinary team, or task force, approach to attacking complex problems. It racked up a number of spectacular successes when applied to World War II battle and supply problems. The development and effective use of radar technology plus the analytical techniques characteristic of OR increased the effectiveness of air defenses during the Battle of Britain an estimated tenfold. Operations research had a strong quantitative analysis orientation that its proponents attempted to apply to government and business administration after the end of World War II with varying degrees of success. Cost-effectiveness analysis was one of the more popular and more widely used techniques after World War II. Operations research, systems management, and management science have much in common even though many purists argue that there are significant differences. All have a systems orientation and, therefore, it is appropriate to examine the basic concept of a system.

The Concept of a System and General Systems Theory

A well-known expression attributed to the Gestalt school of psychology of the 1920s and 1930s was that "the whole is greater than the sum of its parts." Many others have used the same concept since then, including those in systems management, to convey the notion that complete understanding of a complex organization is not possible by analysis of its separate units in isolation or without due consideration of the interrelationships and interactions among individual parts.

Johnson et al. defined a system "as an array of components designed to accomplish a particular objective according to plan."[33] There are some subtleties in this seemingly simple statement. It implies "an established arrangement of materials, energy, and information," that there is goal-oriented behavior in a system, and "inputs of materials, energy, and information are allocated according to plan." Others view a system as a collection of interactive and interdependent components that are focused on a cluster of objectives for an organized entity with well-defined boundaries that aid or impede interchanges with its external environment. An analogy is often implied with *living* systems.

The boundaries that both help to define and constrain a system are likened to the skin of an animal or the geographic borders of a political unit. Within the boundaries are subsystems, with the linkage between two or more such subunits called the "interface." Outside the "skin" of a system is the surrounding environment, that is, forces and factors identified as being "exogenous to the system." The degree of interplay between the system and its external environment is determined by the "permeability" of its boundaries. When inputs from the "outside" are sealed off or difficult to accept, a "closed" system results. Closed systems tend to be unstable over the long run, for signals of the need for a change that are generated in the external environment cannot or have difficulty in penetrating the impermeable boundaries. When there is a high rate of flow of both inputs and outputs to and from the system which are neither impeded nor excessivly filtered by the boundaries that encase it, the system is called "open."

An educational "system" may be conceptualized as a network of interrelated subsystems, each charged with accomplishing part of the overall task of converting inputs into desired outputs. It is a manmade system with an array of resources, with a dynamic interplay with its external environment or community, and with a set of missions or objectives. Its primary purpose is to deliver educational services desired by the community that created, supported, and can terminate it. The major components, or subsystems, follow.

A Goals and Priorities-Setting Subsystem. There is some degree of uncertainty as to who is cloaked with full authority to articulate the goals of public education systems. Concerns over "federal control of education" stem, in part, from efforts of the federal government, rather than the state legislatures or local school boards, to assume responsibility for specification of educational missions and priorities. The allocation of authority for goals determination and specification of mechanisms for arriving at such determinations are not well defined in most cultures, giving rise to much controversy and efforts by various segments of society to control the subsystem.

Educational Resources Subsystem. In contrast to the above the responsibilities for and functioning of this subsystem charged with the identification, procurement, and allocation of human, physical, and fiscal resources required to pursue various educational missions is both structually and legally well defined in our culture.

Thus, state laws spell out taxing authority available for educational purposes, what qualifications shall be demanded of human resources employed for instructional purposes in schools, limits on school borrowing, and so on. There is a tendency to break down further the major elements of this complex subsystem into divisions dedicated to manpower needs, educational facilities requirements, and fiscal resource management.

Operations Control Subsystem. Control over various dimensions of a complex educational institution may be dispersed among several agencies at the local, state, or national levels. It may be vested in a school board, legislature, or a state administrative agency as well as in some internal mechanism within the administrative hierarchy of the institution. The function of this subsystem is to sense the rhythm of operations, assess progress toward realization of objectives, monitor resource utilization patterns, and so on, as well as to institute actions and adjustments necessary to keep the system locked onto targets and to facilitate productive operations.

Client Services Subsystem. This is the most visible subsystem, and traditionally the entire educational system may be projected through it. It is the payload, for its output is a better educated and adjusted student. It is the unit in the overall system that identifies who qualifies, how admitted, how grouped for purposes of instruction, what learning experiences shall be available to each admitted, and what other services consistent with the goals and objectives shall be made available to those recognized as "clients" of the educational delivery system. Its importance is difficult to overemphasize. It is usually well defined and institutionalized by law and supplemented by organizational designs. All other subsystems interface with and support the important client services subsystem.

Educational Manpower Development Subsystem. At one time in the history of American public education the very large city school district (New

York, Chicago, St. Louis, etc.) operated and controlled, in large part, its own educational manpower preparation and development through the creation and operation of "Teachers Colleges." This is no longer true, for the preparation of instructional personnel for entry into the "client services subsystem" of an educational system is presently outside the purview of local and state boards of education. In effect, this is a subsystem of education in society as a whole rather than a subunit of the local school system. The interface between the local district employing qualified teachers and the institution preparing them is important to insure that the competencies needed for effective performance on the job are the ones being developed by an agency external to the local school unit. An imbalance between supply and demand may occur periodically as well.

Environment Relations Subsystem. The education delivery system is only one of many in society and as such must relate to other systems in the total environment. The measure of the effectiveness of the environment relations subsystem is the degree of meaningful and efficient interchange with other systems and subsystems in the environment. This requires special mechanisms and techniques to sense the magnitude and the urgency of exogenous forces and to translate each into adaptive implications for the educational system. These subsystems, unfortunately, are not well defined nor always operationally effective, thus generating unnecessary conflicts between the educational system and its environment.

Student Reentry Subsystem. Eventually all who are served by the educational system will reach the limits of opportunities and programs available within the educational system and reenter the world of productive labor. This is one of the most neglected and poorly defined dimensions of educational systems, for what happens to students who "graduate" seems to be placed in other systems within society or left to the fortune of individuals.

Although it is convenient to examine a total

and complex system in terms of its major components, real understanding awaits integration of the subsystems into a whole that is greater than the sum of its parts. Analysis may help to diagnose specific problems or particular faults in one or more subsystems, but problem resolution rests on synthesis, that is, on recognizing the impact of any change to resolve a problem upon all operating subsystems within the organization. The concept of system, general systems theory, and the perception of education in society as well as particular educational organizations as being a unified system with well-defined boundaries are important for the application of management science approaches to educational administration.

Some Management Science Tools, Techniques, and Approaches

Management science, or systems management, seeks to enhance the capabilities of administrators at various levels in the hierarchy by making "decision making more explicit, more systematic, and *better* by using scientific methodology, principally mathematics and statistics," according to Grayson,[34] and by acquiring a better comprehension of the organization as a systems through the generation and utilization of models. The management scientist working at the university level may have inadvertently contributed to the underutilization of management science tools and techniques in business management, according to Grayson, because the management scientist (1) had an insufficient appreciation of the decision time constraints faced by practitioners; (2) failed to realize that most available data were not in the form necessary to be applied to the decision-making models; (3) lacked the direct experience of what power plays, internal politics, and resistance to change by persons within the organization could do to militate against the use of sophisticated decision tools; and (4) failed to recognize that simplifying assumptions for the generation of an easier to manipulate model often divorced the abstraction from reality.[35] This prompted him to call for the closing of the cultural gap between management thought and management practice.

What Hitch called systems analysis for the military during the 1950s and 1960s has much in common with the concept of management science. Systems analysis included "defining military objectives, designing alternative systems to achieve these objectives, evaluating these alternatives in terms of their effectiveness and cost, questioning the objectives and other assumptions underlying the analysis, opening new alternatives, and establishing new military objectives."[36] Systems analysis emphasized models as frameworks for observation and analysis of the interrelations among variables—particularly between input and output variables—and also consequent quantification of the data, that is, their translation into mathematical models that facilitate further analysis of the system.

The systems approach encompassed such nonexclusive major elements as systems analysis, systems design, systems engineering, systems management, and systems evaluation. These were characteristic and popular designations in the aerospace industry and spilled over to some extent into government administration. The concepts and procedures continued to be applied but under new designations such as management science or systems management.

The limitations of this rational approach to prudent decision making was indicated early on by Fisher who outlined the extreme positions in the use of analysis.[37] At one extreme is the zero analysis position wherein it is argued that the long-range decision problems are too complex and beyond the current capabilities of the analytical art. The implication is that decisions should continue to be based upon intuition, judgment, and experience of the executive. At the other extreme is the "100 percent" analysis position whose proponents believe that all problems can be attacked in purely quantitative terms and through mathematical manipulations the correct decision for each situation can be determined.

The optimum utilization of cost-effectiveness or other types of analysis to enhance the quality of decisions lies somewhere between the two extreme positions on this issue. The most plausible perceptions of the contributions of the trained analyst (or "systems analyst") in the decision-making process are to enhance decision making by administrators, held accountable for results, by: framing issues surrounding the decision problem so that objectives are clear and important environment considerations known; collecting and arranging data relevant in the decision; indicating the decision alternatives and how each may be evaluated; and outlining possible costs and benefits of alternative actions. The decision (or systems) analyst *does not make decisions* but helps those with such authority and responsibility in the organization. The intuition and judgment of the experienced executive will continue to remain important in the decision-making process; analysis is simply a way of sharpening or improving upon the judgments that must be made.

Fisher recognized that in administration "the really interesting problems are just too difficult, and there are too many intangible (e.g., political, psychological, and sociological) considerations that cannot be taken into account in the analytical process, especially in a quantitative sense."[38] Quantitative analysis is not synonymous with management science or systems management; it is a subset within the total approach. One further warning is that a person who is better identified as an information systems analyst and may have some measure of responsibility for the operation or management of a computer-based electronic data-processing system may be referred to as a "systems analyst" as well. This confusion in titles is unfortunate, but should not be compounded further by assuming that an information systems analyst is qualified automatically to be a decision analyst.

Systems analysis, sometimes called "cost-effectiveness analysis," is perhaps better identified as "predecision analysis." From an operational point of view it is a set of objective and often quantitatively oriented activities pursued prior to a decision determination with the hope that a more effective course of action will be implemented. It is one of the general approaches or attitudes consistent with management science.

Other more general administrator organizational behaviors or frames of reference that are consistent with management science or systems administration would include the following:

1. Administrator perception of the educational organization as a unique delivery system, that is, an open system for the delivery of educational services and products to selected participants within specified age ranges.
2. Administrator recognition of the importance of identifying and clarifying long- and short-range objectives for the organization as well as dedication to the realization of educational missions with the most efficient utilization of resources.
3. Administrator recognition of the necessity of change within the organization as both normal and inevitable if the educational delivery system is to remain relevant and to make most productive use of its limited resources.
4. Administrator acceptance of the need for the identification of alternative means or strategies for the realization of the organization's missions.
5. Administrator commitment to the creation and utilization of models for all major dimensions of the educational system.
6. Administrator acquisition of the competencies and understandings related to the appropriate use of quantitatively oriented tools and procedures in the analysis of decision problems.
7. Administrator dedication of a high priority rating to time necessary for planning and programming responsibilities.
8. Administrator willingness to appoint or employ interdisciplinary teams of specialists in decision analysis, new systems design, operations evaluation, and so on.
9. Administrator recognition of the importance of coordinating the activities of the many subsystems within the organization as well as the ever-growing number of educational specialists.
10. Administrator openness in considering the implementation of new and emerging objectives and scientifically oriented procedures for the management of any dimension of the system or for the execution of any of the administrator processes.

During the 1960s and 1970s educational administrators began to implement *some* of the specific tools and techniques related to management science even though that term was relatively uncommon in the education literature and had not gained popularity with practitioners as yet. Some approaches were adopted and then discarded prior to the end of the 1970s. Others fell into disuse as the occasions for their utilization became less frequent. It is difficult to predict how quickly educational administration will embrace a complete array of management science tools and techniques that now characterize the management of other types of organizations in our society.

Not all management science tools and techniques can be reviewed in depth in an introductory text in educational administration. There are texts or special manuals devoted to one or more of these. Not all of the really perplexing problems in educational administration such as those related to accountability, improved race relations, more effective instructional programs, drug abuse on school campuses, militancy of some employed personnel, crime and vandalism on school campuses, and so on, are amenable to resolution or improvement through the application of mathematical models, but there are other approaches in management science that could contribute something. There is always the danger of generalizing from the simple illustrations or cases—those governed by a single objective, clear-cut control over resources, relatively simple output measures, and easily quantifiable data—in which decision analysts using mathematical models and tools of analysis were able to identify the optimum course of action. These are the exceptions in complex systems with a variety of variables where it is not possible to develop a symbolic or mathematical model to analyze or manipulate the educational system as a whole or most of its major units. As Sisson stated, "Mathematics, as advanced as it is, has not developed techniques which permit manipulation of thousands of highly interacting variables required to model a school district."[39]

PERT (NETWORK ANALYSIS) AS AN ADMINISTRATIVE TOOL

PERT (the acronym for "program evaluation and review technique") grew out of the early operations research and systems approach techniques. It was employed elsewhere for some time before it was tried and accepted by educational facilities planners during the 1960s.[40] PERT helped administrators schedule complex projects more precisely, predict where the likely snarls could occur, and how to utilize project resources more effectively. It was credited by the U.S. Navy with making the Polaris missile operational some two years ahead of the previously anticipated schedule. One of its major contributions in education has been in the planning and scheduling of the design and construction of complex educational facilities projects. With the decline of school plant construction during the 1970s, PERT was utilized less frequently even though it has many applications beyond facilities planning.

Essential Elements of PERT

PERT is a systems-oriented technique for reviewing and evaluating progress toward a stated goal. Its primary contributions are in the so-called once through complex projects rather than with more repetitive activities. If a project is not too complex, it can be "thought through" or "planned" with scheduled completion dates for various dimensions in the "well-organized head" of the experienced administrator. PERT is not only an extension of such administrative activities to more complex projects, it is also a formalized, verbalized, diagrammed, and sophisticated statement of a well-organized and orderly way for accomplishing difficult tasks.

An outline of the major steps in PERT is (1) break down the complex project into its significant components or stages; (2) develop a flow plan for the work to be accomplished showing the sequence from one stage to the next (the development of the network); (3) establish the estimated time schedules for the completion of each stage of the interrelated work events; and (4) develop a means of monitoring and analyzing the time required for completing each of the major work events to help ascertain which work objective is on schedule, behind schedule, or ahead of schedule. Effectiveness, or "success," is based not only upon comprehension of PERT as a process, but also upon a clear and detailed understanding of the nature of the project being "PERTed." This implies that those who are to apply PERT to the construction of a large educational facility must know what happens during construction projects or otherwise only a fictitious or an unrealistic PERT schedule may result. It is more realistic to expect an experienced school administrator to apply PERT than it is for an expert on PERT to comprehend the intricacies of educational operations and administration. Usually a team effort represents the optimum approach.

In the design of a PERT network it helps to "think backward," "think small," "think togetherness," and "think time." With PERT one focuses first on the end result or product, and then "thinks" or moves backward while enumerating each of the important steps that must be completed (events that must be realized) before the final result is consummated. The ultimate goal, be it a constructed schoolhouse, a newly published curriculum guide, or an on-going staff development seminar, is always kept in mind in preparing the network of activities and events leading to it. PERT calls for the "retracing of steps" leading to the final outcome.

In PERT it is essential to "think small enough" to permit specific defintion of the significant work events or tasks, as well as related work activities, that must be completed along the way to the final outcome. It is a combination of "thinking small" while keeping an eye on the "big end product." This translation of an identifiable goal into a series of interrelated but specific events and activities is the most challenging, time-consuming, but most necessary phase of PERT. Here is where it is essential to know the details and fundamental nature of the project being PERTed.

The words *event* and *activity* require further analysis. An event is a milestone or evidence of a significant achievement. It occurs at a finite point in time. It is the end product that requires no further time or other resources to complete it. Thus final architectural drawings completed, teachers hired, curriculum guide completed in written form, and so on, represent significant, definable, and measurable events.

There can be no accomplishment of an event without completion of a set of prior activities that made it possible. Activities, in contrast to events, require both time and resources. Thus an event such as "teachers hired" demanded such varied activities as visiting teacher preparation institutions, conducting interviews, preparing contracts, and receiving signed contracts. It takes time and money to pursue such activities. Events and the activities leading to them are key elements and the important building blocks for a PERT network to be meaningful.

The "togetherness" admonition implies that no single event, short of the final outcome, and no single activity can be considered in isolation but rather perceived in terms of what went on before and what followed until the end product is a reality.

PERT is similar to the Gantt Milestone Charts, developed much earlier, in that both record significant events and measure the time required to complete the activity leading to an event. It differs from the Gantt approach by showing or diagramming the sequential flow and relationships between events and activities as well as the importance of certain events that must be completed before others can be expected. The event "roof installed" is not possible without something else occurring first such as "supporting walls completed" and "footings poured."

Much of the usefulness of PERT could be lost if one failed to "think" of, or include, the time it takes to complete a given activity in the network. The time it takes to complete every activity is not always known with a high degree of precision; in some projects the variance of time estimates could be considerable. One of the unique characteristics of PERT, and one that distinguishes it from other network modeling approaches, is its reliance on three estimates for the duration of time required to complete an activity. These are (1) the most likely time, (2) the optimistic time, and (3) the pessimistic time for completion of an activity. An average, or *expected elapsed time,* is calculated from the estimates using the formula $t_e = (a + 4m + b)/6$, where a is the optimistic time, m is the most likely time, and b is the pessimistic time.

The PERT Network

A sequential diagram depicting interrelated events and activities that eventually culminate in the realization of the end product is called the "PERT network" (or model, diagram, or schematic).[41] PERT is one of several systems classified under the general heading of network modeling. In preparing a diagram of a PERT network, the events are designated by circles which are numbered for each significant unit of work, activities by a straight line ending with an arrow meeting a numbered circle, and the time duration of an activity by a number above the activity line. A legend accompanies the diagram to describe each of the numbered (circled) events. Figure 6.2 is a diagram of a simple PERT network.

In this network diagram, Event 2 is dependent upon the prior completion of Event 1 and the activity between them. It is independent of the realization of Events 3 and 4. Activities 1–2, 1–3, and 1–4 are illustrations of parallel (not in the geometric sense) activities. Parallel activities are those that are independent of each other. In contrast, activities 1–3, 3–6, and 6–8 are series-connected activities. The network terminal event is 8.

Time may be expressed in weeks or decimal fractions thereof. In Figure 6.2 the time required to fulfill activity 1–2 is 4 weeks, activity 2–6 is 6 weeks, and activity 4–7 is 7 weeks. More precisely, this is the "expected elapsed time," designated as t_e, which is an important PERT concept as will be developed further later.

An obvious ground rule is that an event cannot be said to have been completed until *all* activities leading to it have been fulfilled. Event 6 must await realization of Events 2 and 3 together with activities leading from them to Event 6. Activity 1–2 requires 4 weeks and activity 2–6, 6 weeks. The total activity time to reach Event 6 is 10 weeks for path (for activities) 1–2–6. On the other hand, it takes a total of 9 weeks to move from Event 1 to Event 6 via path 1–3–6, or one week less than that for path 1–2–6.

The relatively simple mathematical computations determine how long it takes to reach a network-ending event, where slack time can be found in the overall project, and how to identify the path critical to meeting scheduled deadlines for arriving at the final outcome. In very large and complex networks, a computer may be used to save time and insure accuracy of computations.

Identifying the critical path. The critical path concept is one of the most important contributions of PERT. In Figure 6.2 there are four separate paths leading to the network ending Event 8. All start at Event 1 and can be traced as paths 1–2–5–8, 1–2–6–8, 1–3–6–8, and 1–4–7–8. The earliest time, designated as T_E, for the comple-

tion of Event 8 is the sum of the "expected elapsed times" (or sum of the t_e for each activity) along a given path from Event 1 to Event 8. The T_E must be computed for each of the four paths to Event 8. Thus, the earliest time (T_E) to reach Event 8 along path 1–2–5–8 (or $4 + 9 + 6$) is 19 weeks, along 1–2–6–8 is 14 weeks, along 1–3–6–8 is 13 weeks, and along 1–4–7–8 is 14 weeks.

The critical path is defined as the longest time path from network beginning to ending events. In the PERT network diagrammed in Figure 6.2, the critical path would be 1–2–5–8, which takes 19 weeks to complete.

Computing slack time. The slack time is a little more difficult to compute than the critical path, for several computations are necessary. The concept of "earliest time," designated as T_E, has been mentioned and is the initial computation required. The second, or the concept of "latest allowable date," designated as T_L, is computed backward along a path from the network ending event. T_E is a forward computation that starts with the network beginning event. Obviously, for the network ending event $T_E = T_L$.

The determination of T_L for Event 5 is based on the T_L for the following event, which is Event 8, and the activity time (or expected elapsed time, t_e) between these two events.

FIGURE 6.2

A simple PERT network.

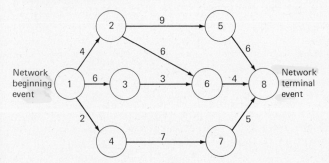

Keep in mind that the T_E, and therefore the T_L, for the network ending event is computed along the critical path, which in this case is 19 weeks for Event 8. Because the t_e, or expected elapsed time, for activity 5–8 is 6 weeks, then the T_L for Event 5 is equal to 13 weeks (19 − 6). That also happens to be the T_E, or earliest time, for Event 5 (4 + 9 = 13). Again, for Event 5 $T_E = T_L$.

The slack time for completion of a given event is equal to the difference between the T_L for that event and its T_E: Slack time = T_L − T_E. For Event 5 the slack time equals zero (13 − 13), meaning that for this particular event in the diagram the planners cannot anticipate any slack time or leeway for its completion. Obviously, there is no slack time for any event where $T_E = T_L$ is true.

Event 6 does have some slack time. Its T_L = 15 (19 − 4), but its T_E = 10 (4 + 6). The slack time equals 5 (15 − 10). This means that Event 6 could be delayed 5 weeks beyond its estimated earliest expected date, and this would still not delay the completion of the network ending Event 8 beyond the scheduled 19 weeks.

The T_L for Event 3 is based on the T_L for Event 6, which followed it, and the expected elapsed time for activity 3–6. By mathematical manipulations the T_L for Event 3 was found to be 12 weeks (15 − 3), and its T_E was 6 weeks. The slack time for Event 3, therefore, is 6 weeks (12 − 6).

PERT as a decision-making tool. The t_e for each activity in Figure 6.2, the T_E for each event, the T_L for each event, and the slack time for each event were computed and arranged in Table 6.2. Note that no, or zero, slack is found for all events on the critical path. The critical path may also be defined as the path with the least amount of slack between beginning and ending network events. This tells the decision maker that resources allocated to activities along this path must not be reduced and progress of the work along this path must be monitored carefully. PERT can facilitate prudent decision making related to resource allocation and utilization, for some resources may be moved, at least temporarily, from events where there is slack time contemplated to events where there is zero or less slack. To illustrate, some of the manpower dedicated to the completion of activity 1–3 could be diverted to activity 1–2 to insure on-time realization of Event 2 that is on the critical path.

The illustration of a PERT network presented is a very simple one, based on a single time estimate for the activities. This is more characteristic of the critical-path method (CPM). PERT networks are used in situations where the precise time span is unknown and, therefore, the three estimates of pessimistic, optimistic, and most likely time schedules are used. Likewise, this brief review was confined to PERT/time; PERT/cost is more complex and less well developed or utilized.

The emphasis thus far has been on the abstract diagram, with the substance of the project being aided by PERT not indicated. Table 6.3 is a legend or special list of a work breakdown schedule for school-plant planning. The major events are shown with the diagramming of the network model, inclusion of activity times, and so on, that follow the preparation of the list.

TABLE 6.2

COMPUTED t_e, T_E, T_L, AND SLACK TIME FOR THE PERT NETWORK DEPICTED IN FIGURE 6-2

Activities	t_e	T_E	T_L	$T_L - T_E$ (Slack time)
1–2	4	4	4	*0*
1–3	6	6	12	6
1–4	2	2	7	5
2–5	9	13	13	*0*
2–6	6	10	15	5
3–6	3	9	15	6
4–7	7	9	14	5
5–8	6	19	19	*0*
6–8	4	14	19	5
7–8	5	14	19	5

Note: Italic indicates critical path (Events 1–2–5–8).

PROGRAM BUDGETING (PPBS) AS AN ADMINISTRATIVE PROCEDURE

Program budgeting, or PPBS, began to attract serious attention around the mid-1950s and then gained more popularity during the 1960s. Its origins can be traced to economists working with the Department of Defense and the RAND Corporation.[42] It spread to other federal agencies and some state governments during the 1960s. Its impact began to be felt in education by the late 1960s, followed by an increase in popularity, and then a significant decline during the last half of the 1970s and into the early 1980s. Relatively little has been heard or written about program budgeting in education for almost a decade now.

Although the word *budgeting* captures most of the attention, this collection of management science related concepts are better perceived as a decision technology. As the early writings of Novick indicated, ". . . the objective is to im-

TABLE 6.3

WORK BREAKDOWN SCHEDULE FOR SCHOOL-PLANT PLANNING

	Event no.	Event described
Network terminal event	25	Start school-plant construction
	24	Contracts awarded
	23	Bids accepted
	22	Bids opened and evaluated
	21	Bids advertised
	20	Specifications and final drawings approved
	19	Start specifications and final drawings
	18	Preliminary drawings approved
	17	Start preliminary drawings
	16	Educational specifications completed
	15	State educational specifications
	14	School site purchased
	13	Start search for school site
	12	Architect hired
	11	Start search for architect
	10	Bond vote approved
	9	Start bond election campaign
	8	Bond vote authorized
	7	School survey completed
	6	Start financial survey
	5	Start plant survey
	4	Start education program survey
	3	Survey team hired
	2	Board approval of facilities study
Network beginning event	1	Start school-plant planning

prove the decision making in real life. . . ."[43] It has little to offer the third and important leg of the so-called budgeting triangle, namely, the "receipts plan." Its focus is primarily on the "expenditures plan" and to some extent on the "educational plan" of the classical budgeting triangle.

From early on there were semantic problems with many different designations for much the same thing such as program budgeting, PPBS, PPBES (where the E stands for evaluation), EPPBS (where the E stands for education), ERMS (educational resources management system), and RADS (resource allocation decision system). Sometimes zero-based budgeting (ZBB) may become confused with PPBS as well. Over the long run the earliest terminology, PPBS and program budgeting, won out not because of being the most precise, but because of popularity.

The economists who developed the concepts and techniques selected terms that tended to confuse rather than communicate effectively with others. As a result, some important dimensions of the system such as analysis, evaluation, and recycling were not included by those implemented PPBS. The letters of that acronym are not of the same order. The first three identify the processes of "planning, programming, and budgeting," but the last simply indicates that the three processes make up a system because of their interrelationships.

Furthermore, the initial phase of the system called "planning" was aimed at producing goals and objectives before initiating any further actions. It was a call to "know and clarify" your objectives for the organization before decisions are made on an expenditures plan. The time frame was expanded to defining outcomes desired for the immediate future (such as the next fiscal year) and also for the "longer range," which usually was interpreted as the next three to five years. The stimulation of the use of sophisticated planning models was not what was sought in the initial phase of the system.

Programming may be the most misunderstood phase of program budgeting insofar as educational applications are concerned. The economists, who introduced the term, defined it as the next logical step of translating the objectives, generated during the first phase, into a series of related activities for the realization of these objectives. This was to be approached rationally, meaning that a number of alternative strategies were to be developed for reaching the objectives before any decision could be reached as to what cluster or "program" of interrelated and objectives-oriented activities were to be selected and supported with resources. It must be reemphasized, because of the frequent misunderstanding in the field of education, that there can be no "programming" in the PPBS sense without first identifying the objectives or without the related activities being connected closely with one or more adopted objectives. In education, unfortunately, it is common to speak of elementary or secondary school programs with the emphasis being placed on the performance of functions, not the realization of objectives, to be supported with dedicated resources. PPBS is outcomes-oriented and can be called budgeting-by-objectives or expenditures-by-objectives. The uniqueness of the system is related in part to the demand that no expenditures be approved unless and until it is known what objectives are likely to be fulfilled as a result of the expenditures. In the traditional approach, functions or activities unrelated to measurable objectives could be supported in the educational budget.

The next phase is called "budgeting," but in reality is better understood as the process of determining what fiscal and nonfiscal resources must be allocated to each of the alternative "program of activities" related to the attainment of one or more objectives. The *complete budget document is NOT produced* at this point in the overall process. It would be better identified as the "costing"-of-program-alternatives phase. There are other important phases even though not suggested by the PPBS acronym or the term *program budgeting.*

Analysis of the generated alternatives is now possible because the objectives are known, alternatives have been specified, and the resources demanded for pursuing each alternative known ("costed out"). Each alternative can be analyzed in terms of its costs (i.e., what resources are demanded for its implementation) and its estimated benefits or effectiveness in satisfying the objectives in whole or in part. Here is where the quantitative analysis tools of management science are applied in the PPB system. Unfortunately, this was the one dimension of the system most likely to be ignored or neglected in educational applications. It also happens to be one of the most necessary to reach the full potential inherent in the PPB system.

The analysis phase supports what PPBS is all about, namely, the rendering of more prudent resource allocation or expenditure decisions according to a single and multiyear plan. The deciding or decision-making phase is where the judgment of the administrator is combined with the data and processing by the analyst to determine which of the alternative programs for achieving objectives will be supported. The expenditure side of the budget document is prepared during and after the decision phase.

At a subsequent point in time the decisions on the expenditures, as summarized in the budget document, are appraised in terms of: were objectives realized within the time frame indicated, was this the most productive use of the limited resources, what implementation problems were experienced, did even better alternatives emerge during operations, and so on. This evaluation phase of program budgeting was seldom implemented in education. The recycling phase makes use of data generated during the evaluation activities by introducing such information in the preparation or modification of expenditure allocation decisions for future budget years. The feedback of evaluative data helps to refine objectives and improve upon program selection as well. The final or recycling phase is the built-in self-correcting feature that is characteristic of management science and all systems-oriented management approaches.

The above disciplined approach probably sounds familiar, for it is essentially the same as outlined in more abstract form as the steps in rational decision making and problem solving.

The application happens to be in the fiscal domain and, therefore, what is called PPBS could be more precisely defined by the acronym RADS, or resource allocation decision system.[44] This approach involves administrators at all levels in the hierarchy rather than being confined to school business managers or other budget officials alone. In short, the PPB system applied to education is a decision technology concerned with clarification of objectives followed by identification, analysis, and appraisal of public school expenditure alternatives through the application of the logic of economics. It can be called "budgeting-by-objectives-and-with-analysis."

Whether PPBS is new or a reincarnation or reconfiguration of previously existing practices depends upon whether the focus is on specific elements or the system as a whole. It is unique in the emphasis on objectives rather than simply the performance of functions to be supported by expenditures. It is not the first to call for classification of expenditures per se. It is a different way of organizing expenditures around program efforts rather than the more common broad educational functions such as instruction, administration, transportation, and debt service. Cost-benefit or cost-effectiveness analysis was recommended, even though seldom used in education, prior to PPBS. These analysis techniques were given new impetus, however. The PPB system differs from the usual unit-cost analysis and the so-called scientific efficiency approaches that were espoused during the early part of this century. In short, it is the system that is unique, for not all aspects of all individual components could be called new.

Zero-based budgeting (ZBB) is sometimes confused with PPBS. ZBB is an alternative approach to the more traditional method of budget preparation called "incremental budgeting." In the latter, one starts with expenditures allocated in the budget for the prior year. To this base established in the prior year one adds, or subtracts, something to suggest the amount for the next budget year. As implied, in ZBB the base for all expenditures becomes zero, not amounts budgeted for any item in previous years. It literally demands that each objective or activity in the educational system be justified anew every fiscal year; no automatic continuation can be assumed simply because only "a little more is asked," or nothing additional, during the next fiscal year. Because it is more a specific budgeting approach rather than a new management science system, it will be considered in the chapter in which fiscal management is reviewed more completely. In short, ZBB is rejected as being synonymous with PPBS.

How many public school systems actually adopted and continue to operate in the PPBS mode depends in part on the perception of the system. About 500 school districts claimed to be operating in the PPBS mode by the mid-1970s. If it were demanded that all dimensions of a comprehensive program budgeting system, including budgeting-by-objectives-and-with-analysis, had to be implemented, then few, if any, school systems could have been found who satisfied all relevant criteria for operation in the PPB mode.

Program budgeting fell on hard times and attracted few new adherents after about 1975. Many who tried at least a few parts of the system later abandoned it because PPBS made demands beyond the existing capabilities or resources. For some strange reason, some extremist groups began to attack PPBS for being a mysterious and nefarious activity alien to a democratic culture. It is argued herein that program budgeting has considerable merit, its present loss of popularity or suffering from the more irrational attacks notwithstanding. Whether it may reemerge in a more disciplined form during the 1980s is open to question.[45]

MANAGEMENT-BY-OBJECTIVES-AND-RESULTS (MBO/R)

A superficial examination may suggest that MBO/R contains some redundant terms, for to some objectives and results are one and the same. An objective represents an intent, desire, or potential outcome. A result, good or bad, represents reality, that is, the actual outcome or consequence. Objectives are not self-executing nor do they end up satisfying fully the potential inherent. This management-science-related technique might have been expressed more precisely as "management-with-objectives-to-obtain-results."

The initial designation was simply MBO, which remains very popular even though many writers added the "R" for special emphasis. It took its rise in the business sector at about the same time PPBS was being accepted in the public sector or in government administration. Its concepts are compatible with and complement many elements found in PPBS. Both place much stress on the importance of identifying, clarifying, and focusing on objectives as the initial step in the administration of institutions.

The basic MBO concepts can be traced to the writings of Peter Drucker and Douglas McGregor as well as the later publications of G. S. Odiorne. There were others as well, but the interpretations and the emphases were not always the same so that new meanings continued to evolve. This management science technique did not begin to attract much attention in education until the early 1970s, or about five years after PPBS.

The two major interpretations of MBO/R are the human relations and the systems orientations. Within the broad human relations interpretations are at least four subsets: MBO/R as a results-oriented administrator appraisal system; a motivation strategy for administrators; an administrator development approach; and a unique sensitivity training program.

Educational systems claiming to implement MBO or MBO/R tend to focus primarily on MBO/R as an administrator appraisal device. This may be responsible for some resistance to it, particularly among principals who appear to be those most likely to be evaluated by it. In its simplest form this type of an appraisal system is based on setting of objectives that the principal or other adminsitrator agrees to accept as realistic expectations for the forthcoming year. At the end of the year there is a determination as to which objectives previously agreed upon were satisfied and to what degree. The final evaluative judgment of the principal's performance is based on objectives that were and were not satisfied. Closely related is the definition of administrative positions in terms of objectives to be satisfied rather than functions to be performed or activities to be pursued. The traditional approach to administrator and other personnel evaluation was to assess personal traits, functions performed, or other input measures rather than the output measures employed in the result-oriented appraisal systems.

The concept of MBO/R as a leadership strategy for motivating administrators is again based on jointly determined objectives. The assumption is that people perform better and are more productive if they know what is expected and if these expectations are considered to be realistic and achievable. This approach places primary emphasis upon internal motivators, that is, upon a sense of achievement based on knowing one's contributions to the organization or pride in accomplishment. Its roots are in promoting self-actualization rather than stimulation through primary emphasis on external pecuniary rewards. Most have found it very difficult to operationalize this conceptualization of MBO/R.

"Managerial development" through MBO/R is closely related to the above. It calls for identification of competencies that an administrator may need to enhance productivity or overcome previously revealed shortcomings. These are expressed as professional development objectives for the administrator with a time frame and a set of special learning experiences identified to facilitate acquisition of the new competencies. A special case of such objectives-oriented-professional-development programs is the sensitivity training conceptualization of MBO/R suggested by some writers.

The systems-oriented conceptualization of MBO/R does not neglect the human relations interpretation, but sees this as only one component in a complex organization. The entire organization is perceived as being a goal-seeking mechanism. It is important that all such outcomes be identified, clarified, and expressed in measurable terms. MBO/R becomes the prime device in the overall planning and control of all dimensions of the organization.

The general systems model for MBO/R is diagrammed in Figure 6.3. It can be seen that neither goals nor objectives are set once and then never modified or changed to any degree. At step 7 in Figure 6.3 objectives are subjected to the test of feasibility. If not feasible in terms of time, money, personnel available, or other factors, there is a recycling back to step 3 to define a more realistic performance objective. Yet another test of feasibility comes to play when the strategies or alternatives for realizing objectives must be generated. If there is no known or realistic way to complete an objective given the existing state of the art, then once more there is recycling to generate the kind of objective that has a high probability of accomplishment.

It becomes clear now that the system is not management-by-any-kind-of-objectives. The relevance, clarity, measurability, and feasibility of the statement of objectives are all important to such a management system. Likewise, it is not only top management that operates in this mode, but also the commitment extends to all administrative levels, from organizational goals to division objectives to operational objectives to performance objectives down to the very specifically targeted objectives where the detail work must be accomplished. Finally, it is more than preparing just any set of objectives and then filing them in some cabinet (a practice not uncommon in education for objectives that are demanded by accrediting or other external agencies). The objectives remain on top of the administrator's desk, are reviewed frequently, and each day progress toward their realization monitored. In short, MBO/R almost becomes a way of administrative life. This disciplined outcomes oriented approach to management has not occurred in education up to this point in time but may before the century comes to an end.

Management-by-objectives-and-results is a participative management style similar to what is called democratic school administration. The manner in which objectives are arrived at can be as important as their quality and relevance. Objectives can and should be jointly determined with full participation from all administrators and other appropriate professional personnel at all levels in the hierarchy. Mutual agreement as well as mutual understanding of the educational organization's objectives are essential, particularly in sensitive areas such as personnel appraisal. In summary, MBO/R gives direction, substance, and style to educational administration.

Education is a public service with multiple and difficult to measure objectives. MBO/R is easier to implement in product-oriented, as opposed to service-oriented, organizations and where there are a limited number of relatively easy to measure objectives. There are some semantic difficulties as well. Professionals such as teachers do not identify readily with "management" and, therefore, may resist introduction

of something called management-by-objectives-and-results. The system could just as easily be called education-by-objectives-and-results (EBO/R) and applied to the instructional as well as management dimensions.[46] If this were to occur, then EBO/R would include MBO/R and IBO/R (instruction-by-objectives-and-results). The MBO/R side would include supervision-by-, personnel-management-by-, planning-by-, budgeting-by-, and so on, and objectives-and-results. The IBO/R side would include teaching-by-, learning-by-, curriculum-by-, and so on, and objectives-and-results.

MBO/R and PPBS as management science-oriented systems have elements in common and others which are not. Both are outcomes-

FIGURE 6.3

General systems MBO/R model.

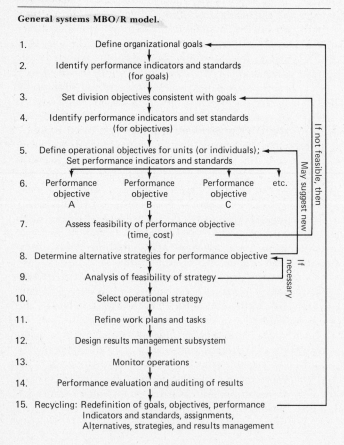

1.   Define organizational goals
2.   Identify performance indicators and standards (for goals)
3.   Set division objectives consistent with goals
4.   Identify performance indicators and set standards (for objectives)
5.   Define operational objectives for units (or individuals); Set performance indicators and standards
6.   Performance objective A   Performance objective B   Performance objective C   etc.
7.   Assess feasibility of performance objective (time, cost)
8.   Determine alternative strategies for performance objective
9.   Analysis of feasibility of strategy
10.   Select operational strategy
11.   Refine work plans and tasks
12.   Design results management subsystem
13.   Monitor operations
14.   Performance evaluation and auditing of results
15.   Recycling: Redefinition of goals, objectives, performance Indicators and standards, assignments, Alternatives, strategies, and results management

If not feasible, then May suggest new

If necessary

oriented; quality and relevant objectives are important to each. MBO/R has something to offer to personnel motivation, management development, and appraisal; PPBS does not. PPBS has much to offer in more productive use of resources and more prudent expenditure allocation decisions; MBO/R has relatively little to contribute to these. Nonetheless, it is regrettable that historically PPBS gained some attention in education before MBO/R. Had it been the other way around, the experience and discipline in generating relevant, quality, and measurable objectives essential to MBO/R would have been a most useful transfer of special professional competence for the more effective implementation and operation of a PPB system. Generating and working with precise objectives sound very easy when in reality they are very difficult and demand discipline to implement in practice.

OTHER MANAGEMENT SCIENCE TOOLS AND PROCEDURES

A system may be conceptualized as a converter of inputs, in an efficient and effective manner, to yield more highly prized outputs. Input-output analysis focuses on the input utilization patterns within an organization and the value realized with the outputs. Educational institutions present an output assessment problem even though the inputs (teachers' salaries, supply costs, operating expenditures, etc.) can be measured precisely in terms of money. The outputs (pupil learning, improvements in society, human adjustments to change, etc.) cannot be measured as precisely and the dollar unit is very difficult to apply to such outputs. The applications of input-output analysis to education have met with varying degrees of limited success.

Over 20 years ago, Miller and Starr writing on business decision problems declared: "Management science is essentially quantitative; however, important problems that cannot be quantified are handled qualitatively."[47] Starbuck noted as well that the "Applications of

mathematics in the social sciences have not lived up to their advance billing, partly because too much has been expected, and partly because too few social scientists are mathematically sophisticated."[48] There is a similar lack of mathematical sophistication among most in educational administration. Nonetheless, there were more quantitatively oriented specialists coming into the field during the 1970s than ever before. An increase in mathematical analysis of various dimensions of educational administration can be expected during the remainder of this century and certainly during the next one as well.

Linear programming, a relatively new mathematical approach developed during the 1940s, has military and industrial applications, but those in educational management do not focus on the critical dimensions of educational decision making. Linear programming focuses on problems with such characteristics as "there is some *objective* to be attained" such as minimizing costs or time as well as maximizing other factors; "there are a large number of *variables* to be handled simultaneously"; "there are many *interactions* between variables" and often there is competition among variables for the limited resources; and "most linear programming problems are also characterized by the presence of objectives that *conflict* with the principal objective of the problem."[49] This mathematical procedure is associated with complex situations because of the many interacting variables, competing objectives, and desire for optimization of some criteria. In educational administration this approach related to the theory of simultaneous equations may be used to optimize transportation, determine the most economical mixture of ingredients in school food services management, and in the resolution of some types of personnel allocation problems. The mathematical equations and graphs will not be developed herein, but may be procured in any one of the many standard references on the use of linear or mathematical programming in management.

Queuing, or "waiting line," theory focuses on "processes which have the characteristics of having random arrivals (i.e., arrivals at random

time intervals), and the servicing of the cos-
tumer is also a random process."[50] It can be
applied to ascertain the number of serving lines
needed for the school cafeteria given the student arrival rate, the length of the scheduled
lunch period, or how long a wait in line would
be tolerated. Monte Carlo techniques which are
based on random sampling of events to design
a model which simulates probable service demands are other mathematical approaches for
the resolution of such problems.

Game theory deals with decision making in
conflict and competitive situations. It is talked
about more than it is used as yet in business or
educational administration. It is based on a
"mathematical model which has its primary application to the relationships between two independent competing entities (i.e., individuals or
organizations)."[51] There are two-person-zero-
sum games (where the gains for one is a corresponding loss for the other) as well as nonzero-
sum games. Perhaps its closest application
would be in collective bargaining and other
types of negotiating situations between parties
that are competitive if not in conflict. The variety of strategies and payoffs for each can be
outlined to facilitate decision making on the
optimum approach.

Decision theory may be considered as "a
game against nature" although "nature does
not think and plot against its opponent."[52] Its
purpose is to enhance the quality of decisions
made under conditions of uncertainty, that is,
where the future consequences as well as conditions can be estimated at best on the basis of
probabilities rather than certainty. In contrast
to scientific experiments where the probability
of error may be measured fairly accurately with
the use of statistics, "the business decision
maker frequently has a situation where objective probabilities are lacking, but the consequences are subject to measurement."[53] This
approach to the enhancement of decision making on probability concepts, measures of utility,
and a variety of other statistical concepts and
procedures as well as related mathematical
models. Such heavy reliance on mathematics
has not had much impact on educational decision making as yet.

SUMMARY

Management in many different fields began to
search for and establish theoretical underpinnings to reinforce and enhance the reflections
and experiences of the more successful practitioners during the late 1950s and early 1960s.
Early perceptions of administration in most
fields tended to emphasize the concrete and the
operational rather than the abstract and the
theoretical. Theories and models of various dimensions of a practice represent the highest
level of abstraction of its substance and operations.

Empiricism places heavy reliance on direct
observation, but does not include theories or
models to organize and interpret the observed
events and activities. Science is based on observation but seeks theory development as well.
The scientific method is essentially an inductive
form of reasoning, that is, moving from discrete
and individual cases or facts to reasonable generalizations.

Although there were many very early efforts
to provide a scientific base for management, the
more disciplined and sophisticated approaches
are relatively recent. The generation and use of
theories and models to guide practice, research, and thinking about educational administration represent the real indication of the
scientific maturity of the field and profession. A
theory (or model) may be defined as a cluster
of interactive and interlocking concepts systematized into an abstracted intellectual framework capable of interpreting and predicting
generalizable trends and relationships within a
set of varied facts within the real world. Although about 30 years have passed, the majority of educational administration practitioners
view what exists as theory as an intellectual exercise with little to offer the improvement of
practice.

A theory should be judged not only in its
contribution to the generation of new ideas,
but also in terms of its ability to explain and
predict future conditions and phenomena. A
theory is not a philosophy, a bold guess, idle
speculation, or simply a classification scheme.
A theory, according to Dewey and others, may

be "the most practical of all things." It may help one to profit from experience and to portray a meaningful mental picture of how an organization works. Some called the so-called common sense a "loose collection of conceptual schemas." There are limitations to all efforts at abstraction, and those who wish to employ them must select the appropriate or relevant situation for such applications.

Many specific theories and models useful in the management of organizations were presented in earlier chapters. These include the Theory X and Y, Expectancy model, Contingency Theory, and Theory of Bureaucracy. Most were developed outside the field of education with some subsequent efforts to adapt them by practitioners in the education field.

What theory exists in educational administration took its rise during the 1950s and 1960s and has a social science orientation. The theory of administration as a social process developed by Getzels and Guba is the prime illustration and also the most popular conceptualization up to this point in time. It postulates that the behavior of persons within an educational organization, pictured as a social system, is shaped by the interaction of psychological factors (individual personalities and needs) and sociological factors (the demands that the institution makes upon occupants of various positions in the organization). The nomothetic or normative axis of the dimension is the sociological component of the model, whereas the idiographic or personal dimensions make up the psychological component. The social process or interaction model of educational administration stimulated much research in educational administration but has had limited impact upon practice in the field. The difficulty in bridging the gap between theory and practice is not confined to educational administration alone.

Models are closely related to theory and represent yet another way to create a bridge between the abstract intellectual activity and performance in practice. It is a representation of reality. As a simplified version of the real world it contains only those variables and concepts judged to be important to better understanding, control, or prediction. As a symbolic approximation it is not a precise miniaturization of the real situation. The simplification is essential to ease of manipulation. The quality of a model is determined by factors that are included and omitted as well as by its ease of manipulation and internal consistency.

There are many ways to classify models; physical, verbal, symbolic, and mathematical represent one pattern. Models can serve and facilitate organizing, heuristic, predictive, and measuring functions. Facts do not speak for themselves but must be interpreted within some conceptual framework. Inaccurate models are better than none, for the effort demonstrates a concern for generating conceptual frameworks which can be refined through further practice.

Models help to strip away the minutiae, or less important variables, and bring the focus on the crucial determinants of a condition or relationship. The organization-oriented (OO) models in educational administration that focus on major dimensions or processes in institutions would include the social-system, economic, decision-rendering or power, communication, service, organizational structure, and change models. The adminsitrator-oriented models (AO) are more concerned with the various major roles played by the administrator such as leader, innovator, policy scientist, mediator, technician expert, "organization man," decision maker, and educational planner models.

The holistic approach to management pictures educational administration as a complex set of interrelated functions and activities, and no dimension should be emphasized at the expense of all others. No single global or universal model of administration can replace all others or portray all major aspects of it.

The absence of a theoretical base and overemphasis upon gathering of facts reported in isolation has lessened the quality of research in educational administration. This in turn may help to explain why research has had such a limited impact upon the field. The professor of educational administration may be conceptualized as an administrator-scientist with special sensitivities to practice in the field along with special competencies in the generation and testing of models.

Management science, sometimes called operations research or systems management, is an approach that seeks to harness the potential in theory and models to the enhancement of administrator performance and greater effectiveness in realizing the objectives of the organization. It should not be confused with scientific management developed earlier in this century and which focused on the level of shop-room production problems. Management science places emphasis on interrelationships within systems, models, the scientific method, and a greater reliance on quantitative approaches for the enhancement of decision making.

A system is a unit or organization with defined boundaries and endowed with an array of interrelated resources dedicated to achievement of stated objectives. A closed system is unstable because its relatively impervious boundary makes it difficult to receive inputs from the surrounding environment. The educational system in society or in a smaller community may be perceived as a network of interrelated subsystems not all of which are well defined; for example, a goals and priority-setting subsystem, educational resources subsystem, operations control subsystem, client services subsystem, educational manpower development subsystem, environment relations subsystem, and student reentry subsystem.

What some called systems analysis has much in common to what is referred to herein as management science. The emphasis is upon models to provide the framework for observations and upon analysis of alternatives generated. In the zero-analysis position it is argued that long-range decision problems are beyond the capabilities of the analytic art, and it is best to rely on the intuition, judgment, and experience of the executive. Proponents of the "100 percent analysis position" believe that all problems can be attacked in quantitative terms to reach the best decision. Optimum utilization of cost-effectiveness analysis lies somewhere between these two extremes.

Perceptions of the organization as a delivery system, its emphasis on objectives, its accept-

ance of the inevitability of change, its demands on the generation of alternative strategies, its commitment to the use of models, its granting of high priority to planning and programming, its willingness to employ interdisciplinary analysis teams, its emphasis on coordination of all specialists, and its recommendations of administrator openness in trying the new are key points in the systems orientation or management science.

PERT, or network modeling, is a systems-oriented technique for reviewing and evaluating progress toward goal achievement. In network design it helps to "think backward," "think small," "think togetherness," and "think time." The critical path and slack time are important PERT concepts. It is a useful approach for "once through" and complex projects.

PPBS, or program budgeting, is better conceived as a decision technology rather than purely a budgeting approach. It contributes little, if anything, to the receipts side of the budget plan, and places primary emphasis on the expenditures plan for one or more fiscal periods. The complete system includes clarifying objectives, programming or generating alternative strategies for realizing objectives, determining the fiscal consequences of each alternative (costing), cost-effectiveness analysis of each alternative, deciding on the expenditures to be approved in the budget document for each alternative and objective selected, evaluating actual results at the end of the fiscal period, and recycling the evaluative data in the new fiscal planning activities. It is better identified as "budgeting - by - objectives - and - with - analysis." Zero-based budgeting is sometimes confused with PPBS, but it may or may not be one of the approaches within the total system. Relatively few, if any, public school systems could be said to have implemented PPBS if to gain such recognition it was necessary to allocate expenditures on the basis of objectives and to complete cost-effectiveness analysis for each alternative related to achievement of each objective.

MBO/R is "management-with-objectives-to-obtain-results." The human relations interpretation of this system includes results-oriented administrator appraisal, a motivation strategy for administrators, an administrator development approach, and a unique sensitivity training program. All rest on the concept that if the objectives of a position were clarified, an administrator would perform more effectively because what is expected is known beforehand. The general systems orientation focuses on the organization as a whole as a goal-seeking mechanism. The relevance and quality of objectives are important; it is not management-by-and-kind-of-objectives. MBO/R is also a participative management approach when objectives are mutually determined and mutually agreed upon. Resistance to the term management might be overcome by using the term education-by-objectives-and-results. The MBO/R system and PPBS have many elements in common but also others that are not.

Other management science tools may include input-output analysis, linear programming, queuing theory, game theory, and decision theory. The more mathematical approaches are more difficult to implement in education. It is easier to quantify input variables in education than the output variables.

NOTES

1. Joseph L. Massie, "Management Theory," in James G. March, ed., *Handbook of Organizations,* Chicago: Rand McNally, 1965, p. 387.
2. Ibid., p. 403.
3. F. N. Kerlinger, *Foundations of Behavioral Research,* New York: Holt, Rinehart and Winston, 1964, p. 10.
4. Frederick W. Eby, *The Development of Modern Education,* 2nd ed., Englewood Cliffs, N.J.: Prentice-Hall, 1952, p. 647.
5. Andrew W. Halpin, "The Development of Theory in Educational Administration," in A. W. Halpin, ed., *Administrative Theory in Education,* Chicago: Midwest Administration Center, University of Chicago, 1958, pp. 7–9.
6. Kerlinger, op. cit., p. 11.
7. Herbert Feigl, "Principles and Problems of Theory Construction in Psychology," in *Current Trends in Psychological Theory,* Pittsburgh: University of Pittsburgh Press, 1951, p. 182.
8. Kerlinger, op. cit., p. 24.
9. Ernest Greenwood, "The Practice of Science and the Science of Practice," W. G. Bennis, R. D. Benne, and R. Chin, eds., *The Planning of Change,* New York: Holt, Rinehart and Winston, 1961, p. 82.
10. John Dewey, *Sources of a Science of Education,* New York: Liveright, 1929, p. 17.
11. Albert Einstein and Leopold Infeld, *The Evolution of Physics,* New York: Simon & Schuster, 1938, p. 23. (Quoted in Andrew W. Halpin, ed., *Administrative Theory in Education,* op. cit., p. 17.)
12. Ibid.
13. James D. Thompson, "Modern Approaches to Theory in Administration," in Andrew W. Halpin, ed., op. cit., pp. 20–24.
14. W. G. Bennis et al., eds., op. cit., p. 194.
15. Jacob W. Getzels, James M. Lipham, and Ronald F. Campbell, *Administration as a Social Process,* New York: Harper & Row, 1968, p. xvi.
16. See J. W. Getzels and E. G. Guba, "Social Behavior and the Administrative Process," *School Review,* Winter 1957, pp. 423–441.
17. Getzels, Lipham, and Campbell, op. cit.
18. Ibid.; italics appear in the original quotation, p. 51.
19. Ibid., p. 53.
20. Ibid., p. 54.
21. Ibid., p. 80.
22. J. A. Lee, "Behavioral Theory vs. Reality," *Harvard Business Review,* March–April 1973, pp. 20–28, 157–159.
23. Quoted in ibid.
24. R. J. Mockler, "Situational Theory of Management," *Harvard Business Review,* May–June 1971, pp. 146–155.
25. William J. Baumol, *Economic Theory and Operations,* Englewood Cliffs, N.J.: Prentice-Hall, 1961, p. 393.
26. Ibid.
27. Irwin Bross, *Design for Decision,* New York: Macmillan, 1953, pp. 161–182.
28. Karl W. Deutsch, "On Communication Models in the Social Sciences," *Public Opinion Quarterly,* Fall 1952, pp. 356–357.
29. Baumol, op. cit., p. 391.
30. Bross, op. cit.
31. M. Cohen, *A Preface to Logic,* New York: New American Library (Meridian Books), 1956, p. 148.

32. C. W. Churchman, R. L. Ackoff, and E. L. Arnoff, *Introduction to Operations Research,* New York: Wiley, 1957, p. 18.

33. R. A. Johnson, F. E. Kast, and J. E. Rosenzweig, *The Theory and Management of Systems,* 2nd ed., New York: McGraw-Hill, 1967, pp. 403–404.

34. C. Jackson Grayson, "Management Science and Business Practice," *Harvard Business Review,* July–August 1973, pp. 41–48.

35. Ibid.

36. C. J. Hitch, "Plans, Programs, and Budgets of the Department of Defense," *Operations Research,* January–February 1963, p. 8.

37. G. H. Fisher, "The Role of Cost-Utility Analysis in Program Budgeting," in David Novick, ed., *Program Budgeting,* Cambridge, Mass: Harvard, 1965, pp. 67, 68.

38. Ibid.

39. R. L. Sisson, "Applying Operational Analysis to Urban Educational Systems: A Working Paper," Philadelphia: Management Science Center, University of Pennsylvania, 1967, mimeo.

40. See D. L. Cook, *Program Evaluation and Review Technique: Applications in Education,* OE-12024, Cooperative Research Monograph No. 17, Washington, D.C.: GPO, 1966, for early illustrations in school testing, and so on.

41. See PERT Orientation and Training Center, *PERT Fundamentals,* Vols. I and II, Washington, D.C.: GPO, 1963, for presentation in programmed instruction format.

42. See the pioneer efforts and reports in David Novick, ed., *Program Budgeting,* A RAND Corporation Sponsored Study, Washington, D.C.: GPO, 1964.

43. Ibid., p. xii.

44. See S. J. Knezevich, *Program Budgeting (PPBS),* Berkeley, Calif.: McCutchan, 1973.

45. See S. J. Knezevich, "Program Budgeting Revisited: Reexamining Its Promise for the Enhancement of Educational Administration During the 1980s," *Institute For School Executives,* Univeristy of Iowa, Vol. 2, No. 1, 1981.

46. See AASA National Academy for School Executives, *Management by Objectives and Results,* Arlington, Va.: The Academy, 1973.

47. David M. Miller and Martin K. Starr, *Executive Decisions and Operations Research,* Englewood Cliffs, N.J.: Prentice-Hall, 1960, p. 9.

48. William H. Starbuck, "Mathematics and Organization Theory," in James March, op. cit., pp. 335–386. (Quotation appears on p. 346.)

49. Robert W. Llewellyn, *Linear Programming,* New York: Holt, Rinehart and Winston, 1964, pp. 1–2; italics appear in the original.

50. Harold Bierman, Jr., Charles P. Bonini, and Warren H. Hausman, *Quantitative Analysis for Business Decisions,* 5th ed., Homewood, Ill: Irwin, 1977, p. 473.

51. Ibid., p. 223.

52. Ibid., p. 94.

53. Ibid., p. 139.

CHAPTER REVIEW QUESTIONS

1. What are the distinguishing characteristics of a theory?

2. Of what value are taxonomies?

3. Why is it said that theories are concerned with what is rather than what ought to be?

4. How does the scientific method of "coming to know" differ from the more formal methods of logic based on the syllogism?

5. What is a model?

6. Why are inaccurate models better than no models?

7. How can models be used to bridge the gap between the abstract and the practical?

8. How does an open system differ from a closed one?

9. What is operations research?

10. Where can PERT be applied most appropriately in educational administration?

11. Why are models important in the systems approach?

12. What changes must take place in educational administration before the systems approach can be implemented?

13. What are the similarities and differences between management science and scientific management?

14. Why have some of the management science techniques failed to gain greater acceptance and utilization among practitioners in the field?

15. Why is RADS a more accurate description of the management science technique more popularly known as PPBS?

16. In what ways are MBO/R and PPBS compatible and complementary management systems?

17. Why is MBO/R more difficult to adapt and implement in educational systems than in

profit-making business and industrial organization?

18. Why would input-output analysis be more diffi-cult to implement in educational institutions than in organizations manufacturing a physical product?

SELECTED REFERENCES

AASA National Academy for School Executives, *Management by Objectives and Results,* Arlington, Va.: The Academy, 1973.

Bierman, Harold, Jr., Bonini, Charles P., and Hausman, Warren H., *Quantitative Analysis for Business Decisions,* 5th ed., Homewood, Ill.: Irwin, 1977.

Cook, Desmond L., *Program Evaluation and Review Technique: Applications in Education,* Cooperative Research Monograph No. 17, Washington, D.C.: GPO, 1966.

Etzioni, A. A., *A Comparative Analysis of Complex Organizations,* rev. ed., New York: Macmillan, 1975.

Getzels, Jacob. W., Lipham, James M., and Campbell, Roald F., *Administration as a Social Process,* New York: Harper & Row, 1968.

Grayson, C. Jackson, Jr., "Management Science and Business Practice," *Harvard Business Review,* July–August 1973, pp. 41–48.

Hanson, E. Mark, *Educational Administration and Organizational Behavior,* Boston: Allyn and Bacon, 1979.

Hoy, Wayne K., and Miskel, Cecil G., *Educational Administration: Theory, Research, and Practice,* 2nd ed., New York: Random House, 1982.

Knezevich, Stephen J., "Program Budgeting Revisited: Its Promise for the Enhancement of Educational Administration During the 1980s," Vol. 2, No. 1, *The Executive Review,* Iowa City: Institute for School Executives, 1981.

Licata, J. W., and Willower, D. J., "Student Brinksmanship and the School as a Social System," *Educational Administration Quarterly,* Vol. 21, 1976, pp. 598–610.

March, James G., ed., *Handbook of Organizations,* Chicago: Rand McNally, 1965.

Schmuck, Richard A. et al., *Handbook of Organization Development for Schools,* Palo Alto, Calif.: 1972.

Sergiovanni, T. J. et al., *Educational Governance and Administration,* Englewood Cliffs, N.J.: Prentice-Hall, 1980.

PART II

THE STRUCTURAL FRAMEWORK FOR ADMINISTRATION OF PUBLIC EDUCATION

"Form follows function" is a truism. The structural framework for public education was influenced by the struggles that molded a nation out of a wilderness as well as the impact of informal agencies and of other governmental units. The pattern for the administration and operation of public education in the United States differs considerably from that found in most countries of the world.

The local school district is the basic structural unit. The numbers of these units continue to decline as local districts become larger and more efficient. The local unit does not and cannot exist alone. The intermediate unit, or regional educational service agency (RESA), is an essential component in a three-echelon state education system. The state education agency also has a leadership role in public education. Federal impact on education started with the need for the collection and dissemination of facts about education on a nationwide basis, but has expanded far beyond that today. It keeps changing but growing in importance with the creation recently of the U.S. Department of Education.

A comprehensive system of public education is the major but not the only component of education in the United States. Private elementary and secondary schools exist alongside the public institutions. A perspective on private education is provided and related to public education. Additional factors influencing public education are the professional education societies and unions. Finally, the rapid development of postsecondary education institutions, many of which are publicly supported as well, is reviewed and related to the basic units.

7

THE LOCAL SCHOOL DISTRICT: THE BASIC ORGANIZATIONAL UNIT FOR PUBLIC EDUCATION

The basic organizational unit for the administration and operation of public education is the local school district. Here is where educational programs and services are delivered to learners of various ages and abilities. Here is where most of the resources society dedicated to public education are consumed. Here is where competencies of professionals in the classrooms and administrative offices are applied and also tested.

The design and development of a comprehensive system of public education is one of the major cultural achievements of the United States. It represented a significant departure from previously existing patterns in other nations of the world. The American pattern of organizing for purposes of delivering educational services was unique, for it called for the transfer of control and authority over public educational institutions from religious authorities or private corporations to public or civil authorities.[1] It gave birth to the concept of education as a function of the state, but also created a pattern of local educational units to keep schools close to the people.

Public education that was provided through what were called "the common schools" grew and prospered in response to "grass roots" efforts, rather than from compliance with the directives or admonitions of central government officials at state or federal levels. A measure of county and state controls over local educational units was developed at a later date to correct some excesses of decentralization. Federal interest in public education has a long history, but was not felt in day-by-day operations until after World War II. The district system placed heavy reliance on the local educational unit for delivery of quality and relevant educational programs and services.

EVOLUTION OF THE DISTRICT SYSTEM OF PUBLIC EDUCATION

The district system of educational organization and administration was ideally suited to a pioneer society where localism was cherished and democracy a passion. It evolved from a

New England town, a geographic entity of irregular shape and with boundaries determined "naturally" by terrain features such as difficult-to-traverse hills, swamps, or rivers. It was a village-centered community, but also included a sizable rural area. Continuing population growth and the hunger for more land stimulated greater population dispersion to areas that were a considerable distance from the New England town center. This led to the formation of districts within the large town unit as each such unit clamored for a school of its own.

The further decentralization was resisted, for the town meeting was where decisions were made on many things besides education such as construction of roads and defense against marauders. The "moving school" represented one of the early efforts to keep administrative responsibility for education within the town meeting while at the same time serving children residing in outlying areas and at a considerable distance from the town school. A "school" that consisted primarily of a schoolmaster with little equipment and few books to transport was a very simple institution that was not too difficult "to move." A rented room in a private home was the "schoolhouse" in most locales. In the town of Harwich, in 1725, there were six widely separated places where the master taught for varying lengths of time. The complete circuit within the town took 3½ years; "school vacations" at that time were two to three years in length![2] The demand for longer periods of instruction (and much shorter vacations) eventually helped spell the demise of the "moving school" concept and the creation of the "district system of educational administration" as the better solution. The rise of the district system also marked the separation of school administration from general municipal administration.

The one-teacher school was also a social invention of considerable consequence. This concept of providing education was carried from New England to other parts of the nation as the pioneers headed westward. The district system of educational administration with its one-teacher school was as important to the early settlers of the Middle and Far West as was the axe that cleared forests, the gun that protected them, and the covered wagons that transported them westward. The one-teacher school persisted for over 300 years before it all but disappeared late in the twentieth century.

The district system of educational administration had some unintended effects as well. It resulted in highly unequal resources to support education as well as unequal interest in its development. Legal action in state and federal courts to redress these historic inequities did not begin to have a significant impact until late in the twentieth century. More will be said about the efforts to counteract the undesirable effects of excessive decentralization of educational operation and control in subsequent sections of this chapter.

The seemingly simple local school district is in reality a complex mechanism that is a political entity, a legal entity, a geographic entity, and a social entity as well as being an educational entity.

The District as a Political Entity

The school district is a civil subdivision of the state created to help the state discharge its educational responsibilities. The state legislature has the power to create, modify, or abolish local school districts; it is restrained only by specific constitutional prohibitions. In short, education is a state function in the United States, and the state legislature is the educational policymaking body that it may share to whatever degree it desires with other subdivisions such as school boards of local districts.

In contrast to the highly centralized, national control of education in other countries of the world, the United States has 50 state school systems plus separate ones for the outlying territories as well. Nor can it be said that all schools in each state are uniform. On the contrary, there is considerable diversity in the size, wealth, and quality of educational services provided through the local school systems within most states. This is true in spite of the fact that

THE LOCAL SCHOOL DISTRICT   167

the school district is a political or civil subdivision of the state, an instrument created by the state to facilitate the realization of a specific governmental purpose.

Nonetheless, members of state legislatures are aware of the long-established tradition of local concern and involvement in the operation and administration of public education. For many years legislators in many states hesitated to modify the existing local school district structure without prior approval of district residents. The political reality is that what is done is what the legislators consider to be politically expedient at the time.

The federal government has no direct legal authority over the operations and administration of local school systems, which puzzles and confuses education ministers in other nations. Federal influence upon the local schools is experienced through federal grants for specific purposes and through U.S. Supreme Court interpretations of how educational operations may impact upon the rights guaranteed to all citizens under the U.S. Constitution. In recent years, local school systems found themselves caught in the legal and political crossfire between federal court orders and local community desires not in sympathy with such orders.

Often strife related to social change within a school system may impact upon its operating policies. Concentrations of minority populations in certain sections of large urban communities generated new political forces to be considered in the organization and control of education in cities and surrounding communities. These triggered recommendations for further restructuring of local districts by merging the separate districts in surrounding suburbs with the central city to create a larger metropolitan school district believed to be better able to cope with racial tensions and achieve a better racial balance within the total metropolitan area. After more than a decade of trying, the issue of crossing political boundaries of local districts in one locale with those of another to realize a better racial balance in one of these state's political subdivisions has not been re-

solved definitively by U.S. Supreme Court decisions.

The District as a Legal Entity

From a legal point of view a school district is defined as a quasi-municipal corporation, that is, it is a special kind of public corporation.

A corporation may be defined as a collection of many individuals united in one legal body that has perpetual succession under an artificial form, that is vested with the capacity to act in several respects as an individual, and whose powers are specified and conferred upon it by some governmental agency. In short, a corporation is a legally created but artificial person that enables many who comprise it to act with the ease of one and to enjoy limited liability as well. In contrast to the ordinary partnership, which ceases to exist after one partner dies, a corporation survives the death of any or all of its members and officers. As a "person," it can be sued or sue others in its corporate name. Limited liability means that school board members, acting in good faith and in the absence of fraud and collusion, cannot be sued as private persons for their acts as corporate officers.

Most charters of incorporation are granted by state governments; some by the federal government. Private corporations are created to engage in activities that will result in economic gain to those who own stock in it. Quasi-public corporations are technically private in ownership and would be classified as wholly private if their activities did not have a significant impact upon public welfare.

Public corporations are created for governmental and political purposes only. They are not only created "persons," but also instrumentalities of the state to facilitate some governmental activities. A municipal corporation is a public corporation that is local in character and exercises some governmental functions within its locale. Incorporated cities, towns, and villages are municipal corporations with charters that specify the extent of their governmental powers. This enables them to facilitate government by people in the local area and also to act as an arm of the state. A more technical definition of a municipal corporation is that "it is a body politic and corporate, established by law or sovereign power, evidenced by seal, and perpetual succession, primarily to regulate the local or internal affairs of the territory or district incorporated, and secondarily to share in the civil government of the state in a particular locality."[3]

A school district, from a legal perspective, is a special kind of a municipal corporation, that is, it is a quasi-municipal corporation. The word *quasi* implies that the school district operates "as if" it were a municipal corporation, but its authority is far more limited. Its authority is limited to that required to perform the education function for which it is expressly created. It, however, enjoys the other benefits of a municipal corporation, which means that, within the limits of its charter, a school district may sue and be sued, can acquire and convey property, and its officers are not personally assessable for corporate acts. This legal structure greatly facilitates the operation and administration of public education.

The school district as a limited or quasi-municipal corporation may exercise the following powers and no others: "(1) those expressly granted by statute, (2) those fairly and necessarily implied in the powers expressly granted, and (3) those essential to the accomplishment of the objects of the corporation."[4] A school district, city, or county are separate and distinct legal entities or corporations even though their boundaries may be exactly the same. The exception is where the specific intent of a law is to grant the city or county authority over the school district; city or county officials have no authority unless the legislature clearly intended that such a condition exist in the operation of school districts.

The District as a Geographic Entity

The school district may be described by the geographic area it encompasses. The most common land-survey system is the rectangular survey, and its major unit is the 6 mile by 6 mile, approximately, geographic or surveyor's township. It was used when the Northwest Territory was first surveyed and continued to be employed as more new lands were opened. The older metes-and-bounds system was utilized in the original 13 colonies.

A base line is determined first from which the survey proceeds north and south as well as east and west. These base lines vary from one area to the next; on occasion a principal meridian is used as the base or range line.

The fundamental unit or geographic township is subdivided into 36 one-square-mile areas or subunits called a section of land. This is shown along with the unique numbering system for identifying each section in Figure 7.1. This was important in the award of the famous "section 16 in each township" by the federal government for the support of public education when each new state from the Northwest Territory was organized formally. In some states, section 32 was awarded in the federal land grant for the support of public education.

The one-square-mile section of land contains 640 acres, which is further subdivided into four quarters of 160 acres each. Each quarter section is identified by its location as the NE ¼

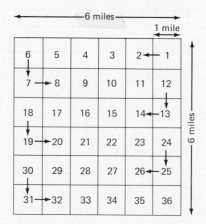

FIGURE 7.1

The geographical township.

(upper right-hand corner), NW ¼ (upper left-hand corner), SE ¼, and SW ¼. Each quarter section is further cut up into four 40-acre parcels. Thus one 40-acre parcel of land could be described as the NW ¼ of the SE ¼ of section 16. It is important to determine precisely the boundaries of a school district, for this specifies what lands can be taxed to support school operations as well as residents who may attend without paying tuition. The above system allows an easier land description than the metes-and-bounds employed in 19 states located in the East and South.

The District as a Social Institution

A school may serve a community in many ways in addition to providing educational services. It served as the social gathering place during pioneer and subsequent days. These interactions between the school as the institution and the people served gave rise to the community school concept. The more popular definitions of a community school district have a predominately rural flavor. It was more than utilization of educational facilities for social or athletic events during after school hours and on non-school days. The curriculum was designed to reflect more closely the needs of the community as well. The original conceptions were more difficult to adapt to the facts of life in densely populated urban and highly mobile populations. School facilities continue to be used as emergency housing centers during serious floods, fires, and earthquakes. Mass inoculations as well as other unusual health activities have called upon educational facilities for assistance.

At various points in time some states passed laws that declared that a merger or reorganization of two or more districts would result in the formation of "community school districts." This does not always produce a community district in spirit as well as in name. Where people tend to go for school services is considered by some to be one criterion for defining or locating a community, but such reasoning tends to compound rather than clarify the determination of community boundary lines for an enlarged school district.

The concept of the school as a social unit or the community school concept was complicated further in very large urban centers. Some self-appointed or special interest groups emerged as spokespersons of a vaguely defined area or neighborhood of a city and claimed the rights of the "community" to control school operations. These "community rights" were to supersede those of the legally elected or appointed board of education for the district as a whole. The "community control" was deemed necessary to enhance the education of the disadvantaged in the core cities, and this meant that the hiring and firing of teachers and principals were to be prerogatives of imprecisely defined community leaders.

Decentralization of this type led to fragmentation of some large urban city school districts into autonomous subdivisions not unlike the "ward school control" systems abandoned around the turn of the century. The New York City school system was closed down by a strike of teachers in September 1968 when decentralization resulted in the local governing board in one community of similar ethnic background firing ten teachers who were of another ethnic background without the concurrence of the central Board of Education for the city as a whole. The crossfire between proponents of centralization and those of decentralization of large urban school systems, ethnic sensitivities or considerations, and teachers' demands that tenure or other assurances of job security not be violated without following due process made the dispute both complex and highly emotional. The other side of the coin is that spokespersons, whether self-appointed or legally recognized, in the large and complex cities have also come to recognize the school as a social institution that should remain sensitive to the needs of students from minority backgrounds as well as those from other social classes or backgrounds.

With the increasing urbanization of the nation's population, the focus of the school as a social entity serving the needs of the community and drawing support from it has shifted from a predominately rural focus to the even more complex urban setting. The school has become a battleground over resolving many of the great social issues of our times such as improving race relations, reducing the negative impact of poverty, and helping individuals to better adjust to the complexity of modern life.

The District as an Educational Entity

School districts vary as to the type and variety of educational services offered. There are elementary, secondary, and unified school districts. The number of students served, the wealth to support education, and the numbers of professional and other staff personnel in the school districts of the nation vary greatly as well.

An oddity in history is that at one time there were thousands of school districts that operated no school nor employed any professional personnel. The school board existed to give legal substance to the unit and collected taxes to pay tuition of resident pupils attending school elsewhere. In many states such school districts degenerated into tax avoidance colonies. Most states in recent years disestablished all nonoperating school districts through the enactment of compulsory closing laws that mandated out of existence districts in which no schools were operational over a stated period of time and laws that required that all areas within the state must be a part of a school district providing secondary school opportunities. By 1983 there were fewer than 300 nonoperating school districts, a substantial reduction from the more than 17,000 in 1948. Thirty-four states have no nonoperating school districts, and only five states accounted for almost 75 percent of the nonoperating administrative units. Most were found in the New England states (54 percent of the total) and Nebraska. Maine had more than any other state, or 18 percent of the total.

The school district as an educational entity may be perceived as an administrative unit and as an attendance unit. The administrative unit, or the basic unit, "is an area in which a single board or officer has the immediate responsibility for the direct administration of all the schools located therein."[5] It is, more often than not, the fiscal unit with authority to tax and raise other revenues for educational operations.

An attendance unit (school or attendance center) is a geographic area with a population served by a single school plant and related professional staff. There are usually several attendance centers within the administrative or basic unit of educational administration. The attendance unit does not have taxing authority nor can it act independently from the administrative unit as some proponents of decentralization of large urban districts have proposed. Changes in the structure or boundary lines of two attendance centers to create a single and larger one is called consolidation. The merger of two or more administrative units into a single and larger new administrative unit is more precisely identified as reorganization. The two terms *consolidation* and *reorganization* are erroneously considered to be synonymous or interchangeable. There can be, however, reorganization for administrative purposes without any consolidation of previously existing attendance units.

School districts as educational entities are known by many different names. Some fairly popular ones through the years are common, city, town or township, county, union free high school, united, unified, and elementary or secondary school districts. The legal designations are usually related to some act of the legislature, with new acts changing the old in favor of another label.

Characteristics and Trends in the Creation of Effective Administrative Units

The effectiveness of a school district as an administrative unit may be related to such factors as the number of students of various ages served, the taxable wealth available in the district, the geographic area encompassed as well as the quality of its professional and leadership personnel. Effectiveness standards are related to the definitions of what constitutes a quality or relevant educational program at a given point in time. The more complex society of today demands a far more advanced conception of a minimum or basic education for all children and youth than the primitive or pioneer societies. School districts of today are challenged to stimulate greater learning among students served to prepare them to perform more effectively in the world of work or in institutions of higher learning. The delivery of a program of education that is relevant for these times calls for a larger tax base, more students, and more efficient utilization of resources available.

School districts that were able to provide quality education programs and insure the most productive use of resources in previous years were found wanting by present-day standards. This fact and other forces within the post-World War II society stimulated the most dramatic reorganization of local school districts in the history of the nation. It was essential for local school administrators to comprehend the significance of an effective local school district organizational pattern and to demonstrate competencies needed to meet the leadership challenges related to forming effective administrative units. It is repeated that it was not reorganization for the sake of reorganization, but rather reorganization necessary for the redesign of administrative units capable of delivering relevant educational programs to satisfy today's demands and to do so with the most efficient utilization of educational resources.

Over the years there developed numerous expressions of what minimum standards were desirable for districts offering elementary and secondary school educational opportunities. Most of the history was focused on efficient district size in rural, as opposed to urban, America. In recent years some began to express concerns over when is a district too large, or what are maximums for the size of administrative and attendance units.

Dawson, one of the early pioneers in the study of district structures, offered some minimum standards for district size related to minimum enrollments in elementary and in secondary school attendance units. He employed a pupil–teacher standard far higher than considered appropriate presently, but which was not too unusual for 1933, namely a 40 to 1 pupil–teacher ratio for an elementary school class. The minimum enrollment for an elementary school with six grades would be 240 students, if it were accepted further that no teacher would have to teach more than one grade level of students in any single class. Dawson's standard for the secondary school attendance unit was based on no fewer than ten teachers at this level to insure that all essential programs would be made available to learners. This was translated into a minimum enrollment from 210 to 300 in the six-year high school and 175 to 250 in a four-year high school.[6]

A different set of minimum enrollments was produced when a lower pupil–teacher ratio was employed in recommendations about 15 years later in 1948. Dawson was also involved in this study that called for no fewer than 175 pupils in grades K to 6 and at least seven teachers for these elementary grades.[7] A more desirable minimum of 300 pupils and 12 elementary school teachers was proposed as well. The same 1948 publication recommended a minimum of 300 junior-senior high school students, or 75 for each of the six age groups, plus no fewer than 12 full-time teachers. For schools with grades 9 to 12, the minimums were 200 students and ten full-time secondary school teachers.

By present-day standards, the above recommendations seem more modest than revolutionary. They did manage to stimulate a significant restructuring of American public school districts. A perspective is necessary to interpret the standards. There were more than 100,000 local school districts at that time, with most being far too small to be justified. Over 60 percent of all elementary attendance units in 1931–1932 were one-teacher schools, that is, one person taught all grade levels and all subjects in grades 1 to 8. Even as late as 1951–1952, 40 percent of all elementary school attendance centers had only one teacher!

The reorganization of administrative units focused on rural areas of the nation during those years. Another standard or criterion was that elementary school pupils should not be required to walk more than 2 miles to reach an attendance center nor ride a school bus each way for more than one hour. High school pupils were to be limited to a 2½ mile walk to a school or a 1½ mile ride in a school bus each way. The National Commission of 1948 preferred a maximum bus ride each way of no more than 45 minutes for elementary school students and one hour for secondary school students.[8] In short, maximum allowable bus riding time was one of the important constraints on the possible geographic size of a newly reorganized school district.

Prior standards dealt with minimums for individual attendance centers and not the administrative unit as a whole. Starting with the 1948 National Commission's minimum of 75 pupils for each of the six secondary grades, the minimum enrollment for the secondary center as a whole would have to be 450 students. Obviously, that would also have to be the minimum found in all of the elementary grades (again six grades). The combined elementary secondary enrollments would have to be at least 900 students, actually more to allow for dropouts at the secondary level. The commission considered other factors as well and recommended a minimum of 1200 students between the ages of 6 to 18 for the basic unit of educational administration.[9] This seemed unusually high for many rural residents and school board members even though it may appear to be much too small by present-day perspectives. During the 1950s other recommendations called for a minimum of 2400 pupils for an administrative unit. Still others noting the greater number of social responsibilities as well as more comprehensive educational programs being added in the decades following the 1940s suggested that the absolute minimum student population for the administrative unit should be 10,000. A 1971 Educational Research Service study revealed widely disparate recommendations on minimum, maximum, and optimum sizes of school districts.[10]

The Regional Service Agency, or intermediate unit, would enable the operation of a basic or local school district at efficient and effective levels with fewer than 10,000 total enrollment. Reorganization of local units must be kept in the perspective of what educational services could be provided by other units such as the Regional Educational Service Agency. A citizen population of 40,000 in the basic administrative unit would result, by and large, in a school-age population of approximately 10,000. District populations of this magnitude in the rural and more sparsely settled regions would cover sizable geographic areas and include several diverse community and/or cultural groupings. Effective intermediate units of educational administration, which are reviewed in greater detail in the chapter that follows, make it feasible to create community school district administrative units with student populations of less than 10,000.

As late as 1971 about 80 percent of the basic and local administrative units enrolled fewer than 2500 students; about 40 percent had less than 300 students. It was stated at that time that "four-fifths of all districts in the country enroll only about one-fifth of all pupils."[11] Progress toward further improvement of the local district structure in American education slowed perceptibly during the 1970s. By 1982 the overwhelming majority, about 75 percent of the nation's school districts, continued to enroll fewer than 2500 students.

Do larger school districts, that is, those with enrollments at or above the recommended minimums, provide better educational programs or is pupil achievement higher in such districts? The answer is a qualified yes, although more research is needed. A U.S. Office of Education, now Department of Education, released a study of educational change in 522 newly reorganized school districts which concluded that the new administrative units with larger enrollments tended to make significant improvements in both elementary and secondary school programs.[12]

Another study concluded that the pupil educated in a rural elementary school and graduated from a small high school with fewer than 100 students suffered a form of double jeopardy. The hypothesized merits of attendance at small schools have little basis in fact, as demonstrated by formal tests of student achievement. Pupil achievement (in social studies, science, English, mathematics, literary appreciation, and vocabulary) in high schools of 100 or less (in grades 9 to 12) was below that in larger schools with enrollments of 200, as well as those with enrollments from 101 to 199.[13]

Stephens and Spiess observed that most studies "pointed to a direct and positive relationship between size of school and pertinent factors: achievement, educational cost, breadth of educational program, extracurricular activities, professional staff qualifications, special services, and school plant"[14] The 1971 Educational Research Service study found that continuation of very small school districts was at least highly suspect.[15]

In 1974 another review of research and related literature by the Educational Research Service concluded that the *optimum* size for a basic administrative unit ranged from no less than 10,000 to no more than 50,000 pupils.[16]

There remain a few dissenting voices such as those of Sher and Tompkins who write about the "myths of economy, efficiency, and equality in district organization" and then declare that small is better.[17]

The Post-World War II Changes in Basic Administrative Units

The changes in the number of school districts in the United States as a whole are summarized in Table 7-1. By 1931–1932 the number of local school districts declined to 127,531 from almost 200,000 about a decade earlier. As late as 1931–1932 there were over 143,000 one-teacher elementary schools in operation, or over five times as many as all the secondary

TABLE 7.1

NUMBER OF LOCAL PUBLIC SCHOOL DISTRICTS AND PUBLIC SCHOOL ATTENDANCE CENTERS IN THE UNITED STATES, 1931–1932 TO 1983–1984[a]

| | | Public school attendance centers | | |
| | | Elementary schools | | |
School year (1)	Local school districts (2)	Total (3)	One teacher (4)	Secondary schools (5)
1931–1932	127,531	232,750	143,391	26,409
1941–1942	115,493	183,112	107,692	25,123
1945–1946	101,382	160,227	86,563	24,134
1951–1952	71,094	123,763	50,742	23,746
1955–1956	54,859	104,427	34,964	26,046
1961–1962	35,676	81,910	13,333	25,350
1965–1966	26,983	73,216	6,491	26,597
1970–1971	17,995	65,800	1,815	25,352
1975–1976	16,376	63,242	1,166	25,330
1976–1977	16,271	62,644	1,111	25,378
1978–1979	16,014	61,982	1,056	24,504
1983–1984[b]	15,000	60,000	800	23,700

Source: National Center for Educational Statistics, *Digest of Educational Statistics 1982,* Washington, D.C.: GPO, p. 61, 1982.

[a]Does not include the single school district for education for each of the five outlying areas: American Samoa, Canal Zone, Guam, Puerto Rico, and Virgin Islands.
[b]Estimates by author for the year 1983–1984 only.

schools in operation in the nation. Some 50 years later the one-teacher schools almost disappeared and accounted for less than 1 percent of all public school attendance units.

By the end of World War II (1945–1946 data) there was a reduction of about 20 percent, leaving about 101,493 school districts in the United States. The most rapid decline in numbers of school districts in our educational history was accomplished during the next 15-year period, that is, from 1945–1946 to 1959–1960. The numbers fell to about 40,500 in 1959–1960, or about 60 percent below that for 1945–1946! The decline continued during the 1960s, but the pace moderated to an annual district reduction rate between 1800 and 2000 as compared with the annual reduction rate of 4000 during the previous decade. The district elimination pace slowed even more during the 1970s to an average of less than 200 per year. About 2000 school districts were eliminated during the 1970s, which is fewer lost through mergers during one decade than was accomplished during only one year of the 1950 decade.

Only Alaska increased the total number of

school districts by 20 or more after 1975. Three other states recorded nominal increases in local school districts of from one to three during that same period.

More than 112,000 local school districts disappeared from the educational scene during the 50-year period following 1931–1932, with the period of most rapid decline being between 1945–1946 and 1959–1960. Nonetheless, more remains to be done. About 40 percent of the number in existence at the beginning of the 1980s can and should be eliminated. The fiscal and other crises facing school districts during the 1970s and early 1980s would have been exacerbated if the vast majority of inefficiently organized and nonoperating school districts had not been eliminated earlier. An even more efficient district structure will be needed to meet the challenges that lie ahead during the remainder of this century.

A comparison of the number of basic administrative units found in each state in 1948 and 1980 is presented in Table 7.2. There is considerable variablity among the basic administrative units. Thus, the Elko County, Nevada, school district is a single basic administrative

TABLE 7.2

STATUS OF SCHOOL DISTRICTS IN VARIOUS STATES OF THE UNITED STATES, 1948 AND 1980

(1) State	No. of school districts		No. of nonoperating school districts	
	(2) 1948	(3) 1980	(4) 1948	(5) 1980
Alabama	108	127	0	0
Alaska	—	52	—	0
Arizona	322	229	0	12
Arkansas	1589	370	20	0
California	2429	1036	39	0
Colorado	1884	181	392	0
Connecticut	172	165	2	0
Delaware	126	16	0	0
District of Columbia	1	1	0	0
Florida	67	67	0	0
Georgia	189	187	0	0
Hawaii	—	1	—	0

TABLE 7.2 *(Continued)*

Idaho	1011	115	320	0
Illinois	11061	1012	315	1
Indiana	1196	305	94	1
Iowa	4856	443	1335	0
Kansas	5643	307	1270	0
Kentucky	256	181	0	0
Louisiana	67	66	0	0
Maine	493	283	21	56
Maryland	24	24	0	0
Massachusetts	351	403	0	55
Michigan	5434	575	1041	0
Minnesota	7606	437	2418	2
Mississippi	4194	153	0	0
Missouri	8422	551	2067	0
Montana	1800	568	327	14
Nebraska	6991	1089	1812	54
Nevada	211	17	22	0
New Hampshire	239	168	7	11
New Jersey	561	606	25	18
New Mexico	104	88	0	0
New York	4609	721	1765	6
North Carolina	172	144	0	0
North Dakota	2267	335	279	39
Ohio	1583	615	24	0
Oklahoma	2664	619	192	0
Oregon	1363	311	336	1
Pennsylvania	2540	504	101	0
Rhode Island	39	40	0	0
South Carolina	1737	92	45	0
South Dakota	3409	196	801	8
Tennessee	150	147	0	0
Texas	5145	1076	900	0
Utah	40	40	0	0
Vermont	268	273	5	26
Virginia	125	139	0	4
Washington	628	300	39	0
West Virginia	55	55	0	0
Wisconsin	6385	433	1074	0
Wyoming	359	49	43	0
Totals	100,947	15,912	17,131	311

Source: Columns 2 and 4 data from unpublished surveys conducted by the Division of Rural Services, National Education Association; columns 3 and 5 from W. V. Grant and L. S. Eiden, *Digest of Education Statistics 1982*, National Center for Education Statistics, Washington, D. C.: GPO, 1982.

unit that embraces a geographic area larger than the combined states of Connecticut, Massachusetts, and Rhode Island.[18] In contrast, there are fewer than 4000 students enrolled from the 17,127 square miles within Elko County, whereas the 608 local school districts in Connecticut, Massachusetts, and Rhode Island enroll almost 1.6 million pupils. The enrollment in the New York City school district is greater than the total found in each of 38 states; enrollments in the Los Angeles Unified School District exceeded those in each of 22 states.

The boundaries of a school district may be coterminous with those of a county as well as a city or township. The county school district may be an intermediate unit more often than it is a basic unit of educational administration. There are 13 states, located primarily in the South, wherein all counties are basic school administrative units. Of these 13, Alabama, Georgia, Kentucky, New Mexico, North Carolina, Tennessee, Utah, and Virginia have independent units not included in the county unit as well as the basic county school district where the entire area is in but is a single administrative unit. The 13 county unit states have relatively few school districts, ranging from a low of 17 in Nevada to a high of 187 in Georgia.

The states in the Midwest traditionally have allowed the largest numbers of school districts to be created, to continue, and their reorganization has been among the most difficult to achieve. As late as 1958 the states of Iowa, Kansas, Minnesota, Nebraska, North Dakota, South Dakota, and Wisconsin with less than 7 percent of the nation's public school enrollment accounted for 44 percent of the public school districts in the nation. At that time over 80 percent of the nonoperating school districts, more than 50 percent of all one-teacher schools, and 55 percent of the districts with nine or fewer teachers were to be found in this region. Progress since then has been impressive. Some 20 years later these same seven states reduced the number of school districts to 3240 from 22,100, which is still about 20.4 percent of all school districts in existence in 1980.

The southern states deserve recognition as having the "most efficient" local school district structure. Only one state in the southeast and southwest has over 200 school districts—Texas with 1076. The average number of school districts per state in the fall of 1980 was approximately 318. In 1960 about 26 percent of the states had more than 2000 school districts in each one. About 20 years later, no state reported 2000 or more school districts and only four remained with 1000 or more. In 1948–1949 Illinois had the largest number of local school districts with 11,061 and seven other states had more than 5000 school districts.

The emotional disputes over school district reorganizations in many states came to an end, by and large, during the 1970s. Progress will continue, albeit somewhat slowly, during the remainder of this century to probably no fewer than 5000 local school districts and no more than about 7500.

Urban School Districts: Structural Patterns and Subdivisions

Historically, the first efforts and emotional responses related to the reorganization of school attendance and administrative units were in the cities that grew by annexing territories where established basic school units existed for the rural or suburban fringe. The growth of cities often resulted in several school districts as separate legal entities that were operating within the same city boundary lines. In other large cities the control and supervision of schools within each ward were delegated to separate "ward boards of education." The initial step away from ward control over school operations was to elect a citywide school board with individual members representing a given ward of the city. About 75 years before more efficient school district structures were realized in the rural and less densely populated areas, city school districts achieved structural unity by placing authority and control over all city schools in a single or unified board of education. This centralization of administration and supervision reduced inefficiencies in operation and eliminated the worst features of political control that characterized the fragmented "ward system of school administration."

For much of history the large urban public school systems were the finest in the nation. City schools attracted the best professionals in education. The special advantages and excitement of city life attracted people in general and provided a variety of employment opportunities. The suburban areas benefited from what the central city had to offer. Following the end of World War II there came into being a large number of school districts in the suburban areas and the rural fringe surrounding the core cities that exhibited unusually rapid growth in enrollments. This prompted a restructuring of administrative units in the suburban and nearby urban areas. Many such districts grew at the expense of the core cities. The so-called white flight to the suburbs increased during the late 1950s, continued during the 1960s, and slowed somewhat during the 1970s.

As indicated earlier, the city was the point of entry for the disadvantaged from minority backgrounds. By the 1970s, most of the largest cities in the country saw students from minority backgrounds become the majority of those enrolled in the core city public schools. The so-called white flight from the cities resulted in predominately white enrollments in the suburban districts surrounding the central city with predominately minority student enrollments. This generated a new set of social and political pressures for reorganization of administrative units in metropolitan areas. In an effort to achieve what is called a better racial balance in public school enrollments, some local leaders and some federal judges called for a merger of the city school district with one or more school districts in the surrounding urban and rural fringe to create an enlarged metropolitan school district. The mechanism selected for bringing about "racially balanced" enrollments in every city school-attendance unit was so-called crosstown busing of students, particularly from the central core where the large concentrations of minority students resided to school buildings in the outlying areas, and, of course, transporting the predominately white students from the outlying areas in return to

the core city schools. The issue of whether a court can set aside the legally constituted quasi-municipal corporations called school districts (which the state legislature created to discharge the state function of education) is as far reaching as it is politically and socially sensitive. The U.S. Supreme Court has not ruled definitively on this specific issue, but the conservative turn during the early 1980s suggests that it may not be an easy resolution of this constitutional dilemma confronting education and broader social issues.

There are metropolitan school districts that came into being before the racial or social issues calling for the creation of more such units began to attract attention. Some examples of metropolitan school districts that include all the land within a county or other metropolitan area plus that of a large city center as well are Savannah and Chatham County in Georgia; the city of Miami and Dade County in Florida; the city of Albuquerque and all of Bernalillo County in New Mexico; the city of Nashville and Davison County in Tennessee; the city of Greenville and Greenville County in South Carolina; and the city of Charlotte and Mecklenburg County in North Carolina. There are others; the above list is not exhaustive but illustrative. Metropolitan school districts are relatively common in the county-unit states (where the county is the basic school administrative unit as well) such as Florida, West Virginia, and Nevada. They are less likely to be found or created where suburban areas are proud of their political independence from the central city, particularly if the school district of the central city is fiscally dependent, that is, must have the school budget or taxing authority approved by the city council.

The administrative complexity in very large urban school systems often raises the issue of whether such units should be divided into more manageable smaller districts, or at least the creation of some type of decentralized internal administrative structure. A study in 1982 prepared for the California legislature considered as one option the division of the Los Angeles Unified School District into a number of smaller and legally autonomous school districts within that sprawling city. The sheer size of the district is awesome. The Los Angeles Unified School District enrolls 13 percent of all students in the state of California, and within its geographic area could be included the cities of Boston, Cleveland, Denver, Detroit, Milwaukee, Philadelphia, Providence, and Washington, D.C. The legislative study concluded, however, that the breaking up of this city school district with over 500,000 students enrolled would solve relatively few of the existing problems and could exacerbate many others such as the attempted resolution of the many so-called racially isolated school attendance units and others that related to overcoming segregation. Such major surgery on one of the nation's largest school administrative units was judged to be impractical and almost impossible. This was not the first try at this. In 1970 the then governor Ronald Reagan vetoed legislation that would have subdivided the Los Angeles Unified School District. The problems of maximum size and bigness of the administrative unit in the large urban areas remain vexing and doubtless the simplistic solution of "breaking up the big ones" will continue to surface in the years ahead.

A more successfully implemented approach is related to an internal restructuring while preserving the ultimate control and authority in the central administrative board and the general superintendent. It is the decentralized administrative plan or simply decentralization. Although much attention was given it during the 1960s and 1970s, decentralization of large city school administration is not new. Bertolaet reported that as early as 1883 the Philadelphia school system created ten geographical divisions for purposes of decentralized administration and appointed ten district (more precisely, subdistrict) superintendents, each with considerable operational decision-making authority over schools within the "districts."[19]

The Board of Education of New York City in 1906 approved the creation of 46 decentralized administrative areas and appointed 26 "district superintendents." Chicago used the title of "district superintendent" in 1898, with the number of such positions varying from 6 in 1902 to 12 in 1913. By 1969 there were 27 "district superintendencies" in Chicago.[20]

The number of subdistricts (often called "districts") within a large urban school system varies from place to place and from one period in time to another. Ten to 30 such operational subdivisions are not uncommon in the larger urban centers. Most have fewer than ten, typically three to eight. With declining enrollments and the financial crises of more recent years the trend is toward fewer such administrative units.

Decentralization of administrative operations facilitates instructional decision making and can involve those who are closer to pupil–teacher interactions in classrooms. Other functions such as personnel management, educational facilities planning, and financial operations remain centralized in the general superintendent's office. Often the decentralization also allows greater community involvement in educational decision making or advisement.

Decentralized operational decision making that is coordinated and supported from a unified and centralized district-wide policymaking agency has many advantages. It may continue to the extreme, however, where the subdistrict approaches autonomous and separate status from any district-wide policymaking and decision-making agency. Often self-appointed lay groups may emerge and claim to speak for the "people" or "community" in the more extreme forms of runaway decentralization. There is then a possibility of fragmentation that once again resembles the evils of the ward system of public education administration. Past experience documents that the ward school administration practice is less efficient in the utilization of limited resources, more prone to partisan political involvement in educational decision making, and less likely to improve the quality of education within the ward schools. It would be unfortunate if the politics of decentralization brought a reversion to the previously repudiated ward politics in appointing instructional and administrative personnel and in awarding contracts to those who do business with the educational system. Community participation has much to offer to the advancement of learning and the improvement of educational programs. It should not be allowed, however, to be the front for the behind-the-scenes manipulation of those whose purposes are more political and related to personal economic gain than are educational in orientation.

The public school enrollments in the large cities grew rapidly until the late 1960s for some and the early 1970s for others. Enrollments have been in a declining trend for about a decade. As indicated previously the composition as well as the magnitude of the public school enrollments in large city school districts changed dramatically. The largest concentrations of the minority and the disadvantaged students are now found in the large urban school districts; the so-called white student population is now the minority group in many such districts.

Some characteristics of the 60 largest local public school systems in the United States are presented in Table 7.3. As late as 1977, the New York City schools enrolled over 1 million students. It was the only school district in the nation with that many pupils. By the fall, 1980 enrollments in New York City dropped to 963,-142, or 16 percent below that of ten years earlier. By 1980 no district had 1 million students and only New York City and Los Angeles reported 500,000 or more. Only six districts enrolled 200,000 or more, and about one-third had 100,000 or more pupils. Most large districts experienced substantial enrollment declines during the 1970s; Cleveland and St. Louis reported enrollment losses over the ten-year period of more than 40 percent. The median decline during the 1970s was about 17.4 percent. In contrast, seven of the very large districts registered modest enrollment gains.

THE NEIGHBORHOOD SCHOOL AND LOCAL CONTROL OF EDUCATION CONCEPTS

The neighborhood school concept was a reflection of the desire of the people to keep schools close to the family unit to insure a relatively high level of parental involvement and interest in the education of children and youths. In addition, there was an economic advantage to locating elementary school attendance centers within walking distance of most who attend. Transportation was justified in rural areas to procure the benefits of larger and fewer attendance units in sparsely settled areas.

During the past two decades the neighborhood concept of long standing came under attack, not because it was deemed wrong to keep the schools close to the family unit or that it was economically unsound, but because the neighborhood or residential patterns in the central cities reflected the clustering of persons of predominately one race or ethnic heritage therein. The segregated housing patterns resulted in racially isolated schools. Busing of pupils who lived within walking distance of school where the enrollment was predominately students of a single race or ethnic heritage to another attendance center that reflected a different racial or ethnic mix was promoted by court order or by sociological reasons rather than educational ones. The local school districts and the structuring of attendance areas within them were impacted heavily by the broader social concerns within society as a whole. When people of one color or a single ethnic heritage reside, for reasons outside the control of the educational system, in a given area of city, then terms such as *ghetto* and *barrio*, with all their undesirable connotations, are used rather than the softer and previously more accepted terms such as *neighborhood* or *community*. In recent years crosstown busing to achieve student integration or to reduce racial isolation has received as much criticism as the neighborhood school concept.

For much of history, local control over public education was cherished and recognized as one of the unique characteristics of the American system of public education. This is now being challenged as well. Some have gone so far as to brand local control of education a myth, an archaic practice, and an encrusted tradition. It is said to inhibit innovation, impede achievement of excellence, make difficult the amelioration of social injustices. It is accused of perpetuating *de facto* segregation and alleged to be a high

TABLE 7.3

FALL OF 1980 ENROLLMENTS, ENROLLMENT CHANGES FROM 1971 TO 1980, AND NUMBER OF SCHOOLS IN 50 LARGEST U.S. SCHOOL SYSTEMS

Rank	School System	Enrollment Fall 1980[a]	Enrollment change Fall 1980 over Fall 1971	Est. No. of Schools[c]
1	New York, NY	963,142	−16.0	989
2	Los Angeles, CA	535,161	−17.5	687
3	Chicago, IL	458,804	−19.8	623
4	Dade County, FL (Miami)	233,100	−5.0	251
5	Philadelphia, PA	220,550	−22.4	272
6	Detroit, MI	213,318	−24.4	289
7	Houston, TX	191,869	−17.3	241
8	Hawaii (entire state)	166,237	−8.9	
9	Broward County, FL (Ft. Lauderdale)	131,851	+7.6	153
10	Baltimore City, MD	129,984	−31.9	203
11	Dallas, TX	128,771	−24.0	195
12	Fairfax County, VA (Fairfax)	127,542	−6.2	181
13	Prince George's County, MD (Upper Marlboro)	118,996	−26.8	217
14	San Diego, CA	110,685	−13.8	169
15	Memphis, TN	109,689	−29.2	179
16	Hillsborough County, FL (Tampa)	109,200	+5.5	131
17	Duval County, FL (Jacksonville)	100,663	−13.4	151
18	Jefferson County, KY (Louisville)	98,669	[b]	65
19	Baltimore County, MD (Towson)	97,664	−27.1	159
20	Montgomery County, MD (Rockville)	96,476	−23.6	185
21	Washington, DC	96,416	−32.5	188
22	Pinellas County, FL (Clearwater)	87,425	+0.6	111
23	Milwaukee, WI	87,000	−34.3	146
24	Clark County, NV (Las Vegas)	85,365	+14.2	112
25	Orleans Parish, LA (New Orleans)	83,105	−22.9	129
26	Cleveland, OH	80,118	−45.0	147
27	DeKalb County, GA (Decatur)	78,890	−10.1	113
28	Orange County, FL (Orlando)	78,787	−9.4	120
29	Jefferson County, CO (Lakewood)	78,068	+8.4	107
30	Albuquerque, NM	76,545	−11.0	112
31	Charlotte-Mecklenburg County, NC (Charlotte)	75,100	−7.3	108
32	Atlanta, GA	72,500	−27.6	124
33	Palm Beach County, FL (West Palm Beach)	71,161	+7.8	88
34	Columbus, OH	70,828	−34.8	149

35	Anne Arundel County, MD (Annapolis)	70,193	−7.5	110
36	Metropolitan School System, Nashville, TN	69,112	−21.6	129
37	Fort Worth, TX	65,848	−18.3	108
38	East Baton Rouge Parish, LA (Baton Rouge)	64,790	−1.9	114
39	Boston, MA	64,319	−33.8	156
40	Mobile County, AL (Mobile)	64,184	−4.0	78
41	Indianapolis, IN	63,856	−37.7	117
42	St. Louis, MO	62,389	−42.5	150
43	Jefferson Parish, LA (Gretna)	61,883	−5.6	85
44	Denver, CO	61,077	−35.6	119
45	San Antonio, TX	61,000	−16.7	91
46	El Paso, TX	60,160	−3.5	65
47	Polk County, FL (Bartow)	58,112	+4.5	93
48	San Francisco, CA	57,883	−30.1	103
49	Granite, UT	57,436	−8.6	81
50	Newark, NJ	57,164	−25.9	90

Sources: Educational Research Service, *ERS Bulletin,* April 1981, p. 9; also *Digest of Education Statistics 1982.*

[a]Data derived from Educational Research Service publications.
[b]Computation not appropriate in view of school district change in 1975.
[c]Estimates derived from National Center for Education Statistics data for 1979–1980.

price to pay for inferior education. This is a serious indictment of a democratic tradition and a distinctly American approach to the administration of public education.

What is attacked as local control is not always the same. Some people criticize the neighborhood school, the existence of the local school district operationally independent from other governmental units, the policymaking powers of school boards, the legislative control of education by the state rather than the federal government, or even the authority of the school board to accept or reject a curriculum idea.

It should not be assumed, however, that there no longer exists any support for the concept of local control. On the contrary, there exists a full spectrum of reaction ranging from unequivocal approval to complete condemnation. Some people judge the system ridiculous, others sublime. Some appraise it a vice, others proclaim it a virtue.

Local control as defined herein means placement of policymaking authority, within legislatively defined limits, for the direct operation of education with the people or their designated representatives within a legally defined civil subdivision of the state known as the school district. It represents an effort to compensate for the removal of absolute control for the educational development of the child from the parent. Under the local control concept, parental concern over the education of their offspring can be effectively expressed even though a preponderance of operational controls rests with the more distant units such as the state or the federal government. The qualifying clause "within legislatively defined limits" is significant in the interpretation of the concept of local control as developed herein.

No serious student of education ever championed the extreme position of unqualified local determination of all dimensions of education operations or implied that education is a local rather than a state function. There never was a time in this century when a local school district could do as it pleased. Nor does the local control concept suggest a return to the inadequately organized school district or the one-teacher school; but it does imply keeping home, family, and patrons actively involved and concerned about the quality and relevance of education.

Minimum length of school terms, teacher certification standards, safety standards for school plants, minimum secondary school graduation requirements, and mandatory courses of instruction are determined often by state law and serve as constraints which local school district policies on such matters must respect. State demands have tempered the actions of lay school board members for over 100 years.

There remains variation in quality among local school districts in spite of state and other efforts to equalize educational opportunity. Those impatient with local control of education tend to generalize from the sorriest examples; those who champion the concept point to the degree of excellence found among the best. Are their more effective patterns for the structuring and control of public education? One might be to move the decision-making authority over educational operations to a more distant unit such as the federal government. Some equate highly centralized control with innovation and with programs more responsive to present and future needs of society. There is little in experience to document that the federal or national unit, as noted in other countries of the world, is the best qualified to operate directly the local schools of the nation. On the contrary, there is overwhelming evidence to demonstrate that confusion and contradictions abound in past and present federal involvements in education that are far less extensive than would be demanded if direct and day-by-day operational control were shifted to this level. The so-called national commitment to education is neither unified in one agency, well coordinated among the many involved, nor consistent from one presidency to the next. Whatever the shortcomings related to qualified local control of education, there is considerable evidence that the transfer of operational decision-making authority for public education to Washington, D.C., would not be in the best interest of education or for the nation.

There is little to suggest that direct state operation of all public schools would generate fresh and imaginative approaches to learning. In short, there is little evidence to recommend the restructuring of the administration of public education to where greater centralization by direct state or federal operations is substituted for the existing pattern of qualified local educational control. Each of the units, namely, local, state, and federal, can contribute that which it is best qualified to contribute to the advancement of public education in the United States.

In the best educational framework, people with vision and competence are free to experiment, to be creative, and to speak out without fear of oppressive reactions. Local initiative can have virtue and be productive if properly nourished. It can degenerate into inertia where local leadership is bankrupt, corrupt, or unstable. State and federal educational agencies have a responsibility to stimulate, recognize, and reward productive educational leadership at the local level. Local control can be visualized as a means for tapping the creative potential that resides within thousands of lay citizens teamed with more than 2 million professionals.

The propensity to castigate inadequate local control where it exists should be sublimated in favor of searching for an approach that would multiply its advantages and minimize its shortcomings. A creative decentralized school administrative pattern for our times calls for local operational responsibility for education supported by adequate resources, blessed with leadership talents, and stimulated by enlightened partners at the state and federal levels. Shortcomings in present school organizations may call for a review but not abandonment of the unique American approach that rests on the democratic premise that the people are the safest repository of governmental controls over something as sensitive and important as public education.

There exists the ever-present danger that schools, as social institutions, may be subverted to the narrow purposes of a dominant power elite, and, therefore, fail to serve adequately the needs of the majority. The church, in previous centuries, paid the price when in some of its missions it became the tool of a favored or wealthy minority at the expense of the masses.

It is far more difficult for a single power bloc to gain control of public education in a system where decentralized administrative units prevail rather than where a high degree of centralization exists. It is reemphasized that the democratic tradition of local control over public education is more likely to achieve excellence in education than centralization and concentration of authority in a state, regional, or federal educational unit. The concept of local control of public education exerts a powerful influence on the administration and operation of schools in the United States.

FISCAL RELATIONS WITH OTHER MUNICIPAL CORPORATIONS

Whether local school districts should be dependent fiscally or independent from the fiscal controls of general municipal corporations in which they are located has been a matter of considerable and long-standing debate. There is less research and debate presently on this issue than was noted during the 1930s and 1940s. But it does reappear every now and then, albeit for briefer periods than in earlier years.

If the legally elected or appointed local board of education has complete and final authority to levy local property taxes and to expend funds according to a budget for education, the local school district is said to be fiscally independent of other local (municipal) governmental units. In other words, in such school districts there is no need to procure prior approval from elected or appointed municipal officials to determine finally and legally the size of the levy for education, the educational tax rate, and/or the size of the educational budget for a stated fiscal period.

If the school district lacks complete fiscal authority over the levying of taxes for education or to implement budgeted expenditures and must obtain prior approval for these from some other local governmental agencies, it is said to be a fiscally dependent school district.

Relatively few new studies on school district fiscal relationships appeared during the past two decades. A 1958 study reported that 54 percent of city systems of education were completely independent of any budget review, 18 percent simply submitted the school budget to a municipality for purposes of information, and the remaining 28 percent were fiscally dependent. In short, of the city systems studied, 72 percent enjoyed a large measure of fiscal independence in deciding the educational budget.[21] The pattern has not changed materially over the years since then. In addition, 62 percent were, for all practical purposes, fiscally independent in determining the amount and rate of school tax rate. The city school districts are the most likely to face constraints on fiscal authority from other municipal bodies. At the time of the study less than 5 percent of the total number of school districts were in a city setting. The overwhelming majority of school districts are fiscally independent from other municipal agencies because it is the rare school district not in a large city setting that experiences such fiscal constraints from town or county governments.

Political scientists have tended to favor fiscal dependence of local school districts, but educators argue in favor of fiscal independence. The arguments most used by those supporting fiscal independence are:

1. Efficiency and simplicity are best measured in terms of realization of the educational function.
2. The ends of education are important to the welfare of our democracy and realized best by those who devote considerable time and effort to their achievement.
3. School boards could become mere appendages unless able to control the fiscal implications of educational planning.
4. Public education in many cities is a large complex organization operating with efficient and professional management.
5. The boundaries of many cities are not coterminous with school district boundaries.

6. Education is a state function and the local board of education represents the state as well as the people living within the district.[22]

Firman defined the basic issue as "whether or not educational policy formulation can be separated from financial policy formulation," that is, control of the purse strings by other municipal agencies can mean control of educational operations as well.[23] He developed eight practical tests to assess the relative degree of fiscal independence to include:

1. Budget. The school board has the power to establish the budget.
2. Taxing Power. The school board has the power to levy taxes to finance, in part, the proposed budget.
3. Adequacy of Tax Base. There is an adequate tax base within the school district to procure funds when local taxing authority is exercised.
4. Tax and Indebtedness Limits. Maximum legal limits on tax rate and indebtedness are sufficiently flexible to raise amounts required for school support.
5. Tax and Indebtedness Leeway. Enough taxing and indebtedness authority remains after satisfying mandatory educational programs to permit the school board to go beyond and toward enriched experiences.
6. Accounting. The board can keep its own system of financial records, including control of auditing and reporting procedures.
7. Responsibility. The citizen can turn to one local governmental authority—the school board—for appeal and for responsibility determination.
8. Response to Educational Needs. Fiscal resources and powers are acceptable and flexible enough to permit the school board to adjust to emerging demands.[24]

Educators declare unequivocally that the agency assuming responsibility for the delivery of quality education programs and services must have the power to finance the implications of its educational policy actions.

Perhaps one of the reasons why the emotional fervor that earlier surrounded the fiscal independence-dependence debates is that local school boards have authority limited to control of local fiscal resources that are contributing less and less to the total school revenues as state aids; moreover, some limited amounts of federal grants make up the majority of educational support funds. On the other hand, earmarked or categorical aids from the state or federal government can make a mockery out of local freedom of choice or of the exercise of judgment by the local board of education.

SUMMARY

The American pattern of organizing for the purposes of delivering educational services was based on the transfer of control over public schools from religious or private authorities to public or civil authorities. The basic organizational unit for the administration of public education is the local school district.

The school district is a civil subdivision of the state with definitive boundaries and with corporate status as a quasi-municipal corporation. Its reason for being is to provide educational opportunities to residents of the district; therefore, when it ceases to perform this function and becomes "nonoperating" it has no further reason for continued existence. The district system of educational administration had some unintended effects such as unequal resources for the support of public education among the various districts of a state.

The concept of the community school was at first predominately rural in flavor, but was later adapted to urban America as well. In the urban areas it led to decentralization that included varying degrees of community involvement in the operation of schools in various area of a city. In its extreme form it led to fragmentation that approached the earlier excesses of the "ward school control" systems.

The effectiveness of a local school district as an administrative unit is related to such factors as the total student population and taxable wealth available to support a quality program of education. The minimum numbers of students residing within a local school district to provide a quality educational program at a reasonable cost has increased over the years. During the 1950s the recommended minimum per district was 2400 pupils within an administrative unit, but presently most suggest that 10,000 students are necessary for the district to meet the educational and social responsibilities of today —particularly if there is no effective regional educational service agency available to complement the local district. As late as 1971 about 80 percent of the basic administrative units enrolled fewer than 2500 students. By 1981 75 percent of these districts had fewer than 2500 students. There is evidence to support the contention that larger school districts have the better educational programs and higher student achievement records.

In 1931–1932 there were 127,531 local school districts, which is less than the more than 200,000 a decade earlier, and 143,000 one-teacher schools. The most rapid decline in the number of school districts took place during the 15-year period from 1945–1946 to 1959–1960 when 60 percent of those existing during 1945–1946 were eliminated. The rate slowed during the 1970s when less than 2000 local school districts were eliminated. By 1983, there were only about 15,000 local school districts in the nation, the number of nonoperating districts dropped to about 300, and the one-teacher school almost disappeared.

There is considerable variability among the states in the number of local school districts in existence. There are fewer in the South than in most other regions. The Midwest made the most impressive reductions in numbers of school districts, but still has about 20 percent of the total in the nation. Some local districts are large in geographic area but are sparsely settled. The emotional disputes surrounding district reorganization came to an end, by and large, during the 1970s. Progress will be slower during the remainder of the century until a level of from 5000 to 7500 school districts is reached.

The cities were the first to go through the throes of reorganization of school districts and more recently the rural and smaller urban communities. The "ward system of school administration" disappeared in most very large cities about 75 years ago. The sociological disputes related to reduction of racially isolated schools and promotion of integration led to crosstown busing of students and recommendations to form a single metropolitan school district comprised of the central city and surrounding suburbs plus the rural–urban fringe in some cases. There were many metropolitan school districts in the nation that came into being before the racial or social issues came to the fore.

There were pressures to break up large districts such as Los Angeles as well as to create larger metropolitan units. These efforts have not been accepted to date and in its place a decentralized internal administrative pattern has been instituted in most of the very large urban school districts. The enrollment growth in the very large cities ended by about 1970 and declines were noted in most of them throughout the previous decade.

The neighborhood school concept, which was a reflection of the desire to keep schools close to the home and family, came under attack in large urban areas where the neighborhoods included large concentrations of persons of a single racial or ethnic group. Local control over education was also criticized. Such control has been constrained in past years by state legislative mandates. There is no feasible alternative to the operation and administration of public education with considerable local decision-making authority.

The issue of whether local school districts should be fiscally dependent or independent from other municipal agencies has been debated for many years, with educators promoting independence and some political scientists recommending dependence upon the city or other municipal government. The control of purse strings can be an effective way to control educational policymaking without assuming responsibility for operations. Earmarked or categorical state and federal grants can make a mockery out of local freedom of choice as well.

NOTES

1. R. Freeman Butts and L. A. Cremin, *A History of Education in American Culture*, New York: Holt, Rinehart and Winston, 1953, p. 253.
2. Newton Edwards and Herman G. Richey, *The School in the American Social Order*, Boston: Houghton Mifflin, 1947, pp. 111–112.
3. Eugene McQuillan, *The Law of Municipal Corporations*, 3rd ed., Vol. 1, Chicago: Callaghan, 1949, p. 451.
4. Newton Edwards, *The Courts and the Public Schools*, rev. ed., Chicago: University of Chicago Press, 1955, p. 146.
5. Howard A. Dawson and Floyd W. Reeves, *Your School District*, Report of the National Commission on School District Reorganization, Washington, D.C.: Department of Rural Education, National Education Association, 1948, p. 47.
6. Howard A. Dawson, *Satisfactory Local School Units*, Nashville, Tenn.: Division of Surveys and Field Studies, George Peabody College for Teachers, 1934, p. 39.
7. Dawson and Reeves, op. cit., pp. 81–82.
8. Ibid., p. 82.
9. Ibid., p. 87.
10. "Size of Schools and School Districts," *ERS Information Aid*, No. 8, June 1971, Arlington, Va.: Educational Research Service, p. 39.
11. Ibid., p. 21.
12. C. O. Fitzwater, *Educational Change and Reorganized School Districts*, U.S. Office of Education, Bulletin 1953, No. 4, Washington, D.C.: GPO, 1953.
13. Leonard S. Feldt, "The Relationship Between Pupil Achievement and High School Size," unpublished paper, Iowa City: University of Iowa, 1960.
14. E. R. Stephens and J. Spiess, "What Does Research Say About a Local School District?," *Journal of State School Systems*, Fall 1967, pp. 182–199.
15. Educational Research Service, op. cit., pp. 7–20.
16. Educational Research Service, "Summary of Research on Size of School and School Districts," *Research Brief*, Arlington, Va.: ERS, 1974, 65 pp.
17. J. P. Sher and R. E. Tompkins, *Economy, Efficiency, and Equality: The Myth of Rural School and District Consolidation*, in *Hearings Before the Subcommittee on Elementary, Secondary, and Vocational Education*, 95th Congress, May 10–11, 1977, Washington, D.C.: GPO, 1977, pp. 67–97.
18. American Association of School Administrators, *School District Organization*, Report of the AASA Commission on School District Reorganization, Arlington, Va.: The Association, 1958, pp. 80–83.
19. F. W. Bertolaet, "The Administrative Functions of the District Superintendent in Chicago as Related to Decentralization," doctoral dissertation, Madison, Wis.: University of Wisconsin, 1964, pp. 3–6.
20. Ibid.
21. National Education Association, "Fiscal Authorities: City School Boards," *Research Bulletin*, April 1958, pp. 46–79.
22. S. J. Knezevich and John Guy Fowlkes, *Business Management of Local School Systems*, New York: Harper & Row, 1960, p. 12.
23. W. D. Firman, "Fiscal Independence of School Systems," *Trends in Financing Public School Systems*, Proceedings of the Eighth National Conference on School Finance, Washington, D.C.: National Education Association, 1965, pp. 117–124.
24. Ibid.

CHAPTER REVIEW QUESTIONS

1. Why is it essential for a local school district to have legal status as a quasi-municipal corporation?
2. What are the major advantages and disadvantages in creating the district system of educational administration?
3. What are the similarities and the differences between the New England town and the surveyor's township used in the mapping of the Northwest Territory?
4. What is a community school district?
5. What is the difference between an administrative unit and an attendance unit?
6. How were the standards for the determination of effective local school administrative units developed at various points in time?
7. During what recent periods of time were there the greatest reductions in the numbers of local school districts? The smallest annual reductions?
8. What factors stimulated the reduction of local school districts in sparsely populated regions of the nation?

9. What factors stimulated interest anew in the reorganization of local districts in very large urban areas?

10. What are the advantages and dangers in the internal decentralization of administration in large urban school districts?

11. In what ways does a fiscally dependent district differ from one that is fiscally independent?

12. Why do educators favor fiscal independence for local school districts, whereas political scientists tend to favor fiscal dependence?

SELECTED REFERENCES

American Association of School Administrators, *School District Organization,* Report of the AASA Commission on School District Reorganization, Washington, D.C.: The Association, 1958.

Firman, W. D., "Fiscal Independence of School Systems," *Trends in Financing Public Education,* Proceedings of the Eighth National Conference on School Finance, Washington, D.C.: National Education Association, 1965, pp. 117–124.

McKelvey, Troy V., ed., *Metropolitan School Organization,* Vols. 1 and 2, Berkeley, Calif.: McCutchan, 1975.

McLoone, E. P., "Advantages of Fiscal Independence for School Districts," *The Challenge of Change in School Finance,* Proceedings of the Tenth National Conference on School Finance, Washington, D.C.: National Education Association, 1967, pp. 137–150.

National Society for the Study of Education, *Metropolitanism, Its Challenge to Education,* R. J. Havighurst, ed., 67th Yearbook of the Society, Chicago: University of Chicago Press, 1968, part I, especially chaps. 1, 4, 5, 8, and 16.

Stephens, E. R., and Spiess, J., "What Does Research Say About a Local School District?," *Journal on State School Systems,* Vol. 1, No. 3, Fall 1967, pp. 182–199.

8

THE INTERMEDIATE UNIT OF EDUCATIONAL ADMINISTRATION: THE REGIONAL EDUCATIONAL SUPPORT MECHANISM FOR LOCAL SCHOOL DISTRICTS

The intermediate unit of educational administration is one of the oldest but also the least understood organizational units in the nation's system of public education. This may be true partly because of this administrative unit's more distant relations with patrons, students, and professionals.

The term *intermediate unit of educational administration* was used in the 1930s; 5223 such units were identified in 35 states (there were none in the remaining 13) in 1934–1935.[1] It gained greater popularity after World War II and replaced the designation "county superintendency" whose origins can be traced back over 150 years. The executive officer of the intermediate unit continues to be referred to in some states as the county superintendent of schools. This contributed to the terminological confusion that surrounds this unit because the executive head of the local school district in the 13 county-unit states may also be called the county superintendent or simply superintendent of schools. Emerging even more recently during the 1960s and 1970s is the more functionally descriptive designation of this unit as

the regional educational service agency (RESA). The terms *RESA* and *intermediate unit* will be used interchangeably in this volume. Both recognize that such units may not be confined to a single county any longer, but may embrace a cluster of basic administrative units whose boundaries go beyond that of one or more counties.

The terminological problems have been compounded recently by the varying uses and connotations related to the term *regionalism*. To some, regionalism suggests the reorganization of local school districts in a very large urban area or region to create a single metropolitan school district. Thus, regionalism is recommended by some as a means of overcoming "white flight" from very large urban school districts under a court order to desegregate and which can be implemented only through substantial crosstown busing to and from racially isolated schools. Whatever the advantages or disadvantages in creating more metropolitan basic units of educational administration, this interpretation of regionalism is unrelated to the intermediate or regional unit of educational administration as a special support and services mechanism for a set of local school districts. To repeat, the key to resolving much of the terminological confusion is the recognition of the intermediate or regional educational service unit as one that supports and provides selected services to basic administrative units where students attend public schools.

CHARACTERISTICS OF THE INTERMEDIATE OR REGIONAL UNITS

The intermediate unit of educational administration is an arm of the state but serves a region that encompasses many local school districts. Structually and functionally, it lies between the state and the local school district and also serves both. The state educational agency provides the legislative approval for the creation of such units and for the performance of specified public education functions. The county superintendency, as an intermediate unit, came into being early in our nation's educational history for the performance of such functions as "overseeing public school lands, accounting for state school money expended at the local level, certifying teachers, and serving as an 'organ of communication' between the state and local district boards of education. . . ."[2]

Early in history and in many states at present, the area of the RESA was coterminous with other political units formed by the state such as the county or township. In the New England states the intermediate unit takes the form of a supervisory union of townships. In many others that operate with intermediate units it corresponds with the geographic area of a county or of a cluster of local school districts.

The identification of this administrative unit as a "betweener" is evident from the following more formal definition: "An intermediate unit of school administration is an area comprising two or more basic administrative units and having a board, or officer, or both responsible for performing stipulated services for the basic administrative units or for supervising their fiscal, administrative, or educational functions."[3]

Cooper and Fitzwater conceived of the intermediate unit in rather much the same way, namely, as "a unit of school administration that performs administrative and supervisory functions and provides supplementary educational services in a designated area composed of two or more local administrative units."[4] More recently Stephens employed the term *regional educational service agency (RESA)* in preference to intermediate unit.[5]

The intermediate or regional unit has no direct authority over local school district operations, that is, it does not specify the nature or comprehensiveness of the educational programs in local districts, which teachers should be employed, or how pupils are assigned to various attendance units in a school district. On the contrary, local districts exert more influence over the intermediate unit and often specify what services shall or shall not be rendered by the regional unit.

Emerson referred to this unit as "the middle echelon of a state school system made up of a state education office, numerous local school districts (public corporations), and less numerous intermediate school districts (also public corporations)."[6] Thirty-two states have a three-echelon public education school governance system with either rudimentary or reorganized intermediate units of educational administration. The intermediate or regional unit is known by many names: intermediate school district (in Michigan), county school district (in California), cooperative educational services agency (in Wisconsin), multicounty educational services unit (in Nebraska), board of cooperative educational services (in New York), educational service regions (in Illinois), area education agency (in Iowa), and regional educational service agency (in West Virginia). The diversity of titles is apparent; most came into being during the 1960s and early 1970s.

Historical Development of Intermediate Units

The local school district and the state education agency emerged as essential elements of a system of public education before even the rudimentary forms of the intermediate units were created. Cooper and Fitzwater noted that a 1795 law that existed for no more than five years in New York contained the seeds of the functions that were later to be assigned to intermediate units, but gave recognition instead to Delaware for being the first state to enact legislation establishing the traditional county superintendency in 1829.[7] New York followed with a continuing law in 1843, Illinois in 1844, Virginia in 1845, Louisiana and Ohio in 1847, New Hampshire and Oregon in 1850, and California in 1852. By 1879, 34 of the 38 states then comprising the nation, and four of the territories, had created the office of county superintendent as an intermediate unit of educational administration. Most new states that followed created local districts, intermediate units, and the state educational agency all at about the same time.

In New England, the town served as the basic administrative unit. A collection or federation of the town school districts was called the "supervisory union."[8] The superintendent of this intermediate unit was commonly referred to as the union district superintendent. About one-half of the New England superintendents in 1950 held such positions.

Permissive legislation prevailed for the creation of the supervisory union. In Massachusetts laws were enacted in 1881, in New Hampshire in 1895, in Maine in 1897, in Connecticut in 1903, in Rhode Island in 1903, and in Vermont in 1906. Local district affiliation was voluntary and frequently of short duration. The transitory character of local school district membership in the supervisory union created an unstable organization. Subsequent revisions in the laws made local district affiliation mandatory for districts that did not employ a superintendent. Supervisory unions in the various New England states represented a pooling of local resources in some instances, a decentralization of state department of education services and leadership activities in others, and a relatively primitive intermediate unit of educational administration in still another state composed largely of urban communities.[9]

The emphasis on supervisory unions in New England is related, doubtless, to the relatively weak position of the county as a political unit in these states. In several New England states, the county exists for little more than to execute come judicial functions.

The township served for relatively short periods of time as a primitive intermediate administrative unit in education in New York and to some extent in Wisconsin, Illinois, and Michigan. In most cases the township is much too small in geographic area, usually no more than 36 square miles, to serve effectively the one-teacher school districts, much less the larger ones, as an intermediate unit. The township no longer serves as an intermediate unit.

For much of history in the United States, until significant changes began to occur after 1960, most intermediate units had boundaries coterminous with the political unit known as the county. The county was the intermediate unit in 27 states in 1950, but only 15 percent of these had a county board of education as well as a superintendent. Approximately 3050 school administrators in the nation about 30 years ago were superintendents of county units, county intermediate units, or comparable units of educational administration.[10] Reorganization of the intermediate unit during the past two decades greatly reduced the total number of intermediate school superintendencies by more than 60 percent, but by the same token, the fewer but larger and more complex intermediate units had substantially more professional positions including second and third level administrators.

The county superintendency was established either by act of the state legislature or by the state constitution. The county superintendency is a constitutional office in 14 states that greatly compounds the difficulties in redefining the functions and responsibilities as well as the geographic area served.

Selection of the County Superintendent of Schools

Historically, the selection of the county superintendent of schools was determined by the vote of the people residing within the county.

This method is now losing popularity and most professional education groups recommend strongly that selection by election be abandoned. Some 25 to 30 years ago most county superintendents of schools in the states of Arizona, Colorado, Illinois, Kansas, Minnesota, Mississippi, Montana, North Dakota, Oklahoma, South Dakota, Washington, and Wyoming were elected by popular ballot.[11]

About 39 percent of the 913 county superintendents in the 13 county-unit states were elected by popular vote in the early 1950s. In contrast, all superintendents of the county basic administrative unit in the following county unit states were appointed to office by the county board of education: Kentucky, Louisiana, Maryland, North Carolina, Utah, Virginia, and West Virginia. All states that utilize the selection by election method were located south of the Mason-Dixon line and west of Indiana. This pattern has been changing slowly in favor of the appointment system of selection in most of the states that formerly relied on the election method.

Election of the county superintendent of schools, whether for the intermediate or basic administrative unit, is difficult to justify. Politics, rather than the welfare of public education, supports this pattern. Before the end of this century it will be the unusual state that continues with the election of the county or the intermediate superintendent of schools.

The term of office for the county superintendent varies and is usually prescribed by law. In 9 states the terms is two years; in 20, a four-year term; in 2 states, a three-year term; and in 6 states, a term of indefinite length. The shorter terms for appointment are carryovers from the political election or appointment system. Appointment by the county board of education for a period of no less than three years, and preferably for an indefinite period, has the support of most professionals in education.

Educational requirements for the county superintendency increased during most of the past 20 years. In most states where the county superintendent is the executive head of the intermediate or basic unit, four or more years of professional preparation in education are now stipulated for employment consideration. Many states require an administrator's certificate based on five or more years of professional preparation to serve as a county superintendent. The county superintendency gained considerable professional stature over the past three decades. There was a time (1880) when "no state required county superintendents to be graduates of college or normal school graduates and none required any definite amount of experience"; as late as 1930 "only four states had enacted laws requiring normal school or college graduation . . . and 14 prescribed teachers' certificates as the only educational requirement."[12] By 1950 12 states demanded at least five years of college preparation and one required six years. An earned doctorate and considerable experience in education are presently common among county-unit and intermediate unit school superintendents. This is an impressive record of growth and a tribute to many leaders in the profession who labored unceasingly for such achievement.

Reorganization of the Intermediate Unit of Administration

The traditional intermediate unit that was dependent upon the county superintendency was subjected to long and continuing criticisms from both within and outside the education profession. Newsom's nationwide study of the county superintendency reported in 1932 that the consensus in the educational literature was "that the office is too much mixed with politics; that the personnel lacks academic and professional training and experience, and is below the standards of district and city superintendents; that the powers, duties, and responsibilities of the county superintendent are not sufficiently definite; that the superintendent lacks clerical assistance and traveling expenses; that the salary attached to the office is insufficient to secure high-grade professional service; and that the position is uncertain, due to the political nature of the office."[13] The office focused more on the one-teacher school districts and other weak and small local school administrative units.

Local school district reorganization during the post-World War II period eliminated over 90 percent of the weak and ineffective local school districts and saw the number of one-teacher schools almost disappear. The remaining and stronger local school districts demanded a more sophisticated set of supervisory and other professional services from the traditional county education offices. The choices were limited: reorganize and strengthen the intermediate unit or abolish it; the latter was recommended by some of its more severe critics.

A variety of approaches was tried. Some states in the years following 1950 removed the county superintendency from partisan politics. County boards were established where none existed previously. Professional qualifications for the superintendency were upgraded as were the salaries paid and the tenure enjoyed.

Unless all school districts are structured so as to serve 10,000 or more students, there is a need for an effective intermediate unit of educational administration. The sparseness of population in most states as well as transportation limitations and desires to form community school districts meant that most reorganized school districts would have fewer than 10,000 students needed to provide a comprehensive and quality program of education at a reasonable cost per pupil. This means that another special unit is necessary to provide special services for a cluster of local school districts either because there are too few pupils in any single reorganized local unit or because the costs for one district alone would be considered to be prohibitive.

Colorado, Minnesota, and Missouri had legislation that provided for eliminating the county superintendency if so desired. By 1966 the county superintendency in education was voted out of existence in most counties of Colorado. Plans were developed in that state to design a revitalized form of the intermediate unit which came to be called the Board of Cooperative Services. With permissive legislation, the state of Colorado established 17 of these "Boards of Cooperative Services" by July 1975.[14] There were other illustrations such as the Idaho law that called for the abolition of intermediate units when local school district reorganization was completed.

The more typical approach was to redesign what was formerly the ineffective intermediate unit to strengthen what Emerson called the "three-echelon" system for public education. The 1960s and 1970s will be remembered as the periods of the most dramatic reorganization of the intermediate administrative units. Stephens reported on the governance, organization, and programs of newly developed RESAs (regional educational service agencies) in 14 states that had "a relatively clear legislative framework" and reflected a "deliberate state policy to promote the concept" of an effective intermediate unit or the "regionalism" he spoke of.[15]

The following illustrate some of the significant reorganizations of the intermediate or regional educational service agencies that were accomplished during the 1960s and 1970s. (An earlier "partial network" of intermediate units was created in New York State under permissive legislation of 1948 which led to the creation of 45 "Boards of Cooperative Educational Services" [BOCES] by 1975.)

1. In 1962 Michigan enacted legislation which led to the formation of 58 revitalized intermediate units from the original 83 county intermediate districts. Fourteen multicounty consolidations came from 38 separate county education districts; most were two-county mergers although one new intermediate district was formed from five counties. At one time there was consideration given to further reorganization with only 20 intermediate units continuing in the future, but by July 1975 some 58 such districts were in operation.

2. In 1963 Oregon approved permissive legislation that facilitated the formation of what Stephens called a "partial network" of 29 "intermediate education districts" by July 1975.

3. In 1965 Wisconsin abolished 72 county intermediate education units through mandatory legislation and only 19 "cooperative

educational service agencies" were created for the entire state as the new middle echelon units.

4. In 1965 Nebraska used mandatory legislation to establish 19 new multicounty "educational service units" for the state as a whole. Counties were given the option of moving out of such units if so desired.

5. In 1965 Colorado developed a "partial network" of 17 "boards of cooperative services" through permissive legislation. The county superintendency was voted out of existence in most counties by 1966.

6. In 1967 Texas passed mandatory legislation that led to the formation of 20 "education service centers."

7. In 1969 the state of Washington approved mandatory legislation for the creation of 12 "intermediate school districts." Earlier, in 1965, legislation called for state board of education planning for the reorganization of intermediate units.

8. In 1971 Pennsylvania passed mandatory legislation that by 1975 led to the formation of 29 "intermediate units." There was earlier legislation as well in 1965 that recognized the need for the reorganization of intermediate units in that state.

9. In 1971 Illinois passed mandatory legislation that eventually led to the creation of 55 "educational service regions."

10. In 1972 Georgia approved mandatory legislation that led to the formation of 18 "cooperative educational service agencies."

11. In 1972 West Virginia used mandatory legislation to help form eight "regional educational service agencies" for the state as a whole.

12. In 1974 Iowa passed additional mandatory legislation on the reorganization of its intermediate units. It all started in 1947 when county boards where permitted to merge two or more adjacent county intermediate units. The first multicounty units was formed in July 1966. The most recent law was not permissive as was the initial one. Its mandatory feature helped to stimulate the formation of 15 "area education agencies" by July 1975.

13. In 1976 Minnesota passed mandatory legislation that led to the creation of ten "educational cooperative units" for the state as a whole.

There were other states that conducted special studies of the need for intermediate school district reorganization. The Elementary and Secondary Education Act of 1965 encouraged the formation of multicounty cooperative educational service programs. Title III of this act provided funding of special projects for regional educational planning and services.

Stephens outlined these four basic approaches for the enhancement of the quality of state systems of public education through structural and operational relationship changes: (1) creation of local school districts with larger student enrollments; (2) provision of selected educational services directly from the state education agency to the local school district; (3) "formation of informal single-purpose and multi-purpose educational cooperatives"; and (4) establishment of "regional educational services agencies."[16] Most states promoted more effectively organized local school administrative units, but also recognized the limitations of this approach alone. The most frequently used additional means for improving the quality of state systems of public education was creating reorganized and revitalized intermediate units of educational administration or the "regional educational service agencies."

Stephens predicted "a bright future for regionalism," defined as the provision of special education services through the revitalized regional or intermediate unit of educational administration, but only under special conditions. The conditions or prerequisites for effective performance by the revitalized regional educational unit included:

1. The existence of a governance mechanism for the RESA to enable it to perform its major functions, to permit shared policy development by all parties in the consortium that includes advisory councils of local school district representatives, and to discourage competitive regional arrangements

for the delivery of educational services to the same cluster of local school districts.

2. The enhancement of educational planning capabilities of each RESA.
3. The existence of a relatively sophisticated level of educational management competencies in each RESA.
4. Each RESA recognizing the importance of and granting a high level of priority to the dissemination and utilization of new knowledge in education generated through research or other means.
5. Each RESA is granted the fiscal resources required to perform effectively the roles assigned to insure its fiscal stability, independence, and integrity. The sources of funding of RESA activities and services could include some degree of taxing authority, state aid, and federal grants.
6. Each RESA accepting as a primary responsibility the promotion of effective intergovernmental relations within its region.
7. The RESA developing and maintaining a set of educational services and functions that are relevant, viable, and related to the priority needs of elementary, secondary, special, and other education programs in the local school districts that comprise the regional consortium.
8. Each RESA discarding the "dysfunctional service-regulatory dichotomy" in favor of a balanced view that recognizes both roles as possible contributors to the enhancement of public education in the region.
9. Each RESA demonstrating a commitment to achieving excellence in staffing.[17]

Program and Services of Revitalized Intermediate Units

As a general rule the intermediate or regional educational service agency provides those services to two or more local school districts that could not be provided by the local units in an efficient manner or at a reasonable cost per pupil. There is less emphasis on regulatory functions and more on quality of educational and administrative services needed by the consortium of local districts served in the region.[18]

The range of the special educational opportunities that could be used to enrich the programs of local districts is almost without limit. They include at least some of the following, which are being provided by one or more intermediate school units somewhere in the United States.

1. Adult education programs for residents of a given region.
2. Educational technology and media services including the operation of equipment rental and film or videotape rental libraries.
3. Cooperative logistical support services ("business management," accounting, large volume purchasing, payroll and other expenditure payment management, etc.) for the consortium of local districts.
4. Curriculum libraries, laboratories, and other leadership services.
5. Educational testing and specialized counseling services.
6. Services for children and youths with varying exceptionalities, including the operation of special attendance centers for children from a cluster of local districts that would benefit most from such selective educational environments.
7. Health services for diagnosis, inoculations, and epidemic controls.
8. Professional development programs, special instructional materials, and preparation laboratories for all types of teachers, supervisors, aides, and administrators.
9. Specialized diagnostic instructional supervision services, and special subject matter consultants or coordinators.
10. Recreation programs.
11. Pupil transportation services and management of bus fleets.
12. Special itinerant teachers in fields such as art, music, and physical education.
13. Research design and development of new programs services.
14. Computer programming and operations services for instructional and administrative uses.
15. State department of education funds distributions, verifications of funds use, and certification review activities.

The variety of education services required by local districts seeking to offer comprehensive educational programs require different numbers of pupils for effective and economical operations. To illustrate, an attendance supervisor with clerical assistants can monitor 6000 students, a health nurse can serve 2000 pupils, and a guidance counselor about 600 students. Many programs offered through a RESA are supported by federal funds. As Stephens noted, "Programs and services offered by RESAs in both metropolitan and nonmetropolitan areas tend to require a high degree of staff specialization, a high degree of specialization of facilities and equipment, substantial start-up and operating costs, research, development, evaluation, and diffusion competencies, and in the case of programs and services for exceptional children, low student prevalency ratios."[19]

The Los Angeles County school district is one of the largest revitalized intermediate units, provides a comprehensive range of educational services to local districts of its county, and is one of the most efficiently organized and professional-administered intermediate units. It serves 95 educational units (of which 13 are community college districts), embraces a 4080 square-mile area within a single county, and responds to the special needs of one-third of all the public school students in the state of California, the nation's most populous state.

It is one of 58 intermediate units in California. Its chief executive officer is appointed as county superintendent of schools by a seven-member Los Angeles County Board of Education. Appointment is followed in only five units, with election to office for the county superintendent continuing in the other 53 intermediate units. The county superintendency was established as a constitutional office in 1852, but county boards were not authorized by statute until 1881.

This illustration of the change in the intermediate unit from being a monitor for the state and gatherer of statistics and other records for a period of over 100 years ago to a dynamic regional educational resource center is not unlike what occurred elsewhere. The magnitude may be different, for the Los Angeles County superintendency has 3000 regular employees and a budget (in 1980) in excess of $170 million. It provides a broad range of more than 300 educational services to the consortium of local school districts. Its film library services are used by more than 900 schools. Its educational programs and classes in special education reach over 13,000 children and youths enrolled at 132 different campuses operated by the intermediate unit. It has responsibility for educational programs in 37 schools for wards of the juvenile court. Its electronic data processing services handle payrolls, retirement contributions, appropriation accounting, grade reporting, class scheduling, test scoring, and attendance accounting for over 70 of the 95 local units served by the county intermediate unit. It also assists the California State Department of Education by receiving and transmitting financial, administrative, and informational reports on the status of public education in the county.

CRITERIA FOR THE FINANCING AND STRUCTURING OF INTERMEDIATE UNITS

There were many weaknesses in the organizational structure for public elementary and secondary education which limited the quality of educational opportunities available and precluded the most efficient utilization of fiscal resources for education. Reorganizations of local districts as well as intermediate units during the last 30 to 35 years corrected many of the most serious shortcomings in organizational structure and administrative operations. Special recognition and credit must be given to the lay and professional leaders who helped make these significant achievements possible.

Past experience demonstrated that most counties as well as supervisory unions were too small to serve effectively as revitalized intermediate units of educational administration. It was best to proceed with the restructuring of intermediate units without regard to the boundaries of existing political units that were not created with the needs of public education in mind. The combined student enrollments in the local school districts comprising the intermediate unit should be no less than 5,000 and preferably 25,000 or more. A few state laws specify minimum enrollments for reorganized intermediate units that approximate the desirable level. Thus the minimum enrollments for reorganized intermediate units in Texas are 20,000; in Wisconsin, 25,000; and in Washington, 50,000 students.

The other organizational dimensions for effective intermediate or regional educational units would include the following:

1. There should be an intermediate board of education and an executive officer with appropriate professional qualifications. This board would be the educational policymaking body and consider the appointment of a professionally qualified executive officer or superintendent as one of its most important functions. Most states with a revitalized intermediate unit provide for appointment of the intermediate unit superintendent of schools, only a few continue with popular election.
2. There should be provision for participation of representatives from local school districts in the administration, operation, and programming decisions of the intermediate unit with which they are affiliated. This could be done through the creation of advisory councils for the intermediate board and for the superintendent. Most recent legislation provides for such participation and in many other states the practice exists even though not mandated by law.
3. The provision for enrollments in affiliated local districts of sufficient size to provide efficiently a variety of educational services was indicated in the previous paragraph.
4. There should be designed the type of intermediate unit structure and programming that can meet varied educational needs and that could be modified or changed efficiently and without encountering serious disruptions in operations.
5. There should be included special mechanisms to facilitate cooperation among intermediate units in a state for providing unique educational services that may be beyond the capability of a single unit.[20]

The financial resources required for the effective operation of an intermediate unit of educational administration can be procured from many different sources such as state appropriations, county allocations, taxes levied upon the geographic area served by the intermediate unit, and from contractual agreements made with individual local districts receiving special types of intermediate unit services. The taxing authority existed among the older county intermediate units. Only 2 of the 11 legislatively mandated and revitalized (during the 1960s or 1970s) regional educational service agencies were granted taxing authority, all but one received direct state appropriations, all were eligible to receive federal funds, and all had authority to enter into contractual arrangements with local school districts.[21]

The following criteria were recommended in previous years to insure the adequacy of the financial base and fiscal stability of intermediate units of administration:

1. The financial base and authority should be of the magnitude that allows the intermediate unit to provide essential services to the consortium of local school districts involved.
2. The state should assume responsibility for at least a share of the total financing needs of the intermediate unit.
3. The state's contributions to intermediate units should insure the implementation of at least a minimum of foundation program and be based on the principle of equalization.
4. Intermediate units should be granted taxing authority over the geographic area served to enable them to go beyond minimum programs of service.
5. The financial structure should be so designed as to allow the implementation of creative and experimental programs.
6. Indirect financing through contractual agreements between the intermediate unit

and a local school district should be allowed for the support services of a temporary or special nature not extended to all affiliated local school districts.

7. A budget should be prepared, covering the subsequent year and those beyond, by the intermediate district superintendent of schools and approved by the intermediate board of education in accordance with state regulations and accepted educational practices.

8. Compensation of professional and other employees should be based upon a salary schedule.

9. The salary of the intermediate district superintendent should be determined annually to reflect current practices among local district superintendents.

10. The financial structure of the intermediate unit should be reviewed at frequent intervals and kept sufficiently flexible and changed in the light of experience and further study.[22]

Emerson recommended a rule of thumb for allocation of educational functions within the state system of public education: "Allocate the function to the echelon of the system closest to the student, where it may be carried out with completeness, equity, efficiency and responsibility. In testing for fit try the closest echelon first."[23]

Periodic reevaluation and reallocation are likewise essential to maintain the efficiency of intermediate unit services and program development at levels of peak efficiency. Many states have demonstrated over the past two decades that a successful and revitalized intermediate unit structure cannot be developed casually or without careful study of needs and conditions as well as designs to satisfy such demands. As Stephens, Isenberg, Cooper, Fitzwater, Dawson, and Cocking along with others who have studied or enjoyed experiences with the intermediate unit have documented over the past 50 years, these units will have a dynamic and an important role to play in the delivery of quality public educational services in the United States during the re-

mainder of this century and for much of the next one as well.

SUMMARY

The intermediate unit of educational administration is one of the least understood and least appreciated dimensions of state systems of public education. It provides certain administrative and supervisory functions as well as supplementary educational programs and services to a cluster of two or more local school districts. It is also identified as the regional educational service agency (RESA). It is an arm of the state, but performs services for affiliated school districts within a given geographic region. It has no direct or operational authority over local school districts, but may facilitate the state's regulatory functions. It is the middle echelon in a state system of education that includes the local school district and the state education agency as well.

Originally, the supervisory union was the intermediate unit of educational administration in the New England states and the county as a political unit performed similar functions for most of the remainder of the nation. There are states without intermediate units, particularly among the 13 county-unit states in which the county is the basic unit of educational administration. Historically, most of the county superintendents were elected to office, but this practice has now changed in states where the county is the intermediate unit as well as the basic unit of school administration.

Much of the work of the early county and intermediate district superintendents focused on supervision and regulation of the weak and ineffective local school districts. This led to severe criticisms and the call by some for the abolishment of all intermediate units. Reorganization of local school districts into larger and more efficient administrative units stimulated the reorganization and revitalization of intermediate units. There were many significant reorganizations of the intermediate or regional administrative units during the 1960s and 1970s.

The new roles for the revitalized intermediate units that may embrace multicounty areas of local school districts include the provision of educational programs and other special services that could not be offered by a local unit acting alone in an efficient manner and at a reasonable cost per pupil. The range of intermediate unit services made available to enrich the offerings of local school units is virtually unlimited. Less emphasis is placed upon the regulatory functions of the intermediate unit and more on the quality of services to local units.

The revitalized intermediate or regional educational unit has an important role to play in a three-echelon state system of public education. Its bright future can be tarnished if there are too few pupils within the local districts affiliated with it, if the chief executive office continues to be elected rather than appointed, if it lacks the financial resources necessary to perform essential functions, and if it fails to involve those affiliated with it in policy and program decisions.

At the beginning of this century there were many weaknesses in the organizational structure of local as well as intermediate units. The impressive reorganizations of both during the last half of this century helped to correct most deficiencies in most states.

NOTES

1. Walter D. Cocking and Charles H. Gilmore, *Organization and Administration of Public Education,* Advisory Committee on Education, Staff Study No. 2, Washington, D.C.: GPO, 1938, p. 60.
2. Department of Rural Education, National Education Association, *The County Superintendent of Schools in the United States,* Yearbook, February 1950, Washington, D.C.: The Department, 1950, p. 120.
3. Howard A. Dawson and Floyd W. Reeves, *Your School District,* National Commission on School District Reorganization, Washington, D.C.: Department of Rural Education, National Education Association, 1958, p. 52.
4. Shirley Cooper and C. O. Fitzwater, *County School Administration,* New York: Harper & Row, 1954, p. 103.
5. E. Robert Stephens, *Regionalism: Past, Present and Future,* AASA Executive Handbook Series #10, Arlington, Va.: The American Association of School Administrators, 1977.
6. W. J. Emerson, "Intermediate School District," *Journal on State School Systems,* Spring 1967, pp. 33–45.
7. Cooper and Fitzwater, op. cit., p. 136.
8. Ibid., p. 120.
9. Ibid., p. 21.
10. Ibid., p. 140.
11. Ibid.
12. Department of Rural Education, op. cit., p. 42.
13. William N. Newsom, *The Legal Status of the County Superintendent,* Bulletin 1932, No. 7, Washington, D.C.: GPO, 1932, p. 1.
14. Stephens, op. cit., p. 6.
15. Ibid., pp. 11–33.
16. Ibid., p. 2.
17. Ibid., pp. 34–59.
18. Robert M. Isenberg, ed., *The Community School and the Intermediate Unit,* Yearbook, Washington, D.C.: Department of Rural Education, National Education Association, 1954, chap. 7.
19. Stephens, op. cit., pp. 20–21.
20. See Isenberg, op cit., pp. 197–198, and also Stephens, op. cit., pp. 21–22.
21. Stephens, op. cit., pp. 12–15.
22. Isenberg, op. cit., pp. 205–206.
23. Emerson, op. cit.

CHAPTER REVIEW QUESTIONS

1. Why is the intermediate unit sometimes called a "betweener"?
2. Will there be a need for intermediate school units after all local districts in the United States have been reorganized into effective school districts? Justify your stand.
3. What are the factors that have created a need for the reorganization of intermediate units?

4. What are the characteristics of effectively organized intermediate units?
5. List some of the educational services that the intermediate unit appears better adapted to sponsor or execute than is the local district. What educational functions should remain with local units rather than being delegated to intermediate districts?

SELECTED REFERENCES

Cooper, Shirley, and Fitzwater, C. O., *County School Administration,* New York: Harper & Row, 1954.

Emerson, W. J., "Intermediate School District," *Journal of State School Systems,* Vol. 1, No. 1, Spring 1967, pp. 33–45.

Fitzwater, C. O., "Patterns and Trends in State School System Development," *Journal of State School Systems,* Vol. 1, No. 1, Spring 1967, pp. 26–32.

Isenberg, Robert M., ed., *The Community School and the Intermediate Unit,* Yearbook, Washington, D.C.: Department of Rural Education, National Education Association, 1954, chaps. 1, 2, 6, and 7.

Rhodes, Alvin E., *Better Education Through Effective Intermediate Units,* Washington, D.C.: National Education Association, 1963.

Stephens, E. R., "A Profile of Exemplary Regional Educational Service Agencies," *Planning and Changing,* Vol. 3, No. 3, Fall 1972, pp. 33–40; also see *Regionalism: Past, Present, and Future,* AASA Executive Handbook Series, Vol. 10, Arlington, Va.: American Association of School Administrators, 1978, 66 pp.

9

EDUCATION AS A STATE FUNCTION: IMPACT OF STATE LEGISLATURES AND STATE EDUCATION AGENCIES UPON EDUCATIONAL ADMINISTRATION AND OPERATIONS

Public education in the United States is recognized today by statutory and ruling case laws as a function of the state. It took, however, parental initiative in local communities to establish and operate school before any serious encouragement of public education come from the state level. State laws and mandates in the original 13 colonies followed and legitimatized the fact that there were public schools in operation and local school districts in existence. Historically speaking, public education was a grass roots phenomenon, an expression of democracy in action, for it was clusters of people at the local level, and without any central direction or guidance, who agreed when a school was necessary and what the form and shape of the local administrative district should be. The local school districts created during the seventeenth, eighteenth, and most of the nineteenth centuries tended to be very small, only large enough to take care of the children of parents who helped to create the unit. There was an absence of careful and long-range educational planning.[1] Localism in its extreme form led to excesses that continued right through the nineteenth century and which were not corrected, in large part, until the second half of the twentieth century.

Although today "Education is mentioned in every state constitution in varying detail," none of the first constitutions for the original 13 states had anything to say about public education![2] It is significant that the federal constitution was silent on matters related to public education as well. In a democracy such as ours, the so-called sovereign powers reside within the people who determine what shall be guaranteed by federal and state constitutions and what shall be awarded by federal and state statutes that must be consistent with the constitutions. The federal government's powers are delegated expressly to it by the people of the state. The states are the plenary sources of governmental power. This is made clear in the Tenth Amendment to the U.S. Constitution which declares:

The powers not delegated to the United States by the Constitution, nor prohibited by it to the States, are reserved to the States respectively, or to the people.

This proviso and the silence of the U.S. Constitution on matters of public education confirmed education to be a function under the jurisdiction and control of individual states.

This was a radical departure from what existed in other countries of the world at the time the U.S. Constitution was being drafted. It was the clear intent of our founding fathers NOT to emulate the structural patterns, the centralized control systems, and the religious domination of school operations that characterized the private systems and the limited public systems of education at that point in time and for all of previous history. The fact that the people were establishing and controlling schools at the local level prior to deliberations and the adoption of the federal constitution may have influenced our founding fathers as well.

All state and federal courts have confirmed and reinforced the prevailing education responsibility pattern. Federal financial contributions to the public schools are made within this context; and in no way can past, present, or future federal fiscal awards to public education of whatever magnitude, be interpreted as the beginning or actual abrogation of the historic doctrine that proclaims education a function of the individual states.

There are presently 50 different state systems of public education in the United States. This is often puzzling to visitors from other nations where there is a single and nationally controlled system of public education. The original 13 states accepted and recognized by law the local public school districts created by action of people in a locality banding together to promote the cause of education. Subsequent to that, states had a tendency to rely on the judgment of the local people in matters of creating schools without regard to size, quality, or efficiency of operations. By the end of the nineteenth century the excessive proliferation of local school districts and the beginning of greater state involvement in the financing of public education led many states to attach conditions to the formation of new school districts and for the granting state funds for the operation of public schools.

Legislatures of every state other than Hawaii continued to follow the American tradition of local control of public education and continue to delegate considerable operational control over public systems of education to the people and/or their representatives (the school board) residing within local school districts. The basic unit of educational administration, however, is only one echelon of a three-echelon system of public education. The state legislatures also created a state education agency, if such was not already stipulated in the state constitution. This state agency usually includes a state board of education, a chief state school officer, and a state department of education. The relationships between the state education agency and the local districts have changed over time and the roles and structure of the state unit redefined to reflect the new challenges.

THE STATE LEGISLATURE AND PUBLIC EDUCATION

The legislature of each state determines basic and general policies for the administration and operation of systems of public education including such matters as how local school boards shall be selected, what specific subjects or experiences shall or shall not be taught in the public schools of that state, how many years of public education shall be made available to various types of pupils or pupils in various age ranges, what criteria or standards shall be applied for the admission or graduation of students from public schools, and even what textbooks may be used in the system of public education. In addition, the state legislature, acting within the constraints or demands of the state constitution, determines how schools shall be financed, what teacher certification standards shall prevail, and what the safety and quality standards for educational facilities shall be. In short, the state legislature is the public education policymaking authority at the state level and makes the decisions as to whom shall be delegated what policymaking authority and who shall have authority or a share in making what types of decisions with reference to the operation and administration of the public schools.

No state legislature may act in an arbitrary and capricious manner in discharging educational or other responsibilities. A citizen may obtain relief through the state judicial system if the legislature exceeds its authority. Relief through the federal courts may be sought when residents feel that operation of the system of public education as prescribed by the legislature deprives or abridges in any way the rights guaranteed to all citizens by the U.S. Constitution.

State legislatures implement the demands of the state constitutions and honor its prohibitions in matters dealing with public education. Most authorities recommend that the legislature refrain from overly detailed operating and administrative demands within the laws passed. These could inhibit local boards of education, as well as impair their status, in coping with the myriad conditions that are beyond the comprehension of those not responsible for day-to-day operating demands. Likewise, the assignment of state executive authority over matters related closely to public schools to state agencies other than the state department of education is a questionable practice not in the best interests of public education.

The system operates more effectively when state legislation focuses on broad policy matters governing the organization, financing, and operation of public education and then delegates establishment and enforcement of defensible criteria to the state education agency. The legislature establishes the defensible minimums in public education, with the proviso that local units may upon their own volition exceed these minimums. There should be a partnership concept between the state legislature which determines policies and basic guidelines for a state system of public education and the state department of education that helps to implement the will of the legislature or the people of the state. State legislative officials respect the prevailing political climate and the wishes of the people with respect to education. In effect, the people of the state speak through laws enacted by their elected representatives sent to the state legislature; through state constitional mandates; and through rules, regulations, and policies enunciated by one or more of the state executive agencies.

All states have come to realize the importance of and have created a state education agency. This agency may be mandated by a state constitution or created through legislative action. The Massachusetts laws of 1642 and 1647 evidenced the willingness of people within an area, later to be recognized as one of the 13 original states, to take governmental action to insure the establishment of a system of public schools. This included the willingness to resort to legal means to compel the recalcitrant parents to respect their obligations for the education of the young. Although not mandated in the constitutions of the original 13 states, this concept of public education was implemented through state legislative actions. The establishment of a state system of public education became one of the conditions to be satisfied in the enabling acts drafted to transform a territory into a state. At first the state role was a limited one, with the legislature and state agencies following rather than leading the activities of local people who stimulated the creation of and controlled the operation of local schools. This changed rather slowly, for, as will be indicated, the development of the state education agency as a dynamic and leadership force in public education did not occur until some time in the twentieth century. This will become more evident in the review of each of the state education mechanisms (other than the state legislature and governor) such as the state board of education, the chief state school officer, and the state department of education.

THE FUNCTIONS AND CHARACTERISTICS OF THE STATE BOARD OF EDUCATION

New York created in 1784 the first state board of education that focused on colleges and academies. It had no authority over public elementary and secondary schools until 1904, or 120 years after its founding.

Federal land grants for the support of public

education are credited with stimulating the formulation of state public education policies as well as the creation of some state mechanism to disburse the funds from and to manage the federal land grants. In 1825, North Carolina established the first state board of education, and ex-officio mechanism, for the management and disbursing of state school funds to local districts. Broader powers over public education were granted to it in 1837. Vermont created a rudimentary state board of education in 1827, abolished it in 1835, and then subsequently recreated it.

Massachusetts in 1837 created what was to be the prototype for modern state boards of education with an appointed secretary or chief school executive. The early boards (created prior to 1900) were relatively weak because "state legislatures had a tendency to scatter limited and executive powers among a considerable number of state boards and officers," the majority were "ex-officio in nature, being composed of several elected state officials and usually included the chief state school officer," and the duties assigned were those the state legislatures "were reluctant to delegate to the chief state school officer alone—duties such as promoting education in the state, supervising legal custody of school lands and funds, determining who should be considered qualified to teach, determining the course of study, selecting textbooks, and handling problems of policy and administration in connection with state operation of special institutions."[3] The typical practice during the nineteenth century was for the state legislature to create a number of special boards whose powers and duties were often limited to a unique purpose such as operation of one type of educational institution, management of the state educational fund, or administration of a specific state educational activity. The poorly defined terminology for the description of state board functions makes impractical a detailed historical analysis of state boards of education prior to 1900.[4]

All states, the District of Columbia, and the outlying territories of American Samoa, Guam, Puerto Rico, the Trust Territory of the Pacific Islands, and the Virgin Islands now have some type of state board of education (see Table 9.1), for federal law requires a state board for vocational education if the state or territory is to be eligibile to receive federal funds for vocational education. Wisconsin is the only state or territory *without* a state board for public elementary and secondary education activities unrelated to vocational education.

In 1945 only 38 of the then 48 states had comprehensive state boards of education. After 1945, state boards were established in Illinois, Iowa, Maine, Michigan, Nebraska, and North Dakota. The total reached 49 when Alaska and Hawaii entered the union with a state board of education concerned with public elementary and secondary education.

Over 25 years ago the Council of Chief State School Officers adopted a policy statement calling for a "nonpartisan lay state board of education" in each of the states. Other professionals in education support this recommendation as well.

Duties of the State Board of Education

Early duties of these state boards were referred to in such general terms as "to promote the cause of education"; there were few resources allocated, however, for promotional activities. Most assumed responsibility for managing school lands (and very few were able to do this effectively as evidenced by the fact that the original federal land grants for education were so poorly managed that today they have relatively minor importance in the financing of public schools). Their duties included broad discretionary powers over such issues as teacher certification, mandating specific courses of study in the public schools, and local and intermediate unit reorganization. Many state boards also assumed regulatory responsibilities for certain state-operated educational institutions that generated administrative and other problems for the full-time or resident institutional administrators, the chief state school officer, and members of the state department of education. "As recently as 1954, 18 state boards of education had regulatory board responsibilities,

TABLE 9.1

CHARACTERISTICS OF THE STATE BOARDS OF EDUCATION (SBE)

State	Designation	Chief method of selecting members			Number of members		Terms of membership (years)	SBE is board for vocational education	SBE is board for vocational rehabilitation
		Elected by people or representatives of people	Appointed by governor	Ex-officio (by virtue of office or position held)	Total	Ex-officio			
Alabama	State Board of Education	—	X	—	10	2	4	Yes	Yes
Alaska	State Board of Education	—	X	—	7	0	5	Yes	Yes
Arizona	State Board of Education	—	X	—	9	1	4	Yes	Yes
Arkansas	State Board of Education	—	X	—	10	1	9	Yes	No
California	State Board of Education	—	X	—	10	0	4	Yes	Yes
Colorado	State Board of Education	X	—	—	5	0	6	No	No
Connecticut	State Board of Education	—	X	—	10	1	6	Yes	Yes
Delaware	State Board of Education	—	X	—	8	2	3	Yes	No
District of Columbia	State Board of Education	X	—	—	12	1	4	No	Yes
Florida	State Board of Education	—	—	X	7	7	4	Yes	No
Georgia	State Board of Education	—	X	—	10	0	7	Yes	Yes
Hawaii	State Board of Education	X	—	—	11	0	4	No	No
Idaho	State Board of Education	—	X	—	8	1	5	Yes	Yes
Illinois[a]	State Board of Education	—	—	—					
Indiana	State Board of Education	—	X	—	19	1	4	No	No
Iowa	State Board of Public Instruction	—	X	—	9	0	6	Yes	Yes
Kansas	State Board of Education	X	—	—	10	0	4	Yes	No
Kentucky	State Board of Education	—	X	—	8	1	4	Yes	Yes
Louisiana	State Board of Education	X	—	—	12	1	6,8[b]	Yes	Yes
Maine	State Board of Education	—	X	—	9	0	5	Yes	No
Maryland	State Board of Education	—	X	—	7	0	5	Yes	Yes
Massachusetts	Board of Education	—	X	—	14	3	5	Yes	No
Michigan	State Board of Education	X	—	—	10	2	8	Yes	Yes
Minnesota	State Board of Education	—	X	—	9	0	6	Yes	Yes
Mississippi	State Board of Education	—	—	X	3	3	4	Yes	Yes

TABLE 9.1 (*Continued*)

CHARACTERISTICS OF THE STATE BOARDS OF EDUCATION (SBE)

State	Designation	Chief method of selecting members			Number of members		Terms of membership (years)	SBE is board for vocational education	SBE is board for vocational rehabilitation
		Elected by people or representatives of people	Appointed by governor	Ex-officio (by virtue of office or position held)	Total	Ex-officio			
Missouri	State Board of Education	—	X	—	8	0	8	Yes	Yes
Montana	State Board of Education	—	X	—	11	3	8	Yes	Yes
Nebraska	State Board of Education	X	—	—	8	0	4	Yes	Yes
Nevada	State Board of Education	X	—	—	9	0	4	Yes	No
New Hampshire	State Board of Education	—	X	—	7	0	5	Yes	Yes
New Jersey	State Board of Education	—	X	—	14	2	6	Yes	No
New Mexico	State Board of Education	X	—	—	10	0	6	Yes	Yes
New York	Board of Regents, University of the State of New York	X[c]	—	—	15	0	15	Yes	Yes
North Carolina	State Board of Education	—	X	—	13	2	8	Yes	No
North Dakota	State Board of Public School Education	—	X	—	7	1	6	Yes	Yes
Ohio	State Board of Education	X	—	—	23	0	6	Yes	Yes
Oklahoma	State Board of Education	—	X	—	7	1	6	No	No
Oregon	State Board of Education	—	X	—	7	0	7	Yes	No
Pennsylvania	State Board of Education	—	X	—	17	0	6	Yes	No
Rhode Island	Board of Regents	—	X	—	9	0	4	Yes	No
South Carolina	State Board of Education	X	—	—	16	0	4	Yes	No
South Dakota	State Board of Education	—	X	—	7	0	5	Yes	Yes
Tennessee	State Board of Education	—	X	—	15	3	9	Yes	Yes
Texas	State Board of Education	X	—	—	24	0	6	Yes	Yes
Utah	State Board of Education	X	—	—	11	0	4	Yes	Yes
Vermont	State Board of Education	—	X	—	7	0	6	Yes	Yes
Virginia	State Board of Education	—	X	—	9	0	4	Yes	No
Washington	State Board of Education	X[d]	—	—	15	1	6	No	No
West Virginia	State Board of Education	—	X	—	11	2	9	Yes	Yes

Wisconsin	No State Board of Education	—						
Wyoming	State Board of Education	—	X	—	1	10	6	Yes	No
American Samoa	Board of Regents	—	X	—	1	10	2,3	Yes	No
Guam	Territorial Board of Education	—	X	—	0	7	3	Yes	Yes
Puerto Rico	Commonwealth Board of Education	—	X	—	2	10	6	No	Yes
Trust Territory of the Pacific	Micronesia Board of Education	—	High Comm.	—	1	7	3	Yes	Yes
Virgin Islands	Virgin Islands Board of Education	X	—	—	1	10	2	No	No
Totals		16	36	2	48	562		46	32

Source: Sam P. Harris, *State Departments of Education, State Boards of Education, and Chief State School Officers*, DHEW Publication No. (OE) 73-07400, Washington, D.C.: GPO, 1973, pp. 60–61.

[a]To be determined by the state legislature.
[b]Three elected for overlapping six-year terms; eight elected for overlapping eight-year terms.
[c]Elected by the legislature.
[d]Elected by members of boards of directors of local school districts.

while 26 had, in addition, governing board responsibilities for one or more educational institutions such as normal schools, vocational schools, and state institutions for handicapped children or delinquents."[5] In more recent years the general state boards of education have been removed from responsibility for operation of special institutions because in most states they "were too involved in administration to become competent and comprehensive in important legislative and policymaking responsibilities, and remnants of this situation can still be detected in a few states."[6]

The recommendations of the Council of Chief State School Officers on the duties and responsibilities of the state board of education submitted over 30 years ago remain relevant today and deserve translation into state statutes. These include the following:

1. Formulate policies and adopt such rules and regulations as are necessary to carry out the responsibilities assigned to it by the constitution and the statutes of the state.
2. Appoint and fix the salaries of the professional staff of the state department of education on the recommendation of the chief state school officer.
3. Establish standards for issuance and revocation of teacher certificates.
4. Establish standards for classifying, approving, and accrediting schools, both public and nonpublic.
5. Prescribe a uniform system for the gathering and reporting of educational data, for the keeping of adequate educational and finance records, and for the better evaluation of educational progress.
6. Submit an annual report to the governor and legislature covering the areas of action of the state board of education and the operations of the state department of education and to support education throughout the state.
7. Consider the educational needs of the state and recommend to the governor and the legislature such additional legislation or changes in existing legislation as it may deem desirable.
8. Interpret its own rules and regulations and upon appeal hear all controversies and disputes arising therefrom.
9. Publish the laws relating to education with notes and comments for the guidance of those charged with the educational responsibility.
10. Provide through the state department of education supervisory and consultative service and issue materials which would be helpful in the development of educational programs.
11. Accept and distribute in accord with law any monies, commodities, goods, and services which may be made available from the state or federal government or from other sources.
12. Designate the extent to which the board is empowered to exercise supervision over public and nonpublic colleges, universities, state institutions and public and nonpublic elementary and secondary schools in accord with the law and sound public policy on education.[7]

To this can be added the responsibility of the state board of education to stipulate the relationships between the executive officer of the state board and members of the department of public instruction.

State Board of Education Membership Selection and Characteristics

The ex-officio committee of state officials was the earliest and most rudimentary type of state board of education. Usually included were such state officials as the governor, secretary of state, and secretary of the treasury. This was justified on grounds of difficulties in travel and communication during pioneer days. Accomplishments of the rudimentary boards were limited because the elected duties of the state officials were granted a much higher priority.

The Indiana State Board of Education of 1852 was a unique type of ex-officio board. Its membership included the president of the university and the superintendents of certain cities on the theory that professionals in education were the best qualified to cope with the complexities of public education. Subsequent experience demonstrated that conflicts of interest were not uncommon, for decisions of the state board were bound to influence the operations and administration of local school districts.[8] Other states had both ex-officio and appointed state board members. The trend since the nineteenth century has been away from both state boards that are either wholly composed of ex-officio members or those with only some ex-officio members. As late as 1890, 20 of the existing 29 state boards of education "were wholly or mostly ex-officio."[9] By 1963 there were only four states with state boards that were completely ex-officio; presently only two states, Florida and Mississippi, have wholly ex-officio membership.

By 1974, 22 states of the 49 with a general state board of education and five outlying territories plus the District of Columbia had one or more ex-officio members. The low point was reached in 1962 when only 16 state boards of education had any ex-officio members, but the number jumped to 27 by 1974 to equal the 1940 level.[10] Most (15 out of 27) had only one ex-officio member; only about 8.5 percent of the total state board membership were of the ex-officio type. The chief state school officer is most likely to be an ex-officio board member and is on 22 of the 27 state boards in the combined state and outlying territories plus the District of Columbia. This is true in spite of the fact that most authorities consider this a questionable practice and recommend that the chief state school officer not be a member of the state board of education. This is based on the belief that there should be a separation between policy formulation by a state board and policy execution by the state school administrator. At one time governors were most likely to be among the ex-officio members of state boards of education. This is less true now than ever before. Thus, as late as 1940 some 15 governors were among the ex-officio state board of education members; but by 1973 there were only five governors as ex-officio members.

At one time persons serving on some state boards of education were appointed to office by the legislature or the chief state school officer. This archaic practice has been abandoned. The prevailing patterns are appointment of individuals by the governor (36 boards), election by popular ballot (16 boards), and by ex-officio status (2 boards). These data include boards in the outlying territories plus the District of Columbia. Popular election was found in only two states in 1945, Nevada and Louisiana, but today election is practiced in 14 states. Election is the approach recommended by professionals in education.

Arguments for appointive boards are based on the belief that the governor should appoint the heads of all state departments. It works best in states with a strong tradition of nonpartisanship in board selection and where governors are receptive and responsive to advice from citizens interested in education. It also can work well if the governor does not have the power to change the entire membership during one term of office. Nonetheless, there is indication of a trend away from appointment toward election (even though this is presently a minority practice) "paralleling the trend toward giving state boards the authority to appoint their chief state school officers. . . ."[11]

As a general rule, the total membership on the state board should be large enough so that it cannot be dominated by a single personality and yet not so large that it becomes unwieldy and inefficient; from 7 to 11 members is recommended most often. At the present time the range varies from 3 members in Mississippi and 5 in Colorado to 23 in Ohio and 24 in Texas. Over half of all state boards of education have from 7 to 9 members, well within the recommended range.

Qualifications or legal requirements for membership on the state board of education are usually not prescribed by law. In spite of this, most state board members have attended college.

Term of Office of Board Members

Four- and six-year terms of office seem to be the most popular; about 60 percent have terms of either four or six years duration. However, the length of term varies from two years to fifteen years (in New York). As a general rule, it is recommended that members of the state board serve long, overlapping terms so that a comprehensive educational program can be developed and carried forward. A term of six to eight years seems most appropriate, for it would provide sufficient time to come to understand the problems and the methods of operation and still provide flexibility and adaptability in membership.

Recommendations for State Boards

The following recommendations with reference to state boards were made by Cubberley in 1927 and are worth repeating. He recommended that the state board of education should be:

1. A lay board representing the people.
2. Neither too small nor too large, with 7 members as the optimum size.
3. Appointed or elected for relatively long and overlapping terms.
4. Appointed by a governor who does not have opportunity to change the entire character of the board during one term.
5. Appointed solely on the basis of ability to serve the people without reference to race, creed, occupation, party, and residence.
6. Elected by the people if this is preferred to appointment.
7. Removed only by action of the governor and then only for such causes as immorality, malfeasance, and gross incompetence.
8. Without ex-officio members, even the governor.
9. Organized so that the state superintendent is not a member of the board.
10. Paid an honorarium instead of a per-diem allotment.
11. Able to consider as its most important function the appointment of a state superintendent.
12. Organized in such a way that the subordinate officials for the state department are selected only on the recommendations of the state superintendent.
13. Empowered to make its own rules and regulations.
14. Organized so that there is a clear distinction between the legislative and the executive functions.[12]

Sound ideas seldom lose credibility with the passage of time. Cubberly's principles applied to state boards of education are as valid today as they were when made over 55 years ago. Although not all states have recognized this nor implemented what was recommended at that time, it keeps cropping up in the professional literature in education.

THE FUNCTIONS AND CHARACTERISTICS OF CHIEF STATE SCHOOL OFFICERS

The chief state school officer is referred to most frequently as the state superintendent of education or of public instruction. Gaining popularity is the title of state commissioner of education. The position is established as a constitutional office in most states. Persons selected for such positions "legally are officers of the state governments as well as professionals in education."[13]

The first chief state school officer position was created in New York in 1812 with the title of superintendent of common schools and a salary of $300 per year. The salary was not to be paid until "he shall give notice of the first distribution of school money." The duties revolved around management of the common school funds and other services related to the welfare of the public schools. This short-lived position was abolished in 1821 and not reestablished until 1854. The secretary of state became the ex-officio "superintendent of common schools" during the interim.

The position was established next in Maryland in 1826, followed by Michigan in 1829. Only three states in existence prior to 1830 created the chief state school officer post. The numbers increased rapidly thereafter, for by 1859 this post was found in 24 states and territories. It is clear that the state education positions came into being many decades after local schools and districts were in operation. More than a century would have to pass before the state education agency would begin to exert a leadership role for the enhancement of public education.

At present all states and territories have a chief state school officer. However, at one time or another the governor, comptroller, secretary of the treasury, state auditor, and other state officials served as ex-officio state superintendents of education in about half the states. It was not unusual to have the position established and then abolished several times in the same state. Iowa is a case in point where the position was created for the first time by the territorial legislature in 1841 and the chief state school officer was appointed by the governor. In 1842 it was considered a needless expenditure and was legislated out of existence. Four years later it was recreated as an elected office with a three-year term. It was disestablished for a second time in 1858, only to be reestablished six years later as an elective office for a two-year term. It continued thereafter, but with changes in method of selection going back to appointment by the governor in 1913, then election again in 1917, and finally by appointment once more in 1953, but this time by the state board of education. Other states had varying degrees of uncertainty about the position lasting all of the nineteenth century and continuing into the twentieth. "To protect the office against abolition, the people often placed it in the state constitution, which gave the office a higher status within most state governments in the nineteenth century than it would have received otherwise, as well as some independence from governors and legislators."[14]

Duties and Problems
Confronting the Position

Early in history duties of the chief state school officer were both limited and primarily clerical, requiring a very small staff for their execution. As local school district enrollments grew and educational programs expanded, during the twentieth century in particular, the responsibilities and contributions of the state office also increased. Unfortunately, the conceptualization and the structural form of the chief state school officer and the state department of education that grew around this office were cast during the years that the functions were clerical, statistical, and regulatory. These early duties, rather than the more recent and educa-

tionally more relevant ones, were crystallized into laws and formed the traditions of the office. Changes were exacerbated further by the fact that in 35 states and three territories the position is thus described in the respective constitutions. The realization of the potential that resided within the office and the related department had to wait until the last half of the twentieth century.

A serious disadvantage to this important position in a state system of public education was that it was more political in the beginning than it was professional. As late as 1920 the chief state school officer was forced to launch a political campaign to be elected in 34 of the 48 states. It follows that where there is an election the choices for this educational leadership post are limited to residents of the state. During the second half of the twentieth century things began to change, for from 1945 to 1974 the number of states electing the state superintendent of education declined from 33 to 19. The election is nonpartisan in only six states. During the first 125 years or so of this office, the most popular method of selecting the chief state school officer was through election, but appointment won out during the past three decades.

Where the position remains to be decided by the ballot, it is recommended that such an election be nonpartisan and held when other primarily partisan-based elections are not being held. The great weight of professional opinion supports appointment of the chief state school officer. Very few—only two states—"ever returned to elected chief state school officers after abandoning that method of selection."[15]

In 37 of the 50 states, the District of Columbia, and the outlying territories, the state superintendent of education is presently appointed to office. (See Table 9.2.) In 28 situations, the appointment is by the state board of education; in the remaining 9 it is by the governor. The latter approach is said to make "the chief state school officer dependent upon the governor," and the person so appointed "may benefit from the governor's power on behalf of education or suffer because of the governor's lack of enthusiasm for it."[16] For most of the

TABLE 9.2

STATUS OF THE CHIEF STATE SCHOOL OFFICERS (CSSO)

State	Title	Method of selection			Term of office (years)	Relation to state board of education (SBE)	
		Elected by popular vote	Appointed by SBE	Appointed by governor		Ex-officio member	Official capacity
Alabama	Superintendent of Education	—	X	—	Indef.	Yes	Secretary and executive officer
Alaska	Commissioner of Education	—	X	—	5[a]	No	Principal executive officer
Arizona	Superintendent of Public Instruction	X	—	—	4	Yes	Executive officer
Arkansas	Director of Education	—	X	—	Indef.[b]	No	Ex-officio secretary
California	Superintendent of Public Instruction	X	—	—	4	No	Secretary and executive officer
Colorado	Commissioner of Education	—	X	—	Indef.[b]	No	Secretary
Connecticut	Secretary of the State Board of Education and Commissioner of Education	—	X	—	Indef.[b]	No	Secretary and executive officer
Delaware	Superintendent of Public Instruction	—	X	—	1	No	Executive secretary
District of Columbia	Superintendent of Schools	—	X	—	3	Yes	Seat on board, no vote
Florida	Commissioner of Education	X	—	—	4	Yes	Secretary and executive officer
Georgia	School Superintendent	X	—	—	4	No	Executive officer
Hawaii	Superintendent of Education	—	X	—	Indef.[b]	No	Executive officer and secretary
Idaho	Superintendent of Public Instruction	X	—	—	4	Yes	Administrative officer
Illinois	Superintendent of Public Instruction	—	X	—	4	Undetermined	Undetermined
Indiana	Superintendent of Public Instruction	X	—	—	2	Yes	Chairman of each of three commissions into which SBE is divided
Iowa	Superintendent of Public Instruction	—	X	—	4	No	Executive officer
Kansas	Commissioner of Education	—	X	—	Indef.[b]	No	Executive officer
Kentucky	Superintendent of Public Instruction	X	—	—	4	Yes	Executive officer
Louisiana	Superintendent of Public Education	X	—	—	4	Yes	Executive officer and ex-officio secretary
Maine	Commissioner of Education and Cultural Services	—	—	X	Indef.	No	Secretary
Maryland	Superintendent of Schools	—	X	—	4	No	Chief executive, secretary and treasurer
Massachusetts	Commissioner of Education	—	X	—	Indef.[b]	No	Chief executive and secretary
Michigan	Superintendent of Public Instruction	—	X	—	Indef.[b]	Yes	Chairman
Minnesota	Commissioner of Education	—	X	—	4	No	Executive officer and secretary
Mississippi	Superintendent of Education	X	—	—	4	Yes	Chairman
Missouri	Commissioner of Education	—	X	—	Indef.[b]	No	Chief administrative officer
Montana	Superintendent of Public Instruction	X	—	—	4	Yes	Secretary

State	Official title				Term	Member of board	Relationship to board
Nebraska	Commissioner of Education	—	X	—	Indef.[b]	No	Executive officer and secretary
Nevada	Superintendent of Public Instruction	—	X	—	Indef.[b]	No	Secretary
New Hampshire	Commissioner of Education	—	X	—	Indef.[b]	No	Chief executive officer and secretary
New Jersey	Commissioner of Education	—	X	X	5	No	Official agent and secretary
New Mexico	Superintendent of Public Instruction	—	X	—	Indef.[b]	No	Chief administrative officer
New York	Commissioner of Education	—	X	—	Indef.[b]	No	Chief administrative officer
North Carolina	Superintendent of Public Instruction	X	—	—	4	Yes	Secretary and chief administrative officer
North Dakota	Superintendent of Public Instruction	X	—	—	4	Yes	Executive director and secretary
Ohio	Superintendent of Public Instruction	—	X	—	Indef.[b]	No	Secretary, executive and administrative officer
Oklahoma	Superintendent of Public Instruction	X	—	X	4	Yes	President and executive officer
Oregon	Superintendent of Public Instruction	X	—	—	4	No	Executive officer
Pennsylvania	Secretary of Education	—	—	X	Indef.[c]	No	Chief executive officer
Rhode Island	Commissioner of Education	—	X	—	Indef.[d]	No	Executive officer
South Carolina	Superintendent of Education	X	—	—	4	No	Secretary and administrative officer
South Dakota	Superintendent of Public Instruction	X	—	—	2	No	Secretary and administrative officer
Tennessee	Commissioner of Education	—	—	X	Indef.[c]	Yes	Chairman
Texas	Commissioner of Education	—	X	—	4	No	Executive officer
Utah	Superintendent of Public Instruction	—	X	—	Indef.[d]	No	Executive officer
Vermont	Commissioner of Education	—	X	—	Indef.[d]	No	Chief executive officer and secretary
Virginia	Superintendent of Public Instruction	—	—	X	4	No	Secretary
Washington	Superintendent of Public Instruction	X	—	X	4	Yes	President and executive officer
West Virginia	Superintendent of (free) Schools	—	X	—	Indef.[d]	Yes	Chief executive officer
Wisconsin	Superintendent of Public Instruction	X	—	—	4	No SBE	No SBE
Wyoming	Superintendent of Public Instruction	X	—	—	4	Yes	Executive officer
American Samoa	Director of Education	—	—	X	Indef.	Yes	Executive officer
Guam	Director of Education	—	X	—	Indef.[d]	No	Executive secretary
Puerto Rico	Secretary of Education	—	—	X	Indef.[c]	Yes	No vote
Trust Territory of Pacific	Director of Education	—	Comm.	High	2	Yes	Executive officer
Virgin Islands	Commissioner of Education	—	—	X	Coterm. with Governor	Yes	Secretary
Total		19	28	9			

Source: Sam P. Harris, *State Departments of Education, State Boards of Education, and Chief State School Officers,* DHEW Publication No. (OE) 73-07400, Washington, D.C.: GPO, 1973, pp. 76–77.

[a] Appointed for a five-year term, but serves at the pleasure of the governor.
[b] Law is silent.
[c] Serves at the pleasure of governor.
[d] Serves at the pleasure of the state board of education.

history of this office until relatively recently, when there was appointment, the power rested with the governor. This was approved by those political scientists who subscribed to the doctrine of centralization of appointment power for heads of state departments within the office of the governor. Professional educators preferred more distance from partisan politics at the state level and rallied to promote election of a state board of education and appointment of the chief state school officer by this state board. It was argued as well that there be separation of policymaking or legislative functions held by the state board of education from the executive and administrative functions of the state superintendent of education. Within the last two decades it became clear as well that "the older practice of authorizing governors to appoint both the state board members and chief state school officers was losing ground, with only New Jersey, Pennsylvania, Tennessee, and Virginia preserving this method of selection."[17]

It is unfortunate that in many states there are no legal qualifications demanded to hold the important office of state superintendent of education. In addition, the historically meager salary, related more to the political dimensions than professional dimensions, of this position continues right up to the present. It has been below that of local district superintendents in cities of 20,000 or more as well as that of university presidents, deans, and professors. The median salary climbed from $7,180 in 1948, to $23,000 in 1969, and to approximately $45,000 in 1981. The spread in 1981 was from a low of $34,000 to a high of $71,100 (New York). The highest salary is far below the $120,000 salary for the Chicago superintendent of schools and the $100,000 salary for the deputy superintendents in that same city for about the same year. Historically, chief state school officers and their professional state department of education staff members received lower salaries than their peers in other local schools or related federal education agency positions.

The Council of Chief State School Officers recommended that the state legislature enact laws defining the relation of the chief state school officer to the state board of education and to the state department of education.[18] These laws should indicate the functions of the chief state school officer in a general way, namely:

1. Keeping the board currently advised about the operation and status of the public schools.
2. Recommending to the board such policies and rules as he deems necessary for educational progress.
3. Serving as executive officer of the board and being responsible for promoting efficiency and improvement in the public-school system.
4. Delegating ministerial and executive functions to members of the state department of education.
5. Preparing a budget for the state education program under the jurisdiction of the state education agency, including the state department of education, and administering the same after approval.
6. Establishing and maintaining a system of personnel administration.

THE STATE DEPARTMENT OF EDUCATION

The state board of education determines policies, and the chief state school officer assumes responsibility for their execution. Given the complexity of the public education responsibility, the execution of board decisions and the implementation of board policies are beyond the capabilities of a single person and demand the creation of a special organization and competent staffing. This important administrative arm of the state education agency is the state department of education that is coordinated by and works under the direction of the chief state school officer.

For over 100 years state education departments were small, with a staff consisting of the chief state school officer and one or two others. Functions were usually limited to enforcing a few state regulations, visiting only a sample of schools on a regular basis, and collecting some meager statistical data. Some notable exceptions were Horace Mann of Massachusetts, Henry Barnard of Connecticut, and one or two others who were the leaders of the early nineteenth century in curriculum improvement, professional training of teachers and administrators, and better design of educational facilities.

Beach and Gibbs outlined with broad brush strokes the major activities and changes in the evolution of modern state departments of education.[19] There were special forces that stimulated the movement from one stage in development to another, and each major shift in priority and emphasis called for substantially different personnel requirements for state departments of education. Their perceptions of the major stages in the evolution of the modern state department of education included the following.

The Statistical Stage. For most this constituted a period from the establishment of the state education agency to roughly around 1900, a little less than the "first 100 years." During this early period the state education department was concerned primarily with gathering, compiling, and publishing some limited statistics on public education; preparing forms; issuing biennial reports on public education; and related activities. Clerks could perform these functions. Most time was spent in the central office completing clerical chores rather than on field visits and relations. There was little growth in the size of the state department of education during the long statistical stage of development. As late as 1900 there was a total in the United States of only 177 employees, of which 47 were chief state school officers. The remaining 130 staff personnel brought the average to less than three person per state plus the state superintendent.[20] In 1900 there were five state school officers with no staff, not even a secretary or clerk.

The Inspectoral Stage. A number of states after 1900 began to pass state standards for public school operation and turned to the state education agency for the monitoring of compliance with legislative demands for local school improvements. The focus began to switch to regulatory (as opposed to statistical) functions and to the employment of the quasi-professional "state education inspector." Such state

department personnel required some degree of professional preparation and knowledge of education that the typical office clerk lacked. Such personnel went out into the field (not at the request of local districts) to determine the degree of compliance with state laws on compulsory school attendance, with the state-mandated or the prescribed courses of study, with the state requirements for the maintenance of safe and healthful educational facilities, and with the state demands for implementation of approved educational accounting systems. This approach was based on the concept that the best way to bring about local school improvement was through state action that established mandatory state educational standards which were to be enforced by state educational inspectors. It was during this period that local school district professional personnel developed the negative image of the state department of education professional as a "snoopervisor"; some state education departments sought to soften the implications of the harsh term *inspector* and used titles such as supervisor or consultant. The image of the office remained during this period as the enforcer of regulations rather than as a professional peer or an educational partner in a total system of public education. The state education department was something more to be feared than contacted for professional assistance by local school systems.

The time period of the inspectoral stage was roughly about three decades—from about 1900 to around 1930—after which many began to see its limitations and sought more positive and professional roles for the state department of education. All the above dates are approximations, there was a degree of overlap among the stages, and not all state departments of education left or entered a development stage at exactly the same time. The size of the median state department staff grew during the second stage from less than 3 to about 28 employees. This is almost a tenfold increase in a 30-year period; nonetheless the typical state department of education some 50 years ago was a relatively small professional organization. Much of the growth during this period could be ascribed to the passage by the federal government of the Smith–Hughes Act and the beginnings of the federal vocational rehabilitation program. As will be shown in subsequent paragraphs, federal education legislation and financial support did much to stimulate the growth of state departments of education during all of the twentieth century.

The Leadership Stage. In neither the statistical nor the inspectoral stages was the state education department designed or committed to lead, stimulate, or assist local or intermediate school districts in improving the quality and relevance of educational programs or services.[21] Recognition of the importance of educational leadership from the state education agency became evident when it was apparent that state mandates and inspection fell short of achieving equalization of educational opportunity among the various local districts as well as in enhancing educational program quality.

The emphasis began to change toward stimulating the acquisition of professional education knowledge and special competencies in instructional or educational administration among local district professionals. New state department personnel requirements emerged. Educational specialists and competent consultants were needed to help the state education agency fulfill its leadership role in the improvement of public education. There came into being, as a result, a new type of state department of education professionals who had special insights into various dimensions of education, competency in research and recognition for being at the cutting edge of the profession, and was able to work with and interact with professionals and lay people at the local and intermediate unit levels.

The leadership stage began sometime after 1930 in many state education departments, but was not evident in some until the 1950s. This resulted in the spectacular expansion of the personnel. The median size of the department quadrupled from 28 in 1930 to 126 in 1950. Some departments grew much faster than others, for the *average* size of staff in 1950 was 200, or significantly higher than the median.[22] This was simply a portent for even more growth. By

the early 1970s the total numbers employed in all state education departments were almost double what it was in the early 1950s. (See Table 9.3.) Much of the growth could be attributed to the tremendous expansion of federal education programs during the 1950s and 1960s.[23] As late as 1949 at least two-thirds of all state education department personnel were either in the federally subsidized vocational education or rehabilitation programs. The federally related program orientation remained, but was not limited to these two fields as a result of more comprehensive federal education programs of the 1950s and 1960s.

State departments of education continue to vary greatly in size. The smallest at the begin-

TABLE 9.3

PROFESSIONAL AND NONPROFESSIONAL STAFFS OF 50 STATE DEPARTMENTS OF EDUCATION, 1890–1972

Year	No. of staff members	Percent increase over preceding reporting year
1890	129	—
1895	155	20
1900	177	14
1905	219	24
1910	534	144
1915	610	14
1920	836	37
1925	1,416	69
1930	1,760	24
1935	2,256	28
1940	3,718	65
1945	5,403	45
1950	9,550	77
1955	15,375	61
1972	18,472	20

Sources: L. M. Thurston and W. H. Roe, *State School Administration,* New York: Harper & Row, 1957, p. 117. Statistical information adapted from Fred F. Beach and Andrew H. Gibbs, *Personnel of State Department of Education,* Washington, D.C.: U.S. Office of Education, GPO, 1952. Sam P. Harris, *State Departments of Education, State Boards of Education, and Chief State School Officers,* DHEW Publication No. (OE) 73-07400, 1973, pp. 42–43.

ning of the prior decade had about 47 full-time professionals, whereas the largest had 1421; the average was almost 370. Growth in personnel was only one factor. The changes in type of personnel are more likely to be found and the tendency of the professional staff to spend more time in the field assisting local and intermediate units are additional characteristics of the leadership phase. This should be contrasted with the older and abandoned approach where the state department supervisor or visitor descended upon the local school system once or twice a year primarily for purposes of evaluation. Violations of the state regulation would have to be gross or ill-disguised to be spotted during the brief "visits" of the old inspectors.

Factors Influencing the Development of State Education Agencies

The last half of this century saw most state education departments come of age in the three-echelon system of public education and gain recognition for leadership within the profession. The stature of state education units increased tremendously during the past three decades in particular.

State legislatures prior to the last of this century often increased the burdens of state education departments without providing the fiscal resources necessary to fulfill the additional challenges. Increased state funding for state agencies helped them to perform more effectively. Likewise, the greatly increased tempo of federal educational activities during the twentieth century contributed to the support and expansion of state education department professional staffs and activities. These were usually related to the discharge of a federal purpose such as for vocational education, elementary and secondary education in general, or the promotion of civil rights.

The passage of the federal Elementary and Secondary Education Act of 1965 was a landmark act for many reasons, not the least of which was that it allocated federal funds for the enhancement of state education agencies. Such special grants stipulated in Title V of that act provided for basic grants, special-project grants, and assistance to allow interchange of state and federal personnel. Title V funds were used to train state department staff members as well as to introduce electronic data processing and research and development activities. Unfortunately, these federal allocations were eliminated after 1981 as the result of the extensive federal cutbacks that were made. Between 1973 and 1980 some $51 million was provided by the federal government on an annual basis to help strengthen state education departments (Under Title V, b of ESEA). This dropped to $42 million in 1981 and to zero thereafter with the implementation of federal "block grants" under the Education Consolidation and Improvement Act of 1981.

A fourth stage in the development of the state department of education may well be the extension of the leadership stage into what can be called the "educational partnership" stage. Its beginnings can be traced to 1970 and is made evident by the more effective and closer working relationships between the state education agency and the state legislature, federal education agencies, intermediate school districts, as well as local school districts. The state units presently have approached the staff quality and "critical mass," or numbers of staff, necessary to earn the professional respect of those agencies with whom they must work. This is a significant achievement, for the state agency was the least adequately supported of the three echelons that constitute a state system of public education even though no level has ever been granted all the funds necessary to perform as effectively as each desires.

For continuing growth in educational stature in the future it is incumbent upon state legislatures to provide more stable and more adequate funding to meet the regulatory demands, state educational funds distribution requirements, and the leadership expectations. State education agencies have played traditionally an important role in providing the state legislature with the information and the alternatives essential to the development of prudent public education legislation and policies. Further improvement of state educational planning, research, and evaluation systems will be essential to satisfy the more comprehensive and complex public education needs of the future. In striving for more realistic fiscal support it is recognized that "education budgets are in competition for state funds with the budgets of all other departments, including many that have strong political overtones and frankly political leadership."[24]

The structure of state education organizations has improved materially during the last half of the twentieth century as well. The trend toward appointment and away from election of chief state school officers is preferred. The increased election costs are evident from the fact that one candidate for a California state superintendency in the spring of 1982 expended over $1.7 million in TV and other campaign expenditures to get elected. It is difficult to justify campaign expenses of such magnitude for a professional position that over the following four years of the term will compensate the person less than $200,000.

The more fully developed and matured state education agency, like its counterparts in the reorganized and revitalized intermediate and local units of educational administration, has come a long way during the twentieth century thus far, and also has a bright future with greater capability to contribute to the enhancement of public education in the United States.

SUMMARY

Public education in the United States is a federal interest, a state function, and a local operation. None of the initial constitutions of the original 13 states made any mention of education, but today all do so but in varying detail. There are presently 50 different state systems of public education in the United States.

The legislature of each state determines the basic and general policies for the administration of public education, but most have followed the American tradition of granting substantial operational control over public education to the people in local school districts. Nonetheless, there is a need for an effective state education agency consisting of the state board of education, the chief state school officer, and the state department of education.

The management of federal lands allocated to the states for the support of public education stimulated the formation of state education agencies. Many state boards of education were organized during the 1820s and 1830s. Massachusetts created the prototype for a modern state board of education with an appointed chief school executive. The early boards were relatively weak and tended to be ex-officio, that is, composed of state officials elected to certain positions unrelated to education. All states have some type of state board of education, and Wisconsin is the only one without a general state board of education.

The early duties of state boards were limited and tended to focus on regulatory functions and the administration of special statewide educational institutions. Most state board of education members are appointed by the governor, some are elected by the people, and only two at present are wholly ex-officio. It is recommended that the boards be composed of laypersons, with a total membership that is neither too small nor too large, and serve as the educational policymaking authority.

The position of chief state school officer was established first in 1812. Its form was cast, often in state constitutions, during the years when the primary functions were clerical and statistical. The office was originally political in nature, with most being elected to serve. The trend since the middle of the twentieth century has been toward appointment with the majority now doing so.

State departments of education moved from the statistical stage (up to 1900), to the inspectoral stage (1900 to 1930), to the leadership stage (1930 to the present). The importance of projecting an educational leadership image emerged when the limitations of state regulations and inspections as an educational improvement strategy became evident. Most of the growth in personnel and educational stature of state education agencies came during the leadership stage.

Federal educational programs for local schools and special funds for strengthening state departments did much to enhance the development of state education agencies dur-

ing the twentieth century. The state education agencies came of age and received recognition as a professional partner in educa-

tional leadership during the last half of the
twentieth century. It has a bright future
before it.

NOTES

1. See Robert M. Isenberg, "State Organization for Service and Leadership to Local Schools," in Edgar Fuller and Jim B. Pearson, eds., *Education in the States: Nationwide Development Since 1900*, Washington, D.C.: National Education Association, 1969, pp. 131–173.
2. See ibid., p. 135, and also George J. Collins, "Constitutional and Legal Basis for State Action," in Fuller and Pearson, eds., op. cit., pp. 7–69.
3. Lerue W. Winget, Edgar Fuller, and Terrel H. Bell, "State Departments of Education Within State Governments," in Fuller and Pearson, eds., op. cit., pp. 71–130.
4. R. F. Will, *State Education, Structure and Organization*, OE-23038, Misc. No. 46, Washington, D.C.: GPO, 1964.
5. Winget, Fuller, and Bell, op. cit., p. 75.
6. Ibid.
7. National Council of Chief State School Officers, *The State Department of Education*, Washington, D.C.: The Council, 1952, pp. 14–16.
8. Ellwood P. Cubberley, *State School Administra-tion*, Boston: Houghton Mifflin, 1927, p. 286.
9. Winget, Fuller, and Bell, op. cit., pp. 77–78.
10. Sam P. Harris, *State Departments of Education, State Boards of Education, and Chief State School Officers*, DHEW Publication No. (OE) 72-07400, Washington, D.C.: GPO, 1973 p. 68.
11. Winget, Fuller, and Bell, op. cit., p. 79.
12. E. P. Cubberley, op. cit., pp. 290–294.
13. Winget, Fuller, and Bell, op. cit., p. 93.
14. Ibid., p. 94.
15. Ibid., pp. 94–95.
16. Ibid., p. 95.
17. Ibid., p. 93.
18. National Council of Chief State School Officers, op. cit., p. 16.
19. F. F. Beach and A. H. Gibbs, *Personnel of State Departments of Education*, U.S. Office of Education, Washington, D.C.: GPO, 1952.
20. Ibid.
21. Ibid.
22. Ibid.
23. Sam P. Harris, op. cit., p. 38.
24. Winget, Fuller, and Bell, op. cit., p. 112.

CHAPTER REVIEW QUESTIONS

1. What were the significant stages of development of the modern state department of education?
2. What arguments would tend to support the election of members of the state board of education? Appointment of members of the state board?
3. What factors appear to support the contention that there is a need for a reorganization within many of the present-day state departments of education?
4. Why should the state superintendent be appointed rather than elected to office?
5. What services can an effective state department provide local school districts?

SELECTED REFERENCES

Beach, F. F., and Will, R. F., *The State and Education*, U.S. Office of Education, Misc. No. 23, Washington, D.C.: GPO, 1955.
Cubberley, Ellwood P., *State School Administration*, Boston: Houghton Mifflin, 1927.
Fuller, Edgar, and Pearson, J. B., eds., *Education in the States: Nationwide Development Since 1900*, Washington, D.C.: Council of Chief State School Officers, 1969.
Harris, Sam P., *State Departments of Education, State Boards of Education, and Chief State School Officers*, DHEW Publication No. (OE) 73-07400, 1973.
Will, R. F., *State Education, Structure and Organization*, U.S. Office of Education, OE-23038, Misc. No. 46, Washington, D.C.: GPO, 1964.

10

FEDERAL EDUCATIONAL ACTIVITIES AND CONTRIBUTIONS: IMPACT OF NATIONAL EDUCATIONAL POLICIES ON STATE AND LOCAL SCHOOL ADMINISTRATION

As indicated in the previous three chapters, education was considered one of the "residual powers retained by the states" when the U.S. Constitution was adopted in 1788. This was reinforced by the addition of the Tenth Amendment and a number of court decisions. Our form of federalism precludes direct participation and control of the 50 state systems of public education by the national government. It does not prevent the federal government from expressing an interest in the growth and development or from contributing to enhance the welfare of systems of public schools. From its very inception as a formally constituted political entity, the federal government expressed a keen interest in and became involved in the promotion of education in the nation. Cubberley referred to the federal government as "an interested and benevolent spectator in the growth of state schools systems."[1] Quattlebaum, an education research analyst in the U.S. government, noted the early efforts of the federal government to encourage the establishment of public schools in the then "territories" and later new states in the Union. He then concluded that "the Federal Government became the founder of the public-school systems in most of the States."[2] There is substance to these perceptions of the contributions of the federal government to the development of systems of public education.

Although public schools were in existence many years prior to the Constitutional Convention, there were some among the founding fathers of our nation who desired to establish a national system of education. Quattlebaum indicated that "Although it appears that at one time during the Constitutional Convention control over education was included in a list of specific powers being considered for assignment to the Federal Government, the duty of administering education was among those items later deleted from the list."[3] Some Constitutional Convention delegates assumed that the federal government had responsibility for at least promoting education under the "general welfare" clause of the U.S. Constitution, an opinion held by Alexander Hamilton no less. Two early U.S. Presidents, namely, Jefferson in 1806 and Madison in 1817, "urged a constitutional amendment giving the Federal Government control over education."[4] But that was not to be and education remained a state rather than a federally controlled function as found in other nations.

There were other efforts to convert to a national system of education in later years. Thus, in 1870 Representative Hoar of Massachusetts introduced a bill in the U.S. Congress to create a national education system calling for appointment of a "state superintendent of national schools" (in each state) by the president, the division of states into school districts along the lines of congressional districts, and the appointment of a "local superintendent of national school(s)" within each such district appointment by the Secretary of Interior. It called for a national system of compulsory education, but the bill never got very far. It was argued that its constitutionality was in question, it would destroy local control over education, and it "would be an insult to white Southerners and inflame racial issues."[5] It did manage to cast suspicion upon subsequent federal activities in education and to suggest that "federal aid means federal control."

The role of the national government in public education has generated much controversy and disagreement. Nonetheless, its contributions have had and continue to have a significant impact upon public education. There were a limited number of federal education acts prior to 1900 in contrast to the large numbers during the twentieth century. A listing of selected and major federal education legislation is presented in Table 10.1. Over 100 laws—not all of which are shown in Table 10.1—influencing some level of education were approved at the federal level during this period of 116 years. Over two-thirds of the federal school-related legislation was passed after 1960! It was not unusual to have over 1000 education bills come before Congress during a single two-year term in the years following 1950.

The sample of laws passed and listed in Table 10.1 demonstrates that what started as a modest (in numbers, but not in terms of contributions and impact) federal education effort over 200 years ago mushroomed into heavy and continuing involvement during the last half of the twentieth century. A very large number of federal agencies other than those specifically assigned responsibilities for education are involved. This large federal bureaucracy has been known to give special interpretations to congressional intent and litigations may result. To compound matters, the federal courts have undone congressional as well as state legislative and constitutional educational policy statements.

MAJOR PHASES OF FEDERAL ACTIVITIES AND CONTRIBUTIONS TO EDUCATION

Congress has had a tremendous influence upon public education without explicit and direct constitutional authorization. One wonders how much more could have been done to promote the cause of education with an express constitutional mandate to do so. The history of federal interest and involvement in public education makes a mockery out of what at times prompted very heated debates such as "Should there be federal aid to education?" What is being debated presently is not whether but how the federal government should be involved and how much to contribute under what conditions. The past two decades were times of massive and continuing federal concern for education. The ardor cooled considerably during the early 1980s as the Reagan Administration sought to reduce materially the size of the federal government and its role in public education.

Federal interest in public education predates the Constitution that formed the Union. In 1785 the Continental Congress passed the Ordinance of 1785 from which "arose a national policy which has resulted in providing the states with vast grants for public education."[6] This was the beginning of federal aid as well as federal involvement in the advancement of public education. A more detailed analysis of this and other phases of federal activities in education follows.

TABLE 10.1

SELECTED MAJOR FEDERAL LEGISLATION AND COURT DECISIONS ON EDUCATION, 1867–1984

1867	U.S. "Department of Education" created	Passed by House, June 1866; by Senate, February 1867; signed into law by President Johnson. Never granted cabinet status. No Secretary of Education; executive head called Commissioner. Attached to Interior Department.
1870	Title change: "Department" became "Bureau of Education"	No changes in personnel, functions, activities, etc. Change made in Appropriations Act of 1870.
1890	Second Morrill Act	Provided federal funds for land grant institutions. The first such act donated lands to encourage formation of land-grant colleges.
1896	*Plessy* v. *Ferguson*	U.S. Supreme Court establishes precedent for "racially separate, but equal schools."
1917	Smith–Hughes Act: P.L. 347	64th Congress provides annual federal grants for vocational education in public schools and encourages preparation program for vocational education teachers.
1935	Agriculture Adjustment Act: P.L. 74–320	Start of federal contributions to school lunch programs, in 1936, with commodities purchased under this act to stabilize agricultural prices.
1936	George–Deen Act	Extended Smith–Hughes Act to education in the distributive occupations.
1941	Lanham Act Amendments	Provided federal assistance for school construction for communities adversely affected by nearby federal activities, such as military bases.
1944	Servicemen's Readjustment Act (GI Bill): P.L. 284	78th Congress provided federal funds to individuals returning to civilian life after military service during World War II; provides educational training benefits for veterans.
1944	Surplus Property Act	Enacted a broad policy governing disposal of federal surplus property used during World War II for the purposes of educational, health, and civil defense organizations.
1946	Vocational Education Act (George–Barden): P.L. 586	79th Congress provided for further development of vocational education in states and territories.
1946	National School Lunch Act	Provided for distribution of federal funds and purchased food for public and nonpublic schools. Extended later in 1954 to include school milk program in all schools.
1950	P.L. 815	81st Congress provided assistance for construction of schools in federally impacted areas.
1950	P.L. 874	81st Congress established operating expenses for schools in federally affected areas.
1953	P.L. 13	83rd Congress created Department of Health, Education, and Welfare with U.S. Office of Education a constituent unit.
1953	Dept. of Health, Education, and Welfare created	Office of Education becomes subdivision within this department.
1954	*Brown* v. *Board of Education*	U.S. Supreme Court overturns *Plessy* doctrine and outlaws racial segregation in all schools.

TABLE 10.1 *(Continued)*

SELECTED MAJOR FEDERAL LEGISLATION AND COURT DECISIONS ON EDUCATION, 1867–1984

1954	Cooperative Research Act: P.L. 531	83rd Congress authorized U.S. Office of Education to conduct cooperative research with colleges, universities, and state education agencies.
1958	National Defense Education: P.L. 85–865	Strengthened national defense and encouraged and assisted expansion and improvement of educational programs to meet critical national needs; set up college student loan funds.
1958	Education of Mentally Retarded Child Act: P.L. 85–926	Authorization of federal assistance for the training of teachers serving children with exceptionalities.
1961	P.L. 87-276	Authorized grants to train teachers of the deaf (combined with P.L. 85-926 by P.L. 88-164).
1961	Peace Corps Act	Established a permanent Peace Corps to supply U.S. teachers and technicians to underdeveloped nations.
1962	Manpower Development and Training Act, Title II, Part B: P.L. 88–164	Authorized U.S. Office of Education to assist in retraining and occupational training programs.
1963	Mental Retardation Facilities and Community Mental Health Centers Construction Act: P.L. 88–164	Expanded P.L. 85-926 and established a program of research and demonstration projects in the education of handicapped children.
1963	Vocational Education Act: P.L. 88-210	Expanded and made more comprehensive vocational educational experiences and benefits.
1964	Civil Rights Act (Title IV)	Allowed the U.S. Commissioner of Education to provide technical assistance, grants, and training institutes to help communities prepare for school desegregation.
1964	Amendments to NDEA, Impact School Aid	Extended and expanded both the National Defense Education Act (NDEA) and the impact school aid program. NDEA institutes for the advanced training of teachers, previously limited to guidance counselors and teachers of modern languages, were broadened to include teachers of English, reading, history, and geography, teachers of disadvantaged youths, librarians, and educational media specialists.
1965	Elementary and Secondary Education Act: P.L. 89-10: Bilingual Programs	Established new federal programs to strengthen education.
1965	Higher Education Act of 1965: P.L. 89-329	Established seven new programs designed to strengthen institutions of higher education and provided student assistance.
1966	Child Nutrition Act	Amended the National School Lunch Act by authorizing a special milk program through 1970, a two-year pilot school breakfast program, and a permanent nonfood assistance program for economically depressed areas.
1967	Elementary and Secondary Amendments: Dropout and Bilingual Programs	Extended ESEA through fiscal 1970; transferred Title III and Title V to state control; established dropout prevention projects and bilingual programs.

TABLE 10.1 *(Continued)*

1967	Education Professions Development Act	Extended Teacher Corps for three years; provided $1.1 billion for broadened training programs for education personnel.
1968	Vocational Education Amendments	Reorganized and expanded federal vocational education programs; making the basic state program authorization permanent and extending others for up to four years. Spending authorization of over $3 billion confirmed.
1970	Drug Abuse Education Act	Authorized $29 million over three years for drug abuse training, materials, seminars, and pilot projects, and $29 million for community-based programs.
1970	U.S. Office of Education FY 1971 Appropriation Act: School Desegregation Aid	Included $75 million to help school desegregation, and Whitten amendment prohibiting use of federal funds for forced busing.
1970	Elementary and Secondary Education Act Amendments: P.L. 91–230	Extended ESEA through Fiscal 1973; consolidated Title III (supplementary service) with NDEA Title V-A (guidance and counseling); increased authorization for Title I; expanded impact aid to include children who live in public housing; however, no funds were appropriated for public-housing children; and extended the 1968 Vocational Education Amendments.
1971	Office of Education and Related Agencies Appropriations Act, 1972: P.L. 92–48	Section 310. "No part of the funds contained . . . shall be used to force any school or school district which is desegregated . . . to take any action to force the busing of students; to require the abolishment of any school desegregated; or to force on account of race, creed, or color the transfer of students to or from a particular school so desegregated as a condition precedent to obtaining Federal funds otherwise available to any State, school district or school."
1972	Education Amendments of 1972. P.L. 92–318: Creation of the National Institutes for Education	Expanded and revised most higher education laws, creating new programs of institutional and student aid; established an Education Division within HEW, composed of the Office of Education and the National Institutes of Education, headed by an assistant secretary for education; increased federal support for career (vocational) education, Indian education, and consumer education; established ethnic cultural heritage studies; and provided financial aid for school desegregation.
1975	Education for All Handicapped Children Act: P.L. 94–142	Provides federal assistance for and requires free appropriate education for all handicapped children in "least restrictive environment."
1978	Education Amendments of 1978: P.L. 95–561	Authorizes broad program of study for educational finance reform and equalization; seeks to assist improvement in basic skills taught in schools.
1979	Department of Education Organization Act: P.L. 96-88	Establishes a cabinet level Department of Education with a Secretary of Education as the executive head.
1980	U.S. Department of Education formally begins operation in May 1980	U.S. Office of Education passes into history.
1981	Education Consolidation and Improvement Act of 1981	Distributes funds to public education under "Block Grants" as opposed to categorical funding. Substantial reduction in federal role and financial allocations to education begin.

Phase 1. Federal Land Grants for Elementary and Secondary Schools

The Ordinance of 1785 was concerned with the survey and disposal of western lands (bounded on the west by the Mississippi River) that were ceded by the original 13 colonies and from which new territories and subsequently states were to be formed. The famous declaration of this ordinance was that "there shall be reserved the lot number 16 in each township for the maintenance of public schools in said township, also one-third of all gold, lead, silver and copper mines to be sold or otherwise disposed of as Congress shall hereinafter direct." The Ordinance of 1787, popularly known as the Northwest Ordinance, supported the land policy of 1785 with the statement that "religion, morality and knowledge being necessary to good government and happiness of mankind, schools and the means of education shall forever be encouraged." This federal land policy has been construed as a means of stimulating land sales to large land companies. Whatever the motives of the Continental Congress, the impact of the Ordinances of 1785 and 1787 on the formulation of state constitutions and the development of public education in the states carved from the Northwest Territory was most significant.[7]

It was federal support of public education *without undesirable strings attached.* It established federal support of education as a policy or activity as old as the nation.

The original federal land grants were awarded to states that came into the Union after 1800. Although Tennessee was admitted in 1796, it did not receive its federal land grant until 1806. Ohio was the first to receive land grants for schools when it entered in 1802. The 13 original states plus Kentucky, Maine, Vermont, West Virginia, and Texas (all five contained no federally owned public lands) did not participate in the original federal land grants for schools. In subsequent federal land grants, allocations were made to these and other states from salt lands, internal-improvement lands, and swamplands. Thirty-nine states (excluding Hawaii and Alaska) received over 154 million

acres of land, estimated to be worth more than $1 billion,[8] for schools from the federal government.

Not all states received equal grants of land upon entering the Union. Starting in 1848 when the Oregon Territory was created, sections 16 and 36 in every township were allocated to states entering the Union for the purpose of establishing public schools. Oklahoma received two sections in each township plus $5 million in gold for land held by Indians. Utah was granted four sections in every township in 1896, and Arizona and New Mexico were given similar allocations of sections 2, 16, 32, and 36.

Enabling acts passed by Congress were the legal means to transform a territory into a state (for those admitted to the Union after 1800). These acts required provisions in the Constitution of proposed states for the establishment of a system of public schools. Munse and Booher joined the earlier similar declaration from Quattlebaum that "in this way the federal government may be regarded as the founder of the public school systems for many of the states."[9]

Estimates on the total amount of federal land granted to the new states for the support of public education vary. Quattlebaum estimated that the early grants to the "30 public land states for the common schools" was "an area ten times as large as the state of Maryland," and that additional lands totaling 76 million acres were to be used in whole or in part for the support of schools.[10] Swift estimated that the total area of land "granted specifically for schools by our national government to its thirty public-land states, 121,110 square miles, is larger than Italy, nearly two and one-half times as large as England. . . ."[11] Unfortunately, most federal school lands were poorly administered by states and their full potential for the support of public education went unrealized. Swift referred to this as "squandering the heritage" and noted "From contemplating the school heritage which might have been, we now pass to the stern reality that even an incomplete record shows that in thirty-two of the states funds totaling many millions of dollars have been lost, diverted, or squandered."[12] Most of the tremendous loss in lands to support public education occurred during the nineteenth century. The result is that today the early federal land grants remain an important source of public school revenue in very few states. The present asset value of what were to be "permanent endowments" for education from the federal government is less than $70 million. The annual federal monetary contributions to public elementary and secondary schools in the 1980s were 100 times greater than the combined asset value of the remaining federal land grants for education. A great idea with tremendous potential turned out to be a regrettable educational finance tragedy for public education, with the states rather than the federal government assuming full responsibility for the waste and mismanagement.

Phase 2. Federal Land Grants for Higher Education

About three-quarters of a century were to pass before another major federal educational policy became a reality. The second major action influenced public institutions of higher learning and not elementary and secondary schools. Federal land grants awarded under the Morrill Act of 1862 were in response to demands for improved and expanded agricultural, mechanical, and scientific educational programs in institutions of higher learning.

Federally owned lands totaling 30,000 acres to each state for each senator and representative then in Congress were granted with the proviso that the income from sale or rental of these lands be dedicated to organizing new agricultural and mechanical arts colleges. Such institutions were to include instruction in military science and tactics as well. States that established land-grant colleges but in which the federal government owned no lands were awarded rights of land ownership in another state where large acreages were available. This second major federal policy in public education, although focused on higher education, set the pattern for conditional grants. Some have suggested that this represents the beginning of some degree of federal control.

The Morrill Act demonstrated that the fed-

eral government could and would take action in education (1) if it were important to common defense or general welfare and (2) if vital areas of education were neglected.[13] All states received land grants from the Morrill Act; 6 million acres of federal lands were donated to the states for the founding of agricultural and mechanical arts colleges.

The second Morrill Act of 1890, the Hatch Act of 1887, and others initiated the federal outlay of money as well as land.

Phase 3. Federal Conditional, Targeted Grants for Secondary Schools

Another 50 years with little federal activity in education were to go by before a new direction emerged. Actually, because the Morrill Act dealt with higher education, it can be said that more than a century was to pass before the federal government demonstrated new concerns for public elementary and secondary education. This is in sharp contrast to the 1960s and 1970s when almost every other year a new major federal thrust in some dimension of education appeared.

The third phase of federal activity in public education came with the *conditional grants for highly specific purposes* in public secondary schools. The Smith-Hughes Act of 1917 provided money grants for agricultural education and other activities. The original act required matching of federal appropriations for vocational education in agriculture, trades, and industry and in homemaking. Federal concern for vocational education in a relatively limited number of fields in public secondary schools was extended by various acts in 1929, 1935, 1937, and again in 1946. The Vocational Education Act of 1963 represented a radical departure from past practices if for no other reason than the act was far more comprehensive in scope, included postsecondary institutions, and the dollars involved were much greater. The 1968 amendments expand the Vocational Education Act of 1963 even further.

The original 1917 federal vocational act represented the entry of the federal government into public secondary education and stimulation of specific educational programs with annual appropriations. At one time federal funds accounted for about one-half the expenditures for vocational education. This intervention came at the time when the public high school was concerned primarily with preparation of students for entry into institutions of higher learning. Federal stimulation of local financing of vocational education was successful for federal appropriations for vocational education in 1955–1956 represented less than 50 percent of the total expenditure.

By 1966 the authorization under the Smith-Hughes Act for the various titles of the George-Barden Act totaled less than $60 million compared with $235.5 million for the more comprehensive Vocational Education Act of 1963. In the 1970s federal funds for various dimensions of vocational education, including postsecondary and adult programs, exceeded $500 million annually. In contrast, state and local funds for these same broad ranges of vocational education in the 1970s exceeded $2 billion annually.

Phase 4. Federal Incidental Aid to Education Through Broader Relief Programs

The fourth phase emerged during the Great Depression of the 1930s. Federal interest in schools at this time was only incidental to the greater concerns for the welfare of youths.

The Civilian Conservation Corps (CCC) was organized in 1933 by the federal government for unmarried males 17 to 23. A very small percent of those who joined the CCC graduated from high school; nearly one-half had never finished grade school; and a substantial number were practically illiterate. These factors precipitated change in the 1937 CCC Act to include appropriations for the education and vocational training of the young men. President Roosevelt indicated at that time that the major purposes of the CCC were to promote welfare and *further training*. Administration of the corps was then transferred from the War Department to the Federal Security Agency. About $5 mil-

lion to $10 million was spent for education in CCC camps in 1938, when $308.5 million was expended for all CCC activities.

More than 2.7 million of the approximately 3 million men enrolled in the CCC participated in some type of educational activity. The CCC was abolished in 1943. Almost a generation passed before the CCC idea was brought back as one part of the Job Corps program of the mid-1960s.

The National Youth Administration (NYA) was established in 1935 as a welfare program for unemployed youths from 16 to 25. Educational programs at first were limited, but by 1938 the NYA was concerned not only with part-time work for youths, but also with training programs.

Most observers were impressed by the lack of cooperation between the NYA and local schools. The NYA did not work through state departments of education until 1940, so complete was the federal domination. A less controversial activity of the NYA was the granting of money to needy students in attendance at secondary schools or institutions of higher learning. The recipients of such aid were to perform some useful function in the school.

The NYA funding came to an end in 1944 and it was disestablished. Many educators during the 1930s expressed alarm over what could have been the development of a federal system of education. In some cases federally supported training programs were in direct competition with programs offered by local school systems with far less financial resources. There is little question that the CCC and NYA did much fine welfare work for youths. Nonetheless, the educational activities of the CCC and NYA programs could have been performed by school systems close to CCC camps if these had been awarded sufficient financial support. The same remark was made later with reference to the Job Corps of the 1960s.

Other federal welfare activities during the Great Depression had a more indirect impact on public education.

Thus, many schoolhouses were repainted and renovated through funds and activities of the Civil Works Administration (CWA), organized to provide work for the unemployed. The Federal Emergency Relief Administration (FERA), established in 1933, allocated funds for the employment of unemployed rural teachers. Under the Works Progress Administration (WPA), which succeeded the FERA in 1935, substantial funds were made available for school-plant construction and repair. The Public Works Administration (PWA), organized in 1933, had granted 30 percent (later 45 percent) of the cost of school construction and made loans for all or part of the remaining costs.

The many communities that participated in CWA, FERA, PWA, or WPA projects for school-plant construction were in a better position to meet the schoolroom shortage after World War II. The matching provisions of the federal grants, unfortunately, made wealthier the districts with financial ability to raise money for matching the greatest beneficiaries. All federal relief agencies were terminated in 1940.

The only continuing federal "aid" that grew out of the relief measures of the 1930s was the school lunch program. The school lunch program was under the jurisdiction of the Department of Agriculture because it was initiated in 1935 under Public Law 320. It was followed by the National School Lunch Act of 1946 which established some degree of permanency for federal school lunch aid and also made available to schools the surplus foods purchased by the federal government to support agricultural prices for the nation's farmers. The contributions continued to grow so that the amount of federal funds for school lunch and milk programs granted in one year during the 1970s exceeded the total granted during the first ten years of the National School Lunch Act. These more recent annual grants were in the billions of dollars, but reductions in school lunch program grants were started in the early 1980s.

The Lanham Act of 1941 provided grants to the so-called federally impacted areas where the federal government owned large amounts of land for military and other activities which provided no or insufficient revenues to help support the local services (such as schools) that benefited those residing or working on such extensive federal projects. This law recognized that often large-scale federal activities in specific areas generated special problems for schools and other community agencies.

The GI Bills. The Servicemen's Readjustment Act of 1944, known popularly as the GI Bill, was an educational "bonus" to returning World War II veterans. Funds allocated for veterans' education and training exceeded $2.7 billion in 1949, and then dropped to $0.56 billion in 1958. Benefits were extended to Korean Conflict veterans and others in following years. This direct aid to the individual veteran benefited institutions of higher learning and special schools as well.

Phase 5. The National Defense Education Act

The launching of the first Soviet Sputnik is generally credited for congressional action leading to the National Defense Education Act (NDEA) of 1958. The importance of education to the national defense was declared in the first section of this act:

> The Congress hereby finds and declares that the security of the nation requires the fullest development of the mental resources and technical skills of its young men and women. . . . The defense of this nation depends upon the mastery of modern techniques developed from complex scientific principles. . . .
>
> We must increase our efforts to identify in education more of the talent of our nation.
>
> The Congress reaffirms the principle and declares that the states and local communities have and must retain control over and primary responsibility for public education. The national interest requires, however, that the federal government give assistance to education for programs which are important to our defense.

This rather broad act granted federal funds for:

1. College and university student loans.
2. Strengthening science, mathematics, and language instruction in schools.
3. Creating graduate-school fellowships.

4. Promoting guidance, counseling, and testing services in elementary and secondary schools.
5. Stimulating the teaching of certain languages which previously had been neglected.
6. Performing research and experimentation in various educational media.
7. Promoting the establishment of area vocational schools.
8. Improving statistical services of state educational agencies.

By 1960, nearly $400 million had been spent in carrying out provisions of the NDEA—about $250 million from federal funds, and $143 million from state agencies, school districts, and institutions of higher education participating in the program.[14]

The NDEA was the first piece of legislation passed by Congress aimed specifically at improving instruction in academic or nonvocational subjects. The NDEA was modified in 1961, 1963, and 1964. The last two changes broadened the scope of the act to include history, civics, geography, English, and reading as critical subjects.

Phase 6. The Elementary and Secondary School Act (ESEA) of 1965

Signing into law the Elementary and Secondary Education Act (ESEA) in 1965, President Lyndon Johnson declared: "As President of the United States I believe deeply no law I have signed, or will ever sign, means more to the future of America." This omnibus bill was part of the "war on poverty and ignorance" and "was one of several legislative initiatives in the mid-1960s which originated in the emerging social policy technocracy of the major universities and the populist equalitarian politics of Lyndon Johnson."[15] It is one of the landmark federal education activities and contributions because of its targeting on those considered educationally disadvantaged, its concern for learners in low-income areas, and the magnitude of annual grants. The annual appropria-

tions for ESEA were in the billions rather than the usual millions.

Of its several titles, Title I commanded the most attention (or criticism), the most dollars, and the most amendments (nine during a period of 13 years). It focused on compensatory instruction for "educationally disadvantaged" students in the low-income or poverty schools and by 1978 had an appropriation of more than $2.7 billion.[16] A little less than $1 billion was appropriated for the first year. The majority of funds was expended on instructional services (such as remedial reading and language arts instruction), and food services (such as hot breakfasts and lunches at school) accounted for less than 2 percent of the funds. Most schools receiving Title I funds were in the core areas of the very large urban areas and in the rural areas of the South. According to Vanecko and Ames there was "no comprehensive or coherent federal policy" in education prior to ESEA and that "with the signing into law of ESEA, the federal government committed itself for the first time to a significant role in education."[17] (Such statements ignore history and the original federal land grants for schools.) Title I alone reached 90 percent of the nation's local school districts (but not all school attendance centers within a school district qualified as "Title I schools") and approximately 5.9 million students. Each school had to have pupils who satisfied the low-income test and who were found to be educationally disadvantaged (as measured by test scores or grade retention). This often resulted in a debate on the priority or direction of Title I, that is, whether it was to be a poverty program award or an educational program.

Title II of the ESEA granted support for three types of educational materials: school library resources, textbooks, and other instructional materials. About $100 million were made available for these purposes during the first two years. Private schools received benefits from the appropriations as well.

Supplementary educational centers and services, sometimes called Projects to Advance Creativity in Education (PACE), were founded under Title III. Over 10 million public and nonpublic school pupils were touched by Title III programs, and 1085 proposals and $75.8 million for their support were approved during the first year of operation.

The Cooperative Research Act of 1954 was amended and made Title IV of the ESEA. From funds of only $1 million annually this program exceeded $100 million for research grants and contracts by the late 1960s. Federal educational research funds in all agencies, not simply the Cooperative Research Act, reached $320 million by 1972.

Title V of ESEA also provided funds for the strengthening of state education agencies, which was referred to in the preceding chapter.

Phase 7. Crisis Orientation with Multifaceted Efforts

Throughout most of recent history federal education activities had a crisis orientation, whether real or perceived. Thus, testimony by some that the Russians are surpassing the United States in science and mathematics could trigger a legislative response such as the National Defense Education Act. Others perceived a link between poverty and basic educational deficiencies of children and youths; ESEA was the congressional response to this perceived national crisis. Whatever the nature of the problems or the times, matters of the quality and quantity of educational opportunities or performances of students come to be matters of national concern.

A number of specific federal educational activities followed some ten years after the landmark ESEA. This includes such diverse federal education thrusts as the Job Corps and desegregation as well as education of the handicapped.

The Job Corps

The Job Corps was a unique federal vocational education thrust that was radically different in the target population to be served and also in the strategies selected for delivering the educational programs and services.

Public school dropouts were identified as the target population for Job Corps programs. Considerable advance publicity accompanied this federal activity with claims that it would succeed where the public and private schools had failed. High school dropouts had been the concern of professional educators at the state and local levels at least 50 years prior to this expression of special interests by the federal government. The timing of the federal interest in dropouts coincided with the positive improvement trends as evidenced by the steadily increasing holding power of the nation's public schools. Thus in 1940, 444 graduated from high school for each 1000 pupils in the fifth grade eight years earlier. About the time Job Corps came into being, there were 710 graduates from public high schools for every 1000 in fifth grade eight years earlier. These significant gains were achieved without federal funds or intervention for these specific purposes.

The Job Corps was to be a system of federally controlled as well as federally supported vocational schools for high school dropouts. This is a significant break with previous traditions, with the closest precedent being the education programs in the CCC during the Great Depression. Even more unusual, Job Corps was operated and controlled by a specially created unit that was outside the federal agency most directly concerned with education—the U.S. Office of Education. It was part of the federal agency created to conduct "war" and put an end to poverty. Job Corps was under the direct control and supervision of the Office of Economic Opportunity. This demonstrates anew that Congress will allocate control and funds for educational purposes without regard for existing education departments within the federal hierarchy. It is politics rather than management science that determines in large part such federal decisions.

Job Corps had two major divisions: the Urban Job Corps Centers and the Conservation Job Corps Centers, which were more numerous but enrolled fewer students. At the time when concerns for women's rights emerged and sexism criticized, the Urban Job Corps in particular abandoned the coeducational concepts and designed and operated separate centers for male and female youths. The contract method was employed to sublet the actual operation of specific Job Corps educational centers to private and a few public organizations. The concept and the subsequent operations were developed with little, if any, consultation with professionals in education. To repeat, no center was operated directly by Job Corps officials in Washington, D.C.

The Job Corps may be conceptualized further as a residential educational program that brought the students to places often a considerable distance from what was called home. It was a compensatory as well as a vocational education program with massive welfare dimensions for school dropouts in the 16-to-21 age group. For all the attendant publicity it was never designed nor able to serve all high school dropouts; only about one-third could meet the qualification tests. To illustrate, one of the provisos for admission to Job Corps was that the dropout came from a low-income family.

About three-fourths of the Urban Job Corps contractors in 1966 were private corporations that anticipated a profit from the contracts with the Office of Economic Opportunity. In 1965 one private Urban Job Corps contractor made a one-year profit of $80,000 for operating a center with a capacity of 300 women (about $266 per enrollee); another reported a one-year profit of $364,000 for a center with 1300 men (a profit of about $280 per enrollee). Some of the private corporations used Job Corps Centers to develop and test educational systems that, if successful, could be marketed to enhance the company's product line and profit potential.

No public elementary or secondary school has been allowed to make a profit on federal funds allocated to it. On the contrary, federal grants to public schools have been conditional upon local and state matching funds or at least substantial contributions.

A double standard appears evident from the federal financing of educational ventures. If the grant was to a public school system, the local school system assumed part of the fiscal burden. Furthermore, additional facilities required to house the part of the educational program being stimulated were to be provided somehow by local educational authorities.

Published statements on the cost of keeping a single boy or girl in the Job Corps for one-year range from $9,100 to $13,000 in one set of estimates and from $17,000 to $235,000 in another. As Oregon's Representative Green asked in 1966, could not public schools make breakthroughs if they were permitted to spend $13,000 each year on each student?

Certain factors must be kept in mind in analyzing Job Corps costs:

1. High starting costs along with unusual problems in some centers inflated many units' outlays.
2. The centers were residential—clothing was furnished and enrollees fed three times a day seven days a week.
3. Extensive medical and dental services were available.
4. The corpsmen received allowances of $30 per month plus a $50 terminal allowance.

A study by the writer, using financial data provided by the Office of Economic Opportunity, indicated that the annual cost was about $12,000 per enrollee for 1965. This was over 20 times the $501 per pupil in the average daily membership in the elementary and secondary schools of the United States in 1965–1966. By 1967 Job Corps expenditures dropped to $7500 per enrollee per year. Administrative costs of locating, screening, assigning, and paying corpsmen, as well as maintaining the Washington, D.C., headquarters operations, were in excess of $1500 per enrollee per year, or about 12 percent of the expenditures for 1965. In contrast, only 3 to 5 percent of the budget of a public school system is allocated to administration.

By late 1967, there were over 123 Job Corps centers (93 conservation, 10 men's urban, 18 women's urban, and 2 special), enrolling almost 40,000 people. The Job Corps program was terminated in 1970 having achieved only limited success in its mission and having become politically too controversial.

What kind of an impact did the Job Corps program have on the dropout problem during its brief existence? To begin with two-thirds of all school dropouts were ignored. After some difficult early experiences, the retarded, the emotionally disturbed, and the incorrigible had to be dismissed or screened out of Job Corps and sent to other social institutions if any existed. Reality must have been a bitter pill for some without any first-hand experience but with a great penchant to criticize the operations of ongoing social and educational institutions.

Job Corps spawned its own set of dropouts as well. The Job Corps was not the first federal venture for youths to experience this problem. About 26 percent of the average annual enrollment in the CCC from 1933 to 1941 terminated their education or training prematurely. The dropout rate in the Job Corps was in the neighborhood of 30 percent, depending upon how the term is defined. It was one of the most controversial of the antipoverty programs and one of the first to be phased out.

Federal Stimulation of Desegregation Enforcement

During the 1960s the full force of the federal government came into play to enforce the U.S. Supreme Court decisions on the desegregation of public schools in all states. The impetus came from the Civil Rights Act of 1964, which included the proviso that all federal programs supported by federal funds—including those allocated to public education—must be administered and operated without discrimination. If clear evidence of intent to desegregate and to operate in a nondiscriminatory fashion was not provided, all federal funds were to be withheld. Federal guidelines were prepared and applied to measure the extent to which the spirit as well as the intent of the law were satisfied. In 1967 enforcement responsibility was shifted from the Office of Education to the Department of Health, Education, and Welfare as a whole, and the Department of Justice also assumed a more active role. As will be reviewed in greater detail in a subsequent chapter, the political pressures and climate changed during the 1970s and early

1980s; and the federal enforcement role in such matters as school busing to achieve better racial balance came to an end and greatly lessened in other dimensions of civil rights as well.

Other Federal Education Programs

As Quattlebaum noted, "From its inception the Federal Government has engaged in two types of educational activities: (1) financing and administering its own educational programs, and (2) aiding the States and Territories in financing and otherwise promoting education."[18] Military training programs were the first federally administered educational activities that led eventually to the establishment and operations of such institutions which continue at present: the Military Academy at West Point, the Marine Corps Institute, the Army Medical School, the Merchant Marine Institute, the National War Colleges, the Naval Academy, the Air University, the Air Force Academy, and the Armed Forces Institute. The overseas schools for dependents of service personnel and specific federal government workers are administered and operated by the Department of Defense because efforts to transfer this "sixth largest public school system" to the Department of Education were not successful. The education of Indians has been in large measure administered and financed by the federal government through the Department of Interior. In short, all direct federal administration and operation of specific educational institutions remain outside the Department of Education.

CRITIQUE OF FEDERAL EDUCATIONAL ACTIVITIES AND CONTRIBUTIONS

The consensus opinion is that there is no long-term, rational, or consistent federal educational policy. This is true unless it is argued that political expediency or crisis (real or imagined) orientation can be construed as a policy posture. There is no evidence that the recent and greatly increased federal involvement in the various dimensions of public education or the many published statements decrying the absence of a consistent federal educational policy will resolve this serious shortcoming and fill the existing policy void.

Federal involvement in education is more specific or narrowly targeted at one time than another. Thus, there was a sharply targeted effort to improve the quality and availability of educational opportunities for the handicapped. The war on poverty, on the other hand, was more general and focused some attention on the need for programs for the educationally disadvantaged. The allocation of school lunch funds through the Department of Agriculture that was concerned less with school improvements and more with the disposition of surplus foods accumulated in the process of supporting farm prices.

The initial national educational policy, enunciated over 200 years ago, reinforced the concept that the control and operation of systems of public education were reserved for the individual states. This policy remains in force. There were times during the nineteenth century when some sought unsuccessfully to change this basic policy and to establish a system of nationally controlled public schools. There were occasions when a given federal agency took a few liberties with this initial educational policy such as was noted with the CCC and the Job Corps, but it was confined to very short periods of time and was limited in scope.

What did change over a period of more than 200 years were national *policies on distribution of federal funds to support public education and also the specific educational targets* deserving federal support. Actions speak louder than the words that may communicate an educational policy. Again, the initial federal "education-funds-distribution-policy" called for federal funds allocation with *no strings attached, no written proposals* to be submitted to any federal agency for the release of the federal educational funds, *no subsequent monitoring* of educational funds distributed, and *no subsequent reporting* to the federal government as to how the educational funds were used (and, of course, *no federal auditing*). This was the federal award of massive amounts of land for the

support of public education during the nineteenth century (and into the early twentieth century) that probably assumed at the time that a one-time effort for the support of public education would be sufficient. In short, there was no attempt to control directly or indirectly the state education function or to regulate public education through a federal agency.

This initial federal educational policy of grants distribution and administration lasted over 130 years, to be amended somewhat by federal land grants for a specific purpose (Morrill Act for higher education) rather than general education support. In all fairness to the federal government, the "hands off" land distribution approach resulted in the "squandering of a heritage" as states failed to realize the full financial potential from the land grants for education.

To repeat, it is helpful to differentiate between the original federal educational policy statement which recognized education as the function of the states, which remains intact today, and the changing and inconsistent targeting and distribution policies of federal education funds. Although it began late in the nineteenth century but in a limited way, the twentieth century is characterized by direct and continuing monetary federal grants to education and the abandonment of land grants or the so-called permanent endowments. This was a significant "education-funds-distribution-policy" shift because: money was distributed, it introduced the concept of annual or continuing (as opposed to one time only) federal contributions, it stipulated a specific purpose or category for funds awarded, and the funds allocated carried additional "strings" (as opposed to the initial "no-strings" distribution polcy). It signaled the beginning of federal categorical education aids targeted on a specific dimension of education. During the early twentieth century vocational education and home economics were the initial beneficiaries of the change in "education-funds-distribution-policies." By the middle of the twentieth century other programs in the public schools such as mathematics, science, counseling, and bilingual education were to benefit from categorical federal aids.

The categorical aids policies allowed for a maximum of federal controls and often placed a premium on grantsmanship. They are more compatible with regulatory functions than with leadership. The federal bureaucracy becomes heavily involved in local educational operations. The maze of regulations, or bureaucratic red tape, leads to the publication of books on how to find your way around the jungle of federal educational grants, seminars on how to write federal educational proposals, and the employment of the "federal grantsman" or person with special proposal writing and marketing skills.

The federal government cannot issue mandates or control directly local, intermediate, or state school operations. It may, however, seek to achieve the same through indirect means such as offering special or additional funding through competitive grants proposals. The present-day crisis in federal relations with education stems in large part from the multiplicity of federal grants, the tremendous paperwork and personnel costs generated at the local and state levels to procure or report on federal grants, the irritations that stem from inconsistent bureaucratic monitoring and auditing, the uncertainty of continuation and often tardiness of recent federal grants to education, and so on.

Perhaps an indication of another type of policy problem is related to the extent to which the federal government should be involved in one or more dimensions of the state systems of education. It is clear that by 1965, at the latest, the federal government embarked upon an activist role in public education. Although the Great Depression of the 1930s demonstrated that the federal government would act in times of economic crisis to assist schools, it did so in more indirect ways. It was not until after 1960 that public schools were being perceived as instruments of national policies not intimately related to the instructional or broader educational functions. Some in the federal government began to perceive the public schools as instruments of the national social and economic welfare policies. The schools were to be one of the major means for breaking the harsh cycle of

poverty that entrapped many, as well as for helping overcome the divisiveness inherent in racial conflict and segregation. Such policies and perceptions made the public schools more controversial and impacted negatively upon the prime educational functions as funds were diverted from instructional to social and other noninstructional activities. The social and economic "revolutions" of past decades, stimulated in part by federal court decisions and legislative actions, impacted heavily upon public education as many social problems were brought to the schoolhouse door.

The federal activist posture with reference to education led to substantially increased annual contributions for the support of a variety of educational programs. As late as 1964–1965 federal contributions to the revenue receipts of public education comprised only 3.8 percent of the total for public education. The most dramatic jump in the history of federal educational contributions occurred with the passage of ESEA, for federal funds accounted for 7.9 percent of the total revenue receipts for public education in 1965–1966. Federal contributions climbed further and hovered around 9 percent of all school revenues during most of the 1970s. "Federal sources accounted for just under 10 percent of public school revenues in 1979, but this was more than twice the proportion in 1960."[19]

Federal grants to elementary and secondary education remained below $1 billion annually through 1965. In 1966 they jumped to almost $2.5 billion, due in large part to the passage of the ESEA. This was a portent of things to come because the federal contributions to the public schools exceeded $7 billion, but a change in the presidency suggested that at least a slowing down if not reduction was in store for the early 1980s. Federal funds for all types of educational activities including higher education, veterans' education benefits, special programs, the public schools, and so on, reached almost $34 billion in 1980.

The presidency of Ronald Reagan began in 1981 with a strong declaration that a reversal in the previous pattern of continuing escalation of federal expenditures in general and for education in particular was necessary. This was followed by reductions in federal contributions to educational programs for fiscal year 1981 by about 10 to 15 percent below that for the previous year. A switch from federal categorical aids to block grants for education was implemented. The rapid annual increase in federal funds for education that started in 1966 was arrested in the early 1980s. Some called the reversal which started during the Reagan Administration the "new federalism," a concept that called for lesser federal involvement and contributions to local functions, but with seemingly more attention to state concerns and funding mechanisms.

Whatever happens to the magnitude of federal funding during the 1980s it will not change the fact that the federal government is a partner in the delivery of quality educational services. The public schools would be unable to meet the challenges of the rest of this century or what lies ahead in the twenty-first century without the federal government increasing its contributions to equal at least one-third of the revenues required to provide quality and comprehensive educational services. If schools are to be part of a strategy related to the realization of national social and economic welfare policies, then federal contributions to education will have to be even greater.

The manner in which federal resources are shared or distributed is of no less importance. The initial federal allocations to education are worth emulating in spirit, but with some modifications, to help relieve the massive paperwork and bureaucracy demanded under the existing system of federal funds distribution

THE U.S. OFFICE OF EDUCATION AND THE U.S. DEPARTMENT OF EDUCATION

Although many different federal agencies (about 11 U.S. Departments and 15 other agencies or units) are involved in some type of educational support or program activities, the U.S. Office of Education was (until the Department of Education was created in 1980) the primary channel through which the federal government demonstrated its commitment, leadership, and cooperation with education. Until the Department of Education became operational in mid-1980 it was the only federal agency whose sole concern was for all aspects of the nation's educational systems.

In March 1967, the Office of Education (OE) celebrated its 100th birthday. Henry Barnard, the first Commissioner, had an 1867 salary of $4,000, a staff of three clerks, and a total budget of $18,592. Congress did not seem overly impressed with what was then called the "Department of Education," for they reduced Barnard's salary and his already minimal staff. From these humble beginnings, and after much controversy, OE grew to about 3800 employees and annual expenditures under its control of more than $11.2 billion in 1980. The biggest growth occurred after 1965, for the OE expenditures climbed from $872 million to over $2 billion in the space of one year.

Development and Functions of the Office of Education

In 1838, Henry Barnard, then Commissioner of Education from Connecticut, came to Washington in search of reliable facts about the nation's school system. He found none, and for the next 30 years dedicated himself to the establishment of a federal education agency. Almost every national education meeting of any importance at that time gave attention to the need for creating a federal office of education which would be the official agency for the exchange of educational information among the states, for diffusing knowledge of the science and art of education, and for organizing and administering education.[20] These early educational leaders contemplated an office which would not only collect and report educational information, but also make comparative studies of schools and school systems in this country.

Activities and discussions among educational leaders culminated in 1866 in a request for the creation of a national bureau of education. James A. Garfield, then Representative from the state of Ohio, presented a bill to establish a "department of education." The bill was passed and President Andrew Johnson signed it, creating the Department of Education on March 2, 1867.

The historic purposes of what was then known as the Department of Education and later the Office of Education were:

1. "Collecting such statistics and facts as shall show the condition and progress of education in the several States and Territories"
2. "Diffusing such information respecting the organization and management of schools and school systems, and methods of teaching, as shall aid the people of the United States in the establishment and maintenance of efficient school systems"
3. "Otherwise [promoting] the cause of education throughout the country"

The Commissioner of Education was appointed by the U.S. President, with the advice and consent of the Senate, and was to "present annually to Congress a report embodying the results of his investigations and labors" and prepare "a statement of the several grants of land made by Congress to promote education."[21]

Nine days after President Johnson signed the act creating the Department of Education, he appointed Henry Barnard as the first U.S. Commissioner of Education, a post which Barnard held until 1870. Even though it was known as a Department of Education, the Commissioner was not a member of the president's cabinet and was never intended to be one.

The original draft of the bill presented by Garfield called for the establishment of a "bureau of education" in the Department of the Interior. In 1868 the new department was attached to the Department of the Interior and officially given the status of a bureau, although it was named "office" rather than "bureau" of education. In 1929 the title Office of Education was adopted once again.

The reorganization of government agencies in 1939 transferred the Office of Education, its functions and personnel, to the Federal Security Agency. On April 11, 1953, when the Department of Health, Education, and Welfare (DHEW) superseded the Federal Security Agency, the Office of Education became one unit in this department.

The Office of Education focused primarily on the responsiblities and functions assigned it by the original act: collecting and disseminating statistics and facts and "promoting the cause of education," up until the late 1950s. Additional responsibilities were added to the historic functions by various acts of Congress or executive order. To illustrate, the conduct of educational and relief work among the natives of Alaska was administered under the Office of Education from 1887 until 1931, when it was transferred to the Office of Indian Affairs. During World War I the Office of Education received appropriations to carry on such war-related educational activities as school gardens, social studies, and the Americanization of immigrants.

During World War II several extensive training programs enrolling more than 14 million people were instituted. The Federal Board for Vocational Education, established in 1917 to administer the Smith-Hughes Act, was transferred to the Department of the Interior in 1933 and later to the Office of Education. The large-scale programs for handling surplus property of the federal government were assigned to the office as well.

The acquisition cost of personal property of the federal government transferred to educational institutions during a more recent ten-year period, 1962 to 1971, was in excess of $2.4 billion, or more than double that for the earlier ten-year period. The estimated fair value of such property at the time of transfer was less than 10 percent of its acquisition cost.

The Office of Education performed its work through

1. Publishing research findings, studies, and survey reports.
2. Participating in conferences.
3. Lectures and writing.
4. Consultation and field work.
5. Contracting with colleges, universities, state departments of education, and others that conduct research.
6. Administering grant funds as stipulated by Congress.
7. Preparing guidelines covering conditions to qualify for federal funds.

Stated another way, functions of the office included:

1. Publishing educational information.
2. Establishing cooperative working relations with agencies and groups interested in education.
3. Engaging in educational research.
4. Providing leadership, consultative, and clearing-house services related to education.

It did not directly administer public education anywhere in the United States; other government agencies do.

During the 1960s and thereafter OE became more of a grant-dispensing than statistics-gathering and publications agency. Its influence grew with the size of federal funds disbursed. Its guidelines for disbursing grants made it more controversial as well. The five largest programs administered by the OE in the decade prior to its termination in 1980 were ESEA, Higher Education Act, assistance to schools in federally affected areas, Vocational Education Acts, and NDEA. Each new decade in the post-World War II period brought to OE new federal program priorities and a greater magnitude of federal funding for administration and distribution.

The U.S. Commissioner of Education

The list of those who served as the U.S. Commissioner of Education started with Henry Barnard (1867–1870) and includes some of the most distinguished educators in the United States. The others were John Eaton (1870–1886), N. H. R. Dawson (1886–1889), William T. Harris (1889–1906), Elmer E. Brown (1906–1911), Philander P. Claxton (1911–1921), John James Tigert (1921–1928), William John Cooper (1929–1933), George F. Zook (1933–1934), John W. Studebaker (1934–1948), Earl James McGrath (1949–1953), Lee M. Thurston (July 2 to September 1, 1953), Samuel Miller Brownell (1953–1956), Lawrence G. Derthick (1956–1961), Sterling M. McMurin (1961–1962), Francis Keppel (1962–1965), Harold Howe II (1965–1969), James E. Allen, Jr. (1969–1970), Sidney P. Marland, Jr. (1970–1972), John R. Ottina (1973–1974), Terrel H. Bell (1974–1976), Edward Aguire (1976–1977), Ernest L. Boyer (1977–1979), and the last was William L. Smith (December 1979 to May 1980). The commissioner position was terminated when the new Department of Education became operational. There were 23 different men (no women) who served as Commissioner during the 113 year history of the U.S. Office of Education. Mary Berry, then Assistant Secretary for Education in HEW, did serve as Acting Commissioner for a brief period of 30 days, the maximum period allowed for holding two federal executive positions at one time.

The shortest term for a Commissioner of Education was two months, caused by the death of the incumbent soon after assuming office, and the longest was the 18 years enjoyed by William T. Harris. The most rapid turnover rate took place during the 1970s when six different persons held the office.

The commissioner was responsible for formulating policy, administering the various dimensions of the OE, and coordinating educational activities at the national level. The major functions were:

1. To determine policy and program objectives.
2. To provide executive leadership for operations.
3. To render consultative services to educational agencies.
4. To coordinate office work with related programs within the Department of Health, Education, and Welfare.
5. To establish liaison with executive, legislative, and judicial branches of the government.
6. To advise national, state, and local officials and international bodies on educational problems.[22]

The commissioner was also an ex-officio member of the District of Columbia Commission on Licensure, an ex-officio representative on the Board of Foreign Scholarships, and the governmental representative on the U.S. National Commission for UNESCO.

NATIONAL INSTITUTES FOR EDUCATION

In 1970 President Nixon proposed the creation of the National Institutes for Education (NIE) as a new federal agency. Established in July 1972, it was almost a year later before NIE was an operational reality. Its first budget, a modest $142 million for fiscal year 1973, turned out to be its largest even though $110 million was new appropriations and $32 million was transferred to NIE from the budgets of other agencies.

National Institutes for Education inherited an assortment of ongoing research and development programs as well as personnel that were previously a part of OE. The Institute Director, like the OE Commissioner, was a presidential appointee. NIE was considered to be parallel to the OE and was within the Department of Health, Education, and Welfare.

Its primary focus was research and the development of research in education. The Cooperative Research Act that was administered within OE from its humble beginnings in the 1950s became an almost $100 million effort. The early years were difficult for NIE, for many in the U.S. Senate were said to be disappointed by NIE's lack of direction and action. Its budgets were slashed below requests made and as late as fiscal 1980 only a total of $91 million was approved. NIE became a part of the new U.S. Department of Education in 1980, thus ending its brief and stormy existence as an independent federal agency concerned with a special focus in education.

THE CREATION AND EARLY HISTORY OF THE U.S. DEPARTMENT OF EDUCATION

Over 100 formal bills had been presented to Congress in the space of 70 years to establish a cabinet level U.S. Department of Education. The early but persistent efforts failed for a variety of reasons. Success finally came in 1979 when the bill to create the thirteenth U.S. Department of Education passed easily in the Senate on April 30, 1979, but with bitter debate and only after defeating many attempts to attach crippling amendments on a very close House vote on July 11, 1979. It was signed into law by President Carter on October 17, 1979, who declared upon that occasion that education was the "biggest single national investment" and the creation of the Department of Education the "best move for quality of life in America for the future." Less than two weeks later, Carter nominated a then California-based federal judge, Shirley M. Hufstedler, to be the first Secretary of the newly approved Education Department. Mrs. Hufstedler won quick confirmation from the Senate on November 30, 1979, and was sworn in to be the first Secretary of Education on December 6, 1979, pending the formal start of the Department scheduled for May 1980.

Much credit for success after 100 defeats belongs to President Carter who followed through on a 1976 presidential campaign promise to create a new Education Department and also to the National Education Association that endorsed Carter's presidential bid in part because of his views on the need for a Department of Education. It was the first time in history the NEA entered partisan politics; it continued to support Carter's reelection bid in 1980 as well. The NEA-led supporters for the Department's establishment totaled some 140 organizations. The American Federation of Teachers, however, orchestrated whatever professional and other opposition to a new department it could muster.

Partisan politics that helped give birth to the thirteenth federal Department of Education was responsible in part for its stormy initial years and helped cast doubt as to how long the new department might survive. Whether or not Ronald Reagan's stand, as the 1980 Republican presidential nominee, was influenced by the NEA's open and active support of his opponent may be debated, but it is clear that Reagan pledged to abolish the new Department of Education (as well as another new Department of Energy) if elected. There were questions following the Republican presidential election victory in November 1980 whether a regular or acting Secretary of Education would be appointed. The last cabinet appointment by President Reagan in January 1981 was that of Dr. Terrel H. Bell to serve as the second Secretary of Education, but in a full and not acting capacity. Dr. Bell is a professional educator with considerable administrative experience at the local, state, federal, and univeristy education levels. He was serving as the Utah Commissioner of Higher Education at the time of the presidential appointment to Secretary of Education. He also served in previous years as Associate Commissioner and later Commissioner of the U.S. Office of Education (1974–1976).

The first Secretary of Education served for about eight months after formal operations began or a little over one year after being sworn into office. The second secretary was in office at this writing (1983), but doubts as to how long the position would remain at the cabinet level came early in 1982. In his first "State of the Union" message to Congress on January 26, 1982, President Reagan reiterated his intent to "dismantle" the Department of Education (and Energy as well). In a nationwide address, the President acknowledged his campaign pledge and stated: ". . . education is the principal responsibility of local school systems, teachers, parents, citizens boards and State governments. By eliminating the Department of Education . . . we can . . . ensure that local needs and preferences rather than the wishes of Washington determine the education of our children." The President's 1983 Fiscal Year Budget submitted in February 1982 provided no funds for the operation of the Department of Education after September 30, 1982. In its place and to start on October 1, 1982 (the beginning date for the federal 1983 fiscal year) was to be a noncabinet-level federal education agency called the National Foundation for Education Assistance. Its director would be appointed by the President and subject to confirmation by the Senate as well. A number of other alternatives to a Department of Education were reviewed as well. By mid-1982 there were many rumors of the impending resignation of the second of the Secretaries of Education, with some being led by those of the far right political persuasion who sought someone "more diligent for the immediate dismantling of the Depart-

ment of Education." None of the changes occurred and the department continued through all of 1982 and 1983.

Reagan was following through on his campaign pledge to disestablish the new Department of Education, but a great deal of reluctance was evident in Congress and the issue was shelved. There remains a strong likelihood that the cabinet-level federal Education Department may be able to survive the early doubts. It is clear that a dramatic political presidential power shift cast a shadow on the fledgling department.

When the department was created, about 120 of its 152 programs were simply transfers from the education division of what was previously known as the Department of Health, Education, and Welfare. The remainder came from five other federal departments. Some science programs were transferred from the National Science Foundation (which some say was the model for the proposed National Education Assistance Agency that was to replace the "dismantled Education Department"). It started out relatively large, the seventh largest in terms of total federal expenditures. Its initial budget was about $12 billion. There were supposed to be about 17,350 employees during the first year, with a large number being the teachers and administrators in the Overseas Dependent Schools (reputed to be the sixth largest school system "in" the United States) that were, and after final deliberations and negotiations (particularly after the efforts to dismantle the new department) came to remain as, a part of the Department of Defense. Reductions in positions came quickly with the elimination of 500 positions in the new Department by the end of the first year. In response to the Education Consolidation and Improvement Act of 1981, the Secretary of Education eliminated "30 sets of regulations that required 200,000 pages of grant applications, 7,000 pages of financial reports, and 20,000 pages of programmatic reports annually." The recommended 1983 budget was about $9.95 billion, of which $8.8 billion was to be for the recommended "Education Foundation" which was to replace, but didn't, the Department of Education, with the rest transferred for education programs handled in other departments or agencies. The 1983 staff level dropped to 4800, or 1400 fewer than in fiscal year 1981; this does not include the very large number of staff in the Overseas Dependent Schools that remained, or "went back," to the Department of Defense.

The economic reality facing federal departments and agencies as the result of Reagan's effort to reduce the size of the federal government should be kept separate from the political battles related to the survival of the thirteenth Education Department. Whether or not yet another new federal education structure is created, the intent of the Reagan administration was to "reduce intrusions" of the federal government in local and state educational operations as well as to limit federal authority to "regulate strictly to what is legally required or necessary." The intent is to abolish regional educational offices, terminate 23 existing federal education programs of low priority, and repeal 11 "unnecessary federal boards and commissions." Under the present education configuration, the Secretary of Education does get to see the president far more often than the Commissioner of Education could gain the ear of former secretaries of HEW. The United States was about the only nation without a prestigious national office or ministry of education until the thirteenth Department of Education was created. This new department does have potential to serve as a better mechanism for assisting in the formulation and the subsequent formulation of national education policies on targeting and distributing funds for federally related educational activities.

The present Department of Education was born of many struggles and remains locked in many battles at present. It was the result of compromises. One may expect changes within it during the years ahead. The magnitude of federal expenditures in education may be seen by a review of Table 10.2. The creation of a new department has not only not resulted in an immediate increase in federal expenditures for education during the 1980s, but it was also unable to prevent substantial reductions in federal education expenditures during the early 1980s.

To summarize, the continuation of the thirteenth Department of Education remains in doubt, but it represents a hope, and what it may become or accomplish is unknown as yet.

SUMMARY

There were some among the founding fathers who sought to establish a national system of education, but public education emerged as a state function. The role of the national government in public education has generated much controversy; nonetheless, its contributions have made a significant impact upon education.

Federal concern for public education started with the federal land grants in the early 1800s, although its roots go back further in history. Federal involvement came in fits and spurts, and substantial time delays between major actions were common until after World War II.

The Morrill Act of 1862 signaled a shift in federal policy with conditional land grants. Monetary grants to public secondary education came with the Smith-Hughes Act for Vocational Education in 1917. The Depression years saw what started as welfare activities turn into educational activities. The CCC and NYA had a profound impact on education. The CWA, FERA, WPA, and PWA helped to build and remodel school plants. The only permanent federal aids for public schools that originated as relief measures during the 1930s were the school lunch acts. The GI bills, the NDEA, the Vocational Education Act of 1963, the ESEA, the Job Corps, the Higher Education Act, Education for All Handicapped Children Act, and the Department of Education Organization Act help to demonstrate the activist role of the federal government in education during the past three decades. The ESEA was a landmark act that greatly increased the annual federal contributions to education measured presently in many billions, whereas before it was usually less than $1 billion. The 1980s began with a strong indication that there would be a reversal in the prior trend of escalating federal expenditures for education and other purposes.

TABLE 10.2

FEDERAL ASSISTANCE FOR EDUCATION PROGRAMS (IN THOUSANDS OF DOLLARS), 1950–1981

Federal agency	1950–1951	1956–1957	1966–1967	1972–1973	1980–1981 Est.
Department of Health, Education, and Welfare (including Office of Education)	$ 111,370	$ 457,277	$4,125,500	$ 6,413,491	$13,526,629c
Department of Agriculture	171,154	398,399	119,500a	1,517,254	3,931,429
Department of Commerce	5,292	2,884	18,100	10,309	—
Department of Defenseb	27,807	73,216	1,534,200	1,078,204	1,657,323
Department of Housing and Urban Development	—	—	600	159,121	8,405
Department of Interior	45,834	90,794	199,600	287,392	497,077
Department of Justice	389	530	8,100	47,589	15,556
Department of Labor	3,927	5,940	403,000	1,594,000	7,000,237
Department of State	—	47,751	61,900	45,215	14,281
Department of Transportation	—	—	25,800	16,140	38,110
Department of Treasury	1,800	3,350	—	1,760	11,680
Veterans Administration	2,120,216	813,955	431,800	2,177,862	2,087,347
Appalachian Regional Development Commission	—	—	—	40,700	24,539
Atomic Energy Commission	18,908	30,717	14,400	9,695	—
National Science Foundation	—	34,952	199,800	58,600	—
Agency for International Development	—	—	204,600	140,529	73,410
Library of Congress	—	—	34,300	74,300	200,975
National Foundation for the Arts and Humanities	—	—	12,000	47,029	—
National Aeronautics and Space Administration	—	—	21,200	6,225	—
Office of Economic Opportunity	—	—	929,300	275,637	—
Research and Development (all federal agencies)	—	—	—	2,770,464	6,310,000
Smithsonian Institutions	—	—	19,200	60,000	151,709
U.S. Information Agency	—	—	7,600	2,227	—
Other (District of Columbia Schools, EPA, Government Printing Office, etc.)	5,132	8,481	96,500	119,113	434,983
Totals	$2,511,829	$1,968,246	$8,467,000	$16,952,856	$35,983,690

Source: Adapted from C. D. Hutchins, A. R. Munse, and E. D. Booher, *Federal Funds for Education 1958–1959 and 1959–1960*, U.S. Office of Education, Bull. 1961, No. 14, Washington, D.C.: GPO, 1961, pp. 14–17. 1966–1967 data based on data compiled by A. R. Munse for the U.S. Office of Education publication, *Digest of Education Statistics* 1971; 1972–1973 data from *Digest* for 1978; and 1980–1981 data from *Digest* for 1981.

aDoes not include $448 million for school lunch program.
bIncludes Canal Zone assistance.
cDHEW divided after 1980 into Department of Health and Human Services ($1.657 billion in education assistance in 1980–1981) and Department of Education ($11.64 billion in education expenditures in 1980–1981).

Although the initial national educational policy, enunciated over 200 years ago, recognized education as a state function, there is presently no long-term or consistent federal policy on public education related to federal funds distribution patterns or federal targeted support areas. At first the federal government distributed lands for the support of education in general with no strings attached. This "policy" lasted about 75 years until the Morrill Act. Monetary federal grants dominated during the twentieth century, whereas land grants for education prevailed during the prior century. Such annual grants were targeted specifically for some dimension of public education and had other strings attached. The categorical aids policies of the twentieth century maximized federal controls and placed a premium on grantsmanship.

Federal contributions totaled only 3.8 percent of revenue receipts for public education in 1964–1965 and presently account for just under 10 percent of that total. To meet future challenges schools will require a federal contribution of about one-third of the revenues needed to provide quality and comprehensive educational services.

For 113 years the U.S. Office of Education was the single most important federal education agency. It was replaced by the cabinet level Department of Education in 1980. Its historic purposes included collection of national statistics on education, diffusing such information, and promoting the cause of education. Its chief executive was the Commissioner of Education who was appointed by the U.S. President. Twenty-three men, and only one woman as an acting commissioner, served as commissioners during the 113-year period.

The most rapid turnover and briefest tenures were noted in the 1960s and 1970s.

The National Institutes for Education were created in 1973 and most research thrusts were removed from the U.S. Office of Education thereby. The early years were very difficult ones for the NIE with its frequent budget reductions. This agency lost its independent status in 1980 when it was placed within the newly created Department of Education.

The passage of bills in the House and Senate during 1979 led to the creation of the thirteenth federal and cabinet level Department of Education. Much of the credit belongs to President Carter and the NEA. The partisan politics that helped to create this new department also contributed to its survival problems after Republicans gained the presidency. The first Secretary of Education was Shirley M. Hufstedler, who served for about a year or so. The second was Dr. Terrel H. Bell, a former U.S. Commissioner of Education, who was appointed in January 1981.

Most of the 152 programs transferred to the Department of Education when it officially began operation in May 1980 were from the USOE. The new department is the seventh largest and remains in a state of flux. Its continuation seems assured at least for the next few years.

Only about 32 percent of all federal monies for education were channeled through the U.S. Office of Education and not much more is likely to be dispensed through the new Department of Education. Thus far, federal efforts in education appear to react more to pressures of the moment than to carefully considered long-term trends.

NOTES

1. Ellwood P. Cubberley, *Public Education in the United States,* rev. ed., Boston: Houghton Mifflin, 1934, p. 739.
2. Charles A. Quattlebaum, *Federal Educational Activities and Educational Issues Before Congress,* 82nd Congress, 2nd Session, House Document No. 423, Washington, D.C.: GPO, 1952, p. 27.
3. Ibid., p. 26.
4. Ibid.
5. Edgar W. Knight, *Readings in Educational Administration,* New York: Holt, Rinehart and Winston, 1953, p. 458.
6. Fletcher H. Swift, *Federal and State Policies in Public School Finance in the United States,* Boston: Ginn, 1931, p. 6.

7. L. M. Thurston and W. H. Roe, *State School Administration,* New York: Harper & Row, 1957, p. 56.

8. Arvid J. Burke, *Financing Public Schools in the United States,* rev. ed., New York: Harper & Row, 1957, p. 241.

9. A. R. Munse and E. D. Booher, *Federal Funds for Education 1956–57 and 1957–58,* U.S. Office of Education, Bulletin 1959, No. 2, Washington, D.C.: GPO, 1959, p. 3.

10. Quattlebaum, op. cit., p. 27.

11. Swift, op. cit., p. 59.

12. Ibid., p. 61.

13. E. L. Morphet, R. L. Johns, and T. L. Reller, *Educational Administration,* 2nd ed., Englewood Cliffs, N.J.: Prentice-Hall, 1967, p. 217.

14. C. H. Moore, "The National Defense Education Act After 18 Months," *School Life,* Vol. 42, No. 6, February 1960, pp. 29–35.

15. James J. Vanecko and Nancy L. Ames, *Who Benefits from Federal Education Dollars?,* Cambridge, Mass.: Abt Books, 1980, p. 15.

16. Ibid. p. 3.

17. Ibid., p. 16.

18. Quattlebaum, op. cit., p. 25.

19. N. B. Dearman and V. W. Plisko, eds., *The Condition of Education,* 1982 ed., Washington, D.C.: GPO, 1982, p. 40.

20. Lloyd E. Blauch, "To Promote the Cause of Education," *School Life,* Vol. 35, May–June 1953, pp. 2–3.

21. Ibid., quotations are taken from the original act.

22. U.S. Office of Education, *Handbook of Office of Education,* OE-11002, Washington, D.C., 1972, p. 14.

CHAPTER REVIEW QUESTIONS

1. Trace the significant federal activities with respect to education beginning with the actions of the Continental Congress to the present.
2. Why were there few important federal contributions to public education for over 100 years following the historic federal land grants to education?
3. Why was the tenure of the U.S. Office of Education's Commissioner of Education so brief and the turnover so great during the 1960s and 1970s?
4. What factors led to the establishment of a cabinet level Department of Education in 1979?

5. Why is it necessary for the federal government to continue to exhibit an interest in and provide support for public education?
6. Why has the federal involvement in education during the past two decades particularly provoked so much controversy and criticism?
7. Should all federal education funds be channeled through the newly created Department of Education? Justify your stand.
8. What should be the national policy with reference to public education?

SELECTED REFERENCES

American Association of School Administrators, *The Federal Government and the Public Schools,* Washington, D.C.: The Association, 1965.

Educational Policies Commission, National Education Association, *Federal Financial Relationships to Educators,* Washington, D.C.: The Association, 1967.

Finn, Charles E., "What the NIE Can Be," *Phi Delta Kappan,* February 1972, pp. 347–351.

Vanecko, J. J., and Ames, N. L., *Who Benefits from Federal Education Dollars?,* Cambridge, Mass.: Abt Books, 1980.

11

JUDICIAL BRANCHES OF GOVERNMENTS AND THEIR IMPACTS UPON SCHOOL OPERATIONS AND MANAGEMENT

Previous chapters described the contributions as well as impact of the executive and legislative branches of state and federal governments on operations and administration of local school systems. Special agencies and departments were created and grew rapidly as the state and federal educational roles and contributions increased. The state and federal educational personnel and programs housed within specially designed units can be called an "infrastructure" to enhance the capabilities of central education agencies to distribute educational funds to local school systems, to monitor progress toward realization of program objectives, as well as to audit compliance with mandated regulations and policies. In short, the creation and existence of infrastructures within the executive or administrative branches of state and federal governments enable these units to satisfy their obligations with reference to education.

The judicial branches of these governments, however, lack the infrastructure, or personnel organized in bureaucratic mechanisms, to administer state or federal grants and programs. The judiciary has more difficulty in ascertaining on a current basis whether mandates are being pursued with the diligence decreed. Yet, in spite of this organic or structural deficiency for follow-through, the judicial branches of state and federal governments have a significant influence on the operation and administration of practically every dimension of public education.

It is a most unusual type of influence or stimulation, for the judicial branches cannot pass legislation, have no funds to distribute to schools (but have authority to demand that other units do so), and have limited personnel to implement decisions decreed. Furthermore, the courts do not take the initiative to identify those acting contrary to laws. They may accept complaints brought to their jurisdiction, reject them, receive evidence, hear arguments, and then render a decision. With all the limitations noted, state and federal courts managed to shape to a considerable degree the course of public education in the United States. The influences are so great that some refer to the U.S. Supreme Court as the "National Board of Education."

The tremendous increase in court actions involving public schools suggests we live in a litigious society where people are unafraid of instigating court actions. It creates a unique climate for educational administration. During the past two decades, educational administrators came to expect being named personally in court actions or as the chief school executive and representative of a local school district. Prior to 1960 the typical school district was not likely to employ a full-time legal staff or expend much during a year on legal fees. That is less true today.

Education cases clogged state and federal court calendars during the 1970s. Educational journals feature court decisions on school issues, and daily newspapers in the districts involved report the same on page one, right-hand column. There are books of substantial size and quality dedicated to the legal ramifications of public education.[1] This chapter summarizes a few significant decisions, outlines some major trends, and reviews the impact of the judicial branches on educational administration and operations.

TRENDS IN THE UTILIZATION OF STATE AND FEDERAL COURTS

The legal status of the school district was indicated in a previous chapter. It is a quasi-municipality; that is, it is a special type of public municipal corporation with authority limited to those necessary for the discharge of its public education responsibilities. School board members of a local district are officers of this corporation. Educational administrators are not corporate officers unless the state law specifically declares to the contrary. Members acting at a duly called board meeting obtain their legal authority and control over public school operations from the state, which is the plenary source of powers. Legal disputes may arise when board members, knowingly or otherwise, make decisions or take other actions on matters of school attendance or admission, regulation of pupil behavior that brings "pupil rights" in question, regulation of teacher or administra-

tor behaviors in and out of school, contracts that bind the district, and so on, that exceed the authority delegated by the state or that deprive someone of rights guaranteed by state and/or federal constitutions or statutes. Litigation is the response from those who feel that a school board or any of the board's administrative or other agents exceeded legal authorities or breached the rights of others.

For much of history, school board decisions, or those of the board's recognized agents such as school administrators, were seldom questioned. The past two decades witnessed a reversal of this traditional unquestioning acceptance of the decisions of those in recognized educational decision-making positions. Perhaps the opposite extreme has been reached, for some may feel that practically anything a school board, superintendent, principal, or other administrator decides deserves legal scrutiny by some court. This may be an exaggeration to dramatize more recent events. It is not an exaggeration to declare that school boards, administrators, teachers, and other professional personnel operate in a very sensitive and complex legal environment that prompts caution and request for legal counsel before a final decision is reached on a controversial issue.

Delon noted that prior to 1960 there was a propensity to turn to state courts in teacher/school board and student rights disputes.[2] During the past two decades similar issues were more likely to be decided by federal courts, with a focus on constitutional grounds rather than on statutory interpretations. In most such cases, except where there was clear abuse of authority, the state courts in past years tended to support the legal authority of the school board and refused to substitute the judgment of the courts for that of the local board. This was particularly true in student behavior control cases, for state courts did not wish to undermine the disciplinary authority of school officials and, therefore, tended to rule against objecting students and parents who initiated the legal challenges. During the past two decades, however, the issue of "student control" became one of "student rights" instead and the cases were brought to the attention of federal courts. What school officials interpreted as "student privileges," the students perceived as "student rights." Furthermore, federal courts demonstrated more concern over alleged transgression of personal rights than for supporting the disciplinary authority of school officials.

A similar trend toward greater utilization of federal courts was noted in teacher behavior disputes. In commenting on the increased tendency of teachers to seek relief in federal rather than state courts, Delon related the marked change "with the federal court's recognition of the teacher's civil and constitutional rights and with the extensive federal civil rights legislation of the 1970s."[3] Dismissed teachers found it relatively easy to introduce complaints to federal courts, there was a relatively high probability of collecting damages or gaining reinstatement through actions related to the Civil Rights Act of 1971, and professional education associations were willing to support litigations by members with direct and substantial legal or financial assistance.[4]

The famous *Brown* v. *Board of Education* (1954) was a well-known landmark case in the battle to end school segregation and for other reasons as well. As Glazer noted, "It is no accident that *Brown* v. *Board of Education,* the case that opened up expansion of law into education, controversially made use of social science findings."[5] The decision that led to a substantial reshaping of public education operations was remarkable in that it probed the effects of some patterns of delivering educational services which took the courts beyond the more traditional legal arguments on precedents and opinions of legal scholars into the realm of recommendations, social scientists, and arguments on what is appropriate social policy. The result was a revolutionary change in the relationship between law and social policy, with the schools being among the social institutions that early felt the full impact of this change in legal posture. Some of the more activist jurists of the 1970s went beyond rendering decisions and sought to influence directly daily operations of a local school system, as happened in Cleveland, Ohio, or demanded frequent periodic reporting from a school district following a court decision to determine whether its edicts were being obeyed. Many school systems during the past two decades operated under extensive and frequent monitoring by courts for varying periods of time.

In a nation committed to local control of education and where public education is a function of the state, it may be difficult to understand how the U.S. Supreme Court came to exert the influence it has upon the structuring and operation of systems of public education. This deserves further and more careful analysis.

THE U.S. SUPREME COURT AND EDUCATION

The U.S. Supreme Court is the ultimate interpreter of the U.S. Constitution wherein are defined the rights and privileges of all citizens of the nation. The Court has not allowed the manner in which public schools are organized, administered, or operated to infringe upon or abridge in any way the civil rights of any person regardless of age. In fulfilling its role as the protector of the fundamental human rights guaranteed under the U.S. Constitution, the Supreme Court, through its many decisions and mandates, has had a more dramatic impact upon public education than have the federal legislative and executive branches. Educational operations provide the setting for testing fundamental constitutional issues such as the relation between church and state, impairment of contracts, freedom of speech, due process of law, and rights of citizens for equal protection under the law no matter where they reside in the nation or in a state. Spurlock's[6] review of 45 decisions of the U.S. Supreme Court dealing with education, and analyses of others since his review, indicate that one-third of the cases dealt with constitutional issues requiring interpretation of the First Amendment to the U.S. Constitution, another third with issues related to the meaning of the Fifth and Fourteenth Amendments, and the remaining third with questions of state or federal powers or functions. It remanded to lower courts or refused to review cases where there were no fundamental constitutional issues. The U.S. Supreme Court does not infringe upon the educational policymaking authority of the legislative branches; it has not declared unconstitutional the concept of education as a function of the state. It interprets educational policies set by others to determine their relationships with the law of the land and the rights guaranteed to all.

Occasionally, the Court may reverse a prior position, as it did in the cases of *Plessy* v. *Ferguson* and *Minersville* v. *Gobitis.* The *Plessy* v. *Ferguson* doctrine, affirmed by the Supreme Court in 1896, determined that so long as educational facilities provided Negroes were not unequal and inferior to those used by white children, separate facilities or separate school systems did not violate any rights guaranteed to citizens under the federal Constitution. In 1954, in the case of *Brown* v. *Board of Education,* the Supreme Court ruled that maintenance of a separate school system was basically unequal and deprived children attending separate schools of rights guaranteed under the Fourteenth Amendment. In the case of *Minersville* v. *Gobitis,* the Supreme Court ruled that freedom of religious expression by members of the Jehovah's Witnesses was not abrogated by the requirement that children salute the flag of the United States as a condition of attendance. Following this decision some children were expelled when they refused to salute the flag. The Jehovah's Witnesses believed a flag to be a graven image and that saluting was a form of bowing down before such an image. Approximately five years later, in the case of *West Virginia* v. *Barnette,* the Court rescinded its earlier decision and declared that people have a right to avoid a practice accepted by others on grounds that it is a violation of their fundamental religious precepts. Thus, public education authorities may not deprive any child of fundamental religious beliefs on grounds of patriotism or what is commonly accepted by others.

Whether the federal government can participate in the financing of public education, even though no mention of education is made in the Constitution presented another set of issues to the Supreme Court. President Buchanan vetoed the Morrill Bill in 1859 on grounds that, in his opinion, Congress had no power to appropriate money raised by taxes that were levied against all the people of the United States for the purpose of educating only some of the people in the respective states. Three years later President Lincoln signed the Morrill Act into law. He evidently disagreed with the legal interpretation of his predecessor in the presidency and recognized no constitutional barrier to the donation of public lands to the several states to help establish a particular type of public institution of higher learning. The constitutionality of federal participation in support of public education has been upheld by decisions of the U.S. Supreme Court.

The *Rodriguez* case *(San Antonio Independent School Districts et al., Appellants* v. *Demetrio P. Rodriguez et al.)* decided by the U.S. Supreme Court on March 21, 1973, has been hailed by some as a significant court statement. In a split 5 to 4 decision the Court rejected the position supported by several state supreme courts that school finance systems, although chaotic and unjust, violated the equal protection clause of the Fourteenth Amendment.

Interpretations of the Fourteenth Amendment's application to educational operations and relationships with students may continue to be the focal point of litigation involving schools. The growing and controversial involvement of the federal government in education is bound to increase the number of cases brought to this tribunal from their educational setting. For example, in 1973 the U.S. Supreme Court by 6 to 3 decisions struck down efforts in New York and Pennsylvania to provide public aid to nonpublic schools by means of a tax credit to parents for tuition payments made to private schools or by means of reimbursing private schools for costs incurred in providing state required services.

In his general summary of trends in federal judicial involvement in deciding controversial education issues, McDermott observed that federal judicial power after *Brown* "loomed large"; "witnessed a considerable expansion and development of that power"; was "decisive in resolving educational disputes arising under the equal protection and due process clauses of the Fourteenth Amendment, the First Amendment protections of religion and expressions, and congressional enactments providing financial assistance to state and local educational agencies"; was expressed "in a prohibitory fashion, that is, to prevent infringement on constitutionally and statutorily created rights and interests"; and only in the case of desegregation did the Supreme Court feel it had "an affirmative duty to integrate school systems" which constituted a "judicial foray into constructive policy-making."[7] McDermott considered the Supreme Court's "affirmative duty to integrate" "not so successful as gallant," for the primary role of any court is to be a "dispute-settler" rather than to act as a "policy body."[8] McDermott was gentle in his appraisal of court involvement in school operations, a source of much controversy. A more realistic appraisal of court-dominated public school operations would show increased school operating costs, heightened confusion, greater controversy, and failure to meet initial objectives. The courts earn poor marks, even though there were only the best of intentions, for attempting to do what they were never designed to do.

RELIGION AND THE PUBLIC SCHOOLS

The First Amendment to the U.S. Constitution sought to insure religious and other personal freedoms with the declaration:

> Congress shall make no law respecting an establishment of religion or prohibiting the free exercise thereof; or abridging the freedom of speech or of the press; or of the right of the people peaceably to assemble, and to petition the government for a redress of grievances.

Interpretations and applications of this amendment to public schools focus upon mandatory prayers in public schools, public financial support of parochial schools, transportation of parochial school pupils with public tax funds, wearing of religious garb by teachers in public schools, limiting mandatory attendance to public schools only, and so on. Intense emotional feelings often surround such issues. Definitive precedents notwithstanding, there are likely to be more legal disputes on religion-related issues and the public schools. Thus, in May 1975, the U.S. Supreme Court once again struck down the state of Pennsylvania's third attempt to award substantial amounts of public support for parochial schools (*Meek* v. *Pittenger*). The Court has consistently and clearly declared that government entanglements in any aspect of religion must be avoided. This has not deterred some from continuing to design new ways of circumventing Supreme Court objections to public support of parochial school systems, but with no success thus far.

The efforts to introduce Bible reading, the saying of prayers at the opening or closing of the public school day, the convening of voluntary Bible study or distribution of religious materials on school premises, and so on, impact more directly on the day-by-day administration of public education. Board policies or the efforts of special community groups have been used to introduce such religious activities in the schools. All have been declared to be contrary to the provisions of the First Amendment.

Delon presented an excellent summary or set of generalizations with reference to church-state relations as decided by the U.S. Supreme Court. They are as follows:[9]

A state may (if permitted by the state constitution):

1. Release pupils to participate in religious instruction off school grounds (*Zorach* v. *Clausen*, 343 U.S. 306);
2. Provide transportation for pupils attending parochial schools (*Everson* v. *Board of Educ.*, 330 U.S. 1);
3. Provide books to pupils attending parochial schools (*Board of Educ.* v. *Allen*, 392 U.S. 236);
4. Provide testing and scoring service in secular subjects for pupils attending parochial schools (*Wolman* v. *Walter*, 433 U.S. 229);
5. Provide diagnostic services for pupils attending parochial schools by public school employees and by physicians who are not employees (*Wolman* v. *Walter*);

6. Provide therapeutic services for pupils attending parochial schools on a religiously neutral site (*Wolman* v. *Walter*).

A state may not:

1. Require all pupils to attend public schools (*Pierce* v. *Society of Sisters,* 268 U.S. 510);
2. Provide financial support for parochial schools (*Lemon* v. *Kurtzman*);
3. Furnish instructional materials and equipment other than books to pupils attending parochial schools (*Wolman* v. *Walter*);
4. Provide parochial school students with transportation for field trips (*Wolman* v. *Walter*);
5. Release pupils for religious instruction on school property (*McCollum* v. *Board of Educ.,* 333 U.S. 203);
6. Require recitation of a school sponsored prayer (*Engle* v. *Vitale,* 370 U.S. 421);
7. Incorporate Bible reading and repetition of the Lord's Prayer as a part of the school's curriculum (*School Dist. of Abington Twp.* v. *Schempp, Murray* v. *Curlett,* 374 U.S. 203);
8. Force pupils to salute the flag (*West Virginia State Bd. of Educ.* v. *Barnette,* 319 U.S. 624).

STUDENT ADMISSION, CONTROL, AND RIGHTS

Courts have tended to support state mandates calling for compulsory education and school attendance, which set conditions to be satisfied to gain school admission and which establish student behavior controls. Courts also place limits on some dimensions of the state's authority over students, apply the rule of reason to prevent abuses of authority, and are willing to step in to protect the constitutional rights of students. The rights of persons are not suspended because of age or the fact of attending an educational institution. The desegregation and civil rights issues are given special treatment in another section and are not reviewed here.

A student may satisfy the demands of compulsory attendance law demands by attending either a private or public school. Early in this century the now famous *Pierce* v. *Society of Sisters* assured parents the right to send their children to private instead of public schools. The other

exception to compulsory education laws came in 1972 when the U.S. Supreme Court held that the free exercise of religion prevented the state enforcement of school attendance by Amish children beyond the eighth grade (*Wisconsin* v. *Yoder,* 406 U.S. 205). Reutter and Hamilton declared this to be the exception to the rule and observed "Except for the Amish, courts have been almost uniform in denying religion-based applications for exceptions to any material parts of the compulsory education requirements."[10]

The state may, within the rule of reason, demand that certain conditions be met to gain admission to a public school such as prior vaccination, reaching a specified minimum age applicable to all, residency in a certain area or district, and so on. The number of litigations in these areas declined in recent decades.

Some sought exemption from compulsory attendance by instruction at home. To be successful in procuring an exemption on these grounds, the courts have demanded evidence of equivalency of instruction. Some states demand home instruction by a certificated teacher, and these statutory delineations of home instructional equivalence with a regular school have been sustained by the courts. States vary in the demands placed upon private schools and what constitutes equivalency of instruction.

Issues of student control, or student rights, were the most frequently litigated during the past 20 years, until issues related to handicapped students emerged during the last few years of the 1970s. Prior to the 1960s, student control disputes were resolved in state courts. As indicated earlier, state courts tended to refuse to interfere with local boards and administrators as long as enforcement was reasonable rather than arbitrary or capricious. Hudgins, as well as others, noted the "legal modification" in the autonomy of administrators during the 1960s and the propensity of judges to look beyond the fairness of the administrative decision per se and into the constitutional issues and applications to student rights.[11]

The case of *Tinker* v. *Des Moines Independent Community School District* (393 U.S. 503) began when John Tinker wore a black arm band to school to support a protest against the Viet Nam War and for a truce. School principals of the district convened and adopted a consistent district-wide school operations policy that did not allow arm bands, but each student coming to school wearing an arm band was to be given an opportunity to remove it without further prejudice. Failure to remove the arm band during school time when requested would result in suspension until the student returned without it. The U.S. District Court refused to grant the injunction requested, which would have restrained school officials from enforcing the adopted policy deemed necessary by educational administrators to prevent disruptions and maintain school discipline. This action was affirmed by the U.S. Court of Appeals only because the court was equally divided on the issue. In 1969, on a 7 to 2 decision, the U.S. Supreme Court reversed and remanded the case to the District Court with these statements which are part of the majority opinion:

> School officials do not possess absolute authority over their students. Students in school as well as out of school are "persons" under our Constitution. They are possessed of fundamental rights which the state must respect, just as they themselves must respect their obligations to the state.
> . . .
> . . . the record does not demonstrate any facts which might reasonably have led school authorities to forecast substantial disruption of or material interference with school activities, and no disturbances or disorders on the school premises in fact occurred.

School administrators must now live with the precedent-setting *Tinker* decision. There is clearly no hesitancy in bringing issues involving students to the courts, for some refer to an "avalanche" of such student cases which have been brought to the judiciary. Some current trends in judicial decisions as summarized by Hudgins are as follows:[12]

> . . . students are now permitted to dress as they wish unless there is a compelling need to restrict their dress. . . .
> The courts have protected students in allowing them to speak and to refrain from speaking. On

the first issue, the courts have found in favor of students who massed for demonstration and rallies that were peaceful and did not disrupt the school program. On the latter issue, courts have upheld students in refusal to salute the flag for a variety of reasons, primarily religious and ideological.

> . . . students have been upheld in cases testing their right to publish and disseminate material that administrators find tasteless or unrelated to education. School officials can, however, restrict libelous, obscene, or pornographic material from being published in the campus paper. . . .
> . . . . It (the Fourteenth Amendment) protects a student threatened with suspension or expulsion in that the principle of reasonableness and fairness must be exercised. . . .
> Courts have consistently ruled that a discipline hearing is an administrative conference, not a courtroom trial. . . .
> Courts have also consistently ruled that school officials can discipline students. Even corporal punishment is not disallowed unless it is otherwise forbidden by law.
> On the question of married students, the courts have viewed them as no different from other students.

"Unreasonable search and seizure" is a violation of the Fourth Amendment. Random searches of student lockers, that is, searches without probable or "reasonable" cause, will not be sustained by the courts and the materials confiscated not allowed as evidence. Where there is reasonable belief that drugs or other dangerous substances will be found in student lockers, the courts have been known to sustain the search action (558 P.2d. 781; Wash.; 1977).

Student claims against a district or teacher for "malpractice" which allegedly deprived the student of some learning or a quality education have not been supported by the courts to date. Teacher and district malpractice suits appear to be on the rise (whether this is related or not to the incidence of medical malpractice suits is not known) and may continue during the 1980s in spite of the adverse rulings to date.

One source reported that although the number of "civil cases involving students was 1734" during the period 1977 and 1981, this was considered to be "an underestimate of the total (about two-thirds)."[13] The impact of Public

Law 94-142 dealing with handicapped children and passed in 1975 was apparent because 44.3 percent of the student civil cases in the 1977 to 1981 period dealt with the handicapped student. Discipline ranked second (16.7 percent of the cases), regulation of sports was third (10.7 percent of the cases), and "equal protection" cases such as segregation or discrimination were fourth (9.5 percent of cases). Religion cases dropped to only 4.2 percent of all cases, freedom and privacy (including dress and grooming codes) were only 3.7 percent, and the lowest on the list focused on academic matters (competency testing, "educational malpractice," right to diploma, etc.) being only 1.7 percent of all cases.[14]

LITIGATIONS INVOLVING TEACHERS, ADMINISTRATORS, AND OTHER EMPLOYEES

The legal framework surrounding litigation by or against teachers is more complex than that for students, because teachers are employees. The many and complex litigation possibilities for teachers begin with the employment act. It includes the employment process, which must provide for equality of opportunity for all applicants or no discrimination, must be based upon evidence of proper certification and satisfaction of other professional qualifications for employment, and finally involves the use of a legal contract of employment with its complexities in wording and methods of execution. Legal counsel is often necessary to minimize a veritable legal thicket of possible employment-related litigation.

Conditions or assignments to be satisfied while employed, performance evaluation, and control of teacher behavior while under contract represent another set of concerns that often give rise to some sort of judicial review. The issues of equal pay for equal work, special dress code demands, insubordination, promotion prospects, off-duty behavior, leaves of absence, and so on are all related to actual employment practices. Collective bargaining and behavior during strikes or other job actions are by education employees relatively new factors that may trigger court cases involving public school districts.

Dismissal of teachers, who do or do not have tenure rights, represents an additional dimension in possible personnel litigation. The basis for dismissal may be related to neglect of duty, inefficiency, immorality, or simply a necessary reduction in force. Here such legal matters as dismissal procedures employed and the due process rights of the teacher enter the picture.

Academic freedom receives more publicity in institutions of higher learning but impacts upon the teacher in the elementary and secondary schools as well.

The major points of case law involving teachers and prevailing trends are summarized below with only a few leading cases cited:

· Teachers, along with other professionals such as lawyers and doctors, must have a valid and current certificate to practice and to enter into a valid contract of employment.
· A certificate of a teacher may be revoked for just cause and after following due process.
· Tenure laws for teachers and for administrators have been upheld as constitutional in all jurisdictions and against a variety of contentions.
· Dismissal is complex and the reasons and procedures vary from state to state. The courts will usually not interfere unless the actions are arbitrary, failed to follow due process, constitute excessive punishment, were inconsistent with civil rights guaranteed to all citizens under the Constitution. In general, just cause includes immorality, incompetence, inefficiency, intemperance, neglect of duty, or other factors which impair the quality of instruction in the school. Dismissal procedures must follow procedures such as giving notice of charges, providing an opportunity for a hearing, convening a hearing, rendering a decision, and allowing for appeal.
· Courts will approve fair and reasonable dress codes.
· Arbitrary and inflexible maternity leave policies have been held in violation of the due

process clause of the Fourteenth Amendment (*Cleveland Board of Education* v. *LaFleur,* 414 U.S. 632;1974).

· Termination of a teacher, after completion of a contract, because of declining enrollments that can be documented does not deprive a teacher of any constitutional rights (350 F. Supp. 1965; 1973).

What is described above as applying to teachers has relevance for the employment, control of behavior, and dismissal of administrators and other employees. The differences for administrators are that tenure status is more strictly construed, tenure is not guaranteed in administrative position and transfer to other positions in the district is deemed satisfactory, collective bargaining laws contribute little to the security of administrators, and courts have been much slower in specifying constitutional protections for administrative posts.[15] A number of cases on superintendent dismissal action without due process and for vague and unsubstantiated charges appeared during the 1970s. More can be expected in the 1980s. In general, a superintendent is entitled to the same rights guarantees and fair procedures that are available to other employees of the district. The courts have ruled in favor of illegally or improperly dismissed school administrators and have awarded damages in such actions.

DESEGREGATION, CIVIL RIGHTS, AND THE SCHOOLS

Brown v. *Board of Education* (1954) triggered a civil rights battle that went beyond public schools. It gave special meaning to the concept of equality of opportunity. As stated earlier it also placed the Supreme Court in an affirmative posture of promoting equality and integration rather than resolving disputed interpretations on these issues. The U.S. Commission on Civil Rights called *Brown* a "momentous decision" that "not only outlawed the system of school segregation," but also "provided the legal basis for attacking racial segregation in virtually every aspect of our society."[16] It called the rul-

ing "the most critical civil rights development in this century."[17] These are strong and very emphatic words and most in education would concur with them. The administration of public education will never be the same because of *Brown.*

Plessy v. *Ferguson* (163 U.S. 537; 1896) established the earlier precedent of court approval of "separate but equal" facilities for whites and blacks in railroad transportation. The *Plessy* doctrine was applied to education in 1927 in *Gong Lum* v. *Rice* (275 U.S. 78,85–86). A Chinese citizen of the United States was classed among the colored races insofar as assignment to a separate public school system in the South. The National Association for the Advancement of Colored People kept trying to attack and upset the *Plessy* doctrine for over 50 years before experiencing success in 1954.

Brown v. *Board of Education* (347 U.S. 483; 1954) outlawed public school segregation on the basis of race as "inherently unequal" and decreed that such practices were unconstitutional. The Court's decision was influenced strongly by social science data and opinion as opposed to actual proof of individual damage or assessment of the differences in quality of specific school situations. As Kirp and Yudof put it, "Apart from criticisms of the specific evidence submitted in *Brown,* scholars have sharply debated the propriety of reliance on social science to justify the desegregation decisions."[18]

Brown I, cited above, started the desegregating process and *Brown II* (*Brown* v. *Board of Education,* 349 U.S. 294; 1955) came a year later with the demand for "good faith compliance" and urged "all deliberate speed." There would be another 11 years before the Supreme Court would provide additional guidance to lower courts on how to handle the many and complex social issues encountered in the implementation phases.

Starting in 1966 and at least every two years thereafter there were series of Supreme Court decisions grappling with various dimensions of desegregation, integration, civil rights, or equality of opportunity, terms that fall easily off the tongue but are difficult to interpret with precision or to obtain agreement upon each's operational implications. The succession of cases as reported by the U.S. Commission on Civil Rights is as follows:[19]

· *U.S.* v. *Jefferson County Board of Education* (372 F.2nd 836,847; 1966) declared that "the only school desegregation plan that meets constitutional standards is one that works."
· *Green* v. *County School Board* (391 U.S. 430; 1968) rejected "freedom of choice" and charged the school board with "the affirmative duty to take whatever steps might be necessary to convert to a unitary system in which racial discrimination would be eliminated root and branch."
· *Alexander* v. *Holmes County Board of Education* (396 U.S. 19; 1969) replaced "all deliberate speed" with "the obligation of every school district to terminate dual school systems at once and to operate now and hereafter only unitary schools."
· *Swann* v. *Charlotte-Mecklenburg Board of Education* (402 U.S. 1; 1971) upheld lower court powers to order busing to bring about desegregation as well as other remedies such as assignment of students according to race.
· *Davis* v. *Board of School Commissions* (402 U.S. 43; 1971) and *North Carolina State Board of Education* v. *Swann* (402 U.S. 43; 1971) were companion cases to the earlier *Swann* which reinforced *Swann* above and recognized that in many situations that there may be no "remedy for segregated schools other than busing."
· *Keyes* v. *School District No. 1* (413 U.S. 189; 1973) upheld the use of busing for desegregation for the first time outside the South because this was a Denver case.
· *Bradley* v. *School Board* (412 U.S. 92; 1974) saw an evenly divided opinion of the U.S. Supreme Court serve to uphold a district court's order for metropolitan desegregation in Richmond, Va. and its suburbs.
· *Milliken* v. *Bradley* (418 U.S. 717; 1974) was another U.S. Supreme Court split decision (5 to 4) which held that the imposition of a metropolitan desegregation plan for Detroit was not warranted.
· *Washington* v. *Davis* (426 U.S. 229; 1976) and *Village of Arlington Heights* v. *Metropolitan Housing Development Corporation* (429 U.S. 252; 1977) are noneducation cases that have implications for what followed in many other fields. Established in these cases was the concept that an action racially neutral in intent even though it may have a discriminatory effect is constitutionally permissible. Proof of racially discriminatory intent appears to be required by the Court to show violation of the Fourteenth Amendment.
· *Austin Independent School District* v. *U.S.* (429 U.S. 990; 1976), *Dayton Board of Education* v. *Brinkman* (433 U.S. 406; 1977), and others in Indianapolis, Omaha, and Milwaukee were cases influenced by the *Washington* and *Arlington Heights* cases, and as a result segregative intent or discriminatory purpose had to be established. This was not done and the Supreme Court found for the school districts in question. Some interpret these cases that the Supreme Court is backing away from its previous "affirmative duty to desegregate."

It appears that the activist posture of the Supreme Court during the 1950s and 1960s with reference to desegregation softened somewhat in the 1970s. That remains to be confirmed in the cases that may reach this Court in the 1980s. Perhaps the "white flight" from urban school systems, community conflict, and changing public sentiments may result in a new balance in the great social reform that saw the public schools caught in the middle. There was an easing of pressures to enforce school desegregation during the early 1980s with few venturing to guess how long this climate may continue.

The federal judiciary represents one dimension and congressional action on school desegregation represents another. Federal involvement beyond the courts can be traced to Title IV of the Civil Rights Act of 1964. Subsequent to that a series of amendments has severely limited the executive branch from fulfilling the desegregation enforcement responsibilities of the Civil Rights Act. As concluded by the Civil Rights Commission,[20] "In enacting the Esch, Byrd, and Eagleton–Biden amendments, the legislative branch has undermined the ability of the executive and judicial branches to guarantee the Nation's children and young people their constitutional rights. It has acted against widely accepted civil rights goals and contributed to a lessening of the national will with respect to equal rights in the vital area of public education."

The nation's struggle to reform the delivery of educational services to remain consistent with constitutional rights, legislative demands, and the will of the people will continue probably through the remainder of this century, but in a more muted form. In mid-1982, the U.S. Supreme Court once again held that the Fourteenth Amendment bars de jure segregation but not necessarily de facto school segregation resulting primarily from residential housing patterns. In a California case (*Crawford* v. *Board of Education*) the change in the California constitution which was interpreted to bar de facto as well as de jure school segregation to correspond with the demands of the federal Constitution, The U.S. Supreme Court held by an 8 to 1 decision that such a state constitutional change approved by its people did not violate the Fourteenth Amendment of the U.S. Constitution. The decision had the effect of putting an end to mandatory crosstown busing in Los Angeles to achieve school desegregation. With a substantial number of large urban (city) school districts containing a majority of the previously identified "minority students," the factor of substantial "white flight" from the core city schools, the political reality that mandatory busing may not be worth the social upheaval and other costs, and the actions of the Supreme Court calling for demonstration of "intentional" school segregation, it appears that there may be less mandatory and cross-district busing of public school students to achieve better racial balance in the schools or integration during the remainder of this century.

THE LEGAL RAMIFICATIONS OF EDUCATIONAL FINANCE

Challenges to the manner in which public schools obtain revenues, spend monies, borrow to meet obligations, or manage fiscal resources have a long history that predates the current crop of litigations. A school district has no inherent authority to levy and collect taxes; it is a power delegated by the state and must be used only as prescribed. It is beyond the scope of this volume to delve into detail in the various ramifications of public school finance. Only a brief summary of more recent legal trends and developments follows.

Historically, legal disputes on educational finance were adjudicated by state supreme courts and focused upon how school revenues were generated or the sources of school funding. During the 1970s the federal judiciary became involved, and educational finance was examined in the light of its consistency with the protections and rights guaranteed by the U.S. Constitution. The legal questions raised dealt with how local and state resources for education were distributed rather than how generated. The disparity in wealth among local districts was related to the social, economic, and ethnic backgrounds of district residents.

In some respects the recent legal reviews of educational finance were extensions of the civil rights revolution and the increased concern for a greater equality of educational opportunity without regard to the magnitude of wealth within the school district where the child or youth resides.

The Educational Research Service outlined approximately 76 court cases in various states during the 1970s but only up to 1977.[21] There appeared to be a tapering off of legal disputes that focused on the distribution of state school funds during the final years of the 1970s. The cases after 1977 revolved around the usual concerns of tax limitations, exemptions, and the use of fees.

An Illinois case (*McInnis* v. *Ogilvie* 394 U.S. 322; 1969) was one of the earliest to generate a constitutional issue of the fact of unequal revenues per pupil being available and expended in districts of the state and to seek relief from such conditions of unequal wealth from the U.S. Supreme Court. The U.S. Supreme Court recognized that fiscal inequities existed but refused to judge that the educational finance system that produced the inequities was in violation of any provision of the U.S. Constitution because of it. This was followed in 1971 by the most publicized state court decision that raised both state and federal constitutional violations as well as equality of educational opportunity being deprived because of the disparities in property tax base among the districts in the State of California. It was the now famous California case of *Serrano* v. *Priest* (487 P.2d 1241; 1971) which served as a precedent for other similar state decisions even though it never reached the U.S. Supreme Court on appeal. Speaking of *Serrano,* Reutter and Hamilton declared:[22]

. . . . In 1971 the Supreme Court of California issued a decision that in the year and a half before its federal constitutional theory was rejected by the Supreme Court of the United States possibly generated more reaction than any other decision of a single state court. The core of the decision was that a funding scheme which makes the quality of a child's education dependent upon the wealth of his parents and neighbors (i.e., the wealth of his school district) invidiously discriminates against the poor in contravention of the equal protection clause of the Fourteenth Amendment and parallel clauses in the California constitution. (The ruling is binding in California, of course, despite the court's misconstruction of the Fourteenth Amendment.)

Another state complaint was lodged in Texas claiming the educational finance system discriminated against the poor because of unequal distribution of property tax wealth among the school districts of that state. The case of *Rodriguez* v. *San Antonio Independent School District* (411 U.S. 1; 1973) was reviewed by the U.S. Supreme Court to determine whether the Texas educational finance system failed to meet the tests of the equal protection clause of the Fourteenth Amendment. The Court noted that education "is not among the rights afforded explicit protection under our Federal Constitution." In a close and split decision of 5 to 4, the U.S. Supreme Court recognized that there is no tax system yet devised "which is free of all discriminatory impact," that "it is equally inevitable that some localities are going to be blessed with more taxable assets than others," but concluded that the Texas school finance plan did not violate the federal Constitution and sa-

tisfied the constitutional standard under the equal protection clause of the Fourteenth Amendment. Given the influence of *Serrano* and the split decision on *Rodriguez* that disagreed with the California Supreme Court's interpretation of the Fourteenth Amendment more litigation on this issue during the 1980s would not be surprising.

The various court challenges to educational finance systems have not demanded that state legislatures spend more for education. The issues raised by the complainants sought to insure that the accident of residency was not the determinant of educational opportunities made available to children and youths. The legal conflicts in the federal courts during the 1970s did serve to stimulate educational finance reform in many states, a process that will continue throughout the 1980s.

As more restrictions are placed on the taxing authority of local school districts (such as the property tax limitations), there is likely to occur a greater reliance on other sources of school income. Thus fees may be charged to offset specific operating costs. The levying of school fees has been subject to much litigation as well. Tuition fees to district residents, as opposed to those charged nonresidents, have been held in violation of state constitutional guarantees of a "free public education." Likewise, no fees may be charged a student as a condition for admission or enrollment in public schools. Fees for nonacademic program participation have been sustained in some jurisdictions. Most states approve the levying of rental fees for textbooks essential to the learning process. Legal restrictions on charging fees and statutory or constitutional limitations on taxation for the support of public education compounded the financing problems facing schools during times of rapidly escalating costs, inflation, and increased expectations from educational systems.

OTHER EDUCATION LITIGATIONS

Traditionally, the older textbooks on the legal aspects of education placed much stress and devoted most space to the kinds of conflict encountered by corporations, and by definition a school district is a corporation. These include the legal authority of the corporate officers, contractual authority, tort liabilities for wrong-doings, acquisition and use of property, and so on. In addition, there were the historic litigations related to students, teachers, administrators, other personnel, and church-state-education relations. The principles enunciated over the years in these areas have not changed as much as others.

The civil rights decisions and legislation, collective bargaining disputes, and challenges to state financial distributions to local school systems added more grist to the legal mills. The public schools have become prime factors in more legal disputes during the past two decades than ever before in history.

Even more recent, appearing during the late 1970s, were the cases dealing with minimum competency testing, alleged teacher malpractice, and sex discrimination. About 20 states demand that high school students demonstrate a minimum level of competency as a condition for receiving a high school diploma. The minimum competency test was devised as the indicator of ability to apply the so-called basic skills. In the case of *Debra P.* v. *Turlington* (No. 79-3074; 5th Cir.; 1981) the Florida minimum competency law was struck down as a violation of the Fourteenth Amendment. The initial applications of the instrument indicated that blacks failed ten times more often than whites. Again, this is not likely to be the final word or final legal challenge of minimum competency testing. Similarly, teacher malpractice suits appear to be on the rise with the courts thus far ruling against plaintiffs.

SUMMARY

The judicial branches of the state and federal governments cannot pass legislation, have no funds to distribute to schools, and have no infrastructure to monitor or operate educational institutions. Despite such limitations court decisions have reshaped the course of public education as the number of litigations involving schools escalated during the past 20 years.

Prior to 1960 most education disputes were resolved in state courts. Since then litigants have turned more often to federal courts, for local and state education issues were perceived in the light of rights and protections guaranteed under the federal Constitution. Constitutional rather than purely statutory demands became factors in cases involving teachers as well as students. Education provided the setting for ruling on such fundamental issues as church and state relations, freedom of expression, due process of law, and equal protection under the law.

The U.S. Supreme Court is the ultimate interpreter of the U.S. Constitution and thereby became involved in the legal issues surrounding public education. In most cases it played a prohibitory role, that is, prevented or overturned any infringement on rights and protections. It assumed an activist role in desegregation cases and sought to integrate school systems as a judicial policy and duty. The most controversial dimensions centered around court-dominated or supervised school operations. The courts have not performed well in this area even though their motives are beyond question.

Religious activities in public schools as well as state legislation to provide various types of public financial aid to sectarian schools have been struck down consistently by the U.S. Supreme Court as being contrary to the spirit and substance of the First Amendment. Efforts to find ways around these constitutional prohibitions continue nonetheless.

The state may compel children and youths of certain ages to attend school, but cannot limit such attendance at public schools only. Courts have denied exemptions from compulsory school attendance on religious grounds in all but one situation. Home instruction may be accepted as a substitute for compulsory school attendance if equivalency of instruction can be demonstrated.

The authority of school boards and school administrators over the education and control of students cannot be allowed to infringe upon the rights of students as U.S. citizens. The *Tinker* decision set the precedent on student rights and limits on the control of student behavior. The courts will sustain student locker searches where there is reason to believe that something dangerous or illegal may be found; random searches and seizures are not likely to be sustained.

Teacher employment, termination, and behavior control raise sensitive and complex legal issues that have been presented to state and federal courts. The courts usually will not interfere in such activities unless there is evidence of arbitrary decisions, failure to follow legal due process, or violation of rights and protections guaranteed all citizens. In general, educational administrators are entitled to the same rights guarantees and protections available to other school employees.

The *Brown* decision overturned the *Plessy* doctrine which was upheld previously for about 50 years, and helped trigger the civil rights revolution. The Court's decision on this case made heavy use of social science data rather than legal precedents and arguments alone. About 11 years after this landmark case, freedom of choice doctrines which attempted to circumvent the decision were rejected, busing to bring about desegregation was approved but not demanded, and speedier progress was required to end dual and segregated public school systems. During the last half of the 1970s there were indications of an easing of the activist Court posture, and proof of racially discriminatory intent became necessary. The nation's struggle to reform the delivery of educational services to be consistent with constitutional rights, legislative demands, and will of the people will continue during the remainder of this century.

The legal challenges of educational finance during the 1970s took place in federal courts, by and large, and focused on how funds were distributed rather than how generated or their sufficiency. The arguments against disparities in wealth of local districts to support education were related to the civil rights disputes. Some authorities felt that the leading California case of *Serrano* was based on a misconstruction of the Fourteenth Amendment by the California State Supreme Court. The recent legal challenges led to many educational finance reforms. The greater use of fees to support educational services may in turn lead to increased legal disputes based on state constitutional guarantees of a system of free public education.

Contractual authority of school officials, tort liabilities, restraints on property acquisition, and personnel disputes dominated the school's legal concerns in prior years. Civil suits brought by students, actions by teachers as individuals and as groups in collective bargaining, and desegregation dominated the judicial scene where education was involved in more recent years, and such matters are likely to be continued in the future.

NOTES

1. See the old classic: Newton Edwards, *The Courts and the Public Schools*, rev. ed., Chicago: University of Chicago Press, 1955, 622 pp. Or more recent comprehensive works such as: E. Edmund Reutter, Jr., and Robert R. Hamilton, *The Law of Public Education*, 2nd ed., Mineola, N.Y.: Foundation Press, 1976, 747 pp. David L. Kirp and Mark G. Yudof, *Educational Policy and the Law*, Berkeley, Calif.: McCutchan, 1974, 749 pp. LeRoy J. Peterson et al., *The Law and Public School Education*, New York: Harper & Row, 1969, 590 pp.
2. Floyd G. Delon, "School Officials and the Courts: Update 1979," *ERS Monograph*, Arlington, Va.: Educational Research Service, 1979, pp. 39 and 66.
3. Ibid.
4. Ibid.
5. Nathan Glazer, "Foreword," for Kirp and Yudof, op. cit., p. xxxvii.
6. Clark Spurlock, *Education and the Supreme Court*, Urbana, Ill.: University of Illinois Press, 1955.
7. John E. McDermott, "Federal Courts and Federal Educational Policy," in Harry. L. Summerfield, *Power and Process*, Berkeley, Calif.: McCutchan, 1974, pp. 199–248 (p. 241).
8. Ibid.
9. Floyd G. Delon, op. cit., p. 91.
10. E. Edmund Reutter, Jr., and Robert R. Hamilton, op. cit., p. 539.
11. H. C. Hudgins, Jr., "School Administrators and

the Courts: A Review of Recent Decisions," *ERS Monograph,* Arlington, Va.: Educational Research Service, 1975, p. 52.

12. Ibid., p. 53

13. N. B. Dearman and V. W. Plisko, eds., *The Condition of Education,* 1982 edition, Washington, D.C.: GPO 1982, pp. 40–41.

14. Ibid., p. 66.

15. Floyd G. Delon, op. cit., p. 30.

16. U.S. Commission on Civil Rights, *Desegregation of the Nation's Public Schools: A Status Report,* Washington, D.C.: GPO, February 1979, p. viii.

17. Ibid.

18. David L. Kirp and Mark G. Yudof, op. cit., p. 298.

19. U.S. Commission on Civil Rights, op. cit., pp. 1–7.

20. Ibid.

21. Educational Research Service, "School Finance Reform and Court Challenges in the 1970s," *ERS Information Aid,* Arlington, Va.: ERS, 1977, pp. 13–30.

22. E. Edmund Reutter, Jr., and Robert R. Hamilton, op. cit., p. 185.

CHAPTER REVIEW QUESTIONS

1. Why is the U.S. Supreme Court sometimes referred to as the "National School Board"?

2. Why have students and teachers taken their legal disputes to federal as well as state courts?

3. What is meant by the "activist" role of the federal courts in public education?

4. Why is the *Tinker* decision considered a landmark case insofar as the administration of public education is concerned?

5. Under what conditions may a teacher be dismissed with minimum likelihood of a reversal in a court of law?

6. What made the *Brown* decision so momentous in the history of public education?

7. Identify and describe the crucial issues resolved in the federal cases on desegregation following *Brown.*

8. In what ways are the *Serrano* and *Rodriguez* cases similar? In what respects were they different?

9. What are the major trends in litigation involving public education?

10. What were the major constitutional issues raised in the challenges to educational finance systems during the 1970s?

SELECTED REFERENCES

Delon, Floyd G., "School Officials and the Courts: Update 1979," *ERS Monograph,* Arlington, Va.: ERS, 1979, 98 pp.

Kirp, David L., and Yudof, Mark G., *Educational Policy and the Law,* Berkeley, Calif.: McCutchan, 1974, 749 pp.

McDermott, John E., "Federal Courts and Federal Educational Policy," supplementary essay in Harry L. Summerfield, *Power and Process,* Berkeley, Calif.: McCutchan, 1974, pp. 199–248.

Peterson, LeRoy J. et al., *The Law and Public Education,* New York: Harper & Row, 1969, 590 pp.

Reutter, E. Edmund, Jr., and Hamilton, Robert R., *The Law of Public Education,* 2nd ed., Mineola, N.Y.: Foundation Press, 1976, 747 pp.

U.S. Commission on Civil Rights, *Desegregation of the Nation's Public Schools: A Status Report,* Washington, D.C.: GPO, February 1979, 90 pp.

12

ALTERNATIVES TO PUBLIC EDUCATION AND SPECIAL AGENCIES THAT INFLUENCE PUBLIC EDUCATION

Nonpublic, or private, schools are major alternatives to public education. Most such educational institutions are related to a specific religion. The magnitude and contributions of systems of private education in the United States are of a different order than those noted in other nations.

Professional societies, and the more recently developed unions, enroll the teaching, supervisory, special service, and administrative personnel employed by public schools and engage in activities that influence educational administration and the operation of public schools almost as much as direct state and federal legislative efforts, local operational policy decisions, and ruling case law.

Last, but by no means least, special educational agencies of various sorts influence much or all of public school decision making and daily operations. Among these are the regional accrediting societies, local taxpayers' organizations, and single issue educational groups that seek to promote or prevent some developments in the schools. The National Congress of Parents and Teachers, one such informal agency with a dynamic national as well as local base, will be reviewed in Chapter 24.

PRIVATE SCHOOLS IN THE UNITED STATES

In most nations other than the United States, control of educational institutions is vested in private agencies, usually religious in orientation, which often have access to public funds. In most countries of the world, private education dominates, but not in the United States. Nonetheless, the private elementary and secondary schools in the United States play an important role in the total educational delivery system. The controversy that surrounds the efforts to provide public support for private education in the United States should not obscure the professional and often close relationships between the public and the private educational sectors in our nation.

Statistics on private school systems are difficult to come by. Those prepared by recognized data-gathering agencies with a high level of credibility such as the National Center for Education Statistics do not always agree. What is presented is best labeled as "best estimates" of private school enrollment and faculty data.

Public school enrollments are very sensitive to fluctuations in the number of live births; private school enrollments are not so closely related to the birthrate. Private schools may limit numbers of students accepted; public schools cannot and must enroll all who satisfy the age standards and other limited requirements. Over the past 30 years, private school elementary/secondary enrollments fluctuated between 10 and 15 percent of the total enrolled in elementary/secondary schools.

Private elementary/secondary school enrollments in 1980–1981 were estimated at about 5.03 million—down from the 1967 peak of about 6 million, but up from the 1973 low of around 4.9 million. The slight upward trend is all the more remarkable because it occurred during a period when public school enrollments were dropping by about 15 percent in response to rapidly declining birthrates.

Private schools are more llikely to serve students in the elementary grades (K to 8) than in secondary grades (9 to 12). The private elementary school enrollments ranged from 11.8 percent of the total in grades K to 8 in 1950 to a high of 16.1 percent in 1959 and then fell to about 11.6 percent in 1980. There are indications that some church-related schools are reducing numbers of elementary schools and placing a higher priority on providing secondary school experiences. Private school secondary enrollments were 8.1 percent of the total found in grades 9 to 12 in 1950, hit a peak of 11.2 percent in 1965, declined to around 9.8 percent through most of the 1970s, and then rose again to 10.1 percent in 1980. Whether the percent of the total found in secondary schools with only four grade levels will exceed those in private elementary schools remains to be seen, but the trends suggest that there is a high probability that this may occur if not during the 1980s (for elementary enrollments may rise during the last half of the 1980s) then sometime during the 1990s.

Conflicting data estimates from various reports issued by the National Center for Education Statistics indicate that in 1950, 10.9 percent of all elementary/secondary school pupils were in private schools and a peak of 14.9 percent was reached in 1959. The estimates of the percent of total elementary/secondary enrollments in private schools were between 13.3 and 14.0 percent in 1960, 10.1 and 11.8 percent in 1970, and 10.9 to 11.1 percent in 1980.

Church-Related Private Schools

In 1980–1981, 77.3 percent of the 21,000 private schools in the nation were church related, and 84 percent of the enrollments were in church-related institutions. Most were schools operated by the Roman Catholic Church, which enrolled about 63.4 percent of all students found in all private schools. The next largest, and a very distant second, were Baptist-related schools with 4.6 percent of students in nonpublic schools, followed by Luthern schools with 4.4 percent of the enrollment. Schools operated by those of the Christian, Jewish, Seventh-Day Adventist, and Episcopalian faiths had the fourth, fifth, sixth, and seventh largest enrollments, respectively, but none had as much as 2.5 percent of the total private school enrollment.

The typical or average private school had an enrollment of 259 and a student–teacher ratio of 18.6. These schools employed 281,150 teachers 1980–1981, with about 52.5 percent of all private school teachers employed in the Catholic church-related schools.

In the early 1970s the Roman Catholic and also some Protestant churches were reevaluating the resources being dedicated to church-operated nonpublic schools. To illustrate, Catholic elementary/secondary school enrollments hit a peak of 5.5 million in the fall, 1964, but then declined to about 3.3 million in 1978. Escalating costs as well as the increasingly complex educational demands being placed upon schools helped trigger the reexamination. Church-related or other private schools have the option to continue or abandon operations of some or all grade levels; public schools have no such options.

During the early 1980s there was a renewal of discussions and legislative efforts to provide some tax relief through tuition-assistance tax credits for parents sending children to private schools. This had the support of the U.S. President as well as some in Congress, but the "tuition tax credit" deduction from the federal income tax had not been resolved by the end of 1983. In addition, the so-called freedom of choice or voucher school finance plan received renewed attention in certain states. Efforts through the early 1980s did not meet with success, but this has not discouraged further efforts from proponents. The voucher would be a fiscal boon and could lead to further expansion of private education, particularly parochial school education. The voucher educational finance plans at the state levels and the "tuition tax credit" at the federal level were opposed by individuals and organizations supporting public education, for these institutions are already hard pressed for adequate funding from public taxes sources without sharing these with private education.

Distribution and Recent Developments in Private Education

Private schools are not distributed evenly through various regions of the nation. The highest proportion of the total elementary/secondary school students enrolled in private schools will be found in the Middle Atlantic states even though "that proportion dropped from nearly 22 per cent in 1960 to just under 17 percent by 1980."[1] In contrast, the smallest proportion likely to be enrolled in private schools, about 5.1 percent, is in the Mountain states region. The private school enrollment percentages declined during 1960 and 1980 in all regions other than the South Atlantic and the East South Central states, where a modest 1 percent gain was registered during this 20-year period. The combined east and west portions of the North Central region had over 23 percent of the total enrollment on private schools.

Private school enrollment is concentrated in the urban centers. Thus, "In 1979, private school enrollment accounted for 16 percent of the total in central cities, but only 10 percent in metropolitan areas outside of central cities (suburbs) and 5 per cent in nonmetropolitan (rural) areas."[2]

In the 1960s, the so-called white academies appeared in several Southern states as an alternative to public schools required by law to desegregate. During the 1970s something similar occurred in the large urban districts outside the South to spur the development of new private schools. Educational organizations convened in large homes or church basements as alternatives to crosstown busing of students from predominately white schools to predominately minority schools in the core city. Such private educational organizations made possible the so-called white flight from the public schools.

More than a decade after creation, the so-called white academies continued to operate, were accepted in many small Southern communities as a way of life, and began to focus as well on the quality of academic preparation. By the beginning of the 1980s the tuition moved to $1000 to $2000 per year per child, with parents indicating a willingness to accept the financial sacrifices involved. Socializing and interaction among white students in the public and private schools located in the same community were at a relatively high level. Some of the political pressures for the voucher educational finance patterns and federal tuition tax credits may be related to the creation of a dual system of private and public education in the South as well as numerous parochial schools in the urban areas of the East, North, and Far West. Some of the schools created to accommodate the white flight from desegregated schools did not survive the initial financial crises, some closed after cross-district busing was deemphasized and students returned to the public schools, but others continued to survive for more than a decade and demonstrated strength and community acceptance.

There were new types of private schools that emerged in large urban areas during the past two decades that were unrelated to the civil rights or desegregation battles. In the large cities of the North and East the so-called street academies and free schools took root in abandoned stores and other spaces of the core city to offer "alternative schools" for those who were prone or actually dropped out of the traditional public and nonpublic schools. A 1973 directory of "free" or alternative schools listed 350 such institutions as entities separate, but sometimes at least informally related, to the public schools. The problems of financing and failure to deliver something beyond rhetoric eventually led to their demise by the early 1980s. Not much has been heard from this rather spontaneous educational movement during the past five years.

The responsibility of the state for regulation of nonpublic schools varies from one region to the next. Some enforce statutes requiring nonpublic schools to meet the legal and appropriate educational standards on attendance, others do not.[3] In some instances the public and nearby nonpublic schools have entered into a type of cooperation referred to as dual enrollment.[4] In such cases, a private school pupil may attend one or more special classes in a nearby public school. Private school pupils in grades 7 and 8 or in grades 11 or 12 are more likely to enroll in public school classes than those in other grades.

The Principal in the Private Secondary School

The study of the senior high school principalship in 1978 included private schools as well.[5] The findings of this report are:

1. The private group makes up more than 13 percent of the nation's high schools, but only about 10 percent of the student enrollments.
2. The private school principal is younger (38), appointed to serve as principal at a younger age (34), has had more teaching experience (16), and held fewer other principalships than his/her counterpart in the public high schools.
3. Substantially more women were high school principals in church-related schools (43 percent of all) than in the public sector (7 percent).

4. Both private and public sector senior high principals "are experienced, mature, and highly educated with diverse educational backgrounds."
5. The private sector group differs markedly in teaching responsibility (over 80 percent in private schools teach, only 10 percent in public schools do), scope of authority (more authority in private schools), priorities attached to various education tasks, and views on whether there should be federal aid to private schools.

The quality of faculty and educational programs varies greatly from one private school to another. There are insufficient data available to allow for definitive generalizations about quality comparisons among private schools or between private and public schools, the so-called Coleman II report notwithstanding.[6]

PROFESSIONAL ORGANIZATIONS AND UNIONS IN EDUCATION

There were about 2.47 million professional personnel—teachers, principals, supervisors, and other administrators—employed in the public and private schools in 1980 according to National Center for Education Statistics' data. Bureau of Census data published in the *Current Population Survey* for 1980 include preprimary, some adult education, and other teachers and report a figure for teachers alone that was 3.157 million.[7] About 2.2 million full-time equivalent personnel worked in the public schools, and almost about 280,000 in private schools during 1980. This is more than twice the numbers reported 50 years earlier. The peak year was 1975–1976, and the numbers of professionals employed have declined since then and will continue to do so until about 1985.

Professional education associations and unions exercise considerable influence in the everyday and long-range administration and operation of public more than private schools. These societies and unions influence schools through the employed personnel who join as members. Teacher militance and strikes will be reviewed more fully in the chapters that follow on personnel administration and collective bargaining. This section shall focus on the history and development of professional educational organizations and unions.

Educators are loyal to their profession, as expressed by membership in a professional society or union, as well as to the school district or state that employs them. Professional workers face the dilemma confronting other individuals in an organized society, namely, few can muster the strength necessary to attain important objectives without cooperative efforts. The propensity of educators to form special societies or unions, to support them, to become committed to their programs and activities is a fact of life in the administration and operation of public schools.

The National Education Association

In the beginning there were state organizations of teachers; the creation of a national organization came later. For about 100 years it was purely a professional society that shunned involvement in partisan politics, frowned on aggressive posturing and teacher strikes, and avoided the image or perception of being a labor union. The 1970s saw a dramatic change in the National Education Association (NEA) as it became heavily involved in partisan politics at all levels, supported teacher strikes, became a labor union according to the ruling by the U.S. Internal Revenue Service, and engaged in relatively few primarily professional conferences and publications. But first some history.

Forty-three persons met in Philadelphia on August 26, 1857, to create the National Teachers Association. The original constitution of this national organization excluded women from membership—a restriction that was eliminated in 1866. In 1870 the National Association of School Superintendents and the American Normal School Association merged with the National Teachers Association to create the National Education Association. The four charter departments of the NEA were the Department of School Superintendance (now the American Association of School Administrators), the De-

partment of Normal Schools (now the American Association of Colleges for Teacher Education), the Department of Higher Instruction (now the Association for Higher Education), and the Department of Elementary Schools (abolished in 1925). It is significant that in 1972, a little over 100 years after its founding, the NEA changed its appearance and thrust to become more like the original National Teachers Organization as several of the charter departments, particularly the administrators, broke their ties with the NEA.

In 1906 an act of Congress gave the NEA its charter, which was accepted in 1907 by its membership; its official title was expanded to the National Education Association of the United States.

The NEA today is a complex organization that annually convenes a representative assembly that at the time decides on resolutions, recommendations on budgets and program thrusts, and any amendments to the association's bylaws. The theme of the 1982 Delegate Assembly, or National Convention, was "Political Power for Educational Excellence," thus indicating that the political orientation fashioned during the 1970s would probably continue during the 1980s as well.

There is an NEA president, board of directors, and executive committee. The Washington, D.C., headquarters staff includes an executive secretary, a deputy executive secretary, associate secretaries, assistant executive secretaries, and other personnel. The officers are elected and for most of history served one-year terms. That changed during the 1970s because the NEA president is elected for a two-year term and may be reelected for only one additional term. The NEA executive secretary is an important position as the chief executive officer of the organization. At one time scholars or those with a research orientation were selected for this important post. The political orientation of the 1970s changed that pattern as well.

In some respects, the NEA acted as a holding company, wherein teachers and administrators of various specializations form groupings known as departments, national affiliates, or associated organizations to serve the needs of specialized personnel.

The various administrator organizations for superintendents, high school principals, and elementary principals, as well as the Association for Supervision and Curriculum Development, were at one time related to NEA but now are completely separate and independent. Significant changes between NEA and its related professional societies were approved in July 1968. In the 1970s several national professional societies in education severed their affiliations from NEA rather than accept new requirements.

Some professional groups receive financial support from NEA for operation of activities, others are fiscally independent. Most related organizations are housed in the NEA building at 1201 Sixteenth Street, N.W., Washington, D.C.

There were 43 NEA members in 1857, but there are over 1.75 million members presently. Around the time of World War I, membership in the American Federation of Teachers exceeded that of the NEA; today the NEA membership is more than three times that of the AFT. The big growth occurred after World War II. Membership exceeded 200,000 in 1930 and reached the 1 million mark in March 1967. It is likely to stabilize or decline during the 1980s unless the long awaited merger with the AFT occurs.

Until 1945 NEA dues were less than $2 annually. The dues increased steadily to reach $45 annually, far below most unions, in 1980, but are projected to climb as the average annual salary paid to teachers does so as well. Its annual budget exceeded $70 million early in the 1980s. During 1982, expenditures of several millions were made for partisan political campaigns, primarily for congressional races. The 1981 salary of the NEA president was $61,668 plus expenses of $23,643, or a total of $85,311. This is substantially less than the $89,716 in salary and $51,018 in expenses for a total of $140,734 paid the AFT president in 1981. It is also less than "the $76,000 average salary of top labor leaders in 1981."[8] Although called by some the second largest labor organization in the United States, its officers and executives earn substantially less than the 1982 salary of $225,000 for the president of the Teamsters'

Union (the largest with 1.8 million members). The highest paid union leader in 1980 received salaries totaling $428,803 as president of two Cleveland union locals.[9]

The NEA may also be considered to be a cluster of state and local affiliated education associations. There are 50 states and about 9300 local affiliated associations. It is said to be the only union with members in every congressional district, with an average of 6000 members in each such district. NEA's strengths, however, are at the state and national level. Its weakest structural link is at the local level; the reverse is true for AFT. Prior to 1967, very few NEA affiliates engaged in strikes; today, as during the 1970s, over 80 percent of the teacher strikes were by NEA affiliated local organizations.

During much of its history the NEA championed the theme and projected the image of "the united profession." The concept of a single professional society for teachers, supervisors, administrators, and other professional workers in education had its critics, for some claimed the NEA to be an "administrator-dominated" organization. Now that administrator organizations have separated from NEA and during much of the past two decades, the NEA president is more likely to be a classroom teacher.

The most dramatic change came in the mid-1970s when the U.S. Internal Revenue Service recognized the NEA as a labor union rather than as a professional society in education and adjusted the tax-exempt status of the NEA accordingly. Equally dramatic was the shedding of the nonpartisan image of the association, its support of presidential candidates, and its granting of political activity a higher priority within the organization than the more traditional professional educational activities, such as commissions, conferences, and publications devoted to some dimension of instruction or education as a whole. During much of the 1970s and early 1980s, the association was viewed as an arm of the Democratic party for its propensity to make contributions and openly endorse the congressional and presidential candidates from that party. History was made when the NEA endorsed and supported financially the presidential campaign of Jimmy Carter in 1976. Carter's election was the high point of NEA's political clout at the national level. NEA continued its support of Carter during the Democratic presidential nominations, which was credited in part for turning back the challenge of Senator Edward Kennedy during the 1980 primaries. When Ronald Reagan won the presidency, the NEA's political clout in Washington was diminished severely. The NEA executive secretary conceded that Reagan picked up 41 percent of the NEA affiliated teachers, but other exit polls showed that 46 percent of all teachers voted for Reagan and only 41 percent for Carter (the remainder went to the third candidate, Anderson). Although some question whether the NEA has any more influence over the vote of its members than any other union, there is evidence that prospective presidential candidates of at least one party vie for the opportunity to speak at NEA national conventions and appreciate the financial contributions.

NEA's concentration on politics has led some critics to declare that NEA equates raising of the quality of education to the simplistic solution of "giving more money to teachers" and "giving more control over various dimensions of education to teachers." NEA's opposition to the use of standardized tests for pupils and improvements in teacher preparation through testing, both of which the AFT support, have helped to project an "antiacademic" or "lack of academic standards" image for the association. "More teacher pay and fewer students per teacher" has likewise been used to summarize the primary NEA goals. There is some substance to the argument that more funds for public education can be procured only through more political action and involvement on the part of the education profession.

The American Federation of Teachers

There were teachers' unions at the local district level prior to 1900. A national teachers' union was created on April 15, 1916, when four locals, in response to a call by the Chicago Teachers Federation, formed a new organization known as the American Federation of Teachers. The AFT became affiliated with the American Federation of Labor (AFL) in the same year.[10]

The Chicago Teachers Federation, formed in 1897, was the first significant independent organization of teachers. The San Antonio, Texas, Teachers Union, was the first to be affiliated with the AFL, although the Chicago Teachers Federation joined the AFL some two months later. By 1916, 20 teachers' groups in ten states organized local affiliates with labor. During the early part of this century Chicago had the Chicago Teachers Federation, the Federation of Women High School Teachers, and the Federation of Men Teachers.

The teachers' union was a large-city phenomenon and was usually found where the labor movement in general was strong. The American Federation of Teachers prospered for a while and at one time saw its membership exceed that of the NEA. Many locals were disbanded under heavy pressure from school boards.

Less than one-fifth of the AFT locals previously chartered were still operating in 1927. By 1925, the membership had dropped to less than 3500. At present, AFT membership is estimated to be around 520,000, or over one million less than that for NEA. It is significant that about 90 percent of all teachers in 1980 belong to the NEA or AFT. This is a very high percentage and reflects some who join both organizations. There are about 1750 AFT locals compared with more than 9300 NEA locals. Some 15 AFT local affiliates constitute substantially more than one-half of the AFT membership. New York City accounts for over one-third of the total number in the AFT.

In the 1960s AFT moved its national headquarters from Chicago to Washington, D.C. The AFT lacks the strong financial base of the NEA. The Industrial Union Department (IUD) of the AFL-CIO has made substantial contributions to the AFT.

Historically, teacher unionism was an urban phenomenon in the United States. Relatively few teachers' unions are found outside the very large metropolitan areas.

Dual membership is not unusual; the same person will join the NEA to receive its publications and alleged professional status and the AFT to take advantage of its concern for the individual teacher's welfare. In many school districts, the AFT has been elected bargaining representative for the teachers even though the NEA membership was significantly higher.

Whereas the NEA is accused of being dominated by administrators, the charge most frequently hurled against the AFT is that it is labor-dominated and therefore cannot serve the total community.

NEA–AFT Merger Possibilities

Prior to 1970 the notion of a possible merger was anathema to many in NEA leadership positions during those years. It became apparent to both sides that limited resources were being dissipated in jurisdictional disputes. The AFT dominated the large-city school districts, whereas the NEA was strong in smaller communities. If certain issues such as the NEA historic opposition to strikes and administrator membership in NEA could be resolved, then the two organizations could be perceived as complementary rather than competitive. These issues were resolved by the early 1970s, namely, NEA's opposition to strikes was replaced with support for striking affiliates and all administrator organizations separated from NEA.

NEA resisted overtures from AFT to merge during the 1960s. The historic 1973 NEA convention put an end to merger resistance and signaled the beginning of a series of negotiations to bring the two educational organizations together. For much of the 1970s there were strong indications that an AFT–NEA merger would occur. During the early 1980s, relations cooled once more, partially as the result of the NEA support for and the AFT resistance to the formation of a U.S. Department of Education. The NEA is now classified as a labor union even though not affiliated with any other general national labor organization. There re-

mains a strong possibility that the NEA and AFT may merge, but whether the merger will take place during the 1980s is not clear at this writing.

The American Association of School Administrators

A handful of men gathered in Harrisburg, Pennsylvania, about four months after the assassination of Abraham Lincoln, to organize the National Association of School Superintendents. In 1870 five years after its creation, the National Association of School Superintendents merged with two other educational organizations to form the NEA. It developed into the NEA Department of Superintendence, as it was known until 1937, when it changed its name to the American Association of School Administrators. The first full-time executive secretary was S. D. Shankland. He was succeeded by Dr. Worth McClure and then Dr. Finis Engelman. Dr. Forrest E. Conner served as Executive Secretary of AASA until 1971. Dr. Paul Salmon is presently the executive secretary of that important and influential organization for superintendents and other administrators.

The influence of the AASA goes far beyond its membership of less than 20,000. Its national conference, with attendance in the 18,000 to 20,000 range and educational exhibits, is one of the largest educational work conferences in the world. The AASA influences public education through its publications; its studies by special committees and commissions; its code of ethics for school administrators; and its series of conferences, seminars, and workshops. Its recent innovation, the AASA National Academy for School Executives, became operational late in 1968 as a continuing professional development vehicle for practicing school administrators.

The AASA Committee on Ethics has been in operation since 1964. The AASA Committee for the Advancement of School Administration (CASA) grew out of the Kellogg Foundation programs of the early 1950s. CASA's programs and recommendations have had a positive impact on school administration.

Up until its separation from the NEA in 1972, AASA continued to seek unity in the education profession. The AASA was fiscally independent from NEA even when headquartered in the NEA building in Washington, D.C. Its headquarters staff of Executive Director, Deputy Director, and Associate and Assistant Directors are now housed in an AASA owned building in Arlington, Virginia.

There are many state administrator associations that for most of their history were departments in state education associations. In 1967 the Michigan Association of School Administrators was the first to call for separation from the Michigan Education Association. Many did likewise in subsequent years, and there were some that were never affiliated with a state education association.

Associations of School Principals

The National Association of Secondary School Principals (NASSP) and the National Association of Elementary School Principals (NAESP) are separate from the AASA. They likewise were at one time departments in the NEA. Both associations separated from NEA in the early 1970s. Each of the principals' associations operates its own national convention, elects its own officers, and has its own governing board.

NASSP was organized in 1916. It now has more than 30,000 members. It sponsors the National Association of Students Councils and the National Honor Society for secondary school students. Its annual national convention attracts approximately 10,000 people. NAESP was founded in 1921. Its present membership totals almost 24,000, and its annual convention attracts approximately 6,200. The state affiliates of each of the national principals' organizations are growing in strength and in memberships.

National School Boards Association

The NSBA had its beginnings as the National Council of State School Boards Association, organized in 1940 in St. Louis. It is significant that this event occurred at a meeting held in conjunction with the annual convention of the AASA.

To Pennsylvania goes the honor of organizing the first state association of school boards in 1896. Progress was relatively slow, for by 1920 there were only seven state school board associations. By 1940 there were 27, and by 1957 there was a state association of school boards in every state.[11]

The National Council of State School Boards Association continued meeting in conjunction with the annual conventions of the AASA for many years after its organization. In 1948 its name was changed officially to the National School Boards Association. In 1949 Edward M. Tuttle was selected as the first full-time Executive Secretary of the Association.

This national organization is essentially a federation of state school boards associations. It held its annual meetings just prior to the AASA meeting from 1950 to 1957. The first independent convention met in Miami in April 1958. The NSBA is supported primarily from dues paid by school boards, rather than by individuals.

ACCREDITING AGENCIES

Schools are accredited by the state department of education in most states, or by a state university or collection of universities in the state. There are, in addition, regional accrediting bodies that have no official relation with the state department of education. Primary emphasis here will be on the regional accrediting bodies.

The regional accrediting agencies include the North Central Association of Colleges and Secondary Schools, the Middle States Association of Colleges and Secondary Schools, the North West Association of Secondary and Higher Schools, the Southern Association of Colleges and Schools, the Western College Association, and the New England Association of Colleges and Secondary Schools. These associations are private and voluntary organizations. Membership of local schools is voluntary and dependent upon meeting membership criteria and paying dues. Recognition of these associations by a state department of education is voluntary as well. Nonetheless, these private agencies have a profound impact on public secondary school accreditation in many parts of the country. Recently the southern association has instituted programs for accreditation of elementary schools as well.

The responsibility for evaluating the quality of education of various schools has typically been a state function. Thus, although regional accrediting agencies do not have the force of law behind their actions, they do have a significant impact in determining criteria for accreditation and which schools shall be admitted or continued on their list of accredited institutions.

OTHER INFORMAL AGENCIES

The National Congress of Parents and Teachers, as well as the various citizens' committees for the improvement of public education are reviewed in Chapter 24. Extremist groups of the right and the left have subjected schools to considerable criticism.

The civil rights movement has often focused on education. Some within this movement have equated the neighborhood school concept with de facto segregation. Through the use of the demonstration, and threatened or actual boycotts, the extremists have attempted to influence the decision-making authority of school boards as well as the structural arrangements of school operation.

The Council for Basic Education, which came into being in 1956, has attempted to influence public education through its publications and the speeches of some of its members. Taxpayers' groups in various communities wax and wane in influence. Some have been organized into state associations and have attempted to curtail the school board's right to levy particular taxes.

The number of informal agencies attempting to influence the organization and administration of public education has been growing in recent years. There is no indication that a reversal of this trend is likely.

SUMMARY

Nonpublic schools are primarily church-oriented institutions. They enroll a larger share of elementary and secondary school students in some Eastern and Midwestern states than elsewhere. Private schools are more likely to be found in urban than in rural areas. About 11 percent of the elementary/secondary school enrollments are in the private schools, with about 65 percent of a total of about 5.1 million in Catholic schools.

Special private schools were created during the late 1960s and the 1970s as alternatives to the public schools required by law to desegregate. These schools are continuing in spite of high tuition and appear to be accepted in many parts of the South. The so-called street academies that developed in the 1970s appear to be doing less well in the 1980s.

The private school senior high school principals are younger, include more women, and devote more time to teaching than do their counterparts in public schools. The quality of faculty and program varies greatly among private schools, and there is insufficient definitive data to make valid comparisons between private and public schools.

Professional education associations and unions have a significant impact through their members upon school operations and administration. The NEA, the largest and oldest, is a complex organization that experienced a significant shift in its primary thrusts and priorities during the past two decades. It is now oriented more toward labor union functions, is heavily involved in partisan politics, and focuses less on academic issues. The AFT, another teachers' union, has a membership less than one-third of that of the NEA. There was increasing talk of an NEA-AFT merger during the 1970s. The AFT's strength is in the large urban centers, whereas NEA's strength is in smaller communities, the state level, and national level.

There are several professional societies for administrators. These organizations were NEA affiliates up until 1972. All have separated from NEA and act independently. The oldest (over 100 years old) and most powerful is the AASA.

The NASSP and the NAESP have larger membership rolls and represent secondary and elementary prinipals, respectively. The NSBA is a recent development and is essentially a federation of state school boards associations.

Regional accrediting agencies are powerful informal forces working toward the improvement of education. They are voluntary associations and their membership criteria have an effect on secondary schools in particular. No state laws require accreditation by regional accrediting bodies, but the better schools seek such recognition.

The number of informal agencies seeking to influence the structure, organization, and operation of public education is increasing. This is testimony to the importance of education to the democratic way of life.

NOTES

1. N. B. Dearman and V. W. Plisko, eds., *The Condition of Education,* 1982 edition, Washington, D.C.: GPO, 1982, p. 39.
2. Ibid.
3. D. A. Erickson and L. L. Cunningham, *Non-Public Schools in the United States,* Chicago: Midwest Administration Center, University of Chicago, 1970.
4. J. E. Gibbs, Jr. et al., *Dual Enrollment in Public and Non-public Schools,* U.S. Office of Education, Circular No. 772, Washington, D.C.: GPO, 1965.
5. Lloyd E. McLeary and Scott D. Thomson, *The Senior High School Principalship,* Vol. III, Summary Report, Reston, Va.: National Association of Secondary School Principals, 1979, pp. 33–42.
6. See Educational Research Service, "Coleman Report on Public and Private Schools: The Draft Summary and Eight Critiques," *ERS School Research Forum,* Arlington, Va.: ERS, 1981, 47 pp.
7. Dearman and Plisko, eds., op. cit., p. 85.
8. *Business Week,* "Rank-and-File Austerity Filters Upward," May 10, 1982, p. 118.
9. Ibid.
10. Commission on Educational Reconstruction, American Federation of Teachers, *Organizing the Teaching Profession,* New York: Free Press, 1955, pp. 21–29.
11. Edward M. Tuttle, *School Board Leadership in America,* rev. ed., Danville, Ill.: Interstate Printers and Publishers, 1963, p. 169.

CHAPTER REVIEW QUESTIONS

1. What influence do nonpublic schools have on public education in the United States?
2. Where in the United States are the nonpublic schools the most numerous?
3. Should the state attempt to regulate some or all aspects of nonpublic education? Justify your stand.
4. In what ways do professional societies have an impact on public education?
5. Should administrators' organizations at the state or national level be a part of an education association which includes teachers as well? Justify your stand.

SELECTED REFERENCES

Educational Research Service, "Coleman Report on Public and Private Schools: The Draft Summary and Eight Critiques," *ERS School Research Forum,* Arlington, Va.: ERS, April 1981, 47 pp.

Gibbs, J. E., Jr., Sokolowski, C. J., Steinhilber, A. W., and Strasser, W. C., Jr., *Dual Enrollment in Public and Non-public Schools,* U.S. Office of Education, Circular No. 772, Washington, D.C.: GPO, 1965.

Lieberman, Myron, *Education as a Profession,* Englewood Cliffs, N.J.: Prentice-Hall, 1956.

McCleary, Lloyd E., and Thomson, Scott D., *The Senior High School Principalship,* Vol. III, Summary Report, Reston, Va.: National Association of Secondary School Principals, 1979, chap. 3.

Rich, W. B., "Approval and Accreditation of Public Schools," *Responsibilities and Services of State Departments of Education,* U.S. Office of Education, OE-20013, Washington, D.C.: GPO, 1960.

PART III

EDUCATIONAL POLICYMAKING AND ITS IMPLEMENTATION THROUGH THE ADMINISTRATIVE HIERARCHY: SPECIAL ROLES AND POSITIONS IN EDUCATIONAL ADMINISTRATION

Administration is a set of processes executed within a unique organizational structure designed to facilitate the delivery of educational services. The people involved within it are assigned various professional roles and responsibilities. Their titles often reflect these special roles as well as suggest the authority carried within the administrative hierarchy. Educational policies are generated by responsible lay groups but must depend upon the time and talents of administrators and supervisors for their implementation. Part III identifies the major players in the administrative hierarchy and analyzes the roles and contributions of each within the educational delivery system.

To begin with, the local board of education has both legal authority and general policymaking responsibilities at the district level. As a part-time and lay body it turns to full-time professional administrators to execute policies. The school superintendency functions as the chief executive arm of the board of education. The interface between the chief executive officer and the primary policymaking body is crucial to the success of the educational operation. The chief school executive is also viewed as the educational leader of the faculty. As the complexity of schools increased it became necessary to create additional supervision and administration positions and thus the central-office administrative and supervisory staff came into being.

The principal is the chief executive officer at the attendance-unit level and rounds out the administrative team. There is considerably more emphasis now than ever before on the administrative team. One of the exciting developments in the period following World War II has been the growth of

274 EDUCATIONAL POLICYMAKING AND IMPLEMENTATION

postsecondary institutions—notably the community junior college and the vocational-technical school.

School administrators function at various levels in the educational system. Some are concerned with problems and decisions that are system-wide in scope; others are responsible for a segment of the program as it operates throughout the system; still others are involved with educational problems in a given area or population sector of the district.

The chapters that follow emphasize that the various major policy implementations and the operational levels of school administration are complementary rather than competing. The team concept of school administration requires each level to perform those activities that are best suited to its place and role in the system and to the time and talents available.

13

LOCAL BOARDS OF EDUCATION AND EDUCATIONAL POLICYMAKING

Some public body must assume responsibility and be granted authority to develop local educational policies (the state legislature and also the state education agencies are educational policymaking bodies at the state level), determine that policies are implemented, monitor the quality of educational operations, and in other ways oversee the delivery of educational services in the most efficient and effective manner. In American public education that body is the local board of education. It is consistent with the concept of local control over public education. It carries awesome responsibilities and plays a key role in the administration of public education.

The precise title varies with the region of the nation and it may be board of education, the school committee, the school board, the school commissioners, or school inspectors. The most popular designations are school board or board of education. Its authority, method of selection, term of office, and roles are determined, by and large, by the state legislature.

Early in this century there were over 200,000 local boards of education in the United States.

The reorganization of local districts after 1950 also resulted in a tremendous reduction of school boards as well; there are now about 15,000 local school boards. Membership on these boards presently totals over 100,000—far fewer than the more than 700,000 who served earlier in this century.

The local school board is an American invention. Considerable debate swirls around this unique mechanism; it is as controversial today as it was 100 or 200 years ago. Laypersons and professional educators differ on their purposes and roles, what are defensible operating procedures, and/or what limitations should prevail on individual or group board behavior.

From a legal point of view, school board members are officers of a government corporation known as the school district. Although residing in and being concerned for education in a local district, each is a state officer performing duties related to the state function of education. Although state statutes define in a general way the responsibilities and administrative powers, an even greater number are left to the board's discretion. This legal and discretionary authority lies at the root of much of the controversy and debate. The manner in which a particular board interprets and exercises its authorities and responsibilities has a significant impact upon educational administration, the morale of the professional staff, as well as the quality of educational services delivered.

To illustrate, only the school board has the legal authority to determine salary and working conditions for teachers within the general guidelines spelled out by state legislation. Likewise, it is the board of education that decides which functions shall be delegated to the professional chief executive and which it prefers to retain, the recommendations of experts or the revelations of experience notwithstanding. Under the Hamiltonian concept of division of responsibilities between the legislative and executive branches, the school board is conceptualized as the local legislative or general policymaking body. The *execution* of a determined policy should be delegated to a full-time person with professional preparation, competencies and experience to do so, that is, policy-implementation should not be attempted by such boards. Delegations or single-issue pressure groups seek to influence or temper the general local policymaking authority of local boards of education.

HISTORY AND DEVELOPMENT OF LOCAL BOARDS OF EDUCATION

The school committee or board grew out of the New England town meeting and the committee of selectmen. Selectmen besieged with increasing local governmental responsibilities appointed, in turn, a temporary committee to perform functions such as recommending appointment of a schoolmaster or construction of a schoolhouse. This eventually led to a permanent committee on school visitation such as the one appointed in Boston in 1721.[1] It was later referred to as the school committee. The school committee was, at first, an agency of the selectmen of the town or of another governing body. Dispersal of population from the

New England town and the rise of the district system led to a separation of the school committee from other municipal governing bodies.

Legislation by the state was necessary to validate what existed in practice. Massachusetts legislation on education demonstrates the evolution of such laws. In 1693 a law was enacted that jointly charged towns and their selectmen with maintaining schools and that required selectmen to levy taxes for school support if so directed by vote of the people in the town meeting.[2] More than 100 years were to pass before school committees of Massachusetts were recognized by a law approved in 1798 as a group devoted to school problems. The final step came with the law of 1826 which established school committees as separate from other governing authorities. These committees were delegated general governance over all public schools in Massachusetts.[3] The school committee, as the governing body for public schools separate from other governing bodies of a city or town, was an early nineteenth-century product. Early in history, the local board of education was entrusted with considerable legal authority. It served as an executive as well as a legislative body.

It was the magnitude and complexity of the educational task, rather than laws or the will of the people, that precipitated a reexamination of the school board's role.

Development of General Responsibilities

Powers delegated to a board by the legislature cannot be redelegated or allocated by the board to others. In other words, the school board cannot grant authority to committees or employees or other governmental officials to perform acts which the law demands must be performed by the board as a whole. The discretionary powers of the board are reserved for it and no others.[4]

The school board can exercise those powers that (1) are granted in express words, (2) can be fairly implied as necessary or incidental to powers expressly granted, and (3) are essential to realization of purposes of educational institutions. State laws or state department regulations on such matters as certification requirements for teachers, length of the school term, submission of annual reports, and teaching of specific subjects must be implemented and their violation cannot be excused on the grounds that refusal to comply represents an exercise of discretionary authority of the local board of education. School board members must know the statutory and regulatory requirements or at least have a ready source of reference or legal counsel on such matters.[5]

There has never been a time in this century when the school board could do whatever it wished. The school board's judgment on what can promote the cause of public education can be constrained severely by highly detailed state statutes, federal laws, or court decisions demanding specific educational programs, activities, or behaviors.

There are informal external and internal constraints upon a board's responsibility and authority, such as subtle political pressures or conflicts of interest. In addition, expectations of the community or of other school board members, speaking at a state or national meeting of school board members, may influence individual behavior.

Expectations may be codified as a formal statement of ethics for school board members. A code of ethics may be expanded to define appropriate relations with other board members, the superintendent, the school staff, parents, and children. The effectiveness of such ethical constraints upon board members' behavior is influenced by the machinery for investigation, disposition, and implementation of judgments by committees concerned with promoting high standards of behavior.

Early in the nation's history individual board members interviewed all candidates prior to their employment as teachers, purchased all instructional and building maintenance supplies, supervised through a program of frequent visitations all employed personnel, and evaluated by frequent and continual observation all personnel and instructional activities. Today, direct board involvement in the myriad of operational instructional and administrative details is beyond the time and talents of individual board members and is considered to be inconsistent with effective and efficient educational administration. Boards in complex districts have important roles to play in the delivery of quality educational services. The educational policy-making function of school boards is demanding and time-consuming, and should preclude preoccupation with "administrivia" (such as debating what specific brand floor wax to buy for the school system) during board meetings. Many professional school administrators, experienced and effective school board members, as well as others, have stressed the importance of each board determining how best to utilize the time and talents of each member as well as how best to organize and utilize the time allotted for formal meetings.

The significant responsibilities of the local school board can be summarized as follows:

1. To satisfy the spirit as well as the word of state laws dealing with education and of the regulations of the state education authority.
2. To ascertain goals or objectives of public education and to prepare general policies in tune with them.
3. To select a superintendent of schools, designate him as the chief executive officer, and work harmoniously with him.
4. To strive continuously to develop further and improve the scope and quality of educational opportunities for all children and youth in the district.
5. To create policies that will attract and retain professional and other personnel needed to realize educational objectives.
6. To provide educationally efficient and safe school-plant facilities.
7. To plan for and obtain financial resources necessary to achieve educational goals.
8. To keep the people of the district informed and aware of status, progress, and problems of their schools.
9. To appraise activities of the school district in the light of its objectives.
10. To discharge its responsibilities as a state agency by participating in statewide efforts to promote and improve public education.[6]

Policymaking

Frequent and often loose use of the term *policy* compounds problems of developing its clear understanding. Policymaking may be equated with state and federal legislative activity. Far more afield, however, is the unfortunate use of the term *educational policy studies* to designate what was previously known as educational philosophy, history, and/or sociology. These foundation areas may provide basic value orientations, but do not contribute any more to the study of educational policies than do other fields outside educational administration or political science. The professors in departments titled "Educational Policy Studies" are not likely to be greater experts in the public or private policymaking process or in defining policy content.

A "policy" may be defined as a general and goal-oriented statement of intent to act, or behave, in a particular manner when confronted with a given situation or to achieve a given result within some point in time. It is enunciated as a guideline or a recommended course of action to insure either consistency and/or fairness in dealing with a situation or in achieving promised results. Policies written, published, and disseminated inform persons interacting with boards what the likely disposition is of an issue related to a policy pronouncement of the board, assuming the board acts in a manner consistent with previously agreed upon policies. A policy, therefore, is a means of coping with a myriad of specific demands with a consistent and a well thought out plan of action, and is often expressed in a general and goal-related statement.

A policy statement, therefore, should be phrased broadly enough to include the conditions or issues likely to confront a board, but at the same time specific enough to facilitate its application to particular situations that may arise. One value in preparing a policy statement, even though this may be a difficult and time-consuming process in communities where there are diverse value systems and objectives, is that it may help project the image of consistency and also fairness.

Rules and regulations evolve from and should be consistent with adopted policies. A policy does not confine one to a single strategy to achieve its objective or intent; it sets directions but does not handcuff administrative action to one way of doing things. A clear-cut distinction between the general policy and the specific rule or regulation is not always possible; there is a gray area where one leaves off and the other begins.[7] The distinguishing characteristic of a rule or regulation is its greater detail or sharper focus in defining the specific actions to be pursued in implementing part or all of a policy.

Contributions of Policies

Policymaking is a difficult, time-consuming but challenging agreement-reaching process. It requires discipline and the ability to rise above minutiae to perceive the broad picture of interrelationships in socially sensitive situations. Those with conflicting views and values demand to be heard, and should be allowed to do so, before the board determines finally the policy. In many cases how a policy is arrived at, that is, the execution of the public policy development, may be more important than the culminating act of voting on its adoption.

Most agree that written statements of educational policy adopted by the local board of education are essential to effective educational administration. In policy statements a board can express what actions should be pursued under what conditions, unify the complex system, monitor progress of educational operations, and evaluate the effectiveness of the organization. More specifically, educational policies are valuable in the administration because they:

1. Help clarify responsibilities among board, administrative staff, teaching staff, and community.
2. Help promote more consistent and prudent decision making or, stated negatively, they minimize embarrassing inconsistencies in school-board action.
3. Provide continuity of action.

4. Can save the board time, money, and effort, for many specific questions deal with similar principles, that is, repeat themselves in a variety of forms, and therefore can be handled in a manner suggested by a single policy.
5. Help improve public relations.
6. Help reduce pressure on the board from special-interest pleaders.
7. Help reduce criticism of board action when it becomes apparent to the community that board decisions are based on well-defined and consistent policies rather than on expediency.
8. Give the board a sense of direction.
9. Facilitate orderly review of board practices.
10. Ensure a better-informed board and staff.[8]

Policies are more likely to fulfill their potential if reduced to writing.[9]

One study concluded that as late as 1946 relatively few boards were concerned with written policies.[10]

Boards have been slow in translating into practice the many exhortations to prepare written statements of policy to govern school operations.

Content of policy statements. A review of local school-board policy manuals revealed little consistency of content.[11] Nearly all manuals specified bylaws governing board operation and organization as well as school business management. A majority had provisions relating to school-community relations. Lists of personnel duties and responsibilities similar to those commonly set forth in job descriptions were prominent features in most manuals examined in a U.S. Office of Education study.[12]

In general, carefully written school board policies should speak out on:

1. Legal status, functions, organization, and ethical conduct of the board of education.
2. Selection, retention, and duties of the chief executive officer or superintendent of schools.
3. Relations among personnel in the school system.
4. Scope and quality of the instructional program and school services within the system.

5. Function and operation of the school food services.
6. Procedures and other aspects of budgeting, accounting, auditing, and management of school property.
7. Operation of the pupil-transportation system.
8. Selection, retention, and other matters related to the professional personnel.
9. Selection, retention, and other matters related to the nonprofessional personnel.
10. Identification, admission, promotion, discipline, and so on, of pupils.
11. Public relations.

Policy statements should encompass all aspects of school operations that command the attention of the school board.

Approaches to Policy Development by School Boards

The steps recommended by the American Association of School Administrators and the National School Boards Association are as follows:

1. List problems that should be solved: This includes difficulties that seem to demand a large portion of the school board's time during regular meetings.
2. Review the minute book: Often records of previous decisions taken by the board shed light on items that should be included in statements of written policy.
3. Study what other boards have done: This does not imply that one school board can successfully adopt *in toto* the policy statements of another, but policy practices of other boards can be a valuable source of ideas.
4. Consult studies and writings concerned with policy development.
5. Check established practices: Some traditions of the school which were never reduced to writing previously can inspire policies.
6. Solicit suggestions from the school staff.[13]

Some boards set definite dates or times, such as once a year, to review policies and consider what revisions are necessary in the light of experience. If policies are to be a means by which the board can more effectively discharge its responsibilities, rather than a device that unduly restricts board deliberations, they must be flexible.

There is a considerable body of opinion that supports the notion that one measure of a board's effectiveness is the existence of relevant policies to govern educational affairs. Working with and living by such policies is another measure of effectiveness.

EFFECTIVENESS OF SCHOOL BOARD MEETINGS

The meeting of the corporate officers of the local school district is legally as well as educationally important. The law demands that board members meet face-to-face to decide the destiny of the district, and, therefore, an individual board member absent from a scheduled meeting cannot make decisions that bind the district. One mark of a mature and experienced board member is not engaging in individual supervisory acts or issuing public statements that seemingly commit the district to actions not established previously at regular school board meetings. Meetings are the legal way members may discharge their responsibilities for public education. Skills developed at such meetings, when coupled with a clear understanding of their appropriate role in administrating public education, determine to a considerable degree the effectiveness of individual members.

Time and Place of Board Meetings

The board has the authority to schedule meetings to suit the convenience of its members with the exception of the few dedicated to its formal organization or for other reasons specified in state statutes. About 82 percent meet in the evenings, 10 percent in the afternoon, 6 percent in the morning, and 2 percent at midday.[14]

Most boards meet about once or twice a month. Large systems enrolling 25,000 or more have board meetings typically on a Tuesday but never on a Friday.[15] There may be too many as well as too few meetings. The meeting place is usually the office of the superintendent or a special board meeting room if one exists. During recent decades the media demonstrated increased interest in school board sessions. Board meeting plans must now give consideration to the presence of TV and reporters from other media, consider who will speak for the board, what prepared statements will be issued (if any), and so on. This may tempt special-pressure groups and single-issue board members to engage in political posturing to attract media attention.

Planning for School Board Meetings

Many boards find informality a comfortable way to transact the affairs of the institution. The informality should not go to the extreme where members are unable to ascertain with certainty what was accomplished during the meeting. An informal tone can be maintained during discussion, but final disposition of the issues should follow more formal parliamentary procedures.

The order of a typical business meeting of the school board might be as follows:

1. Call to order by the presiding officer.
2. Roll call and establishment of a quorum (a quorum is usually the majority of the total board).
3. Reading, approval, and signing of minutes of the previous meeting.
4. Reporting of communications to and from the board.
5. Hearing of any scheduled delegation.
6. Report of the superintendent.
7. Unfinished business from previous meeting.
8. New business.
9. Other activities.
10. Adjournment.

An effective school board meeting (defined as one where desired accomplishments are realized with the least amount of difficulty, time, and/or effort) usually is guided by some type of an agenda—a written statement of issues, items, or decisions to be discussed or rendered and their order of consideration during the scheduled meeting. The agenda may be as simple as a one-page, or less, outline of matters reviewed or as complex as a substantial multi-page document, wherein each item of consideration is supported by detailed data related to it as well as an explanation of the consequences likely for each of the possible courses of action.

Agenda preparation is assigned usually to the superintendent, but items or topics for consideration may be submitted by board members, school personnel, or lay groups. Some boards, as a matter of policy, do not take action on items not included in the agenda on grounds of insufficient time or data for careful consideration prior to prudent decision making; others are more flexible.

The agenda is most useful when mailed to board members about a week in advance of the meeting. An agenda issued at the time of meeting is better than none. An agenda helps the board comprehend the ground to be covered and the time required to discharge the business at hand.

The laws of some states demand that all business meetings of school boards be open to the public. One study showed that 68 percent of school boards permitted the public to attend all meetings, 6 percent held only closed or executive sessions, and 26 percent held both kind. Other studies completed over 25 years ago reach similar conclusions. An Educational Research Service review in 1966 showed that over 80 percent of the large city school boards held executive sessions to discuss personnel matters, land acquisition, and cases involving individual pupils.[16]

Occasionally a school board may find it advisable to move into an executive session to deliberate on matters that might prove embarrassing or harmful to an individual or costly to the school district. For example, if a teacher is accused of wrongdoing and the evidence requires careful scrutiny and interpretation, public discussion could prove embarrassing if the teacher was innocent of the charges. Similarly, discussion of pupil disciplinary problems could prejudice the case of those involved. Anticipated purchase of a particular school site might justify deliberation in an executive meeting where the public is excluded. Executive meetings can be held at the request of the majority of members. Their continual use invites criticism and suspicion. The purpose of executive session is discussion rather than decision.

Boards may exercise discretion in selecting the time and place of special meetings, unless there are specific statutes that demand otherwise. When there is evidence that an agreement or conspiracy took place during an executive session to determine how each board member would vote in the open meeting, courts have ruled that such agreements are illegal and unenforceable.[17]

There is no legal compulsion for boards to act immediately on requests made by a delegation or for that matter even to hear out a self-appointed delegation. The board does owe local groups the courtesy of listening and informing the delegation when to expect an answer from the board or superintendent of schools. Picketing has become a frequently used tactic to force board decisions to be in harmony with the demands of the pickets. Disagreements and even violence in a community or state may find their way into board sessions. Board members cannot avoid or run away from conflict; their challenge is to manage conflict situations to minimize dysfunctions in the educational enterprise.

Role of the Superintendent in Board Meetings

Presence of the superintendent, and other key administrative staff members, at the school board meeting is desirable for a variety of reasons. One important reason is that the superintendent is the chief executive officer of the school board whose professional counsel on the administration and operation of the system is essential to the board's policymaking, decisions, and other actions. In about 44 percent of the large districts (25,000 or more enrolled), the superintendent also serves as board secretary with no vote. In general, the superintendent has no legal status at meetings, cannot vote, and is not an official board member. His/her presence at all meetings is recommended with the exception of those where the superintendent's employment status and salary are under consideration.

Minutes of School Board Meetings

The minutes constitute the official record of board actions. Courts will not admit extrinsic evidence that adds or detracts from officially approved minutes or records of board action.

School board minutes are public records and are open to examination by taxpayers or other persons with good reason to examine them. It is common for board minutes to be duplicated and copies distributed to all board members, the administrative staff, newspapers, and other interested persons. The minutes become official records and evidence after formal approval by the board and when signed by the secretary and the president of the board.

Recorded in the minutes of the board are facts such as:

1. Type of meeting and its date, place, and time.
2. Name of presiding officer and/or who called the meeting.
3. Names of members present and absent, as well as of other individuals in attendance in some official capacity.
4. Complete record of each motion, showing the vote of each board member.
5. Identification of all reports, documents, and contracts brought to the attention of the board.
6. Name and number of delegations appearing before the board and description of petitions or complaints submitted.
7. Time meeting was adjourned.
8. Signature of the secretary and president to acknowledge date of approval of minutes.
9. An addendum to show any corrections to the minutes.

A system of indexing board minutes simplifies identification of the time and nature of past board actions. These documents should be kept in a fireproof vault adjoining the board room.

ORGANIZATION OF THE SCHOOL BOARD

The local school board includes a chairman (commonly designated president), a vice-president, a secretary, and a treasurer. Duties of each of these vary in different states.[18] Boards may also create standing or permanent committees.

There were board standing committees before there were superintendents and other professional administrators. Standing committees were found in cities where board membership was very large. Thus by 1849 Boston had 214 school board members, elected by wards, serving on its various committees.[19] Philadelphia as late as 1905 was reported to have 559 school board members. The present size of school boards throughout the United States is much smaller, with most being composed of five to seven members.[20] Boards in large districts (25,000 or more) typically have seven members, only 25 percent have more.[21]

The growth and decline of school board committees can be illustrated by what occurred in Chicago. The Chicago board of 1861 constituted itself into ten standing committees. This number grew to 19 "functional committees" by 1872, 70 by 1885, and 79 somewhat later. The trend was reversed in the twentieth century, so that by 1912 the board had reduced its standing committees to 13. There were only seven permanent committees by 1922.[22]

A 1962 nationwide study of school boards[23] indicated that nearly a third of the responding systems had one or more standing committees of the local school boards. Another 22.5 percent indicated operations through special committees but no standing committee. A 1972 study confined to large school systems, which are more likely to have standing committees than smaller districts, revealed that 61 percent do not have standing committees.[24] The most common type of standing committee is the finance committee. Others include permanent committees for legislation, buildings and grounds, complaints and appeals, public relations, publications, subdistricts, audit, salaries, school supplies, community use of school buildings, insurance, libraries, designated special-subject areas, curriculum and instruction, textbooks, cafeterias, transportation, and school activities.[25]

Most boards have assigned executive functions, previously assumed by board committees, to the superintendent. The prevailing practice is operation of the school board as a unit, with technical and professional assistance provided by the professionally prepared and full-time personnel. The key to effective control is who authorizes and adopts prevailing policies and practices rather than who is delegated responsibility to implement policy.

Standing committees can lead to fragmentation of the school board. As Reeves stated:[26]

It is no more logical to have committees of laymen dealing with technical education matters, such as promotion and grading, courses of study, curriculum, school supplies, and school buildings, than it would be for a hospital board to have committees of laymen dealing with technical matters such as skin and heart diseases, gynecology, pediatrics, and operations.

CHARACTERISTICS OF SCHOOL BOARDS

The size of school boards, methods of selection, length of terms, qualifications for membership, and other characteristics have changed over the years. Membership size presently ranges from 3 to 19, and the trend is away from the extremes in size, with most being in the 5 to 9 range. The size level in the 66 large urban school districts in 1977–1978 was from 5 to 15, a range much narrower than that reported in previous studies.

Boards should be large enough to minimize the chances of domination by a single personality, but not too large to become unwieldy. A strong personality needs only one additional follower to control a three-member board.

Most board members serve for a specified term, with no statutory limitations on the number of successive terms one can continue in office, and during terms that are staggered to preclude replacement of the entire membership at a single election or appointment occasion. Most members are granted a four-year term if elected and five if appointed. Vacancies are filled, usually, through a vote among remaining members. The replacement continues in office for the remainder of the unexpired term or until the next regular election for board members completing a full term.

In 33 states, all school board members are elected by popular ballot; in the remaining states some may be elected and the others appointed. Appointive boards predominate in only three states: Indiana, Maryland, and Virginia. The appointing authority may be a mayor, governor, county court, city council, grand jury, or judge of the court of common pleas.[27] Ninety percent of elected boards were in the Northeast, North Central, and West. The larger the city the more likely it is that board members will be appointed, but even in the large systems about 80 percent of board members are elected to office.

Any qualified voter is eligible to seek board membership in most school districts. Reference to educational qualifications of board members are found in statutes of 11 states. Thus, Kentucky requires a minimum of eighth grade education or its equivalent. In other states such vague expressions as a "fair elementary education," "able to read and write," and "practical education" are employed. Maryland and North Carolina laws require "character and fitness" of those who aspire to board membership. Arizona board members must be taxpayers or have a child in school. In New York, board members of all except city districts must satisfy the following qualifications: (1) own, hire, or lease property within the district; (2) be a parent of a child who attended school for some time; (3) have a child attending school in a district residing with him. A 1946 report by the National Education Association indicated that 61 percent of the school board members had children attending school during their period of service, while 26 percent had children attending school at one time or another.[28] Only 13 percent of the school board members did not have any children attending school at any time.

Most school boards (about 82 percent) are elected to office at nonpartisan elections and from the district-at-large instead of by wards. Selecting board members from the district-at-large is used exclusively in 17 states and to some degree in 26 others. There is general agreement among authorities that boards should be elected-at-large and at nonpartisan elections. A reverse trend is evident in some states experiencing a considerable amount of reorganization which involves a partnership between rural and urban areas.

Compensation of board members is neither a rarity nor a common practice. Where compensation is allowed and practiced the amounts paid have increased in recent years. In 1972 those that paid a salary to board members ranged from a high of $5500 in Florida to a low of $36 in Ohio. The majority of systems paid no annual salary (57.5 percent), although mileage and expenses were permitted as incurred.[29]

A National School Board Association study of 66 urban school districts in 1977–1978 revealed a significant change in remuneration policies for board members over a ten-year period.[30] The majority received no remuneration in 1967–1968, but ten years later two-thirds did receive monthly or weekly payments. The amounts paid previously also increased over that period. In 1980 the annual salary for school board members in Washington, D.C., was $17,500. The majority of school boards in California have not approved member compensation, but some such as those in the Los Angeles Unified School District may receive up to $1000 per month. In general, it can be said that for the United States as a whole the traditional no payment for board members was modified significantly during the 1970s, and there is a strong possibility that before the end of the century most boards may receive compensation. Participation in school board activities is a public service and compensation should be of little or no importance to those selected. Some argue that salaried board members are more likely to assume executive prerogatives in attempting to justify the compensation received.

A composite profile of the typical school board in a large system in 1972 showed it to be:[31]

1. Representative of the entire district.
2. A seven-member board.
3. With members serving four-year staggered terms.
4. Elected.
5. Male-dominated.
6. Meeting once or twice per month.
7. Operating with standing committees.
8. Operating with no salary compensation to members.
9. Served by a superintendent designated as board secretary.
10. Filling vacancies by board vote until next election.

More recent data near the end of the 1970s (1977–1978) revealed some modifications in the 1972 board profile:[32]

1. The majority still represented the district as a whole, but more tended to represent an area within the district (about 23.5 percent in 1977–78 compared with 13.7 percent in 1970–71).
2. The 7 member board remained most popular; there were a total of 506 board members in the 66 urban districts.
3. The length of terms did not change.
4. Election continued as the dominant pattern, only 1 in 6 appointed.
5. Male domination of urban boards was reduced significantly by 1977–78 but still continued; women accounted for 42 percent of urban board members in 1977–78 compared with only 24 percent in 1970–71. (Nationally, women account for only 1 in 4 board members.)
6. Meeting once or twice a month continued as the prevailing pattern. The percent of boards meeting 48 or more times per year

doubled over a ten year period to almost 24 percent of all urban boards by 1977–78.

7. About two-thirds of the urban districts operated with standing committees.

8. The big shift near the end of the decade was that two-thirds of all board members in urban districts received some compensation; this is a reversal from the pattern of a decade earlier.

9. By 1977–78 only a minority appointed the superintendent as board secretary, and there was an increase in separate board staff resources and found in 90 percent of the urban districts.

10. Filling vacancies remained pretty much the same throughout the decade.

The typical urban school board member near the end of the preceding decade was white, male, married, earned some type of college degree, was likely to have school-age children, and was between ages 45 and 50. Minority representation shows an upward trend from 14 percent of total membership in 1967–1968 to 24 percent in 1970–1971 to 31 percent in 1977–1978.

EFFECTIVENESS MEASURES FOR SCHOOL BOARD MEMBERS

The following criteria were suggested as measures for determining the performance effectiveness of school board members:

1. Acceptance of the principle of board unity and subordination of self-interests. This demands that a board member set aside personal desires in favor of realization of the board's objectives and priorities, adhering to the legislative and policymaking functions of the board, and refusing to speak or act on school matters independent of board meetings.

2. Effective understanding of the executive function and willingness to support it during the implementation of policies. This means recognizing the importance of delegating executive responsibilities to the chief school executive officer, supporting the executive officer in authorized functions, and encouraging team work between the executive officer and the school board.

3. Demonstrating initiative and formal leadership on the board.

4. Effectiveness of social and personal relations in spite of personality differences or value orientations noted in board members or others.

5. Effectiveness in staff and group relations.

6. Courageous action for the good of the school system in spite of pressure groups and criticisms. This means being able to weather periods of intense criticism, maintaining valid and firm convictions, taking sides in the face of possible controversy, and sharing responsibility for whatever board actions.[33]

SCHOOL BOARD AND SUPERINTENDENT RELATIONS

The school board and superintendent are members of the same administrative team, share common desires for enhancing the quality of education in the district, and frequently experience the same pressures and criticisms that face the public schools. They work together closely and continuously during the employment period of the superintendent. Differences of opinion should be expected to arise occasionally, but need not precipitate conflict. The complexity of public education today demands a competent professional manager. Likewise, professionals must keep in touch with the community and their perceptions of the effectiveness of the public schools in the district. Board members are essential for that purpose as well as others. In short, the possibilities of conflicts notwithstanding, school boards need superintendents and school superintendents need school boards.

There were some in previous times who questioned the need for school boards. The late C. H. Judd, Dean of the School of Education at the University of Chicago, wrote in 1934 that school boards were an obstruction to good school administration and were survivals from an age when professionalization of schools was less advanced.[34] He was not the first, nor the last, to question the need for school boards. Mark Twain is reputed to have said: "First God made idiots. That was for practice. Then he made school boards." This unwarranted generalization from some inept rural boards in the last century persists despite its lack of substantiation.

Dr. Judd held that no private corporation could be successful if its board of directors behaved toward managers and operatives as boards of education commonly behaved toward superintendents and other members of the school staff. He concluded that there would come a day when school boards would be abolished. (There is no evidence some 50 years later to even hint at the probability of school boards being abolished in any state). His position was an extreme expression of professional impatience with school boards.

An almost immediate rebuttal came from another educator, Dr. Fred Engelhardt, Professor of School Administration at the University of Minnesota, who proclaimed that the general indictment of school boards contained in Judd's article was unfair, prejudiced, and not founded on fact.[35] He went on to say that if professional leaders in schools had been required to face the period from 1930 to 1934 without the assistance of lay school boards, the status of public education during the early depression years might have been much worse than it was. Many superintendents today would be the first to admit that public schools would have suffered more than they did from the vicious attacks upon public education immediately following World War II as well as the militant actions of the 1960s if there had been no school boards.

The Judd–Engelhardt debate is of historical interest, but few today question the significance or importance of school boards in the administration and operation of public education. Boards have gained stature during the past two decades. Many communities are blessed with truly outstanding school board members. The primary emphasis today is on identifying what characteristics lead to effective board leadership, developing orientation programs for people newly elected, and preparing guidebooks to enhance the quality of what some call "boardmanship." The American belief in keeping schools close to the people by vesting educational control in representatives of the people or school boards remains sound and has served the country well.

The relationships between school boards and superintendents during the past two decades have shown signs of serious strains as evidenced by the shorter tenure of school superintendents in larger communities and the propensity of boards to acquire professional staff assistance apart from the superintendent of schools. The conflicts between the two important top level positions in a local district tend to increase as board members focus less on policy formulation and more on managerial functions.

The school superintendent is the board's chief executive and should be used as chief counsel in educational decisions. A board of education that almost ignores professional workers and tries to operate schools on opinions of school janitors or of alarmed and upset parents will continue to experience unnecessary problems. Everybody feels qualified to criticize the schools, but it is the board's *duty* to appraise the school. This appraisal must be based on facts and sound judgment.

The administrative team concept is rapidly gaining hold, whereby schoolboard members, superintendents, principals, and teachers are regarded as members of a team. Each has a specific function to perform, with one depending upon the other.

NEW DIRECTIONS FOR THE SCHOOL BOARD

The stress and strain confronting boards of education are related to the unusual demands facing public education. Board members in some cities have endured physical harm as well as emotional strain. The role and influence of the school board in public education have changed to cope with factors as:

1. The increased emphasis upon instructional quality, the growing expectations for public schools, and the greater complexity of educational operations.
2. The increasing militancy of teachers and the greater use of collective bargaining with teachers' groups. Work stoppages in the public schools are more common and serve to compound greatly the problems of board members.
3. The increased involvement of the federal government as an enforcer of specific kinds of court decisions or laws, such as those dealing with civil rights, and as a stimulator of special programs in which the federal government has an interest.
4. The conception of the school as an institution capable of ameliorating social injustices.
5. The increased number of pressure groups, sometimes violent, and the greater use of protest and demonstrations in and out of school board meetings to influence school policies.
6. The increased emphasis on innovations rather than on the continuation of operations as usual.
7. Changing expectations for public education at the local, state, and federal levels. Criticisms of public education wax and wane, but seldom disappear.
8. The involvement of many informal and formal agencies and professional and non-professional groups in the operation of public education.
9. The difficulty in obtaining additional resources for the operation of public education at the very time expectations are increasing and programs are becoming more complicated.

It is heartening to see efforts of state and national school board associations to improve the leadership quality of school board members by operating clinics, workshops, and conferences.

THE RESOLUTION OF CONFLICT

James[36] summarized the conclusions reported in a number of doctoral dissertations at Stanford University examining school board conflict with the superintendent, the teachers, the community, the state, and the federal government. One concluded that rapid growth of the community was related to the greater likelihood of earlier than anticipated termination of relationships between the school board and its superintendent. Another reinforced a previous discovery that board members improve with experience, and members with long board service are better at managing conflict. A third study concluded that the recall election was not a satisfactory means for resolving board-community conflicts. Recall election campaigns tend to intensify conflicts and polarize the community. The power of the board is misunderstood, and most citizens believe that the board has more authority and discretion than actually exists. A further study revealed that the traditional rule-making responsibility of the school board has degenerated into rule application and rule adjudication. James concluded that conflicts are inevitable, and therefore one mark of a vigorous and healthy school board is successful management of conflict.

Fowlkes presented a series of generalizations drawn from University of Wisconsin studies on citizens' perception of boards of education. These include:

1. Citizens have little knowledge of how school boards function.
2. Citizens' expectations vary on what a board should do.
3. Members of boards of education disagree on school functions.
4. Board membership is valued differently by people who are and are not on school boards.
5. Citizens have little knowledge of the functions of the superintendent and his importance to schools.
6. School board meetings may fall short of potential value.
7. Citizens' knowledge and the specificity of their expectations of schools seem to be related

closely to whether they have children attending school.

8. Teachers generally have little knowledge about school board operations.[37]

McCarty[38] reported that a board of education tended to exhibit the same kind of power structure as its community. He developed a model that depicted the school board as either dominated (looking to one member for a decision), factional (dependent on a majority for a decision), status congruent (dependent on discussion), or sanctioning (dependent on the recommendations of the superintendent).

SUMMARY

The local board of education is an American invention. It is the basic administrative agency for public education in the United States. The numbers of such boards have declined from over 200,000 to about 15,000. It represents the general policymaking level in school administration. The board evolved out of the town meeting and special committees of selectmen of the town. During colonial days and the early part of the nineteenth century, the board served as a legislative and an executive body. The growing complexity of educational institutions demanded a separation of these functions. The board of education is presently regarded as the legislative rather than the executive agency.

The most important contribution of a board of education to the administration of public education is the formulation of policies to guide the institution toward its goals. A "policy" is the general statement of intent to act in a particular way when confronted with a given situation or to achieve a given result at some future point in time; rules and regulations are more specific statements derived from the general policy. Although there has been agreement among authorities on the desirability of written policies, most school boards have not as yet satisfied this requirement.

The board of education carries out its responsibilities at the school board meeting. Board authority to allocate district resources is restricted to actions consummated at authorized meetings. The agenda, prepared by the superintendent beforehand, is a key to effective board meetings. The superintendent should be present at all meetings but has no vote.

Standing committees were more numerous when boards served executive as well as legislative functions. The numbers declined, but there are a majority of urban school boards that operate with them today.

Most school boards are elected on a nonpartisan ballot and from the district-at-large. Only in a few states are all boards of education appointed to office. Most school board members serve without fiscal compensation. In those districts where board members receive stipends, the total amount paid increased substantially during more recent years. The typical school board has from five to seven members, although some have as few as three members and others as many as 19.

One of the fundamental responsibilities of the board today is the management of conflict. The traditional rule-making responsibility of the board has degenerated into rule application and rule adjudication. A board tends to exhibit the same kind of power structure as its community.

NOTES

1. Charles E. Reeves, *Schoolboards: Their Status, Function, and Activities,* Englewood Cliffs, N.J.: Prentice-Hall, 1954, p. 17.
2. Ibid.
3. Ibid., p. 20.
4. Robert R. Hamilton and E. Edmund Reutter, Jr., *Legal Aspects of School Board Operation,* New York: Teachers College, 1958, p. 6.
5. Ibid., p. 4.
6. S. J. Knezevich and H. C. DeKock, *The Iowa School Board Member,* Des Moines, Iowa: Iowa Association of School Boards, 1960, pp. 17–18.

7. Alpheus L. White, *Characteristics of Local School Board Manuals*, U.S. Office of Education, Bulletin 1959, No. 14, Washington, D.C.: GPO, 1959, p. 3.
8. American Association of School Administrators and National School Boards Association, *Written Policies for Schoolboards*, Washington, D.C.: The Association, 1955, p. 6.
9. Ibid.
10. White, op. cit., p. 1.
11. Ibid.
12. Ibid.
13. American Association of School Administrators and National School Boards Association, op. cit.
14. Reeves, op. cit., p. 195.
15. Educational Research Service, *Local School Boards: Status and Structure*, Circular No. 5, August 1972.
16. Educational Research Service, "Local School Boards: Status and Practices," Circular No. 6, November 1967.
17. R. L. Drury and K. D. Ray, *Principles of School Law*, New York: Appleton-Century-Crofts, 1965, p. 18.
18. Reeves, op. cit., chap. 8.
19. Ibid., pp. 20 and 27.
20. Morrill M. Hall, *Provisions Governing Membership on Local Boards of Education*, U.S. Office of Education, Bulletin 1957, No. 13, Washington, D.C.: GPO, 1957.
21. Educational Research Service, "Local Boards of Education: Status and Structure," op. cit.
22. Reeves, op. cit., p. 25; National Education Association, "Status and Practices of Boards of Education," *Research Bulletin*, Vol. 25, No. 2, April 1946, p. 62.
23. L. White, *Local School Boards: Organization and Practices*, Washington, D.C.: GPO, 1962, p. 41.
24. Educational Research Service, op. cit.
25. Reeves, op. cit., p. 121.
26. Ibid., p. 125.
27. Educational Research Service, op. cit.
28. National Education Association, "Status and Practice of Boards of Education," *Research Bulletin*, Vol. 24, No. 2, April 1946.
29. Educational Research Service, op. cit.
30. National School Board Association, *Public Education in the Nation's Urban School Districts*, Washington, D.C.: The Association, 1979, 101 pp.
31. Educational Research Service, op. cit.
32. National School Board Association, op. cit.
33. Richard E. Barnhart, "The Critical Requirements for School Board Membership Based on Analysis of Critical Incidents," doctoral thesis, Bloomington, Ind.: University of Indiana, 1952.
34. Charles H. Judd, "School Boards as an Obstruction to Good Administration," *The Nation's Schools*, Vol. 13, No. 5, February 1934, pp. 13–15. Also note William McAndrew, "School Boards from Below" and "A Disease of School Boards," *The Nation's Schools*, Vol. 3, No. 5, May 1929, pp. 21–23; and Vol. 3, No. 6, June 1929, p. 30.
35. Fred Engelhardt, "In Defense of School Boards," *The Nation's Schools*, Vol. 13, No. 5, May 1934, p. 21.
36. H. T. James, "School Board Conflict Is Inevitable," *American School Board Journal*, Vol. 154, No. 3, March 1967, pp. 5–9.
37. John G. Fowlkes, "What Does the Public Expect of the Board?" *American School Board Journal*, Vol. 154, No. 3, March 1967, pp. 10–12.
38. Donald J. McCarty, *Myths and Realities in School Board Research*, Washington, D.C.: American Educational Research Association, 1966.

CHAPTER REVIEW QUESTIONS

1. Can an agency serve adequately as a legislative as well as an executive body? Justify your stand.
2. What conditions led to the development of the concept that a board of education should confine its activities primarily to the formulation of general policy?
3. What is a policy?
4. Why should a board prepare written policies?
5. What is the significance of the statement: "A board speaks through its minutes"?
6. Why are school board meetings so important in the administration of public education?
7. What should be the role of the superintendent and other professional staff members at the school board meeting?
8. How can school board meetings be made more productive?
9. What is the best method of selecting school board members?
10. What are the functions of the school board?

SELECTED REFERENCES

Educational Research Service, "Orientation Programs for New School Board Members," *ERS Information Aid*, Arlington, Va.: ERS, 1975, 33 pp.

Fowlkes, John G., "What Does the Public Expect of the Board?" *American School Board Journal*, March 1967, pp. 10–12.

James, H. T., "School Board Conflict Is Inevitable," *American School Board Journal*, March 1967, pp. 5–9.

McCarty, Donald J., and Ramsey, Charles E., "Community Power, School Board Structure, and the Role of the Chief School Administrator," *Educational Administration Quarterly*, Spring 1968.

National School Board Association, *Public Education in the Nation's Urban School Districts*, Washington, D.C.: The Association, 1979, 101 pp.

Reeves, Charles E., *Schoolboards: Their Status, Function, and Activities*, Englewood Cliffs, N.J.: Prentice-Hall, 1954.

14

THE SCHOOL SUPERINTENDENCY: THE CHIEF SCHOOL EXECUTIVE AND EDUCATIONAL LEADER

The professionally prepared chief school executive or general administrator is referred to most frequently as the superintendent of schools, as the general superintendent, or the school district administrator. The designation of the chief executive as "president" is more common in institutions of higher learning.

The superintendent is usually the only professional employee in the administrative hierarchy who reports directly to the board of education. The authority within the superintendency is a delegated authority. The board determines what authority shall reside within the superintendency to implement board policies and to operate the system in an efficient and effective manner. Superintendents are held accountable for realizing educational objectives and the delivery of quality educational programs and services. No longer a one person operation, the superintendency in today's complex school systems comprises a cluster of positions. The administrative team at the general executive level functions to enhance the quality of educational programs and services. More will be said about the administrative team in the chapter that fol-

lows. What follows here is an analysis of the roles and responsibilities of the chief school administrator as a leader, decision maker, educational planner, and change agent.

EVOLUTION OF THE SCHOOL SUPERINTENDENCY

The professional school superintendency is a relatively recent development, being only about 150 years old; it emerged many years after other administrative positions were established and continues to change to meet the challenges of the times. It evolved as a new administrative position in educational systems only after other approaches failed to administer effectively the dynamic and complex systems of public education. There were no school superintendents when the national Constitution was adopted. The primitive accommodations that served as the "schoolhouse," the simple curricular fare, and the few students made possible relatively successful school management as a part-time activity that required only limited experience and no professional preparation. Policymaking and policy execution were not separated during the town hall meetings in this early period of the nation's history.

The rapid growth of populations and enrollments during the nineteenth century demonstrated that an administrative and operational system that worked well in isolated rural schools failed in the larger and more dynamic urban communities. A strong antiexecutive attitude prevailed among American colonists—an attitude evident in the state constitutions adopted from 1775 to 1800.[1] It is not surprising, therefore, that the appointment of a full-time administrator as an executive officer for the school system as a whole was delayed almost 200 years—two centuries after the start of the American system of public education.

By 1850 many school boards in large cities were ready to admit that executive problems such as supervising instruction, grading schools, and keeping track of school property in rapidly growing systems were beyond the capabilities of a lay, part-time administration agency.[2] This started the search for alternatives. The creation of the American school superintendency was the alternative destined to survive in spite of resistance.

Thirteen school systems established the city school superintendency between 1837 and 1850. Buffalo and Louisville are credited with the creation, in 1837, of the first superintendencies in public education. The number of teachers at the time of appointment of the first superintendent ranged from only 4 in St. Louis in 1839 to 2168 in Philadelphia in 1883. The dates of establishment (and in some cases reestablishment) of the superintendency in 39 cities are presented in Table 14.1. Only about a dozen cities created the school superintendency prior to 1850. Before the nineteenth century came to an end, the superintendency concept was to be recognized as the only promising solution to the administrative problems confronting public education.

Some of the early city school superintendents were elected to office by popular vote. This approach was short-lived and soon most were appointed to office by school boards. The county and state superintendents, in contrast,

started as elected officials also, but this method of selection persists today in many states.

The school superintendency was well established in many jurisdictions by the time of the Civil War. For a time there existed a full-time professional executive as well as some part-time lay standing committees that continued to be involved in managerial or operational responsibilities. The existence of two agencies with administrative responsibilities precipitated misunderstanding and conflict then as it does today. The origins of many school board–superintendent controversies can be traced back to how the position was created and how long board committees continued to assume operational functions.

Brief tenure for board members meant the same for the superintendent as well.[3] The early superintendent was the administrative assistant of the board; there was not any question then as to "whose man" the superintendent was. Board executive committees continued to exercise considerable administrative authority during all of the nineteenth century.[4] This greatly inhibited the demonstration of the professional skill and leadership ability of the school superintendent then as it does during the late twentieth century. Only a few nineteenth-century school boards were ready to grant the status of chief school executive officer to the superintendent.

Most early superintendents focused on instruction. The delegation of responsibilities for fiscal affairs or schoolhouse construction and maintenance did not come until early in the twentieth century.[5] These functions were retained the longest by boards in fiscally dependent districts or where the city council controlled school finances. The superintendent was pictured as the instructional leader concerned with developing a graded organization for schools, designing new courses of study, and organizing pupil promotion procedures. Many boards held opinions that the "scholarly executive" did not have "a head for business" and had "little interest in many of the supplementary executive activities."[6]

Few state statutes defined the school superintendency, most simply authorized creation of the position in districts of a certain size. It is

TABLE 14.1

ESTABLISHMENT OF THE SCHOOL SUPERINTENDENCY IN 39 CITIES

City	Year of establishment	Year of reestablishment	Population as of nearest census	Population at time of reestablishment as of nearest census
Buffalo	1837		18,213	
Louisville	1837		21,210	
St. Louis	1839		16,469	
Providence	1839		32,171	
Springfield	1840	1865	10,985	15,199
Philadelphia	1840	1883	93,665	847,170
Cleveland	1841	1853	6,071	17,034
Rochester	1841		20,191	
New Orleans	1841		102,193	
Brooklyn	1848		96,838	
Memphis	1848		8,841	
Baltimore	1849	1866	169,054	267,354
Cincinnati	1850		115,435	
Jersey City	1851		6,856	
Boston	1851		136,881	
New York	1851		515,547	
San Francisco	1851		56,802	
Nashville	1852		10,165	
Newark	1853		38,894	
Los Angeles	1853		1,610	
Chicago	1854		29,963	
Indianapolis	1855		8,091	
Detroit	1855	1863	21,019	45,649
Worcester	1856		24,960	
Minneapolis	1858		2,564	
Milwaukee	1859		45,246	
New Haven	1860		45,267	
Savannah	1866		28,235	
Kansas City	1867		32,260	
Pittsburgh	1868		86,076	
Washington, D.C.	1869		109,199	
Richmond	1869		51,038	
Wilmington	1870		30,841	
Denver	1871		4,759	
Atlanta	1871		21,789	
Omaha	1872		16,083	
Portland	1873		8,293	
Seattle	1882		3,533	
Salt Lake City	1890		20,768	

Source: Theodore Lee Reller, *The Development of the City Superintendency of Schools in the United States,* Philadelphia: published by the author, 1935, pp. 81–82. Selected cities that were over 100,000 in population in the 1930 census.

more likely to be defined in states where it is a constitutional office. Thus, in Florida, the position of county superintendent of schools (which is the local school district superintendent, since the county is a basic unit of school administration) is rather well defined in terms of authority, responsibility, and relations with the county board of public instruction. McCann reported that the school codes in only about half the states define the relationship between the board and the superintendent.[7] The courts of 13 states have declared superintendents to be officers of the board, whereas 6 others ruled they are employees.

Experience and recommendations of authorities on school management have done more to shape the superintendency than did state or federal legislation or agency directions. A recodification of state statutes to define more clearly the status, authority, and responsibility of the superintendent of schools in public education would be desirable.

DEFINING THE ROLE AND RESPONSIBILITIES OF THE CHIEF SCHOOL EXECUTIVE

The superintendent's close working relationship with the board and the fact that he/she serves at the pleasure of the board are enough to indicate the importance of effective superintendent–school board relationships. The superintendent is professionally obligated to either implement board policies, even though opposed to them, or resign. The superintendent cannot expect the board to shield the position from all criticism, but is entitled to board public support when carrying out board directives or policies.

The American Association of School Administrators (AASA) suggested that the superintendent has a right to:

1. The support of his board members as long as he is superintendent.
2. Provision of the tools and clerical assistance necessary to carry on the work of his office effectively.

3. Protection from work days that are too long and from too close attention to his job (vacations should be provided for him as well as his staff).
4. Protection from an unreasonable termination of his contract.
5. Protection from people who would use his office for the personal gain of prestige.
6. Protection from factions.
7. Protection against excessive or unfair criticism.
8. Appreciation of the board when his work is satisfactory.[8]

Collective bargaining is a relatively new responsibility for the school superintendent. A third party, namely, the chief negotiator for the school board, could be placed between the board of education and the superintendent. Earlier in history, business operations were delegated to a school business manager who reported directly to the board of education rather than to the superintendent of schools. A dual system of administration fraught with conflicts and problems was thus born, and over 50 years were needed to reestablish the unit system of administration with one executive officer responsible to the board. If the chief negotiator reports directly to the board, he/she will be coordinate with the superintendent, and once again a dual system of administrative organization results.

If the school board seriously questions the professional leadership of the superintendent, the situation should be discussed forthrightly, not clandestinely at meetings involving school board members only. In some states, the state school board association in cooperation with the state administrator association attempts to help an individual board discuss differences with its superintendent. Reluctance to discuss openly an unpleasant situation should be overruled by the responsibility of both parties to act in the best interest of the children and youth of the district. Board members have an obligation to evaluate the effectiveness of their superintendent and to make their findings known. If, after exhausting all reasonable efforts toward corrective action, the board still finds the performance of the superintendent unsatisfactory, he/she should be informed of the decision and be permitted to resign. The board has an obligation to present to the superintendent the specific reasons that have led to dismissal.

The board's delegation of special authority to other members of the administrative hierarchy is especially important to the superintendency, particularly where others are allowed to report directly to the board. A board may openly or inadvertently opt for the *unit system* or *multiple system* of administrative organization.

In the *unit system of educational administration* the board delegates responsibility for executing all dimensions of the system to a single or chief executive officer. The chief executive is usually the superintendent of schools, who is accountable to the board for educational administration and operations. All other professional employees are subordinate in administrative authority to the superintendent and submit information or reports for the board of education through the superintendent.

In the *multiple system of educational administration* two or more persons report directly and independently to the board of education. Each of the administrators has equal authority, that is, the positions are considered coordinate. A few boards have gone so far as to divide responsibilities in separate domains for independent administration such as instruction; auditing; logistical support and finance; building planning, construction, and maintenance; and public relations. An administrator who has coordinate status with other top executives may be appointed to head each of these major divisions. The superintendent of instruction, with whom most professional employees would interact, would require a very strong personality to assume a position of leadership in the multiple system of administrative organization.

The *dual system of educational administration* is the most common of the multiple systems. It usually consists of a director of business affairs, who reports directly and independently to the board, and therefore has coordinate administrative status with the superintendent of schools, whose authority is limited to instructional activities. Most management specialists recommend the *unit system* as the most effective mode. The right kind of organizational structure can facilitate the leadership, decision making, planning, and change agent roles of the superintendent of schools. Working relations between the teaching faculty and the superintendent can become confused if there are too many layers of administration between the two, if there are communication gaps or breakdowns between them, and if the superintendent lacks the status of chief executive officer of the board of education.

PROFESSIONAL AND PERSONAL CHARACTERISTICS OF SUPERINTENDENTS

About every ten years since the early 1920s the American Association of School Administrators (AASA) has reported on the characteristics of the American school superintendent. The first such reading was based on 1921–1922 data and published in 1923; others appeared in 1933, 1952, 1960, 1971, and 1982. (World War II interrupted the study of the superintendency in 1940–1941.)

Mobility and Tenure

The various AASA studies reveal that school superintendents, in general, are not highly mobile. During 1969–1970, about 71 percent served in only one or two districts; seven out of eight had experiences in no more than three systems.[9] Movement from state to state at that time was even more limited, for better than nine out of ten completed their administrative careers in a single state. The superintendents in large urban school systems are more likely to move across state borders; almost two-thirds in 1969–1970 in districts with enrollments of 100,000 or more were superintendents in two or more states. The 1982 AASA study confirmed that not much had changed during the past decade and reported there was "Little interstate mobility: 1.1 states is the median".[10]

The smaller the school district enrollment the greater the likelihood that the superintendent's contract will be limited to only one year.

In contrast, districts with 25,000 or more are likely to issue contracts with terms of 4 years or more. The average contract or appointment period for superintendents was 2.6 years in 1982.

Superintendency turnover increased during the past two decades as a result of greater pressures on the position and heightened tensions between boards and superintendents. The 1982 AASA study reported that nearly half the superintendents accepted another position because it was viewed as a promotion or a higher salary was offered. About 15 percent cited conflict with the board as the reason for leaving.

Death of a superintendent while on the job is an unusual occurrence in any given year. The majority of states reported no deaths; one state, however, during 1969–1970 reported the deaths of five superintendents. About 2 to 3 percent of the superintendents retire from their positions.

Entry into Administration

The 1982 AASA study revealed that superintendents were a little over 23 years of age when appointed to the first full-time position in education. This changed little from the data based on the 1969–1970 year. About 95 percent reported classroom teaching experience compared with the 74 percent of the superintendents who had teaching experiences in 1921–1922.

No single discipline can be called a breeding ground for future superintendents, although teaching courses in the natural sciences, social studies, and mathematics were among those commonly experienced. The 1982 AASA study noted that more had elementary school teaching experience, fewer were from the secondary social science fields, and more indicated English teaching. The data from the two most recent AASA studies of the superintendency dispel the slowly dying myth that the typical superintendent is an ex-physical education instructor.

The typical future educational administrator devoted about 6 years or so in the classroom prior to entry into administration. There is no indication as yet that there are many who move directly from graduate study at a university (without any previous education or other employment experiences) into an administrative or supervisory position. About 79 percent in 1969–1970 (but only 42 percent of the superintendents in 1982) indicated they coached some type of an athletic team as part of their extracurricular responsibilities.

The 1982 AASA study revealed that the superintendent-to-be was about 29½ years of age when appointed to his/her first administrative/supervisory position, whereas the 1969–1970 study showed this age to be 30.4 years and the 1960 data only 27½ years. The entry position into administration was most likely to be the principalship (assistant principal or principal); almost 71 percent used this as a beginning in 1969–1970 and almost 75 percent did so in 1982. The assistant superintendency was the initial administrative appointment in less than 3 percent of the cases. Ages 26 to 34 were prime periods for the initial entry into administration/supervision; over two-thirds of those who were part of the 1982 AASA study started their management careers during this age range. Less than 14 percent entered into an administrative/supervisory position at age 25 or younger; only about 6 percent of the superintendents were appointed to their first management post at age 40 or later. Appointment to the superintendency came later with the mean age for attaining this position being about 35, according to the 1982 AASA study. Less than 5 percent in 1969–1970 and only 3 percent in 1982 were appointed to their first superintendency at age 50 or later.

OTHER PERSONAL CHARACTERISTICS

Data released in 1982 confirmed what was indicated in 1969–1970 and earlier, namely, that the superintendency continues to be male dominated, for almost 99 percent are men. Only 2.1 percent in 1982 were from minority backgrounds. Most superintendents come from rural or small city communities. Some increase in the numbers coming from large cities or their suburbs was noted in the 1982 AASA study. Superintendents serving districts with enrollments of 100,000 are more likely to come from the very large cities.

In 1982 the median age of the superintendent was found to be 48.7 years or about the same as that reported from 1969–1970 data but a little younger than the median of 49 in 1950–1951 and 51.8 in 1958–1959. The typical superintendent in 1921–1922 was about 43 years of age and the age level increased in each subsequent decade until 1958–1959 when the increasing age trend appeared to hit a peak and then started a slight reversal. As late as 1958–1959 there were no big city superintendents under the age of 40, but by 1969–1970, 3.6 percent were under 40.

About 75 percent of the local district superintendencies in 1982 were in districts with enrollments of less than 3000. Only 1.3 percent of the school districts enroll 25,000 or more, or a total of 189.

Professional Preparation

In 1922 about 13 percent of the superintendents had no degree and 65 percent attained a bachelor's degree or less. In 1982 there were no superintendents without an earned degree and almost 99 percent earned a master's or higher degree. There were substantial increases in the level of professional preparation among educational administrators during recent decades.

The 1982 AASA study reported the following distribution of preparation achievements for superintendents: bachelor's degree, 1.1 percent; master's degree, 48 percent; specialist degree, 17.1 percent; and doctor's degree, 33.4 percent (with 2.5 percent of the respondents giving no indication or other status).[11] The percent with earned doctorates was more than double that indicated for 1969–1970. The percent pursuing further study beyond the doctorate almost doubled during the same period (2.9 percent in 1969–1970 compared with 5.4 percent in 1982). The earned doctorate was particularly evident among superintendents in the very large systems. By 1969–1970 a majority

(almost 65 percent) of superintendents in systems with 25,000 or more enrolled had earned at least a doctorate; this increased in 1982 to 77 percent with an earned doctorate or even more graduate study.

An earned doctorate may be the minimum preparation level for the school superintendency in most large districts during the 1980s; there may be demands for postdoctoral specialization at the beginning of the next century.

The typical superintendent devotes more than 55 hours per week to official duties. This includes three or more evenings per week, two or more Saturdays a month, and at least one Sunday a month to educational responsibilities.

PROFILE OF THE 66 LARGEST URBAN SCHOOL SUPERINTENDENCIES

An increase in the percent of superintendents from minority backgrounds was noted in the large urban school districts during the 1970s. By 1977–1978, 16.4 percent of the superintendents in the 66 large urban districts were black; in 1973–1974 about 9.5 percent were black.[12] The status of women did not change as dramatically for only two were reported in the 66 large urban districts in 1977–1978 as compared with one in 1973–1973 and none prior to 1969–1970.

More surprising is that less than half (43 percent) of superintendents in these large districts had earned doctorates in 1977–1978. Some ten year earlier about seven out of eight districts with 100,000 or more enrolled had superintendents with earned doctorates. Admittedly the samples taken during the two periods are not the same, but the results for the period near the end of the 1970s were not anticipated. Almost 20 percent of the 66 districts reported the master's as the highest degree in 1977–1978; more than 80 percent, however, had a degree beyond a master's or higher accomplishment.

There appeared to be a higher incidence of internal promotion to the superintendency in the 66 largest districts, for well over one-half (57.4 percent) had six or fewer years experience in the chief executive position. The median level of experience as superintendent for this group was only about five years; more than 31 percent had three or fewer years of experience in the top managerial position.

There were indications of a relatively high turnover rate in the large urban superintendencies during the 1970s. Over 60 percent had served four or fewer years as superintendent, the median length of service was only 3.5 years. The high turnover is not surprising given the declining enrollments, desegregation conflicts, rapidly escalating operating costs, teacher militancy, and other sensitive problems facing the great cities and their school systems.

COMPENSATION TRENDS FOR SCHOOL SUPERINTENDENTS

The median salary paid school superintendents at the end of selected decades since 1920 is presented in Table 14.2.

The 1950–1951 salary was only slightly more

TABLE 14.2

MEDIAN SALARY OF SUPERINTENDENTS 1920–1921 TO 1980–1981

Year	Median Salary
1920–1921	$ 3,390
1930–1931	$ 4,050
1950–1951	$ 6,804
1958–1959	$10,733
1969–1970	$17,310
1978–1979	$39,344[a]
1980–1981	$43,055[a]

Source: S. J. Knezevich, *The American School Superintendent,* Arlington, Va.: The American Association of School Administrators, 1971, p. 39.

[a]Educational research data based on districts with 300 or more enrolled as reported in Educational Research Service, "Scheduled Salaries for Professional Personnel in Public Schools, 1980–81," *ERS Report,* Arlington, Va.: The Service, 1981, p. 25 and 40.

than double the 1920–1921 median salary. At the end of the next 30-year period the median salary for superintendents increased sixfold, with the most dramatic gains occurring during the 1970s. A salary of $50,000 appeared to be a psychological barrier until the beginning of the 1970s when the highest superintendent's salary reached $56,000. A decade later the $120,000 salary for the Chicago superintendent and $100,000 for deputy superintendents for the 1980–1981 year were among the most dramatic in the history of compensation for those in the superintendency. There was a tremendous gap between that paid in Chicago and the next highest superintendent's salary of $71,225 for that same year. All others were below $70,000, but 26 superintendents received salaries in the $60,000 to $69,999 range. At the beginning of the 1980s over two-thirds of superintendents in districts with enrollments of 25,000 or more were paid $50,000 or more; the mean was $53,565. The mean salary for all superintendents (where enrollments were 300 or more) in 1980–1981 was about $43,000.

The so-called fringe benefits are an important part of a compensation package. The superintendent receives the usual benefits accorded other employees in the system, such as sick leave, disability insurance, retirement contributions, and health or hospitalization insurance. The most common additional benefit to the superintendent is a transportation allowance which is provided in almost 96 percent of the districts. Less than half of the districts provide a car for the superintendent; providing a chauffeur is a rarity. An overwhelming majority also provide expenses to attend state, regional, or national professional meetings.

The overwhelming majority of districts *do not* provide the following benefits: housing (almost 98 percent do not), country club or other social club dues (98 percent do not), sabbatical leave with pay (86 percent do not), or paid-up life insurance policy (94 percent do not). Only a minority appear to pay for required physical exams (about 23 percent do), dues to professional organizations (37 percent do), and severance pay (almost 26 percent do).

THE SUPERINTENDENT SELECTION PROCESS

The process used by school boards to select a new superintendent of schools changed significantly during the past two decades. The complexity of educational administration was the primary force that brought to an end what was previously a relatively informal set of search procedures. Laws dealing with affirmative action in personnel employment also demanded more carefully orchestrated procedures.

Prior to 1960 it was the unusual school board that employed a consultant or team of consultants to facilitate the superintendent search process. Today this is a relatively common procedure even though the selection of consultants may be relatively informal. The superintendent search procedures outlined in previous editions of this volume have not changed significantly over the past decade. What has changed is the number writing about and recommending the implementation of more formal search procedures.

In general, the steps to follow in the formal superintendent search process, with or without assistance from consultants, would include:

1. Identification and description of the primary roles, responsibilities, and status of the superintendency—with special emphasis on professional relationships with the board of education—within the specific district. This should be a realistic and somewhat detailed "position description" or "role analysis" representing the beliefs of the board as a whole and agreed to by all. The external consultant(s) may or may not be involved in this step of the process, but usually may make their most important contribution to the process in this step if consultants are to be employed.

2. Determination of the professional and personal preparation levels, experiences, competencies, and other qualifications desired in persons who will receive consideration for the superintendency. These qualifications should recognize the needs of the district at this point in time and should be related to the "position description" or "role analysis" developed in step one. The procedures for making the position qualifications determination include gathering data from the community, professional staff, as well as school board members. This may be done by holding hearings to which various community and education groups or organizations may be invited to present diverse points of view on the educational leadership needs of the school system. Such procedures demand additional time, expenditure of resources, and often patience to listen to all with something to say. Consultant(s) may or may not be involved at this stage, but can make a contribution and relieve the school board of a time-consuming responsibility. The process may be condensed if a community-wide search committee is organized with diverse community and professional representation. The objective of step two is to generate a set of criteria relevant to the needs of the district and that may be employed in assessing the qualifications of position applicants.

3. Determination of the date for the formal announcement of the superintendent position vacancy, salary range for the position, desired employment starting date for the new superintendent, and other pertinent search issues as the prelude to the dissemination of the position vacancy notices. Consultants usually assist in the design of the position-announcement brochure.

4. Distribution of the formal position-search announcement brochures to appropriate persons and agencies, along with requests for nominations and indications of application cutoff dates, and so on. This is often viewed as the "beginning" of the formal search process; important planning activities should precede this phase. Consultant(s) often are delegated responsibility for this phase of the search.

5. Screening of applications received based upon criteria and agreements developed in (1), (2), and (3) above. The screening may be done by a community-wide search committee, a subcommittee of the school board, or consultant(s).

6. Development of special competencies in applicant interview procedures and in applica-

tion materials analysis may be desired in some situations. This may be done through board interview and sensitivity-training seminars usually designed and conducted by consultant(s) when such special services are requested and included in the contract of employment. The extra time taken to develop effective interviewing techniques, what to look for in letters of application and those of recommendation, how the board can gain consensus on various candidates, and so on, may prevent subsequent conflicts and delays in completing the search process.

7. Initial or screening interviews of the more promising applicants by the search committee or consultant(s) on board subcommittee.

8. Interview of five to ten finalists by the board as a whole with visits to the communities of those candidates receiving more serious consideration.

9. School board deliberations in postinterview sessions to obtain preliminary agreement on one or no more than three possible finalists. Intraboard conflicts may emerge with special private (nonpublicized) meetings with consultant(s) who may try to frame the issues and suggest means for their possible resolution.

10. Selection by the board as a whole of the successful candidate for the superintendency and agreements on compensation to be paid and any conditions related to the beginning of employment. The consultant(s) should not be involved in the final determination of the successful candidate.

11. Board offering of the position through formal and written communication. If position is accepted under the conditions stipulated, then there is the formal preparation and signing of a contract of employment by the new superintendent of schools.

12. Public announcement released by the school board and press conferences introducing the new superintendent of schools.

One of the ever-present issues is whether the board should select from within or seek outside talent as well. In 1982 about 38 percent of those selected were "insiders"; 62 percent were "outsiders." It is not prudent to announce a decision before the search process begins, for all worthy applicants deserve serious consideration. Harvis wrote about the superintendent selection process from the board member's perspective.[13]

CERTIFICATION REQUIREMENTS FOR SUPERINTENDENTS

Superintendent certification is a post-World War II development by and large. As late as 1966 four states required only the equivalent of a bachelor's degree for certification. By 1970, however, all but one state requiring some type of certification demanded a master's degree, or its equivalent, or higher. Certification requirements are summarized in Table 14.3.

Only Florida, Michigan, and the District of Columbia issue no certificates for superintendents. In contrast, some states have two or more certificate levels.

Professional preparation is only one requirement for certification as superintendent. Some states specify that the experience shall be in education. Others declare it must be in teaching. In some cases, experience as a principal is necessary for a superintendency certificate. In 1953 and again in 1970, five years of experience was the most common requirement for certification as superintendent; three years was the next most common.

Typically the initial certificate as superintendent is valid for five years, three years, or life, in that order. Certificates after the initial one are valid for life in most states.

There was considerable discussion of the competency-based approach to administrator certification in the 1970s. The competency-based certification issues may be resolved by the end of this decade.

Trends in certification requirements for superintendents clearly indicate that higher professional preparation standards are being incorporated into laws or board of education regulations.

The answer to improving the quality of school administration in public education is to upgrade the quality of preparation programs and to increase the period of preparation. As the professional preparation requirement for the superintendency increases to six years or beyond, an internship program will be necessary to provide practical administrative experience.

APPRAISAL OF THE SUPERINTENDENT OF SCHOOLS

Informal and nonobjective evaluation of the superintendent has been and continues in many

TABLE 14.3

PROFESSIONAL PREPARATION REQUIREMENTS FOR CERTIFICATION OF SUPERINTENDENTS, 1972

State or territory	Years of preparation	State or territory	Years of preparation
Alabama	5[a]	Montana	5
Alaska	5	Nebraska	5
Arizona	6[b]	Nevada	5 + 15 hrs.[d]
Arkansas	6	New Hampshire	6
California	7	New Jersey	5
Colorado	6	New Mexico	5
Connecticut	6	New York	6
Delaware	6	North Carolina	5
District of Columbia	5, NC[c]	North Dakota	5
Florida	NC	Ohio	6
Georgia	5	Oklahoma	5
Hawaii	5 + 20 hrs.[d]	Oregon	6
Idaho	5	Pennsylvania	7[e]
Illinois	6	Puerto Rico	5
Indiana	6	Rhode Island	5
Iowa	6	South Carolina	6
Kansas	6	South Dakota	5
Kentucky	6	Tennessee	5
Louisiana	5	Texas	6
Maine	5	Utah	6
Maryland	6	Vermont	5
Massachusetts	4 + 15 hrs.	Virginia	6
Michigan	NC	Washington	6
Minnesota	5 +	West Virginia	6
Mississippi	5	Wisconsin	5
Missouri	6	Wyoming	5 + 15 hrs.[d]

[a]Five years is a master's degree or at least a bachelor's degree plus 30 hours.
[b]Six years is a master's degree plus 30 hours or a specialist degree.
[c]NC = No certificates for superintendents issued. District of Columbia issues no administrator's certificate but requires a master's degree for all position holders.
[d]Designates a master's degree plus additional hours of study beyond that degree.
[e]Designates a doctorate or 70 semester hours of work including at least a master's degree.

places an almost daily and popular pastime. What was new during the 1970s were the efforts to produce a fair, objective, and relevant system of appraisal for all types of administrators including the superintendent. Prior to 1970 there were thousands of articles on teacher evaluation but "only three articles on evaluating the superintendent."[14]

The initial focus of formal administrator evaluation was the principalship and not the superintendency. Principals had professional educators as their "superiors" which permitted implementation of the "superior evaluates subordinate" concept, but the superintendent's superiors were members of the lay board of education. The observation phase of teacher evaluation begins with classroom visits to observe teaching behaviors and performances with students. The observation phase of administrator evaluation is less meaningful, for viewing what goes on in the superintendent's office is less productive and meaningful than watching teacher behaviors in the classroom.

Management - by - Objectives - and - Results (MBO/R) that came into education during the early 1970s offered another approach to the appraisal challenge. It emphasized the outcomes-oriented appraisal of managers based on the so-called MBO or MBO/R contracts. In this approach the school board, not some self-appointed community or professional group, assumes the primary appraisal responsibility, designs the instrument to be used in evaluation, identifies procedures to be employed, and determines when the process will be consummated in a fair and equitable manner. Personal traits of the superintendent or activities analysis that show the superintendent to be busy, a hard worker, and so on, become less important than the results achieved and for which the chief executive could be held accountable.

Results-oriented appraisal, sometimes called MBO or MBO/R, starts with specifying job targets for the year, is based on mutual agreement and understanding between evaluatee and evaluator that these targets are relevant and realizable, focuses on the results obtained at the end of the year, and concludes with a written report on the degree to which previously set objectives were satisfied by the evaluatee. These results may serve as the initial step toward further professional development and improvement of the superintendent.

The 1982 AASA study of the superintendency reported that performance evaluation occurred annually among 69.5 percent, semiannually among 7.7 percent, at contract renewal time among 10.9 percent, and "never" among 4.9 percent (with 7 percent indicating "other" or "don't know").[15] Only 45 percent of the superintendents favored the so-called "formal approaches." In actual practice almost 30 percent were evaluated formally, 42.5 percent informally, 25.5 percent both formally and informally, and the remaining 8.6 percent didn't know or failed to respond as to what procedures were used.[16]

Some superintendents continue to resist formal assessment, and thereby by implication accept the subjective approaches by self-appointed groups or the board of education. Superintendents are visible and cannot avoid appraisal; they can, however, influence the development of more objective instruments and procedures for appraisal. By the end of the 1980s it will be the unusual school district that does not have a formal, annual, more objective, and continuing system of administrator appraisal that will also include superintendents.

SUPERINTENDENT CHALLENGES AND PROFESSIONAL GROWTH

The American school superintendency is complex, sensitive to social as well as educational forces, and dynamic. It demands professional growth as an integral part of the position to insure the quality of public education, the prudent use of educational resources, the ability to cope with the many conflicts and pressures, and maintenance of a high level of professional competence and personal responsibility.

A quality preservice professional program that terminates with an earned doctorate in educational administration provides the school executive with the entry level of competencies required for successful performance. Preservice preparation is the beginning of a lifetime dedicated to continuing professional development. This makes it necessary for the profession as a whole, as well as graduate institutions of higher learning, to design and implement a new set of vehicles to provide the quality of professional growth experiences required for today's administrator.

During 1967–1968 an operational model for the AASA National Academy for School Executives was developed specifically to respond promptly to some pressing educational needs and to provide national leadership for the continuing professional education of practicing school administrators. It was the first time that a well-defined, sharply focused, multidimensional, and operationally feasible national in-service institution for school administrators had been translated into an action plan. The affiliation of the National Academy with AASA provided it with a national and professional base needed to gain credibility with the profession. The academy continued to grow and gain acceptance during the 1970s and into the 1980s. It served as the model for similar efforts by professional associations for supervisors, principals, and other administrators as well as for special state efforts by universities and associations.

Although the superintendency is the same in principle in whatever size school district, the manner in which the superintendent executes responsibilities in a large district is distinctly different from what happens in a small district. In a small school district, the superintendent comes to know in a face-to-face relationship most members of the administrative and supervisory staff. From such contact comes considerable information about how the system is operating and where incipient trouble spots may be. In a large and complex district it is physically impossible to have frequent personal contacts with the large professional staff. The superintendent must instead depend upon oral and written reports from members of the adminis-

trative team. Knowing what kind of information an executive officer needs to gauge progress and problems within a school district and who is best qualified to supply it is a significant challenge to the superintendent in the large urban district.

The superintendency is being recognized as a complex cluster of leadership, decision making, planning, and change responsibilities that have a profound impact upon the operation and outputs of the educational organization. It is no longer a one-person operation. The concept of the superintendency and administrative team was developed in response to the many challenges in educational administration. This is the substance of the chapter that follows. It presents a modern-day perception of the American school superintendency.

SUMMARY

The American school superintendency is a relatively recent administrative development, being only about 150 years old; it emerged many years after other administrative positions were established and continues to change to meet new challenges. It evolved as a new administrative position only after the failure of other approaches. It was a position born of conflict and in the face of traditional antiexecutive attitudes. School boards attempted to cope with the complexity of educational administration by forming standing committees to implement policies, but by the time of the Civil War most saw the futility of this approach and the superintendency was created.

The superintendency evolved without much legislative direction from the state level. Problems in the relatively new post were compounded by the propensity of board executive committees to continue to exercise administrative responsibilities during all of the nineteenth century.

Basic to effective school administration is a clear understanding of the difference between policymaking and policy execution. There is a need for a specific enumeration of the superintendent's functions. The superintendent has a right to the support of the board as well as to the provision of the necessary tools and clerical assistants to accomplish tasks. The management of disagreements between the board and the superintendent is essential for effective school operations.

The superintendent is also the professional leader of the staff. The relations to the staff are defined by the board of education. The unit type of administration is more effective than other types.

The typical superintendent is a man 48 years old who started as a classroom teacher at age 23. His first administrative position, typically a principalship post, was gained by age 29 and his first superintendency by age 35. The majority have at least a master's degree; the larger the district the more likely it is that the superintendent will have a doctorate. The superintendency in the 66 largest urban districts changed during the 1970s. By the end of the 1970s about 16 percent of urban district superintendents were black, whereas in previous decades

there were none. Very few women as yet are employed in this capacity. Compensation for the superintendent increased markedly during the 1970s. A superintendent's salary of $120,-000 was reached in 1980–1981, and over two-thirds received annual salaries of $50,000 or more when employed in districts with enrollments of 25,000 or more.

The superintendency selection process has become more formal, and consultant(s) may be employed to facilitate the process. Certification standards now exist for school superintendents in most states. More demand six or more years of professional preparation for entry into the superintendency than ever before.

The 1970s witnessed the development of more formal, objective, and result-oriented superintendent appraisal to fill a void that existed previously. The emphasis on continuing professional development of all administrators is increasing and special mechanisms such as the AASA National Academy for School Executives are in full operation to facilitate realization of the professional development objectives.

NOTES

1. Leonard D. White, *Introduction to the Study of Public Administration*, rev. ed., New York: Macmillan, 1939, p. 20.
2. Thomas M. Gilland, *The Origin and Development of the Power and Duties of the City-Superintendent*, Chicago: University of Chicago Press, 1935, chap. 9.
3. Ibid., p. 124.
4. Arthur B. Moehlman, *School Administration*, Boston: Houghton Mifflin, 1940, p. 246.
5. Ibid.
6. Ibid.
7. Lloyd E. McCann, "Legal Status of the Superintendent of Schools as a Public Officer," unpublished doctoral dissertation, Greely, Colorado: Colorado State College of Education, 1951.
8. American Association of School Administrators, *School Board-Superintendent Relationships*, 34th Yearbook, Washington, D.C.: The Association, 1956, pp. 63–65.
9. S. J. Knezevich, ed., *The American School Superintendency, an AASA Research Study*, Arlington, Va.:

American Association of School Administrators, 1971, pp. 39–41.
10. L. L. Cunningham and J. T. Hentges, *The American School Superintendency 1982: A Summary Report*, Arlington, Va.: American Association of School Administrators, 1982, p. 23.
11. Ibid., p. 39.
12. National School Board Association, *Public Education in the Nation's Urban School Districts*, Washington, D.C.: The Association, 1979.
13. Nancy F. Harvis, "Recruiting and Selecting a Superintendent—as Viewed by a School Board President," *ERS Monograph*, Arlington, Va.: Educational Research Service, 1977, 55 pp.
14. Educational Research Service, "Evaluating the Superintendent of Schools," *ERS*, Circular No. 6, Arlington, Va.: ERS, 1972, 35 pp.
15. L. L. Cunningham and J. T. Hentges, op. cit., p. 33.
16. Ibid.

CHAPTER REVIEW QUESTIONS

1. Enumerate the conditions that stimulated the creation of the post of school superintendent. Enumerate those that inhibited its development.
2. Why are standing committees of the board in fundamental conflict with the functions of the superintendent?
3. What factors were responsible for an increase in the maturity and professional preparation of superintendents?
4. Should certification standards for the superintendent be based on no less than seven years of professional preparation? Justify your stand.
5. Why is involvement in programs of continuing professional development essential for all educational administrators including those with earned doctorates?
6. Debate: Resolved that formal evaluation of the superintendent should be illegal, for it may undermine the effectiveness of the chief school executive.
7. Who should evaluate an administrator—community, teachers, administrative colleagues, or the school board? Justify your stand.
8. What would be a fair package of compensation (salary and fringe benefits) for a superintendent?

SELECTED REFERENCES

Cunningham, Luvern L. and Hentges, Joseph T., *The American School Superintendency 1982: A Summary Report,* Arlington, Va.: American Association of School Administrators, 1982.

Educational Research Service, "Evaluating the Superintendent of Schools," *ERS,* Circular No. 6, Arlington, Va.: ERS, 1972, 35 pp.

Harviss, Nancy F., "Recruiting and Selecting a Superintendent of Schools—as Viewed by a School Board President," *ERS Monograph,* Arlington, Va.: ERS, 1977, 55 pp.

Knezevich, S. J., ed., *The American School Superintendent,* an AASA Research Study, Arlington, Va.: American Association of School Administrators, 1971.

Reller, Theodore L., *The Development of the City Superintendency of Schools in the United States,* Philadelphia: published by the author, 1935.

15

THE ADMINISTRATIVE TEAM AT THE CENTRAL-OFFICE LEVEL: SPECIALIZED MANAGEMENT AND SUPERVISORY PERSONNEL IN THE HIERARCHY

During the past 50 years over 90 percent of local school districts were eliminated, school enrollments almost doubled, and the number of school teachers increased by 250 percent. In addition to the significant quantitative changes, there were qualitative improvements. Thus, more comprehensive and varied educational programs were made available in more schools, and more different types of learners, including those with severe learning problems and other exceptionalities, were being served in regular classrooms and special schools. The setting for the delivery of expanded educational opportunities became more challenging with rapidly escalating price inflation, collective bargaining demands of teachers and support personnel, and with many sensitive social problems brought to the schoolhouse door.

Given the major educational revolution during past decades in our society and the continually rising educational expectations, it is essential for the continual well-being of the educational enterprise that the quality of administrative and supervisory staff be improved, expanded, and reconceptualized where neces-

sary. This is necessary at the central-administrative level (including the superintendency), the special management and supervisory levels, as well as at the school site or principalship level. The last will be reviewed in the following chapter. This chapter will focus upon the superintendency and supervisory levels.

EVOLUTION AND DEFINITION OF THE ADMINISTRATIVE TEAM CONCEPT

The development of a central-office administrative staff began with what shall be called the "one-person-office-of-superintendent." It was not unusual to find the individual at the top administrative level teaching a class or two, coaching athletic teams, and working with little or no clerical support services. As late as 25 years ago, the superintendent in many small districts served as the elementary and secondary school principal.

The initial advance occurred when the chief

school administrator was allowed to focus on leadership and management by being relieved of nonadministrative functions such as teaching and coaching. The next came with the authorization of full-time clerical and other "nonprofessional" resources to enhance operational effectiveness. The third phase in the evolution was evident when full-time and separate elementary and secondary principals, where enrollments were of the size to warrant such actions, became a part of the total administrative staffing for the district.

Districts with large enrollments were the first to complete the initial three steps toward developing the administrative team concept. The next phase took a long time coming even in the very large school systems. The "one-person-office-of-superintendent-of-schools" continued during the 1950s even in school districts with a total population of 75,000 or more. Sometimes the development of the administrative team concept was retarded by the ego of the individual personality who believed "if you want something done right, do it yourself." In other cases, the school board and many community leaders were concerned about having "too many chiefs and not enough Indians" and, therefore, had trouble accepting the importance or need for an administrative team. As a result, for most of the history of the American school superintendency, there were no, or very few, specialized line administrators between the superintendent and principals.

It was the extremely rapid growth in size and complexity of school districts during the 1950s and 1960s that helped to break down the resistances to and triggered interest in the team administration concept. As M. J. Rathbone, former board chairman of Standard Oil Corporation, put it: "Investment for modernizing plant and equipment is often wasted unless there is a corresponding investment in managerial and technical talent to run it." The typical school central-office administrative staff is barely adequate (in size) to keep the system operating efficiently and less than adequate to cope with social issues, implement promising practices, and engage in professional negotiation.

Some boards were quicker to sense the need for administrative team staff strength than others, but shied away from full implementation because of fiscal restrictions on the district. The multiplier effect of administrative leadership is impressive but not always recognized; one person at any of the top two or three administrative echelons can influence the development of 1000 teachers and at least 20,000 students.

Identification of administrative team members (those between the superintendent and principals) by title is not easy, for little uniformity exists among districts. The designations include "central-office administrators," "superintendent's staff," "administrative or instructional specialists," or "administrative team members." The last has some merit because it conveys the notion of a network of interactive professional relationships among specialists who facilitate the effective administration of complex educational systems.

Analysis of the Team Concept

A team is a unit, that is, it is more than a collection of individuals in physical proximity to each other because of office location, frequent attendance at the same meetings or other reasons. The test of a team concept occurs during the performance of functions that require the intimate interplay of specialized talents and a high degree of precise communication among team members. A team may be described in terms of its functions, structure, or the strength of one or more individual personalities.

Relatively few studies on the administrative team concept have their setting in educational institutions. From an organizational and structural point of view, bureaucracy gives form to the team. The team, however, is described better in the human relations context than in Weber's bureaucratic context. The unifying factors are the social system with its communication networks as well as personal values, commitments, and abilities. Each team can be characterized by its unique set of values, commitments or objectives, behavior norms, rewards systems, recognition patterns, and so on. Within this unique social system the concerted action of many reinforces the efforts of each to achieve what each acting separately could not hope to accomplish.

The administrative team may be perceived as differentiated staffing applied to management rather than instruction. It is differentiation based on specialized talents as well as varying degrees of authority as suggested in Weber's bureaucratic theory. The team is molded into a unit that is bound together by mutual acceptance and agreement on goals, mutual respect for the need for each other's talents, and mutual acceptance or loyalty to the team leader and chief executive.

Differences in backgrounds, experiences, and preparation are welcomed. When the superintendency began to evolve as a cluster of leadership and management positions, the initial approach to expansion was to employ another administrative generalist with a professional profile similar to that of the superintendent. This occurred in the early stages of the principalship team development as well. This was based on the belief in the desirability of interchangeability of functions among team members, that is, everyone should be prepared to handle anyone's responsibiliies within the system. Homogeneity of professional competencies led to the initial conception of the administrative team as a cluster of people trained in pretty much the same way, to do pretty much the same things, and to complete assignments in pretty much the same fashion. Replication was the approach, it was believed, to administrative team development.

This, however, is not the perception of the administrative team projected in this volume. It is argued here that an administrative team is conceptualized better as a unified cluster of diverse specialists rather than as similar generalists. Analogies with baseball and football teams may help make the point. An effective baseball team is not one where all players can hit well but no one can pitch or field well. Not every player is required to play every position on the team equally well. Likewise, few would bet on a football team composed of 11 "quarterback types." Recognition of the need for clusters of persons with varied abilities to perform the many but different and essential roles well is the first step in building the effective team in any endeavor.

It follows that it is not necessary for everyone on the administrative team to be able to teach any subject well, to prepare budgets with great skill, or to manage well all dimensions of change. The team leader must know the special talents and limitations of each team member and how to coordinate the contributions of each to enhance the productivity of the educational organization as a whole. There is no reason why a computer specialist should have ten years of classroom teaching experience simply because this is desirable for other educational supervisors or directors who are more intimately involved in instructional and curriculum development.

The educational management, or "superintendency," team may be summarized as follows:

$$EMT = \text{Relevant Specialized Talents} + \text{Differentiated Role Assignments (or Specialized Functions)} + \text{Leadership}$$

Collective and coordinated actions of team members can result in more productive use of resources and a higher probability of achieving objectives.

The more complex the team the more vital becomes the concern for the flow of information that influences prudent decision making among the variety of coordinated administrators. Practically all wrong decisions in history from Darius' attack on Marathon to the birth of the Edsel can be traced in large part to inefficient or inadequately processed knowledge.

Each team has a personality. It may reflect the impact of a dominant chief executive, the uncertainties of a community in ferment, or individual hangups. The personalities of professionals selected for key positions are as important as the total number of positions available. Administrative assistants can make the general superintendent look good or bad.

More than one ex-superintendent can tell the story of how demise was hastened by some key assistants who failed to give 100 percent support and commensurate efforts.

Team skills do not come naturally. In some large corporations as much as 20 percent of a manager's time may be devoted to further training to sharpen team skills.

RESEARCH ON THE ADMINISTRATIVE TEAM

What many refer to as the "administrative revolution" is in large measure the emergence of professional managers and also the use of team administration, that is, establishment of cooperative efforts among a variety of administrative specialists.

A 1971 AASA publication viewed the team as a "cluster of supportive administrative positions . . . created to enable the superintendent to amplify his efforts" and this leadership team was "composed of administrative specialists who hold the titles of deputy, associate, assistant and district, or area superintendent."[1] In relatively fewer instances, the team concept embraced personnel at lower levels such as supervisors, directors, and coordinators.

Often formal designation of membership on the administrative team was appointment to the superintendent's cabinet. The cabinet is an advisory body to the superintendent as well as a strategy planning group.

Principals were included as members of the administrative team, as witnessed by their involvement as formal participants in the "superintendent's cabinet" in smaller school systems. There were a few large systems where principals were represented in the cabinet. The AASA study revealed that approximately 44 percent of school systems included those holding rank of assistant superintendent or above within the superintendent's cabinet.[2] The heads of the four educational functions typically included instructional activities, business administration, pupil services, and staff personnel. Public relations and general administration were included less frequently.

The Educational Research Service (ERS) reported that only a limited number of systems considered the principal and the heads of such newer school district functions as research, federal projects, negotiations, intercultural education, and data processing to be members of the administrative cabinet.

The three functions of instruction, business administration, and general administration tended to hold higher rank positions on the leadership team than other functions such as staff personnel, public relations, and pupil services.

The larger the district, the larger is the size of the superintendent's cabinet. Membership of the cabinet ranges from 2 to 28, but the median size for districts of various enrollment groups is narrower from a low of 5 to a high of 12.

Some writers use *teaming* as the new term for the older concepts of democratic administration, participative management, or shared responsibility for decisions. In another case, the interest of some principals in a few states to engage in direct collective bargaining with school boards on matters of wages and working conditions caused some to recommend an administrative team configuration that included principals as members. Whether the limited or the more general conceptualization is used, neither should be confused with a leadership style such as democratic school administration or participative management. Not everyone agrees at this point in time on a basic definition or the limitations that apply to the management team concept.[3]

Operational Impact of the Administrative Team

The superintendency may be an "impossible" position if practices inconsistent with realities are continued, such as those which tolerate operation with fewer administrative posts than warranted. A rapidly expanding and radically changing school district needs more administrators than one that is less dynamic but is of similar size. A general superintendent maximizes leadership potential by selecting the right combination of administrative and/or supervisory talents; conversely, best efforts may not help improve quality if assistants lack the necessary competencies or loyalties needed for effective teamwork.

There is the added implication that when the superintendent, as team leader, is dismissed, other key administrators on the team must be prepared to resign. A board that fires its superintendent implies dissatisfaction with the entire administrative team, not simply with the captain. "Fire me, fire my assistants" may sound brutal to some, but it is not unrealistic.

The newly appointed chief executive should be free to appoint key administrative team members. Some incumbents may be reappointed if appraisal of the situation shows this to be in the best interests of the new team and the school system. Loyalty is then due to the newly appointed chief and not to the predecessor. Failure to support the superintendent by withholding or delaying key information, slowing down the decision process, or covertly planting doubt in minds of superiors as to the superintendent's effectiveness becomes a threat to the tenure of administrative assistants as well. If this seems overly harsh on other administrative personnel, the existing pattern is unusually harsh on superintendents. This concept of employment or disemployment of the administrative team is what prevails presently in the executive branch of the national government. The cabinet, or key members of the president's "administrative team," resigns when the president leaves office for whatever reason.

Determining the composition and formally appointing qualified persons to the administrative team are among the more crucial decisions to be made by a new superintendent.

New Designs for the Administrative Team

The administrative and leadership style of the chief school executive will be reflected in the kind of team created, how well it functions, and the esprit de corps within it. The primary thrusts should be on instruction or the delivery of high quality educational programs and services. A variety of specialists in education have emerged to facilitate the improvement of the curriculum and instruction. Instructional leadership specialists should be key members of the educational management team.

Administrative specialists are needed as well to cope with other dimensions of the educational organization such as conflict management, effective use of computers and educational data, collective bargaining with teachers and other organization personnel, identifying and implementing new approaches, and more productive uses and better protection of educational resources.

There is an art to being number two or three in an administrative hierarchy, and there are competent professionals who experience difficulty in performing such roles in the team situation. There are organizational prima donnas with the intellectual ability and special training and experience who perform well as number one in simple situations but who somehow manage to confound the productivity of teams in larger and more complex operations. Even assembling the best possible people may on occasion result in various personalities going their separate ways with little concern for the functioning of the team as a unit. Creating an administrative team may appear to be relatively simple; experience, however, has demonstrated that a number of unknowns related to human interactions in sensitive social and professional situations make it a difficult and challenging assignment requiring careful monitoring and the courage to make the personnel changes that are in the best interests of the organization.

It can also be argued that the racial, ethnic, social, or economic backgrounds of the community being served as well as personnel characteristics should be considered in forming the effective management team. This suggests that team members are selected in terms of their special competencies to communicate or relate to various segments of the community or employed personnel.

It is incumbent upon educational administrators to remain sensitive to internal and external forces that may necessitate a change in the configuration of the management team. The administrative staff should be at the cutting edge of the profession and the community. Form follows function. The team, its size and its shape, should reflect the functions of importance to be performed.

TITLES AND TYPES OF ADMINISTRATIVE TEAM MEMBERS

Members of the administrative team include personnel with such diverse titles as deputy, associate or assistant superintendent; director; supervisor; administrative assistant; coordinator; and consultants, all of whom are attached to the office of the superintendent of schools. Individuals in such posts are charged with responsibilities that are system-wide in scope but limited in range within the institution. Thus, the supervisor of music functions are system-wide in scope but confined to music; the assistant superintendent in charge of elementary education is responsible for elementary education only, but in all parts of the system. The central-office administrative staff concept does not include itinerant teachers of art who are called erroneously "art supervisors" but actually teach in several buildings rather than supervise in any one.

Dividing the work of the superintendent among the central-office staff should include delegating authority to accomplish tasks. Delegation involves the following: assignment of duties by an executive to subordinates, the granting of permission to make commitments, utilize resources, and determine other actions necessary to perform delegated duties; and the creation of an obligation on the part of each subordinate to the executive for satisfactory performance of duties.

The laws of some states call for the establishment of assistant administrative and supervisory positions when there are 30 or more teachers in a system, others when there are 50 or more, and others when there are 100 or more. Specialized positions vary with the characteristics of the system; these are discussed later in this chapter. It is useful here to review some of the basic concepts of organization and to apply them to central-office personnel.

When the span of supervision of the superintendent becomes so large that he/she is unable to act in an effective manner, a subordinate position is needed. Effective span of supervision is related to such factors as:

1. Time available for supervision.
2. Mental capacity and personal adaptability of the executive responsible for supervision.
3. Complexity of the situation being supervised.
4. Other duties of the executive.
5. Stability of the operation.
6. Capability and experience of the individuals appointed to subordinate positions.

Functions of an advisory nature can be performed by personnel in staff or in line positions. There is considerable question about the value of differentiating between staff and line on anything but a very broad basis.

The majority of professional central-office staff personnel are supervisors or consultants (an arrangement that appears to be gaining in popularity). These include elementary school supervisors and secondary school special-subject supervisors (for instance, in art, music, physical education). Individuals in these posts supervise activities of personnel in attendance centers.

The appropriate size of a central-office staff cannot be determined only on the basis of number of pupils and teachers within a district. As long as districts grow at varying rates, have pupils with significantly different social, cultural, or intellectual backgrounds, and are not likely to accept innovations in the same way or at the same speed they will need different numbers and types of central-office personnel to operate effectively.

The Deputy and the Area Superintendent

The deputy superintendent is superordinate to assistant superintendents. The deputy superintendent accepts any responsibility delegated as the immediate representative with operating authority. Unlike the assistant superintendent, the deputy superintendent is not responsible for a particular division of the school system, such as elementary or secondary education. Closely related to the deputy superintendency is the area superintendency in very large school systems organized to achieve some measure of decentralization. The term *district superintendent* may be synonymous with *area superintendent* if the district is thought to be a portion of a large city school system. The area superintendent is responsible for all aspects of administration of public education within a subdivision of a district in very large and populous school systems such as those in New York, Los Angeles, and Chicago. The area or "district" superintendent is a special type of deputy superintendent with general administrative responsibilities in a specific geographic area of a local district.

The deputy and the area ("district") superintendency should not be confused with the "assistant to the superintendent," sometimes called the "administrative assistant." Deputy and area ("district") superintendents are delegated line, or operating, responsibilities, whereas an administrative assistant is a staff position. In 1982 the number of subdistricts within the 48 large urban school systems so organized ranged from a low of 2 to a high of 37, and about 60 percent had either 3 or 4 subdistricts.

The Assistant Superintendent

The assistant superintendent is the most common of the major administrative positions at the top level of the hierarchy. The assistant superintendent's responsibility may be assigned on the basis of (1) large divisions of educational activity, such as elementary and secondary education, business affairs (educational resources management), professional personnel, pupil services, special services, curriculum, school plant, ør combinations of these; (2) instructional areas, such as elementary education, secondary education, curriculum, or special services concerned with instruction; or (3) auxiliary or service functions such as business and/or school-plant services. The assistant superintendent is directly responsible to the superintendent (or to the deputy or area superintendent, if such exist).

The assistant superintendency was created as early as 1854 in New York, 1868 in St. Louis, and 1870 in Chicago.[4] The position was established after the principalship and superintendency.

The first assistant superintendents were concerned with supervision and coordination of instruction in various buildings of the large system, as well as with advising principals and teachers. Friction between assistant superintendents and principals was relatively common. Subsequent organization considered the principal as the administrative head of the building, but subordinate to the assistant superintendent in charge of the instructional area.

The Director or Coordinator

The director, or coordinator, is subordinate to the assistant superintendent, the deputy superintendent, and the area superintendent, as well as the general superintendent. The title "director" in some quarters is unpopular because it is thought to connote autocratic direction instead of leadership. Other school systems, however, use the term "director" in place of "assistant superintendent." A director of secondary school supervisors would be responsible to an assistant superintendent in charge of secondary education or an assistant superintendent in charge of curriculum.

The assistant superintendent in charge of business services is sometimes called the "school business manager," but there appears to be a movement to replace this title with "assistant superintendent in charge of business services," "director of business services," or better, "educational resources manager."

Supervisory Positions

In business and industry the level immediately subordinate to middle management is referred to as "supervisory management." The supervisory positions in public education are staff rather than line positions.

GROWTH IN NUMBERS OF CENTRAL-ADMINISTRATIVE OFFICE POSITIONS

There have been central office administrative/supervisory positions in the very large school systems for more than 100 years. Their development in smaller systems is more recent but remains inhibited by community lack of understanding of their importance. The relatively small school districts turn to the staff in the intermediate school district for the kinds of functions performed by central-office personnel.

A significant expansion in central-administrative staff accompanied the enrollment boom of the 1950s and 1960s. One 1959 study reported that almost one-fourth of the central-office positions identified in 1959 were in positions newly created during the previous five years, and about 71 percent of the districts anticipated further expansion in the number of new administrative positions during the ensuing five years.[5] The expansion did continue beyond the five years and through most of the 1960s. This expansionary mood was curtailed sharply when the financial crunch and the beginning of the enrollment declines hit in the early 1970s. The number of the usual types of central-office positions declined during the 1970s, but this was offset by an increase during the 1970s of directors of federal programs. The increase in federal contributions helped swell the numbers of directors and special project managers during the 1970s and early 1980s to reach an estimated 28,500 by 1982–1983. A decline in the number of central-administrative staff positions is expected during the 1980s.

In New York City there were 2544 full-time administrators with district-wide responsibilities working under the supervision of the general superintendent. No correlation exists between the number of central-office administrative positions and the size of school district, whether the size is measured by enrollments or numbers of school buildings.[6] Other factors such as scope and variety of educational services available, rate of district growth, and propensity to implement educational or administrative innovations have a greater impact upon the size of the central-office staff than the sheer magnitude of the local district. The pattern of staffing for those positions that are related to average enrollments and numbers of school buildings is shown in Table 15.1. The averages

shown obscure the great variation within each category. Thus, in the 66 districts with four central-office administrators, the enrollments per district ranged from 100 to 29,290 and the number of buildings from 1 to 52.

The estimates reported in various publications tend to be conservative and may underestimate the actual numbers. The numbers of central-office administrators are exceeded only by principals and vice-principals. It is estimated that the typical school district of today may have about seven central-administrative/supervisory staff personnel. The largest numbers are likely to be found in the districts that were forced to expand services such as school bus-transportation management, food services coordination, and federal programs administration as a result of court order or other reasons. Such central-office administrative personnel are often classified under "Financial and Business Services," which are better described as "Logistical Support Services." Administrators/supervisors engaged in providing leadership and special support for instructional programs and services make up the next largest numbers of central-office staff positions.

The above data exclude school secretarial and clerical level personnel. Estimates prepared by the writer, and based on a variety of published and nonpublished sources, are that

TABLE 15.1

NUMBERS OF CENTRAL-OFFICE ADMINISTRATIVE STAFF POSITIONS RELATED TO ENROLLMENTS AND NUMBERS OF SCHOOL BUILDINGS (Based on 1959 data)

No. of central-office administrators	No. of school districts	Average enrollment per district	Average no. of school buildings per district
1	80	1952	6.5
2	74	2442	7.0
3	61	2973	8.4
4	66	4191	10.5
5	37	4751	12.8

Source: Georgette N. Manla, "Administration in Transition," *American School and University, 1960–61*, 32nd ed., New York: Buttenheim, 1960, pp. 144–154.

there are about 135 central-office administrative personnel in the very large districts with 25,000 or more enrolled, but only 1.7 such positions in the small districts with 300 to 2499 enrolled. Districts in the largest enrollment category have almost 80 times the number of central-office administrative personnel as those found in the lowest enrollment category.

In one exceptional case, the deputy or associate superintendents received salaries of $100,-000 per annum during 1980–1981; the median salary for such positions in 1980–1981 was $41,589.[7] However, one-fourth of all such top level administrative personnel in districts with enrollments of 25,000 or more received at least $50,000. The 1980–1981 median salary for assistant superintendents was $37,341, for directors of instruction, $31,935, for finance managers, $29,041, and for subject area supervisors, $26,500.

Not all central-office administrators with similar sounding titles perform the same functions. In 1980, according to one reliable source of educational data, there were five times as many "supervisors" in public elementary and secondary schools as there were 50 years ago. There is some confusion in interpreting such national data, for often the deputy, associate, and assistant superintendent positions may be grouped in the "supervisor" category.

The writer's best estimates of the number of central-office administrative personnel during 1980 are presented in Table 15.2. These are based on data released by the ERS, the National Center for Education Statistics, and Quality Education Data, Inc., but these sources should not be held accountable for the interpretations which led to the data presented in Table 15-2.

SUPERVISION OF INSTRUCTION

"Supervision," as used in educational circles, is interpreted narrowly and related to teaching and learning activities and hence implies instructional supervision.

Supervision, as an administrative activity, is a controlling and coordinating device. It is not an end in itself. As such it may be viewed as a strategy to stimulate others toward greater effectiveness or productivity. The added expense in terms of organizational time and money can be justified only to the extent that the institution can function more efficiently with the adopted supervisory strategies than without them.

The functions of those engaged in supervision may include designing and implementing

TABLE 15.2

ESTIMATED CENTRAL-OFFICE ADMINISTRATIVE STAFF POSITIONS IN PUBLIC ELEMENTARY AND SECONDARY SCHOOL DISTRICTS WITH ENROLLMENTS OF 300 OR MORE, 1980

Title or Type of Position	Estimated Numbers
1. Asst., Assoc., or Deputy Supt.	9,800
2. Directors or Managers of Financial and Business Services	9,000
3. Directors or Managers of Instruction	9,500
4. Subject Area Supervisors (Inst. Sup.)	13,300
5. Directors of Public Relations	1,250
6. Directors, Supervisors, etc., of Specialized Administrative Support Services for Health, Transportation, Food Services, Research, Facilities, Federal Programs, etc.	48,500
7. Administrative Staff Assistants	3,300
8. Other Administrative Personnel, not covered in any of the above	6,000
Grand Total	100,650

programs of in-service professional development; direction and stimulation of professional instructional efforts of selected personnel; observation of classroom instructional activities; and appraisal of instructional progress and outcomes. The more controversial aspects of supervision, at least in education, are those related to direction, control, observation, and appraisal.

The supervisor of instruction may enhance the quality of learning by working with and through classroom teachers. Such close and continuing interactions with professional personnel point to the importance of developing special competencies in human relations. This includes gaining the acceptance and respect of professional personnel such as teachers and principals, having the ability to motivate adults to higher levels of professional performance, and stimulating personnel to accept and implement more promising instructional practices. This is in addition to a high level of knowledge in the subject matter field, special expertise in teaching or instructional strategies, and competencies in diagnosing instructional problems others may be experiencing and prescribing approaches for resolving them.

There is a decided preference in education for softer terms such as stimulating, motivating, or leading instead of direction, which management writers in other fields consider to be an essential step in administration. Direction starts action and without it little or nothing would happen in the organization. Whatever the preferred terminology, the administrative or supervisory purpose is the continuing improvement of the performance capabilities of personnel. Subordinates deserve specific information (instructions or communications) on what is expected and recommendations as to preferred modes of operation.

Effective supervisory leadership, or "good direction," is based upon mutual understanding and agreement between the supervisor and the person being supervised ("supervisee") on the instructional objectives or outcomes given the types of learners, the resources available, the existing state of the instructional art, and the abilities of the in-structor. Clarity of information or "instructions" sent is measured by the person receiving the communication. It is the supervisor's obligation to explain in whatever detail necessary the purposes and procedures consistent with the instructions. Even Napoleon with the reputation of being one of the most autocratic of commanders never issued an order without explaining its purpose and making sure that all understood it. Following through to insure that what was recommended was indeed implemented is of no less importance.

Control, in its broadest and best sense, is a means of assuring that the organization is not straying too far off course from previously agreed upon goals. Control of organizational direction and outcomes should not be confused with negative controls on individual behavior.

Control in the organizational context merges with direction at one point and with appraisal at another. It requires an understanding of what is to be accomplished and the quality level desired. It is achieved by means of observation and reporting. Appraisal may trigger in-service development of personnel, allocation of special resources to those being supervised, and similar activities. It is unfortunate that the personnel appraisal function has acquired a very negative image and that it generates fear or apprehension. Personnel evaluation may be misinterpreted as the first step to possible personnel reprimand and perhaps to dismissal. The facts demonstrate otherwise because less than 5 percent of those appraised face any type of subsequent personnel action. Nonetheless, the emotions generated are more powerful than facts. Recognition of the "evaluatee's" reluctance does not allow any administrator to shirk the direction, control, and appraisal functions. The issue is how best to discharge these broadly defined supervisory functions of administration.

Supervision is a means of ascertaining how well the assigned responsibilities are being discharged. Board members are supervisors of the performance of the superintendent to whom they delegate specific educational and administrative functions. The superintendent supervises the performance of all deputy, area, and assistant superintendents, principals, directors, and so on. The principal and special instructional supervisors are responsible for the performance of teachers, who in turn "supervise" the learning of their pupils.

Those held accountable for what transpires in the institution require current and reliable data on student learning and the performance capabilities of instructors. Effective supervision is a continuing and important responsibility of administrators-supervisors at all levels of the hierarchy. Supervision of instruction helps administrators held accountable for instructional and other organizational objectives to "know what is going on" or "what's happening."

The Organization Structure for Instructional Supervision

Eye, Netzer, and Krey defined supervision of instruction as "that phase of school administration which focuses primarily upon the achievement of the appropriate instructional expectations of educational systems."[8]

As more people become involved in supervision there arises the problem of how they are to be related and actions unified. One approach is to place all concerned with supervision of elementary and secondary schools under the direction of an assistant superintendent in charge of curriculum. This type of organization permits better articulation among elementary and secondary school supervisors and simplifies the management of broad problems of curriculum, such as scope and sequence of subject matter and instructional materials, as well as methods of teaching.

Another approach is to place special-subject supervisors under the direction of an assistant superintendent for elementary education and an assistant superintendent for secondary education. This pattern may lessen conflict between the principal (who also has a role in instructional supervision) and special-subject supervisors, because both are serving under the assistant superintendent in charge of a particular division of education. It can be argued that curriculum is as much a concern of an assistant superintendent for elementary or secondary education as of an assistant superintendent in charge of curriculum.

In a small district, with too few special-subject teachers (for music, art, etc.) to warrant special-subject supervisors, the problem may be solved by seeking such services from the regional educational service agency (intermediate unit). Several such districts, federated as parts of a regional educational service agency, would have sufficient special-subject teachers to justify employment of a special-subject supervisor.

Prevailing opinion recommends that state department personnel not be used as "supervisors" to evaluate performance on the basis of a brief visit. Supervision of instruction is a local function supplemented as needed by certain intermediate-unit supervisory services; it is not a state department of educational function. The role of the state department of education is one of providing consultant services for highly specialized problems that cannot be managed by local or intermediate units.

Changing Perceptions of Instructional Supervision

There were at least four major phases in the evolution of instructional supervision. The first phase, from the colonial era to about the Civil War, was characterized by instructional supervision being a function of laypersons such as clergymen, school trustees, and town selectmen. The supervisory techniques and procedures were crude, highly subjective, inspection-oriented of questionable validity and contributed little to instructional improvement but may have helped to insure orthodoxy on values and/or religion. The ineffectiveness of lay supervision stimulated the search for other alternatives. Many of the negative images of and fears attached to instructional supervision can be traced to the crude and questionable approaches employed during the first phase of the evolution of this function.

The second phase, from the Civil War to the early part of the twentieth century, witnessed the transfer of instructional supervisory responsibilities from lay and part-time individuals to professional and full-time school officials such as state, county, and local superintendents and principals. Supervision continued to be equated with inspection and dedicated to insuring compliance with rules and regulations. This reinforced the perception of the supervisor of instruction as an inspector and evaluator of teacher performance. In short, there was transfer to different types of people, but the focus remained much the same.

In the third phase, from the early twentieth century to about 1935, the emphasis moved away from inspection and compliance toward a professional study of instructional problems and the means available for the enhancement of instructional performance at the classroom level. The professional literature increased markedly and projected the concept of instructional supervision as a means for improving instruction. It emphasized the importance of more objective and relevant observational techniques for the supervisor, more productive conferences between the supervisor and teacher, and the use of demonstrations as a means to help teachers improve instructional functions. The emphasis was on the professionalization of the instructional supervisor as an educator with special talents, experiences, and competencies. Primary responsibility for instructional supervision was assigned to principals and special-subjects supervisors at the local level, with a diminished role for county and state level supervisors.

The fourth phase, from 1935 to the present, was characterized by a further broadening of professional horizons, with special emphasis on group dynamics or human relations competencies, continuous professional development programs for all educators, and special curriculum studies, together with newer approaches to classroom instruction.

Eye, Netzer, and Krey developed yet another perspective for viewing the development of instructional supervision through five major changes in its purposes and functions:

1. The period of administrative inspection, 1642 to 1875, was the period when the supervisor was literally an inspector whose functions were more judicial than executive in character. There was established at that time a forbidding relation between the supervisor and the supervised.
2. The period of efficiency orientation, 1876 to 1936.
3. The period of cooperative group effort in the improvement of instructional learning, 1937 to 1959.
4. The period of research orientation, 1960 to the present time.
5. An emerging new period for the 1970s that may include systems analysis.[9]

Development of Special-Subject Supervision

The introduction of special subjects beyond the so-called basics eventually led to greater reliance on the special supervisory personnel to supplement the activities of principals, assistant superintendents, superintendents, and other general supervisory officials. There were a few special-subject teachers at the elementary school level prior to 1850, but their broader utilization was not evident until later. Thus, Cincinnati had a special teacher for handwriting in 1842 and two music teachers by 1845. Music was taught in the Chicago schools as early as 1850.

Chicago attempted to utilize principals and other general supervisors to oversee teaching of special subjects, but the project was abandoned in favor of special-subject supervisors. There were supervisors in drawing, handwriting, physical education, and primary instruction in Cleveland by 1873. St. Louis employed supervisors of kindergarten by 1890.[10] The situation is difficult to interpret precisely because some regular classroom teachers taught special subjects and were supervised by special-subject teachers. Sizable staffs of special-subject supervisors even in large cities are a twentieth-century development. Such personnel may be called curriculum specialists.

Responsibility for instructional supervision is often divided among principals, department heads, and superintendents, as well as special supervisors. The functions and techniques of instructional supervision are the same, by and large, in elementary and secondary schools. Supervision is concerned with professional personnel—how to motivate and assist them to perform more effectively.

The general instructional supervisor assumed to be capable of improving instruction in any and all academic and nonacademic courses for all types of pupils and at all grade levels is less likely to be found in the public schools today. The supervisor or curriculum specialist who focuses on a limited set of programs, a limited range of grades, and a limited type of learners (such as those with exceptionalities or atypical learning problems) has replaced the so-called general elementary and/or secondary school supervisor or curriculum specialist. One reliable source identified over 28,500 supervisors, curriculum specialists, or curriculum administrators in the nation's public schools during 1982–1983.[11] There are more reading specialists (almost 50 percent of the total) than those in any other field, other than those related to various dimensions of special education. Wiles's prediction of about 20 years ago is evident in practices of today, namely, "The number of people with the label of general supervisor . . . will probably decrease. . . . It is being recognized that more specialized assistance is needed."[12]

The Continuing Evolution of Instructional Supervision

Instructional supervision has come a long way since the early days of inspection and compliance demands. It is a specialized body of knowledge within education in general as well as educational administration. About 25 years ago the many facets of instructional supervision were perceived as including:[13]

1. A planned program for the improvement of instruction.
2. All efforts of a designated school official toward providing leadership to teachers and other educational workers in the improvement of instruction.
3. A program of in-service education and cooperative group development.

4. The efforts to stimulate, coordinate, and guide continued growth of teachers in school, both individually and collectively.
5. Assistance in the development of a better teaching-learning situation.
6. A means of maintaining existing programs of instruction as well as improving them.

Only limited improvement is possible where instructional supervisors continue to be perceived as "snoopervisors." To diagnose ineffective instruction is only the beginning; the most important phase follows, namely, generating the strategies and programs to help the individual teacher to become an effective instructor. More research and development in the art and science of teaching are necessary to generate ways of overcoming instructional problems. Perhaps before this century comes to an end teachers will ask for the assistance of an "instructional consultant" to help them work out a special instructional problem.

How long instructional supervisors will be able to shy away from some degree of involvement in teacher evaluation is open to question. Personnel appraisal, in its best professional interpretation, provides the basic data required in the design of individualized programs of professional development. This is not to say that personnel appraisal should be the prime function of an instructional supervisor. It is a prime function of the school principal, but the supervisor can assist in collecting performance data and interpreting the significance of such information. It is hard for many supervisors to accept such functions, particularly when appraisal is perceived as a negative force in pinning labels on professionals rather than as a positive first step in determining the instructional improvement needs of a teacher.

The change agent role of the instructional supervisor received considerable emphasis after 1960. The supervisor does more than help maintain the status quo at efficient levels; the supervisor must also keep abreast of new developments and be able to manage the introduction of instructional changes with a minimum of dysfunction.

Yet another new role emerged during the

early 1970s, and which shall continue for the rest of the century. This is the role of the supervisor in educational auditing. Its purpose is to verify teaching-learning outcomes. The emphasis on accountability generated considerable interest in auditing learning outcomes.

The supervisor must depend more upon "functional authority" than the power that may reside in the position in the administrative hierarchy. It is performance-based authority. It is the competencies possessed rather than what authority inheres in the position that makes for success or failure. Supervisors are not immune from performance appraisal. Failure to perform essential roles and responsibilities that lead to instructional improvement can lead to the demise of a nonproductive position in the hierarchy. It is a difficult challenge because supervisors must work with and through others to achieve objectives; that is, the measure of the person is how well others are performing and students are learning.

SUMMARY

The administrative team concept is a relatively recent step in the evolution of effective top level school leadership and management. It all started with a single person in the superintendency who often assumed nonadministrative functions and had no professional or clerical support personnel for much needed assistance. Some boards in larger districts were quicker to sense the need for a school management team than others.

A team is a unit; a collection of individuals with diverse talents and differentiated roles. A team has a structure and a human side. The people in the social unit must be able to mesh their talents with diverse personalities.

Although very large school districts had assistant superintendents between 1850 and 1870, only in recent years have central-office administrative and supervisory personnel been common in most urban school districts. The growing complexity of education signaled the passing of the one-person-office-of-school-superintendent. The administrative team is now more important than ever before.

Division of responsibilities with other executives can result in the creation of such positions as deputy or area superintendent to whom general administrative functions have been assigned. An assistant superintendent is often granted responsibilities for a division of the school system such as elementary education, secondary education, curriculum, or business. Immediately subordinate to the assistant superintendent are directors or coordinators of major bureaus or divisions within a given area of the school system.

Need for supervision arises whenever there is more than one administrative or nonadministrative worker in a system. In education it is equated with instructional supervision. Instructional supervision began as a lay function that focused on inspection and compliance. Professionals in education assumed the supervisory tasks after the Civil War but did not change the focus. It was not until early in the twentieth century that supervision was perceived as a means for instructional improvement. The fourth stage in development that came after 1935 further broadened supervisory horizons and stressed in-service programs as part of an improvement strategy. The special-subject supervisor at the local level has replaced the general supervisor of all subjects and grades as well as the county and state supervisors.

The evolution of this concept continues, and the era of the professional colleague with special abilities who deserves to be called an instructional consultant may not be too far away. Instructional supervisors tend to shy away from personnel appraisal, and few view it as providing data important to designing individualized professional growth programs for teachers. The change agent role of the supervisor is receiving greater emphasis at present. During the 1970s more supervisors of instruction became involved in educational auditing, that is, in the verification of teaching-learning outcomes. The effective supervisor depends more upon "functional authority" than the power that resides in the position.

NOTES

1. American Association of School Executives, *Profiles of the Administrative Team,* Arlington, Va.: The Association, 1971, p. 11.
2. Ibid., p. 19.
3. ERIC Clearinghouse on Educational Management, "The Management Team," *The Best of ERIC,* No. 28, Eugene, Ore.: University of Oregon, May 1978, 4 pp.
4. Paul R. Pierce, *The Origin and Development of the Public School Principalship,* Chicago: University of Chicago Press, 1935, pp. 90–95.
5. Georgette N. Manla, "Administration in Transition," *American School and University, 1960–61,* 32nd ed., New York: Buttenheim, 1960, pp. 144–154.
6. Ibid.
7. Educational Research Service, "Salaries Paid Professional Personnel in Public Schools, 1980–81," *ERS Report,* Part 2 of National Survey of Salaries and Wages in Public Schools, Arlington, Va.: ERS, 1981, 145 pp.
8. G. G. Eye, L. A. Netzer, and R. D. Krey, *Supervision of Instruction,* 2nd ed., New York: Harper & Row, 1971, pp. 30–31.
9. Ibid., pp. 22–29.
10. Pierce, op. cit., pp. 105–115.
11. Based on data provided the writer by Jeanne Hayes, President, Quality Education Data, Inc., Denver, Colorado. The actual number and interpretations are the writer's.
12. Kimball Wiles, *Supervision for Better Schools,* 3rd ed., Englewood Cliffs, N.J.: Prentice-Hall, 1967, p. 305.
13. Kimball Wiles, "Supervision," in C. W. Harris, ed., *Encyclopedia of Educational Research,* 3rd ed., New York: Macmillan, 1960, p. 1442.

CHAPTER REVIEW QUESTIONS

1. Why is it that the "one-person-office-of-superintendent" is passing from the urban school scene?
2. Differentiate among the following posts on the basis of functions or responsibilities: (a) deputy superintendent, (b) director, (c) assistant superintendent, (d) supervisor.
3. Who should be on the administrative team?
4. When is it preferable to use the title "director of elementary education" instead of "assistant superintendent in charge of elementary education"?
5. Trace the evolution of the supervision of instruction.
6. Debate the following: Resolved, that supervisors of instruction shall never be permitted to evaluate teachers they supervise.

SELECTED REFERENCES

Eye, G. G., and Netzer, L. A., "Educational Auditing: From Issue to Principle," *New Directions for Education,* No. 1, Spring 1973, pp. 63–75.
Eye, G. G., Netzer, L. A., and Krey, R. D., *Supervision of Instruction,* 2nd ed., New York: Harper & Row, 1972.
Newell, Clarence A., *Human Behavior in Educational Administration,* Englewood Cliffs, N.J.: Prentice-Hall, 1978, chaps. 1–3, 5, 8–10.
Sergiovanni, Thomas J., and Carver, Fred D., *The New School Executive,* 2nd ed., New York: Harper & Row, 1980, chaps. 5–8, 10.
Wiles, Kimball, "Supervision," in Chester W. Harris, ed., *Encyclopedia of Education Research,* 3rd ed., New York: Macmillan, 1960.

16

THE PRINCIPALSHIP: THE EXECUTIVE
TEAM AT THE SCHOOL SITE LEVEL

The effectiveness of educational administration at all levels in the hierarchy is measured best at the school site level. Here is where educational services are delivered. Here is where material resources are utilized by teachers and others to promote learning.

The principal is the educational leader and executive officer of the school attendance center. The executive or management team, led by the principal, at the building level influences to a considerable degree how well teachers perform, how well students learn, and how easily and rapidly innovations are introduced into the school. It takes more than one person to provide the leadership, the management talents, and special instructional expertise required in today's complex educational organizations. The limited effectiveness of the "one-person-principalship" is now recognized and is being replaced by the "principalship team."

The principalship is the oldest administrative position in public education. Like other administrative posts, it took its rise in complexity and with the development of the multiroom school operation. There were very few princi-

pals during the colonial period of our nation's history and not all that many until the twentieth century. Early data are hard to find and even more difficult to interpret because only a few were full-time (nonteaching) principals; most were teaching principals who devoted part time to educational administration. It is equally difficult to ascertain whether vice-principals were included in the early data for 1919–1920 released by the National Center for Education Statistics that reported 14,000 public school principals at that time—the first national data available on the position. Ten years later the numbers more than doubled to 31,000. Relatively minor changes were noted during the Great Depression years of the 1930s. Even as late as 1949–1950 there were only 39,000 school principals—only an increase of about 25 percent during two decades. This was a very modest gain compared with the more than 120 percent increase during the ten years from 1920–1930.

The most significant growth in the principalship occurred during the 1950s and 1960s. The numbers increased by 25,000 or more during each of the two ten-year periods to reach 91,-000 (principals and assistant principals) by 1969. This 20-year growth rate exceeded 133 percent (compared with 25 percent in the preceding 20 years) and about 52,000 new positions were established. This unusually rapid growth rate slowed during the 1970s when enrollment declines began and continued to do so in the early 1980s. The peak number was probably the 107,000 reported for the fall of 1980,[1] but the numbers in the principalship remained above 100,000 throughout the 1970s. The writer estimates that because of abandoned school sites (there were 2,240 fewer school buildings in operation in 1982–83 compared with 1981–82), declining overall enrollments, and fiscal cutbacks, the numbers in the principalship will remain between 100,000 and 104,-000 during the 1980s.

The most numerous are elementary school principals. The secondary school principalship is more complex and includes many assistant (or vice) principals, whereas relatively few such positions are found in elementary schools. School organization patterns have much to do with the functions and numbers in the principalship and therefore are reviewed as a background for understanding the challenges facing the principalship.

EVOLUTION OF ELEMENTARY SCHOOL ORGANIZATIONAL PATTERNS

The size and structure of elementary school attendance centers are influenced by the purposes, programs, enrollments, age range of pupils served, instructional strategies pursued, and the nature and educational expectations of the community in which the school is located. The one-teacher school attendance unit was an organizational pattern that reflected the simple educational fare and limited educational expectations of a rural and pioneer society. More students often meant replication of the existing structual pattern and so another one-teacher school unit was created. The two-teacher

schoolhouse was another response, but not a radical departure because each teacher was confronted by wide age ranges of pupils and there were no "grades" established as yet. The one- and two-teacher elementary schools were until almost the end of the nineteenth century ungraded instructional organizations.

The Development of the Graded Instructional Organization

The first significant instructional organization change came with the grading of pupils. Graded elementary schools emerged first in the larger urban school districts. Its distinguishing characteristic was the classification of pupils of similar (not necessarily identical) age into groups or "grades" for purposes of instruction. This required a professional understanding of the learning process as well as human growth and development that were beyond the ability and time available to lay groups that administered public education. The desire to establish the "graded" school stimulated boards in larger cities to create the professional school superintendency, and much of the time of the early superintendents was devoted to the instructional reorganization of the elementary school.

The graded system of instructional organization was the most significant educational innovation of the midnineteenth century. It replaced the chaos and confusion that reduced learning effectiveness in the prevailing ungraded school patterns. It provided teachers with the opportunity to design instructional strategies geared to the level of students of relatively similar maturity and life experiences. It was a better way of organizing educational opportunities in large urban centers faced with rapidly growing enrollments for which the one-teacher pattern was poorly suited.

By the end of the Civil War graded elementary schools were established in most urban communities. Almost 70 more years were to pass before this instructional organization approach was accepted in rural areas. The first graded elementary school building was the Quincy School in Boston, erected in 1847 at a cost of about $60,000. It had 12 separate rooms, with a total capacity of 660 pupils (more than 50 per room); for the first time a separate seat and desk were available for each student. Each classroom was assigned a single teacher who had about 55 pupils!

Although there is some dispute among scholars as to precisely what was borrowed from the system of schools operating in Prussia during the first four decades of the 1800s, it is clear that a number of distinguished American educators, including Horace Mann, did make a special trip to visit the Prussian schools. They were impressed with the extensiveness of the curriculum and the classification of "scholars" in what must have been a "graded" German "Volksschule." The eight-grade common school of Prussia was adapted and became the model for the eight-grade elementary school organization in the United States. The number of grade levels per building is less important than the fact of classifying students into specific grades for purposes of instruction and determination of promotion to the next level.

During the early part of the twentieth century, the child study movement in the United States called for the termination of the elementary school at the end of grade 6 rather than 8. It developed the concept of the elementary school as the instructional center for children (prepuberty) and the secondary school for adolescents. The trend since then has been toward formation of six-grade (plus kindergarten) elementary school attendance centers. The emergence of the middle schools after the late 1960s did not affect this trend, although some middle schools started with grade 6 and some with grade 5. At present (the 1980s) about 80 percent of the elementary schools terminate at grade 6, 15 percent at grade 8, and the remaining 5 percent with other arrangements. Unfortunately, the National Center for Education Statistics continues to report elementary school enrollment data on a K to 8 or 1 to 8 format.

Downward extension of educational opportunities to include kindergarten and nursery school, children in the three to five age group also called the "preprimary" enrollment, has had an impact on the elementary and special

"preprimary" school. In 1960 only 4.5 percent of the urban communities maintained a public nursery school, and the overwhelming majority of existing nursery school programs were financed by private funds or a combination of private and public funds.[2] Kindergartens were far more likely to be found in urban centers then (70.4 percent maintained them) and the great majority were supported entirely by public funds. Only about one in four school systems in rural counties supported public kindergartens in the mid-1950s.

Considerable progress in the acceptance and establishment of nursery and kindergarten education was evident during the 1970s. The percent of three- and four-year-olds enrolled in some type of school jumped from 20 percent in 1970 to 37 percent by 1980. Furthermore, 69 percent of the five-year-olds were in a nursery school or kindergarten in 1970 compared with 85 percent in 1980. Enrollments in preprimary schools (three- and four-year-olds) tripled in metropolitan areas to about 42 percent of this age group during the 15-year period of 1965 to 1980. In nonmetropolitan areas only about 26 percent of the three- and four-year-olds were enrolled in nursery schools in 1980.[3] There were more working mothers in 1981 than in 1966, which helps to explain at least part of the increase in preprimary and kindergarten enrollments. In contrast to limited kindergarten opportunities in rural areas, by 1980 almost 90 percent of school districts with 300 or more enrolled provided such opportunities. Increased federal support of the Headstart program also helped to increase preprimary school enrollments.

Flexible Grading and Departmentalized Instructional Organizations

The 1950s and 1960s witnessed an increase in the interest in the so-called ungraded elementary school instructional organization. It is not a reversion to what existed in one-teacher schools more than 100 years ago. It is better to use the term *nongraded* to indicate that the pattern is markedly different from the *ungraded* schools of the nineteenth century and earlier. *Nongrading* is a relative term implying less rigid (or more flexible) classification of pupil-learning achievement and pupil promotion practices rather than no classification as to level of student accomplishments. The term *flexible grading,* which never gained much popularity, is a more precise description of the modification recommended for the then prevailing instructional organization. The volume of published material on the concept expanded during the 1970s as well.

By 1958 less than one in five of urban districts adopted the flexible grading approach. Subsequent samplings showed limited progress during the 1960s, which prompted one of the founders and proponents of the concept to declare that "there are, indeed, precious few nongraded schools."[4] Interest flagged during the 1970s, and there probably are fewer now than there were ten years ago.

The departmentalized elementary school instructional organization is a pattern in which students report to a different teacher for each of the academic subjects in the school program (e.g., mathematics, science, social studies, and English or reading), and each teacher is responsible solely for instruction in a specific subject or closely related subjects. Departmentalization is most likely to be practiced for grades 7 and 8; to a lesser degree in grades 4, 5, and 6; and least likely for the primary grades (1 to 3). Complete departmentalization in elementary schools is the exception rather than the rule. A degree of departmentalization may be created to enhance learning and instruction in special subjects such as art, music, and physical education and in only a few regular subjects that require special instructional equipment such as science.

In short, there was a time during the last three decades when much was written about new instructional organization approaches such as "nongraded schools" and departmentalization of elementary schools. Only a minority of elementary schools continue to implement such instructional approaches. The typical elementary school today continues to operate as the so-called self-contained graded elementary school instructional organization.

There were other approaches to the individualization of instruction that incorporated team teaching and other instructional strategies. They were often reactions to departmentalization as well as the self-contained classroom organization. Some individualized instruction strategies, such as Individually Prescribed Instruction (IPI), had a lesser impact on large numbers of elementary schools than did others such as Individually Guided Education in the Multiunit School—Elementary (IGE/MUSE). The pioneer work of Klausmeier and others led to the design of the multiunit school that combines many of the instructional and organizational components into a unified package such as:

1. Organization of learners into units of 75 to 150 pupils for purposes in instruction.
2. Multi-age and cross-grade grouping of learners in units.
3. Nongrading.
4. Continuous promotion (progress) for students.
5. Team teaching.
6. Appointment of unit leaders for each learner unit.
7. Cooperative instructional planning by teaching teams.
8. Implementation of an instructional programming model to guide teaching efforts.
9. Emphasis on the use of behavioral objectives in all instructional activity.
10. Use of criterion referenced evaluation approaches.
11. The sharing of instructional leadership responsibilities in each school through the creation of an Instructional Improvement Committee.[5]

ADMINISTRATION OF THE ELEMENTARY SCHOOL

The one-room school with a very small number of pupils had little need for a principal or a site management team. The school committee of laypersons supervised and saw to the operating details of the primitive educational instituions (by today's standards). The teacher cared for the building to some extent, but had few other responsibilities that could be called administrative.

Evolution of the Principalship

The principalship was designed to cope with instructional leadership complexities of urban school systems. Some urban systems simply created more one-teacher centers as enrollments grew, whereas others established a "doubleheaded" school system, with authority divided between the grammar master, who taught reading, grammar, and geography, and the writing master, who taught other subjects and particularly writing. Still others opted to unite teachers in larger attendance centers and under a single head—the school principal. Although the Quincy School, established in Boston in 1847, is usually cited as the first to have all teachers and departments united under a single principal, Pierce pointed out that Cincinnati placed all departments under a single head prior to 1838.[6]

The establishment and further development of the public elementary school principalship received encouragement from the following forces:

1. The rapid growth of the cities and the increase in numbers of pupils in each building.
2. The grading of schools.
3. The consolidation of the "writing" and "grammar" school departments.
4. The freeing of principals from teaching duties.
5. The recognition of the principal as a supervisory head of the building.
6. The establishment of specialized departments of the NEA concerned with elementary school administration.[7]

First there were teachers; then teachers with some administrative responsibilities; still later the principal-teacher, who was more of an administrator than a teacher; and finally a principal. It was not unusual to find one teacher in a multiroom building designated as the principal-teacher for purposes of controlling and managing school affairs. The early functions of the principal-teacher were:

1. To be recognized and function as head of the school attendance unit charged to his care.
2. To regulate classes and courses of instruction for all pupils in the building.
3. To discover any defects in the building and apply remedies.
4. To report defects to the trustees of the district if he is unable to remedy the conditions.
5. To give necessary instructions to other teachers in the building (such teachers being classified as his assistants).
6. To classify pupils.
7. To safeguard the schoolhouse and furniture.
8. To keep the school clean.
9. To instruct the other teachers referred to as his assistants.
10. To refrain from impairing the standing of other teachers especially in the eyes of pupils.
11. To require the cooperation of all the assistant teachers.[8]

The term *principal* became a noun rather than an adjective that modified "teacher." By the middle of the nineteenth century the duties of the typical principal in a large city were limited largely to discipline, routine administrative acts, and grading of pupils. As late as 1881 principals of Chicago schools were required to devote as much as one-half time each day to regular classroom instruction. In other large cities principals were relieved of responsibilities for classroom teaching prior to 1870.[9]

Released from teaching duties, the principal was able to visit other teachers and supervision became an important function of this position. Supervisory techniques were rudimentary until well after the start of the twentieth century.

A sampling of duties assigned to principals prior to 1845 showed that 58.8 percent were concerned with record keeping and reporting, 23.5 percent with organization and classification, 11.8 percent with care of the equipment and building, and 5.9 percent with discipline and care of the pupils.[10] Administrative, or nonsupervisory, responsibilities shifted in the last half of the century from records and reports to organization and general management.

Early in the twentieth century, functions of the principal were expanded to include participation in selection of teachers and assistants assigned to the school center. More clerical help was provided urban elementary school principals during the early part of the twentieth century, but many principals in small school systems in urban and rural areas still have an inadequate number of clerical assistants.

Functions of the Principal

By 1870 the typical elementary school in urban communities was an attendance center with 8 to 16 teachers under the direction of a principal who frequently taught part time. The curriculum included the three Rs and, in large cities, music, physical education, and art. The kindergarten movement was received with little enthusiasm by principals in the 1890s.

Urban districts began to experiment with various types of organization for elementary instruction such as departmentalization or the self-contained classroom type of organization. The former plan was called the Gary, Platoon, rotary, shift, or departmentalized plan. It, along with others, will be examined in greater detail in a subsequent chapter.

The principal was recognized as the building-level supervisor by 1900. Employment of special-subject supervisors created problems of relation between the building principal and the central-office staff. The supervisory role of the elementary principal changed from being the only instructional supervisor in the building to a position that relies more and more on specialized supervisory personnel attached to the central office. The supervisory role of the present-day principal involves determining what specialized resources teachers need to perform more effectively.

The functions of the principal are to provide leadership, facilitate change that can enhance school quality, and to manage efficiently and effectively all professional and instructional activities within an attendance center. There is the constant reminder that purely management functions and clerical chores, which can be demanding and time consuming, must not be allowed to dominate the time schedule or priorities.

Leadership that focuses on motivating pro-fessional personnel to achieve optimum performance is the most important single function. Like all administrators, the principal can make things happen only with and through the efforts of others related to the school. Selection and assignment of instructional personnel along with continuing supervision of instruction and/or monitoring of learning progress rank among the highest priority concerns. Related to that is the fact that teaching and learning consume resources, and the principal must be able to identify and then procure resources needed at the building level to reach the agreed upon objectives.

Curriculum and instruction leadership responsibilities are usually publicized in the literature as deserving top priority; unfortunately, the analysis of the time schedules of administrators indicates they have great difficulty in meeting these expectations. Faculty motivation and understanding learner needs follow in relative importance. Working with parents, patrons, and citizens in general to develop better home-school relations are included as well in the established consensus of the more important pressures and most frequently cited leadership roles for principals.

Characteristics of Elementary School Principals

Profiles of the elementary school principal started in 1928 and are updated every ten years by the National Association of Elementary School Principals (NAESP), formerly the Department of Elementary School Principals. The major trends and selected characteristics of elementary school principals based on 1978 data were:[11]

1. About 31 percent of all principals in 1968 were teaching principals, compared with less than 5 percent in 1978. Teaching principals may all but disappear by the end of this century.
2. In 1978 about 82 percent of the elementary principals were men; 50 years earlier the majority of all such principals were women (55 percent). The post-World War II trend

toward male domination is evident from the facts that 59 percent were men in 1948, 62 percent in 1958, and 78 percent in 1968. More women elementary principals are found in urban districts, but even here they account for only 25 percent of the total for 1978.

3. Most had elementary classroom teaching experience before appointment as principal; about 18 percent in 1978 did not.

4. Over 96 percent had an earned master's degree or higher, compared with only 15 percent of the principals 50 years earlier. Almost 5 percent of principals in 1978 reported an earned doctorate, whereas only 2 percent did in 1968.

5. About 82 percent of principals serve in only one school.

6. The median age was 46 years in 1978; the same as in 1968.

7. Almost 90 percent in 1978 were married; 5 percent never married.

8. About 83 percent would do it all over again, down from the 90 percent who said the same thing in 1968.

9. The principal's office work week is about 45 hours.

10. Only 57 percent saw the principalship as the ultimate career goal; 26 percent set the superintendency as the final professional goal.

11. The majority enter the principalship before age 35 (at age 33); less than 10 percent make it after age 45.

12. In 1978, 93 percent of principals were employed 10 months or more, compared with 78 percent in 1968. The majority in suburban districts have a work year of 11 months or more. Where there is collective bargaining by teachers, principals tend to have shorter work years.

13. The median salary of $21,500 in 1978 was more than double the $9700 in 1968 and more than triple the $6237 in 1958. (Other data showed the 1980 median salary to be $27,807 with almost a third receiving $30,-000 or more.)

14. Formal collective bargaining to determine the principal's salary was found in 15.7 per-

cent of the systems in 1978. The opinion of 28.8 percent of the principals was that collective bargaining was the "preferred practice" for salary determination! The majority of principals preferring principal negotiation were in the Northeast and more likely to be older than most in the group.

To summarize: In 1978 the typical elementary principal was a middle-aged married man with at least an earned master's degree who served a single attendance center with about 490 pupils. He taught in the elementary grades before becoming a principal, put in a 45-hour work week, would choose to become a principal if he had to do it all over again, and was employed for ten months or more.

A 1970 study of elementary school assistant principalships concluded: The most popular title for this position was assistant principal; almost 62 percent were men, the median age was 42, over three-fourths were married, most had previously been elementary classroom teachers (72.5 percent), median classroom experience was ten years, and almost seven out of eight had at least an earned master's degree.[12]

The 1978 study of the elementary principal reported that only about 19.5 percent of the principals had administrative assistants. The assistant principalship position is found only in the largest attendance centers. A majority of schools with 700 or more enrolled employed an assistant principal. Those with 1000 or more pupils are the most likely to establish such posts; about 80 percent in 1978 operated with an assistant principal.[13]

A recommended standard for the creation of an assistant principalship position is that such positions would be warranted when the school enrollment reaches 400. Typically, duties and functions of this post are defined by the principal or in the case of very large school districts by system-wide policies. Often this position serves as the training ground for those likely to be considered for the principalship. In contrast to the more specialized assignments usually given to secondary school assistant principals, the elementary school assistant principal assumes more general and varied responsibilities.

ORGANIZATION OF THE SECONDARY SCHOOL

The early and pioneer elementary schools were not copies of any European model, although the Dame schools in England came close. It was much later that the Prussian system of pupil classification into grades served as the instructional organization model, but not the program model. In contrast, the colonial secondary schools were copies of the English Latin Grammar School. It was highly selective and not open to all secondary age youths. Some entered the colonial Latin, or "grammar schools," as early as age seven or eight. Inability of the Latin Grammar School to adjust to rising educational expectations in the United States led to the formation of a new and competing form of a secondary institution called the academy. It, too, was short-lived, even though its science program and other innovations represented an improvement over the limited curriculum of the Latin grammar school. The radically utilitarian studies suggested for the academy by Franklin eventually lost out in favor of the Andover program. The Andover curriculum included English grammar, practical geometry, logic, geography, and "such other liberal arts and sciences or languages" which may be permitted, as well as Greek and Latin grammar. It became the model for the academy movement.

The American high school made its first appearance when the academy was at its peak of popularity. Originators of the high school in 1821 adopted the curriculum offered by the academy, but added public support for programs of secondary education. It evolved as the extension of what was called the "common-school education."

Public high schools grew very slowly during the remainder of the nineteenth century. There were only a little over 2500 high schools in the nation by 1890 with a total enrollment of about 200,000. Rapid development started early in the twentieth century, for by 1910 there were

10,000 high schools with more than 900,000 enrolled. Thereafter, public high school enrollment, grades 9 to 12, would be recorded in the millions. A peak of 14.31 million was reached in 1976 before relatively modest declines began in the late 1970s. It is estimated to fall below 12 million by 1986. The United States became one of the few nations in the world with public support for a comprehensive and compulsory secondary education program. Secondary education for all youths was a twentieth-century development in the United States.

Grading Patterns

The transition point between elementary and secondary education is most likely to occur at the end of grade 6. Secondary institutions are designed for adolescents; their terminal point has long been considered grade 12. Recently, the last year of community (junior) college (grade 14) has come to be recognized as the terminal point in some states. There is some question whether the word *terminal* is appropriate, because continuing education is generally considered desirable.

The traditional pattern for secondary education consisted of four grades beyond the traditional eight-year elementary school curriculum. It became known as the 8-4 system (K-8-4 if kindergarten is included). As late as 1920, 94 percent of the 14,300 public elementary and secondary schools were organized on an 8-4 or K-8-4 basis.[14] Furthermore, 83 percent of the 2 million pupils enrolled in secondary schools were in 8-4 or K-8-4 system.

A significant change in the number and pattern of grades included in a public elementary and secondary school was to occur over the following 30 years. By 1959 only 24 percent of the 24,000 public secondary schools were a part of an 8-4, or K-8-4, organization and about 18 percent of the enrollments of 11 million public secondary students were in such patterns. About 85 percent of the public elementary attendance centers in 1982 terminated with grade 6 rather than 8. The initial division of secondary education was into junior and/or senior high schools. Then the present day version of the middle schools emerged. The relatively recent expansion of community colleges complicated the picture further for a brief period in some parts of the nation.

In 1920 only about 5 percent were organized on a 6-6 (or K-6-6) basis, but about 30 years later 36 percent of all public secondary centers enrolling about 35 percent of such students implemented a six-grade secondary school. A decline in popularity followed, for by 1965 only 19 percent of public secondary attendance centers were organized with grades 7–12. More recent data based on different study samples are not in agreement, for one study based on 1978 data reported that only 6 percent were organized as 7–12 attendance centers, whereas another based on 1982 information indicated that about 12.7 percent still continue with a six-grade secondary school pattern.

The reorganization of the secondary school into a separate junior high school center (for early adolescents) and a separate senior high school building (for older adolescents) with a principal for each, or a K-6-3-3 pattern, gained popularity after 1920, the year only 1 percent of the public secondary schools implemented it. By 1959, however, 34 percent of the public schools and 50 percent of the secondary enrollment operated in the K-6-3-3 mode. A 1966 study of the junior high school principalship revealed that 67 percent were in a public system with a 6-3-3 organization pattern.[15]

During the 1970s the tide shifted rather dramatically once again to the four-grade high school, grades 9 to 12, as the most prevalent pattern. The grade organization pattern common at the beginning of the century gained popularity again for by 1977 63 percent of all public high schools operated with grades 9 to 12 and only 26 percent with grades 10 to 12.[16] The primary difference between what existed 50 years ago and now is a two- or three-year junior high or middle school intervening between the elementary and senior-level secondary school.

Fall 1982 data compiled by Quality Educational Data, Inc. revealed there were operated by public school systems 79,346 elementary and secondary centers, 1,937 special education schools, and 982 vocational/technical centers for a total of 82,265 public schools. This is down about 2200 schools, or about 2.7 percent, from the numbers reported for 1981–1982. (These data do not include 897 Alternative Education or 473 Adult Education Centers.) In 1982 there were 50,119 schools that provided elementary education only, 27,662 secondary education only, and 1565 combined K-12 education opportunities. Of the secondary centers only some 47.1 percent focused on the junior high grades, about 39.5 percent offered senior high grades only, and 13.4 percent provided both or 7–12 grade levels.

The Middle School

Middle schools attracted attention around the turn of the century. The concept or pattern failed to catch hold, lost favor, and disappeared for almost 50 years. Understanding today's middle school is complicated further by the fact that the U.S. Office of Education, now the Department of Education, used the term to designate the upper elementary grades.

The present-day versions trace their origins to the 1950s. The growth was very slow until 1965–1966 when the New York City schools proclaimed that all junior high schools in the system would be replaced by intermediate or middle schools. Like the junior high school, the middle school (true to its name) serves students who completed elementary education that terminated at either grade 5 or 6 but who are not destined to enter a senior-level secondary school until grade 8, 9, or 10. There is no single pattern, for a middle school may include one or two grades below grade 7 plus one or two grades above grade 7. The middle school is more popular in the eastern states from Maine to Maryland and also in Texas.

Middle school proponents argue that the instructional organization pattern permits greater subject matter specialization through departmentalization for pupils in grades 5 and 6 than would be found in the traditional self-contained elementary school. The same argument was used 60 years earlier to justify creating the junior high school. Research to date fails to support strongly the claims of either the supporters or critics of the middle school concept.[17]

Between 1965 and 1971 the numbers of new middle schools established, or retitled, were said to have quadrupled to hit a peak of about 2000.[18] Interest slackened during the late 1970s and early 1980s.

One reason for the renewed interest in these schools appears related to the desire for racial integration without busing or other costly maneuvers. Another is to include in grades 5 and 6 laboratory experiences, particularly in home economics and industrial arts. In some situations, the desire for a four-year senior high school remained strong and the middle school was an excuse to maintain it.

Sanders summarized various grading patterns as shown in Table 16.1. Sanders concluded:

> Grades six through eight do not constitute a more heterogeneous group than seven through nine in the characteristics of mental and educational development measured by instruments, and the former could not be judged to be less satisfactory than the seventh, eighth, and ninth grade junior high school in this respect. Most differences which exist are too small to be educationally significant. . . . What differences were found tended to favor grades six through eight as the more homogeneous. No combination of grades removes the need to provide for every substantial differences in intellectual development within each grades.[19]

ADMINISTRATION OF THE SECONDARY SCHOOL

The secondary school principalship in other countries has been traced as far back as 1515. Johann Sturm was the most famous secondary school administrator (of the German Gymnasium) of that century. Sturm did not teach much and had many assistants under his direction to carry out the extensive, but largely classical, curriculum of the school for boys from ages 10 to 19 or 20. The great headmasters of English Latin Grammar School fame are direct descendants of Sturm. Headmaster (literally, "head" of the schoolmasters or master teachers) was the title given to a building-level administrator and was granted considerable responsibility for control over the Latin schools. Always a male, he was required to be a great teacher and also an effective disciplinarian.

The first American secondary schools were also Latin Grammar Schools, but they had small enrollments, which meant that the administrators also had to teach. These schools

TABLE 16.1

GRADING PATTERNS OTHER THAN 8-4 AND 6-3-3

Grading pattern	Year advocated	Advocates and occurrence
6-6	About 1900 by early reorganization committees	Always common in small communities as a substitute for 6-3-3.
7-5	Existed in early 1900s	Prevalent in the South where 7-year elementary schools were common.
6-2-4	Late 1800s	Constantly common through the years.
6-4-4	1940s	Leading advocate: Koos; much recommended, seldom adopted.
4-4-4	1950s	Leading advocate: Woodring; receiving more attention in the 1960s.
5-3-4	1950s	Most common in Texas and some cities of the Northeast; now receiving support as more than an expedient.

Source: Stanley G. Sanders, "Differences in Mental and Educational Development from Grades Six Through Nine and Implications for Junior High School Organization," unpublished doctoral dissertation, Iowa City: University of Iowa, 1960, p. 68.

were headed usually by a highly competent schoolmaster such as the famous Ezekiel Cheever. At the height of the development of the academy as a secondary institution, about 1850, the average number of teachers per school was only two. The Latin Grammar Schools and the academies were much too small to lay the foundations of secondary school administration. Their legacy was one of implying that all administrators should teach, and discipline or control was the most important function of the headmaster.

The American secondary school principalship emerged with the spread of the high schools during the nineteenth century, but did not come into its own until the twentieth century. Principals were relatively independent of other district administrators, often conferring directly with the school board and, in some cases, considered coordinate with the superintendent. Early superintendents were given little or no authority over secondary schools of the district, and concentrated on problems of grading and coordinating the activities of elementary school principals. Relations between secondary school principals and superintendents were not always cordial during the nineteenth century and the early part of the twentieth. It was not until well into the twentieth century that there were serious efforts to improve the articulation between elementary and secondary schools.

The headmaster of the small secondary schools of the eighteenth and nineteenth centuries was the best teacher and the most knowledgeable in most, if not all, subjects offered within a very limited secondary school curriculum. The comprehensive secondary school in the United States with enrollments many hundred times greater than those of their early counterparts makes it impossible for the present-day secondary school principals to know each subject better than each and every teacher employed. Nonetheless, the "headmaster concept" of the secondary school administrator dominates the profession. Most headmasters were great teachers rather than great administrators of large and complex institutions. The American secondary school principalship demands curriculum and instruction understanding along with special leadership and management competencies.

Characteristics of Secondary School Principals

The typical public senior high school principal by the late 1970s was a white, middle-aged married man with at least an earned master's degree.[20] About 93 percent were men as compared with 89 percent in 1965. Most were between the ages of 45 and 49. Fewer than 5 percent came from minority ethnic backgrounds. At the time of the most recent survey in 1977, about 65 percent had served six or more years in that position, which is about the same as that noted in 1965. Over one-third served in attendance centers with enrollments in the 1000 to 2000 range; only 12 percent were in schools of such size in 1965.

An impressive 99 percent earned a master's degree or higher in 1977 compared with 90 percent in 1965. Nine percent had an earned doctorate in 1977; only 1 percent did in 1965. The majority appeared to be reasonably well satisfied with their present roles, which is the same as noted about 12 years earlier. A substantially higher percent indicated aspirations for the superintendency in 1977 than in 1965. Principals are a highly motivated, professional, and upwardly mobile group who view their present post as a stepping stone to other administrative challenges.

The median salary for senior high school principals was $25,600 in 1977 and climbed to $32,206 by 1980. The 1980 median salary for secondary assistant principals was $30,372.

During the mid-1960s about 96 percent of the junior high school principals were men. Their profile was similar to their senior high school counterparts in 1965. The typical junior high principal in that year was a married man in his early forties with an earned master's degree or higher (93 percent).[21]

The Assistant Principal

Senior high school principals are four times more likely to have at least one assistant principal than their counterparts at the elementary level. Administrative personnel subordinate to the principal are given many different titles, among which are assistant principal, dean, vice-principal, and administrative assistant: Assistant principal seems to be preferred. A single assistant principal is usually considered second in command; when there are more than one, the title may be specific, such as assistant principal in charge of attendance and scheduling or in charge of student-body activities.

There is some debate about the optimum size of the administrative staff for a high school. A rough standard is one administrator for 400 pupils. The actual number will doubtless be influenced by the financial ability of the district, the complexity of student services, the number and turnover among staff, the total enrollment, the types of students served, and the nature of the area served. Justification for administrative staff increases must be based on an improvement in the quality of instruction or services.

What assistant principals do appears to be determined by what the principal delegates. Functions assigned to most assistant principals include:

1. Assuming responsibility for the operation of the school in the absence of the principal.
2. Serving as a representative of the school in lieu of the principal.
3. Participating in parent conferences in matters of school discipline.
4. Performing special assignments delegated by the principal.

The position may be considered as an internship for the principalship only if specifically designed for this function. A principal overseeing the professional experiences and development of an administrative intern is assuming an added burden and should not anticipate any relief that comes with the addition of administrative personnel.

The Department Head

The department head is at the classroom level of school administration in the large high school centers. The department head was found in more than three-fourths of the large California high schools.

The position's usefulness is subject to debate. Communication difficulty owing to lack of coordination among departments is the most pressing problem. The formation of a principal's cabinet composed of department heads has been suggested to facilitate communication.

The duties of the department heads are usually those delegated by the principal and include:

1. Participation in budget planning at the building level by submitting needs of the department to the principal.
2. Detailed supervision of instruction primarily by working with central-office supervisors.
3. Organization and conduct of departmental meetings.
4. Recommendations of courses or educational experiences to be offered within the department.
5. Orientation of teachers within the department who are new to the system.
6. Investigation and recommendation of texts and other instructional materials.
7. Procurement, coordination, and distribution of departmental equipment and supplies.

To give department heads administrative responsibilities such as gathering appraisal data on the performance of teachers in their departments would call for the removal of department chairpersons from the bargaining unit for teachers.

Department heads are justified when there are at least three and preferably five or more teachers for a given subject area.

Forces Changing the Principalship and Emerging Leadership Roles

There is a close relationship between district size and numbers serving in the principalship. In 1980 about 60 percent of all principalships were located in only one-fourth of all school districts. The 30 largest school systems in the nation employ one out of eight principals.

The conceptualization of the principalship as a cluster of administrative positions united into an administrative team at the school site level has been slow to develop—even slower than the management team at the superintendency level. It was an accomplishment for most districts to relieve the principal of nonadministrative responsibilities and then to add a professional assistant or two. It may take the remainder of this century for most districts to advance to the principalship team stage. Not all districts move with equal speed from one phase in the professional evolution of the position to another. Even at present the principalship has been arrested at one of the earlier phases of development in some communities.

The most frequently mentioned of the many and complex roles of the secondary school principal are the classic ones such as serving as the headmaster model, performing as an instructional supervisor, acting as a professional counselor to teachers and others, fulfilling leadership demands, rendering decisions at the site level, and identifying what needs changing and then implementing the new programs, methods, or technology. The instructional leadership role cannot be satisfied simply by teaching a class or two, that is, serving as the role model of the effective teacher. It is better realized through demonstrating competencies related to marshaling and distributing the resources, human and material, that classroom teachers require to perform more effectively. To illustrate, the principal makes great teaching possible by helping teachers procure instructional materials or the services of an instructional specialist in a specific field.

The administrator of the attendance center makes things happen with and through other people. What is prized most is the ability to organize, to allocate, and to stimulate action among those working in the attendance center. These managerial and leadership responsibilities may be difficult for a principal to fulfill if bogged down with the kind of work that is better assigned to clerical staff. Inadequate clerical assistance results in a great waste of professional time and talent.

A frequently heard remark is "as the principal, so the school." This may be an exaggeration to prove the point that the person in the principalship exerts considerable influence on the climate, morale, and learning productivity. The reverse of this cliché is no less true, namely, "as the school, so the principal." The challenges within a school and society shape the principalship, reorder priorities, and redefine what constitutes effectiveness in the position.

Among the many forces that have had a significant impact upon the elementary and secondary school principalships during the 1970s and which are expected to continue to some degree during the 1980s are:

1. Declining enrollments started in the early 1970s to reverse the growth trends of the previous 25 years and which are expected to continue during the first half of the 1980s at the secondary level. Elementary enrollments are likely to increase once again during the last half of the 1980s, but declines will continue at that time at the secondary levels.

2. Management of retrenchment replaced the administration of rapid growth. Reductions in the teaching force replaced the previous administrative concern of how to attract more qualified personnel. Substantial enrollment losses also mean reductions in resources and fewer students against which to allocate and justify program costs. This could impact negatively on program quality during the 1980s.

3. The redefinition of professional relationships and practices as the result of collective bargaining conflicts will persist during the 1980s as well. How principals will relate to teachers is often defined in the negotiated personnel contract. These issues are complicated further by some principals requesting formal bargaining with school boards and/or superintendents to determine salary and working conditions.

4. Continuing inflation, tax revolts, and less willingness on the part of the public to allocate more essential resources for the support of public educational work compound the prob-

lems of providing quality educational programs that are expected but not willingly supported with additional resources. Principals are being asked to fulfill growing educational expectations in the form of improved rates of learning among all students, satisfying a broader range of learning needs than ever before, coping with the special problems of society that spill over into the schools such as more prevalent abuse of drugs by students and increasing crime and violence on school campuses, and so on, but with less resources. Doing more with less will remain one of the big administrative challenges of the 1980s.

5. Desegregation and considerable court monitoring, or other court strategies, of school operations were more prevalent during the 1970s than ever before. There is small likelihood that the civil rights battles which focus so much upon public education will be reduced substantially during the 1980s.

6. Mandated community involvement in direct administration of attendance centers exacerbates the problems related to the "politics of the principalship." This has been and will remain, more than likely, true in large urban districts and with particular types of federally supported programs. Citizen participation in educational administration that came out of civil rights activists efforts, antipoverty programs, and some consumer movements generated greater public questioning of "education experts" and "administrative office holders." The principal was the first to feel, and will continue to do so, the negative as well as the positive impact of all this.

7. Alternative schools became more common during the 1970s. How to relate to or stimulate the formation of in-school "alternative educational models" (which are not uniform and encompass a whole range of possibilities) will remain to challenge principals and other administrators during the 1980s.

8. Facilitation of educational changes will continue to be a pressure on principals even though the 1970s produced a mixed bag of results where some changes were implemented and others abandoned shortly thereafter. Change for the sake of change is less likely to be accepted as the "in thing" during the 1980s, but this is not likely to reduce the importance of the change agent role of the principal searching for better ways of doing things and greater productivity in promoting learning results.

9. Competency testing as one basis for awarding diplomas to secondary school graduates, increasing academic study requirements and the enrollment of pupils in more academic courses, reemphasis on grade standards as the basis of promotion from grade to grade as well as participation in athletics or other extracurricular activities, "back to basics," and similar accountability thrusts that came to a head during the 1970s will remain as challenges to the instructional and professional leadership role of the principal.

10. Vandalism, crimes of violence against students and professionals, and other school security problems reached high levels of concerns during the 1970s. Never before in American educational history was security of persons and property at schools a matter of greater concern and priority.

11. Program or project management competencies of principals were in great demand during the 1970s as the result of the proliferation of special projects supported by state, federal, or foundation funds. Principals will continue to be held accountable for the efficient expenditure of special program funds and for the achievement of objectives set for them.

12. Developing and working with an educational management team at the site level, and those at the system-wide level, will require the time and special talents of principals during the remainder of this century.

In short, there are forces such as those related to inflation, declining enrollment trends, and collective bargaining that are beyond the control or influence of the principal. There are other forces such as facilitation of prudent change, sensitivity to the community's changing needs, effective utilization of resources, improving instruction, enhancing the academic image of the school, effective student-faculty relations, and school climate for which a principal can be held accountable, at least to some degree.

Much of what confronted principals during the 1970s could not have been anticipated, and preparation to meet such challenges was not available in institutions of higher education during that period. Likewise, no one can forecast with certainty what additional, unexpected, or new crises will confront the principalship during the remainder of this century. This places a premium on persons with quickness, that is, quickness of mind to know that additional competencies must be acquired somehow if professional effectiveness is to be maintained, quickness to diagnose the nature of the new concerns confronting the schools, and quickness to sense the most promising directions and strategies to pursue. Obviously, a quick mind, quality preservice preparation, profitable experiences, and dedication to a lifetime of continuing professional development are important for success in the principalship. The image of the principal moving to defuse one crisis after another, until being late in resolving the one crisis that can destroy a career, is perhaps one of the more unfortunate signs of our times.

Many special-interest or single-issue groups pressure the principal to act on their concerns without regard to what might happen to others. Maintaining a professional perspective is not easy in the face of continuing pressures of vocal and dedicated critics. Threats to personal or job security are not uncommon.

There are many ways to define or describe the many complex roles, responsibilities, or functions of the principalship. The more traditional ones of leadership, decision making, planning, and change management were presented in earlier chapters. Some other perceptions of important roles would include at least the following:

1. *Linking-Pin Role.* The principal may be perceived as the linking-pin (or communication link) between teachers and the system as a whole, the community and the school, the learner and the educational program, and so on. The principal is often referred to as the "person in the middle" of many interactions in public education.

2. *Instructional Leadership Role.* Frequent reference has been made to this important role, but it would not be prudent to omit it from any list. Everyone agrees with its importance; how to fulfill it is often vaguely or poorly defined and accompanied by considerable conflict.

3. *The Catalyst Role.* To motivate professional personnel, to stimulate better student performance, and in general to make good things happen through the efforts of the principal in the education equation is what is meant by the word *catalyst.*

4. *Resource Manager Role.* The principal is held accountable for the protection, best use, and auditing of resource use in the instructional process. No principal can directly influence the quality of learning for every pupil in the school. The principal, however, can exert tremendous influence on learning quality through the resource manager role.

5. *Security, Control, or Discipline Roles.* Each of these concerns is interrelated and may be perceived as several sides of the same role. Learning cannot take place in an environment of fear, disruption, or chaos. Recent events have pushed the security, control, and discipline roles of principals into matters of considerable and high priority.

6. *Project Manager Role.* This was described in earlier paragraphs.

7. *Student Ombudsman-Counselor Roles.* These more traditional roles may be seen as the balances to the control or disciplinarian functions. Fairness, objectivity, and maintaining perspective help to minimize the apparent conflicts with other roles.

The administrative style and favored strategies when confronted with challenges and conflicts will often typecast the person in terms of the the roles preferred. Performance appraisal, however, should not be based on gossip or hearsay, but rather upon results or impact of the person and position in the light of challenges faced, resources available, quality of faculty, and so on.

Dean conceptualized the principal's office as a service center for the school.[22] The ten important services of this office were considered to be:

1. A communications center of the school.
2. A clearing house for the transaction of school business.
3. A counseling center for teachers and students.
4. A counseling center for school patrons.
5. A research division of the school for the collection, analysis, and evaluation of information regarding activities and results.
6. A repository of school records.
7. The planning center for solving school problems and initiating school improvements.
8. A resource center for encouraging creative work.
9. A coordinating agency cultivating wholesome school and community relations.
10. The coordinating center of the school enterprise.

He also reported that there is a need to transfer more administrative authority (such as assignment of pupils to classes, improvement of instruction, selection of educational materials, evaluation of staff, curriculum improvement, community relations, pupil promotional policies, selection of staff, budget preparation, and pupil transportation from the central office to the individual elementary school center.

The greater the amount of change in instructional procedures and the smaller the urban community, the more likely it is that the elementary school principal carries a high degree of responsibility for policy administration.

Selection of the Principal

The American Association of School Administrators recognized that the responsibility for selection and assignment of principals should reside in the superintendency and not the school board.[23] Some of the major observations and recommendations of an AASA Committee on Selection of Principals were:

1. That the school board, as a matter of policy, elect only those persons recommended by the superintendent for a principalship.

2. That the superintendent execute his responsibility for principal selection with the consultation of professional administrators and/or instructional staff members.
3. That a better conceptualization of the principalship consistent with present demands maximizes the chances of selecting the right person.
4. That the uniqueness of each attendance center be recognized and defined with clarity; that expectations of the principalship vary with the times and referent group and help to define the demands in a given attendance center.
5. That no person be excluded from consideration as principal on the basis of sex alone.
6. That personal variables such as age, sex, marital status, intelligence, health, personality, and value patterns may be considered in the selection process, but that most systems ignore the existing research on the appropriate use of these factors.
7. That the issue of how much prior experience is necessary to become a principal remains unresolved, but unusually long periods are not recommended.
8. That each system may have its own group of "principal makers"—people who have the ear of the superintendent or contacts with the selection committees and those individuals whose recommendations carry weight.

Not all selection information or devices used in principal selection have equal value. Biographical information blanks reveal the obvious characteristics; it has been remarked that the latest horoscope for the candidate may be as valid and reliable as letters of recommendation or credentials. Some of the factors used in principal selection and devices used in measurement are summarized in Table 16.2. No single device is perfect, nor can it provide all data necessary for prudent selection.

SUMMARY

Pupils learn and teachers instruct in the attendance units of the system. It is at this level that the efforts of the administrators at other levels are tested to determine their influence on the teaching-learning process and thus their value in the attainment of educational objectives.

The administrator of the attendance center is commonly referred to as the principal. The importance of his role in the administration of public education is difficult to overestimate.

The trend in the organization of elementary and secondary school attendance centers was away from the traditional 8-4 pattern after 1920. About 85 percent of elementary schools now terminate at grade 6; secondary education is now conceded to start at least at grade 7, and earlier in some middle schools. Considerable progress in the acceptance and establishment of nursery and kindergarten education was evident during the 1970s as indicated by 37 percent of the three- and four-year-olds and 85 percent of the five-year-olds now in such programs. Interest in the nongraded ele-

mentary school (better called flexible grading) peaked during the late 1950s and early 1960s and then fell during the 1970s and early 1980s.

In 1978 the typical elementary school principal was a middle-aged married man with at least a master's degree who served a single attendance center with about 490 pupils and put in 45 hours per week. Very few elementary schools have an assistant principal.

By 1960 most secondary schools were reorganized to include a junior and senior high school. A switch back to the four-year senior high school was noted during the 1970s, with 63 percent of the schools including grades 9 to 12 by the late 1970s. The primary difference between what existed 50 years ago and now is

TABLE 16.2

FACTORS USED IN PRINCIPAL SELECTION AND SOME RELATED MEASURING DEVICES

Factors used in selection	Devices used in measurement
1. Age, experience, family history	Biographical information blank, interview.
2. Breadth of general knowledge	Achievement tests, transcript, ratings by competent observers, interview, letters of recommendation.
3. Breadth of specialized knowledge of education	Achievement tests, transcript, ratings by competent observers, interview, letters of recommendation.
4. Command of the English language and ability to articulate thoughts	Tests, interview, ratings by competent observers.
5. Dependability, drive	Ratings by competent observers.
6. Emotional stability and other characteristics of personality	Tests, ratings by competent observers, letters of recommendation, interview.
7. Human relations skills	Ratings by or conversation with competent observers, letters of recommendation, interview.
8. Interests	Interview.
9. Likely administrative behavior or creativity	Situational performance tests, interview, letters of recommendation.
10. Mental ability or intelligence	Intelligence tests.
11. Moral fitness	Ratings by or conversation with competent observers, letters of recommendation.
12. Scholarship	Transcript, letters of recommendation.
13. Value patterns	Tests of value, ratings by or conversation with competent observers, interview.
14. Physical fitness or health	Health examination.

Source: American Association of School Administrators, *The Right Principal for the Right School*, Washington, D.C.: The Association, 1967, p. 44.

that a junior high or middle school intervenes between the elementary and senior high schools. The middle school movement flourished for a while, but interest has slackened considerably during recent years.

The early secondary administrators were independent of other administrators, but this changed during the twentieth century. The typical secondary school administrator during the later 1970s was a white, middle-aged married man with at least a master's degree. The profiles of junior and senior high principals are similar. Secondary principals are far more likely to have assistants than their elementary school counterparts.

The principal influences the school climate and productivity, but the school community also influences the person. Many forces are reshaping the roles and responsibilities of principals.

NOTES

1. W. Vance Grant and L. J. Eiden, *Digest of Education Statistics, 1981,* National Center for Education Statistics, Washington, D.C.: GPO, 1981.
2. Stuart E. Dean, *Elementary School Administration and Organization,* U.S. Office of Education, Bulletin 1960, No. 11, Washington, D.C.: GPO, 1960, pp. 15–17.
3. N. B. Dearman and V. W. Plisko, eds., *The Condition of Education,* 1982 edition, National Center for Education Statistics, Washington, D.C.: GPO, 1982, pp. 3–4.
4. J. I. Goodlad, "Editorial," *The National Elementary School Principal,* November 1967, pp. 2–3.
5. H. J. Klausmeier et al., *Individually Guided Education and the Multiunit Elementary School: Guidelines for Implementation.* Madison, Wis.: The Wisconsin R and D Center for Cognitive Learning, 1971.
6. Paul R. Pierce, *The Origin and Development of the Public School Principalship,* Chicago: University of Chicago Press, 1935, p. 9.
7. Ibid., p. 7.
8. Ibid., p. 12.
9. Ibid., p. 210.
10. Ibid., pp. 210–211.
11. W. L. Pharis and S. B. Zakariya, *The Elementary School Principalship in 1978,* Arlington, Va.: National Association of Elementary School Principals, 1979, 119 pp.
12. National Association of Elementary School Principals Association, *The Assistant Principalship in Public Elementary Schools-1969, a Research Study,* Arlington, Va.: The Association, 1970, 96 pages.
13. W. L. Pharis and S. B. Zakariya, op. cit., p. 55.
14. Edmund A. Ford, "Organizational Pattern of the Nation's Public Secondary Schools," *School Life,* Vol. 42, No. 9, May 1960, p. 10.
15. D. A. Rock and J. K. Hemphill, *Report on the Junior High School Principalship,* Reston, Va.: National Association of Secondary School Principals, 1966, p. 14.
16. David R. Byrne et al., *The Senior High School Principalship,* Reston, Va.: National Association of Secondary School Principals, Vol. 1, 1978, p. 38.
17. Educational Research Service, *Summary of Research on Middle Schools,* Arlington, Va.: ERS, 1975, 40 pp.
18. Ibid.
19. Stanley G. Sanders, "Differences in Mental and Educational Development from Grades Six through Nine and Implications for Junior High School Organization," unpublished doctoral dissertation, Iowa City: University of Iowa, 1960, p. 68.
20. David R. Byrne et al., op. cit., pp. 1–18.
21. D. A. Rock and J. K. Hemphill, op. cit.
22. Dean, op. cit., p. 376.
23. American Association of School Administrators, *The Right Principal for the Right School,* Washington, D.C.: The Association, 1967.

CHAPTER REVIEW QUESTIONS

1. What factors influenced the organization of elementary school attendance centers? Of secondary school attendance centers?
2. What should be the professional relations between the building principal and the central-office supervisor?
3. How can a principal fulfill the role of instructional leadership?

4. When does it become necessary to add assistant principals at the building level?
5. Why should elementary school attendance centers terminate at the end of grade 6? What arguments would tend to support termination at grade 8?

6. What is the profile of the typical elementary school principal? Secondary school principal?
7. Should the department chairmanship be eliminated? Justify your stand.

SELECTED REFERENCES

American Association of School Administrators, *The Right Principal for the Right School,* Washington, D.C.: The Association, 1967.

Blumberg, Arthur, and Greenfield, William, *The Effective Principal: Perspectives on School Leadership,* Boston: Allyn and Bacon, 1980

Cohen, Michael, "Effective Schools: Accumulating Research Findings," American Education, January–February 1982.

Ensign, Forest C., "Evolution of the High School Principalship," *School Review,* Vol. 31, March 1923, pp. 179–190.

Lortie, Dan C. *Elementary Principals In Suburbia: An Occupational and an Organizational Study,* draft report to the National Institute of Education, Washington, D.C.: GPO, 1982.

Manasse, A. Lorri, "Effective Principals: Effective at What?" *Principal,* March 1982.

McCleary, Lloyd E., and Thomson, Scott D., *The Senior High School Principalship,* Vol. III, *Summary Report,* Reston, Va.: National Association of Secondary School Principals, 1979, 63 pp.

Pharis, William L., and Zakariya, Sally B., *The Elementary School Principalship in 1978: A Research Study,* Arlington, Va.: National Association of Elementary School Principals, 1979, 118 pp.

17

ORGANIZATION AND ADMINISTRATION OF POSTSECONDARY SCHOOLS

Educational opportunities in the typical public school district during the eighteenth and most of the nineteenth century terminated at the completion of the elementary school, usually grade 8, if not sooner. Secondary education was a rare opportunity for a few who attended the Latin Grammar School or academy until the American high school began to grow rapidly after 1890. For much of the twentieth century completion of grade 12 was considered the terminal point for all except a relatively small percent that went on to attend an institution of higher learning.

The educational history of the United States documents the rising expectations for public schools and their continuing extensions beyond previous limits of public support. A universal and comprehensive system of public education that includes learning opportunities from kindergarten to the end of grade 12 was a reality for many places at the beginning of the twentieth century and for all by the middle of this century.

The upward extension of education persisted after the end of World War II with the creation of some new postsecondary public education institutions such as regional vocational schools and tremendous expansions in others such as the public junior college. Like the high school, the junior college existed for a half century before it gained widespread acceptance in the American system of public education. The organization and administration of postsecondary schools impact upon the public elementary and secondary school districts.

THE COMMUNITY JUNIOR COLLEGE

Some report the first community college to be Monticello College, established in 1835, and the second, Susquehanna University, established in 1858.[1] These were private schools. Many nineteenth-century four-year universities had rudimentary programs and often the first two years were what is now considered to be of the secondary school level.

It was not until late in the nineteenth century that the term *junior college* referred to the first two years in the undergraduate university program.

Growth of the Community College

Only a handful of junior colleges existed in the world in 1900; eight of these were in the United States.[2] Each had an enrollment of about 100 pupils. All were private schools. The first public junior college in the United States was established in 1901 at Joliet, Illinois. By 1925 the number had reached 325, of which 42 percent were public. It is significant that although the number of private junior colleges exceeded the number of those publicly supported, enrollment in public junior colleges was greater following 1925.

McDowell suggested the following as the four main stimulators of junior college development early in the twentieth century.

1. Encouragement from universities to create a junior college division.
2. Expansion of programs in normal schools to include studies in addition to education courses.
3. Extension of high school programs.
4. Decision by many small colleges too weak to satisfy the accreditation standards of a full four-year institution to concentrate resources on the first two years of collegiate instruction.[3]

The concept of the junior college as encompassing adult education and community service as well as occupational training and the courses found in the first two years of a four-year institution did not gain recognition until after 1945.[4] The dramatic growth paralleled acceptance of the comprehensive concept of the community junior college.

During the first quarter of the twentieth century, enrollment in private junior colleges exceeded that in public ones. By 1931 enrollment in public junior colleges was more than twice that in private junior colleges, by 1941 more than three times, and by 1971 more than 15 times the enrollment in private junior colleges. Enrollment in all types of junior colleges exceeded 1 million students for the first time in 1965 and exceeded 2 million only five years later. It took only seven years to double again when enrollments exceeded 4 million for the first time in 1977. The feverish growth rate began to ease during the mid-1970s, with small declines noted in some years of the late 1970s and the early 1980s. Private two-year colleges set a record high in 1978 with 154,451 enrolled. This is only a small percent of the total; 96 percent of two-year college enrollments are found in publicly supported institutions. The number of men enrolled exceeded that for women in 1976 and prior years. Since 1977, however, the number of women enrolled exceeds that for men.

As late as 1964 ten states had no public junior colleges; this was true only in three states in 1974. By 1980 all states supported one or more public junior community colleges.

Gleazer, in 1966, noted the tremendous development of junior colleges in California and Florida as follows:

California's goal is for all of its high schools to be within a junior college district. This is now the case for 90 percent of the high schools. Florida aims for a junior college within commuting distance of 99 percent of its population. Publicly supported junior colleges are now within commuting distance of 80 percent of the population and will be within commuting distance of 95 percent when the junior colleges already authorized are established.[5]

The Education Policies Commission, the President of the United States, and the President's Committee on National Goals have called for the establishment of a nationwide system of free public education through two years beyond high school.

The number of two-year institutions in 1982 was 1213, or almost double the number of 634 in 1963. The largest growth was in the public sector, climbing to 936 in 1980 from 375 in 1963; private institutions (about 269 in 1980) did not change much during that period. Only modest changes in numbers are anticipated during the remainder of this century; the heady growth days are over.

Characteristics of the Community College

The community college has at least three main purposes. The first (and the one that gave rise to the term *junior college*) is the provision of courses found in the first two years of the typical four-year, baccalaureate-degree-granting college or university.

The second function is adult education. Such programs are open to nonmatriculated students, and typically the only admission requirement is personal interest.

The third function is technical education to develop special occupational skills that require more than a high school education but less than four years of college.

Thornton identified the generally accepted purposes of the community junior college as:

1. Occupational and technical education at the post-high school level.
2. General education for all students.
3. College transfer or preprofessional education for the baccalaureate-degree-oriented student.
4. Continuing educational opportunities for part-time students.
5. Community services.
6. Counseling and guidance of students.[6]

Yet another function emerged, namely, remedial instruction for some students. Most states require by law that public junior colleges admit all high school graduates and others of postsecondary school age who can profit from some type of instruction. This open-door admission policy, one of the more controversial issues in junior college education, necessitates one of the least publicized functions of the junior college—remedial instruction. It is to be expected that increasing numbers of the full-time student body will be low-ability students.[7] Results of remedial instruction have been somewhat less than encouraging in terms of students' subsequent educational accomplishments.

Fields suggested that the uniqueness of the community college could be traced to the following five characteristics:

1. It is democratic, having low tuition and nonselective admission policies, and is geographically accessible to large numbers of people.
2. It is comprehensive, serving a wide range of abilities, aptitudes, and interests.
3. It is community-centered, being locally supported and controlled, and strives to serve community interests.
4. It is dedicated to life-long education and is concerned with learners of all post-secondary school ages.
5. It is adaptable, being concerned with differences in clientele and changing needs of society.[8]

Although some college-parallel courses may be useful for students of technical education, by and large, the various branches of the community college exist side by side, each having its own admission standards and staff requirements. It is possible for a public community college to become purely a preparatory school for a four-year degree-granting college.

The community college grants an associate in arts degree to designate the completion of the two-year college-parallel program. Usually the standards of admission to a college-parallel program in a community college are more flexible than those to a four-year, baccalaureate-degree-granting institution.

An important characteristic of the community college is accessibility. A frequently mentioned goal is the location of a campus within driving distance of every pupil in the state. This implies that the junior college is not a residential institution. Whether or not residential facilities should be provided for students is becoming an issue in community college administration.

Administrative Patterns of the Community College

Martorana and Morrison[9] reported on public junior college organizational patterns in the mid-1950s. The three predominant patterns were the junior college being (1) an integral part of and unified with public elementary and secondary schools in a local district (41 percent), (2) controlled by a specially created and separate junior college district (27.2 percent), and (3) operated as a two-year extension center of a state university system (18.3 percent). The state two-year college (5.8 percent) and the county normal school pattern (6.3 percent) represent other approaches. Regional differences were noted early in the history of public junior colleges: The separate junior college district was preferred in the South and West, the unified school and junior college district in the North Central region, and the off-campus university center in the Northeast and some North Central states.

The pattern in Florida up to 1968 exemplified the community college as part of the local school district (and each local district in Florida is coterminous with a county). The junior college represents an upward extension of the total educational opportunities provided in the basic unit of school administration. Although a special budget and separate state support were available, the community college was under control of the county board of public instruction, which is the local board of education in Florida

The community college president was subordinate to the chief executive officer of the local school board (the superintendent of schools). The primary policymaking body was the local board of education, although a special community college advisory committee may make recommendations. Florida abandoned the concept of public junior colleges as an upward extension of a statewide system of elementary and secondary education. A public junior college system separate from other public schools came into being on July 1, 1968.

In California the public junior college may be organized as (1) a part of a high school district, (2) a part of a unified city school district, or (3) a separate junior college district with an independent junior college board. Authorization to extend secondary school programs for an additional two years was passed in California as early as 1907. Educators who argue that the junior college is a collegiate rather than a postsecondary school institution subject to local jurisdictions appear to prefer a separate organization for junior colleges.

The trend during the 1970s and 1980s is moving toward separation of public community college administration from the control of local school districts. The public's perceptions of the purposes and contributions of community colleges to a system of public education will determine in the long run its structure, organization, and relationships with other units of a total system of public education. If conceptualized as a junior-level collegiate institution whose primary function is to feed students into four-year degree-granting institutions, then a separate status with a state junior college board and closer working relationships with baccalaureate-degree-granting schools could be justified. If, however, it is perceived as a multipurpose postsecondary institution in which college parallel courses are a part of, but necessarily the dominant feature of, a community-oriented comprehensive program of public education, then it could be argued that this segment should be related more closely or be an integral structural part of intermediate or local school districts. The community college movement may be viewed as the upward extension of the system of public education during the last half of the twentieth century just as the high school movement was the upward extension of the common schools during the last half of the nineteenth century. The contrary view holds that these institutions are offshoots of institutions of higher learning and not upward extensions of the common schools.

The appearance of high schools in greater numbers near the end of the previous century caused some to argue in favor of a separate and special status for secondary schools. The arguments were persuasive, for thousands of "union-free" and other special high school districts were created separate from existing elementary districts during the early years of the twentieth century. Reorganization of local school districts during the last 30 years brought an end to most of the separate secondary schools districts in favor of "unified" K to 12 local districts. Junior college "specialists" have contended during the past 25 years that separate and special status for junior community colleges is likewise essential. This has happened in most states. Time alone will tell whether "false prophets" prevailed, and whether 20 years hence there will be yet another battle to integrate once again such special units into a new form of an expanded local school district.

The major sources of funding for support of public two-year colleges are tuition, state contributions, taxes on the property within a community college district, and gifts. More and more states assumed the major share for capital outlay and operation of community colleges. In a few states community college "tuition" was not allowed to be levied against residents of the district on the same grounds as that found for the elementary and secondary education of residents.

The 1970s generated new challenges and caused many to begin to rethink the fundamental purposes as well as means of financing. This often happens when a period of very rapid development comes to an end, as it did for community colleges during the late 1970s. Community colleges began to experience a serious financial squeeze near the end of the 1970s and into the 1980s. This prompted many opposed previously to community college tuition charges made to residents as well as others to think more kindly of this source of revenue. Confronted with declining enrollments in four-year collegiate institutions, these schools began to compete for qualified students who might have in former years opted to complete freshmen and sophomore studies in community junior colleges. There is every indication that competition for the college-bound student will intensify during the 1980s. In short, the combination of financial pressures, declining enrollments, and competition for certain students with four-year institutions on the one hand and with adult education and other postsecondary programs on the other hand presents today some unusual challenges to community college administration and operation.

Administrative Staffing for Community Colleges

The chief executive officer of a community college is referred to most frequently as a president and less often as a dean.

Staff members usually carry titles common in four-year institutions of higher learning rather than those in use in elementary and secondary schools. Thus, there is a vice-president or a dean (but never a supervisor) for instruction, a dean or a director for technical education, a dean of students, and a vice-president or dean (but not assistant superintendent) for administrative or for business affairs. Department heads are the rule rather than the exception in the junior college.

As yet professorial rank has not been awarded commonly to junior college instructors, but this may change.

Community colleges have emulated universities rather than elementary and secondary institutions. In most states, however, junior college teachers are certified by or through the state department of education as are elementary and secondary school teachers. No state requires the certification of four-year college and university teachers.

THE AREA VOCATIONAL-TECHNICAL SCHOOL

The community college represents only one type of postsecondary school school center. The Vocational Education Act of 1963 stimulated formation of the area vocational-technical school that serves the needs of senior high school students, postsecondary school students, and adults. Federal funds provide resources for a variety of purposes related to these schools.

Because the vocational-technical school is a specialized institution, it usually serves a geographical territory larger than the local school district. Thus, in Wisconsin there are over 440 local school districts, but only 15 or 16 area vocational-technical school districts that are controlled by a special board and operate with a separate set of administrators from local schools.

The area vocational-technical school was created to provide young people and adults with the skills necessary to gain and hold a remunerative job. Some of the schools provide complex vocational-technical training for senior high school students; others serve high school graduates and young adults seeking to learn specialized skills in such fields as automobile mechanics, culinary arts, refrigeration mechanics, data processing, and electronics. These functions overlap to some extent with technical education programs of the community college.

In a few cases the area vocational-technical school and the community junior college are merged into one institution. In some instances the expansion of the educational program of an area vocational-technical school to include liberal arts courses as well as vocational and technical makes it operate as if it were a community college even though this name is not applied to it.

INTERRELATIONS OF THE POSTSECONDARY SCHOOL CENTERS

The community college may be evolving in many respects in a pattern similar to that of the secondary school. The Latin Grammar School offered only college-preparatory programs. The academy and then the high school appeared, providing more diversified, but nonvocational, courses to meet the needs of more students. The inclusion of vocational courses followed in spite of resistance from those who considered vocational instruction beneath the academic standards of the school. Federal funds stimulated comprehensive vocationally oriented programs. At present there are few who challenge the comprehensive secondary institution in the United States; there is general agreement that education for all youths can be achieved only through comprehensive secondary education programs that include vocational training.

Whether there shall be one or several postsecondary education institutions to satisfy the needs of the American society in the last of the twentieth century has yet to be resolved. The multipurpose community college, providing college-parallel, adult education, and technical educational programs, represents one approach. The area vocational-technical school

represents another. The strictly collegiate, degree-oriented junior college is a third.

ADMINISTRATION OF THE POSTSECONDARY SCHOOL CENTER

The past few decades witnessed a dramatic decrease in the number of basic administrative units in the public school system. This trend might be reversed, not by an increase in local school districts but by the creation of specialized educational administrative units for a variety of postsecondary school purposes, such as junior college districts and vocational school districts.

Inefficient and overlapping school-district structures may reappear if postsecondary school institutions are managed by specialized administrative units rather than incorporated in a comprehensive local school district or intermediate unit. The enthusiasim for upward extension of educational opportunities beyond the secondary school level must be tempered with sound organizational procedures or the precious resources of the state, already strained to support expanding commitments in education, may be dissipated by duplication of administrative effort.

SUMMARY

What was once considered terminal education —completion of the elementary grades and graduation from high school—is being revised upward with the growth of the community junior college. The concept of terminal education should be abandoned in favor of continuous learning programs for all ages.

The handful of junior colleges in 1900 grew to 1213 by 1982. Private community colleges were dominant early in this century, but the publicly supported ones emerged as the most numerous, the largest, and the strongest during the last half of the century. Junior college enrollments topped the 1 million mark in 1964 and went beyond 4 million by 1977. The growth phase has run its course, with stability and some decline anticipated during the remainder of the century.

The community junior college is a multipurpose postsecondary school institution offering college-parallel occupational, and adult education programs. A remedial function is now recognized as well. An important characteristic is the college's accessibility to the people being served.

Whether the public community junior college is an upward extension of the secondary school or a part of higher education is an unresolved issue. The many different functions have attributes of both. At one time most public community junior colleges were a part of the local school district. Separate junior college districts are becoming the most common organizational pattern.

The chief executive officer of a community college is referred to as president or dean. It is apparent from the titles of officers that community colleges have emulated universities rather than elementary and secondary schools.

The area vocational-technical school created by the Vocational Education Act of 1963 represents the new postsecondary school institutions. To some extent its functions overlap with the community college's, but the latter institution seldom assumes comprehensive vocational instruction.

Whether there shall be one or several postsecondary school institutions has yet to be resolved. The organizational implications of new educational extensions may precipitate problems of proliferation of organizational units.

NOTES

1. C. E. Blocker, R. H. Plummer, and R. C. Richardson, Jr., *The Two Year College: A Social Synthesis*, Englewood Cliffs, N.J.: Prentice-Hall, 1965, p. 25.
2. W. Thornton, *The Community Junior College*, 2nd ed., New York: Wiley, 1966, p. 45.
3. F. M. McDowell, *The Junior College*, U.S. Bureau of Education, Bulletin 1919, No. 35, Washington, D.C.: GPO, 1919.
4. Thornton, op. cit., pp. 51–56.
5. American Association of Junior Colleges, "Emphasis," *Junior College Journal*, Vol. 37, No. 3, November 1966, p. 5.
6. Thornton, op. cit., pp. 58–70.
7. J. E. Roueche, "The Junior College Remedial Program," *Junior College Research Review*, UCLA Clearinghouse for Junior College Information, Vol. 2, No. 3, November 1967.
8. R. R. Fields, *The Community College Movement*, New York: McGraw-Hill, 1962, pp. 63–95.
9. S. V. Martorana and D. G. Morrison, *Patterns of Organization and Support in Public Two-Year Colleges*, U.S. Office of Education, OE-52000, Washington, D.C.: GPO, 1957.

CHAPTER REVIEW QUESTIONS

1. Are there other educational institutions better suited to assume adult education functions than the community junior college? Justify your response.
2. Why did the public community junior college grow so rapidly after 1945?
3. Should the open-door admission policy of public junior colleges be revised? Justify your stand.
4. How does the public community junior college differ from its private counterpart?
5. Debate the following issue: Resolved, that all community junior colleges in a state be under the control of a state junior college board, not the local board of education.

SELECTED REFERENCES

Blocker, C. E., Plummer, R. H., and Richardson, R. C., Jr., *The Two Year College: A Social Synthesis*, Englewood Cliffs, N.J.: Prentice-Hall, 1965.

Bushnell, David S., *Organizing for Change: New Priorities for Community Colleges*, New York: McGraw-Hill, 1973.

Fields, R. R., *The Community College Movement,* New York: McGraw-Hill, 1962.

Gleazer, Edmund J., *Project Focus: A Forecast Study for Community Colleges,* New York: McGraw-Hill, 1973.

Monroe, Charles, *Profile of the Community College,* San Francisco: Jossey-Bass, 1977, 435 pp.

Roueche, J. E., "The Junior College Remedial Program," *Junior College Research Review,* UCLA Clearinghouse for Junior College Information, Vol. 2, No. 3, November 1967.

Thornton, J. W., *The Community Junior College,* 2nd ed., New York: Wiley, 1966.

PART IV

THE PRACTICAL DIMENSIONS AND OPERATIONAL CHALLENGES IN EDUCATIONAL ADMINISTRATION

The basic educational structural units described in previous chapters, such as local school districts, intermediate units of administration, state education agencies, and federal education agencies, provide the setting for the execution of the many functions of various management and supervisory personnel.

The delivery of educational programs and services to students gives rise to the so-called practical dimensions of educational administration. These include such practical administrative challenges as the admission, counseling, classification, and so on, of pupils for the purposes of instruction. These are the student or pupil personnel administration functions. The instructional leadership dimension of school management includes defining learning objectives, developing and offering an educational program or curriculum consistent with the objectives, defining the achievement standards and related means of measuring student learning progress, introducing and managing changes in instructional strategies to be utilized within the system, and so on.

Professional personnel, or what economists prefer to call "educational manpower," make it all happen. Professional personnel administration today is more complex than ever before. Teachers, supervisors, administrators, consultants, aides, and so on, must be recruited, oriented, assigned, motivated, appraised, and so on. Organized personnel now demand the right to bargain to influence salary and working conditions, to participate in those decisions that affect their welfare and that of the school, and to be consulted on a regular basis in other educational issues.

Without adequate resources schools would be unable to deliver the quality of services and programs to a wide range of learners. Administrators are charged with the procurement, protection, allocation, and efficient utilization of equipment, supplies, building, grounds, money, and other resources. The so-called business management function has long been identified with administration with its true significance not always appreciated.

Finally, included are the chapters that probe the politics of education, policy development, public relations, accountability, and future dimensions in the practice of educational administration.

18

STUDENT PERSONNEL ADMINISTRATION: THE QUANTITATIVE AND QUALITATIVE DIMENSIONS OF SERVING THE LEARNER IN THE SCHOOL SETTING

Some use the term *schooling* to describe that which is learned through formal educational mechanisms such as the public schools. Obviously, much behavior can be learned and knowledge acquired outside formal schooling, but that in no way diminishes the importance of special mechanisms. Students, or pupils, are the specific clients of educational institutions and society as a whole is the general beneficiary. Laws are passed to insure that educational opportunities are available to all and mandated for those within a given age range.

Obviously, without students there would be little need for schools. A first and important challenge to educational administrators is to identify the numbers of potential pupils of mandatory school age residing within the district, develop procedures for their admission to appropriately located school attendance centers, counsel and classify students in terms of personal characteristics and any special educational needs, and cluster students into grades and/or classes. This is referred to as "student personnel administration." It includes those administrative and supervisory functions and

services, other than classroom instruction, that are concerned with (1) identification, admission, registration, and classification of school-age children and other learners; and (2) the comprehension and development of the abilities, interests, and needs of individuals at various levels of maturity. The first or quantitative dimensions of student personnel administration are the focus of Section 1 of this chapter. The second section examines the qualitative dimensions of this phase of administration. Section 3, which has been added to this edition, deals with student security on or near campuses. This challenging dimension of pupil personnel administration reviews and analyzes school vandalism, violence, and disruption.

SECTION 1: QUANTITATIVE DIMENSIONS OF STUDENT PERSONNEL MANAGEMENT

Early in this century student personnel administration was equated with "child accounting," that is, keeping track of pupils. As late as

1951, one writer defined it as "the recording of all administrative, instruction, and appraisal information necessary to keep a pre-school, school, or post-school record of each student."[1] Ayres[2] in 1915 stressed the record-keeping dimensions—particularly locating, grouping, keeping track of, and reporting progress of students.

The qualitative dimensions emerged when records were analyzed and interpreted as a means of improving pupil adjustment and learning in the school situation. The qualitative emphasis stimulated the expansion of special-school services, but it was not until after World War II that it overshadowed completely the quantitative orientation of pupil personnel administration.

IDENTIFICATION OF PUPILS: THE SCHOOL CENSUS

Early in educational history school census data were the basis for the distribution of state funds to local districts. Distributions of state or federal educational grants today are rarely based on such raw data. During the late 1940s the following were identified as the primary purposes for the school census, and all continue to have value to some degree today:

1. Ascertain the nature and scope of educational services needed in the school district.
2. Provide data basic to planning school-plant programs.
3. Evaluate enforcement of compulsory-attendance laws.
4. Determine the number of children who will enter school for the first time and report any unusual characteristics of this group.
5. Locate children who move into, out of, or about the district.
6. Discover the employment of a child.
7. Check enrollment and absences in public as well as private and parochial schools.[3]

The priority attached to each of the above will vary from district to district. In addition, school census data can help to identify pupils with special education needs and to insure compliance with state and federal program requirements. The school census is the official record of all persons residing within a school district. Numerous studies reported that in prior years the school enumerations were notoriously inaccurate. One nationwide study revealed that 25 percent of school-age children were not reported in the school census. The reverse may result when census takers are paid in proportion to the number of persons counted; one study indicated overreporting of children by as much as 15 percent.[4]

The census appears to be fairly accurate for children between the ages of 7 and 13. The count of the preschool (under age 5) population is the least accurate.

The census begins with a house-to-house canvass. Those who are to be counted are usually specified in state laws. By 1910, 33 states required an enumeration of school-age children, and by 1940 all states except Nevada did so. Culbertson reported a reversal in the trend, for by 1953 only 38 states required a census, 5 had permissive laws, and 5 had no laws.

In most states children between 6 and 21 were reported; this includes pupils under the jurisdiction of the compulsory-attendance laws.

Identifying children for the census roster immediately following birth is now recommended practice. There is some argument for not reporting those over 19 if no community college experience is anticipated.

Minimum information would include name of child, date of birth, authority for birth information, address of child, names and occupations of parents, name and location of school attended, reasons for nonattendance, notation of physical or mental handicap, and movements within or out of the district. Whether a child is likely to attend a private school is useful in a district having a large percentage of the school population enrolling in private or parochial institutions.

The Continuous Census

The continuous system starts with an initial house-to-house canvass, as does the periodic enumeration. The continuous census records changes in student population either weekly or monthly. By keeping track of pupil movements within, into, and out of the district, it increases the chances of discovering those missed in the initial house-to-house canvass.

The continuing census demands more personnel, more work, and careful organization: New data must be posted at the end of each week or month to update the original enumeration; additional clerical personnel and machines are required to gather and record such data. The additional expense is justified if the continuous census system makes possible more accurate counting of the preschool-age population and compensates for the incompetencies of the enumerators.[5]

The continuing census system has been recommended since at least the early 1920s. Its adoption has been slow. No district is too small to install it. A continuous system requires validation by a periodic house-to-house canvass, but such canvassing can be spaced much farther apart than the usual one or two years.

Processing of Census Data

Manual procedures were used in collecting and filing census data prior to the establishment of computer-based information systems. Computer-based electronic data processing has greatly reduced the drudgery of census operations and improved the accuracy and accessibility of information.

There are a large number of programs available at present for use with a variety of electronic data-processing hardware to expeditiously handle the school census, attendance, registration, and similar reports.

ADMISSION OF PUPILS TO SCHOOL

Requirements for Admission

Admission to a public school is not an absolute right. It can be exercised only upon meeting qualifications established by legal authorities.

Thus, a child must usually attain a given age before being admitted to a public school. Although there are exceptions, research supports the contention that a child who enters first grade with a mental age of six years or older is more likely to experience academic success than a child with a younger mental age.[6]

One study pointed out that four times as many under-age children had difficulty in school than did normal-age children. Both under-age and over-age children had more adjustment problems than those of normal age.[7]

Many administrative problems are encountered when all students who have not reached a fifth birthday by the fall-opening date for school are disallowed automatically from admission to kindergarten. This is a very sensitive decision with parents, and research to date has not helped to resolve it. First time admission either to kindergarten or first grade generates highly emotional complaints. Rigidity rather than flexibility tends to compound the difficulties.

Administrators search for objective bases to undergird such decisions and therefore tend to be sympathetic to policies that base school entrance upon such objective factors as mental age plus indicators of physical, social, and emotional maturity. Unfortunately, the instruments available to measure such indicators are not as precise or reliable as would be desirable. The result is that there is wide variation among public school systems as to the minimum age attained for admission of pupils to kindergarten; the same is true for first grade. This is less true in states that mandate uniformity in minimum age requirements among all districts.

Publicity about admission standards are often accompanied by parent education to reduce emotional reactions toward exceptions to rules which permit some children, particularly girls, to enter school sooner than others of the same chronological age.[8]

A second requirement for admission is residence within the district. A child's residence is normally where the father lives. The definition of residence for school purposes is much broader than that for domicile, which is the basis for determining the right to vote in a given area. A district has the option to refuse admission to non-resident pupils.

Certain health requirements must be met for entry into school. Thus, courts sustained vaccination requirements for admission to a public school. The elimination of small pox in the United States may bring modifications in this requirement if it is tested once again in court.

Effect of School Integration

For most of the history of public education the assignment of pupils to attendance centers was relatively noncontroversial. Predetermined boundary lines designated the attendance area for a given school building, and all residing therein were directed to register at that school center. The neighborhood school concept is based upon attendance centers within walking distance of potential pupils and this held pupil-transportation costs to a minimum in most urban school districts. The few requests for pupil transfers to attend other than the assigned school seldom generated much disagreement.

The image of the neighborhood school changed after the *Brown* decision even though the U.S. Supreme Court never intended to bring into question the neighborhood school concept. The clustering of racial and ethnic populations in specific areas caused some to perceive the neighborhood school as a strategy to insure racial isolation if not segregation. Cross-district busing of pupils from neighborhoods that were predominately of a single race or ethnic background to others to obtain a better racial or ethnic mix was the relatively common strategy ordered by some courts. Pupil assignment to specific schools became a social and legal issue rather than an education decision for efficient operation and administration. "White flight," that is, the movement of predominately white families with school age children out of a district with a substantial minority student enrollment, was the response of parents who objected to court-ordered cross-district busing to achieve integration in school attendance centers. The counterresponse to

this was the effort to create much larger metropolitan school districts by court orders—an effort that has had little success to date.

The difficult situation confronting school administration eased somewhat during the mid-1970s when congressional action was used to temper the activism of some federal agencies that promoted more rapid desegregation of urban school systems. These legislative efforts succeeded to the point where it prompted the U.S. Commission of Civil Rights to declare in 1979 that congressional amendment of certain bills "severely limited the ability of the executive branch to carry out its desegregation enforcement responsibilities." The commission developed its own indicators of the extent of school segregation and concluded that "the average level of segregation of all minority pupils in the country was moderate in 1976."[9]

Black leaders shifted strategies from accommodation to protest, from subservience to challenge. Many organizations, formed at least initially to further the civil rights of blacks, focused on schools. Havighurst[10] depicted the many phases in the schools' involvement in civil rights issues as follows:

Phase I: Response to the court, 1954 to 1958;
Phase II: Rise of controversy, 1958 to 1963;
Phase III: Black revolution, 1963 to 1966;
Phase IV: Drive for integration, 1966 to 1970.

A Phase V may be described as a drive for black control of schools where the majority of the student body in the district is black. This includes more black school board members and black administrators as well as more black teachers. The number of black school superintendents increased for a while during the 1970s and then leveled off.

A Phase VI would be the increasing acceptance of integrated schools and perhaps a lessening of tensions related to the desegregation process. The nation has come closer than ever before to this ideal.

The school desegregation focus shifted around 1970 from the South to urban districts in the North. There was no intent, or basis in law, on the part of most states outside the

South to operate separate schools for blacks and whites. Blacks outside the South lived in residential neighborhoods where most others were blacks, which meant that the schools serving such neighborhoods would have predominately black or minority student enrollments. Civil rights-oriented groups sought legal relief from what were called racially isolated school or de facto segregation. Cross-district busing for racial balancing of school enrollments became a state and national political campaign issue during the 1970s and into the 1980s. Mandated busing for purposes of desegregation dominated school board and other elections at the local level as well. It prompted Californians to approve a statewide initiative to have its state constitution correspond to the federal Constitution on issues of desgregation that had the net effect of lessening the demands for court-ordered cross-district busing. The U.S. Supreme Court in 1982 upheld the constitutionality of the California initiative. Court mandates and other efforts to ameliorate any existing racial imbalances in some schools, for whatever reason, remained an unresolved and very controversial issue over 25 years after the landmark *Brown* decision.

Hauser and Taitel[11] reported demographic factors related to the movement of blacks into large urban centers. In 1910, 89 percent of the blacks of the nation were in the South. By 1950 the migration of blacks from the South to other regions left only about two-thirds in the South. By 1960 less than 60 percent of all blacks remained in the South. This trend continued and by 1970 there were as many blacks in other regions as in the South. In a single 35-year period about 4.5 million blacks migrated north and west.

Southern blacks tended to be rural residents. In 1910, prior to the migration of blacks to the North and West, only 27 percent lived in urban places, defined by the census as places of 2500 inhabitants or more. By 1960, 58 percent of the blacks in the South, and 95 percent of those in the North and West, lived in urban communities. Blacks settled in the central core of the metropolitan areas rather than in suburbs. Hauser and Taitel described the central core of

the city as the blacks' port of entry into northern regions and into urban America. Recently a movement toward the suburbs has been in evidence.[12] In many large cities the majority of residents are blacks. In many urban school systems black students constitute the largest proportion of those enrolled in the public schools.

National data for 1978 revealed that 76 percent of those enrolled in public elementary and secondary schools were white, 15.5 percent black, 6.4 percent Hispanic, 1.2 percent Asian or Pacific Islander, and 0.8 percent American Indian or Alaskan native. There was a tremendous variation in the ethnic and racial mix of public school populations from state to state. Thus in 1978, 99.2 percent of all public school students in Vermont, 99.1 percent in Maine, and 98.9 percent in New Hampshire were white. Ninety percent or more of the students in 17 states, or over one-third in the nation, were white. In contrast, less than half of the public school students in Hawaii and New Mexico were classified as white. Only about 3.5 percent of the students enrolled in the Washington, D.C. public schools were white.

Viewing distributions from the local district point of view, the students from minority backgrounds make up the majority of those enrolled in the public schools of the five largest urban school systems in the nation. Students from minority backgrounds comprise 90 percent or more of those enrolled in public schools of the cities of Washington, D.C., Newark, N.J., and Atlanta, Ga. In addition, minority students make up more than 80 percent of total public school students in the cities of San Antonio, Detroit, New Orleans, Oakland, and Richmond. At present the percent of the school enrollment that is white in the 29 largest school systems is substantially less than what it was ten years earlier. Eight of the 29 went from enrollments that were predominately white to those that were predominately of minority backgrounds in the space of a single decade. Thirteen of the 29 were predominately black ten years ago, and the disparity increased as minority enrollments increased faster than those for whites in the subsequent ten years. It is the unusual large city school

TABLE 18.1

HISTORICAL SUMMARY OF PUBLIC ELEMENTARY AND SECONDARY SCHOOL ENROLLMENT AND ATTENDANCE, 1869–1870 TO 1972–1973

	1869–1870	1899–1900	1919–1920	1929–1930	1939–1940	1949–1950
K-8 enrollment	6,792,000	14,984,000	19,378,000	21,279,000	18,833,000	19,387,000
9–12 enrollment	80,000	519,000	2,200,000	4,399,000	6,601,000	5,725,000
Total K-12 enrollment	6,872,000	15,503,000	21,578,000	25,678,000	25,434,000	25,112,000
Percent of total population enrolled	17.3	20.4	20.6	21.1	19.4	16.9
Percent of school-age population (5–17) enrolled	57.0	71.9	78.3	81.7	84.4	83.2
Percent of total enrollment in high school	1.2	3.3	10.2	17.1	26.0	22.7
Percent of enrolled pupils attending daily	59.3	68.6	74.8	82.8	86.7	88.7
Average length of school term in days	132.2	144.3	161.9	172.7	175.0	177.9
Average number of days attended by each pupil enrolled	78.4	99.0	121.2	143.0	151.7	157.9

system that has fewer than 30 percent of its enrollments represented by minorities.

The initial study by Coleman reported the results of a study of racial segregation in public schools and the effect that school characteristics have on student learning.[13] Done at the behest of the U.S. Congress, the report was based on 1965 data. It concluded that the great majority of American children were segregated, the blacks being the most segregated of the minority groups. The report declared, and in great opposition to other educational research, that the amount of money spent per pupil for books, buildings, and other resources had little direct effect on achievement. The report stated: "The achievement of minority pupils depends more on the schools they attend than does the achievement of majority pupils" and "improving the school of a minority pupil will increase his achievement more than will improving the school of a white child."[14]

Some critics contended that the Coleman report was based on relations among factors that were not isolated and that the methods used to measure the background of "black" students were inadequate.

By the fall of 1978, 40 percent of the nation's schools had enrollments that were predominately white, 30 percent minority, and 30 percent classified as "racially isolated" in which 90 percent or more were minority students. A higher percent of schools in the Northeast and Midwest (in excess of 43 percent) were identified as racially isolated. Although 76 percent of the total 1978 public school enrollment in the United States was white, 82 percent of the graduating classes was white.

ENROLLMENT AND ATTENDANCE OF STUDENTS

Data presented in Table 18.1 are based on reports issued by the U.S. Office of Education (presently the Department of Education) and a federal division of the department called the National Center for Education Statistics. Enrollment in public nursery, elementary, and secondary schools totaled only 6.872 million pupils in 1869–1870. Most were elementary school pupils, for only 1.2 percent of the total enrollment was in high schools. Fifty years later, in 1920, public school enrollment tripled

TABLE 18.1 *(Continued)*

	1959–1960	1969–1970	1975–1976	Fall, 1979[a]	Fall, 1980[a]
K-8 enrollment	27,602,000	32,597,000	30,487,000	28,037,000	27,560,000
9-12 enrollment	8,485,000	13,022,000	14,304,000	13,762,000	13,360,000
Total K-12 enrollment	36,087,000	45,619,000	44,791,000	41,799,000	40,920,000
Percent of total population enrolled	20.1	22.4	21.0	DNA	DNA
Percent of school-age population (5–17) enrolled	82.2	86.9	88.9	DNA	DNA
Percent of total enrollment in high school	23.5	28.5	31.9	DNA	DNA
Percent of enrolled pupils attending daily	90.0	90.4	90.3	DNA	DNA
Average length of school term in days	178.0	178.9	178.3	DNA	DNA
Average number of days attended by each pupil enrolled	160.2	161.7	161.1	DNA	DNA

Source: K. A. Simon and W. V. Grant, *Digest of Educational Statistics 1986*, (various editions), Washington, D.C.: GPO, 1981.

DNA = Data Not Available at this writing.
[a]Data for fall of 1979 and fall of 1980 are estimates released by the U.S. Department of Education, August 31, 1980.

to 21.578 million. Enrollment increased again during the next decade.

A decline was evident, particularly at the elementary school level, during the Depression decade of 1930 to 1940. Although elementary school enrollment increased during the 1940s, secondary school enrollment declined, so that once again total enrollment dipped. Total enrollment in public schools in 1939–1940 and 1949–1950 was lower than in 1929–1930. Enrollment during the 1950s and 1960s set new records each year. There was an increase of over 9.5 million pupils in the 1960s. The peak enrollment was hit in the fall of 1971 with 46.081 million pupils. A reversal of growth patterns started thereafter. The 1970s will be remembered in history as the decade of substantial decline in public school enrollments. By the middle of the previous decade the enrollments in the nation's public schools dropped to 44.791 million. By the beginning of the present decade, the fall of 1980, enrollments tumbled to only 40.920 million. A further decline to about 40.664 million was noted in the fall of 1982. Enrollment totals for each of the last three years of the 1970s were below those of the comparable last three years of the 1960s. Public school enrollments are projected to remain between 39 and 40 million for most of the 1980s; it is not likely to exceed 40 million again until 1988. Enrollments by 1990 will be slightly less than 1979, but more than for 1980. Elementary school enrollments are predicted to rise after 1985, and in the ten years thereafter to rise in numbers to equal or exceed the drop during the previous 15 years.

During the nineteenth century less than 2 percent of the total enrollment in public schools was found in high schools. By the end of the first decade of the twentieth century only about 5 percent of the total enrollment was in high schools. Since the end of World War II enrollment in public high schools has constituted approximately 22 percent of the total in public elementary and secondary schools. About 88.5 percent of the school-age population is enrolled in the public elementary and secondary schools.

Enforcement of Attendance

Part of the dramatic gains in public school enrollment can be traced to compulsory-education laws. The first modern public school compulsory-attendance law, enacted in Massachusetts in 1852, required three months' attendance in public school during the year; in 1873 this was extended to five months.[15] By 1890, 27 states and the District of Columbia had enacted similar compulsory-education laws, and by 1914, all but six Southern states had such laws. Mississippi, in 1918, was the last state to enact a compulsory-education law. It was not until the early part of the twentieth century that most states enacted child-labor laws compatible with compulsory-education laws. As a result of the Supreme Court decision on school integration, South Carolina and Mississippi repealed compulsory-attendance laws in 1955 and 1956,[16] and Virginia did the same in the late 1950s.

Establishment and enforcement of compulsory-education laws were accompanied by debate and difficulty. Early compulsory-education laws placed school-leaving age at 13 or 14 years. By 1954 school-leaving age was 16 years in 39 states, 17 years in 4 states, and 18 years in 5 states.[17]

Most state departments of education have some responsibility to enforce compulsory-attendance laws. The most common age at which a pupil must begin regular attendance is 7 years, and the most common school-leaving age (or exemption from compulsory school attendance) is 16 years. By 1977, 43 of the 50 states specified age 7, or earlier, through age 16, or older, as the compulsory school-age range, with most opting for the 7 to 16 age period.

The case of *Pierce* v. *Society of Sisters* established that a pupil may satisfy legal education requirements by attending a parochial or private school. An individual completing the highest grade offered within a district is likewise exempt from further conditions of the compulsory-attendance laws in some states. Exemptions have been recognized for illness, physical or mental handicap, and special religious reasons. On the other hand, the courts have repeatedly held that a married pupil cannot be excluded from school on the grounds of marriage alone. Although a married pupil is excused from conditions of the compulsory-education law, she has a right to attend school if she chooses. Board action cannot override the law.

The present-day attendance officer relies less on police power (although it is still employed where necessary) and more on discovering or understanding reasons for not attending and applying corrective measures to minimize recurrence of chronic nonattendance.

Individuals charged with enforcement of school attendance during the 1920s had such occupations as police officer, real estate agent, meat cutter, glass blower, painter, and electrician; only about 14 percent could be classified as professionally trained; the majority were 51 years of age or older.[18] The White House Conference on Child Health and Protection in 1932 suggested an attendance officer for every 1500 to 2000 children enrolled in public, private, and parochial schools. It also suggested that the office should be oriented toward social work rather than policing.

The visiting-teacher whose origins can be traced to the early part of the twentieth century (1906 to 1921) was a type of school attendance officer. Visiting teachers were to provide services that would help the child adjust better to school and to attack such problems as nonattendance, juvenile delinquency, and tardiness.

In a large school system an assistant principal may be in charge of attendance services at the building level and work with attendance officers in the central office.

There is greater need for a social worker, supplemented by a psychologist, psychiatrist, school nurse, and school counselor than for the traditional truant officer. The attendance worker retains police powers, being able in most states to pick up truants, enter and inspect places of employment, prepare cases, and, in some circumstances, prosecute cases.

The six major functions of attendance personnel in a school system are:

1. Determining causes of absence through interviews at home and school.
2. Providing liaison between home and school.
3. Providing liaison between school and a law-enforcement agency.

4. Offering intensive casework on social and emotional problems.
5. Providing liaison with other social agencies in the community.
6. Interpreting the program to the community.

Length of School Term and Daily Attendance

The average length of the school term has ranged from 132.2 days in 1869–1870 to about 179 days at present. The average number of days attended by each pupil enrolled has ranged from 78.4 in 1869–1870 to about 162 at present. The average length of the school term and the number of days attended by each pupil enrolled increased by significant amounts until about 1939–1940; since that time very small gains have been registered. Only 59.3 percent of enrolled pupils attended daily in 1869–1870; at the end of the nineteenth century the figure was only about 64.1 percent. Average daily attendance, as a percent of average daily membership, is presently around a high 90 percent. Investigations document that 50 to 80 percent of absenteeism is due to illness. These data also indicate that primary grade pupils are absent for illness more often than older children, and girls more than boys. Most absences are for two days or less. Truancy, or willful absence, accounts for only about 2 percent of absenteeism. Attendance at school varies with the month of the year and the age and sex of the child. Girls appear to have a slightly better attendance record than boys.

The public schools increased steadily their holding power over the nation's youth. About 30 percent who entered fifth grade in 1924 continued and graduated from high school 8 years later; only 39 percent who graduated from high school entered college in the fall of 1932.

Dropouts, those who terminate their education prematurely, declined in number in the years following 1932. About 98 percent of all fifth graders enrolled in public schools in the fall of 1970 entered high school, or ninth grade, in the fall of 1974; 88 percent then continued as far as grade 11; 75 percent graduated from high school in 1978; and 44 percent went on to some type of postsecondary school or college by the fall of 1978. About 23 percent of those who started as fifth graders in 1970 are expected to graduate from a four-year collegiate institution in 1982.

The public school dropout rate in 1932 was 70 percent; in 1970 it was about 25 percent. These are national figures and there is considerable variation in this rate from state to state and among school districts within a given state.

The comprehensiveness of the program, availability of remedial instruction, and improvement of instructional methods and guidance services contributed to the improvement of the holding power of the secondary school. More remains to be done, however.

CLASSIFICATION OF PUPILS

After admission and enrollment, pupils must be classified for instructional purposes. Grading is the initial step in grouping pupils for purposes of instruction. Further classification may be necessary if there are more than enough pupils to fill a one-grade room or one high school class section.

Heterogeneous grouping can be defined as class sectioning on the basis of chance factors or arbitrary standards unrelated to the students' learning ability or past performance. Homogeneous grouping implies placement of pupils into class sections on the basis of some measure of ability or special talents. "Homogeneous" implies *approximately* the same kind and quality of ability as measured by some instrument. Stated another way, the range of some type of student ability is less in a homogeneous than in a heterogeneous section.

Implicit is the assumption that a considerable amount of some type of ability or aptitude is related to facility in mastering a skill or gaining special knowledge. Homogeneous grouping through what might be called "natural selection" occurs at the secondary level in advanced courses in specialized fields of learning. The highly interested or who possess special aptitude in a given field are most likely to enroll in advanced and elective courses.

General learning ability is commonly used in sectioning elementary school classes and required classes at the secondary level. General learning ability is measured usually with one of the standard intelligence tests and is reported in terms of mental maturity as indicated by mental age or intelligence quotient. It can also be inferred from the pupil's past achievements as determined by scores on a standardized test, by grade-point averages, or by informal evaluation by teachers. A pupil's general aptitude for learning may be influenced by such factors as social maturity and emotional stability as well as intelligence. A combination of factors, such as mental age, reading skills, grade-point average, and emotional stability, provides a better indication of general ability to learn than does intelligence alone. The most frequently reported bases for grouping pupils are intelligence quotient from a group mental test, scholarship marks in all subjects, an average of several teachers' ratings of the pupil's academic ability or intelligence, scores on group intelligence tests, mental age, and average scholarship marks in certain and related subjects.

Grouping is most advantageous for those at the extreme ends of a curve of normal distribution of ability or intelligence. Thus, the very dull and the very bright appeared to succeed better under homogeneous rather than heterogeneous grouping, although the evidence was less positive for the bright than for the dull children. Differentiation of those pupils in the broad normal range was more difficult to relate to learning ability.

Grouping does not solve educational problems. It is an administrative device that can facilitate learning only if teaching techniques are adapted to the group's potential.

Following a survey of research on the effects of ability grouping, Goldberg et al. made the following comment: "Many of the issues concerning grouping remain unresolved and most questions are still unanswered despite 70 or 80 years of practice and at least 40 years of study. Insufficient and conflicting data are being used to support partisan views concerning the consequences of grouping rather than to resolve the persistent issues."[19] An effective class organizational pattern for instruction is far more complex and elusive than the champions of specific approaches would have us believe.

SECTION 2: QUALITATIVE DIMENSIONS

Education for all demands adequate resources and services to meet the varied needs of a heterogeneous student body—some bright, others dull; some mature, others immature; some emotionally balanced, others disturbed; some sound of body, others physically handicapped; some highly motivated to learn, others apathetic or even antagonistic to school and learning; some from privileged socioeconomic backgrounds, others from deprived areas. The qualitative aspects of pupil administration concern the educational institution's responsibility to serve students of almost infinite variety by providing special instructional, counseling, health, welfare, and other services (in addition to classroom teaching).

By the early 1980s there were almost 2.2 million classroom teachers, but only about 95,000 full-time equivalent educational specialists providing student services other than full-time teaching in the public elementary and secondary schools. Included within this number of educational specialists were guidance counselors, school social workers, attendance supervisors, school psychologists, speech and hearing clinicians, and school nurses and other health personnel. Guidance and counseling personnel were the most numerous, totaling almost 64,000, but these numbers are more likely to drop than increase in the 1980s. Psychological personnel accounted for about 14,000 of the total. The most rapid growth and development of each of these areas occurred during the 1960s with a lesser gain in the 1970s. Some retrenchment began to be noted in the late 1970s and is projected to continue through at least the early 1980s.

Guidance Services

Comprehensive educational-guidance services trace their origins to vocational guidance activities during the beginning of this century. The development of objective tests added impetus to the movement. The growing concerns for sound mental health and the emergence of special knowledge and skills related to the counseling process helped to extend further the potential of the field.

Guidance focuses upon individual needs, concerns, and problems. It seeks to help each person better comprehend and interpret potentials and limitations and to also plan realistic life goals. It is defined more formally by the American Personnel and Guidance Association in cooperation with the National Education Association as "services available to each student to facilitate his academic success in school; to help him better understand his strengths and limitations; to identify his interests; to aid him in planning for and attaining realistic goals. The emphasis is always on the individual even when students meet in groups for guidance purposes."[20]

Guidance—a cluster of particular kinds of services to individuals—should not be confused with one of its most common techniques—counseling. Guidance is the responsibility of many different kinds of professional persons: teachers, counseling specialists, psychologists, psychiatric specialists, social caseworkers, and administrators.

Counseling in a Guidance Program

Counseling is the central service of guidance. The counselor employs special understanding of human behavior, skill in interpreting data, and knowledge of interview techniques to understand and perhaps subsequently to direct efforts of the counselee. So important is counseling to the entire guidance program that often the two are held to be synonymous.

As Bishop put it, "Whoever counsels touches the delicate web of individual deci-sion-making, personal adjustment, and self-image. Those who counsel may beckon, consult, or direct."[21]

The teacher's concern for the development of the individual learner is as much a part of guidance and counseling as the work of those who identify themselves as specialists in the field. Counseling is not solely the prerogative of the guidance counselor.

Recognition of the teacher's role in the process suggests the importance of the teacher's gaining skill in guidance techniques.

The guidance program includes appraisal of students, placement of school graduates, and related services, as well as counseling. Guidance and counseling can help pupils in elementary as well as in secondary institutions.

Guidance and counseling services expanded rapidly after 1958 owing to the provision of federal funds, primarily through the National Defense Education Act (NDEA). The number of public school counselors increased during the early 1960s by 143 percent over the pre-1958 or pre-NDEA numbers. The numbers in such positions reached almost 64,000 in 1981.

The typical school counselor was a former classroom teacher with special preparation in guidance, educational psychology, and/or social work. The number of such specialists on state departments of education staffs increased significantly during the 1960s as well. Again, here as elsewhere the need for an increased numbers of such specialists diminished during the 1970s.

The counselor–student ratio in secondary schools declined from 1:960 in 1958–1959 to 1:320 in 1980. The recommended counselor–student ratio at the secondary school level varies from 1:250 to 1:400.

The desired counselor–student ratio for elementary schools has been estimated from the low range of 1:300 to 1:600, depending upon the characteristics of the student body and availability of other services. Guidance needs increase with school size, for with the availability of greater learning opportunities comes the difficulty of determining what is the most prudent choice of educational and development programs.

If several specialists in guidance and counseling services are employed in one building, they may be attached to the principal's office, with an assistant principal assuming responsibility for supervising such services. In large school operations, a person of central-office rank may be concerned with supervising the work of guidance and counseling experts at the building level and developing programs for their continued professional growth. There were about 7000 district level guidance directors or coordinators in 1982.

Certification of school counselors is provided in all states, although the requirements vary from a few hours of graduate credit to a master's degree or more.

It is well to recognize the limitations as well as the contributions of counseling. The counselor may apply techniques to understanding problems confronting the counselee and, if necessary, recommend therapy by professionals in the treatment of human behavior problems.

SOCIAL WORK SERVICES

Like guidance and counseling, school social work began at the turn of the present century. Visiting teachers were the first specialized school personnel with a social work orientation. They were part of the program for enforcing attendance at school and worked primarily with children who were unable to adjust to school and refused to attend. In the course of enforcing compulsory-attendance laws, they became involved in juvenile court activities to determine the scope and nature of the child's problem. Their interest extended to unmarried mothers of school age who sought special services.

The early school social workers dealt primarily with disadvantaged youngsters from socially and economically deprived areas of the district. Today, school social workers are concerned also with able students from high socioeconomic backgrounds who suffer from the stress of high social and academic expectations and develop internally directed rather than overt patterns of maladjustment.

School social work and guidance services overlap; the former arose from concern with attendance and absenteeism in the school, and the latter from concern with adequate vocational choices after leaving. The close relation between the two services is illustrated by the following enumeration of the social worker's responsibilities. The social worker is described as:

1. A caseworker who counsels with students and their parents.
2. A collaborator concerned with working with teachers and other members of the school staff.
3. A coordinator who serves as a liaison agent between school and home and school and community in order to bring each into a better working relation.
4. A consultant available to other school staff members to add his perceptions to problems that students may have and that may not directly involve the social worker.

By 1950 nearly all states that certified attendance workers required a minimum of a bachelor's degree.

One study reported 29 different titles. The two most frequently used were school social worker and visiting teacher. Other terms are adjustment teacher, welfare worker, caseworker, and attendance officer.

Case loads vary greatly and there is little uniformity in reporting the number of pupils served.

PSYCHOLOGICAL SERVICES

School psychological services were inaugurated just before the turn of the century, but were confined primarily to large cities and a few wealthy suburban districts until after World War II. They became more common during the 1950s. One study reported that there were only 520 school psychologists in the nation in 1950.

The number jumped to 2724 in 1960, an increase of more than 500 percent. This is corroborated by the fact that in 1950 there were no school psychologists in 22 states, whereas in 1960 only in 4 states was this true. By 1980 about 14,000 "psychological personnel" were employed in the public schools.

Most cases referred to the school psychologist deal with learning, disciplinary, and other special-school adjustment problems. The emphasis is primarily on diagnosis of difficulties with special testing and other diagnostic instruments. The school setting is not conducive to extended therapy, and the serious cases are referred to parents with recommendations for possible private therapy or any other special assistance. Diagnosis and special placement recommendations for children and youths with various exceptionalities are frequently based on the analysis and judgment of the school psychologist.

Most states and the District of Columbia have some type of certification requirements for school psychologists. The American Psychological Association recommended that full certification of a school psychologist be contingent upon attainment of a doctor's degree in psychology and that the minimum certification requirement be two years of graduate work. For certification as psychological assistant, $1\frac{1}{2}$ years of graduate work are required; such personnel may work only under the supervision of a certified school psychologist.[22]

The employment of school psychologists is not yet widespread. Only a fraction of the schools have adequate services, and usually the psychologist's time must be carefully budgeted. In 1980 there was one school psychologist employed for every 2400 students enrolled in public schools. There were almost five times as many counselors as school psychologists.

PSYCHIATRIC SERVICES

Psychological services are limited in most schools, but psychiatric services are even more limited. This is true even though approximately 7 to 14 percent of the children attending school each year have an emotional, behavioral, or psychosomatic disturbance or a learning problem of psychological origin which is clearly beyond the capabilities of teachers to cope with. Usually psychiatric services are limited to examination and consultation. The greater concern for the mental health of the child may some day increase the number of child psychiatrists and other mental health workers in schools. Direct therapy for disturbed children under school auspices is still a long way off.

The larger the system, the more important the psychiatrist becomes in the school's physical and mental health program. One estimate is that a school system of 5000 or more children may encounter almost daily behavioral, emotional, and psychosomatic disturbances in its students and staff.

The school psychiatrist can also serve as a consultant to teachers, parents, and school administrators. The development of special psychological clinics, school social-casework divisions, and guidance services may help maintain mental health of those served by or serving in the school.

SPEECH AND HEARING SERVICES

By far the most common services available in schools are those related to remediation of disorders of communication. These services are concerned with impairment of speech, hearing, or language, or some combination of these. One survey reported that 76 percent of elementary schools provided services in speech and hearing.

The typical case load for a specialist in this area varies. It is estimated that a child with a significant communication handicap should be seen at least twice a week for 20 to 25 minutes. A total of 12 such children would require the full-time services of a speech clinician. By grouping, the efficient clinician could work with as many as 100 children per week. Thus, depending upon the work performed, the case load will be more than 12 but less than 100.

NURSING SERVICES

School nursing began around the turn of the century. In 1952 there were over 6300 school nurses; today there are many times that number. A defensible nurse–pupil ratio has yet to be defined. Such a ratio depends on many factors such as the availability of nonprofessional assistants to handle clerical and housekeeping duties.

MEDICAL SERVICES

The physician's participation in school health services is limited to periodic visits for diagnosis and referral and for immunization. The need for physicians in the public schools is far greater than for psychiatrists but far less than that for nurses. Typically the school medical advisor acts as physician to the athletic teams, examines pupils not examined by their personal physicians, and consults with the school administrator on a variety of health problems in the school. Medical advisors are paid on a fee-for-service basis.

SERVICES FOR EXCEPTIONAL PUPILS

Public schools may not refuse schooling to pupils who satisfy general admission requirements unless their presence would be disruptive to the learning of others. A wide variety of human talents and exceptionalities clamor for attention in the public schools. The intellectually gifted present one set of challenges and the mentally retarded another. In addition, there may be students who are physically disabled, visually handicapped, and hearing impaired. The autistic and emotionally disturbed children and youths are even more difficult to serve in the typical public school setting.

The numbers enrolled with some type of exceptionality more than doubled between 1948 and 1958, but remained less than 1 million. By 1978 total enrollment climbed sharply to almost 3.5 million, or 8 percent of the total public school pupils. The learning disabled (1,281,973) made up the largest single group, followed by the speech impaired (1,188,973) and the mentally retarded (881,739). Prior to Public Law 94–142 there was a tendency to organize separate attendance centers for most pupils requiring special education services. Mainstreaming modified that practice and led to reduced numbers of separate special education centers; the practice continued for those who needed treatment or for education of the more severe exceptionalities that were not likely to benefit from learning in a typical classroom.

There were about 1937 special public education centers serving the handicapped in 1982; about 2.4 percent of all public school attendance centers. During 1978–1979 about 69.4 percent of the handicapped population received instruction in regular classrooms, 23.7 percent in special class situations, 4.9 percent in special schools, and 2 percent in other schools. Those most likely to be placed in separate special education schools are the trainable mentally handicapped, seriously emotionally disturbed, educable mentally retarded, and those with other severe and multiple exceptionalities.

The passage of Public Law 94–142 by the federal government was a significant milestone in the development of special education. This 1975 law mandated appropriate educational experiences "in the least restrictive environment" for all students with exceptionalities for districts seeking federal funding for such programs. This complex law popularized "mainstreaming" of many with exceptionalities, that is, provided for including such pupils in regular programs whenever and wherever possible. Identification, evaluation, and assignment of such pupils to specific learning environments represented a challenge to the instructional leadership capabilities of the administrator. PL 94–142 helped trigger a number of civil suits involving school districts and the largest number of such legal disputes during the period 1977 through 1981 dealt with the handicapped pupil; these comprised 44.3 percent of all civil cases involving students. Only about $72,000 in federal funds during its 1960 fiscal year were allocated to special education compared with

$47.846 million in 1970 and an estimated $762.119 million in 1981!

ADMINISTRATIVE IMPLICATIONS OF SPECIAL SERVICES FOR PUPILS

Specialists in guidance, social casework, speech and hearing, health, and psychological services serve students with learning, adjustment, and self-image problems. They have a commitment to work with teachers, parents, and school administrators as well as pupils. The coordination of the ever-increasing number of specialists represents a significant challenge in educational administration. The specialist perception may be limited in some cases to consider such contributions as an end rather than as a means to help teachers reach more students and students to learn more. The effectiveness of such special services is evaluated best in terms of their impact upon individual pupils and teachers at the classroom level.

Adding support services increases operating costs without reducing class size. Such additions are justified as quality improvements and better ways of meeting the needs of more pupils. More diversified and specialized educational services reduce the significance of the pupil–teacher ratio as an indicator of educational quality. The pupil–teacher ratio was more relevant when students were instructed by only one teacher unassisted by special-services personnel. The pupil–professional staff ratio (number of pupils per professional staff member or number of professional staff members per 1000 pupils enrolled or in average daily attendance) is a more meaningful index. Professional staff members include full-time equivalent nurses, doctors, psychiatrists, psychologists, guidance counselors, and special consultants, as well as teachers.

Many years ago the Institute of Administrative Research at Teachers College, Columbia University, developed a comprehensive measure called numerical staffing adequacy or professional staff per 1000 pupil units.[23] Mort and his students completed many studies of the relation of numerical staffing adequacy to other quality-related criteria.

SECTION 3: STUDENT SECURITY DIMENSIONS OF PUPIL PERSONNEL ADMINISTRATION

Prior to 1960 few considered the protection of students at school or going to and from school a pressing problem in educational administration. There were safety concerns then, but the focus was on accident prevention, that is, on bicycle and traffic safety. The situation changed dramatically in recent decades as more students became victims of crime and violence on school campuses. School security came into being as "frequenters" and students attacked other students and teachers, destroyed or defaced property, and disrupted the learning process as well.

Protection and prevention represent one side of the security concerns. Control or management of the disruption is the other side. Both have an impact upon pupil personnel administration.

Traditionally, the school administrator was considered "in loco parentis" (literally, in place of parents) and was assumed to have authority control and curb unruly behavior. As indicated in a previous chapter, prior to 1965 the courts chose not to interfere with the disciplinary actions of school administrators as long as there was no evidence of arbitrary or excessive punishment. The significant shift in court attitudes during the 1970s placed student rights above student control at a time when campus violence was increasing to further complicate the situation.

Most schools have codes of student conduct that could be enforced by teachers. The school principal was expected to and usually did reinforce teacher disciplinary actions or became involved more directly in the more difficult or unusual behavior problems. The principal's authority, however, is now more limited than before. A pupil may be suspended for cause but not expelled; expulsion demands the exercise of certain procedures as well as a decision from a higher level of authority in the school system.

Present limitations notwithstanding, maintaining discipline in schools remains an important administrative responsibility. For most of history the prime disciplinary or pupil control issues were as follows: should a student be forced "to stay after school"; how can smoking regular cigarettes on school grounds be suppressed; is corporal punishment (spanking) justified or necessary; when should a student be expelled; and so on. Much debate swirled around the forms of punishments appropriate for various types and frequency of infraction of school rules of conduct by students. There were concerns as to how "strict" an administrator should be. In the so-called good old days, the majority of student offenses were tardiness, talking out of turn, "skipping school," throwing spitballs, not completing work on time, smoking cigarettes on school premises, "talking back" to teachers (or insubordination), fighting with other pupils on school grounds, misbehaving at a school dance, and so on. These are rather tame when compared with the more malicious offenses of recent decades.

Unrelated to legal challenges and new interpretations of the appropriate procedures and limits in exercising controls over students were other events during the 1960s and 1970s. These ranged from the emergence (and then disappearance) of mostly secondary school student activism to violent crime and the use of drugs on school premises. The school campus became a significantly different environment in many parts of the nation. This introduced challenges never previously faced in pupil personnel administration.

Student Activism

First came the general civil disturbances in the middle to late 1960s when the country was in an unpopular war in Viet Nam. The demonstrations were noted throughout the nation and the popular gathering places for protestors were campuses of universities, not public elementary and secondary schools. College student protests accompanied by some disruptive and destructive behavior on the part of some groups

not enrolled in collegiate institutions gained considerable media attention and precipitated confrontations with university administrators and clashes with the police and, in a few cases, the National Guard. The large university that experienced no student-originated campus protests during the 1960s was the exception.

By the mid-1970s with the Viet Nam War over, disruptive campus behavior seemed to have run its course. Many of the basic causes of such actions were removed or ameliorated with the termination of an unpopular war and the modification of restrictive and arbitrary dress and behavior codes. Communications between campus administrators and students improved with more "rap" sessions as well. The emergence of drug-oriented subcultures was part of the atmosphere that surrounded the protest and violent demonstrations. Unfortunately, these drug-oriented subcultures survived even though student demonstrations disappeared.

In general, what is labeled as "student activism" is characterized by a relatively high degree of organization, a strong financial base in some cases, and leadership. It is not a spontaneous occurrence as some tried to project. It is carefully orchestrated with full consideration of the impact on the media covering the event. It may be connected with a political event or a larger social protest both outside or inside the university or school campus.

It was inevitable that junior and senior high school students, particularly those near university campuses, would emulate their older counterparts, albeit in a milder form. By the end of the 1960s one survey of over 1000 secondary school principals reported that a majority experienced some kind of protest. This marked the beginning of an unusual challenge for school administrators. Discipline, or school pupil control measures, focused primarily on individual rather than group or crowd behavior. There were occasions when an intense athletic rivalry led to a large-scale disorder following a bitterly fought game.

The appearance of student "underground newspapers" and student walkouts to protest undesirable school food services, dress and discipline codes, and actual or purported denial of civil rights to minority students are of a different order of student discipline concern. Administrators were hard-pressed to cope with the tactics of secondary school activists during a decade of dissent. It led to greater involvement of students in the secondary school government, in the formulation of school building policies, and on local boards of education.

The student activism-related confrontations in the secondary schools during the early 1970s were relatively short-lived. Most lasted no more than half a school day. Seldom was it carried on for more than one or two days. To repeat, the now famous *Tinker* decision which set the student rights precedent grew out of the wearing of black arm bands by some high school students as a form of protest against the Viet Nam War.

School Crime and Violence by Students and Against Students and Others

Crime, violence, and vandalism on school property began to be reported with alarming frequency prior to the advent of secondary school student activism. These more serious disruptions were overshadowed for a brief period of time by student activism. Protest behavior disappeared by the mid-1970s, but crimes and campus violence did not. Some declare with a degree of optimism that there has been a "leveling off," but there is little hard evidence to support such optimism. School crime and violence are more costly, more frequent, and of more concern to the public today than they were during the 1960s.

No school is an island, and no attendance center can insulate itself from the realities around it. If there is significant growth in violent crime and the abuse of a variety of drugs in society in general, then it can be expected to spill over into the schools as well as other social institutions, as unfortunate and regrettable as that may be. What happens in the home or is accepted on the street corner may be tested in the school situation as well. The wisest of professionals and "futurists" in education dur-

ing the 1930s, 1940s, and even as late as the 1950s were unable to forewarn educators, who might have been hard to convince without first going through such experiences, of the seriousness and magnitude of crime, violence, drug abuse, and vandalism that would strike public school campuses during the 1960s, 1970s, and 1980s. Each administrator had to learn "on the job" and under fire how to cope with the disruptions and destructions.

The various types of severely disruptive, harmful, or destructive antisocial actions classified as school "violence and crime" include at least the following:

1. *Physical attacks or assaults,* with or without weapons, with the intent to do bodily harm in a school-related or school-controlled situation that are committed by those who are or may not be students (this includes "frequenters," dropouts, or others not enrolled at the time of the action) and that may be inflicted upon other students, teachers, administrators, or other employees or volunteers while the victims were on school premises. These may range from simple assault, serious physical harm resulting in disability, and rape, to murder. The sex-related crimes are often reported separately in another category.
2. *Robbery* (deprivation or damage of property or other valuables owned by school-related persons and doing so by unlawful force or threats of violence), or attempted robbery, of students, teachers, and so on, while on or near school premises.
3. *Vandalism* (wanton and illegal damaging, defacing, or destruction) through marring of surfaces, painting of unauthorized messages, arson, and so on.
4. *Drug abuse* (unauthorized use or sale of dangerous and/or controlled substances as defined by state or national statutes) by students or others while in, on, or near school facilities, activities, travel, and so on.
5. *Violent clashes or confrontations among racial, ethnic, or interschool groups* while on school premises or during school-sponsored activities.

By 1975 more than one in eight teachers reported being attacked or their property maliciously damaged by students. During a 12-month period of 1980–1981 an estimated 110,000 teachers faced physical attack, but an estimated 650,000 reported being sometimes or often afraid of being attacked. Such attacks on teachers and others could take place in classrooms, school corridors, or large group-meeting rooms; on school grounds or adjacent public places; in school-sponsored or school-controlled conveyances; and during school activities held away from school-owned or school-leased premises.

About 8 percent of the nation's school districts appear to have the most serious problems of crime and violence, but the largest numbers of these systems are found in predominately suburban and rural locales. Some studies support the generalization that ethnicity and/or race as well as urban versus rural school settings DO NOT correlate highly with the greater incidence of crime and violence on school premises. Some argue that the so-called growth in school crimes can be explained in large part by more sophisticated data-gathering and reporting techniques. Others question the accuracy and usefulness of data collected ten or more years ago given the absence of uniform definitions and the use of untrained reporters. These data limitations should not be allowed to detract from the seriousness of school crime and violence.

A California report released in 1973 contained the following generalizations about school crime and violence in that state:[24]

1. "Although most acute in the inner city, campus disorder and violence exist throughout the state."
2. "School conflict is not associated with any single racial or ethnic group of students."
3. Vandalism is the most frequent, widespread, and expensive problem.
4. "Conflicts arising as a result of student activism seem to have reached their peak between 1968 and 1970 and now appear to have declined in frequency."
5. "The incidence of crime on school campuses has been increasing in recent years." (This was made in 1973 and another made in 1981 confirmed that the increase continues.)
6. "Gang activity is a campus problem in a few concentrated areas."
7. Students, faculty, and staff as well as community leaders differ significantly on the causes of situational conflict in the schools. Students tend to blame "uneven application of discipline," school smoking regulations, "authoritarian administration practices," poor counseling, lack of student involvement in school decision making, and so on. Teachers and administrators point to excessive administrative paperwork, poor facilities, teacher disinterest, use of drugs by students, and breakdown in home values. Parents cite crowded schools, lax school discipline, irrelevant curriculum, outside agitators, and "poor communication" as the prime causes of the crime problems in the schools.
8. "The causes of criminal behavior on the school campus are complex, reflecting problems of the larger society."
9. "Misuse of drugs, alcohol, gang violence, and similar highly visible problems do not function as causes of crime in schools but rather as symptoms."
10. Involvement of all related to the school in all school programs is the most frequently cited and significant preventive measure for such conflicts.
11. "Coordinated cooperation among the school officials, the police, and community agencies can help reduce the incidence of crime on school campuses."

The findings and recommendations reported in the late 1970s and early 1980s were similar to those described above in the 1973 California study. The situation was of such concern that hearings were held on school crime and violence by the U.S. Senate and also by the House of Representatives during the 1970s. These helped to focus attention on the magnitude of the problems, led to the collection of important data on the extent of crime and violence facing the schools, and stimulated the release of federal funds to help combat the situation.

The cases of vandalism account for between 80 and 85 percent of all school crime. Burglary and larceny ranked second with about 5 percent of the incidents. Of great concern are the growing assaults upon teachers. These incidents numbered fewer than 50 per year by the mid-1960s, exceeded 1000 in 1968, and continued to increase throughout the 1970s. The attackers were not limited to students. Parents and intruders were instigators of such attacks as well.

Drug abuse by students increased significantly throughout the 1970s, although some felt there was a leveling off of the growth rate late in that decade. Data based on 1978 national surveys revealed that almost two-thirds of high school seniors used an illicit drug at one point in time. Alcohol is used most frequently (to some extent by 87.7 percent of the senior class of 1978), followed by marijuana (tried by about 50 percent), cigarettes (about 18.8 percent), and the drugs known as stimulants (about 17 percent). Cocaine, hallucinogens, tranquilizers, and sedatives were ingested by between 9 and 10 percent of the seniors. Heroin was employed or tried by less than 1 percent. These data document that drug abuse by students is a serious problem on school campuses.

Glass breakage is the most common form of vandalism and such damage occurs in about 95 percent of school districts. Equipment theft is the next most common (in about 80 percent of the districts), followed closely by other types of property damage. Arson-caused school fires were reported in about 25 percent of the districts. It is five times more likely to occur in large urban areas than in districts within the smallest enrollment classifications. Deliberately set multiple-school fires within a single school year are no longer classed as rare occurrences.

The costs of school crime and violence are difficult to measure and all such data must be interpreted with care. By the mid-1970s it was estimated to have skyrocketed to about $500 million per year, or about the same as the total spent on providing textbooks to all students. By the early 1980s these additional costs that contribute nothing toward enhancing the quality of education, but merely prevent their further deterioration, exceeded $1 billion annually! This includes costs for maintaining security forces as well as expenditures to repair damages.

By the mid-1970s school districts were forced to employ a new type of staff person in rather large numbers. One of the things that may be remembered about the previous decade is that it was the time of the great increase in the size of school security forces created to cope with the the crimes, violence, and vandalism. The majority of school districts with 5000 or more students enrolled employed security guards by the mid-1970s. In 1974–1975 New York City schools expended $15 million for school security personnel alone and Los Angeles spent about $5 million. By 1980–1981 the Los Angeles unified school district more than doubled the 1974–1975 expenditures and devoted $10.5 million to operate its security forces for schools. The total number of school security guards in New York City was estimated at 2400. Los Angeles had substantially fewer with 324 agents, 23 supervisors, 4 assistant chiefs, and one chief of security. This is the fourth largest security force in Los Angeles County; it is exceeded only by the Los Angeles Police Department, the Long Beach Police Department, and the Los Angeles County Sheriff's office. By 1980 there was one security guard for every 1800 pupils in public schools.

In the relatively brief period of a few decades, school crime and violence moved from an unusual or occasional problem for the school principal and superintendent to a frequent, serious, and ever-present danger in public school operations. The public and educators alike rank school crime and violence among the top educational problems. Cooperation with community police forces, involvement of parents and community leaders, participation of students, as well as the efforts of all educators are essential for a successful resolution. Silent alarms, patrols, better fencing, improved lighting, guard dogs, and so on, are useful in minimizing some incidents. But participation of people in the community can help even more. New organizational arrangements such as design of attendance centers with fewer students may assist as well.

SUMMARY

The administration of pupils has moved from the quantitative aspects of accounting and reporting the whereabouts of pupils to the qualitative aspects of interpreting all data available on pupils and providing special services to help them adjust in the school situation. So great has been the emphasis on the qualitative aspects that pupil personnel administration for some was synonymous with guidance and counseling.

All enumeration starts with the house-to-house canvass. Periodic census taking is notoriously inaccurate and the data become progressively more obsolete. The continuous system of reporting is recommended. The advent of computer-based electronic data processing greatly facilitates the operation of a continuous census system.

Admission to school is not an absolute right. Admission is contingent upon satisfying certain conditions of age, residence, and mental and physical health. It is generally agreed that pupils who start school too soon may experience difficulties throughout the school career. Assignment of pupils to attendance centers has become controversial since 1954.

Cross-district busing for racial balancing of school enrollments became a state and national political campaign issue during the 1970s and 1980s. Court mandates and other efforts to ameliorate racial imbalances in school enrollments remained a controversial issue more than 25 years after the *Brown* decision. In 1978 about 76 percent enrolled in public schools were white, 15.5 percent black, 6.4 percent Hispanic, 1.2 percent Asian or Pacific Islander, and 0.8 percent American Indian or Alaskan native. There was a tremendous variation in the ethnic and racial mix from state to state.

Public school enrollments increased steadily until 1971–1972 and then declined through the rest of the 1970s and first half of the 1980s. Elementary enrollments are predicted to rise after 1985 and ten years thereafter to make up for the drop that occurred during the previous 15 years.

The attendance of pupils is improving, as evidenced by the fact that approximately 94 percent of those enrolled now attend school daily. The length of the school term has been extended as well. The school dropout rate has improved dramatically from the 70 percent in the early 1930s to less than 25 percent in the early 1970s.

The most common cause of absenteeism is illness. Truancy, or willful intent to be absent, accounts for about 2 percent of the absenteeism in public schools. The emphasis in administration of attendance has shifted from the truant officer to the social worker and the identification of causes and correction of truancy predispositions among students.

Attempts to classify pupils into more or less homogeneous groups based on ability is a refinement of grading practices. Research in this area has been inconclusive. The advantages of homogeneous grouping may be dissipated if instructional techniques and materials are not developed to take advantage of the reduced range of abilities and interests of learners present in class.

There are 95,000 full-time equivalent public school personnel working as guidance counselors, school social workers, school psychologists, speech and hearing clinicians, school nurses, and other personnel who are part of the qualitative dimension of pupil personnel administration that seek to help develop better learners and more effective social beings.

Educational guidance services grew out of the narrower field of vocational guidance and expanded greatly after 1958 due in large part to federal support through NDEA. Guidance is a cluster of functions and many educational personnel contribute to their realization.

School social work began around the turn of this century and was related to the enforcement of compulsory-attendance laws. Counseling is an important technique for school social workers, as is casework. School social work focuses on the fundamental causes of a pupil's difficulty in adjusting to school, which often manifests itself as absenteeism or premature termination of education.

The number of school psychologists increased dramatically after 1950. Often decisions about placing a child in a special school or excusing him from school are made by the school psychologist. Psychiatric services are even more limited. The school setting does not always permit therapy for emotionally disturbed children.

By far the most common special services available to schools are those of speech and hearing clinicians. The school nurse was one of the early service experts. Relatively few physicians, however, participate in school health services beyond diagnosis and immunization programs.

The passage of PL 94-142 in 1975 greatly enhanced the quality and availability of educational services for the handicapped in the "least restrictive environment." It also stimulated a tremendous number of civil law suits on behalf of students with exceptionalities. Federal funds for special education increased from about $70,000 annually to over $762 million annually in the space of 20 years.

The increasing numbers of educational specialists compound the problems of coordination of diverse efforts by the educational administrator. The large number of support-service personnel make the pupil–teacher ratio less meaningful and the introduction of other indicators such as pupil–professional staff ratio more necessary to measure the qualitative aspects of school staffing.

Student disciplinary problems changed from the relatively harmless pranks, truancy, and insubordination to more damaging actions, such as physical assaults, robbery, vandalism, and drug abuse. Court cases supporting student rights and legal challenges to school disciplinary practices further complicated the discharge of the traditional disciplinary control role of the administrator. Better reporting practices may have contributed to the increased incidence of school crime and violence.

Student activism of the 1960s was characterized by a relatively high degree of organization and leadership, a connection with political action or social protest, and relatively short-lived periods of disruption. It appeared to have run its course by the mid-1970s.

School crime and violence include such antisocial behavior as physical assaults on teachers, students, administrators, and others; robbery; vandalism; drug abuse; and intergroup clashes. Such problems can be found in suburban and rural districts as well as in the core city of the large urban area. Vandalism is the frequent, widespread, and costly problem. Assaults on teachers now exceed 110,000 per year, but attacks on students are three or four times more common. Alcohol and marijuana are the drugs of choice among high school seniors who use drugs.

School security forces now number in the hundreds in some large districts, and expenditures are in the millions annually. Total costs to schools for security forces and for repair of damages now exceed $1 billion annually.

NOTES

1. A. B. Moehlman, *School Administration,* 2nd ed., Boston: Houghton Mifflin, 1951, chap. 14.
2. L. P. Ayres, *Child Accounting in the Public Schools,* Philadelphia: William F. Fell, 1915.
3. William A. Yeager, *Administration and the Pupil,* New York: Harper & Row, 1949, p. 71.
4. Jack Culbertson, "Attendance," in Chester W. Harris, ed., *Encyclopedia of Educational Research,* 3rd ed., New York: Macmillan, 1960, p. 95.
5. Ibid.
6. Harold G. Shane and James E. Polychrones, "Elementary Education: Organization and Adminis-

tration," in Chester W. Harris, ed., *Encyclopedia of Educational Research,* 3rd ed., New York: Macmillan, 1960, p. 425.

7. Ibid.
8. Ibid.
9. U.S. Commission of Civil Rights, *Desegregation of the Nation's Public Schools: A Status Report,* Washington, D.C.: GPO, 1979, pp. 8 and 20.
10. R. J. Havighurst, "Schools Face New Desegregation Phase," *Nation's Schools,* Vol. 77, March 1966, pp. 80–82.
11. P. M. Hauser and M. Taitel, "Population Trends: Prologue to Educational Programs," *Perspective Changes in Society by 1980: Designing Education for the Future,* Denver, Colo.: The Eight-State Project, July 1966, pp. 23–55.
12. Ibid.
13. U.S. Department of Health, Education, and Welfare, *Equality of Educational Opportunity,* Office of Education Summary Report, OE-38000, Washington, D.C.: GPO, 1966.
14. Ibid., p. 21.
15. Culbertson, op. cit., p. 93.

16. Ibid.
17. Ibid.
18. Yeager, op. cit., p. 77.
19. M. L. Goldberg, A. H. Passow, and J. Justman, *The Effects of Ability Grouping,* New York: Teachers College, 1966, pp. 21–22.
20. American Personnel and Guidance Association and National Education Association, *Answers to Questions About Guidance,* Washington, D.C.: The Association, 1963, p. 3.
21. L. J. Bishop, "Who Is the Counselor?" *Educational Leadership,* January 1967, p. 301.
22. James I. Barden and Division 16 Committee on Training Standards and Certification, "Report of Division 16 Committee on Training Standards and Certification," *American Psychologist,* Vol. 18, 1963, pp. 711–714.
23. B. H. McKenna, *Staffing the Schools,* New York: Teachers College, 1965, p. 4.
24. California State Department of Education, *A Report on Conflict and Violence in California High Schools,* Sacramento, Calif.: Bureau of Publications, the State Department, 1973, 30 pp.

CHAPTER REVIEW QUESTIONS

1. Differentiate between the qualitative and the quantitative aspects of pupil administration.
2. What are the advantages of the continuous census system over the traditional periodic census systems?
3. How does the present-day attendance officer differ from the truant officer of the past?
4. What are the advantages of homogeneous grouping? Disadvantages?
5. What were the major conclusions of the Coleman report?
6. Should counseling be restricted to guidance specialists? Justify your stand.
7. What were the significant historical developments in the school social work movement?
8. What services can be provided by a school psychologist?
9. Why has the advent of more supportive services

complicated the administration of public education?
10. What factors have been responsible for the lessening of the significance of the teacher-pupil ratio?
11. Is it better to dedicate special buildings or special classrooms within a building for regular pupils, or to enrich regular classroom work for the following types of pupils: (a) the mentally gifted, (b) the mentally retarded, (c) the physically handicapped, (d) the emotionally disturbed?
12. Debate: Children with exceptionalities are better served and are happier as the result of mainstreaming than when placed in special schools.
13. What impact have recent court decisions on students rights had on the disciplinary and control functions of the administrator?
14. What are the most effective strategies for coping with school crime and violence?

SELECTED REFERENCES

American Association of School Administrators, *Reporting; Violence, Vandalism, and Other Incidents in Schools,* National School Resource Network, Arlington, Va.: AASA, 1981, 39 pp.

Bishop, L. J., "Who Is the Counselor?" *Educational Leadership,* January 1967, p. 301.
California State Department of Education, *A Report on Conflict and Violence in California's High Schools,*

Sacramento, Calif.: The State Department, 1973, 30 pp.

Goldberg, M. L., Passow, A. H., and Justman, J., *The Effects of Ability Grouping,* New York: Teachers College, 1966.

Marvin, Michael et al., *Planning Assistance Programs to Reduce School Violence and Disruption,* U.S. Department of Justice, Law Enforcement Assistance Administration, Washington, D.C.: GPO, 1976, 160 pp.

Vestermark, S. D., Jr., and Blauvelt, P. D., *Controlling Crime in Schools,* West Nyack, N.Y.: Parker, 1978, 354 pp.

Walden, John C., and Cleveland, Allen D., "The South's New Segregation Academies," *Kappan,* December 1971, pp. 234–239.

Yeager, William A., *Administration and the Pupil,* New York: Harper & Row, 1949.

19

PROFESSIONAL PERSONNEL
LEADERSHIP AND MANAGEMENT: I.
SELECTION, ASSIGNMENT,
COMPENSATION, AND EVALUATION

Professional personnel stimulate pupil learning, translate instructional plans and strategies into reality, and influence the realization of predetermined educational objectives. Until such time as instructional technology evolves to where it is possible to motivate student learning with a minimum of human intervention, teachers and the instructional support staff will continue to be the most important professional resources in education. The effectiveness of an administrator as a leader, decision maker, planner, manager, and so on, is determined by how the instructional personnel perform and the educational results of their efforts. Professional personnel leadership and management are among the oldest and most important of the traditional administrative responsibilities and focus upon the identification, selection, assignment, motivation, professional growth, and evaluation of all educational personnel, most of whom by far are teachers.

These more traditional personnel responsibilities have not lost any of their importance even though the 1960s saw the development of the dramatic new dimension of collective bargaining, that is, the greater involvement of professional staff in decisions affecting their economic welfare and work conditions. During the 1960s the term *professional negotiations* was preferred as it seemed "softer" and disguised better the "union image" or harsh realities of collective bargaining. By whatever name it may be called, it stimulated a revolution in personnel administration and impacted strongly on other dimensions of educational administration as well. Collective bargaining is reviewed in the chapter that follows; the more traditional dimensions are presented first in this one.

PROFESSIONAL PERSONNEL IN EDUCATION: NUMBERS AND TRENDS

The sheer numbers, variety of specializations, and deployment of professional personnel are influenced by many factors. These include student enrollments, class size, comprehensiveness of available educational programs, and types of students being served. The sizable enrollment increases between 1956 and 1969 (that brought 9.5 million more students to public schools) triggered a concomitant increase (of over 610,000) in teachers employed during the same period. The enrollment decline during most of the 1970s, particularly at the elementary school level, did not lead to an immediate and continued growth in number of elementary school teachers, which hit a peak of 1.195 million in 1975. A reduction in teacher numbers started thereafter, but it was modest, for there were 1.17 million teachers in public elementary schools in fall 1981. The discrepancy in student enrollment and teacher employment trends may be explained partially by what happened to the elementary school pupil–teacher ratio; it dropped from 24.9 pupils per teacher in 1971 to 20.5 in 1981, and is projected to drop to 20.0 after 1983. The outlook for elementary school teachers during the 1980s is much brighter and will reverse the pattern of the previous decade. Enrollments in elementary schools will begin to rise in the last half of the 1980s, so that by the end of the 1980s more rather than fewer elementary teachers will be needed.

There was an increase in enrollments and teachers employed in the public secondary schools during most of the 1970s. The peak of 1.024 million secondary teachers came in 1977 with a subsequent drop to 980,000 in fall 1981 to reflect the public secondary enrollments declines near the end of the 1970s. Continuing secondary school declines are projected for all of the 1980s with an estimated 876,000 secondary school teachers by 1988, which is below that recorded for 1969.

During the 1960s, about 70,000 to 80,000 additional persons were being added annually to teaching rosters. Personnel administrators during this period of a teacher shortage that lasted almost 25 years were hard pressed to identify and attract new and qualified professionals. The teacher employment picture changed as the shortage came to an end in the early 1970s and teacher layoffs began during the last half of that decade. The peak came in 1977 with 2.209 million public elementary and secondary school teachers. By 1981 there were 2.150 million classroom teachers; the bottom is predicted as early as 1983 and no later than 1985 after which a small upturn in employment is projected. There were about 280,000 nonpublic grades K to 12 teachers in 1981, bringing the public and nonpublic total to 2.430 million. These data are derived from various reports released by the National Center for Education Statistics (NCES) of the U.S. Department of Education. There are slight variances for the same year from one publication to another. The figures shown herein are far below the 1980 figure of 3.175 million elementary/secondary teachers published by the U.S. Bureau of Census Current Population Survey, because this report includes "preprimary teachers, some adult education teachers, and otherwise unclassified teachers" that are not in the NCES figures.[1]

Spot shortages of teachers with specific competencies such as mathematics, science, and special education persisted throughout the 1970s and into the 1980s. These were exceptions to the oversupply of teachers, particularly during the last half of the 1970s when only about one-half of those prepared to teach were actually employed on a full-time basis.

The total of all types of *professional personnel* in public schools reached 2,476,487 in 1975–1976, of which 2,195,740, or about 89 percent, were classroom teachers. The annual increase in instructional staff employed during the 1960s fluctuated between 4 and 5 percent, but dropped to only 1 to 2 percent during the first half of the 1970s. After that, annual declines rather than rates of increase characterized public education.

Secretarial and clerical workers, custodians, maintenance employees, transportation workers, food-service employees, and others account for at least an additional 1 million public school employees. Approximately one noninstructional person of some type is employed for every 2.4 professional personnel (teacher aides are not included). Board members add another 115,000 and there are about 75,000 part-time noninstructional personnel; the grand total for all types of personnel related to the public schools is over 4.3 million.

Teachers are not distributed equally among

the 15,000 or so local school districts. Thus, about 1 percent, or the 187 largest, of the school districts employ 27 percent of all teachers. At the other extreme, the approximately 4200 school districts with fewer than 300 pupils, about 27 percent of all districts, employ only 2.7 percent of all teachers. The 20 largest school districts, which account for less than two-tenths of 1 percent of all districts, employ almost 10 percent (9.6 percent) of all teachers.

The numbers employed changed significantly during the past decade, but the sex and racial and ethnic mix did not; for by 1979 about 70 percent of all teachers were women and 88.9 percent of all teachers were white. In 1979, 8.6 percent of all teachers were black and 1.8 percent were Hispanic, but there was great variation from state to state. The southern states had the highest percentage of black teachers, with Mississippi having 35.7 percent and Louisiana with 34.3 percent. In contrast, states such as Iowa, Maine, Minnesota, New Hampshire, North Dakota, South Dakota, and Vermont had less than 1 percent of their teachers from black minorities.[2] About 83 percent of all elementary teachers are women, but 54 percent of all secondary school instructors are men. The proportion of male public school teachers almost doubled over a period of three decades. The number of male teachers in 1978 was over 4.6 times what it was 30 years earlier. During the same period the number of women elementary teachers slightly more than doubled.

CERTIFICATION

A teaching certificate is a license needed to practice, but carries no guarantee of employment. From 1900 to 1920 the elementary teacher's certificate preparation standard was such that no state required the attainment of a bachelor's degree. Today all states demand at least a bachelor's degree for such certification. In 1930 less than half the states required a bachelor's degree for high school teacher certification; by 1964 this was the minimum degree level in all states. The nondegree teacher is a relic of past ages, for presently over 99 percent

of all employed public school teachers have earned at least a bachelor's degree. Those who would criticize the preparation or intellectual development of teachers have shifted the attack from the absence of at least an earned degree to how the Scholastic Aptitude Test (SAT) scores of education majors compare with others enrolled in a college or university; the scores for education majors are lower.

Teacher certification has changed and the trends show that certification is:

1. Centralized at the state level whereas during the early part of this century and before local boards and the county issued certificates.
2. Based on completion of a professional preparation program at an institution accredited to do so. The use of special tests made a comeback during the late 1970s as part of "competency-based teacher certification," which is reviewed later.
3. Granted or made valid for a specified period of time, usually two to five years; the so-called life or unlimited teaching certificates are no longer issued.
4. Limited to special areas or subjects; the general certificate that allowed the holder to teach any subject or grade is not issued.
5. Based on recommendations of members of the teaching profession as well as other professionals interested in the quality of requirements for entry into the profession.
6. Confined to fewer different types of teaching certificates issued.
7. Beginning to recognize teacher certification in one state as being acceptable in another; reciprocity in teacher certification among states is often hampered by variations in standards but facilitated by the accreditation efforts of the National Council for the Accreditation of Teacher Education (NCATE).

During the 1970s greater interest developed in relating preparation more closely with performance, which gave rise to what is known as competency-based teacher preparation and competency-based teacher certification. The latter gained operational reality during the late 1970s and early 1980s in the form of new state laws demanding that those who would qualify for a teaching certificate must submit to one or more special state-developed or state-approved examinations in addition to completing a special preparation program and an earned four-year degree at a recognized institution. By 1981 there were 17 states with new laws demanding competency-based teacher certification; 10 states implemented the law by 1981 and 3 more are expected to do the same by 1982. The majority developed their own state examinations; a few used the National Teacher Examination (NTE).[3] All states other than New York were in the South, Southwest, or West.

EMPLOYMENT OF TEACHERS

The school board, as officers of the corporation, may employ only those teachers who meet state certification standards. The school board may require higher standards but not less than what the state demands.

It is physically impossible for boards in large school districts to identify, interview, and formally appoint all teachers personally. The operational dimensions of applicant screening and employment are delegated to the superintendent, who in turn relies heavily on the recommendation of the professional personnel administrator and school principals. The board remains the legal authority to employ all personnel, doing so only upon the recommendation of the chief school executive. As early as 1950, 84 percent of city school systems delegated the responsibility for nominating the appointment of all school personnel to the superintendent of schools. Politics has been removed, by and large, from the teacher appointment process.

Professional Qualifications for Employment

In 1923 a two-year normal certificate was the minimum requirement for elementary teachers in 79 percent of the cities; 20 percent had lower requirements. Remember that 100 years earlier there were no teacher training institutions, and

for much of the ninteenth century elementary school teachers either attended high school for a short period or actually graduated from high school. Signicantly higher professional preparation standards were demanded as a condition of employment during the last half of the twentieth century. By 1951, 99 percent of the city systems required four or more years of preparation for senior high school teachers. By 1970 it was the unusual large or small system that did not demand at least a four-year degree. With a surplus of applicants during the 1970s, many systems were demanding master's degrees at the secondary level. There were, however, other factors that restrained school districts from demanding higher professional preparation levels than a four-year degree. Escalating costs was one factor, for teachers with a master's or higher degree command higher salaries in the professional salary schedules. Some districts sought to reduce the impact of the financial crunch being experienced by searching for new teachers with four-year preparation and no experience to balance off a faculty that was increasing in large numbers at the high end of the salary scale.

Prior Experience and Personal Factors Related to Employment

Over 50 years ago the National Education Association (NEA) expressed forceful opposition to experience as a condition for employment. It was the severe teacher shortage, however, that forced even the largest school systems to employ the inexperienced. Today, it is the quality of professional preparation and special competencies that far outweigh prior teaching experience as conditions related to employment. Large as well as small systems today actively seek the inclusion of some inexperienced new teachers in the total faculty profile.

Age. Age limits for new teachers are less important today than they were during the times when nondegree teachers were employed. By 1951 less than 12 percent of city systems reported minimum or other age limits for new teachers. The college degree requirement eliminated the need for a minimum age stipulation and the temper of present times prevents any type of age discrimination in personnel employment.

Marital Status. Discrimination against the employment of married women teachers was fairly common prior to 1950. In 1931, 77 percent of the city school systems refused even to consider employing qualified married women as teachers. This dropped to 58 percent of the systems in 1941 and to 8 percent in 1951. First the teacher shortage and later the emphasis upon equal employment opportunities brought to an end the professionally unjustifiable and discriminatory practices. Any school system refusing to employ a qualified person on the grounds of marriage alone would face legal action. About 80 percent of all teachers are married; the "old maid" school teacher image has gone the way of all stereotypes. About the same percent of men and women teachers were married at one time during their professional careers.

Sex. There was a time when school masters outnumbered the "school marms." By 1880 some 43 percent of all teachers were men and 57 percent were women. By 1920 only 14 percent of all teachers were men. As indicated earlier, a tremendous increase in the proportion of men in the profession occurred during the past 30 years. Conflicting data exist for more recent years, for the U.S. Bureau of the Census reports that in 1980 about 70 percent of all employed teachers were women, whereas The National Center for Education Statistics noted that in 1978 only about 66 percent of all teachers were women.[4]

Description of the Typical Teachers

The National Education Association has compiled a profile of the typical teacher every five years since 1961.[5] The typical teacher in the years following 1961 kept getting younger as the median age dropped from 41 years in 1961

to 36 years in 1975 but then increased slightly by 1980. This is supported by other data which showed that the proportion of teachers "under the age of 25 dropped by half between 1970 and 1980," but "the proportion in the 25- to 34-year-old age group rose from 28 percent to 38 per cent."[6] Only about 10 percent were in the over 55 age group in 1980 compared with a little over 16 percent in 1970. Although less experienced than their counterparts of 20 years ago, teachers today are better prepared, with those having an earned master's degree (about 35 percent of all) being far greater than those without any degree (less than 1 percent).

The typical teacher in 1980 was a married woman in her late thirties, with at least a bachelor's degree, was likely to be teaching elementary school, reported to a male principal, worked in a school with a teaching staff of 25, and put in a 46-hour work week.

Teachers are remaining in current positions longer, and this reduction in mobility placed upward pressure on salary schedules. The reduction in new hires resulted in the drop in the proportion of teachers under 25 noted previously. The opinion polls that asked teachers if they would select teaching as a career "if they could go back and do it all over again" reported a tremendous drop in those who responded "certainly would" from 49.9 percent in 1961 to only 21.8 percent in 1981. Those who responded "certainly would not" jumped to 12 percent in 1981 compared with only 2.8 percent in 1961. There evidently are many more factors presently that are having a negative effect on teacher morale; doubtless, the declining enrollments, teacher layoffs, and the financial squeeze facing public education have not helped build positive attitudes.

ASSIGNMENT AND TEACHING LOAD

The contract signed by the board of education and the teacher consummates the formal employment act. Seldom is the name of the building, the specific grade level, or a schedule of classes to which a teacher is assigned mentioned in the contract. The contract is supplemented by executive action to determine the teacher's specific assignment and teaching load. Usually, the teacher is informed prior to employment the general type of grades or cluster of courses likely to be taught. The working conditions for all teachers within a system may be also developed through a collective bargaining agreement between the board of education and the organization representing teachers.

After the formal contract signing and the general assignment from the central-administration level, the focus of personnel administration shifts to the attendance center and involves principals to a greater extent. Teaching locale is predicated on general and central-office decisions that are consistent with existing negotiated agreements. Implementation of operational policies on numbers and types of pupils and/or grade levels or subjects assigned to each teacher is the domain of the principal.

Many factors influence the measurement of load. Among these are student-teacher ratio; classes per day; total enrollment in classes taught; number of different subjects taught or preparations required; total clock hours for the school day; nature of students in classes (particularly if the mental ability is unusually low or high or if the pupils have handicaps); nonclassroom responsibilities such as corridor or playground supervision, extracurricular activity commitments, and administrative responsibilities.

In elementary school, number of pupils in the classroom, ability range in the room, nonclassroom supervisory chores, number of special subjects taught by the regular teacher, and number of grade levels within a room are considered in measuring teaching load. The average work week of an elementary school teacher is about 46 hours per week.

Computation of work load for secondary school teachers is more complex. A formula developed by Douglass in 1932 and revised in 1950 took into consideration number of classes per week; length of class period; amount of time spent in class sections of the same subject and grade level; time per week spent in study hall supervision, classroom teaching, prepara-

tion, and other activities. The Douglass formula attempted to compensate for difficulties in preparing and teaching certain subjects by developing a "subject matter difficulty" coefficient.

Various surveys show that the average secondary school teaching load diminished from six to five sections per day. The average work week for secondary school teachers was 48 hours, of which 29 hours were spent in classroom instruction, 8 hours in out-of-class instructional duties (correcting papers and preparation), and 11 hours in miscellaneous functions such as supervising study halls, sponsoring clubs, monitorial duties, and community service.

Some states enacted legislation that prescribed a duty-free lunch period for classroom teachers. As late as 1971 over 30 percent of the teachers ate lunch with their pupils. The percentage of elementary teachers without a duty-free lunch period is twice as high as that for secondary teachers (40.5 percent versus 19.6 percent). The duty-free lunch is more common in larger districts.

Teacher assignment has been complicated further in some instances by court orders and other mandates related to desegregation or a reduction in "racially isolated" schools. Some districts have been forced by court order to progress toward a "racial balance of teachers" as well as students. Some teachers resisted transfers to core city schools because of a fear of being unable to teach effectively or control students in such situations. Substantial salary inducements have been offered to encourage the acceptance of teacher reassignments to more challenging situations. This proved effective for some and became known as "combat pay." The use of such incentives remains very controversial.

CONTINUING PROFESSIONAL DEVELOPMENT OF TEACHING PERSONNEL

A teaching career may be pursued over a period of 40 or more years after completing the entry-level preparation programs. Many changes can occur during a five-year period that could necessitate acquiring new knowledge or special competencies. In-service education, more appropriately titled "continuing professional development," is not unique to education; it is a challenge facing all professionals in all professions to keep abreast of new developments and to maintain or improve upon professional performance.

Effective professional growth programs represent one of the major unmet needs of the profession, the rhetoric that surrounds the issues notwithstanding. Universities control preservice preparation, whereas local school systems dominate in-service educational activities. Universities tend to be more information-oriented and hope that the application of the added information can be made successfully by practitioners. Local systems are performance- or competency-oriented and desire to bridge the gap between professional development programs and improvement of classroom learning outcomes.

Teachers, by and large, have been very critical of most in-service programs. An experienced classroom professional demands an even more competent professional to serve as the instructional leader and motivator plus relevant program content that may contribute to further professional growth. A tremendous infusion of state and federal funds during the past decade helped improve the quality of professional growth programs, but the results to date have been mixed. Additional money represents potential that must be blended with new ideas, better structures, more effective planning, and more sharply focused programs on individual needs of teachers to translate potential into reality.

The previous and more traditional approaches include creation of a professional library; providing time off to observe promising practices in other schools; providing special consultants to work directly in the classroom with teachers; special workshops; and faculty meetings. Sabbatical leaves for elementary and secondary teachers are relatively rare. Involving faculty members in selecting new texts or curriculum revision are additional ways to stimulate growth. Some systems relieve certain teachers from all instructional responsibilities to participate in curriculum projects that may continue for several months; then substitute teachers are employed and paid by the district during the interim.

The faculty meeting is perhaps the most abused instrument, often called with little serious planning or known objectives, and is criticized most often by teachers. The end of a hard day in the classroom is not the best time to try to stimulate professional development. Those with clearly developed purposes that are planned just before or after the school year appear to be more productive. There is a difference between a "faculty meeting" in which faculty may be involved in planning and implementation and a "principal's meeting" that includes faculty members but satisfies the principal's purposes and not necessarily those of the faculty. The design of productive faculty meetings, usually scheduled about once per month, is one of the more difficult but important challenges facing the principal.

TEACHER ORIENTATION, MORALE, TURNOVER, AND REDUCTIONS-IN-FORCE

Orientation of the new teacher to the school system is a specific professional development program of relatively short duration, certainly not contemplated as a "continuing" development effort. Teachers new to the system encounter a variety of problems such as adjusting to assignments; getting acquainted with the community as well as students; understanding the regulations of the system, how to procure instructional materials, and whom to contact for what; knowing the texts and instructional strategies recommended in the system; getting to know professional colleagues in the building and throughout the system, and so on.

Responsibilities for orienting the new teacher to the system are shared by many including the experienced teachers of the system, the principal, special-subject or grade supervisors or consultants, assistant superintendents, the personnel administrator, as well as the superintendent; it is the personnel administrator, however, who assumes responsibility for coordinating the efforts of all as well as assessing the effectiveness of the program.

The great reduction in teacher turnover rates and in new position availability during the past decade and the early 1980s meant fewer new personnel; this, however, did not bring to an end the need for orientation programs that grew so rapidly during the 1950s and 1960s. About three-fourths of all school systems continued school building and/or district-wide orientation programs during the 1970s. The costs were nominal, seldom more than $2500 per district, and the benefits were far greater than the costs. Most held multiple-day orientation sessions and some continued the effort throughout the first year of employment for new personnel.[7] The battery of techniques and activities to facilitate orientation include preschool opening workshops (of one day to two weeks); special letters of welcome to new teachers from community and school board leaders as well as key administrators; assignment of one existing staff member or special supervisor to be on call to meet any requests from the new teacher; carefully prepared handbooks for new teachers; reduced work loads for new teachers for periods ranging from one semester to one year; and monthly workshops for one or two semesters during the new personnels' first year. What started as a relatively new development in personnel administration during the very rapid expansion of school faculties during the 1950s and 1960s will doubtless become a permanent fixture in school personnel administration.

Morale is difficult to define and even more difficult to measure with any degree of precision. It is a state of being that is more likely to be felt intuitively than expressed verbally. Although not necessarily an end in itself, it is a means for promoting a smoothly functioning and productive institution. It is possible to have a high level of morale and low productivity or limited accomplishment.

Many factors influence feelings of high or low morale such as reputation of the system; community reactions to the system and public education in general; relationships with students and colleagues; and that catch all "conditions of employment." Conditions of employment encompass such items as work load; types of assignments; availability of a planning (sometimes called "free") period; sick leave policy; provision for substitute teachers; and, of course, the compensation package that includes salary, retirement contributions, and other so-called fringe benefits. Salaries are important, but more pay may not always reduce emotional pressures related to discipline problems, fear of appraisal, criticisms from a principal, or unfriendly relations with colleagues. The feeling of being wanted and appreciated, being a contributing member of an effective organization, and being able to communicate freely with colleagues and superiors in the hierarchy helps build better morale. Teachers need a brief respite during the day which can come from a planning period, duty-free lunch period, and freedom to escape on occasion to the "teachers' lounge." Participative management, or democratic school administration, that attempts to tap the creative abilities of teachers is also conducive to better morale. Sensing and building better morale are a never ending challenge in educational administration.

Teacher turnover was less of a problem during the 1970s (as well as at present) than it was during the periods of the greatest teacher shortages. During the 1950s out of every 100 teachers who started in one year, 83 returned the following year, 6 moved to another teaching position, and 11 left the profession. During the 1960s the teacher turnover rate fluctuated between 11 and almost 14 percent, which was a little lower than that for the 1950s. The turnover rate among child welfare caseworkers during that period was 28 percent and among nurses almost 67 percent. The rate is obviously much lower in education, but education had even lower rates prior to 1950. Teacher mobility during the 1970s and at present was far below that of the 1950s and 1960s; the annual turnover rate during the 1970s was less than half that for the 1960s. Continuing fiscal cutbacks and reductions-in-force suggest there will be a relatively high degree of occupational stability in education (low turnover rates) through at least 1985.

Reductions-in-force reappeared in the late 1970s, after an absence of about 40 years when it was necessary during the Great Depression years of the 1930s, in response to declining enrollments, financial emergencies, and reduced teacher mobility. In some cases the entire attendance center was closed. Retirement and other turnovers helped ease the situation for a while; it was inevitable that nonemployment of faculty desirous of continuing was necessary as well.

Layoffs during 1979 in both public and private schools reached 23,900, which represented less than 1 percent of the total teaching force.[8] About one-third were in the elementary schools; English and social studies teachers at the high school level were the hardest hit.

There are statutes in about 41 states that define procedures to follow in cases of involuntary termination of qualified personnel for just cause such as enrollment decline or fiscal exigencies. There is a body of ruling case law that applies as well.[9] It is essential for administrators to implement with care district policies and legal demands in all matters dealing with involuntary termination of qualified personnel. Reductions-in-force will continue through the first half of the 1980s and may not be necessary much beyond that point unless more serious fiscal crises confront public education during the 1980s.

SALARY SCHEDULES AND COMPENSATION FOR TEACHING PERSONNEL

The authorization of a contract for personal services is the initial step in the management of salary payments. The amount of payment can be an arbitrary figure or part of an overall salary policy.

One of the significant developments in personnel administration has been the salary schedule. A "salary schedule" may be defined as a formal and detailed statement, in writing, of the remuneration policy of the organization. In appearance it is a matrix that places the key criteria, such as professional preparation, which influence variations in amount of annual compensation along the horizontal dimensions. Placed within the vertical dimensions of the matrix are such factors as the initial or entry-level compensation amount plus additional increments for each period of experience within the system or elsewhere. The alternative to some type of formal schedule of monetary remuneration is annual bargaining with each employee with or without regard to any objective and measurable criteria upon which to base the compensation decision.

Prior to 1920, fewer than one-half of the city school districts (those most likely to have schedules) implemented salary schedules for instructional or other personnel. Very shortly thereafter, by 1922–1923, approximately 65 percent of such systems inaugurated a compensation schedule for teachers. At present most school systems have some formalized means of salary determination for teachers and others who have different preparation levels, experience, and/or unique responsibilities.

Collective bargaining in education had a significant impact upon approaches used in developing and revising salary schedules as well as their implementation; but no better way could be found to cope with the complexity of remuneration policies in large systems. The salaries to be paid as defined in the schedule are presently a major item of discussion in collective bargaining sessions. Using 1976–1977 data, the Educational Research Service declared: "Today approximately 70 percent of the school systems in the United States have a negotiated teacher salary schedule."[10]

Planning for a salary schedule begins with some important board of education policy statements as well as the hard data collected and the recommended decisions from school administrators. To begin with there are the policies related to minimum or starting salaries. Again, collective bargaining may influence that as well. The initial salary for teachers with a bachelor's degree and no experience rose from less than $1000 during the Great Depression years of the 1930s to $11,562 in 1980–1981 (this is the mean of all minimums in U.S. school districts). The 1973 NEA convention called for a starting salary of $12,500 for qualified beginning teachers.

At the opposite end is the determination of the maximum or top salary to be paid for those under the district's compensation schedule. In 1980–1981 the mean of all maximum-scheduled salaries for teachers was $22,703.[11] The rule of thumb is that the maximum should be at least twice the scheduled minimum salary. There was a tremendous range in the maximums paid, with the highest being $37,956 paid in Alaska.

It is generally felt that the number and size of annual increments should permit a teacher to move from minimum to maximum salary in 12 to 15 years. Prior to 1950, $50 to $100 was considered a reasonable annual pay raise. Most school systems presently award annual increments of five to ten times these amounts. The average size of the increment may be determined by dividing the difference between the minimum and maximum salaries by the number of steps in the schedule. There is some argument for allowing smaller increments during the earlier period of employment and much larger increments subsequently to career teachers. The single salary schedule, that is, a schedule in which salary is based on professional preparation and experience, without regard to position in the system, replaced the differentiated salary schedule that was far more common and popular in the early years of this administrative innovation. Prior to 1920, no city system employed a single salary schedule. By 1956–1957 the proportion that did not implement a single salary schedule was negligible.

An examination of other trends in teacher salary scheduling reveals the following: Salary differentials between men and women teachers have been decreasing and should disappear soon to put an end to a questionable practice; the cost of living bonuses so popular during the 1950s almost disappeared by the mid-1960s only to make a small comeback and in a differ-

ent form in the mid-1970s in response to double digit inflation; minimum salaries escalated more rapidly than did maximums; the number of annual increments before reaching the top level remained constant; schedules are revised upward more frequently than originally intended when the salary schedule was conceived; collective bargaining precipitates more frequent changes in salary schedules; and scheduled salaries for teachers have increased sharply.

Among the more controversial issues encountered in developing a salary schedule is differentiated payments based on special functions or unequal responsibilities. Thus, there are separate salary schedules for each of the following specialized professional groups within a school district: administrators (usually principals and supervisors), counselors, librarians, and school nurses. These may be tied to the salary schedule for teachers by creating an index or ratio between them rather than specifying absolute dollar amounts between the separate schedules. It usually is not recommended that schedules for administrators be indexed or related closely to teachers, particularly where the schedule for teachers is the product of collective bargaining.

Another debate in scheduling is extra pay for extra work. Teachers may have professional assignments that go beyond the classroom. Some, but not all, may request salary supplements above and beyond the base schedule for such extra duties during after-class hours as coach, drama director, yearbook supervisor, or department chairperson. The size of the additional remuneration varies from district to district and creates as much controversy as the concept.

Even more controversial is inclusion of merit pay for teachers. This issue has been argued for more than 60 years without any letup in sight. The term *supermaximum payments* may on occasion be preferred to merit pay, but it does little to resolve the basic arguments pro and con. The typical salary schedule assumes that all teachers are competent or they would not be employed or retained. From this flows the argument that any compensation distribution should be based on objective and easily measured data such as those related to preparation or experience levels.

On the other side, those supporting the merit pay concept argue that the best indicator of a teacher's quality is actual performance in the classroom or school rather than the years of service or degrees acquired. Teaching is a practical art and the best teachers deserve special recognition with a special increment or super-maximum salary. The merit pay controversy first peaked during the 1920s, died down for a while, surfaced briefly once more in the 1950s; the arguments receded one more time, and then periodically flared up during the 1960s and 1970s, but without much real or prolonged conviction and controversy noted in previous years.[12]

Part of the problem with merit pay is that it cannot be implemented or operated without appraisal of teacher performance. Those who oppose the concept are equally opposed to existing evaluation systems that they contend fall far short of objective and accurate measurements of teacher performance. The concern is that favoritism or politics rather than actual and evaluated performance will be the prime determinant of merit salary increments.

A 1970 Gallup Poll revealed that 58 percent of the general public polled were of the opinion that teachers should be paid on the basis of the quality of work (merit) rather than on a standard scale. In contrast, the pooling teachers' opinions demonstrated that 67 percent of the teachers favored payment on the basis of a standard scale and only 28 percent supported the quality of work (merit) criterion as the basis for determining remuneration.

Does merit pay work in practice? The concept was tried in many districts and then abandoned. There were operational problems encountered in determining what constitutes meritorious performance, what instruments provide the most precise data, and who should be the final judge of merit. Implementation also encountered faculty resistance and generated staff dissension. It was estimated that during the 1960s only about 10 percent of the school districts had merit plans in operation. There

was a decline to only about 5.5 percent by 1972 and dropped further to only 4 percent by the late 1970s.[13] As late as 1938–1939 about 20 of the large urban school systems had merit pay or superior service maximums. During 1977–1978 fewer than 2 percent of the nation's largest school districts in urban areas declared that there existed merit or incentive pay plans along with the regular salary schedule.[14] It now appears that smaller districts are more likely to implement the merit pay concept, but again less than 5 percent said they did in the late 1970s. This is an historic reversal, for through most of its 60-year history, the largest of the school districts were the most likely to put the merit pay concept into practice. Whatever the reasons, the generalization is justified that the merit pay concept sounds enticing, but it does not seem to work well in practice.

The schedule was developed as an alternative to the time-consuming individual bargaining over salary. This led some to reason that the process of group bargaining might spell the doom of the salary schedule or at least modify it considerably. To illustrate, every salary schedule has built within it an annual salary increase. This, it was felt, could weaken the bargaining power of the school board and the administrator in the salary-agreement-reaching process. The worst case, however, did not happen and the teacher salary schedule is now more strongly entrenched than ever. The experiences of the 1970s, a time of considerable growth in teacher-board-administrator bargaining, demonstrated that an objective and written salary schedule is essential even during the age of collective negotiation. To repeat, the major changes were that the teacher remuneration plan is hammered out at the bargaining table and approved by all parties present. It is no longer constructed for teachers by school administrators and then implemented after receiving formal approval by the school board.

Salaries paid teachers increased over the years when measured in current dollars. The average annual salary hovered around $1400 to $1450 from 1929 to 1940. As late as 1960 the average annual salary reached only $5088. More sizable increases over a decade followed, hitting $9269 in 1971, exceeding $10,000 for the first time in 1971, and was $17,264 in 1981. Although the dollar amount almost doubled during the 1970s, the buying power of these salaries "decreased by nearly 15 per cent during the 1970s."[15] The reduction in buying power is expected to continue as long as the teacher oversupply and financial crises persist, but may be lessened if inflation is brought under control during the 1980s.

There is a great range among districts, for the average of the lowest salary likely to be paid was $11,676 and the mean of the highest was $24,073; the "mean of the average" salary for 1980–1981 was $17,678, or slightly above the figure compiled and reported by the National Center for Education Statistics.[16] The percent of change in teachers' salaries during the last half of the 1970s was slightly higher than that for the salaries of administrators during the same period.

OTHER COMPENSATION OR BENEFITS: FRINGE BENEFITS, RETIREMENT, AND LEAVES

Retirement provisions for teachers are a twentieth-century development, but some states had only meager provisions until after World War II. All local school systems are presently covered under some type of state retirement plan; about 60 percent also provide federal Social Security coverage as well.

The so-called fringe benefits were slowly introduced as part of the total compensation package for teachers in the years following 1950. It was the unusual school system during the first half of this century that provided anything more than a modest retirement contribution (in most cases funded completely by state funds) and only a few days sick leave without loss of pay. In contrast, today it is the unusual school district that does not include a fairly comprehensive package of benefits as part of an overall compensation plan.

The Educational Research Service publishes an annual report on the types of fringe benefits available to teachers. The types of special benefits include at least the following:

1. About 11 days of sick leave per year with most permitting accumulation of unused sick leave days for use in subsequent years.
2. Some provide emergency/personal, religious, and sabbatical leaves with pay under certain conditions.
3. Federal Social Security coverage to supplement the state teachers retirement plans.
4. Group hospitalization plans with almost two-thirds of the districts paying the full premium for teachers and over one-third do the same for all members of the family.
5. Major-medical-surgical group insurance plans with over 60 per cent paying the full premium for teachers.
6. Dental and visual (optical) services group insurance plans are presently found in only a minority of school systems.

Leaves of absence for other than illness may be granted with or without pay and no loss of employment status. As indicated earlier, sabbatical leaves are relatively rare in local school districts as a whole but are allowed in some states and some large districts.

A tenure law guarantees continued employment indefinitely after completion of a probationary period; discharge can occur for only specific causes that are stipulated in the tenure law and if certain procedures are followed as well. Some states have approved continuing contract laws rather than tenure. A continuing contract law merely specifies that a teacher must be notified of employment status by some definite date (usually in March or April). Failure to notify by the stipulated date means that the teacher's contract is renewed automatically for the following year. Collective bargaining has reduced the significance of tenure and continuing contract laws insofar as teacher organizations are concerned. Such organizations at one time were the chief proponents of teachers' tenure laws.

Absenteeism and Substitute Teachers

Absenteeism emerged as a professional personnel problem during the last half of the 1970s. A 1977–1978 Pennsylvania study, to illustrate, reported a 106 percent increase in teacher absenteeism over a 16-year period. Monday and the first work day after a holiday period appear to be the "bad days" for faculty attendance. The Los Angeles unified school district dedicated $9 million in its 1974–1975 expenditures for the salaries of substitute teachers who covered for the absences of certificated personnel. This was equivalent to salaries for 600 elementary teaching positions in that district. Absenteeism has become a relatively high cost item in school budgets.

A 1977 Educational Research Service publication on the use of substitute teachers noted:[17]

1. About half of the school districts operate a centrally controlled organization for assigning substitute teachers with the rest using a decentralized approach or employing elements of both.
2. The overwhelming majority of districts require applications for substitutes and maintain a central roster.
3. About three-fourths of the substitutes have professional qualifications that approach the quality of preparation and certification status of the regular personnel.
4. The building principal usually receives the notification or requests from the regular teachers and triggers the process for the employment of a substitute.
5. Most school districts maintain a roster of about 26 to 35 for every 100 regular teachers employed.
6. Large systems (25,000 or more students) employed 143 substitutes per typical day, medium size systems 34, small districts (2500 to 9999 pupils) 13, and very small 3.
7. During 1976–77 on any given day about 4.3 percent of the total teaching force was classed as a substitute. This means that teachers had a 95.7 percent attendance average.
8. Salaries for substitutes vary widely from district to district. In 1976–77 it ranged from a low of $10 per day to about $55 per day, with the average rate being about $26 per day. The rates in 1980 were up substantially and were in the $75 to $100 per day bracket.
9. About 1.8 percent of the budgeted instructional salaries was spent on salaries for substitutes.
10. Only in a few situations, about 5 percent, are provisions for substitutes covered in a collective bargaining agreement.

TEACHER APPRAISAL

As indicated earlier, evaluation is a means to an end; it is essential to the continued productivity of the organization and for the continued performance effectiveness of personnel. It provides data useful in the design of individualized and more relevant programs of continuing professional development. The negative image of faculty evaluation systems can be traced to poorly designed instruments of evaluation, poorly implemented systems of appraisal by inadequately trained evaluators, and misuse of evaluative data to brand people as good, bad, or indifferent rather than as the base for further improvement of personnel. It bears repeating that evaluation of teacher performance can be a positive force for teacher and organizational improvement.

Mitzel reported: "More than a half century of research effort has not yielded meaningful measureable criteria around which the majority of the nation's educators can rally. No standards exist which are commonly agreed upon as the criteria of teacher effectiveness."[18] Redfern concurred: "The appraisal of teaching performance has baffled both teachers and school administrators for half a century."[19] The 1950 edition of the *Encyclopedia of Educational Research* concluded that, although research has added materially to an understanding of abilities, traits, and qualities desirable in the teacher, the identification and definition of competency are as yet unsatisfactory. There is no "adequate definition of teacher efficiency and consequently no satisfactory means of measuring this variable."[20] These were typical statements prior to 1965.

More recently, Redfern claimed to see some "light at the end of the tunnel" with reference to performance evaluation of teachers. There is a definite move toward modifying traditional unilateral rating schemes in favor of results-oriented and competency-based evaluation.[21] More state legislatures are mandating teacher evaluation.

Great strides in the improvement of teacher evaluation were noted during the 1970s, but this still remains one of the more sensitive challenges in professional personnel administration. The public demands personnel appraisal as evidenced by special state laws directing that this be carried out. The teaching profession's reaction ranges from resistance to outspoken opposition. Involving faculty representatives in the design and interpretation of appraisal results has not helped much to reduce the resistance to appraisal. Educational administrators have a responsibility to implement fair, objective, and meaningful faculty appraisal systems. The principal has a major responsibility in the implementation but many others should be involved in the appraisal process.

OTHER PERSONNEL ADMINISTRATION ISSUES

Faculty integration continued to be a professional personnel issue during the 1970s in most major cities with large minority enrollments. As indicated earlier, the racial and ethnic mix of the teaching force did not change much during the 1970s. More minority teachers are found at the elementary school level and in the South. The oversupply of qualified personnel and faculty layoffs during the late 1970s and early 1980s made it difficult to confront this sensitive employment issue. The achievement of a better racial balance in the composition of the total teaching force in the public schools would necessitate employing several hundreds of thousands of teachers from minority or special ethnic backgrounds.

Team teaching (also called cooperative instruction or cooperative teaching) gained popularity during the 1950s and 1960s which was not sustained to the same degree during the 1970s and early 1980s. It is another way of deploying professional personnel that results in creating a hierarchy of teaching positions headed by a team leader. The team leader coordinates the work of several others responsible for instruction and guidance of as few as 50 to as many as 200 pupils. Although the leader does some teaching, the majority of time is devoted to curriculum planning, staff leadership, and pupil evaluation. Some controversy occurs when the team leader receives more salary than others with similar experience and preparation (the range may be from as little as $400 to several thousand dollars more). Team membership usually consists of a master teacher, an auxiliary teacher (usually a trainee or student teacher), and an aide. The complexity and numbers on the team vary from place to place.

The team leader is a product of differentiated staffing for purposes of instruction and can be likened to the department chairperson in secondary schools. The effectiveness of team teaching remains a matter of controversy. It demands the matching of teacher personalities as well as special or differentiated capabilities to form a team. Not all competent teachers relate well to each other or enjoy working closely with all other teachers in the same building. Team teaching will not reduce the number of teachers needed in a school. It may necessitate more personnel, although the increase may be in auxiliary teachers or teachers' aides. Relatively few teachers, perhaps no more than one in eight, are found in team-teaching situations and most of these are at the elementary school level. It has not made the same impact at the secondary level.

Teachers' aides, sometimes called paraprofessionals or paraeducators, are, as a rule, noncertificated or nonprofessional personnel who assist or relieve teachers of some duties related to classroom instruction and may or may not be paid for their time and contributions. The use of lay readers and lunchroom aides as well as parent helpers has a long history in public education. The availability of federal funds during the 1960s greatly increased the use and payment of teacher's aides.

The functions of aides range from entering marks on report cards (or on forms for subsequent computer processing of report cards), correcting tests, distributing instructional materials, helping young children put on or take off clothes, interpreting for students whose mastery of English is as yet inadequate, supervising playgrounds or lunchrooms to assisting in the preparation of some kinds of instructional materials. These aides numbered 279,000 in 1976 with most resulting from federally funded projects.

Most volunteer aides work less than six hours per week. Aides that receive some type of compensation, usually an hourly rate, put in about 20 hours per week. Paid teachers' aides may be retired teachers, former substitute teachers, as well as others. Mothers receiving aid to dependent children are given priority in some large urban centers. Educational requirements vary, with high school education being the most common. A few states have established certification requirements for teachers' aides. The teacher surplus in the 1970s created a most unusual situation when some unemployed teachers who qualified for a full teaching credential accepted employment on an hourly basis as an aide.

Some controversies in the payment of aides began to gain attention by the late 1970s. There were some demands that aides deserve hourly wages equivalent to that of other "nonprofessional" workers in the system such as painters or other craftsmen. What began as a modest cost personnel service supported in large part by federal funds could generate more fiscal problems for local systems if federal funds are withdrawn and higher hourly wage demands are met.

SUMMARY

There are over 4.3 million persons involved in some way in teaching, support services, and administration of public education. A peak of about 2.2 million classroom teachers was reached in 1977 with declines thereafter projected to bottom out around the mid-1980s. The personnel administration challenges are many and diverse.

The teacher shortage lasted almost 25 years, came to an end during the 1970s, but there continued to be evidence of spot shortages in some fields.

Teacher certification standards have been upgraded to demand at least a bachelor's degree, are centralized at the state level, are valid for a specified period of time, and reciprocity among states is more common. By 1981 there were 17 states that approved laws establishing competency-based teacher certification.

Personnel policies are developed by the board but implemented by members of the superintendency team. The board is the legal-employing authority, but the nomination for employment of all personnel is delegated to the superintendency.

Employment discrimination based on age, sex, or marital status began to disappear after World War II and is no longer tolerated or practiced today in the public schools. Few require prior experience as a condition of employment. The typical teacher in 1980 was a married woman in her late thirties, with at least a bachelor's degree, and teaching in an elementary school. Teacher mobility was reduced during the 1970s. The proportion of teachers in 1981 who declared they certainly would enter teaching again dropped significantly to only 21.8 percent, whereas those declaring they "certainly would not" jumped to the highest level yet to 12 percent.

The principal has considerable responsibility for determining the teaching load. This load is affected by class size, number of class preparations, time spent in study hall supervision, ability range of pupils, and similar factors. Some attempts have been made to develop more objective procedures for measuring teacher load. By 1980 the salary paid to beginning teachers with a bachelor's degree exceeded $11,500. The average annual salary in 1980 for teachers was $17,678, or about triple the approximately $5500 that was registered 20 years earlier.

Salary schedules are a statement of board policy with reference to salary payment. Most school systems now employ salary schedules based on professional requirements only. Merit increase provisions remain a point of controversy. During the 1970s and continuing into the 1980s, salary schedule development and revisions were influenced strongly by collective bargaining.

Effective professional growth programs for employed personnel represent one of the major unmet needs of the profession, with teachers being among those most critical of such programs. Orientation of new teachers emerged during the period of the great teacher shortage but still continues in practice today. Morale is difficult to define, and is influenced by many factors including the conditions of employment.

There was less concern about teacher turnover and more about reductions-in-force during the 1970s. Layoffs affect less than 1 percent of the total teaching force at present. The so-called fringe benefits were introduced slowly after 1950, but today it is the unusual system that does not include these in the total compensation package for teachers.

Teacher absenteeism emerged as a more serious personnel administration problem during the past two decades. Teacher evaluation can be a positive force for both teacher and organizational improvement. The public demands that such appraisal and administrators must implement the systems. Improvements in appraisal were noted during the 1970s.

Faculty integration, team teaching, and the great use of teacher aides increased the number of personnel administration challenges during the past two decades.

NOTES

1. N. B. Dearman and V. W. Plisko, eds., *The Condition of Education*, 1982 edition, National Center for Education Statistics, Washington, D.C.: GPO, 1982, p. 85.
2. Ibid., pp. 85 and 94.
3. Ibid., pp. 88 and 114.
4. See ibid., p. 85; and also W. V. Grant and L. J. Eiden, *Digest of Education Statistics 1981,* National Center for Education Statistics, Washington, D.C.: GPO, 1981, p. 57.
5. National Education Association, *Status of the American Public School Teacher, 1980–81* (or 1960–61, 1965–66, 1970–71, or 1975–76), Washington, D.C.: The Association, 1982.
6. N. B. Dearman and V. W. Plisko, op. cit., p. 91.
7. Educational Research Service, "Orientation Programs for New Teachers," *ERS Report,* Arlington, Va.: ERS, 1977, 85 pp.
8. Dearman and Plisko, op. cit., pp. 86 and 100.
9. P. A. Zirkel and C. T. Bargerstock, "The Law on Reduction-in-Force: A Summary of Legislation and Litigation," *ERS Monograph,* Arlington, Va.: Educational Research Service, 1980, 74 pp.
10. Educational Research Service, "Methods of Scheduling Salaries for Teachers," *ERS Report,* Arlington, Va.: ERS, 1978, p. 2.
11. Educational Research Service, "Scheduled Salaries for Professional Personnel in Public Schools, 1980–81," *ERS Report,* Arlington, Va.: ERS, 1981, 123 pp.
12. Educational Research Service, "Merit Pay for Teachers," *ERS Report,* Arlington, Va.: ERS, 1979, 126 pp.
13. Ibid.
14. Ibid.
15. Dearman and Plisko, op. cit., pp. 102 and 103.
16. Educational Research Service, "Scheduled Salaries for Professional Personnel in Public Schools, 1980–81," op. cit.
17. Educational Research Service, "Practices and Procedures in the Use of Substitute Teachers," *ERS Report,* Arlington, Va.: ERS, 1977, 86 pp.
18. Harold E. Mitzel, "Teacher Effectiveness," in Chester W. Harris, ed., *Encyclopedia of Educational Research,* 3rd ed., New York: Macmillan, 1960, p. 1481.
19. G. B. Redfern, *How to Evaluate Teaching,* Worthington, Ohio.: School Management Institute, 1972, p. 6.
20. A. S. Barr, "Teaching Competencies," in Walter S. Monroe, ed., *Encyclopedia of Educational Research,* rev. ed., New York: Macmillan, 1950, pp. 1453–1454.
21. G. B. Redfern, "Competency-Based Evaluation: The State of the Art," *New Directions for Education,* Vol. 1, No. 1, Spring 1973, pp. 51–61.

CHAPTER REVIEW QUESTIONS

1. What factors influence the numbers, variety, and deployment of personnel?

2. What is competency-based teacher certification?

3. Why is in-service education one of the major unmet needs of the profession?
4. What factors should and should not be considered in determining the employment qualifications of prospective candidates?
5. What is the role of various educational administrators in the employment and assignment of professional personnel?
6. What impact does collective bargaining have on salary schedules?
7. What are the major controversies in the development of salary schedules?
8. Does merit pay for teachers work in practice? Justify your stand.
9. Why is teacher evaluation essential to the teacher and the organization?
10. What is team teaching?

SELECTED REFERENCES

Bolton, Dale L., *Selection and Evaluation of Teachers,* Berkeley, Calif.: McCutchan, 1973.

Castetter, William B., *The Personnel Function In Educational Administration,* New York: Macmillan, 1981.

Educational Research Service, "Methods of Scheduling Salaries for Teachers," *ERS Report,* Arlington, Va.: ERS, 1978, 56 pp.

Educational Research Service, "Merit Pay for Teachers," *ERS Report,* Arlington, Va.: ERS, 1979, 126 pp.

Knezevich, Stephen J., ed. "Creating Appraisal and Accountability Systems," *New Directions for Education,* Vol. No. 1, Spring 1973.

Zirkel, Perry A., and Bargerstock, Charles T., "The Law On Reduction-in-Force: A Summary of Legislation and Litigation," *ERS Monograph,* Arlington, Va.: ERS, 1980, 74 pp.

20

PERSONNEL LEADERSHIP AND MANAGEMENT: II. COLLECTIVE BARGAINING AND NEW RELATIONSHIPS

Collective bargaining by professional personnel, previously referred to as professional or collective negotiations, has wrought a revolution in personnel administration in education. It modified significantly the previous pattern of professional relationships as well as the way in which administrators and teachers, school boards and teachers, and professional societies or unions and teachers perceive each other and work together.

Other revolutionary concepts were introduced in professional personnel management during this century, such as the design and implementation of salary schedules, elimination of discriminatory employment practices, and the delegation of teacher screening and employment recommendation to the superintendent of schools; however, none was as dramatic in impact on previously existing personnel relationships as collective bargaining. None of the others depended upon angry rhetoric, long strikes, or other threatening postures for their introduction. The suddenness and intensity of real or threatened strikes, sanctions, and work slowdowns among teachers caught the nation

as well as school boards and administrators by surprise during the 1960s and 1970s. Professional teacher organizations were transformed into militant labor unions during a relatively brief period of time.

The significant modification in professional and working relations among educational personnel shall be analyzed in terms of its impact on educational administration. The basic concepts and trends will be reviewed along with the urgency to develop additional administrative competencies to cope with these personnel challenges.

UNDERSTANDING THE KEY CONCEPTS

Professional negotiation was the new and preferred term in the vocabulary of employer-employee relations in education during the 1960s. Collective bargaining is the much older description that was preferred in labor and industry; it was used for a century in the United States and even longer in Britain.

Stinnet et al. defined "professional negotiation" as a "set of procedures written and officially adopted by the local staff organization and the school board which provides an orderly method for the school board and staff organization to negotiate on matters of mutual concern, to reach agreement on these matters, and to establish educational channels for mediation and appeal in event of an impasse."[1] The significant factors in professional negotiation are:

1. A written and officially adopted set of personnel procedures.
2. An orderly method through which to negotiate matters of mutual concern.
3. An established pattern for resolving an impasse.

"Collective bargaining" is a way of arriving at decisions that influence terms and conditions of employment, that is, "governance of the shop." It is an agreement-making process involving give and take by both sides. It begins with flexible positions from which both sides can retreat with honor. It presumes a similar degree of bargaining power for representatives on each side of the table. The debates and discussions may be peppered with varying degrees of histrionics to impress the public, that is, to win public opinion to a given side of the bargaining table.

It is an art and not a science. It is conflict management at its most basic level, for the parties involved proceed from contrary, often antagonistic, viewpoints and concepts of self-interest to collective agreement.

The National Labor Relations Act (Sec. 8d) declared that, in its perception of bargaining, employer and employee representatives have a "mutual obligation" "to meet at reasonable times and confer in good faith with respect to wages, hours, and other terms and conditions of employment, or the negotiation of an agreement, . . . but such obligation does not compel either party to agree to a proposal or require the making of a concession." Lieberman and Moskow defined "collective negotiation" in operational terms to be "a process whereby employees as a group and their employers make offers and counteroffers in good faith on the conditions of their employment relations for the purposes of reaching mutually acceptable agreement."[2]

At one time the NEA preferred "professional negotiations," AFT preferred collective bargaining or collective negotiations, and AASA simply negotiation. By the late 1970s it was clear from the literature that collective bargaining was the most popular and most commonly used. For the purposes of this volume the three terms are considered synonymous.

There was an abortive attempt by some in educational administration, particularly during the 1960s or early years, to substitute informal negotiation procedures, or "to meet and confer" as an informal or collaborative effort, which did not end with a formal and official work contract, carried no threats of force or strikes to enforce one's demands, and did not bother with mediation or arbitration procedures. This informal problem-solving approach among professional peers never got very far, and was abandoned almost as soon as it was recommended in favor of the more formal and complex machinery of collective bargaining.

EVOLUTION AND DEVELOPMENT OF COLLECTIVE BARGAINING

The factors stimulating the development of collective bargaining in education are many and complex. They include: the high teacher turnover rate of the 1950s and 1960s; teacher dissatisfaction with economic rewards and lack of access to the school's power structure; the rampaging inflation of the 1970s; and the testing and tacit approval of negotiation rights in the public employment sector.

Increased economic reward is often cited as the primary motivator of collective bargaining in education. However, significant increases in the average teacher's salary were gained prior to the outbreak of militancy and for reasons other than those related to threatened strikes. To illustrate, teacher salaries more than doubled between 1949 and 1965, which was a rate faster than that for other workers, other than civilian federal government employees. What is more, most teacher job actions were in the wealthiest states that were paying better salaries. Nonetheless, many felt that the salaries were still unjustly low then, as they remain today, and represented the failure of society to recognize the contribution of professional personnel in education. It can be argued further that if greater economic rewards and security were the most important motivators, then teachers in rural rather than urban areas and those in the South rather than the North would have been the first to engage in strikes. Economic factors were important, but there were many others as well that motivated teachers toward more aggressive actions to improve their lot.

In 1960 the United Federation of Teachers (UFT) began collective bargaining with the New York City Board of Education, which resulted in the calling of an election in December 1961 that recognized the UFT as the systemwide bargaining agent for teachers. The subsequent bargaining broke down in April 1962 when the UFT called a strike.[3]

The Norris–LaGuardia Act of 1932 guaranteed labor the right to engage in strikes, boycotts, picketing, and other activities in labor disputes and limited the role of federal courts in labor affairs. The National Labor Relations Act (Wagner Act) of 1935 recognized the rights of employees to form, join, or assist labor organizations to bargain collectively through representatives of their own choosing and to engage in concerted activities for purposes of collective bargaining.

Most gains for labor were made during the presidency of Franklin D. Roosevelt. It is interesting that President Roosevelt in 1937 did not consider collective bargaining appropriate for public employees. He stated:

The process of collective bargaining, as usually understood, cannot be translated into the public service. It has its distinct and unsurmountable limitations when applied to public personnel management. . . . Particularly I want to emphasize my conviction that militant tactics have no place in the functions of any organization of government employees.[4]

President John F. Kennedy, in Executive Order 10988, took the opposite view and authorized collective bargaining as a way of reaching agreements between organizations of federal employees and federal administrators.

State laws define employer-employee relations in public education. The drive by the NEA and the AFT to have negotiation laws covering teachers enacted in every state will continue during the 1980s.

Wisconsin was the only state that had a comprehensive law regulating negotiation in public education prior to 1965. Between 1965 and 1967, 14 states—Alaska, California, Connecticut, Florida, Massachusetts, Michigan, Minnesota, Nebraska, New Hampshire, New York, Oregon, Rhode Island, Texas, and Washington—enacted legislation guaranteeing the right of teachers to participate in professional negotiation. By 1972, 29 states enacted legislation defining in some manner teacher-school board negotiations. Maguire reported that "many state statutes have taken major portions of their collective negotiations acts verbatim from the Taft-Hartley Act (1947)" and "used precedents established by the National Labor Relations Board in deciding disputed cases in teacher negotiations before state appeals board."[5]

The basic elements of a comprehensive collective bargaining law would include key definitions and purposes of the law; rights of teachers to join a professional organization; prohibitions against coercive actions by school districts; methods of ascertaining the composition of negotiation groups; what constitutes "good faith" negotiation; conditions conducive to negotiation, resolution, or impasses; stipulation of fact-finding procedures; what constitutes unfair labor practices; prohibition against strikes and work stoppages; development of agreements and contracts; and periods of duration of negotiated agreements.

By 1982, 33 states and the District of Columbia approved laws granting bargaining rights to teachers; only one new state instigated between 1978 and 1982.[6] Bargaining occurs in 8 states without a law authorizing it, two states permit consultation, and there is no bargaining in only 8 states. The AASA prepared a "model" state-collective bargaining law for education.[7]

State laws may stipulate the right of public employees to join unions or related organizations. Compulsory membership is not likely to be upheld by the courts without statutory approval. Several states require a "no strike" pledge from public employees for recognition as the bargaining agent for employees. Violation of the no-strike pledge may be mild or as severe as termination of employment for those engaging in such strikes. The lack of legal authorization or penalties for teacher strikes has not prevented teacher unions and organizations from engaging in strike actions.

THE COLLECTIVE BARGAINING OR NEGOTIATION PROCESS

The collective bargaining process is a conflicts reduction, group-interaction situation which hopefully will result in the production of a labor agreement or contract which will detail the conditions of employment, compensation package, and working relationships that shall prevail for one or more years. As one set of writers put it, "The conditions under which negotiations take place, the experience of the participants on each side, the goals they are seeking to achieve, and the strength of their relative positions" will set the tone and the likely time for completion of the unique bargaining sessions.[8]

Each side enters the process with varying degrees of preparation or advanced planning that determines as accurately as possible the proposals likely to be considered, the financial conditions facing the organization, the problems and successes of past labor contracts, the bargaining strategies likely to be employed by both sides, the key data essential for review of proposals, and how pressures and deadlocks are likely to be handled. Some conditions and procedures that should be clarified either prior

to or as soon as possible during the agreement-making or negotiating process are:

1. Who is to represent the teachers and who is to represent the board of education.
2. What is the scope of the subject matter of the negotiations.
3. How the negotiating sessions are to be structured, conducted, and scheduled.
4. How agreements are to be reached and reported (in oral or written form).
5. Whether, if an impasse is reached, mediation or arbitration shall prevail, and under what conditions.

After an agreement has been concluded, the conditions that govern the execution of the negotiated contract, the person responsible for its execution, and the rights and responsibilities of parties during the term of the negotiated contract must be determined.

Choosing Representatives

Determining who is to represent the professional staff involves defining who is a classroom teacher, specifically whether the principals are part of the teachers' group, as in Canada, or part of administration, as is likely in the United States.

The advantages of empowering one organization to speak for the professional staff in the negotiating sessions are: It simplifies the process, it is consistent with the majority rule concept, and it provides for the most efficient use of negotiating organizations resources.[9] The disadvantages are that exclusive recognition may exploit nonmembers and that in the absence of state laws, boards are legally prohibited from recognizing an exclusive representative.

Typically, the teachers' representative is chosen in an election called and supervised by: the board of education, a special state labor agency, or an independent group experienced in holding negotiation elections.

In the past considerable sums have been expended by rival organizations battling to gain exclusive representation rights for teachers.

This is one of several reasons why merger of the NEA and AFT should be attractive to both. Each questions the wisdom of teachers battling each other. The NEA-AFT rivalry continued unabated in the early 1980s with each attempting to organize the unrepresented or to wrest one represented group from another. Some teachers joined and supported both.

Determining or Limiting the Content of Proposals to Be Negotiated

Some negotiators say flatly that everything affecting the teacher is negotiable. Others argue that certain matters are part of "management rights" and not subject to negotiation. State legislation may define dimensions of the subject matter for negotiation in a general manner (as in Wisconsin, where questions of wages, hours, and conditions of employment are negotiable) or specifically (as in Oregon, where only salaries and related economic policies are negotiable). Washington state allows discussions to include "school policies related to but not limited to curriculum, textbooks selections, in-service training, student teaching programs, personnel hiring and assignment practices, leaves of absence, salaries and salary schedules and noninstructional duties." As many as 45 different items could be subject to negotiation.

The NEA believes that decisions affecting what the teacher does in the classroom and working with pupils, as well as economic interests, are subject to negotiation. The AFT similarly refuses to limit the scope of bargaining.

Board selection of a superintendent is not negotiable with a teachers' organization, nor are other administrative decisions that are clearly prerogatives of the board and administrators and with which teachers are not concerned.

What is negotiable must be agreed on by both parties prior to entering into discussions. In private industry and commerce, there seldom are legislative guides to the scope of negotiations. The substance of bargaining is not prescribed in the Wagner Act or other labor legislation.

Collective bargaining can and does limit administrative discretion. Therefore, the content of proposals needs to be analyzed to determine its likely impact on administrative prerogatives and inhibition of leadership activities.

The Schedule and Locus of Bargaining or Negotiating Activities

Once considered a sporadic activity of relatively short duration, planning for or actually engaging in collective bargaining is perceived presently as a year-round activity. The initial or opening negotiating session on a new contract is often vital and may establish the tone or climate of sessions to follow. Some proposals may be submitted before the initial face-to-face meetings.

Redfern referred to organizing data into a "negotiation book" which included board policies in general; board policies for making salary adjustments; salary, fringe benefit, and working condition improvements of the past five years; data on practices in other systems; dollar value of fringe benefits; number of certificated employees and average salary of each type of employee; approximate amount of money available for salary adjustments; items to be presented by the board in negotiation; items not granted in previous negotiation and why, and a prognosis.[10] The Educational Research Service also prepared a series of publications to aid school administrators in the collective bargaining process. These were entitled "Negotiation Aids" and each focused on a special topic such as class size or teacher evaluation.[11]

Bargaining Roles and Tactics

Collective bargaining in education involves human relations skills, knowledge of the issues confronting the organization, facts about operations, and sensitivity to the existence of a third party to negotiations, namely, the students. It occurs in a pressure-packed environment, if not a crisis atmosphere, and ability to operate effectively under such conditions is essential.

The roles of all those around the bargaining

table should be specified at the start of the process. Someone on each side must be designated as chief negotiator. Usually this is more than one person for each organization who may speak across the negotiating table; the size of the negotiating committee varies but should be limited in number to facilitate the process.

In addition, there may be nonnegotiating advisers who deal only with personnel on one side of the negotiating table, that is, do not participate in across the table or formal discussions. The presence of an attorney should be clarified because some are bargaining representatives and others are simply legal advisers. A statewide or national representative from the state or national NEA or AFT may be present as a member of the negotiating committee, advisor, or observer. Management may have various members of the administrative hierarchy present at some but not necessarily all sessions. The observer role is one of listening and noting what goes on.

Those who play negotiating roles need the competence to perform effectively as well as the knowledge to participate intelligently. Educational management has been relatively slow in developing personnel with negotiating skills, and there has been a tendency to employ those outside the system to perform the management-negotiating role. It is not unusual to find law firms or independent consultants who specialize in collective bargaining to be employed at various times as chief negotiators for the management side. Very often they are competent in the general process of bargaining or performing in conflict situations but have less sensitivity to the unique problems and issues of the school district. It is essential in the years ahead that the educational management team of the district include full-time and specialized personnel in the art and science of collective bargaining.

A bargaining position may be enhanced by the appropriate use of a number of tactics. Thus, calling for a recess when unusually laborious discussions that seem to be going nowhere are evident may help to resolve the differences when the teams reconvene. Requesting delays or referral to a special negotiating subcommittee are other tactics. Sooner or later there will be times when a series of counterproposals may be introduced to overcome knotty problems. Sometimes waiting for a deadline or crisis may be an appropriate tactic to hasten the agreement process on a sticky item or the package as a whole. If not, then the use of impasse resolution procedures may be called for; timing of the call for mediation or arbitration or fact-finding is also helpful in bargaining.

When the negotiating process begins in earnest, there are no rules. Psychology as well as sudden shifts in community and national sentiment influence the process. The points raised in early discussions are seldom the concluding points. Just when concessions begin, that is, when modifications of initial offers start to appear, is difficult to ascertain. Application of pressure and other tactics may create shifts. When firmness sets in is likewise a crucial point, but is difficult to pinpoint.

Resolving an Impasse

When each side has yielded maximum concessions (from its own point of view) and conflicting viewpoints have polarized some distance apart, an impasse has been reached. Impasses can occur even though both parties are bargaining in good faith and are represented by skillful negotiators.

Mediation is the term used when the third party intervention is agreed upon voluntarily and the third party opinions are used only in an advisory capacity. Mediation differs from consultation in that the mediator recommends settlement terms, whereas the consultant only assists parties to arrive at some point of agreement. The question of who should be the mediator is controversial.

Fact-finding is another procedure for resolving an impasse. Independent fact finders may investigate and search out true conditions. In 1965 Massachusetts, Michigan, and Wisconsin were the only states providing for fact-finding in employment disputes involving public school teachers. Many more have joined that list since then. Public approval of the fact finders' objective and independent recommendations provides a strong incentive for the disputants to agree to the terms recommended. The process is voluntary, and either party is free to reject all or part of the fact-finding report.

Binding arbitration may be used to resolve an impasse. Its acceptance may be compulsory or voluntary. In either case, once accepted, the recommendations are binding on each group involved in the negotiation. There is opposition to compulsory binding arbitration on the grounds that if it becomes common practice, it will diminish the usefulness of collective bargaining.

Bernstein challenged the point of view that collective bargaining in industry is breaking down because of its lack of "social vision," the change in the nature of the work force, and the impact of automation in a stagnant economy.[12] He claimed a misreading of collective bargaining was responsible for the accusation that it was too limited for the solution of current problems. To Bernstein, collective bargaining cannot be equated with an academic collective search for truth.

Others argue that government must step in because the public interest is often ignored by selfish groups. It is interesting that education became involved in an agreement-reaching process at the very time many experts were questioning the appropriateness and effectiveness of that process.

Reporting and Administering the Negotiated Agreement

The traditional point of view is that the board cannot delegate its discretionary authority without specific statutory permission. This had been interpreted to mean that negotiated agreements cannot be substituted for the board's discretionary authority. New laws have changed this traditional conception.

Once the agreement is reached, a zipper clause may be included to insure that negotiation will not be reopened for a specified period of time.

Lieberman and Moskow state that until the first agreement was signed between the UFT and the New York City Board of Education, the AFT was little concerned with written agreements. As late as 1962, only 12 local affiliates of the AFT had written agreements with school boards. Since 1962, and particularly since the 1965 edition of the NEA *Guidelines on Professional Negotiations,* considerable emphasis has been placed on developing written contracts that set out the term and other conditions of agreement. These written agreements can be voluminous and contain detail that requires 100 pages or more of explanation. Such documents then form the basis of future operations with copies available to many as a basic reference source.

The execution of policy is an administrative concern, and, therefore, the administration of the negotiated contract between employer and employee is the responsibility of school administrators, the principal, and the superintendent. Grievance procedures must be developed to handle conflicting interpretations of an agreement or a direct violation of it. Arbitrators are called in when discussions cannot produce agreement about interpretation. Binding arbitration is the terminal point in approximately 95 percent of all grievance procedures in private industry. It is relatively uncommon in education. School boards generally oppose the concept of binding arbitration, that is, resolution of the conflict between board and teachers by referring it to a third party whose decision is accepted without appeal by parties to the conflict.

Grievances and Their Disposition

Strictly speaking a grievance is an expression of employee dissatisfaction with a real or an imagined violation of a negotiated contract. Many writers in personnel administration, however, interpret it more generally as any valid or invalid expression of employee dissatisfaction (sometimes called complaint) about any dimension of working conditions.

Grievances may occur because of conflicting interpretations of a written bargaining agreement due to vagueness of the wording of the labor contract or omissions caused by the failure to anticipate all possible situations. Others may be explained by the inability of the employee to satisfy position requirements or some personal problems. Whatever the cause, effective personnel administration demands that any and all personnel complaints be heard promptly and acted upon with dispatch.

The best way to deal with such situations is, of course, to prevent grievances from occurring in the first instance. Because this is not always possible, the strategy is to minimize the possibility of employee grievances and to treat them before they blow up to unmanageable proportions. Many organizations have created formal grievance-disposition systems consisting of formal and written procedures for submitting grievances; carefully defined systems for processing all grievances received as soon as possible; delegation of managerial responsibilities for the monitoring of grievances at various levels in the hierarchy; and well-designed strategies for resolving grievances including intraorganizational committees and extraorganizational approaches such as arbitration.

The school principal is located where grievances are experienced, filed, and considered initially. The implementation of the negotiated agreement is felt first and continually at the building level. This provides the justification for involving the site-level administrators as part of the negotiating team and grievance-disposition committee of the system.

Trends in Collective Bargaining in Education

Many leaders in public education kept insisting throughout the 1960s that collective bargaining "would never happen" in education. The concept of bargaining was either ignored in the hopes that it would go away or treated with hostile contempt by administrators, school boards, and many others in the profession because it was considered to be "bad" for education and unprofessional as well. By the mid-1970s collective bargaining in education was accepted as part of the new reality, a new approach in educational personnel administration. It is easy to criticize the early views as being

shortsighted, but the temper of the times was consistent with the desires for professional unity. Witness the landmark National Labor Relations Act, which specifically excluded negotiations for public employees. No new federal legislation on collective bargaining in the public sector has been passed to upset this exclusion even in the face of strenuous lobbying by some organizations in education to do just that.

Newer approaches unique to education such as multiarea bargaining were being developed during the 1970s and tried out during the 1980s. In Michigan and Oregon some smaller school districts banded together to form a larger single bargaining unit. These "Multi-Area Bargaining Organizations" were reputed to be more efficient and productive. Participation of teachers in such units is purely voluntary. Michigan reported a positive response in about 33 regions with experience in this approach. School boards in such districts tended to resist the large area bargaining units as a further threat to local control.

Time and experience helped the profession to gain a measure of maturity in the negotiation process. Many on both sides of the bargaining table acquired sophisticated negotiating competencies. Some noted that social relationships as well as professional interactions among teachers and administrators changed as a result of negotiations. The "after-bargaining" impact of the process is only beginning to be understood.

Cresswell and Murphy noted that by the mid-1970s "fewer and fewer articles appear as the years go by dealing with the evils of bargaining and how it must be exorcised from the body of education."[13] They noted the following trends as well:

1. The social and political environment seems to be growing more open to collective bargaining in education.
2. Teacher militancy as a movement seems to be giving way to teacher unionism as an institution.
3. Courts, legislatures, and boards of education seem as yet to be unsure of appropriate responses to the teacher militancy movement and the institutionalization which seems to follow.

4. There is movement from a fragmented, pluralized system of educational decision making to one in which the principal relationship is between two strong parties.

5. . . . teacher militancy occurring at this time is in part attributable to the growing militancy of society.[14]

The initial focus of collective bargaining in education was on salary and fringe benefits for teachers. This was followed in order by an emphasis on working conditions, job security, and other educational policy issues. Teacher collective bargaining behavior has resulted in teachers having a greater impact upon economic and noneconomic decisions in education at the expense of authority held and exercised by school boards and administrators. To illustrate, principals today have less discretionary authority than they did in the days when there were no negotiated agreements that spelled out in great detail many noneconomic or school operating provisions. The RAND Corporation submitted a study which showed a sharp increase during 1975–1976 in teacher union activities influencing what previously were considered to be "management prerogatives."[15]

STRIKES, SANCTIONS, AND WORK STOPPAGES

A serious breakdown in bargaining fueled by high emotions over the lack of ability to generate a working agreement may lead to the exercise of raw power to influence the actions of another party. Power implies access to or possession of resources—physical, personal, or psychological—coveted by others. Boards and administrators desire to keep schools operating and to avoid unseemly controversy. The strike is a union's most powerful weapon and is based on the refusal of employees to continue to perform in positions deemed essential for continued and productive operation of the organization. The mere threat of its use may on occasion generate the pressure desired to overcome bargaining deadlocks. Job actions or relatively brief work stoppages are used commonly in education. Sanctions by the NEA during the 1960s was the "softer alternative" to strikes based on the hope that no new persons would seek employment in a district or state under NEA sanctions. Sanctions proved to be too mild and relatively ineffective; the strike weapon replaced it during the 1970s and thereafter.

Legal control over public systems of education is placed in the hands of boards of education and never with teacher associations or unions. Efforts of organized teachers, or others without legal authority, to control important decisions and resources in an organization must be directed through other channels. The success of such group efforts lies in their ability to bring an organization's work to a halt by refusing to work and by inhibiting others from working. This is the power of the strike or slow-down. The show of such force is effective during times of teacher shortage, in locations where democratic traditions flourish, and when community opinion, existing laws, and other associations or unions at the state and national level support the strike. When protesters lack access to the conference table, or when the conference fails to bring capitulation of holders of legitimate power, then wielders of nonlegitimate power take to the streets to demonstrate in behalf of the social change desired. There are limits to nonlegitimate show of force as a means of influencing an organization's policies: It must stop short of a complete takeover of the administration of the organization.

For much of its history the NEA condemned strikes by professional educators. This traditional posture was changed in 1962 when *condemnation* was replaced by the softer term *opposition* to teacher strikes. By 1965, NEA went further and deleted all references to strikes. The complete abandonment and reversal of its historic position came in 1967 when the NEA went on record with full support for striking NEA local affiliates. It took only five years of debate for an historic reversal and to bring an end to the use of euphemisms such as "withdrawal of services" and to call a strike a strike. Yet another step was taken during the 1970s when the NEA lost its favored tax status as a professional organization, and was classified by the U.S. Internal Revenue Service as a labor union.

The American Association of School Administrators (AASA) continues its traditional posture and does not condone teacher strikes under any condition. It is highly improbable that this position will change.

The founding fathers of AFT also took the position that teachers should not be allowed to strike. It moved away from the antistrike posture earlier than did the NEA. Although AFT local strike actions preceded it, the 1964 AFT convention formally recognized the right of locals to strike under certain circumstances. The AFT president wrote a 1970 article for the *Saturday Review of Literature* entitled "Needed, More Teacher Strikes."

By 1970, Hawaii and Pennsylvania approved legislation that allowed teachers to strike under certain conditions; two other states later joined them. In the overwhelming majority of states there is no legislative recognition of the teacher's right to strike; nor is there any national support of strikes by public employees.

The absence of legislative authorization for strikes by public employees has not deterred the use of the weapon of last resort. Court decisions have supported the concept that public employees provide essential services, and therefore upheld public policies opposed to public employee strike actions. It was not court decisions that made it clear that public employees have no right to strike in the absence of permissive legislation or that could explain the relatively few work stoppages by teachers prior to 1945, which were less than a dozen. The rare strike that captured so much attention when it happened was contrary to the prevailing professional mores, but such attitudes were destined to change during the 1960s, prevailing laws and court decisions notwithstanding. Early in the 1960s teacher strikes were averaging two or three a year. By 1969–1970 there were 183 strikes involving 105,000 teachers and 412,000 days of work were lost. Teacher strikes were averaging 142 per year during the last three years of the 1960s—a significantly higher rate than noted early in that decade. There was a brief period of decline during the first half of the 1970s to 130 in 1970–1971, 89 in 1971–1972, and 143 in 1972–1973. A new record of teacher strikes (203) was set in 1975–1976. The NEA called 1978–1979 a "normal" year for strike actions as 176 took place at that time. After more than two decades of significant numbers of strike actions by teachers there is no indication of any hesitancy to use this weapon or that the actual number per year may decline soon.

Prior to 1966 the majority of teacher strikes were sponsored by AFT rather than NEA affiliates. The majority of teacher strikes during the 1970s and presently are conducted by NEA local affiliates. (The NEA experienced several actual and threats of strikes by its own employees as well.) AFT-sponsored strikes tend to last much longer, however. Over 81 percent of teacher strikes during 1978–1979 were by NEA local affiliates and 16 percent by AFT locals. Despite predictions that uncertain economic conditions would lessen the probability of strikes during 1982–1983, there were 68 by October 1, 1982, compared with 59 by October 1, 1981.

Strikes occur more frequently in some states than others. Less than half the states have one or more teacher strikes in a given year. Over one-half of all teacher strikes in 1978–1979 took place in four states that included Michigan (the leader with 34 strikes), Pennsylvania (22), Illinois (21), and Ohio (20). The opposite side of the coin is that in any given year there are no teacher strikes in almost 99 percent of the local school districts. About 89 percent of school superintendents have never experienced a teacher strike as of 1982. Teachers are among the more strike-prone public employee groups, for in 1980–1981 one-third of all strikes in the public sector were by teacher organizations.

A review of the incidence of teacher strikes in Pennsylvania during the past decade revealed that one out of four teacher strikes in the nation was in Pennsylvania, 160,000 employees were affected, a typical strike lasted about 12.6 days, over 2.4 million did not attend school because of the strikes, and the strike-action cost to taxpayers amounted to $12 million.[16] Additional management costs for implementing negotiated contracts came to $328 million. Teacher dues paid to associations or unions since the emergence of collective bargaining in that state was estimated at $110 million.

September seems to be the most popular month for strikes; May is next in popularity with December being the least likely month. The majority of strikes are of relatively short duration, lasting from one to five days. Over 80 percent continue for ten days or less. Only about 10 percent of teacher strikes involve 1000 or more school personnel.

Administration alternatives to a strike, with or without picketing, are to continue operations with substitutes and supervisory personnel or to shut down all schools. It is now common for the administrative team to prepare strike contingency plans to minimize pupil learning loss, protect possible damage to resources, and reduce ill-will during and after the work stoppage. The poststrike planning may help heal wounds in a shorter period of time and enable the system to move more quickly to higher levels of learning productivity.

ROLE OF THE ADMINISTRATORS IN COLLECTIVE BARGAINING

Collective bargaining calls for an administrative style that bears some resemblance to participative management or democratic school administration insofar as the noneconomic issues are concerned. The important differences are that collective bargaining guarantees teachers the right to influence many dimensions of educational operations, whereas democratic administrative style simply provides a permissive environment for teachers' participation in vital educational decisions. Collective bargaining is part of the new reality and the roles of key administrators must be analyzed in the light of the new conditions.

The Superintendent and Collective Bargaining

During the early years of this personnel revolution there were many who pictured the superintendent in the role of a special resource person for both the board of education and the teachers' association, supplying information to both sides or acting as a referee without being a formal representative of either side. The superintendent in this role was depicted as being above and aloof from any bitter intergroup conflict.

There were others who demanded that the superintendent could not remain in an uncommitted role when confronted with sensitive personnel issues and still survive as the chief executive officer of the school board. Furthermore, this point of view argued that the status of the superintendent as an educational leader would be jeopardized if not intimately involved in an agreement-making process of which teachers were a part.

The aloof versus involved role of the superintendent has been resolved, but the fact that it was an issue for about a decade can be understood by examining the temper of the times and historical precedents. Prior to 1960 the great theme was the unity of the educational profession as evidenced by the fact that teachers, supervisors, and administrators were members of a single professional association. If the superintendent was aligned with the board, then this adversary role in collective bargaining would result in de facto fragmentation of the educational profession. The NEA's initial position was that the superintendent's role was to be an information supplier for both negotiating groups but not an active representative of either. The NEA Research Service provided data that most superintendents of that time in the early 1960s perceived themselves as advisors rather than as negotiators; those in the states of California and Michigan were the exceptions in that they viewed themselves as negotiators with full authority. The AASA as late as 1966 expressed a position that was very similar to that of the NEA by declaring that the superintendent "should be an independent third party in the negotiation process," but then added, "In no instance should the responsibility for negotiations be delegated outside the profession."[17] There was a division on this issue among its membership and headquarter's staff at that time; AASA quietly backed away from its initial position during the 1970s.

The AFT declared from the very beginning that the superintendent was not an acceptable spokesperson for teachers and boards at bargaining sessions; it put the superintendent clearly on the board's side of the negotiating table. NEA did likewise during the 1970s. Both groups insisted that teachers could speak for themselves through unions and were not dependent upon administrators to improve their lot. What was a sensitive professional issue is now resolved along with any further concern for a "united profession"; the superintendent is the chief school administrative officer and is a member of the board or administrative-negotiating team.

School board members, as laypersons representing the community, seldom have the special preparation needed to be effective negotiators nor do they have the time to participate directly and daily until the conclusion of collective bargaining. Some argued that the superintendent is better off if removed from the bargaining process or from its coordination and direction. This position is contrary to the best interests of the superintendency. The superintendent and the administrative team at the central office and building levels must assert a dynamic and leadership role in the collective bargaining process to insure that its outcomes are in the best interests of the students, the school system, and the efficient administration of the organization. Educational administrators at all levels, superintendents and principals in particular, must acquire the competencies needed for the effective direction, completion, and implementation of the results of collective bargaining in education. Others with the special time and talents may be involved in the direct and daily bargaining, but such personnel report to the school board through the superintendent and work under the direction and supervision of the superintendent.

Board delegation of negotiating responsibilities to someone other than the superintendent, who is granted coordinate status with the person formerly recognized as the "chief school executive," would result in the dual or multiple system of educational administration and all its attendant problems. The dual- or multiple-headed administrative monster has been condemned as inimical to the best interests of effective administration when other specialists sought coordinate or superior status to that of the chief school executive. Of no less consequence is what happens to the superintendent's relations with teachers when the specialist in bargaining makes unilateral decisions concerning the welfare of teachers or the operation of the school system during some difficult bargaining sessions. Teachers and others come to respect and work with those who have stature and have the authority to make decisions essential to the welfare of the system.

The superintendent's responsibility for district negotiating responsibilities should not imply personal and daily participation by the chief executive in all bargaining activities. In large school systems additional specialized personnel facilitate the negotiating responsibilities. Any and all persons engaged in negotiations on behalf of the school board should be considered subordinate to the chief executive so as to maintain the integrity of the unit system of administration. The superintendent is held accountable for the actions of the administration's negotiating team, and the team's authority during negotiating sessions is confined by the policies and prior agreements of the school board.

The 1982 AASA study of the superintendency reported considerable variation in who assumed the chief negotiator role for the board and administration. The chief negotiator was the superintendent in 36.1 percent of the districts, a professional negotiator from within or outside the district in 29.2 percent of the cases, board members in 23.6 percent of the districts, the board attorney in 5.6 percent of the cases, and "don't know" or no response was recorded for the remainder.[18]

In all bargaining, the end product must be ratified by all parties involved. Thus, representatives for teacher groups must submit the agreement to the vote of the entire membership; the superintendent and staff must receive approval of the agreement from the school board.

The Personnel Director

The personnel director in the large school system is concerned more with preparing for and developing a negotiated agreement than with other activities. Complexity of the school personnel director's office has greatly increased as a result of staff negotiation.

The Principal

The principal's role in negotiation is less controversial now than it was in the 1960s. As a member of the total administrative professional negotiation strategy team, the principal advises the superintendent on matters of concern at the attendance-unit level such as the implications of particular concessions for the operation of a school system.

Whether or not the principal has a dynamic role in bargaining is related to the responsibilities delegated to the superintendent for such functions. The exclusion of principals from significant administrative roles may lead to the dissatisfactions that prompted some principals in large cities and the eastern part of the nation to talk seriously about forming unions for principals for the purposes of bargaining directly with school boards and/or the superintendent. The 1978 study of the elementary school principal revealed a rather large percentage of principals who believed that the formation of special bargaining units for principals was desirable.

THE FUTURE OF EDUCATIONAL PERSONNEL RELATIONSHIPS

By the early 1980s the education profession had experienced two decades of rather traumatic change insofar as the development of new professional relationships was concerned. Some dire predictions of the destruction of public education as the result of bargaining and strikes happily did not come to pass. Educators on both sides of the negotiating table gained maturity, and some added wisdom and sophistication in a fashion appropriate to professional responses during a new era in personnel relationships. In short, considerable adjustment to the new realities occurred by 1980.

In 1979 the Bureau of National Affairs offered the following predictions on the future of labor relations in the public sector:[19]

1. Public employee unions and organizations will continue to increase.
2. There will be more interunion conflict as competition for employee members increases.
3. A federal bargaining law for the public sector may be passed.
4. Strikes by teachers and other public employees will not increase, but each may be more intense.
5. There will be increased use of binding arbitration in the public sector.
6. Grievance arbitration will increase.
7. Although employer-employee confrontations will not disappear, the differences will be ameliorated by more sophistication in the bargaining process.

Perhaps the worst is over. Teacher strikes may decline over the next 50 years as the limitations of this weapon in the public sector become more obvious and other tactics come to the fore. Teacher groups favor binding arbitration and boards may lessen their opposition to binding arbitration as a means to overcome serious obstacles and impasses toward reaching a mutually acceptable agreement.

About 20 years ago a radical in the profession was one who discussed openly the forthcoming revolution in personnel relations, the increased probability of strikes and personnel strife, and the likelihood of a separation of administrator organizations from those for teachers. The nonradicals argued for the importance of a "unified profession," resisted the new reality of bargaining, and questioned whether teacher strikes would occur.

The controversy is still unsettled and many remain unsure whether all segments of the profession can yet come together. Time proved the alleged radicals to be realists in projecting the course of personnel relations. The time is ripe for teachers and administrators to put aside the conflict and the confrontation of the past two decades. It is predicted that teachers and administrators will come together again during the 1980s because joint action by the profession is essential if public education is to acquire the added resources required for quality programs as well as for professional salary levels for educators. The 1980s, in contrast to the 1970s, will be a decade of healing and "rejoining" of separate efforts and forces (not to be confused with "reunification" or any other suggestion of reverting to pre-1960 personnel relations). The crisis in educational finance, the attacks on public education, the fact that neither teachers nor administrators can exist or function effectively without the other, and so on, will help provide motivation to bring together previously warring elements of the profession. Each will come to recognize soon that continued divisiveness will bring more harm than benefit to each group. Each side will begin to find ways to establish new lines of professional communications and professional working relations on the local, state, and national levels. The future will be brighter for it.

SUMMARY

Collective bargaining produced a revolution in school personnel relationships. Its origins may be traced to the 1960s. Professional negotiations and collective negotiations were preferred terms for a time, but collective bargaining is presently the most commonly used term in education.

Factors stimulating the development of collective bargaining in education are many and varied with low teachers' salaries being only one. The National Labor Relations Act excluded bargaining by public employees, and President Kennedy issued, much later, an Executive Order authorizing collective bargaining for federal employees. Over 60 percent of the states enacted statutes governing negotiations in education. These laws may stipulate what is or is not subject to negotiation, how representatives in behalf of teachers shall be se-

lected, and the nature of the negotiated agreement.

Bargaining in education involves human relations skills, knowledge of the issues and operational dimensions, and sensitivity to the existence of learners as silent parties to all activities. At the negotiating table is a team of negotiators representing each side plus advisors and observers. The role of each person present should be clarified. A number of tactics come into play such as demanding a recess, requesting a delay in controversial items, submitting counterproposals, and waiting for a deadline or other special timing for the introduction or resolution of a problem.

The goal is to reach a mutually satisfactory agreement, which is not always possible. Discussions may reach an impasse that may necessitate the use of mediation or arbitration. Mediation is based on third party intervention whose opinions are advisory. In binding arbitration, the recommendations of the third party intervenor are binding on all parties in the negotiation. Technically, a grievance is an expression of employee dissatisfaction with the implementation or interpretation of the negotiated agreement, but generally it may apply to any type of employee complaint. Grievances may not be prevented completely, but they can be minimized. The principal is the initial recipient and processor of grievances.

By the mid-1970s bargaining in education was accepted as a part of the new reality and fewer articles appeared about its evils. The initial focus of bargaining was on salary and fringe benefits and expanded later to include working conditions, job security, and educational policy issues.

Strikes by teachers grew rapidly during the late 1960s and all of the 1970s, with most occurring in four states. About 1 percent of the school districts experiences a strike by teachers in any one year. Most strikes are supported by NEA-affiliated groups. Strikes persist without statutory or ruling case-law support for such actions.

The role of the superintendent in negotiations was resolved in favor of leadership and direction of the process rather than in being an interested observer who worked both sides of the negotiating table. Principals and the personnel administrator have important roles on the administrator's negotiating team.

The 1980s is predicted to be a time of healing in the profession, with teachers and administra-

tors joining forces once again to promote the cause of public education. A new set of professional relationships is being fashioned to expedite the process and adjustments are being made to the changes made necessary by collective bargaining.

NOTES

1. T. M. Stinnet, J. H. Kleinman, and M. L. Ware, *Professional Negotiation in Public Education,* New York: Macmillan, 1966, p. 2.
2. M. Lieberman and M. H. Moskow, *Collective Negotiations for Teachers,* Chicago: Rand McNally, 1966, p. 1.
3. Ibid., pp. 35–40.
4. Letter from Franklin D. Roosevelt to L. C. Stuart, President of the National Federation of Federal Employees, August 16, 1937. Reprinted in Charles S. Rhyne, *Labor Unions and Municipal Employee Law,* Washington, D.C.: National Institute of Municipal Law Officers, 1946, pp. 436–437.
5. John W. Maguire, "Professional Negotiations: State or Federal Legislation?", *School and Society,* Vol. 98, No. 2324, March 1970, pp. 176–177.
6. Education Commission of the States, *Cuebook II: State Education Collective Bargaining Laws,* Denver: The Commission, 1980, 78 pp. See also: *NEA Today,* April, 1983, p. 6 for more recent changes.
7. American Association of School Administrators, *AASA Model Public Employee Collective Bargaining Law,* Arlington, Va.: AASA, 1976, 36 pp.
8. H. J. Chruden and A. W. Sherman, Jr., *Personnel Management,* 5th ed., Cincinnati: Southwestern, 1976, p. 391.
9. Stinnet et al., op. cit., pp. 167–168.
10. American Association of School Administrators, *The School Administrator and Negotiation,* op. cit., p. 55.
11. See Educational Research Service, "Negotiating the Teacher Evaluation Issue," *ERS Negotiation Aid,* Arlington, Va.: ERS, 1979, 76 pp.; and similar *ERS Negotiation Aid* publications.
12. Irving Bernstein, "The Cockeyed World of Paul Jacobs," *AFL-CIO American Federationist,* May 1964, pp. 20–22.
13. Anthony M. Cresswell and Michael J. Murphy, *Education and Collective Bargaining,* Berkeley, Calif.: McCutchan, 1976, p. xiv.
14. Ibid.
15. See RAND Corporation, *Organized Teachers in American Schools,* Santa Monica, Calif.: The Corporation, 1978, 103 pp.; and also Education Commission of the States, *Impacts of Collective Bargaining Policy in Elementary and Secondary Education,* Denver: The Education Commission, 1981, 98 pp.
16. See *Government Union Review,* Vienna, Va.: Public Service Research Foundation, 1981, 69 pp.
17. American Association of School Administrators, *School Administrators View Professional Negotiation,* Arlington, Va.: AASA, 1966, p. 54.
18. L. L. Cunningham and J. T. Hentges, *The American School Superintendency 1982 A Summary Report,* Arlington, Va.: American Association of School Administrators, 1982, p. 50.
19. Bureau of National Affairs, *Negotiating the Future: Labor Relations in the Public Sector, 1979–2029,* Washington, D.C.: The Bureau, 1979, 20 pp.

CHAPTER REVIEW QUESTIONS

1. What forces stimulated teacher militancy in the 1960s?
2. Should teachers be allowed to strike? Justify your stand.
3. Are sanctions more effective than teachers' strikes? Justify your position.
4. What is collective negotiation?
5. What should be the role of the superintendent in the negotiating process? The role of the principal? The role of the supervisor?
6. Why is single representation for teachers' groups recommended over a proportional representative council?
7. What is mediation?
8. Should compulsory arbitration be a part of all state laws governing negotiation with teacher groups? Justify your stand.

SELECTED REFERENCES

American Association of School Administrators, *The School Administrator and Negotiation,* Washington, D.C.: The Association, 1968.

Cresswell, Anthony M., and Murphy, Michael J., *Education and Collective Bargaining,* Berkeley, Calif.: McCutchan, 1976, 513 pp.

Education Commission of the States, *Impacts of Collective Bargaining Policy in Elementary and Secondary Education,* Denver: The Commission, 1981, 98 pp.

Lieberman, M., *Public-Sector Bargaining: A Policy Reappraisal,* New York: Lexington Books/D. C. Heath, 1981, 180 pp.

Lieberman, M., and Moskow, M. H., *Collective Negotiations for Teachers,* Chicago: Rand McNally, 1966.

Maguire, John W., "Professional Negotiations: State or Federal Legislation?" *School and Society,* Vol. 98, No. 2324, March 1970.

21

INSTRUCTIONAL LEADERSHIP AND MANAGEMENT: I. CURRICULUMS, PROGRAMS, AND MATERIALS DEVELOPMENT

Instructional leadership is one of the most important challenges facing educational administrators at all levels of the hierarchy. Its central focus is learning in the school setting, that is, what should be learned or program definition, how learning effectiveness may be enhanced or instructional strategies, and what resources are essential to the learning process or the instructional materials. Instruction and learning are two sides of the same coin; instruction defines the educational process from the instructor's or teacher's perspective, and learning is the related activities from the student's point of view. There is interaction between parties involved and the materials and strategies utilized.

Instruction may be defined as the process, usually involving teachers performing with or without special devices or materials, which seeks to promote or actually results in the acquisition of knowledge, skills (or special competencies), or attitudes by one or more learners. Modification of learner behavior may be an outcome of instruction. Self-instruction is learning without benefit or intervention of another party. There are limitations to the process, for not all instruction results in learned behavior or insights to the degree desired.

Educational administrators are held accountable, at least in part, for the quality, quantity, and effective delivery of instructional services; the nature of the learning environment provided by the educational system; and the learning outcomes. The instructional leadership and management responsibilities of the administrator are discharged by motivating teachers and other personnel involved in the instructional process; procuring and allocating resources necessary to enhance learning; stimulating the development of or introducing new and more promising learning systems; monitoring and appraising learning outcomes; designing and implementing professional development programs for instructional personnel; arranging time schedules and school terms to facilitate the teaching-learning process; designing and operating the most effective instructional organization patterns; and so on. Teachers are directly involved in the learning process and interact directly with learners; administrators are at least once removed from the classroom but are concerned with what transpires in each. The myth persists that the administrator demonstrates instructional leadership best by teaching a class or two, that is, serving as the model of an effective teacher for others to emulate. This, however, is the least effective way of influencing learning in all classrooms in the school or system.

The most difficult instructional leadership and management challenge is to exert positive influence on learning at some distance from where it actually takes place (the classroom), when it is stimulated by some person other than the administrator, and when it occurs in an environment in which many other important responsibilities distract or compete for the administrator's attention. The administrator must work with and through others to realize instructional leadership and management objectives.

This chapter focuses on only part of the instructional responsibilities related to what is to be learned or taught as defined by the school's curriculum and its materials of instruction. The next chapter examines the management dimensions such as scheduling the school day and year, instructional organization patterns, monitoring and appraising pupil progress in learning, and promotion policies.

THE CURRICULUM AND THE ADMINISTRATORS

Curriculum is defined as all learning experiences provided by an educational institution. Broadly conceived, it is the "means of instruction used by the school to provide opportunities for student learning experiences leading to desired learning outcomes."[1] "Means of instruction" include classroom studies, guidance and counseling programs, school and community service projects, school-related work experience, school health services, school camps, and school libraries, as well as those activities called "extracurricular" or "cocurricular." Curriculum planning includes identifying and stating educational objectives, developing the all-school program, teaching and learning, providing curriculum guides, and providing instructional aids and materials.[2]

Curriculum includes the scope and sequence of learning experiences that are provided in the school, as well as the teaching-learning process (commonly referred to as methods of instruction) and instructional aids and materials. That which is to be learned can be separated from methods to promote learning (pedagogy). The curriculum is the operational statement that defines the school's program or offerings. Administrative and supervisory personnel are held accountable, as well, for maintaining a relevant program of educational offerings and the development of a conceptual framework for the study and improvement of curriculum and instructional strategies.

Taba observed that "one is struck by a seeming lack of rigorous, systematic thinking about curriculum planning."[3] She commented that the literature about curriculum development is eclectic in quality and lacks a conceptual framework to determine crucial elements and their relation to each other. These complexities and shortcomings within the curriculum field complicate the discharge of the leadership responsibilities of administrators.

The principals and superintendents of 150 to 200 years ago were concerned primarily, if not solely, with determining the appropriate courses of study within the school's curriculum, supervision of instruction, and grading and related instructional organization problems.[4] As indicated earlier, other responsibilities such as those for buildings and finance were not delegated to superintendents until many decades later.

When an administrator is criticized for spending "too much time on buildings, bonds, and budgets," there is often the implication that these have little to do with curriculum and instruction. There is always the danger of overemphasizing a few dimensions of educational administration to the neglect of others that may be equally or even more important. It is equally unfortunate, however, when one fails to comprehend that functional educational facilities, the so-called buildings, cannot be planned and designed without understanding the nature of the curriculum and instructional methods and materials. A physical facility, or "building," is the physical expression of the school curriculum; the size, shape, and arrangement of educational spaces are dictated by the educational program and approaches to instruction. The planning and design of functional educational facilities, presently occurring at a far slower rate than that noted during the 1950s and 1960s, set the stage for better instruction and allow for including special learning experiences as well. It is one of the many ways the administrator fulfills the curriculum and instructional leadership and management roles.

Securing and protecting educational funds, the so-called "bonds" dimension of the cited previous criticism, are necessary for the procurement and retention of qualified teachers, for purchasing necessary instructional equipment, and so on. The school budget is the fiscal interpretation of the educational program because everything that is planned for a quality curriculum and an instructional program must be translated, sooner or later, into their dollars and cents equivalent.

Criticism is justified when facilities are planned and constructed and also budgets developed and accepted without regard to what goes on at the classroom level. This is an argument for control as well as involvement by professional educators in facilities and finance. The so-called buildings, bonds, and budgets represent significant resources for the fulfillment of comprehensive educational programs and that support the functions of teachers in the learning process.

A leader can be defined as one who knows where the organization is and should be headed, and also knows how to reach the targets. The content of the curriculum is related to the performance of public education in a democratic society, a society that may be experiencing unusual challenges both now and in the near future. An instructional leader must know, therefore, why the curriculum includes what it does and what needs changing.

The setting of objectives is the first step in instructional leadership. Knowing what kinds of learning experiences (curriculum) at what levels of human development can be attained by pupils to satisfy objectives is also a part of the total picture. Of no less significance is the ability to translate the objectives and the related curricular experiences into an effectively operating organizational pattern. The administrator must demonstrate a knowledge of objectives and curriculum, and also the competency to design and operate a system that will deliver these promises.

RESPONSIBILITY FOR CURRICULUM

The public school curriculum is far too important and complex to be the sole responsibility of only one agency. Involved in determining what should be taught and how it can be taught most effectively are the state department of education, classroom teachers, local school administrators working at various levels, and local boards of education.

Role of the State Education Agency

Responsibilities of the state education agency for curriculum planning, development, and change are:

1. Ensuring that a minimum educational program is available in all public schools of the state.
2. Sponsoring leadership and coordinating activities to bring together large numbers of persons with first-hand experience to plan state educational programs. Developing curriculum guides is preferred to specifying required courses of study prepared by a few people or a single specialist.
3. Employing supervisors or consultants in special subjects to improve general educational programs for schools in the state.
4. Organizing programs for continuous statewide evaluation of curriculum.
5. Planning changes and possible improvements in curriculum through development of workshops, conferences, meetings, and committees.
6. Sponsoring research and experimentation on curriculum as a means of promoting new ideas that could be of value to local school programs.

7. Selecting textbooks in those states in which the same textbooks are used throughout the state. In too many school systems a textbook is considered equivalent to the course of study, and, hence selection of textbooks has considerable influence on the educational experiences provided in local districts.[5]

Role of Local School Administrators

The local board of education is responsible for determining policies governing scope, sequence, continuity, and integration of the curriculum organization and for procuring resources necessary to realize goals. The superintendent, at the general administrative level, is concerned with executing these policies and organizing, coordinating, stimulating, and allocating human and material resources necessary to achieve curriculum and instructional goals. The central-office staff is responsible for coordinating curriculum study among teachers, organizing demonstrations on new methods of teaching, and supervising execution of teaching responsibilities. Principals have functions similar to those of central-office staff members, but confined to the building level. It would be difficult, however, for central-office staff and attendance-center administrators to realize their aspirations for curricular improvement without guidance and direction from superordinate officials who control allocation of necessary resources.

Superintendents and principals are generalists who look to curriculum specialists for data and counsel on, for example, strategies to be used in introduction of new learning experiences; elimination of nonrelevant content; and value of such developments as team teaching, nongrading of schools, or computer-assisted instruction.

Activities of administrators in curriculum programs include:

1. Stimulating staff members and others to study cooperatively new approaches to instructional improvement.

2. Helping staff members to become more skillful in research or problem solving in curriculum.
3. Providing staff members and others engaged in study and research with resources needed.
4. Obtaining from such study groups the kinds of information required for prudent decision making on changes in the curriculum, for allocation of various resources within the system, or for introduction of new approaches.

Curriculum planning and development is a continuous process, with activities becoming more intense as new data or situations warrant. In large systems, this may be the duty of the assistant superintendent in charge of curriculum or instruction; in others, of the director of elementary or secondary education; in still others, of a cabinet of principals or an individual principal or even an organization of classroom teachers.

Eye and Netzer placed the instructional leadership roles of principals and superintendents in a dynamic perspective related to the pressure of the times.[6] In the most definitive statement yet, these writers called for development of valid indicators of instructional improvements that went beyond the usually laudatory self-appraisal of projects and accumulation of new but seldom used curriculum reports.

CLASSIFICATION SCHEMES FOR EDUCATIONAL EXPERIENCES

What the task of the schools should be has been debated for thousands of years. Technology and science, the knowledge explosion, and the social revolution have complicated issues and intensified debate. Even if there were agreement on "what knowledge is of most worth" or what function deserves the highest priority, only part of the many difficulties would be solved. Purposes are important, but may be expressed in terms so general as to fail to reveal precisely the practical ways of achieving them. Identifying specific learning experiences to be provided from a statement of general objectives is a difficult task. After a pattern of courses is determined, the specific problems related to each instructional field must still be solved.[7]

Educational programs or fields of study must be systematically organized and then scheduled to be completed by the learner over a given period of time. Taba[8] declared that scope, sequence, continuity, and integration are central problems of curriculum organization. The most widely used curriculum-classification schemes are based on (1) subjects, (2) broad fields, (3) problems or areas of living, and (4) experiences.[9] Other patterns, such as the programmatic curriculum format, may yet emerge.

The Subject Curriculum

The traditional and prevailing pattern defines educational experiences in terms of subjects, or categories of knowledge or skills, arranged in a particular sequence and with a defined scope for the purpose of teaching.

The traditional emphasis in curriculum can be stated succinctly as "teach the disciplines." Those opposed to a broad or comprehensive set of learning experiences within the public schools rally around the "back to basics" slogan. This translates into emphasizing intellectual and cognitive development of learners to the limitation or exclusion of other personal, social, or vocational needs for students with greatly varying abilities, interests, and cultural backgrounds. The so-called basics never left the school curriculum; more experiences were added to educational programs to cope with the wide range of learners that come to public schools. The so-called subject matter-oriented curriculum emphasizes the pursuit of knowledge in readily understood packages and labels or the transmission of the great cultural heritage. Taba indicated that "part of the philosophy of subject organization is that there is a hierarchy of priority among the subjects according to their value as mental disciplines."[10]

Thus, there are "hard" or "soft" courses. Some are called "solid" subjects. Implied is the repudiated notion that certain, difficult-to-learn subject matter actually "toughens" or sharpens the human mind or ability to think.

Despite its shortcomings, the subject pattern continues to be the most popular because of certain practical advantages: It is backed by long tradition, it makes the counting of educational progress clearer, and it is related to teacher training. Much of the current curriculum reform, particularly that sponsored by the National Science Foundation, focuses on the revitalization or increased relevancy of the subject matter content to produce the "new" mathematics, science, social studies, and so on. It is a laudable effort, but it cannot claim to be a radical departure from the traditional curriculum of subject matter.

The Broad-Fields Curriculum

A reaction to and significant departure from the compartmentalization (or fragmentation) of the store of human knowledge and skills into discrete and artificial subjects or courses, with either the "old" or "new" and more relevant subject matter content, led to the broad-fields classification for educational experiences. This pattern emphasizes correlation among subjects to permit greater integration of substantive knowledge. Correlation is more easily accomplished if the identity of the subjects related to each other is maintained; thus, American history as a subject can be correlated with American literature. This approach is feasible in the self-contained, or undepartmentalized, elementary school classroom, where one teacher teaches both subjects. In the departmentalized secondary school, where two or more instructors teach these subjects, correlation is more difficult to operationalize. The broad-fields classification is, in effect, a modification of the subject organization. The difference between the two is one of comprehensiveness of the division of knowledge and skills for purposes of teaching geography, history, sociology, and economics.[11] High school biology is a fusion of botany, zoology, anatomy, physiology, and other life-science subjects.

Only when the field becomes so broad that the subject content is not readily identifiable or when too many subjects are being fused is debate stimulated. Such terms as *social living* or *senior science* create "curriculum conglomerates" that may precipitate controversy and resistance.

The Areas-of-Living Curriculum

Organization of school studies on the basis of problems or areas of living is a radical departure from the traditional subdivisions of the curriculum. Learning experiences are grouped on the basis of human needs, such as selecting and preparing for an occupation, selecting a mate and getting ready for marriage, developing skills for more effective human relations, and becoming an effective citizen. Proponents argue that the areas-of-living curriculum is intimately related to the pupil's day-to-day life pattern. It is also closely related to Herbert Spencer's categories of common features of life in any culture.

The pattern represents a shift from a classification designed for the convenience of scholars and teachers to a classification directed to the learner. The pattern is difficult to implement, due primarily to the traditional teacher-oriented outlook and secondarily to the difficulty of deciding whether problems to be discussed should be selected by adults or learners.

The Experience Curriculum

The experience curriculum is a long distance away from the traditional curriculum-classification schemes. The curriculum is conceived as a series of experiences which are not fixed; hence, the experience curriculum is said to be "in a continuous process of development in which the learner participates."[12] For these reasons, this classification is called the "emerging" curriculum. The vagueness and elusiveness of the terms *experience, interaction,* and *improvement of human growth* make definition and illustrations of the emerging curriculum difficult.

Programmatic Curriculum

Learning experiences may be organized around realization of a set of specific outcomes. A program may be defined as a set of activities related to the fulfillment of certain objectives; hence the name "programmatic curriculum." In this curriculum format, the clustering of learning experiences is by objectives to be achieved rather than by the more traditional subject matter to be learned. The profession has been flirting with this concept under the guise of the instructional objectives approach to stimulating learning. It bears a kinship to and would facilitate the implementation of program budgeting and management-by-objectives-and-results. It could be called instruction-by-objectives-and-results.

The Core Curriculum

During the 1930s the term *core curriculum* or *core classes* came into popular usage. Unfortunately, it acquired several unrelated definitions, such as (1) the required subjects in a program of studies, (2) any high school class combining two or more subjects, and (3) "common learnings organized not around subjects, but around common problems and needs of children and youths regardless of subject lines."[13] The last definition is accepted in this volume. The nature of the core curriculum can be understood from the following list:

1. It seeks to establish relations among areas of living by the study of problems that challenge the pupil to explore and utilize the knowledge and skills of more than one subject.
2. It aims at larger objectives than would characterize any single subject area.
3. It involves the joint planning of those objectives, and of means of achieving them, by both teachers and pupils.
4. It requires a block of time longer than the traditional period.
5. It involves either a single teacher for two or more periods or a team of teachers who work together.
6. It is dedicated to improved guidance of individuals and groups of pupils.

7. Its basic emphasis in instructional planning is the present psychobiological and social needs of the pupils themselves.[14]

The core curriculum has had a brief but stormy history. Its death knell has sounded many times, but it continues to resurface somewhere every now and then. The success of the core approach in some places cannot be denied. One writer claimed that the "most damaging one-two punch to the existence of core programs is the combination of the Conant reports and the current emphasis on college-preparatory secondary school programs."[15]

The core curriculum may be revived in the 1980s as an integral part of efforts to individualize instruction.

THE HUMANISTIC CURRICULUM

The 1970s saw a new or renewed emphasis on the humanistic school based on a humanistic curriculum. The learning activities are designed to focus on person-centered values; self-growth and self-learning are major missions. The individualization of the school program is seen as one way to achieve a humanistic school that looks to people and not inanimate subject matter.

This was a theme sounded by Dewey and his followers early in this century. The revival was more in the form of discussions and publications describing its substance and merits rather than in operational interpretations.

FACTORS STIMULATING CURRICULUM CHANGE IN THE PUBLIC SCHOOLS

Although the subject matter curriculum format continues to dominate and survives recent and past curriculum "reforms," there have been and probably will continue to be "internal" modifications within that format. Hardly a decade passes without some course being added, dropped, or substantially modified in an effort to better meet the needs of elementary or sec-

ondary school students. Shifts in grade level for essentially the same subject also occur; for example, biology has moved from the tenth to ninth grade, algebra moved from tenth to ninth and even eighth grade in some cases, reading-readiness may be at the kindergarten level rather than first grade, and calculus is now found in some high schools as well as universities.

Developments in science and other fields often trigger a change in subject matter content of some courses or in the emphasis attached to various topics. Nuclear physics, space exploration, gene splicing, and so on, have had a significant impact on the teaching of science and mathematics. It is not unusual that there is examination of a curriculum change about a decade or so after it occurred; witness the reactions to SMSG mathematics.

Content changes were less frequent outside the sciences and mathematics. Nonetheless, more emphasis was sought during the 1970s on teaching writing and composition skills in English classes as well as literature. More foreign language classes may be found at the elementary school level, apart from the bilingual-bicultural concerns. In short, practically every subject matter course has been or is presently undergoing some degree of study and modification.

The format and the substance of the school curriculum are not controlled by professionals in education, much less educational administrators acting alone; nor are changes always limited to rational arguments or careful evidence that supports such changes. Politics or public policies of the moment as expressed by some social movement, financial crisis, or political upheaval may speed up or prevent some significant curricular changes. The launching of the "Sputnik" by the Russians was a powerful stimulus for changes in the amount and content of science and mathematics instruction. Social movements brought "black history," "Chicano studies," "women studies," and bilingual-bicultural education into the public schools. Goodlad noted that "Curriculum planning is a political process. . . . Proposals either find their way to the political structure in educational institutions or slip into obscurity."[16] Curriculum leadership must be sensitive to the political dimensions of curriculum reform; perceptions by parents and the public often determine the fate of a curriculum or instructional change. At present the enthusiasm for curricular change remains high, but interest in the evaluation of such changes remains relatively low as well.

Goodlad reported at least three different weaknesses following his survey of the current curriculum-reform efforts:

1. Program development in social sciences, humanities, especially the arts, health and physical education is as yet only embryonic at both elementary and secondary levels.
2. Many subjects that could be included in the curriculum are not included as part of the reform efforts.
3. There is an absence of experimental effort to fit together the various subjects or combinations of subjects into a reasonably unified curriculum.[17]

Present curriculum-reform efforts are far more conservative than those noted during early parts of this century. The traditional subject matter mold is assumed, and no radical curriculum reorganizations are being recommended.

Changes in the curriculum influence the size and design of school buildings, the number and type of personnel to be employed, the size of the budget, and the means of financing schools. Unless the administrator gives primacy to matters of curriculum, classrooms may fail to function because of being based on an outmoded concept of teaching, instructors may be employed who lack the ability to teach pupils to meet the problems of today's world, or budgets may be planned for educational experiences of another era.

NEW METHODS FOR PROGRAM DEVELOPMENT

A variety of new agencies at the local, state, and federal level, along with private groups such as foundations, are required to produce the creative curricular and instructional innovations ca-pable of promoting more effective learning as well as learning in tune with the challenges of the time.

Regional Education Laboratories

The federally sponsored and supported regional education laboratories were created under Title 4 of the 1965 Elementary and Secondary Education Act (ESEA). Twenty regional laboratories were established by 1965; by 1973 less than half that number survived the many federal evaluations and budget cuts. The founding legislation specifies that the laboratories are to identify specific problems confronting public education today, conduct and coordinate research and research-related activities in problem areas, and disseminate finding for implementation in the schools.

The debate continues about the effectiveness and contributions of regional educational centers for the improvement of curriculum and instruction in the public schools. There is little uniformity of purpose or effort among centers. Financial problems worsened in the early 1980s; there are fewer operating centers than ever before and the continuing federal support for the centers during the remainder of the 1980s appears to be in doubt.

Pilot Programs

Curriculum and instructional leadership may be demonstrated by accepting the opportunity for the local district to serve as a pilot center to field test a promising set of strategies, instructional organization package, or other curriculum or instructional materials. There is a risk involved, for not everything will generate improved results and may heighten confusion or controversy within the district. On the other hand, the pilot program may work out so well that it becomes the first step in implementing curriculum and instructional innovations.

Alternative Schools

Reference was made earlier to the so-called free schools, street academies, and other alternatives to the established patterns of educational operations. They appeared to be having less acceptance by the end of the 1970s and into the early 1980s than noticed a decade earlier. Most were in competition with established school systems, although some were designed to operate within an established district. Those within existing school systems were most often inclined to emphasize the "basics," college-preparatory programs, and stricter controls over student behavior through dress codes and honor systems. "Alternative" schools are easier to talk about than implement as something unique and productive over the long run. The survival rate following the first flush of enthusiasm and rhetorical promises of "something really different and better" is very low. The life span of specific alternatives outside existing public or private schools is even shorter. In 1982 there remained about 897 alternative education centers which represent about 1 percent of all public schools.

INSTRUCTIONAL ORGANIZATION OF THE ELEMENTARY SCHOOL DAY

The minimum length of the day is often specified in state laws, state department of education regulations, and general local school board policies. The number of hours in the elementary school day varies with grade level. Thus, kindergarten pupils attend only a half day, or from 2 to 2½ hours. Pupils in grades 1 through 3 attend for shorter periods than do pupils in grades 4 through 6; those in grades 7 and 8 attend for longer periods than those in grades 4 through 6. A study of urban school districts indicated that, nationally, 85 percent of elementary schools have a school day of between 5 and 6 hours.[18] No primary school pupils and few intermediate-grade pupils are in school longer than 6 hours. In general, it can be said that the length of the school day for pupils in grades 1 through 6 is 5½ hours; for those in grades 7 and 8 it is 6 hours. A change in the length of the school day is not likely, although there might be an increase in length of the school year.

Double sessions were common until their disappearance in all but a few districts in the 1970s. The abandoned elementary school was more of a symbol during the 1970s than the overcrowded school on double sessions.

ELEMENTARY SCHOOL CURRICULUM FORMATS

The elementary school curriculum includes seven broad subject fields: language arts, arithmetic, science, social studies, art, music, and health and physical education. The challenge confronting administrators at this level is how much time to allocate to each subject in order to achieve a balance relevant to individual learning and development. The curriculum and instruction priorities are revealed by the number of minutes per week allocated to each subject field and in each grade.

Reading comprehension and skill development appear to be granted the highest priority, particularly in the primary grades; more time during the school day is devoted to reading than to mathematics, science, and social studies combined. In grades K to 3 about 95 minutes per day are dedicated to reading, where the self-contained instructional organization prevails, compared with 41 minutes for mathematics, 17 for science, and 21 for social studies. The time allocations are different in grades 4 to 6 where 66 minutes of instruction per day are devoted to reading, 51 for mathematics, 21 for science, and 34 for social studies. Art, music, and physical education are allocated relatively less time and seldom are taught every day.

The grouping of pupils in a graded or nongraded (actually flexible grading) configuration as well as self-contained versus departmentalized instructional organization patterns was reviewed in a previous chapter. Although the grouping and grading of pupils was a controversial issue some 100 to 150 years ago, it is not presently considered to be a major administrative problem. The self-contained instructional organization, with some modifications, prevails in most elementary schools. In the modified (or enriched) self-contained classroom, specialists may teach art and music, but the general or regular classroom teacher instructs in most other subject areas, particularly the language arts (reading), arithmetic, and social studies. This may also be called the "partially departmentalized" plan. In this instructional organization, the pupils, usually during the second half of the school day or afternoon, move to various classrooms to receive instructions from special teachers of science, art, music, and physical education. More complete departmentalization, where each teacher is a specialist in one and no more than two subjects, is the usual plan of instruction for the seventh and eighth grades that may be part of an elementary school, junior high, or middle school. Over three-fourths of the schools with only grades K to 6 implement the self-contained (usually with some modification) instructional organization plan.

Curriculum changes influence instructional organization. Greater demands made upon the general elementary school teacher as a result of an enriched program of studies spur use of special teachers and stimulate creation of an instructional organization of a different type. Use of school-plant facilities at the elementary school level is affected by instructional patterns. Thus, departmentalization results in more efficient utilization of the school plant. At the primary school level, however, the maturity level of the pupils may necessitate special teachers coming to the classroom, rather than the elementary pupils moving to the special teachers. In other words, building utilization notwithstanding, a self-contained organization is more likely to create a desirable learning situation.

INSTRUCTIONAL MATERIALS

Administrative leadership carries the responsibility for obtaining and allocating instructional materials necessary to promote educational program development and student learning. The proliferation of instructional devices and aids has complicated the job greatly. Today there are FM radios, television, sound and color motion-picture projectors, slide projectors, teaching machines, and computers, as well as the traditional textbooks, maps, globes, charts, and models. The availability of federal funds during the past two decades greatly increased the amount of teaching materials available in the schools. Fewer federal dollars are likely to be available for such purchases during the 1980s.

Audiovisual Instructional Materials

The post-World War II era saw a veritable explosion in the purchase and use of audiovisual instructional materials in the public schools. Hundreds of thousands of 16-mm. motion-picture projectors and millions of films are owned or used by the schools. It is the unusual school that does not own or have access to such basic equipment and materials.

By the 1960s a number of the larger school districts owned and operated educational TV (ETV) stations and most others utilized the TV instructional programs. The typical ETV station is on the air an average of 71 hours per week. Videotape recorders that emerged in greater numbers during the 1970s further extended the use of ETV stations and regular TV station programs for instructional purposes. The relatively inexpensive videotape recorder may someday replace the projector as the most common piece of instructional equipment. The TV receiver found its way into practically all school buildings and many of them have more than one. A sizable inventory and substantial annual expenditures for this instructional material continue in most school districts without much question, for considerable experience has demonstrated their value.

Computers and Teaching Machines

The late 1970s and the early 1980s witnessed a tremendous expansion in the number of computers, more specifically microprocessors or microcomputers, used for instructional purposes. One source claimed there were more than 90,000 microcomputers in the schools by June 1982, that number would double by June

1983, and that 150,000 microcomputers per year would be purchased by schools by 1985.[19] A survey by Quality Educational Data, Inc. reported that 38.2 percent of school districts had microcomputers in 1981–1982 but 56.8 percent had them during 1982–1983, a 44.9 percent increase. The number of schools with microcomputers in 1982–1983 (30,859) was more than double that found in the previous year. By 1983, 27.4 percent of all elementary schools, 46.2 percent of all junior highs, and 62.5 percent of all senior highs used microcomputers. QED estimated that 115,000 microcomputers were purchased by school during 1982, a 32 percent increase over the previous year. The larger the enrollments the more likely it is that a district will have microcomputers.[20]

The greatly reduced cost and technological improvements speeded the introduction of microprocessors into the supply of instructional materials. These devices help students to know and use computers and also serve as teaching or learning machines for student knowledge and skill development. The primarily mechanical teaching machines have lost out to the computer-controlled instructional mechanisms. The computer will be to the last quarter of this century what the more familiar audiovisual devices were to the third quarter of the twentieth century.

Laboratory facilities

The laboratory approach to teaching has extended beyond the science courses. There is a growing demand for foreign language, as well as chemistry, biology, and physics laboratories. The laboratory approach might well be employed in social studies, English, and mathematics as well. The library is recognized by English and social studies teachers as a laboratory.

Library facilities

About 70 percent of the schools (nearly all the secondary, but less than half the elementary, schools) have centralized libraries serving about 75 percent of the pupils. Elementary school pupils use the public library and the mobile library more often than junior or senior high school pupils do. The major users of the library materials are English and social studies teachers, followed closely by science teachers.

Large systems are likely to have a paid librarian. Title II of ESEA provided funds for the improvement of school libraries in the years following 1966. In 1982 there were an estimated 6426 library services personnel. The library has been reconceptualized as the Instructional Materials Center (IMC) and has become an integral part of the educational process at all levels. The facilities have been attractively designed and made more functional.

Textbooks

The textbook continues to be an important part of the instructional program despite the proliferation of microcomputers and other instructional aids. The selection of textbooks is determined in different ways by various states and territories. Local school authorities in 27 states selected textbooks without recommendation or control from any state authority. In the remaining 23 states, the local school authority was required to select books from an approved list of texts adopted by a state committee, particularly if state dollars are to be used to buy texts. This pattern has not changed much during the past 20 years. State selection and adoption of public school textbooks are practiced in Alabama, Arizona, Arkansas, California, Florida, Georgia, Idaho, Indiana, Kentucky, Louisiana, Mississippi, Nevada, New Mexico, North Carolina, Oregon, Oklahoma, South Carolina, Tennessee, Texas, Utah, Virginia, and West Virginia.[21]

The shift from local and county to state adoption occurred between 1897 and 1927. In 1897, 21 states permitted local school districts to adopt textbooks, but by 1927 the number had dropped to 17. The number almost doubled after 1927.

Some of the arguments for statewide uniformity of textbook adoption are:

1. It ensures a uniform course of study.
2. Textbooks may be purchased at lower prices because of large orders.
3. The mobility of the population makes statewide uniformity of textbooks helpful for children who change school often.[22]

The arguments against statewide uniformity of textbook adoption are:

1. No state is a homogeneous unit, so neither uniform text nor uniform courses of study will satisfactorily apply to all districts.
2. The state text-adoption plan will stifle local initiative and irritate teachers.
3. State adoption involves long periods of time during which new and better books cannot be adopted.

A higher percent of elementary pupils have free texts (about 90 percent) as compared with secondary pupils (about 73 percent). Title II of the Elementary and Secondary Education Act accentuated this trend to free use of texts. Where the rental plan is used, the students pay a nominal fee. Philadelphia in 1818 was the first district to provide free textbooks to pupils. Massachusetts in 1848 was the first to have a statewide free textbook law for all public schools. All states except one have legislation which provides that a textbook must or may be furnished to students. Free textbooks are mandatory for some or all grades in 30 states and permissive in 18 others.

The fiscal crises facing schools mandated districts in some states to stretch out the life of a school text from about five years to seven or eight years prior to replacement. The average expenditures for school texts declined by about 30 percent during the period of 1966 to 1981.[23] One state put on spending restrictions, another delayed pending renewals, and a third delayed all textbook adoptions for 1981–1982. The delaying of textbook replacements resulted in the continued use of obsolete textbooks in many states.

State textbook lists are prepared by the state board of education, a state textbook-purchasing board, or a state textbook-selection committee. Ten states do not specify the number of texts in any given field that may be placed on the state approved list. One state has as many as ten texts in each field on the approved list and the local agencies may select one or all. Most states place five texts in one field on the approved list for local adoption. The multiple listing of texts is a recent development that has displaced the more traditional single textbook list.

During the 1970s and early 1980s the state textbook review committees examined books in terms of educational merit and also "legal compliance." The latter determines whether the books accorded "fair treatment" to women, minorities, the disabled, the elderly, and any other special social groups that may be inadvertently maligned in stories or subject content. There is a great deal more concern about the social content of books than ever before. Censorship propensities by some lay groups in some states compounded the long and difficult task of selecting school texts.

SUMMARY

Educational administrators are held accountable, at least in part, for the quality, quantity, and effective delivery of instructional services and the nature of the learning environment. The difficult challenge of instructional leadership is to influence learning at some distance away from where it transpires, when it is stimulated by others, and when other important challenges also confront the administrator. Insisting that the administrator teach a class or two contributes little to the realization of the many dimensions of instructional leadership and management. Educational facilities are translations of the school's curriculum into functional spaces arranged to facilitate instruction. The budget is the fiscal interpretation of the educational program. The so-called buildings, bonds, and budgets are resources essential to the fulfillment of educational programs and to support quality instruction by teachers.

Curriculum refers to all the educational experiences provided under the auspices of a school, including the scope and sequence of educational experiences as well as methods of teaching and instructional materials. Educational programs can be classified by subjects, by broad fields, by areas of living, and by experiences. Recent developments have given birth to the programmatic and to the humanistic curriculum.

The development of instructional materials is part of the instructional leadership responsibilities of the administrator. This includes providing adequate textbooks, supplies, and equipment as well as special devices such as audiovisual materials, microcomputers, and other so-called teaching machines. Over half of the school districts used microcomputers for instruction by 1982. Special facilities, such as libraries and laboratories, are larger aids for instruction. Very little change has occurred in state textbook-adoption patterns. The trend among the 32 states that now use the same textbooks statewide is toward the preparation of multiple listings of textbooks. Legal compliance, "fair treatment" of special groups, and social content are considered along with the educational merit of texts to be adopted.

NOTES

1. Edward A. Krug, *Curriculum Planning*, rev. ed., New York: Harper & Row, 1957, pp. 3–4.
2. Ibid.
3. Hilda Taba, *Curriculum Development*, New York: Harcourt Brace Jovanovich, 1962, p. 3.
4. T. M. Gilland, *The Origin and Development of the Power and Duties of the City Superintendent*, Chicago: University of Chicago Press, 1935, chap. 9.
5. Howard H. Cummings and Helen K. Makintosh, *Curriculum Responsibility of State Departments of Education*, U.S. Office of Education, Misc. No. 30, Washington, D.C.: GPO, 1958.
6. G. G. Eye and L. A. Netzer, *School Administration and Instruction*, Boston: Allyn and Bacon, 1969.
7. Krug, op. cit., p. 132.
8. Taba, op. cit., p. 382.
9. Krug, op. cit.
10. Taba, op. cit., p. 386.
11. Krug, op. cit., p. 105.
12. Ibid., p. 106.
13. Ibid., p. 108.
14. Roland C. Faunce and Nelson L. Bossing, *Developing the Core Curriculum*, Englewood Cliffs, N.J.: Prentice-Hall, 1951, pp. 8–9.
15. Earl W. Harmer, "Le Mort de Core?" *Phi Delta Kappan*, Vol. 42, No. 2, November 1960, p. 67.
16. J. I. Goodlad, *School Curriculum Reform in the United States*, New York: Fund for the Advancement of Education, 1964, pp. 10–11.
17. Ibid., section 3.
18. Stuart E. Dean, *Elementary School Administration and Organization*, Bulletin 1960, No. 11, U.S. Office of Education, Washington, D.C.: GPO, 1960, chap. 5.
19. Dan Watt, "Selling Micros To Schools," *Popular Computing*, February 1983, pp. 48–54. See also special issue of *Today's Education*, "Microcomputers in the Classroom," April–May 1982, p. 21, which gave a more conservative estimate of 52,-000 computers in the schools of which 60 percent were microcomputers, based on 1980 estimates.
20. Mimeographed data presentation sent to the writer by Jeanne Hayes, President, Quality Education Data, Inc.. Data based on telephone calls to every school district and intermediate unit.
21. See Nancy R. Needham, "Textbooks Under Fire," *NEA Today*, December 1982, pp. 4–5.
22. L. W. Burnett, "Schools Are Gaining in Battle Against State Control of Textbooks," *The Nation's Schools*, Vol. 45, No. 5, May 1950, pp. 49–50.
23. See: Carl Luty, "Tight Budgets Keep Outdated Texts In Use Past Normal 'Retirement' Age," *NEA Today*, December 1982, p. 5.

CHAPTER REVIEW QUESTIONS

1. Why is the curriculum of such importance to the administration of public education?
2. What is the role of the school board in curriculum planning and improvement?
3. How should a superintendent fulfill the instructional leader role? The building principal?
4. What are the characteristics of a core program?
5. What factors have compounded the problems of

providing instructional aids and materials for schools?
6. What are the advantages and disadvantages of the use of the same textbooks statewide?

7. What are the advantages and disadvantages of the following curriculum-classification schemes: (a) by subject, (b) by broad fields, (c) by areas of living, and (d) by experiences?

SELECTED REFERENCES

Needham, Nancy R., "Textbooks Under Fire," *NEA Today,* December 1982, pp. 4–5.

Taba, Hilda, *Curriculum Development,* New York: Harcourt Brace Jovanovich, 1962.

Tanner, D., and Tanner, L. W., *Curriculum Development,* 2nd ed., New York: Macmillan 1980, 776 pp.

Today's Education, "Microcomputers in the Classroom," April–May 1982.

VanTil, Wm., ed., *Issues in Secondary Education,* 75th Yearbook, Chicago: University of Chicago Press, 1976, 350 pp.

The School Administrator, "Annual Technology Issue," April 1983, pp. 1, 11–26, 33–34.

22

INSTRUCTIONAL LEADERSHIP AND MANAGEMENT: II. ORGANIZATION, TIME MANAGEMENT, AND LEARNING PROGRESS

Determining what is to be learned as defined in the school's curriculum precedes the development of instructional organization patterns as well as management of other facets of the teaching-learning process. Instructional management includes determining optimum class size for learning, designing time schedules for a day or year, developing marking systems to reflect the level of learning progress, and specifying learning promotion standards and policies.

Many factors in the learning process interact with each other to compound the problems of ascertaining the impact of a single variable, such as the instructional organizational pattern implemented, upon student learning or teacher performance. The crucial question in determining which instructional organization to adopt is: What is it that teachers or other instructional personnel can or cannot do better to realize educational objectives in one pattern as opposed to another? Those who seek to promote novel instructional patterns are quick to use phrases that carry the most favorable connotations (such as "enriching learning," "in-

dividualizing instruction," "education of the whole child," or "developing the humane school"). Rhetoric may be substituted, unfortunately, for hard data born of actual experiences.

News releases proclaim when an instructional mode is adopted; they, however, do a less adequate job of reporting discontinuance. In short, many are tried, but few endure. What exists represents an eclectic pattern of parts of many different organizations that withstood the test of harsh reality and really worked in practice.

The large numbers of learners who come to public schools with diverse abilities necessitate some type of grouping for purposes of instruction. The administrative challenge is how pupils of similar chronological age, or with other characteristics such as maturity or ability levels, are to be clustered and then assigned to the care of one or a team of teachers. How many are placed in a single group allocated to one or more teachers at about the same time is of no less importance. Of no less concern is what types of pupils shall be placed in what types of instructional centers, and how these instructional centers shall be articulated (related to each other) to produce a unified and effective educational and instructional system.

Time is an important factor in the learning process, and its effective management is a special concern of the administrator. The organization of the school year, scheduling of classes during a given semester or quarter, and allocation of periods during the school day to various subjects or activities are all parts of the time management challenges.

ORGANIZATION OF THE SCHOOL YEAR TO FACILITATE LEARNING AND INSTRUCTION

The length of the school year increased steadily during this and the previous century. The school year in 1869–1870 was only 132.2 days; in 1909–1910, 157.5 days; in 1929–1930, 172.7 days; and presently almost 180 (actually about 178.9) days. School terms during the 1700s and much of the 1800s were three- or four-months duration. Pupil attendance was even shorter during the early years of our educational history; less than 90 days per "school year" was common until about 1890. There was far more pupil vacation than "in-school" time until the twentieth century.

Demands for organized educational experiences during summer months were practically nonexistent in the beginning of the twentieth century. The traditional school calendar was molded when there was no shortage of teachers, when school facilities were not crowded, and when the pressures for quality education were not as intensive as they are today.[1]

There were exceptions to the relatively brief "school years" during the nineteenth century. Before 1840, schools in some cities were conducted almost all year round: Buffalo operated schools for 12 months, Baltimore and Cincinnati for 11 months, New York for 49 weeks, and Chicago for 48 weeks. The school year was divided into four terms of 12 weeks each, with 1 week of vacation at the end of each term. Gradually the pattern was altered to 1 week of vacation at Christmas, 1 week at Easter, and 2 weeks in summer. In the 75 years following 1840, cities gradually adjusted programs, shortened the school year, and increased the vacation period. At the same time rural areas, which held school primarily during the winter months (except for the very young), slowly lengthened the school year to approximate the shortened year in the cities. By 1915 most of the nation had a nine-month school year.[2] Between 1924 and 1931, again between 1947 and 1953, and again in the 1960s and 1970s interest in year-round school was renewed. Present year-round programs should not be confused with the nineteenth-century practices in some large urban school districts. The present year-round pattern results in a 12-month utilization of educational facilities, but students follow a staggered vacation and attendance format that result in no more than nine months of total attendance in any one "school year." It is more accurately titled the "staggered vacation" plan, but the "year-round" designation seems to be preferred.

Present-Day "Year-Round" School Plans

Interest in present-day "year-round," or extended year, school operations waxes and wanes in about seven- to ten-year cycles. It is much less common than the nine-or-ten-consecutive-months-of-attendance-plus-extended-summer-vacation-school-year, or traditional school year. Under the new or present-day year-round school the educational program and facilities are operational for about 52 weeks more (there are some vacation days when no one is actually in attendance at the school facility). Extended vacation periods that are briefer (from a few days to no more than three consecutive weeks) and more frequent are the distinguishing characteristics of student attendance in such plans. Continuous class attendance by a group of students lasts for a period of usually no more than nine consecutive weeks (45 school days) rather than the traditional nine consecutive months of instruction (broken up, of course, by brief intermittent vacation periods). The year-round plan is based on a school year of approximately 12 months divided into regular cycles of 45 days of school instruction followed by 15 days of vacation. The accumulated or total vacation days during the 12-month year for any pupil is pretty much the same as that for the traditional school year of 9 months plus an extended summer vacation; only the spacing and durations of vacation are different.

Teachers are employed usually for nine- or ten-month stints under both plans. The year-round plan calls for staggered vacation periods for teachers as well as students. It is the unusual teacher who teaches 12 consecutive months without an extended vacation; to do otherwise is to run the danger of "teacher burnout" within a few years.

The time span for the traditional school day remains much the same in present-day year-round operations. Students do not complete the necessary grade levels for elementary or high school graduation in a shorter period of time; the same amount of time is required to complete a diploma in the traditional and year-round operations. Usually about three-fourths of the total student body is occupied in formal instruction at any one time in the year-round schools. The advantage lies in more efficient school-plant utilization, particularly where new construction is not a feasible alternative for whatever reason, because about one-fourth more students can be accommodated within the same facility under this mode. By the same token air conditioning of facilities and greater energy utilization are part of the year-round costs of operation.

The enthusiasm of some devotees of year-round school calendars goes far beyond those cited thus far to claim improved pupil attendance, reduction of vandalism, and easier curriculum reform. Claims of the committed are not adequate substitutes for results based on disciplined and objective research.

During 1981–1982 while under litigation to reduce the number of inner city "racially isolated" schools, the Los Angeles City schools greatly increased the number of schools operating under the year-round calendar. Additional construction on inner city school sites was not acceptable to the Court, and cross-district busing of pupils from crowded inner city sites to underutilized school centers encountered other opposition. Considerable social protest erupted from some segments of the community opposed to mandatory pupil attendance at the year-round scheduled schools, particularly at those not air conditioned, but these disappeared after a few weeks. The majority of Los Angeles schools continued with the traditional calendar.

The following support the implementation of the year-round calendar for school operations:

1. It allows fuller utilization of school-plant facilities with less demand for new construction at specified sites.
2. It reduces certain unit operating costs, such as those for fixed charges and administration.
3. The staff could be utilized more fully.
4. Urban youngsters could be engaged in constructive programs during the summer.
5. Some nonacademic experiences, such as driver education and typing, could be moved to the summer, allowing more time for the pursuit of academic subjects during the year.

Student attendance periods during an extended or full 12-month school year calendar may follow any number of formats, limited only by the imagination of the designer. Saville outlined the major and specific year-round schedule formats as follows:

1. The Four Quarter Plan
   1.1 Standard four quarter
   1.2 Quadrimester
   1.3 Staggered quarters
2. The Trimester
   2.1 Standard Trimester
   2.2 Split Trimester
3. Summer School Program
   3.1 Extension of regular year (standard) (voluntary)
   3.2 Modified summer program
4. The Multiple Trails Program
5. The 45-15 Plan

6. Other Combinations
   6.1 Continuous Progress Plan
   6.2 Split Semester Plan[3]

The Four-Quarter Plan

The most frequently suggested year-round plan is the four-quarter system with rotating attendance. This is sometimes called the "staggered quarter plan" because vacations are staggered with a different group enjoying time off during each quarter. Each pupil spends only nine months attending classes. Teachers are employed for three or four quarters.

The first four-quarter plan with rotating attendance was put into operation in Bluffton, Indiana, in 1904 but was discontinued in 1915. Some systems employing this plan by 1925 were Gary, Indiana; Mason City, Iowa; Eveleth, Minnesota; Omaha, Nebraska; Albuquerque, New Mexico; Ardmore and Tulsa, Oklahoma; Ambridge and Aliquippa, Pennsylvania; Nashville, Tennessee; Amarillo and El Paso, Texas.

Under the standard quarter plan the school year is 48 weeks, as opposed to the more traditional 36 weeks. Each quarter may be called a quadrimester. If all four quarters are attended, a student could theoretically complete five traditional school years in three years. Most extended year programs were designed primarily for secondary schools.

The advantages claimed for the four-quarter plan with rotating attendance are:

1. Each child continues to receive as much instruction time as under the traditional school year, but theoretically 25 percent more pupils are cared for by approximately the same staff and with the same facilities.
2. A double shift or a shortened day is unnecessary.
3. Teachers have an opportunity for full-year employment and, therefore, better annual salaries, which should reduce teacher turnover.
4. Fewer books are needed at any one time.
5. Pupils have a better opportunity to make up lost work because of extended absence or failure since they can attend school an additional quarter.

6. The work of the pupil is evaluated more often and his progress is reported more frequently to his parents.[4]

The disadvantages inherent are:

1. Districts with relatively small enrollments would experience difficulty in registering equal numbers during each quarter.
2. Families with two or more children in school would want them all to attend school during the same quarters; relatively few would opt for long winter vacation periods or long summer school attendance.
3. Increased costs for air-conditioning installation and increased teacher salaries would reduce some of the claimed initial economies.
4. Additional community recreation programs would have to be scheduled and financed, such as the more traditional summer work opportunities and recreational or camping activities, during each quarter of the 12-month school year.
5. Student activities administration would be complicated under the staggered term approach.

The Trimester

The trimester of 14-weeks duration, roughly one-third of the 12-month year, has enjoyed less popularity and success. It is more likely to be implemented at the university level, but even here special problems are encountered with the summer trimester.

Summer Schools for Pupils and Summer Programs for Personnel

The voluntary summer school extension of the traditional school year has a long history, but its purposes have changed over time. Summer school was designed originally for students who experienced little or limited learning success during the regular traditional school year. It was a time for remedial work, repeating courses failed, or overcoming other special learning problems. It carried an undesirable stigma and was avoided by students whenever possible.

A more recent conceptualization of summer school, apart from the year-round plan, is as a time for learning enrichment for all learners—the bright and the average as well as the unsuccessful learners. Remedial and make-up work is a small part. The major emphasis is upon enrichment through advanced courses in the sciences, creative writing, music, and the crafts. Student driving opportunities are more likely to be available as well. In addition, there may be supervised recreation programs.

Enriched programs increased summer school attendance and helped ease the stigma attached to it. This pattern of year-round school operation demanded increased fiscal expenditures. The enriched summer school was one of the early casualties, with substantial curtailment if not elimination, during the severe fiscal crises that confronted public schools during the last half of the 1970s. Special tuition charges were assessed in some cases, but legal problems were encountered when this was tried.

Special professional development programs were available during summer vacations when most if not all students were away from school campuses. Teachers were paid additional salary for participation in an 8- or 12-week professional development program, but the opportunities were optional. Such summer programs for professional personnel added about 10 to 20 percent to the current expense budget and were likewise among the first to be eliminated during times of fiscal difficulties for the school district.

The 45-15 Plan of Year-Round Operations

The most highly publicized and most frequently implemented year-round operational plan by far is the 45-15 plan. It is a variation of the staggered-quarter plan; about a fourth of the students at any one time are on vacation. The duration of the vacation period at any one time is for 15 school days (3 weeks) rather than the full quarter of 60 school days (12 weeks). In short, the pupil attends for 45 school days (9 weeks) and has a 15 school day-vacation (3 weeks); this pattern is repeated four times during the total school year with 180 days of pupil school attendance.

It appears to be an acceptable alternate to double sessions rather than to the traditional school year in systems with adequate facilities.

The Economies of Year-Round School Operation

Johns reviewed the literature and research on the extended or year-round school calendar that developed during the 1960s.[5] He reported:

1. When initially installed such plans will increase school costs a maximum of 10 to 11 percent.
2. After a transition period there may be no increase or even a small reduction in costs while providing better quantity and quality of services.
3. Enrichment with no pupil acceleration may increase operating costs more than can be saved through more intensive building utilization.
4. If designed primarily to save classroom space, such plans will have a short life, for operating cost increases will exceed building cost decreases.
5. There will be no substantial increase in the number of districts operating in the extended year mode in the next ten years.

Major gains in the improvement in efficiency of school operations will come from improvements in the productivity of its professional work force, namely, teachers and administrators. Eighty-five percent of the school budget goes for personnel and it is there that the largest efficiency gains are to be made.

Energy and the School Calendar

The school calendar may be viewed as an instrument for conserving energy. An initial, but not long-lived, call for extensive conservation by schools as well as others followed the Arab Oil Embargo of October 1973. Many alternatives were proposed, including the closing down of schools during the harsh months of winter, but the duration of the near-panic was less than a year and there was little follow-through on most conservation proposals. Another energy scare appeared in 1978, but this time because of unusually high and rapidly increasing energy costs rather than shortages. The price increases leveled off (and declined for a while) during the oil glut of the early 1980s. Energy problems are predicted for the remainder of this century; whether they will be of sufficient severity and duration to prompt more serious energy-conservation practices in schools is open to question.

The year-round calendar may compound rather than alleviate school-energy conservation and energy cost reductions. When the facility must be in operation during periods of heavy heating and extensive cooling, then costs as well as utilization of fuel and electricity will be at their peaks.

The traditional calendar with starting time around Labor Day and termination shortly after Memorial Day was not set with the conservation of nonhuman energy and costs in mind. A winter energy-saving schedule for schools in climates experiencing severe winters would call for elimination of a spring recess (or long Easter vacation) because school operations during such usual recesses would demand nominal energy consumption. Long winter vacations during periods of the severest winter weather could help to conserve energy. Winter vacations would be shorter in warmer climates, and the concern for such schools would be the operation during times when the least amount of cooling would be demanded.

Another contingency plan would be a school calendar based on a four-day week and extending each day from the typical 6 to 6½ hours to 8½ hours. The important point is the total number of minutes of instruction per week and the total number of schools per academic year rather than the distribution in any fixed pattern. Schools could start as early as 8:30 A.M. and conclude as late as 5:00 P.M. when four-day weeks are employed. It may not be necessary to operate four-day weeks during the full nine or ten months of the total school term or academic year. Thus, an energy-saving schedule calling for a four-day week could operate between November 1 and March 1.

Reducing the number of buildings in use may

or may not be a viable alternative depending on whether the majority of students walk to buildings or are transported. Likewise, whether or not buildings are operating at capacity will determine whether this is a viable option.

Busing for school transportation may demand such adjustments as the use of shoestring routes, which call for students who live at the end of the route, or the shoestring, being selected as drivers. Fewer and larger capacity buses may also be needed. An administrative arrangement may be needed that requires pupils who live as much as two miles away to walk to school.

In short, events during 1973 and 1978 demonstrated the real need for energy crisis plans, generation of energy budgets, and more careful control of energy utilization within schools. The great variation in climatic conditions and the maturity of learners preclude setting up one plan for the nation. Emotional reactions are likely to be generated, as evidenced by what happened when the switch to daylight savings time during the winter months meant that pupils had to leave for school in the dark.

INSTRUCTIONAL ORGANIZATION PATTERNS

Grading and grouping of pupils within grades were introduced and reviewed from various perspectives in other chapters. The emphasis here will be on various efforts to overcome the more inflexible implementation of graded instructional organizations and the relationships between continuous-promotion policies, or no-failure systems, and grading of pupils. All pupils may be required to learn a specific quantity of subject matter information or a given level of skills (as determined by a teacher or as measured by objective and standardized tests) before being permitted to move up to the next grade level. This could result in a significant amount of nonpromotion or so-called pupil failure. Repeating a grade has been construed as a form of social punishment, which in turn may generate behavior problems and a propensity among students with learning problems to drop out of school to avoid the stigma of failure.

The educational and social consequences of student failure to learn in a rigidly implemented and interpreted graded-school instructional organization prompted many professional educators to search for alternatives. Some early efforts modified standards but did not eliminate grading. The St. Louis plan, introduced in 1868, sought to lessen grade rigidity by classifying students at six-week intervals. The Pueblo approach, in operation from 1888 to 1894, required all children to complete all grade levels, but allowed each to progress through the grades at own rate. The Gary plan was a continuation of the original platoon school and represented refinement of principles first tried out in Bluffton, Indiana in 1900. The Winnetka plan of 1919 provided enrichment opportunities in addition to commonly accepted elementary school studies; each pupil was allowed to progress at own rate through the standardized grades. The Burke approach of 1913 represented one of the earliest efforts to permit individual rates of progress in promotion. The Dalton contract system of 1919 permitted the student to move to another contract upon completion of requirements according to own rate of learning. The modern and more sophisticated development of the contract plan is known as Individually Prescribed Instruction (IPI) at the elementary level and "unipacks" at the secondary level. The Cooperative Group plan of 1930, a forerunner of the team-teaching approach, provided for a group of teachers to work together, each offering one part of the curriculum but all trying to coordinate efforts.

More recent efforts to overcome the educational and social problems generated by grading focused on what was called "nongrading" but is more accurately described as "flexible grading." The verb "to grade" means to classify according to some appropriate standard; in education it means to classify pupils for the enhancement and measurement of learning. There is the need to determine where a pupil is to start to learn to read, write, or cipher, and to ascertain whether any progress has been made in such learning. No proponent of the nongraded school recommends the distribution of pupils on the basis of pure chance from kindergarten to senior high school level. Proponents of the nongraded school prefer using the pupil's reading level rather than chronological age for classifying and grouping learners. All recognize the importance of some designation such as grades as a bench mark against which to measure progress.

After World War II, the term *nongraded* designated an organizational pattern first used in schools in Western Springs, Illinois, in 1936, and in the Maryland Avenue Elementary School in Milwaukee in 1942.[6] Goodlad and Anderson did much to stimulate the development of the nongraded instructional pattern for elementary schools.[7]

The lack of organizational uniformity among districts makes it difficult to ascertain when a school is or is not nongraded. Anderson in 1967 commented: "For all the publicity it has received, nongradedness apparently remains a somewhat nebulous, even confusing, concept."[8]

If the term *nongraded* were interpreted literally, not only would grade designation disappear from the classroom, but no books with graded designations, obvious or disguised, could be employed. If no standards are allowed in any educational activity, we can never know where a pupil is, much less how far the student progressed.

To some, nongrading is another name for a continuous-promotion, or no-failure, policy. Because promotion implies that a child must learn a given amount within a specified period of time (a semester or a school year) and failure suggests that a child has not learned the standard amount there can be neither promotion nor failure if no time limit is placed upon learning a certain amount or acquiring specific skills. A major idea behind what is called "criterion-referenced" evaluation is that evaluation of learning need not always be based on some predetermined norm but on whether a criterion level of performance has been satisfied. How long it takes to satisfy the criterion is not as relevant for pupils allowed to learn at their own rate. At some point, however, those who require five years to learn to read and cipher and those who acquire the same level of reading and ciphering in two or three years must be separated in different learning situations lest one impede the progress of the other.

There is a subtle difference between continuous promotion under flexible interpretation of grade norms in a graded school and continuous promotion in the nongraded school. In the nongraded school, there is no failure because a child works at own pace or within the confines of ability to learn. This works better in the primary and elementary grades than it does at the secondary school level. There is at least the implied assumption that any pupil may learn anything if given enough time and appropriate motivation. This premise is open to question. Very few people have the physiological makeup to run one mile in less than four minutes no matter how long or hard they practice; likewise, there may well be certain types of reasonings and specific intellectual skills that cannot be learned by individuals without the intellectual makeup to do so, no matter how long or hard they work.

This assumes present methods of instruction and insights into learning will prevail. Obviously, if new pharmacological, electrophysical, or electronic devices are generated to carry us beyond present knowledge, then new and higher standards will have to be used. Further research is needed to determine what human limitations are; there may be far fewer than presently suspected.

The no-failure policy in the graded school pattern is based on promotion whether or not the student has learned what is required within the allotted time. The justification is that social development would be inhibited if the pupil were not allowed to accompany peers into the next grade level. The problem is that at the next grade level it is assumed that pupils promoted for social reasons have achieved as much as those promoted for academic achievement, and instruction at the new grade level proceeds on that basis for all pupils. Thus, it is imperative that remedial programs be provided either during the summer or continuously during the year in the next grade.

CLASS SIZE AND ITS IMPACT ON INSTRUCTION AND LEARNING

Class size controversies swirl around the optimum numbers of pupils per teacher to achieve high levels of learning, the most effective levels of teacher performance, and most productive use of educational resources. Class size has been subjected to considerable research, with more attributed to this single instructional variable than can be justified by hard data. Interest in and publications on this topic showed no signs of abating during the 1970s and 1980s.

Unfortunately, the terms employed in debates going on for at least 100 years of recent educational history have lacked precision and this has further fueled the emotional arguments both pro and con. A "small class size" has been perceived by some writers as anything less than 40 students per class, whereas others think of it as being only 10 to 15 pupils per teacher. There are others who perceive "small" as being between these extremes; the 20 to 25 range is commonly cited as "small classes of desirable size." A similar problem is encountered in defining when classes become "too large" for a single teacher. Difficulties are compounded further in interpreting the research and writing on class size by:

1. The confusion related to the failure to differentiate between student–staff ratio and pupil–teacher ratio.
2. The fact that some teachers with so-called large classes may receive assistance from aides and other support personnel.
3. The fact that what is learned in a "large" as compared to a "small" class may not be of the same complexity for the students involved.
4. The fact that the learner characteristics are not always comparable.
5. The fact that the teaching styles, strategies, or competencies are not similar.
6. The fact that it is not always possible to isolate a single variable such as class size from other factors influencing learning outcomes.

In one of many recent and comprehensive research and other publications summaries on class size, the Educational Research Service concluded in 1978 that "research provides no clear-cut guidelines for an 'optimum' class size covering all types of students at all grade levels."[9]

In general, teachers and their state and national organizations call for "small" classes, usually defined as less than 30 per teacher with 20 to 25 as the preferred range. School boards and administrators are more sensitive to the relationship between class size and "budget size." They tend to question whether there is an optimum size that applies to all teachers and all groups of pupils, object to management being forced to bargain with teacher organizations on the class size issue, and prefer setting a goal of 25 pupils per teacher which could be moved upward if demanded by fiscal or other pressures.[10] "Large" classes appeared as an issue in some teacher strikes where there were 40 or more per teacher. The employment of an aide where enrollments exceeded 35 per class was usually sufficient to settle the "too large" issue.

Economic reality confronting public schools may be the most decisive determinant of class size. Teacher and also public opinion follow as forces likely to influence outcomes on this issue. The extreme positions of 40 or more as well as 10 or fewer per teacher are not likely to be the prevailing standards for pupils in the normal learning ranges. Fewer than 5 percent of the classes in 1980 had 40 or more per teacher. Classes in grades K to 3, for handicapped students and for others with special needs, are likely to be 20 or fewer.

Declining enrollments during the 1970s, rather than bargaining or any other factor, had the most significant impact upon elementary/-secondary student–teacher ratios. Enrollments declined faster than annual reductions in the teaching force. As a consequence, pupil–teacher ratio at the elementary school level fell to 21.3 by 1978 from 24.8 in the fall of 1969, and is projected to drop further to 18.9 during the 1980s. The ratio was even lower at the secondary school level, declining to 17.2 in 1978

compared with 20.0 in 1969, and 16.5 is projected by 1988.

The combined elementary/secondary student–teacher ratio in the 20 largest public school systems during 1978–1979 was 20.1 compared with the overall national ratio of 19.4. Considerable variation was noted. Thus, Detroit and Cleveland reported ratios of 25.6 and 23.8, respectively, representing the high side, whereas San Francisco with 16.1 and Boston with 16.9 were on the low side. There were state-by-state variations as well. Thus, the high side of statewide pupil–teacher ratios was 23.2 in Nevada and 24.6 for Utah, whereas the low side was 15.6 in Vermont and 16.2 in Wyoming during 1978–1979.

Reducing class size has significant fiscal and school-plant implications. Teacher salaries constitute the largest single item in the budget of a school district. Reducing the average size of classes by only one or two students may increase school budgets by tens of millions of dollars in the largest school districts and by hundreds of thousands of dollars in the smaller school districts.

SECONDARY SCHOOL PROGRAMS, ORGANIZATION, AND SCHEDULES

The comprehensiveness of the secondary school program and the number of grades within the secondary school organization increase the complexity of instructional programming or course scheduling. Prior to 1900 the secondary curriculum was limited, by and large, to English, mathematics, social studies, a few of the natural and physical sciences, and foreign languages. Commercial education, industrial arts, home economics, fine arts, and other non-college preparatory subjects were added by 1930. Extra class or cocurricular activities began around 1920 and increased rapidly after 1930. As high schools grew in size and complexity, guidance and counseling were added. Cafeteria, health services, and transportation were included as an integral part of a comprehensive program by no later than the 1940s.

In general, the history of the secondary school curriculum unfolded over time and revealed four major patterns:

1. The single fixed curriculum, in which all subjects are prescribed for all students.
2. The multiple curriculum, with two or more "tracks," each of which offers a sequence of subjects designed to help the student toward common as well as specific objectives.
3. The constants-with-variables curriculum, in which certain subjects are required of all students but other subjects may be selected.
4. Combination plans that include features of both the constants-with-variables and the multiple programs.[11]

Instructional Programming (Class Scheduling)

Instructional programming, or class scheduling, is the process of relating learning opportunities available to secondary school pupils enrolled and the instructional resources such as time, space, and instructional personnel. The objective is to enhance learning outcomes while making the most productive uses of resources essential to the learning process. The class schedule developed may facilitate or retard the realization of curriculum objectives. It is a means to an end rather than an end in itself.

The length of the typical secondary school day varies from 4½ to 7½ hours, with the median being 7 hours, including interclass intermissions and lunch period. The traditional program schedule was based on an eight-period day, with each period being 40- to 45-minutes duration. These relatively brief time periods generated instructional problems in such fields as physical education, industrial arts, and in academic subjects where laboratory work was essential. The advent of the supervised study movement also stimulated the adoption of longer but fewer class periods per day.

Today the typical secondary school class schedule consists of six or seven periods, of which one may be an activity period. The length varies, with the median being 53 minutes in junior or middle schools and 56 minutes in senior high schools. There is no inherent virtue in a 40-, 55-, or 65-minute period, a rotating or floating schedule over a set of fixed daily class periods, or in a modular schedule over one that is nonmodular. One schedule is superior to another to the extent it helps to enhance or facilitate the instructional process or to extend the number of learning opportunities available in the curriculum.

Modular Schedules

The computer was tapped initially during the 1960s to facilitate the design of school schedules with variable length periods during one or more school days. A basic time period of 10, 15, 20, or 30 minutes is selected as the unit or time module. Most such schedules are based on time modules of 15 or 20 minutes. The number of such basic time modules dedicated to instruction in a given subject during any given day may vary, that is, it is flexible from one day to the next. The titles of modular, flexible, or flexible modular schedules are derived from the fact that the scheduling of classes starts with a basic time module and that the number of modules in a given instructional period for a specific subject is not fixed or required to be precisely the same from one day to the next. In addition, there is no expectation that classes in all subjects will be taught every day of the week and for the same amount of time each day as designed in the more traditional secondary school schedules.

A specific illustration may facilitate understanding. A number of assumptions must be made to determine when the school day starts, when the day ends, and the length of the unit or basic time module. Assume a basic time module of 15 minutes, school starting time at 8 A.M., and dismissal at 3 P.M. The total school time would be seven clock hours of 60 minutes each, which translates into a 28-module day. If desired, a single subject could be scheduled for three modules (45 minutes) one day and five modules (75 minutes) the next day. The flexible schedule is often linked with the team-teaching approach and the rotating schedule discussed below. The issue is not whether it can be done; there exists technology in the form of hardware and several computer programs to create an extremely flexible schedule for instructional activities. The issue is whether it should be done and whether it is necessary to vary the length of the instructional period from one day to the next or one month to the next. There are some case histories that purport much "success" and superiority for the flexible modular type of scheduling. There are others who tried and then abandoned the approach. There is no well-designed research, which suggests that the flexible modular produces greater learning than other types of school scheduling.

Enthusiasm for the so-called innovative secondary school modular scheduling waned considerably during the 1970s and 1980s from the high points of the 1950s and 1960s. Considerably less writing was noted about scheduling during the 1970s, and that which did focused more on the problems encountered and difficulties experienced by some secondary principals who sought to implement modular schedules.

Other types of schedules. The rotating schedule is a variation of the six- or seven-period schedule with the innovation of alternating times when classes meet. Thus, period one meets during the first time slot during one week, the second time slot during the next week, the third time slot during the third week, and so on. Other periods are rotated so that the time slots each occupies are changed each week. The rotation of period meeting times may be done daily as well as weekly. Thus, if there are seven periods per day, the same period would be in the same time slot only on every seventh school day.

In the floating schedule one period during each day "floats," or is not convened each day. Thus, what starts out as a six-period schedule actually has only five class periods meeting each day. It permits five periods from 60 to 75 minutes to occupy a time schedule where six or more could convene. Variations of this schedule are shown in Tables 22.1 and 22.2.

Schedule Preparation Procedures

The following are the kinds of data and activities that are essential to schedule construction:

TABLE 22.1

HORIZONTAL VERSION OF THE FLOATING SCHEDULE: A WEEKLY CLASS SCHEDULE FOR A COLLEGE PREPARATORY SOPHOMORE

Time	Period	Monday	Tuesday	Wednesday	Thursday	Friday
65 min.	1	English 10 Rm. 108	English 10 Rm. 108	English 10 Rm. 108	English 10 Rm. 108	X-Pd.[a] Typing 10 Rm. 5
65 min.	2	German 10 Rm. 11	German 10 Rm. 11	German 10 Rm. 11	X-Pd.[a] Typing 10 Rm. 5	German 10 Rm. 11
65 min.	3	Plane Geom. 10 Rm. 203	Plane Geom. 10 Rm. 203	Z-Pd.[b]	Plane Geom. 10 Rm. 203	Plane Geom. 10 Rm. 203
65 min.	4	Biology 10 Rm. 115	X-Pd.[b] Typing 10 Rm. 5	Biology 10 Rm. 115	Biology 10 Rm. 115	Biology 10 Rm. 115
65 min.	5	X-Pd.[a] Typing 10 Rm. 5	World History 10 Rm. 103	World History 10 Rm. 103	World History 10 Rm. 103	World History 10 Rm. 103

[a]X-periods can be scheduled for the first or fifth period each day, if desired, to avoid interrupting extended periods.
[b]Z-period: First and third Wednesdays, science club; second Wednesday, assembly; and fourth Wednesday, class meeting or guidance.

1. Identify policies that may influence the schedule making.
2. Register students.
3. Determine courses or other educational experiences to be offered.
4. Determine student choices of subjects offered by grade, that is, enrollments in courses.
5. Compute number of sections needed in all courses with sizable enrollments.
6. Determine number of faculty needed and areas of expertise.
7. Assign faculty to courses and class sections.
8. Determine school day starting and ending time.
9. Determine instructional period or modules length in time and number per school day.
10. Identify rooms available for various classes.
11. Assign courses and teachers to available rooms.
12. Identify potential scheduling conflicts, that is, when two or more courses with one or a few sections desired by students that may be offered during the same period.
13. Resolve or minimize schedule conflicts or have students seek alternative choices when confronted by irreconcilable conflicts.
14. Construct preliminary schedule.
15. Try out schedule with shortened time period sessions.
16. Revise final schedule for the ensuing year.

Trends in scheduling. Trends in scheduling during the 1950s revealed that:

1. The schedule is no longer developed by an administrator only; the judgment and experience of all members of the staff are sought and used.

TABLE 22.2

VERTICAL VERSION OF THE FLOATING SCHEDULE[a]: A WEEKLY CLASS SCHEDULE FOR A NONCOLLEGE PREPARATORY STUDENT

Time	Period	Monday	Tuesday	Wednesday	Thursday	Friday
65 min.	1	Work Expr.	Work Expr.	Prob. of Democ. 12 Rm. 105	Short-hand 11 Rm. 3	X-Pd.[b] Phys. Ed. 12
65 min.	2	Work Expr.	Work Expr.	Prob. of Democ. 12 Rm. 105	X-Pd.[b] Chorus	English 12 Rm. 109
65 min.	3	Work Expr.	Work Expr.	Z-Pd.[c]	Short-hand 11 Rm. 3	English 12 Rm. 109
65 min.	4	Work Expr.	X-Pd.[b] Spanish 10 Rm. 13	Prob. of Democ. 12 Rm. 105	Short-hand 11 Rm. 3	English 12 Rm. 109
65 min.	5	X-Pd.[b] Spanish 10 Rm. 13	Work Expr.	Prob. of Democ. 12 Rm. 105	Short-hand 11 Rm. 3	English 12 Rm. 109

[a]The square pattern of the schedule facilitates a shift from horizontal position to vertical position. Pupils scheduled for work experience may be scheduled to work all day without interruption in the vertical plan. In such a schedule, the X-periods involved are either eliminated or rescheduled.
[b]X-periods: This pupil has chosen Spanish for 2 periods (120 minutes) per week, chorus for 1 period, and physical education for 1 period.
[c]Z-period: First and third Wednesdays, commercial club; second Wednesday, assembly; and fourth Wednesday, class meeting.

2. The traditional practice of scheduling each class to meet five times per week no longer confines the schedule maker. The floating period, the two-week cycle, and the "5 by 5" plan illustrate this trend. The last allows one class to meet in an all-day session, permitting long consecutive study of one project or participation in a lengthy field trip.

3. Two or more periods are often allotted for a given teaching situation. This is common practice in junior high school and its use is increasing in senior high school.

4. An increase in total length of the period, allowing more laboratory time or more study time with a given teacher is generally accepted as desirable.

5. The assignment of teachers to otherwise unscheduled classrooms is recommended as a temporary expediency for increasing building utilization.

6. The difficulty of feeding many students in a short time has stimulated much lunch-hour experimentation. Successive groups of classes are scheduled to the service area as facilities become vacant. Instead of several distinct lunch periods, there is a constant flow of students and teachers to keep facilities in constant use.

7. In large high schools a departmental program schedule is made through the leadership of the department chairman and then related to the total school program in order to avoid conflicts.

8. The large amount of clerical work involved in preparing a schedule, whether decentralized or not, is being simplified through use of punch cards or electronic equipment.[12]

The complexity of human learning defies attempts to control or improve it by manipulation of a single variable such as the sheer quantity of time devoted to learning; frequency of specific learning activities during the school day as dictated by a formal schedule; the division of the academic year into either quarters, trimesters, or semesters; or through more frequently interrupted consecutive learning periods through the staggered vacations that characterize the year-round school calendar. Prevailing preferences rather than research results determine the type of instructional programming that should be applied in a given secondary school.

There is relatively little evidence to support the notion that one type of scheduling or school calendar is far superior to all others.

Size of Instructional Centers

Most research on high school size has concentrated on minimums required to achieve a comprehensive program at a reasonable cost per pupil. Wright[13] summarized 18 research studies on high school size. Variables involved in determining optimum size were curricular offerings, extra class activities, staff qualifications, relations, and pupil achievement. The variety of curriculum offerings increased with enrollment up to approximately 2000 students. Beyond that point, there was duplication rather than more program variety. An enrollment of at least 1000 in a four-year high school was considered essential for a minimum variety in educational course offerings.

Some studies found little or no significant relation between pupil achievement and school size. Three reported that student achievement in school with a minimum enrollment of 500 was superior to that in schools with a smaller enrollment. There was general agreement that small schools provided greater pupil participation in extra class activities; the most active participants in extra class activities were pupils in schools of fewer than 300. Studies that considered school community, staff, and teacher-pupil relations recommended enrollments of 1200 to 1600.

The optimum size of the high school for all-around educational effectiveness appears to be less than 2000 pupils, but how much less is not clear.

In the past three or four decades there has been evidence of a movement away from the very large high school. The three largest high schools in 1934 enrolled more than 10,000 pupils each; three others had from 9000 to 10,-000 pupils each. No high school in 1946 had as many as 9000 pupils and not one in 1952 enrolled as many as 7000.

The "great high school," like the educational-park concept, appears to be more closely related to attempts to deal with social conditions within large urban areas than improvement of educational opportunities.

The 6-3-3 structural pattern was the dominant form until the 1970s. As reported earlier, the previous decade saw a shift back to the four-year senior high school. A two- or three-year junior high or middle school for early adolescents preceded the senior high school attendance center.

The very large high schools are introducing the school-within-a-school concept. Thus, one large high school of 4500 pupils on the same site organized three 1500-pupil units with each being given a special identity. It was one way to cope with the problem of school bigness where an individual pupil could be lost easily.

EVALUATION OF LEARNING AND PUPIL PROGRESS

National Education Assessment

National assessment of educational performance was one of the most actively debated issues in American education during the 1960s, but less so in the 1970s and 1980s. The major purpose of the national assessment project was to provide the lay public with censuslike data on educational levels for various sections of the population.

The national assessment did not focus on individual students, classrooms, schools, or school systems; it did not evaluate the effectiveness of a given teaching method or type of school or classroom organization.

Those opposed to national assessment were concerned that it really meant "national testing." Even though based on a sample in a given region, it could indict all schools and pupils, good or bad, within the area. Some felt that national testing would create a national curriculum. There would be a great likelihood that teachers would teach to help youngsters do well on the national tests of achievement. It was also feared by many that national assessment was a coverup for a whole host of nefarious purposes. Experience proved subsequently that the worst

did not happen, that is, there is no national curriculum now that can be blamed on national assessment, most teachers do not teach for these tests, and the testing has had comparatively little impact upon the public school curriculum or teaching. Much of the emotionalism that surrounded national assessment died down before the end of the 1970s.

Marking Systems

Pupil markings generally were based on a percentage system up to approximately 1920. After 1920 the percentage system began to be replaced by letters or other symbols representing a range of percentages. The ABCDF symbols, or their equivalent, remain based on the quantitative approach to marking. Percentage and letter marks are quite different from the descriptive system, which attempts to measure progress made in relation to the individual's ability. Descriptive systems are less easily interpreted by parents and other lay persons than are the quantitative systems.

Marks and reports on pupil progress were developed to inform parents, to enable school and home to work together, to motivate and stimulate learning, to form an administrative shorthand to measure learning, and to serve as a means of comparison among schools. Too much emphasis on marks as a means of stimulating or measuring learning can lead to student short cuts to good marks through such devices as cheating.

Studies of marking and report cards show considerable concern over the validity of marks and their lack of objective meaning. For example, the same English test, graded by 142 different teachers, received marks from 50 to 98 percent; the same history paper, examined by 70 teachers, was marked from 43 to 90 percent; a model-answer paper made by a teacher was awarded 40 to 90 percent by other teachers; and even the same geometry paper was scored from 28 to 90 percent.

School board policies on marking, reporting pupil progress to parents, as well as methods of maintaining permanent student records changed in response to new knowledge and experience as well as criticisms over the past 200 years. The development of new technologies such as the computer and microfiche record systems contributed much to new approaches. Not all the controversies and criticisms surrounding pupil marks and promotion policies have been stilled; nor is this ever likely to occur. During the 1970s over 50 percent of elementary schools and about 30 percent of secondary schools modified previously existing pupil grading, reporting, and promotion procedures. Such changes are expected to continue during the 1980s as well.

In the national study of prevailing student marking and reporting practices completed by the Educational Research Service during 1977, it was reported:[14]

1. For Kindergarten Students
   a. Over half the systems used a checklist or rating scale; only about 8.5 percent employed letter grades (A, B, C, etc.) or percentages as descriptors of learning progress. In 1966 (in contrast to 1977 data cited above), about 26 percent used letter grades on kindergarten reports to parents.
   b. Almost 78 percent held parent-teacher conferences, and about one-third had student-teacher conferences as well. In contrast, in 1966 about 66.5 percent had parent-teacher conferences.
   c. About 84 percent included separate ratings on behavior, work habits, citizenship, or other indicators of personal or nonacademic development.
   d. Only about 31 percent used pass/fail or satisfactory/unsatisfactory indicators of pupil progress on the report cards.
   e. Almost 56 percent issued pupil progress reports every 9 weeks.
2. Primary Grades (1–3)
   a. Not quite one-half (about 46 percent) had a checklist or rating scale; over 42 percent employed letter grades or percentages as descriptors of learning progress. In 1966, however, over three-fourths utilized letter grades, percentages, or similar "classified" scales.

   b. Almost 73 percent held parent-teacher conferences; about 34 percent also held pupil-teacher conferences on learning progress. In 1966, only 54 percent included parent-teacher conferences.
   c. Over 91 percent used separate ratings, as well as the above, on behavior, citizenship, etc.
   d. About 37 percent indicated a pass/fail or satisfactory/unsatisfactory on the report cards.
   e. Over 69 percent issued pupil progress reports every 9 weeks.
3. Upper Elementary Grades (4–6)
   a. Only about one-third used a checklist; about three-fourths employed letter grades or percentages as indicators of pupil learning progress. The current practice represents a drop from the 89 percent who implemented the letter grades or percentages.
   b. About 70 percent operated with parent-teacher conferences as well; less than a third held student-teacher meetings on learning progress. Back in 1966 only 46 percent held parent-teacher conferences.
   c. Over 92 percent also added separate rating scales for behavior development, etc.
   d. About one-fourth used indicators such as pass/fail, etc. on the report card.
   e. Again, the 9-week interval was the most popular for completing pupil progress reports; almost 70 percent did.
4. Junior High/Middle School
   a. Letter grades are most likely to be used at this level for indicating learning progress; almost 91 percent did so. (If number or percentage indicators were added, the total would exceed 100 percent for some used letters and numbers on the report card.) In 1966, about 92 percent employed letters, percentages, numbers, etc., to indicate learning quality.
   b. About 35 percent continued with pupil-teacher meetings; only 22 percent had pupil-teacher conferences as well. Less than 30 percent in 1966 held parent-teacher conferences.

    c. About 78 percent also continued with separate behavior rating scales at this level.

    d. Less than 20 percent utilized the pass/fail, etc., as progress indicators in place of letters or numbers.

    e. Over 70 percent reported pupil progress every 9 weeks.

5. Senior High School

    a. Ninety percent use letter grades and the remainder percentages or other numbers (instead of or along with letters) as the indicators of learning progress. This is similar to that noted in 1966 when 92 percent used letters or numbers for grades.

    b. Relatively few had parent-teacher conferences (less than 26 percent) and even fewer held student-teacher meetings (less than 22 percent).

    c. About 68 percent utilized separate behavior rating scales as well.

    d. About 23.5 percent employed the pass/fail, etc., method of indicating learning progress on report cards.

    e. Over two-thirds sent out reports every 9 weeks and about one-fourth every 6 weeks.

The so-called passing mark ranges from 60 to 75 percent for no apparent reason. "Marking on the curve" is not as uniform as it may appear. For example, in some systems, 3 percent of pupils receive As, in others, 7 percent, and in still others, 10 percent. In some systems, 50 percent of pupils receive Cs, in another, 38 percent, and in still others, 40 percent. The curve of normal distribution is derived from an adequate and representative sampling of a characteristic that is amenable to objective and precise measurement.

Marks can reflect achievement only or incorporate such ideas as effort, attitude, or neatness. Most schools consider only achievement in awarding grades. Some use a dual mark that includes two symbols such as a large letter with a small numerical subscript. The letter indicates achievement only, and the numerical subscript, attitudes such as effort.

Ability grouping compounds the problem of marking. Some students in high ability groups receive low marks when in competition with all mentally gifted pupils. These same students could have received much higher marks in a heterogeneous group.

Some school systems use the same letter but award a higher honor point-count for a B in sections of the gifted than for a B in regular sections. Thus, the honor point-count in regular section is A = 4 points, B = 3 points, C = 2 points, and D = 1 point; in gifted sections it is A = 5 points, B = 4 points, C = 3 points, and D = 2 points.

Promotion and Failure

Current thought on pupil failure and nonpromotion in the elementary grades is as follows:

1. Since 1900 there has been a decrease in the rate of pupil failure leading to repetition of a course of study.
2. Threats of failure do not necessarily motivate children to work harder.
3. Nonpromotion and subsequent repetition of the subject do not always increase mastery of subject matter.
4. The fact that boys fail more often than girls, despite insignificant differences in scores on intelligence and achievement tests, raises the question whether promotion is based on factors other than academic achievement, such as deportment and neatness of written work.
5. Failure of an individual pupil is usually caused by a number of factors sometimes beyond his control.[15]

Nonpromotion in elementary schools dropped from approximately 16 percent in 1909 to about 5 percent in 1949. Most failures in elementary school occurred in the first grade, and the next most in the second grade. The fewest failures were in the eighth grade. The situation was alleviated somewhat when under-age children were prevented from entering, because these pupils experienced the greatest difficulty in learning. At present almost all systems report that a very high percent of pupils in each of the first two grades are promoted at the end of each year; in many districts the rate of promotion is somewhat lower in grade 1 than other grades. A prominent reason for demanding repetition of a grade is irregular attendance.

The "modal grade" is defined as the level in which most children or adolescents of a given age range are likely to placed in a school. Those older than the majority in a modal grade can be assumed to have repeated one or more grades. By 1950 almost 7 percent of all 8-year-olds were found to be below their expected or modal grade level. This percentage increased with each successive age group so that by age 15 about 26 percent were enrolled below their modal grade. The data for 16- and 17-year-olds are less meaningful because of the propensity of this age group to drop out of school.

Nonpromotion declined in public schools over the next 25 years following 1950. In 1976 only 10 percent, compared with 26 percent about 25 years earlier, of 15-year-olds were enrolled below the modal grade. Schools provided remedial classes, operated summer schools, and increased counseling services to help reduce the incidence of nonpromotion and dropouts. According to the U.S. Department of Education "changes within school systems between 1950 and 1976 were in large part responsible for the decrease in the number of children enrolled below the modal grade."[16] There are data which infer that such factors as level of family income, education level of parents, sex, racial-ethnic backgrounds, and region of residence are related to the progress of a pupil through school with the modal group and to persist until high school graduation.

Early studies of the rates of failure in secondary schools showed the range to be from 2 percent in one school to 80 percent in another; more recent data showed the range to be only 0.02 per cent to 10.6 percent. Promotions at the end of a quarter or semester rather than the end of the full year were instituted to reduce the impact of failure. This worked well for secondary school subjects but was too cumbersome at the elementary school level. By 1948, 93 percent of public school systems returned or continued to operate with annual elementary school promotions.

Continuous-Promotion Policies and Practices

The continuous-promotion policy is based on the concept that success is a better regulator of conduct and learning motivator than failure. Failure often leads to frustration rather than the desire to perform more effectively. Thus, data indicate that elementary pupils not promoted one or more times were rated by both teachers and pupil peers as having more undesirable personality and behavior traits than do regularly promoted students.

Continuous-promotion policies work best if there is understanding of and adjustments for the following:

1. Some teachers can only motivate learning through the constant fear of failure for those "who don't study." Such teachers must be helped to acquire alternative motivation strategies before implementing continuous-promotion policies.
2. The curriculum must be adapted to the needs, interests, and abilities of pupils served.
3. Formal and continuing remedial programs are essential.
4. Smaller classes, definitely less than 30 per teacher, are necessary.
5. There must be a formal program of public information about the advantages of and adjustments used in continuous-promotion policies if community resistance and conflicts are to be minimized.

MINIMUM COMPETENCY TESTING FOR GRADUATION

During recent decades, most high schools increased requirements in mathematics, science, English, and social studies as one set of conditions for graduation from high school. Most of the nation's high schools offer only one type of diploma. Some offer a certificate of attendance for those members of the graduating class who are unable to meet the requirements for this diploma.

The 1970s saw the development of minimum competency testing for teacher certification as well as student promotion and high school graduation. Such testing of students was a negative reaction to the "social promotion" concept in which the adolescent is promoted with peers, even though intellectual achievements would not warrant it, as well as to the issuance of "certificates of high school attendance" in lieu of the high school diploma based on academic standards. Legislation was approved in 38 states by 1980 requiring minimum competency testing of pupils and "was passed in an atmosphere of declining test scores on national assessments and college entrance exams . . . and during a period when many people were demanding a return to basic skills instruction."[17]

It is difficult to ascertain as yet the full effects of such legislation in view of the fact that the starting date for testing was 1980 or later. In addition, there is relatively little uniformity in the nature of the testing, what basic competencies were to be evaluated, and how competency standards would be determined and implemented in schools. The state department of education, or state board, is assigned responsibility for setting competency standards for grade levels in slightly more than one-half the states. This function is shared with local agencies in about 20 percent of the states.

The most frequent application is in secondary schools and focuses on graduation from high school. Although about 25 percent of high school seniors were required to pass a minimum competency test to qualify for graduation, five states specifically prohibited the use of such testing for determination of graduation or promotion. About 42 percent of states in the West, 36 percent in the Northeast, and 23 percent in the South require competency testing for graduation, but less than 7 percent of the states in the Midwest do so.

Indications show a slowing of enthusiasm for minimum competency testing for students as evidenced by the fact that all such legislation, with the exception of two states, was approved prior to 1979. The jury is still out on its workability and legality. There have been several legal challenges to minimum competency testing where it was used to deny a high school diploma to a student who satisfied all other requirements for graduation. Such testing generates a tremendous amount of paperwork. Its application to the handicapped learner or one with special needs is not clear.

Some relate the minimum competency efforts to a more conservative swing in the population and the "back to basics." The so-called basics never left the curriculum; a more accurate statement would be increased emphasis on basics even if this means eliminating time and courses devoted to personal growth experiences, vocational or career education, the visual or musical arts, and so on. The implementation of the impressive phrase "Education for all" will continue to generate much controversy in the operation of a system of public education.

Inflation in the grades awarded students generated much concern during the 1970s within universities as well as secondary schools. Grade inflations between 1972 and 1980 were relatively low in public high schools as compared with private secondary schools. Thus, the percent of public high school seniors receiving As and Bs increased from 28.4 in 1972 to 32.5 in 1980; whereas Catholic high school seniors increased from 37.2 percent in 1972 to 38.6 percent, and seniors in other private high schools jumped from 23.7 percent receiving As and Bs in 1972 to 41.6 percent in 1980. Those receiving grades of D or lower were about 1 percent of the seniors and almost 4 percent of the sophomores, with public schools awarding more of these low grades than private schools. Grades awarded to sophomores in 1980 were lower than those for seniors.[18]

PERFORMANCE CONTRACTING FOR INSTRUCTIONAL SERVICES

During the 1960s experiments were designed to determine if the instructional responsibilities, traditionally the most important challenge confronting a school, could be better discharged by agencies in the private sector by employing special contractors who would be paid according to how much the pupils actually learned. Teachers are employed typically under a contract calling for performance of specified services over a given period of time without regard to actual learning outcomes. The so-called performance contract for instructional services is actually a variable payment contract with the payment scale increased or decreased according to how much pupils actually learned.

Results reported and audited in the early 1970s demonstrated that the highly publicized claims of private contractors could not be translated into results. More was promised than could be delivered. Much less is heard now about performance contracting as a viable alternative for instructional leaders. Nonetheless, under special conditions the concept may prove to be worthy of further considerations. Performance contracting served to place the focus on learning outcomes rather than simply on inputs such as teacher salaries or books.

SUMMARY

Instructional organization is a means for the enhancement of learning and the most productive use of instructional resources. There is relatively little evidence to indicate whether this variable has more, equal, or less impact than other variables influencing the teaching-learning process.

Time management is another important factor which includes determination of the school year and developing the daily schedule. It took about a century for the school year to increase from about 132 school days per year to almost 180 days, which continues to be the present length.

The year-round school idea is debated anew, but it is not a new concept. Some variations are the four-quarter year with rotating attendance, the 48-week school year, 45–15 plan, and summer school.

Summer sessions have been broadened to include remedial work, developing avocational interests, enriching educational experiences, and providing special opportunities for study on the part of professional staff members.

The length of the typical elementary school day is between 5½ and 6 hours. The typical school day for the secondary school is approximately 7 hours. Most elementary grades (1 through 6) are nondepartmentalized, whereas most junior and senior high schools follow departmentalized programs. Rigid interpretation of grading generated educational and social problems that led to the search for alternatives such as nongrading, which is better called flexible grading. The pupil's reading level may be used more often than chronological age for purposes of classifying and grouping learners in the nongraded school. There are similarities and subtle differences between continuous promotion and flexible interpretation of grade norms in the nongraded school.

The issue of class size continues to generate controversy, and research has not provided the answer to optimum class size as yet. Declining enrollments helped to reduce pupil–teacher ratios, but there continue to be wide variations in such ratios from school to school and state to state. The extreme position of 40 or more and the opposite extreme of 10 or less are not likely to be the prevailing class size standards; the present level is less than 20 per teacher.

Instructional programming or scheduling relates available learning opportunities with resources such as time, space, and instructional personnel. Enthusiasm for innovative schedules such as the flexible, modular, and floating schedules waned considerably during the 1970s.

National assessment of educational performance stirred much controversy during the 1960s, but much of the emotionalism around this issue died down by the end of the 1970s. It helped to stimulate the minimum competency testing for pupil promotion and graduation that became law in 38 states by 1980. The jury is still out on the workability and legality of such testing. Pupil marking has moved away from percentage marks to letter grades plus more emphasis on description of student growth and development. The nonpromotion rate in public schools has declined, with a higher percent of students found in the modal grade. Grade inflation was less severe in public high schools than in private ones during the 1970s.

NOTES

1. American Association of School Administrators, Year-Round School, Washington, D.C.: The Association, 1960.
2. National Education Association, "All-Year School," Research Memo, 1958-7, Washington, D.C.: The Association, 1958.
3. A. Saville, Instructional Programming, Columbus, Ohio: Chas. E. Merrill, 1973, p. 178.
4. Ibid., and American Association of School Administrators, op. cit.
5. R. L. Johns et al., Dimensions of Educational Need, Gainesville, Fla.: National Educational Finance Project, 1969, pp. 203–204.
6. R. I. Miller, ed., The Nongraded School, New York: Harper & Row, 1967, pp. 3–5.
7. J. I. Goodlad and R. H. Anderson, The Nongraded Elementary School, New York: Harcourt Brace Jovanovich, 1963.
8. R. H. Anderson, "The Nongraded School: An Overview," The National Elementary Principal, vol. 47, no. 2, November 1967, pp. 4–10.
9. Educational Research Service, "Class Size, a Summary of Research," ERS Research Brief, Arlington, Va.: ERS, 1978, 84 pp.
10. Educational Research Service, "Negotiating the Class Size Issue," ERS Negotiation Aid for School Management, Arlington, Va.: ERS, 1978, 93 pp.
11. William G. Brink, "Secondary Education Programs," in Harris, ed., Encyclopedia of Educational Research, 3rd ed., New York: Macmillan, 1960, p. 1262.
12. American Association of School Administrators, The High School in a Changing World, 36th Yearbook, Washington, D.C.: The Association, 1958, pp. 202–203.
13. Grace S. Wright, Enrollment Size and Educational Effectiveness of the High School, U.S. Office of Education, Circular No. 732, Washington, D.C.: GPO, 1964.
14. Educational Research Service, "Reporting Pupil Progress: Policies, Procedures, and Systems," ERS Report, Arlington, Va.: ERS, 1977, 115 pp.
15. National Education Association, "Pupil Failure and Non-Promotion," Research Bulletin, Vol. 37, No. 1, February 1959, pp. 16–17.
16. N. B. Dearman and V. W. Plisko, eds., The Condition of Education 1979 Edition, National Center for Education Statistics, Washington, D.C.: GPO, 1979, p. 46.
17. N. B. Dearman and V. W. Plisko, eds., The Condition of Education 1982 edition, Washington, D.C.: GPO, 1982, p. 41.
18. Ibid., p. 76.

CHAPTER REVIEW QUESTIONS

1. Why is the design of an instructional organization important in administration?
2. What are the essential elements of the nongraded school?
3. Trace the history of significant efforts aimed at overcoming rigidity in the implementation of the graded school pattern.
4. What are the advantages and disadvantages of year-round school operation?
5. What is flexible scheduling?
6. What is the difference between the no-failure policy in nongraded and graded schools?
7. What is meant by national assessment of education?
8. What are the major problems likely to be encountered in the implementation of mandated minimum competency testing for graduation or promotion?

SELECTED REFERENCES

Anderson, R. H., "The Nongraded School: An Overview," The National Elementary Principal, Vol. 47, No. 2, November 1967, pp. 4–10.
Carbone, R. F., "A Comparison of Graded and Nongraded Elementary Schools," The Elementary School Journal, Vol. 62, No. 2, November 1961, pp. 82–88.
Carpenter, Polly, and Hall, George R., Case Studies in

Educational Performance Contracting, Conclusions and Implications, R-90011 HEW, Santa Monica, Calif.: RAND Corporation, 1971, p. 51.

Educational Research Service, "Class Size, a Summary of Research," *ERS Research Brief,* Arlington, Va.: ERS, 1978, 84 pp.

Educational Research Service, "Reporting Pupil Progress: Policies, Procedures, and Systems," *ERS Report,* Arlington, Va.: ERS, 1977, 115 pp.

Saville, Anthony, *Instructional Programming,* Columbus, Ohio: Chas. E. Merrill, 1973, p. 219.

23

EDUCATIONAL RESOURCE PROCUREMENT AND MANAGEMENT: SCHOOL FINANCE, LOGISTICAL SUPPORT, AND EDUCATIONAL FACILITIES

Administrators are charged with special responsibilities for identifying, procuring, and managing the variety of resources essential in the delivery of quality educational services and programs. Fiscal resources are needed to translate curriculum and instructional objectives into reality. The school finance system and the school curriculum are interrelated. The teacher may pay little attention to the former in order to focus energies on the latter. The educational administrator can ignore neither and must demonstrate leadership and management expertise in procuring and protecting educational resources as well as providing and propelling curriculum and instructional objectives and programs.

School finance was at one time primarily a local matter, but today is heavily dependent upon state and federal educational contributions. After the essential resources have been procured, what has been called school business management becomes important. The terms *logistical support services management* or *management of educational resources* are more precise even

though less frequently used than the term *school business management*. "Business" management encompasses all administrative activities of a business and not only those related to financing the business, preparation of budgets, accounting for all funds, and so on. The educational facilities which must be designed, constructed, and/or maintained represent the largest set of educational resources essential to the support and delivery of learning activities and services.

THE FINANCING OF PUBLIC EDUCATION IN THE UNITED STATES

The nation's support level for public education reflects the value placed on education and its ability to pay for educational services and programs. Educational finance approaches never remained fixed for long; they have been modified frequently at various periods of time to reflect the educational needs of society and the ability of various school finance systems to deliver the magnitude of resources required for a comprehensive and relevant educational program for all.

Early in our history a large part of school support came from nonmonetary sources. Patrons provided services to schools (supplying fuel or wood, boarding teachers, or making repairs to the school building) in lieu of money. Later there was an attempt to support public education from income derived from land endowments and rents, lotteries, and gifts and bequests. (Lotteries appear to be making a comeback.) During the early part of the nineteenth century, it was hoped that income from lands received from the state and federal governments would provide all money needed to operate schools. The futility of this hope became evident as the nation grew and demands upon public schools exceeded expectations.

Limiting school support to nontax resources created a financial crisis, and a new method was tried—financing education almost entirely by means of a local property tax. It made sense during a period of our history when local units of government, such as school districts, were the predominant tax-collecting and tax-spending bodies. Prior to 1930 the total taxes collected by state and federal governments combined were less than those collected by local governments.

By the last quarter of the nineteenth century, the local property tax became the backbone of public school support. Reliance on the local property tax enabled school districts to meet the educational challenges of the times that were confined, by and large, to elementary school education. The nineteenth-century school finance system was not designed to cope with expanding secondary education and the more comprehensive educational programs that developed during the first quarter of the twentieth century. Early in the twentieth century there emerged the concept of more significant state support of public education to complement the local educational tax resources. State contributions were relatively modest to begin with, but began to be an increasingly larger percent of the total school revenues throughout the twentieth century as public

school enrollments and program quality increased. The "baby boom" following the end of World War II generated another educational finance challenge. The rampaging inflation of the 1970s, the justifiable demands for higher teacher salaries, and the demands of a broader range of learners than ever before when coupled with social pressures facing schools during the 1970s generated intense fiscal pressures on the public schools even though enrollments were declining.

The resources allocated to public schools doubled or tripled during each of the post-World War II decades in an effort to keep pace with the educational expectations of the nation. Even a cursory review of the history of educational finance in the United States will reveal that public school fiscal crises are not confined to the present period. Educational finance problems are the price paid for rising educational expectations.

Past and Present Magnitude of Public School Expenditures

Schools expend resources for a variety of purposes; some are necessary to meet the demands of current operations such as as salaries for instructional personnel and purchase of materials, others are for one-time, large-scale costs for buildings or other construction that continue to be used long after payments are complete. Total educational expenditures include current (the annual and recurring costs for salaries, services, and materials), capital outlay (the costs for buildings, sites, and long-lasting equipment), and debt service (payments for interest on the school debt or bonds) expenditures. In analyzing and comparing data on school expenditures, it is essential that the same type (total or current, capital outlay, and debt service) of expenditure classification is employed. Unless otherwise specified, the annual current expenditure figures will be employed here to indicate the magnitude and trends in public school expenditures.

Prior to 1920 current expenditures for public elementary/secondary education for the nation as a whole were less than $1 billion. It reached over $1.84 billion in 1929–1930, and increased slightly to about $1.94 billion by the end of the next decade, or 1939–1940. That was the end of relatively minor gains in public school expenditures for current expenses during the period of a decade. By 1949–1950 the current expenditures for the nation's public schools more than doubled during a decade to reach almost $4.69 billion. That signaled the beginning of a series of decades during which current expenses at least doubled or almost tripled. The strain on educational finance systems increased and the growing magnitude of current expenditures was a portent of fiscal exigencies to come. The hard evidence is in the following record of current expense totals for the last year of the various decades: $12.33 billion in 1959–1960 (almost triple the amount at the end of the prior decade); $34.22 billion in 1969–1970 (not quite triple in 1959–1960); and an estimated $87 billion in 1979–1980 (more than 2.5 times 1969–1970). The estimated current expenditures for 1980–1981 were $90 billion.

The reported taxpayer resistance to escalating school taxes should not have generated surprise given the magnitude of current expenditures increases over the 40-year period of 1939–1940 to 1979–1980 of about $80 billion, or more than 4200 percent!

Capital outlay expenditures for buildings, sites, and large equipment showed a rising trend as well, but at a rate below that for current expenses. Capital outlay payments totaled $153.5 million in 1919–1920; $370.9 million in 1929–1930; $258 million in 1939–1940; $1.014 billion in 1949–1950; $2.662 billion in 1959–1960; $4.659 billion in 1969–1970; and an estimated $6.5 billion in 1979–1980 (only slightly different from 1975–1976). The amount of school construction was down substantially during the 1970s, but this was offset by rapidly rising construction and equipment costs. Capital outlay expenditures are likely to remain flat during the 1980s, whereas current expenditures will continue to show substantial increases during that decade.

Annual interest payments on the school debt showed more dramatic rises than did those for capital outlay. Interest paid by public schools

totaled $18.2 million in 1919–1920; $92.5 million in 1929–1930; $130.9 million in 1939–1940; $100.6 in 1949–1950 (reflecting the drop in construction during the depression decade and slowdown during World War II); $489.5 million in 1959–1960; $1.171 billion in 1969–1970; and $1.9 billion in 1979–1980.

Total public school expenditures, of which current expenses are the largest by far, are reported for various decades of this century as follows: $426 million in 1909–1910; $1.04 billion in 1919–1920; $2.32 billion in 1929–1930; $2.34 billion in 1939–1940; $5.84 billion in 1949–1950; $15.61 billion in 1959–1960; $40.68 billion in 1969–1970; and $96 billion in 1979–1980. The total of all educational expenditures for public schools exceeded $100 billion in 1981 (from an estimated $98.5 billion 1980). There were some who considered the prediction of $100 billion in public school expenditures by 1980 as outlandish when made in previous editions of this book about ten years ago. A public education finance system must be designed to generate $250 billion annually for the nation's schools by the beginning of the next decade (the 1990s). This is a prodigious challenge and test of the nation's commitment to quality systems of public education. Those who argue that there was "declining support for public education" during recent decades must have difficulty explaining public support in dollars that grew from about $2.34 billion to $100 billion annually during the space of only about 40 years.

Another indicator that education in the United States is "big business" is the magnitude of expenditures for all levels of education (from kindergarten to graduate programs in institutions of higher learning) in both private and public institutions. Expenditures for all educational programs exceeded $100 billion by 1974–1975; it was almost $200 billion in 1981–1982. The private elementary/secondary schools expend about 11 percent and the public elementary/secondary schools about 89 percent of total funds allocated for these educational levels.

Yet another measure of the willingness of the people to support education at all levels (public and private from kindergarten to university level) is the percent of wealth of the nation as measured by the gross national product (GNP) dedicated to all types of educational expenditures. The percent of the GNP devoted to all levels of public and private education ranged between 3 and 4 percent during the 1930s and then dropped below 3 percent during most of the 1940s. It then began a period of increases, being above 3 and 4 percent during the 1950s and hitting what was then an all-time high of 5.1 percent of the GNP in 1959. It continued upward, exceeding the 5 and 6 percent ranges during the 1960s to reach 7.5 percent of the GNP in 1969. A high of 8 percent of the GNP dedicated for educational expenditures was attained in 1975; a decline followed during the last half of that decade to settle at 6.8 percent of the GNP in 1981, which was below that registered for 1967.[1] The recent decline notwithstanding, the nation invests presently twice as much of its resources, as measured by the GNP, than it did 50 years ago. The nation dedicates a slightly higher percent of the GNP to health than it does to education.

Data on gross expenditures or total dollar amounts expended on public elementary/-secondary education fail to reveal the impact of increasing or decreasing enrollments or how much is being devoted to each pupil. A unit-cost figure such as "current expenditures per pupil in average daily attendance" (ADA) is a better indicator of trends in amounts devoted to educate each pupil in public schools. Such data must be interpreted with great care, for not all use the same base or units. Thus, the base may be the total rather than current expenditures, and the unit may be "per pupil enrolled" or "per pupil in average daily membership" as opposed to "per pupil in ADA" used herein.

Current expenditures per pupil in ADA were $88 in 1939–1940; $209 in 1949–1950; $816 in 1969–1970; and $2275 in 1979–1980. The 1979–1980 per pupil expenditures are 25 times greater than what they were in 1939–1940 when unadjusted for the impact of inflation; they were only five times greater when adjusted to reflect the decline in the purchasing power of the dollar. The ravages of inflation during the past decade in particular are demonstrated by the fact that the Consumer Price Index (CPI) "rose by more than 81 percent" between 1970 and 1979.[2] The current expenditures per pupil in ADA increased 2.6 times—from $860 to $2275 —between 1970–1971 and 1979–1980 when expressed in unadjusted dollars; the increase was only 1.35 times—from $1680 to $2275—the 1970–1971 level when expressed in the 1979–1980 purchasing power of the dollar.[3] Expenditure increases during the past decade were exaggerated by inflation, that is, by the decline in the purchasing power of the dollar.

There is considerable variation among states in the amount spent per pupil in ADA: from lows of $1574 in Arkansas and $1625 in Georgia in 1979–1980 to highs of $3462 in New York and $4728 in Alaska for current expenditures. The national average for current expenditures per pupil in ADA in 1979–1980 was $2275. By 1979–1980, 27 states were spending more than $2000 per pupil in ADA and none less than $1500 per pupil in ADA, as compared with only 11 states above $2000 per pupil in 1977–1978 and 15 states below $1500 per pupil. The national average current expenditures per pupil in ADA exceeded $100 during the 1940s, $1000 in 1972–1973, and $2000 in 1979–1980; it should reach $3000 per pupil during the late 1980s.

Sources of Revenues for the Support of Public Education

The challenge facing educational finance systems is the generation and distribution of school revenues in an equitable and responsible manner to support the level of school expenditures essential for delivering quality educational programs and services. The sources of operating funds for public schools have changed from nonmonetary contributions, to monetary but nontax sources of funds, to taxes levied primarily by local school districts, to tax sources that include state and federal government contributions as well. Before further elaborations, some basic concepts related to revenues and receipts require clarification.

All school revenues are receipts but not all receipts are revenues. Revenue receipts produce additions to assets without increasing school indebtedness and without reducing the value of or degrading school property; they include money from taxes and tuitions. Nonrevenue receipts accrue to the district as the result of incurring an obligation that must be satisfied at a future date or of reducing the value of school property through the exchange of a property asset into a cash asset.[4] Revenue receipts are derived from local, federal, and state sources.

Taxation for the support of public education is only about 100 years old; over the decades the percentage of tax- and nontax-generated school-revenue receipts that have come from various units of governments has varied. This is evident from the data summarized in Table 23.1. In general, for most of history and until 1978–1979 the local school district (plus those of any intermediate unit) contributed the largest portion of school-revenue receipts; but that portion declined throughout this century as the total revenue receipts increased. State contributions remained between 16 and 17 percent until the 1930s, then remained between 30 and almost 40 percent until 1972, and reached 45.7 percent in 1978–1979 to exceed local contributions for the first time. State contributions and

percentage of the total revenue receipts increased as did these receipts; the state will continue to be the major source of public school support during the rest of this century and beyond.

Federal contributions, other than those of the original land grants of the early 1800s that gave rise to the so-called state permanent school funds, were relatively insignificant compared with the total revenue receipts during the first half of this century, but began to climb rapidly after 1960 to reach almost 10 percent by the end of the previous decade. A significant shift in federal support of public education was noted in the early 1980s. The "new federalism" of the Reagan Administration may reduce the federal contributions to the 6 or 7 percent level, at least during the 1980s. This could mean that states will be forced to assume an even larger portion of 50 percent or more during the 1980s. The federal government collects the lion's share of the taxes in the nation but contributes the least amount for the support of public education. This must be changed if $250 billion needed annually to support public elementary/secondary education by the early part of the 1990s is to be generated. The state moved during this century from a relatively minor to the major fiscal role in the support of public education.

TABLE 23.1

PERCENTAGE CONTRIBUTIONS OF FEDERAL, STATE, AND LOCAL GOVERNMENT UNITS TO PUBLIC ELEMENTARY AND SECONDARY SCHOOL-REVENUE RECEIPTS: 1919–1979

School Year	Total School-Revenue Receipts	Percentage Distribution by Government Level		
		Federal	State	Local (including Intermediate units)
1919–1920	$ 970,120,000	0.3	16.5	83.2
1929–1930	2,088,557,000	0.4	16.9	82.7
1939–1940	2,260,527,000	1.8	30.3	68.0
1949–1950	5,437,044,000	2.9	39.8	57.3
1959–1960	14,746,618,000	4.4	39.1	56.5
1969–1970	40,266,923,000	8.0	39.9	52.1
1979–1980	96,580,940,000	9.8	46.8	43.4

Source: W. V. Grant and L. J. Eiden, *Digest of Education Statistics 1982*, National Center for Education Statistics, Washington, D.C.: GPO, 1982, p. 75.

The Property Tax

The property tax is the source of most local funds for public education. School property taxes generate billions of dollars annually, which were in excess of $35 billion during 1978–1979. For all its shortcomings, the property tax is one of the few—and perhaps the best means of generating large local revenue receipts—taxes efficiently and effectively administered by small governmental units such as the local school district. It is one of the most productive and stable revenue producers for local units, and will continue to be used by local school districts for many years to come.

The local property tax has been criticized because (1) it is very slow to respond with additional revenues during times of rapid economic growth (by the same token its revenues do not fall as rapidly during depressed economic periods); (2) it correlates poorly with ability to pay; (3) it is notorious for the inequities in assessment practices and tardiness in realistic reassessment of individual property valuations (the computer and more professional preparation for tax assessors helped in recent years to cope with the many property tax assessment problems); (4) it is saddled with a variety of exemptions, which reduce the taxable value of property by billions of dollars, because of being a homestead, veteran's status of owner-occupant, or being a special class of property (such as personal or intangible personal property); (5) there are psychological limits placed on the size of the tax rate levied on real property in particular; and (6) it is subject to periodic "taxpayer's revolts" because direct payments of this tax makes it difficult to disguise or to render payments less painful through monthly withholding features.

Significant improvements in property tax assessment, collection, and administration during recent decades helped to reduce some of the criticisms. There is no adequate direct substitute for it (short of complete state financing of public education) insofar as local school districts are concerned. During the 1970s there were severe restrictions placed upon property tax rates in several states, with others likely to follow suit during the 1980s. The net effects of such restrictions were to compound school fiscal problems and to greatly increase the level of state aid for public education. The so-called taxpayers' revolts more often than not focus on property tax rates and less frequently on other forms of taxation.

Nonproperty Taxes

Nonproperty taxes may be employed to support public schools, are seldom administered by a local school district, have failed to yield as much as the property taxes until recently, and are more often administered efficiently and effectively by a larger governmental unit such as the state or federal government. The expansion and improvements in nonproperty taxation contributed to the growth of states as important tax-collecting government agencies. Nonproperty taxes are levied on such items as income of state residents, retail sales within the state, tobacco, admissions to entertainment and other events, gasoline, deed transfers, and mercantile licenses.

The two most productive nonproperty taxes are those on income and retail sales. Such taxes respond quickly to business trends, with yields rising and falling according to prosperity or recession. Nonproperty taxes produce a far greater yield with less administrative cost when the taxing unit encompasses a large area that minimizes the chances of tax avoidance or evasion. Authorizing local school districts to levy a host of nonproperty taxes would not be as productive as having such taxes collected by a larger unit (such as the state or federal government) and then distributing those receipts in whole or in part to local school districts.

All but a few states tax *individual* incomes. More states tax corporate income rather than individual incomes. Most but not all levy a general state sales tax. All states tax gasoline and alcoholic beverages; all but one tax cigarettes. State property taxes produce a very small percentage of state revenues.

At one time customs duties accounted for the

largest share of federal tax collections. The advent of the federal income tax during the early part of this century changed all that. Personal and corporate income taxes generate over 80 percent of federal government revenues. Other federal taxes such as special sales or gross receipts taxes and those on alcoholic beverages are distant third and fourth largest producers of federal revenues.

Wealth and Taxes to Support Public Education

The United States is the wealthiest nation in the world; some smaller ones may show more impressive per capita wealth data, but none can match the sheer magnitude of our gross national product. This wealth enabled the nation to design and support a quality system of public education for all children and youths, present educational finance problems notwithstanding.

Education does not take the lion's share of the consumer's dollar. More is spent each year on automobiles; expenditures on recreation and on alcoholic beverages and tobacco approach those devoted to public elementary/-secondary education. Nor do most of the nation's tax dollars go to the public schools; of the $564.3 billion spent by all governments in 1978 only 21 percent went to education. About 44 cents of every local government expenditure dollar and 38.8 cents of every state government expenditure dollar are allocated to public education.

The nation has the wealth to continue to support the most comprehensive and highest quality system of public education the world has ever known. Overcoming the present and future educational finance crises is primarily a matter of priorities and design of educational finance systems that are productive, equitable, and efficiently administered. Such systems require a satisfactory tax base; reliance on a mix of property and nonproperty taxes; efficient and effective tax-collecting procedures; and an equitable and legally defensible system of distributing educational funds for the equal educational treatment of all learners in each state.

THE DESIGN, TRENDS, AND CHALLENGES FOR EDUCATIONAL FINANCE SYSTEMS

Educational finance may be defined in broad terms as that dimension of public or government finance concerned specifically with the procurement, distribution, management, and disbursement of fiscal and material resources essential to the delivery of quality and relevant public educational programs and services. A narrower interpretation is found in education. The general field of educational finance can be divided into (1) educational finance systems that are designed to raise and distribute public education funds and (2) educational finance management, more often referred to as school business management, which comes into play after the educational revenues reach the local school district and includes such activities as budgeting, accounting, and auditing. The latter will be reviewed in a subsequent section of this chapter. What follows will focus upon the receipts-generation side of the finance equation, namely, the procurement and distribution of fiscal and material resources. It bears repeating that there is no single, unified, national-educational finance system. What exists are 50 different state-educational finance systems with some similarities but considerable variation from one state to another. Differences in wealth, and some degree of differences in commitment to various types and kinds of educational opportunities, among the states contribute to the uniqueness of state educational finance systems. Probable federal contributions to the support of public education are not as yet significant factors in the design of state-educational finance systems.

Each state designs its own educational finance system in terms of its educational needs, wealth, or ability to pay for public education, as well as its values or response to its own social and political pressures. Educational needs are not always defined with precision in all states, but these are usually expressed in terms of minimum or desired educational goals; who or what age groups will be served by the system of public elementary/secondary and/or other schools; to what degree or what grade levels shall education be provided through the public schools; how many are likely to be enrolled and their distribution in the public elementary/secondary schools; and what special problems and adjustments will be made for learners with exceptionalities, who may reside in sparsely populated areas, or who may be found in the core of large urban centers. The educational needs within a given state will change over time with rising educational expectations the norm, with enrollments increasing or declining, with social pressures related to civil rights, or as the result of special sensitivities for the education of children and youths with special needs. The focus of most state-educational finance systems is upon the current expenditures that constitute about 90.4 percent of total public-school disbursements. The financing of capital outlay and school debt service may be added as a separate and distinct element of a more comprehensive state-educational finance system.

Sooner or later the educational needs to be supported at minimum or desired levels in each state must be translated into dollars and cents equivalents. It was indicated earlier that the total school expenditures during the 1980s for the nation as a whole would be in excess of $100 billion annually and around $250 billion annually likely during the early part of the 1990s. These national estimates fail to reveal the great variation among states. Analysis of 1979–1980 current expenditures that totaled about $87.0 billion showed Vermont with $189.8 million and Wyoming with $222.1 million at the low extremes, whereas New York expended $8.76 billion and California expended $9.17 billion at the other extremes. About 52 percent of the states had current expenditures in excess of $1 billion in 1979–1980, whereas 48 percent had less than that. Whatever the present levels in each state, they are likely to be 2 to 2½ times such amounts by the early 1990s, and the existing state-educational finance systems will have to be redesigned to

generate such revenues, or most of that, if the federal government cannot be depended upon to absorb any more than 6 to 10 percent of the total public-school revenue production.

After educational needs are translated into likely and annual dollar needs of public school districts within the state the next issues become: what are the likely sources of such dollars; what will be the likely state and local contributions to the total; how shall the amounts collected by the state or other central sources be distributed among the local school districts of the state; and so on. The traditional approach for the financing of private education was to establish endowments through gifts, with the rents or other investment yields from such endowments used annually to support private school operations. This private school finance model was the basis of the early efforts at financing public schools, witness the hope expressed that the income from the huge federal land grants for education made during the early 1800s would support the needs of public education. Unfortunately, there was what Swift referred to as "squandering the heritage," for "even an incomplete record shows that in thirty-two of the states funds totaling many millions of dollars have been lost, diverted, or squandered."[5] Today, the school revenues from the old federal land grants amount to only a small fraction of 1 percent of the total. Income from endowments grows slowly at best and probably never would have been able to keep pace with rising expectations and the great enrollment growth of public education. Even the relatively stable private schools had to turn to escalating tuition and other fees to keep pace with increasing operating costs; public schools do not have the option to levy tuition on residents. The use of nontax sources to support public education had limited success in the early years of educational finance, disappeared for a long while, and then some, like the state-run lotteries, returned in more recent years, but must be considered as supplements rather than major sources of funds for the public schools. Property and nonproperty taxes, outlined earlier, are the major sources of revenues for public education in each of the states. Over-reliance on a single tax source, such as occurred initially during the late nineteenth century with the local school district property tax, will not work; the full range of tax sources must be utilized at the state and local levels to generate the magnitude of revenues needed to support adequately public elementary/secondary education now and in the future. The choice of taxes is a political decision and is also related to the productivity of each source. As one wag put it, "The fine art of taxation is to get the most amount of feathers with the least amount of squawking." That is easier said than done.

The initial educational finance systems were relatively simple and depended upon the resources of local school districts (with the sole exception of income from federal land grants). The authority to levy taxes on the property wealth of the local district reinforced this position, for about 98 percent of the local contributions to school revenues come from this tax. There was a great disparity in wealth among individual districts. The inequality in taxable property wealth resulted in great differences in the quality of public education. In short, the accident of birth or residence in a particular school district of the state determined the quality of schooling likely to be received.

This disparity in the ability to support quality education led to greater state contributions, and to some extent, but much later, federal assistance for the public schools. Education is a function of the state and, state mandates required the employment of qualified teachers, construction of safe school facilities, enforcement of compulsory attendance, and instruction of a given quality for no less than the decreed numbers of school days per year. These state demands contributed substantial increases in local school-district operating costs. Most states recognized the price tag for quality education and developed more comprehensive and sophisticated state-educational finance systems.

After the taxing and other fiscal powers generated monies for public education, there arose the problem of fair and equitable distribution of these state dollars to local districts to be expended for educational programs and services. Initially, relatively crude bases, such as the number of children of school age reported within the school census, were utilized to allocate or distribute state school funds to local districts. These state flat grants were later refined and allocated on the basis of pupils in average daily attendance (ADA) or average daily membership (ADM) in each district. Refinements in flat grants failed to compensate completely for the differences in taxable property wealth among local districts and the wide disparities in the tax rates to support public education. Even the weighting of per capita grants to reflect differences in costs of educational programs for the elementary school pupil, the secondary school student, or handicapped pupil could not overcome fully the inability of flat or per capita grants alone to reduce the local disparities.

The "weighted pupil unit" was one way to cope with the cost differentials in various educational program operation levels. It did so by allocating the weight of 1.0 to costs for educating pupils in grades 3 to 8, 1.20 to costs for students in grade 9 to 12, 3.25 to costs for physically handicapped students, 2.30 for remedial reading pupils, 2.13 for agriculture enrollees, and so on.[6] These weights reflect the reality that the cost of educating a pupil in remedial reading is 2.3 times that of costs for other subjects in grades 3 to 8, educating a student in secondary grades is 1.2 times more costly than that for a regular elementary school pupil, and so on. There isn't complete agreement on the precise weight for each dimension of education supported by state aid formulas. To illustrate, some use the weight of 1.5 rather than 1.2 for secondary school students. This helps to explain in part the rising costs during the 1970s while enrollments were declining. Actually, the elementary enrollments were declining while secondary enrollments increased during most of the 1970s to constitute a larger proportion of total public school enrollments (about 29 percent in 1970 compared to about 32 to 34 percent by the end of the 1970s). This is projected to change during the 1980s as the secondary enrollments continue to decline throughout the present decade, while elementary enrollments increase during the last half of the 1980s.

The "foundation program" concept, developed early in this century, became the cornerstone of state-educational finance systems for more than 50 years because of its value in equalizing among local districts, to some degree, the costs of supporting a "minimum" or "foundation" educational program even though there may be widely varying assessed valuation of taxable property behind each student residing within the district. With "state equalization aid" wealthier school districts (as measured by the amount of assessed taxable property behind each pupil) receive fewer state dollars than the poorer districts with similar numbers of weighted or "raw" pupil units. Usually, the state requires that a specific school tax be levied in each district against the property valuation for the state as a whole as measured by a state agency (to guard against under-valuation of property by local assessors) to constitute the local contribution to the state-defined and -approved "foundation" educational program.

In some cases, the local tax is computed to pay for the entire cost of the minimum educational program, and if this tax fails to do so, then the state aid makes up the difference. The added cost of educational programs outside the state "minimum" or "foundation program" is supported completely by local effort; it represents a program equalization that does not always result in equalization of the school tax burden. The so-called power equalization or equalized percentage grant approach to the distribution of state educational funds seeks to do a better job of equalizing the school tax rate in all districts of the state, and the state contributions are included in all educational programs provided in a school district, not simply the foundation program.[7] It is beyond scope of a comprehensive introductory text to analyze all elements of state-educational finance systems and the reader is referred to special sources cited or other volumes in this field.

Full state funding of public education began to be talked about seriously and more frequently during the 1970s. The increases in the states' share of public school support are evident from the data in Table 23.1 with the historic turnaround in 1978–1979 when the percent of state contributions exceeded that of the local district contributions. The restrictions on the local property tax approved in some states during the late 1970s plus the court challenges bring many states closer to full state funding, which is defined as being close to or actually is 100 percent educational financing from state fiscal sources. It has the advantage of achieving complete equalization of public school education programs and taxes, but it may also restrict local educational initiative. It is more probable that the states' share of public education costs will continue to rise during the rest of this century, but complete state financing is not likely if for no other reason than that the $40 billion raised annually from local resources is not likely to be eliminated in the days ahead. As the role of the state becomes even more important in educational finance, local board members and administrators will become even more involved in state legislative activities.

The wealth of the big cities and the quality of their educational programs were the envy of rural and suburban school districts for much of our history until the middle of this century. Some changes occurred as the more affluent of the population moved to the suburbs along with some business and industrial development. In their place came many deprived and disadvantaged to reside in the core of the cities. Superhighways cut through the cities and removed more property from the tax roles at a time when the new populations demanded more municipal services. The term *municipal overburden* appeared to explain in part why a city school district with property wealth equal to a noncity district had difficulty in dedicating equal amounts to public education. This prompted the cry for increased state support to compensate for the concentrations of low-income families in the big cities just as in previous years state-educational finance systems compensated for the reverse or sparsity of population to be educated in rural areas.

The twentieth century witnessed a complete reversal in educational finance that was predicated initially upon most of the public school funds, coming from local financial resources. Today, the majority of revenues for schools are generated from state resources. The upper limits of local contributions appeared to have been reached by the 1980s and the same may be true for the states by the end of this century. The only resolution to successful generation of the magnitude of fiscal and material resources needed to support quality programs of public education is greater, consistent, and annual contributions from the federal government. This is being written at a time during the early 1980s when there were substantial federal funding reductions and a reversal of previous trends. Nonetheless, there are public education financing needs that cannot be denied. Education is vital to the defense and economic development of the nation as a whole. There will be a new approach to educational finance that will see state contributions to the support of public education of no less that 50 percent, federal contributions of about 30 percent, and local contributions of no more than 20 percent to generate revenues in the magnitude of $250 to $300 billion annually before the end of this century.

DISTRIBUTION OF STATE EDUCATION FUNDS THROUGH "EDUCATIONAL VOUCHERS"

What some called the "voucher system of educational finance" is simply an approach for distributing state and federal education funds directly to parents of school-age children and youths by means of a voucher. Its proponents were relatively unconcerned about how education funds are generated, power or foundation program equalization, or what proportion of the total education revenues should be satisfied by local, state, or federal contributions. It would be erroneous to consider the voucher proponents as designers of a complete educational finance system. They promise no relief to the fiscal crises facing education now or in the future. Their goal is to change the method of distributing state education funds (and whatever applicable federal funds) from going directly to the approximately 15,000 public school districts that existed around 1983 to more than 15 million parents of school-age children and youths. The parent would take the educational voucher to a public or private school of choice willing to accept the pupil and the voucher as full or partial payment for schooling for the year. It is assumed that any parent could take any student to any school in the state without regard to attendance or school district boundaries; that is, there would be no such thing as resident pupils of a given school district.

Beyond the concepts of the voucher that goes directly to parents and "freedom of choice" (given to the parent and not the student) to select any public or private school, there is little further agreement on operational details. Some voucher proponents would peg the value of a "basic educational voucher" at 90 percent of the public school "per pupil cost" (being fuzzy as to which weighted or unweighted per pupil unit would be selected) to "force economies" in educational operations. The latter point was evidently an attempt to garner the support of certain segments of society without further clarification how or why this could be done in practice.

The administrative costs of distributing and recording of vouchers for 40 million or more students would be far greater than any hoped-for "forced economies." Welfare payments are made directly to individuals and the cases of welfare fraud are reported frequently by the media with losses measured in the billions. The voucher proponents have not even recognized the potential for fraud, or additional administrative costs for its prevention, related to direct educational voucher payments.

It is assumed further that parents could assess quality educational program differences between competing public and private school systems or between competing school attendance centers in the same system. The educational program assessment is difficult for professionals to complete in a fair and objective fashion. The idea purports to use the market-place (as in the sale and purchase of commercial goods and services), by virtue of parental choice, as the determiner of which schools and programs deserve financial support and continuance. Education is a social good and not primarily an individual benefit. Society suffers from poor educational choices as well as the person and family. Social goods are not well regulated by the market mechanism, and for that reason governments and special governmental units are created to insure that important social goods are not slighted by individual oversight.

Efforts to install educational vouchers through statewide initiatives have not been successful to date. Obviously, it is a means of providing state funds for the support of private education by distributing educational vouchers to parents rather than directly to private schools, which would be clearly unconstitutional. Whether the voucher plan would meet the tests of constitutionality if actually used to support private schools is open to question. Lively debate continues and the lack of success by voucher proponents thus far has not seemed to dampen their enthusiasm for their version of educational finance reform.

Educational Finance Crises, Reforms, and Court Challenges

There were many manifestations of fiscal crises in the public schools during the 1970s including program cutbacks and staff layoffs. Perhaps the most dramatic were the near bankruptcies of three big city school systems: Chicago, Cleveland, and New York. Bankers stepped in to protect previously issued loans to support continuing school operations (not capital outlay projects that require loans). In 1979 the entire Chicago city school board was removed from office and three top administrators quit in face of the system's deepening financial plight. Other large city operations experienced fiscal problems of varying degrees, and it was not unusual to find the school year shortened to cope with the situation. The fiscal health of sev-

eral large city school systems remains tenuous; the threat of school bankruptcy through default on debt payments or failure to meet contractual obligations during the 1980s is a very uncomfortable reality unless new approaches to educational finance are made operational.

During the 1970s relief from the wide disparities in local property wealth and ability to support public education was sought through the courts as well as the legislative branch of state government. The legal action sought to quicken the pace of needed educational finance reform. It was argued that inequality in the distribution of property tax wealth among school districts resulted in discrimination against the poor and disadvantaged in violation of the equal protection clause of the Fourteenth Amendment to the U.S. Constitution. Thus the design of public-educational finance systems became a legal or constitutional issue as well as an educational, economic, and political matter.

Serrano v. *Priest* (1971) set the stage, for the California State Supreme Court decided that inequities in the ability of local school districts to support education was a violation of that state's constitution and also the U.S. Constitution's equal protection clause of the Fourteenth Amendment. That this inequity was unintentional was rejected as a valid defense and a reform of that state's educational finance system was ordered. This precedent influenced similar decisions by other state courts. This was not the first time courts influenced the development of educational finance systems as evidenced by the historic "Kalamazoo" case of 1872.

As indicated in Chapter 11, the Texas educational finance system was challenged on constitutional grounds in the case of *Rodriguez* v. *San Antonio Independent School District*. It reached the U.S. Supreme Court in 1973, which in a split decision, 5 to 4, found no tax system "free of all discriminatory impact" and concluded that the Texas educational finance plan did not violate any part of the U.S. Constitution. It is interesting that the *Serrano* decision that did not reach the U.S. Supreme Court appears to have had greater impact on other state decisions than the *Rodriguez* decision that did get federal level attention.

The 1970s may be remembered as a decade of court challenges on educational finance and when legislatures were stimulated to begin serious school finance reforms. The legal challenges did not demand that the states spend more on public education, but rather that the quality of public education available to students in a given district be more a function of the wealth of the state as a unit than of a specific school district. There were special educational finance initiatives, propositions, and constitutional amendments brought before the people of 20 states during 1980, and each of these could have had a significant impact on the support patterns for public education.[8] The vast majority of the states considering proposed property tax restrictions or limitation proposals were rejected by the people during 1980. During the 1970s school revenues from local sources almost doubled, whereas those from state sources almost tripled, thus giving indications that the court challenges and the local property taxpayers' revolt were having an impact on educational finance reform.

CONTRIBUTIONS OF EDUCATION TO ECONOMIC DEVELOPMENT

Although the classical economists Adam Smith and Alfred Marshall believed "the most valuable of all capital is that invested in human beings,"[9] most economists thereafter failed to stress the relation between economic growth and education. Most of the nation's economic growth was credited to physical capital investments (instruments of production) and very little to improvements in human capital until about the middle of the 1950s.

Today economists recognize readily that economic productivity is affected not only by the quantity of physical capital, but also by the quality of human capital a society possesses.

Education expenditures are investments in human capital development, just as expenditures for physical tools and machines used in the production of goods and services are investments in development of physical capital.

Local, state, and federal taxes allocated to educational purposes can be viewed as funds to promote economic growth of the nation as well as to promote other benefits an educated populace contributes to society. As Harbison and Myers put it, "Progress is basically the result of human effort. It takes human agents to mobilize capital to exploit natural resources, to create markets and to carry on trade."[10]

This broader view of factors related to economic development grew out of the realization that only about 20 percent of the economic growth of the United States could be traced to increases in size of work force and amount of tools and machinery use in production.[11] The other 80 percent was first credited to improvement in quality of physical capital goods. But qualitative changes in physical capital goods failed to explain all unaccounted-for gains in economic output. Education began to be perceived as a process of building human capital, and investments in education were granted a more prominent place in economic analysis.

Schultz examined the relation between educational expenditures and income or capital formation for the period 1900 to 1956. He computed that the total "stock" of educational capital rose in the United States labor force from $63 billion in 1900 to $535 billion in 1957. He considered that investment in education included not only actual outlay for operation of educational institutions, but also "opportunity costs." The opportunity cost of education was the possible earned income given up by the person who chose to go to school during years he could have been working and earning.

Schultz estimated that 21 percent of the $152 billion increase in real income between 1929 and 1957 could be attributed to additional education.[12]

This and other studies led to the American Association of School Administrators to conclude:

If all of technological progress could be attributed to education, then our school system would be responsible for about 40 percent of economic growth (20 to 23 percent through improvement in labor skill and 20 percent through technological progress). No other field of human endeavor can claim so large a share.[13]

Harbison and Myers further suggested that underdeveloped nations of the world must generate a strategy of human-resource development to move forward in political, social, and economic modernization. They analyzed qualitatively the problems of education and training faced by various types of undeveloped, partially developed, semiadvanced, and advanced countries and outlined a human-resource-development pattern related to economic growth.

Education benefits the individual as well as society as a whole. The evidence continues to mount that the level of education of a person is related to his ability to earn. Miller[14] summarized the lifetime earnings as related to education as ranging from $143,000 for a person with less than eight years of schooling to $454,000 for a person with five or more years of college. The disparities in earning power in various years for persons completing various levels of schooling are shown in Table 23.2.

Although the dropout may start to work two or more years earlier than a high school graduate, the graduate of 1980 will earn an estimated $200,000 more over a lifetime. By 1980 the median annual income (not to be compared with the mean shown in Table 23.2) for a male high school graduate was $19,469 and for females $11,537.

The benefits that accrue to most persons through education include higher income levels, a broader range of job opportunity, greater job security, and happier family life. The rate of unemployment is lower for those with higher levels of education. Johnson provided the following data to support the above generalizations:[15]

1. Unemployment among male dropouts in 1979 was 8.3 per cent, among high school graduates 5.5 per cent, and college graduates 1.8 per cent.
2. The unemployable, many of whom are dropouts, are supported by welfare programs whose costs are measured in billions or about $1800 per person in 1979.
3. Sixty per cent of all jail inmates have fewer than 12 years of school and a median of 10.2 years of schooling.
4. Incarceration at the Joliet, Illinois, maximum security prison cost in 1979 $28,835 a year per inmate or more than 10 times the cost of educating a public school student per year.

Johnson concluded that schools made a positive contribution to the creation of the type of environment important to social and economic

TABLE 23.2

ANNUAL MEAN INCOME (OR EARNINGS) FOR MALES 25 YEARS OF AGE AND OVER, BY YEARS OF SCHOOL COMPLETED

Year of school completed	1939	1949	1961	1968	1978
Elementary:					
Less than 8 years	—	$2,062	$2,998	$ 3,981	$7,149
8 years	$1,036	2,892	4,206	5,467	9,367
High school:					
1 to 3 years	1,379	3,226	5,161	6,769	11,784
4 years	1,661	3,784	5,946	8,145	15,152
College:					
1 to 3 years	1,931	4,423	7,348	9,397	16,708
4 years	2,607	6,179	9,342	12,418	22,010
5 years or more	—	—	9,987	13,555	25,687

Source: W. V. Grant and L. J. Eiden, *Digest of Education Statistics 1981,* National Center for Education Statistics, Washington, D.C.: GPO, 1981, p. 203.

progress; failure to invest in public education means greater social costs of another variety later on.

Education benefits business as well. It generates sales receipts for firms through enlarged markets; it reduces production costs. Furthermore, schools produce a talent pool from which private industry recruits personnel.

Almost a century ago the English economist Alfred Marshall remarked that the cost of educating a generation of children in a whole city would be repaid amply by one important scientific discovery by one graduate of the city schools. The payoff in agricultural research and development in this nation is a case in point. For all types of research expenditures, the annual rate of return is between 100 and 200 percent.

Abundant natural resources represent potential, but educational development of people is necessary to translate potential into per capita income. A frequently quoted illustration shows Brazil and Colombia rich in natural resources but low in educational development, and Switzerland low in natural resources but high in educational development. Analysis of wealth in these countries reveals that the per capita GNP in Switzerland was over eight times that in Brazil and Colombia.

Quality schools contribute to economic development and their absence can adversely affect the economy and other aspects of a nation. To deny the educational system the resources to reach ever-growing numbers of students and/or to improve its quality is to starve the goose that lays the golden egg.

SCHOOL FISCAL MANAGEMENT OR LOGISTICAL SUPPORT SERVICES

What traditionally was referred to as school business management—the planning, expenditure, and management of the school's financial resources—is a significant part of educational administration. The term *business management* is misleading because, as used in fields other than education, it refers to administration of all aspects of an organization known popularly as a business and operated usually for a profit. The term may connote concern with money rather than quality of education.[16] This in turn may give rise to a flurry of old wives' tales such as: "When business practices come into the school system the quality of education goes out the window," "Efficiency is a cult that destroys a fundamental purpose of school," or "The dollar bill dictates educational decisions."

The terms "logistical support services" and "fiscal and material resource management" more precisely describe the nature of the activities involved and minimize the chance of misconception of the importance and contributions of these activities. "Logistics," as used herein, refers to the process of supplying, maintaining, transporting, storing, accounting, and renewing the human, fiscal, and material resources necessary to initiate, sustain, or modify activities of organized institutions in pursuit of predetermined goals. The term has a military connotation, but military organizations are not alone in requiring coherent logistical systems.

The one-room, one-teacher school is the classic illustration of a "self-contained logistical pattern." The teacher in the one-room school gathered wood, started fires, swept floors, created rudimentary instructional devices, and copied materials out of textbooks. Children walked to school. Financial records were limited if they existed at all.

Keeping professional and other personnel in complex educational organizations supplied with consumable and nonconsumable materials; housed in clean, safe, esthetically attractive, functional facilities; and satisfied with prompt and accurate monthly salary payment requires a more sophisticated logistical system.

Fiscal and material resource management is one part of educational logistics and one of many responsibilities of an educational administrator. It includes such activities as budget making, procuring and handling funds, purchasing or expending funds, controlling inventory, accounting, auditing, financial reporting, analyzing costs, maintaining property records, insuring against unexpected financial losses, providing security, operating school food services, and operating transportation systems.

Fiscal and material resource administration should be subordinate to the purposes of the educational institution and to general school administration. If the business official is coordinate with the superintendent of schools, there is a real danger that the quality of public education may be subordinated to business management objectives. General executive responsibility for all fiscal or business management affairs should remain with the superintendent of schools; all others should report to the board of education through the superintendent.

Budgets and Budgeting as a Process

The budget is the heart of the fiscal management system. It is the fiscal interpretation of the educational programs and services. Therefore, expenditure reductions or inability to generate revenues stipulated in the budget document impact upon the quality and quantity of educational programs and services. The budget as a planning device is future-oriented; as a management device during a fiscal period its purpose is control to insure that expenditures are authorized and do not exceed money available.

The development and use of budgets as a disciplined approach to handling school expenditures can be traced back to 1920. Prior to that time local school-district budgetary practices were rudimentary and were not likely to be a statewide standardized practice. Many of the smaller local school units did not give serious attention to annual budgets until the 1930s, and some not until the 1940s. Local school districts were among the last of the governmental units to operate with budgets, and governments were far behind private industry and business in the implementation of such management practices.

The Budgetary Process

The major phases in the budgetary process are preparation, presentation, adoption and authorization, administration, execution, and appraisal. Budget preparation responsibility lies with the superintendent with delegation to and involvement of the associate or assistant superintendent for business services. The three major stages during the preparation phase are (1) determination of educational objectives and related educational programs; (2) estimate of expenditures or costs related to realization of objectives and operation of programs; and (3) estimate of revenues and other receipts anticipated from local, state, and federal sources. These may be referred to as the educational, expenditure, and revenue plans.

The organization and expression of the educational objectives and programs plan are the most important, the most difficult, and the most likely, unfortunately, to be omitted from the final budget document. During the 1970s there were indications that more serious attention was being given to a declaration of an educational plan in the budget process. The three stages in preparation are interrelated and considered as a unit even though one may precede another. The end product of the preparation phase which may take a few months to 12 months (where there is continuous fiscal planning) is the budget document organized in a format demanded by state law or local district preference. Within the budget document is a declaration of educational objectives and a balanced statement of estimated revenues and expenditures essential to the realization of educational objectives for the fiscal period to come. It may also include special exhibits that detail the sources of operating funds, any unusual expenditure plans, current financial condition of various school funds, and so on.

Formal presentation of the budget document or plan for the next fiscal year is an executive responsibility. Disposition of the budget presentation by formal adoption, rejection, or request for modifications or further consideration is a legislative responsibility fulfilled by board action. The adoption includes formal authorization to implement the educational and expenditure plans.

Administrative authority over the adopted budget is delegated to the chief school executive officer. As long as expenditures are kept within the formally adopted budget, there is no need for formal board approval prior to purchase. A different set of circumstances prevails on extra budgetary matters; it is appropriate under such conditions to seek prior and formal approval prior to any extra budgetary expenditures that may have a profound impact on the fiscal operations for the year.

Appraisal of the budget document is an ongoing process that receives special attention at the end of the fiscal period of the budget. It is a joint responsibility of the board and superintendent, but primary responsibility lies with the policymaking authority. All dimensions of the budget document are appraised, including preparation or planning, accuracy of estimates, care in implementation and administration, and any special monitoring or other control procedures.

The term *balanced budget* is relative and usually means that a balance between, or better, an excess of revenues over expenditures, income, and outgo was achieved.

PPBS or Program Budgeting

PPBS, or the planning-programming-budgeting system, attracted considerable attention in education during the late 1960s, but was almost forgotten and considered "passé" about ten years later. As indicated in a prior chapter it is a decision technology, and it focuses mainly on the educational and expenditures plan with relatively little consideration of the receipts or revenue plan. It is, therefore, more accurately labeled as a "resource allocation decision system" (RADS), but many continue to think of it as primarily a new approach to budgeting.

PPBS does give rise to a different looking format for the budget document for several reasons. This format stresses outcomes rather than functions or activities apart from results, emphasizes planning sophistication, uses analysis of alternative strategies as well as cost-benefit analysis, involves a broader range of administrative expertise beyond those related to fiscal management, and looks beyond the next fiscal year to include the fiscal impact over the next three to five years. The planning di-

mensions of the budget receive more emphasis in PPBS than the monitoring or control dimensions, which are the more traditional aspects. The PPBS budget format is part of the outcomes-oriented management approach.

Zero-based budgeting, or ZBB, is equated, erroneously, by some with PPBS. It has a unique contribution to the budgetary process that goes beyond PPBS, that is, it may be implemented with other decision technologies or budget approaches. The preparation of a new budget usually begins by recording expenditures approved for the current year. From this base a specified additional increment, or decrement, may be made for each item in the new budget. The new budget may also introduce entirely new programs and eliminate some of prior years. This is called "incremental budgeting," for the assumption is that a little something, because of inflation if nothing else, is added for the next budget year, and because of this the so-called deadwood may be continued from one budget year to the next. In ZBB, as the name implies, the base is zero rather than what was allocated in any current or previous budget year. It is assumed that nothing survives that cannot be justified for the next or subsequent fiscal years. It sounds better than it works in practice. It requires a tremendous amount of additional time and paperwork even for items that are demanded in schools by law, that is, are outside the discretion of the board or professional staff. ZBB has generated more talk than action.

Accounting

Accounting focuses upon financial transactions and their reporting and interpretation.[17] It is based upon recording, classifying, summarizing, and reporting in terms of money, activities and events affecting the financial character of the administrative unit and its programs. The exact records to be kept and the manner in which fiscal information is to be classified and summarized depends upon (1) purposes of the institution, (2) financial information required for prudent administration, and (3) principles and practices of accounting.

Although some principles and standards

apply both to public school and commercial accounting, there are fundamental differences between the two.

Purposes of accounting. Purposes of public school accounting are:

1. To safeguard school-district funds from loss, theft, waste, or misuse.
2. To promote budgetary control.
3. To provide information to management that is necessary in policy formulation.
4. To provide information necessary to the public and the school board to appraise the management of the local school system.
5. To provide data required for state reports.
6. To show that legal mandates have been complied with.[18]

The United States Department of Education, formerly Office of Education, financial accounting manual, which has been revised several times, provides a basis for such uniformity among school districts in the United States.[19]

If operations analysis and cost-effectiveness studies are to be facilitated, present education accounting systems must be redesigned to reflect outputs as well as inputs.

Fund Accounting

A fund is a sum of money and/or other fiscal resources segregated to support specified activities within limits set by laws or other regulations. Each fund is an independent fiscal and accounting entity. Those related to receiving and safeguarding money to be used for various purposes are classified as receipt accounts; those more closely related to the disbursement, or spending, of money are called expenditure accounts. In common parlance "funds" may be considered to be synonymous with money; in accounting the term *fund* has a more precise meaning to include not only money but other fiscal resources, as well as a means of relating these resources to specific purposes through the establishment of special classifications or entities. The following types of special accounting entities or funds may be established, as needed, by local public school systems: General Fund, Special Revenue Fund, Debt Service Fund, Capital Projects Fund, Food Services Fund, Pupil Activity Fund, and the Trust and Agency Funds.[20]

Receipt accounts. Receipt accounts for public schools may be classified as revenue-receipt accounts, nonrevenue-receipt accounts, and incoming transfer accounts. Revenue-receipt accounts record money that increases assets without increasing school indebtedness by reducing the value of, or by depleting, school property. Included is revenue from local sources, from intermediate governmental units, from state sources, and from federal agencies. Most tax funds and grants received are classified in revenue-receipt accounts.

Nonrevenue-receipt accounts record money produced as a result of incurring an obligation to the district which must be amortized at some future date or money produced from the sale of school property. In such accounts are recorded sale of school bonds, loans, and similar financial transactions.

Incoming transfer accounts record money received from other school districts for services rendered. Incoming transfer accounts avoid duplication of data on school receipts and, therefore, insure more reliable and more comparable state and national figures on receipts.

Clearing accounts. Clearing accounts or "revolving funds" record gross amounts of money received for various school activities and allowed to accumulate for a specified period of time before being disbursed to appropriate agencies or other accounts. In the conduct of school business affairs certain financial transactions involve a double handling of money. To illustrate, money may be received from the operation of a given activity and then spent again for the same activity in a cycle of operations.

Clearing accounts are used when the single-entry system of bookkeeping is employed. They are not required in the double-entry system; in the double-entry system a profit-loss statement is prepared and either profit or loss is transferred to another fund at the end of a given accounting period.

Expenditure accounts. Schools incur liabilities through the purchase of materials and supplies and through contracts for personal services. Procurement of school materials begins with a requisition—a request by the teacher for approval of the purchase of supplies and equipment. It in turn leads to the purchase order, a document authorizing the seller to deliver described merchandise or materials at a specified price. When accepted by the seller, the purchase order becomes a contract. After materials specified have been shipped to the school system, the seller submits an invoice, a document calling for payment for merchandise delivered. The invoice activates expenditure of funds from the school treasury.

Expenditure accounts for schools classified according to function may include:[21]

Code 1000: *Instruction.* Includes expenditures for activities concerned directly with or aiding in the teaching of students or improving the quality of teaching, such as salaries for teaching, such as salaries for teachers aides, and assistants.

Code 2000: *Supporting services.* All of the instructional support services such as administration, guidance, media, etc. are collected under this broad umbrella of accounts.

The major subfunctions within Code 2000 are:

2100: Support services—Pupils. This must be subdivided further into: Attendance and Social Work Services; Guidance Services, Health Services; Psychological Services; Speech and Pathology Services.

2200: Support services—instructional staff. This may be subdivided into Improvement of Instruction Services and Educational Media Services.

2300: Support services—general administration. This may be subdivided into Board of Education Services and Executive Administration Services.

2400: Support services—school administration. Includes primarily the principals' office expenditures.

2500: Support services—business. This large category is usually subdivided into the following services: Direction of Business Support; Fiscal; Facilities Acquisition and Construction; Operation and Maintenance of Plant; Pupil Transportation; Food; and Internal.

2600: Support services—central. This may be broken down into the following types of services: Direction of Central Support; Planning, Research, Development and Evaluation; Information; Staff; Statistical; and Data Processing.

Code 3000: *Community services.* This major account classification includes expenditures for services not directly related to instruction such as community recreation and other services, public library, child care or custody programs, and nonpublic school services.

Code 4000: *Nonprogrammed charges.* This classification is designed primarily to cope with payments or transfers to other governmental units in or outside the state.

Code 5000: *Debt services.* As the title implies the payment of the principal and interest on bonded indebtedness is included herein.

Each state may design its own and unique classification system for school receipts and expenditures without regard to the recommendations of the U.S. Department of Education. Unique state definitions of school accounting practices that are a great variance from national agreements on uniform accounting standards compound the problems of precise comparisons of educational receipts and expenditures among the states.

Encumbrance accounts. An encumbrance is a commitment of resources prior to actual disbursement of funds to liquidate a liability. It insures that the money cannot be used for anything else until the expenditure has been realized. Encumbrance accounting enables a school district to know how much money has been expended or committed to be spent at any given time. Without encumbrance accounting, the exact financial situation at any period of time can only be estimated.

Auditing

The audit is a systematic investigation, verification, and critical review of financial operations within the school district. Its primary purpose is to verify the financial status of the school system.

They may be classified as general or special audits, or complete or limited audits. A general audit encompasses all fiscal transactions and records for every school fund; it is a comprehensive review. A special audit focuses upon a particular aspect of school fiscal transactions. A complete audit is a thorough analysis of operations, necessitating a careful study of the system of internal control and of all books and accounts, including subsidiary records and supporting documents. A limited audit reviews only selective items; it is based on sampling rather than a complete review of every financial transaction. There are complete general audits, limited general audits, complete special audits, and limited special audits.

Preaudits, continuous audits, and postaudits are classifications based on time. A preaudit is an investigation and critical review prior to consummation of a transaction. It is a means of avoiding expenditures of borderline validity and preventing money appropriated for one purpose from being used for another. A postaudit takes place after the transaction has been completed. It is the most common type of audit and is frequently referred to as the "annual school audit." The most common type of audit required by state law is the annual independent audit, which is a postaudit.

An auditor functions most effectively as an expert in accounting or auditing and least effectively as an expert in educational philosophy and curriculum.

Relatively few laws stipulate the time and scope of the audit, or the qualifications of the school auditor. The school district, rather than the state department of education, is the most suitable agency for directing the school audit.

Cost Accounting and Unit-Cost Analysis

The purposes of unit-cost analysis are to ascertain the costs of operating a given school facility, to judge the efficiency and practicality of certain school activities, to help in the budgeting of activities that can be reduced to measurable units, to estimate costs of proposed projects, and to compare educational costs among communities. Perhaps the most dangerous of these steps is comparison. The temptation to compare costs of educational programs of various districts and among states is very great despite the many chances of misinterpretation.

Unless units are comparable for the area under investigation, unit-cost analysis is of questionable value. Cost accounting for schools is limited by the financial information available and the design of procedures in accounting. A well-designed and well-kept accounting system will facilitate the gathering of cost data but cannot guarantee correct interpretation of such information.

Unit-cost figures for different school systems should be qualified if not based on the same educational program. It is erroneous to assume that the same educational program is being purchased with the same or differing amounts of money in all school systems.

Cost accounting may be confused with cost-effectiveness or cost-utility analyses. The cost-accounting procedures may provide basic data in the cost-effectiveness analysis.

Financial Reporting

Financial reports are a means of informing the school board, professional administrators, and public and state officials of the fiscal state of the school. It is usually the function of the school superintendent to prepare the financial reports. The form and content of a report vary with its purpose.

Legislation and/or policies should spell out which records should be kept and which destroyed. Microfilming is useful to reduce storage requirements of permanent records, but the high cost and possible legal problems cannot be overlooked. As long as there are no specific statutory requirements to the contrary, many school records and reports can be disposed of after ten years without adversely affecting school administration.

Management of Student-Body Activities Funds

The Association of School Business Officials and the United States Office of Education each developed a financial accounting handbook for student-body activities funds. It has been proposed that these funds be placed under school board jurisdiction in clearing accounts. Although students can formulate policies related to management of student-body activities funds, actual business operations, such as purchasing, disbursing, accounting, and reporting, should be performed by professionally prepared adult members of the school staff.

Management of the School Debt

The school debt is part of the total public state and local government debt which is presently about 15 times greater than it was in 1945. The increase in private debt since the end of World War II exceeded the meteoric rise in public debt. School indebtedness is incurred to pay for the construction of educational facilities. School construction financed as capital outlays leveled off and declined during the 1970s; capital outlays during 1980–1981 came to about $6.7 billion and interest on the aggregate school debt came to about $1.85 billion.

Most school-plant construction is financed through the sale of bonds although some districts use pay-as-you-go procedures. A "bond" is a written financial instrument issued by a corporate body authorized by law or its articles of incorporation to borrow money with the following conditions stipulated: the timing of release, rate of interest to be charged, method of principal payments, and length or term of the debt are stipulated in the financial document. A school bond is not a mortgage; bondholders cannot assume ownership of school property if the district or the state defaults on interest or principal payments. The assurance given bondholders is the levying of an irrevocable tax, allowed in most states, for the payment of interest and retirement of the debt.

There are legal restrictions on how much a district may borrow, what type of bonds it may issue, how long the term of the school debt, what procedures must be followed (such as popular elections to approve issuance of bonds) for a legally authorized school debt, and so on. These statutory regulations may enhance the marketing of school bonds at a favorable interest rate and promote better management of school indebtedness by insisting on the issuance of term bonds only. Others that peg the school indebtedness to an unrealistically low percentage of the assessed value of district property compound problems of providing much needed educational facilities.

In most cases, school bonds may not be issued without prior approval of the district's electorate. During the early part of the 1960s at least 72 percent of school bond issues were voted approval; that success ratio for school bond approvals dropped thereafter, so by 1969–1970 only 53.2 percent of bond elections were successful. School bond approvals fell below 50 percent levels during some years of the 1970s, for only 46.7 percent of the issues submitted in 1970–1971 and 46.2 percent in 1974–1975 were successful; nonetheless, the approval rate exceeded 50 percent during most years of the prior decade. Maguire observed that success in bond and millage elections "was associated with absence of controversy and low voter turnout."[22] He noted as well that the voters were more likely to be parents, professional people, and those satisfied with their own education.

Limitations on indebtedness vary among states. Debt limits, as percentages of the assessed value of taxable property, range from 2 percent in some states to 50 percent in others. Because property value for tax purposes is not assessed at the same rate in all states, the debt-limit percentages are difficult to interpret.

All school bonds are debenture bonds (a type not secured by collateral or the tangible assets of the district). Bonds are most frequently classified according to the maturity of principal and the method of making principal payments. Straight-term bonds were used widely to finance the construction of school buildings 50 years ago. Principal payments for this type of bond are not made until the complete issue reaches maturity. Failure to set aside a certain amount of money voluntarily each year for principal payment, or the mismanagement of sums accumulated for principal payment, often necessitated issuing new bonds to pay the principal on the old bonds. This often led to a vicious fiscal circle.

To correct the difficulty inherent in deferring principal payment until maturity date, the voluntary annual principal payment was changed to mandatory accumulation. This did not resolve the problem completely because the amount accumulated to pay principal could be mismanaged or diverted to other purposes.

The serial bond proved the best solution to principal management. A serial bond issue is a collection of many term bonds so organized that a certain number of term bonds reach maturity each year. In other words, the total issue is broken down into several bonds of $1000 or larger denominations, which are numbered serially and which mature periodically in serial order. Principal payments are made on certain numbers of the series each year, along with the interest.

Bonds can also be classified as callable and noncallable. Callable bonds include a special provision which gives the district the privilege of paying the entire debt earlier than the maturity date stipulated at the time of sale of the issue. Noncallable bonds can be paid only at the stipulated date of maturity.

The advantages of issuing serial bonds can be negated if careful scheduling of debt amortization is neglected. Prudent debt management is based on the knowledge of existing and future debt requirements, as well as of the size of issues to be amortized.

The annual interest on the school debt reached $1.87 billion by 1979–1980. Interest rates on school bonds rose during the last two decades. The lowest average interest rate on school bonds was 1.29 percent in February 1946. The highest is yet to be seen, for new high records were set during the 1970s and early 1980s.

Accounting for School Property

The total value of school property exceeds $40 billion. This tremendous investment must be safeguarded and carefully identified with a system of property accounting.

School property accounting is at least 50 years behind accounting for other school financial transactions. Inadequate property records characterize most school districts. This is in stark contrast with the capital-accounting procedures in a business or industry. Property accounting for schools is necessary, but for different reasons from those which prompt it in the business and the commercial world.

The development of the Office of Education property accounting handbook[23] eliminated most reasons for delaying the establishment of property accounting in most schools. A property account can be defined as a descriptive heading under which is posted specific information about land improvements and buildings and equipment owned and/or controlled by the school district. The term *account* is used in the sense of a formal record rather than a descriptive classification of a financial transaction.

The various types of property accounts can be classified under the following headings:

1. Type of plant (elementary, secondary, or other used for instructional or noninstructional purposes).
2. Land facilities.
3. Improvements to school sites.
4. Building facilities (type, kind, cost, and size of building).
5. Equipment (instructional as well as noninstructional).

Protection of School Personnel and Property

At one time attacks on teachers and vandalism of school property were a rarity or not a significant concern. This changed dramatically during the past two decades and continued into the present one, as described in more detail in a previous chapter. The cost of school security forces along with property losses from vandalism, arson, and so on, is presently estimated at $1 billion annually.

School insurance. Insurance is one means of protection against sizable financial losses in the event of some catastrophe that may result in destruction of school property, someone else's property, or life. Insurance companies serve as professional risk bearers, and rely on the mathematical theory of probability and the law of large numbers to spread out annual payments for actual losses suffered. The insurance premium is determined, at least in part, on statistical experience with losses inflicted on properties of any given classification, location, and actual use.

Special studies completed prior to 1960 documented that school insurance payments against fire losses were but a small fraction of premiums collected from school districts. This changed dramatically after 1960 with riots in urban centers and the increased incidence of vandalism and arson against school property. School districts, however, continue to be preferred risks with a relatively low loss experience with fidelity bonds and transportation insurance.

Self-insurance. Self-insurance is practical in the very large district with ample financial resources and with a large number of school buildings scattered throughout the district. The various systems of self-insurance can be classified as no-insurance, insurance reserve, or partial insurance. Under the first system, the school has no insurance payment to make and does not attempt to accumulate reserves to pay for losses; this is practical if losses are so infrequent that they can be met by tax payments or bond issues. Under the second system, the school district creates a reserve fund to defray future financial losses suffered through destruction of property; the school system becomes its own insurance company and losses are covered from the reserve. Under the partial insurance plan, the district insures only the most hazardous risks and carries no insurance on the select risks.

Coinsurance. The insurance rate actually charged a school district is influenced by factors within the community and the nature of the risk.

The coinsurance concept was developed when investigation showed that the sum of partial losses paid exceeded the aggregate sum of total property losses. In other words, in the great proportion of fires, the property damage and loss incurred are a small percentage of the total value of the property.

The insurance company agrees to lower the rate per unit of insured value if the insured promises to carry a given amount of insurance stated at a certain percentage of the full insurable value of the risk. The coinsurance clause is an inducement to keep insurance in force equal to at least a certain percentage of the insurable value of the building. If partial loss occurs and commitments of the coinsurance clause have been satisfied by the district, the latter will receive full payment for the partial loss. If the district failed to keep the correct amount of insurance in force, only a percentage of the partial loss will be paid by the company. This does not apply if total loss occurs, for then only the amount indicated on the face of the policy will be paid. Most authorities recommend that districts take advantage of 80 to 90 percent coinsurance rate reductions.

Management of Transportation

Pupil transportation and school food services are among the more rapidly growing school operations. About 56 percent of the 1978–1979 enrollment, or about 21.8 million students, are transported to a public school at public expense on a daily basis; about 50 years ago only 1.9 million were transported daily. Transportation expenditures rose from about $54.8 million in 1929–1930 to almost $3.2 billion in 1978–1979; present expenditures are over 58 times what they were 50 years ago. The unit cost per pupil transported more than quintupled from $28.81 in 1929–1930 to $146.9 in 1978–1979.

School transportation started as a response to population sparsity, that is, to bring rural area pupils to a central and larger school attendance center. In prior years, few large urban districts were involved in any great degree with pupil transportation. By 1980, however, about one-fourth of the urban school districts transported some high school sophomores to achieve a better racial balance. School transportation is used more frequently now as part of a court-ordered strategy in integration cases, particularly in the southern states and urban communities. For the United States as a whole the overwhelming amount of transportation, in about 91.6 percent of all school districts, is unrelated to efforts to achieve a better racial balance.

In many cases the school district may own school buses and operate directly the school transportation system. In other districts, school bus transportation may be operated by private carriers under contract to a school district to provide such services.

CONSTRUCTION AND MANAGEMENT OF EDUCATIONAL FACILITIES

The 1950s saw the beginning of the most impressive school-plant construction boom in the history of the nation as well as the start of the "golden era" for the design, construction, and management of educational facilities. There were significant breakthroughs in functional design and creative approaches to the development of visual, sonic, thermal, acoustic, and other environments related to school-plant architecture. The sheer magnitude of school construction should not obscure the qualitative improvements that facilitated instruction.

It was indicated previously that the purchase of school sites, construction of buildings, and equipping of educational structures are part of what is known as capital outlay expenditures. They are accounted for separately from those that recur annually for salaries of personnel, textbook purchases, transportation costs, and so on. The costs for educational facilities are large, one-time, rather than recurring, expenses financed through the sale of bonds, usually, whose interest and principal payments are amortized over a period from 20 to 30 years.

The school construction boom ended during the 1960s, but capital outlay costs kept rising during the 1970s even though the amount of construction was down. Expenditures for capital outlays are projected to fall during the 1980s to about $5 billion by 1985 as compared

with the more than $6.5 billion in the late 1970s, continuing inflation notwithstanding.

Most new construction during the 1950s were elementary schools, whereas during the 1960s there were nearly twice as many new secondary school plants constructed as those for lower grade levels. During the 1970s more school plants were abandoned or sold than were constructed. During the 1980s there may be modifications to increase energy efficiency or to make existing facilities more functional, but there is not likely to be the pace of new construction noted in the prior three decades. The diminishing concern for new school-plant construction prompted the substantial reduction in the space devoted to such activities in this edition compared with prior ones.

Nature of the School Plant

The school plant is the space interpretation of the school curriculum. The curriculum finds its physical expression in construction and arrangements of the school plant. The size, proportions, and relations of learning spaces influence the type and quality of instruction. The school site and school building are part of the broad concept known as the school plant.

This functional concept of the school plant emphasizes the effect of plant facilities on educational experiences provided and educational methods employed rather than on materials used in construction. An educational facility may be perceived as a controlled environment that enhances the teaching-learning process while it protects the physical well-being of occupants. Caudill suggested that school planning starts and ends with the pupil and that the building should be designed to satisfy the pupil's physical and emotional needs.[24] Physical needs are met by insuring a safe structure, adequate sanitary facilities, a balanced visual environment, an appropriate thermal environment, a satisfactory acoustical environment, and sufficient shelter space for work and play. Emotional needs are met by creating pleasant surroundings, a friendly atmosphere, and an inspiring environment. This humanistic, pupil-oriented approach to school planning and construction views design and equipment as means of enhancing the pupil's learning and comfort.

Not a single line should be sketched until the curriculum to be housed has been defined. Determination of the educational program precedes designation of the physical pattern and materials of construction. The amount of each kind of space needed for learning depends upon the size of the school enrollment. In addition, the total area, shape, and special design of a classroom are determined by the curriculum offered and instructional methods used. Thus, the lecture method of teaching requires an entirely different type of classroom than does the activity or laboratory method of instruction.

Fredrickson identified the essential information to be described in an educational specifications document as: statement of philosophy; grade levels to be accommodated; enrollment capacity expectations; curricular programs and activities; specific utilization plans; instructional procedures; teaching space requirements; specialized instructional facilities; auxiliary areas; miscellaneous concerns; and summary statement.[25]

School-Plant Needs

Despite the greatest rate of new school-plant construction in history that took place in the 1950s and 1960s, there were in the fall of 1972 over 422,000 pupils on curtailed sessions because of inadequate school housing. This improved dramatically by 1980 so that only a few problem pockets remained. During the early years of history the public school system was plagued with overcrowded and inadequate school plants.[26] As early as 1848, Barnard wrote that almost all school plants were badly located; were exposed to the noise, dust, and danger of highways; and built at the least possible expense of labor and material. He criticized them for being too small, badly lighted, poorly ventilated, imperfectly warmed, and not furnished with seats and desks suitable for pupils.[27] Barnard's indictment does not hold true today.

School-Plant Planning and Cost Controls

The major steps in new school-plant planning and construction include:

1. Analyzing present and future educational needs of the district and relating these to facilities required to satisfy program demands.
2. Assessing the adequacy of existing facilities to satisfy program and enrollment needs at present and in the future as part of a district-wide facilities master plan which describes in detail what is available and what is required at various points in time.
3. Identifying new construction sites and acquiring these sites which are part of or consistent with the educational facilities master plan.
4. Preparing the educational specifications for each school plant needed and as defined in the master plan; the educational specifications should indicate the size, shape, and special characteristics of classrooms and other spaces essential for the curriculum and instructional strategies to be pursued within the school plant.
5. Employing architectural and other planning services to design and prepare drawings required to facilitate future construction that will reflect the needs described within the educational specifications.
6. After completion and adoption of architectural plans, there are the securing of bids, letting of contracts to the successful bidders, and construction in accordance with the approved working drawings.
7. Equipping the completed structure, accepting the completed construction following careful inspection, and using the facility.

The cost of school-plant construction increased rapidly following World War II, particularly during the rapid inflation of the 1970s. There is evidence, however, that construction costs for other types of facilities increased at a far greater rate. School administrators dedicated much careful planning and cost control procedures to accomplish this end.

The Council of Educational Facility Planners did much to promote economy in school-plant planning and construction. They identified the following 13 factors or principles that could influence the achievement of economy in planning and construction:

1. Carefully selecting consultants, architects, and school sites.
2. Careful educational planning.
3. Tailoring the school plant to facilitate functioning of the educational program.
4. Planning the building so that internally it is easily adaptable to changing educational conditions.
5. Planning the building so that it can be enlarged or extended at a reasonable cost.
6. Preparing complete, exact, and accurate drawings and specifications.
7. Using a simple design.
8. Making the building as compact as practicable.
9. Planning certain areas or rooms in the building for multiple use.
10. Designing the building according to a system of modular dimensioning.
11. Using recurring structural units and repetitive installation procedures.
12. Using materials that minimize future maintenance and replacement costs.
13. Having standardized parts of the building prefabricated at the factory.[28]

A building whose initial cost is low is not necessarily economical. Indeed, there appears to exist an inverse relation between the initial cost of a building and its subsequent maintenance cost. In other words, the lower the initial cost of a building, the greater the likelihood of early and continued high maintenance expenses during the lifetime of the structure. A study of Zimmerman indicated a correlation between initial price and subsequent maintenance cost which is greater than can be accounted for by chance.[29]

TRENDS IN SCHOOL-BUILDING DESIGN

Buildings are a tribute not only to the creativeness of architects who employ a variety of materials and construction techniques, but also to the many school superintendents and consultants who devoted much time to school-planning and design. The significant trends in school-plant planning and construction are:

1. Planning the school building from the inside out. The present-day concept of the school building as the physical expression of the curriculum calls for the preparation of educational specifications prior to the creation of working drawings and physical specifications of the building.

2. The team approach to planning. No longer is planning the domain solely of the school board and the architect, with the superintendent acting as an informed bystander. Teachers who use the building and laypersons who help pay for it are involved in advisory committees.

3. Greater use of specially trained resource persons in the planning process. The architect, who has the necessary architectural design and engineering services available is only one of many specialists involved. Services of the school-plant consultant as well as specialists in other areas are used to a greater extent than ever.

4. Increased size and more specialized design of instructional spaces. Classrooms now are larger and are designed around the functions performed within them. The typical elementary school classroom of the 1920s and 1930s measured 600 to 750 square feet; today, the size is 900 square feet or more. The use of laboratory and activity methods of instruction has resulted in larger general-purpose and special-purpose classrooms at the junior and senior high school level as well.

5. Flexibility in design. Buildings are long-lasting structures, and the educational program may change several times during the physical lifetime of a building. Planning for change calls for consideration of such things as classroom areas that are square, end walls or partitions that can be moved readily, and building design that facilitates expansion of the structure in many different directions.

6. Concern for shape and form of the building. The relative merits of one-story and multiple-story structures are still debated. The consensus seems to be that in most cases a one-story building costs from 3 to 5 percent less than a multiple-story structure.[30] However, some schools, particularly secondary schools, are so large as to be unmanageable on one floor. Also, the amount of land available and needed for recreational and instructional purposes may dictate whether a single- or multiple-story structure is used. Nevertheless the trend appears clearly in favor of the single-story structure for both elementary and secondary schools.

7. *Use of larger sites.* The minimums recommended by the Council of Educational Facilities Planners are accepted. No longer is an elementary school built on a half-block or block area, and no longer is a secondary school constructed on a crowded downtown site. The elementary school with 5 to 10 acres and the secondary school with 30 to 40 is no longer unusual.

8. *Concept of the building as more than a collection of classrooms.* Classrooms are no longer all exactly the same size, but vary in area and design in accordance with the instruction carried on in them. Highly specialized spaces such as auditoriums, gymnasiums, swimming pools, shops, and laboratories are considered an integral part of secondary schools.

9. *Concern with quality as well as quantity of lighting.* The importance of a "balanced visual environment" is now almost universally recognized, although implementation lags far behind. Contributions of the Council of Educational Facilities Planners cannot be overlooked in this field.[31]

10. *Concern with thermal environment (temperature, humidity, and air flow) and research to determine conditions most conducive to human comfort for learning.* This includes adequate heating and ventilating in winter and air-conditioning in summer. Air-conditioned schools are now commonplace in all regions of the country not simply the South.

11. *Use of a variety of materials and techniques of construction.* Brick and wood are no longer the basic or only construction materials. Glass (in various forms, such as glass block, plain plate glass, tinted glass) is used extensively. Steel and other metal panels for curtain walls are replacing solid masonry exteriors. New materials are being coupled with new techniques of construction.

12. *Concern for esthetics.* Treatment of masses within the structure as well as blending building design and site have enhanced the appearance of many school structures. The beauty of a school is a tribute to the artistry of the architect who is able to blend educational demands, structural requirements, and building materials into an esthetically pleasing structure.

13. *Use of carpeting.* Carpeting in libraries, classrooms, cafeterias, and administrative suites became common during the 1960s and widely accepted thereafter.

14. *Improved design of components.* The establishment of the School Construction Systems Development (SCSD) in the early 1960s by Educational Facilities Laboratories led to improved design for various components used in school construction.

Construction of new facilities in the core city, where land values are usually high, calls for novel approaches. Some solutions include the high-rise school building, the incorporation of instructional centers in commercial high-rise apartment structures,[32] and the incorporation of instructional centers in large downtown office buildings.

The educational park concept, a revival of the idea of combining facilities for kindergarten through grade 12 on a single site, gained popularity during the 1960s—not because any unusual advantages accrue in terms of building construction but because of a desire to hasten the end of de facto segregation. Unless the site is large enough (about 100 acres) and access roads are adequate to handle sizable traffic volume, however, the educational park concept can precipitate many problems in a congested urban area.

OPERATION AND MAINTENANCE OF FACILITIES

The time it takes for a building to become physically obsolete depends on the quality of the original construction and materials as well as the quality of housekeeping and maintenance. Some buildings have a useful physical life of less than 50 years, whereas others have functioned effectively for more than 75.

Operation includes cleaning, disinfecting, heating, caring for grounds, and similar housekeeping duties, which are repeated somewhat regularly. Maintenance is concerned with keeping grounds, buildings, and equipment in their original condition of completeness or efficiency. Repair and replacement are an essential part of maintenance. Operation and maintenance have the common objective of keeping school property in the best possible condition for effective education at all times. Because housekeeping activities can be looked upon as preventive maintenance, separation of operation and maintenance is rather artificial; new terminology is needed.

Employment of custodians by the school board without consideration of recommendations by administrators responsible for their performance is poor personnel procedure. In some states, employment of all nonteaching personnel is subject to civil service rules, and permanent employees are selected only from a list established as a result of examinations. This is an encouraging development, for it removes a post vital to preservation of school property from political favoritism or sentimentality.

At the building level the principal is the immediate superior of the building custodian. The director of plant operations and maintenance for the district and staff is a source of professional aid to the custodian in solving technical problems related to the cleaning and care of the building. They also direct the in-service programs for custodial personnel. It is not the function of teachers to command activities of building custodians. Failure to define lines of authority can result in conflicts among teachers, principals, school-plant supervisors, and building custodians.

Custodial work schedules can save work, simplify tasks, and improve performance. The custodial requirements of a school building vary with the type and age of the structure.

Studies have shown that custodial manpower needs of a building can be determined on the basis of (1) the nature and number of school tasks of the custodian; (2) the setup time and total time required for each and all tasks; (3) the accepted standards for the number of minutes in a man-unit; and (4) the computation of man-units by dividing (2) by (3).

Systematic inspection of each school building at least annually is an important first step toward an effective maintenance program. Regular inspections can detect small difficulties. Record keeping is necessary to obtain the full benefit of periodic inspection.

The question sometimes arises whether maintenance work should be done by custodians, special maintenance crews, or through contracts with outside agencies. The general rule is that the more out of the ordinary the maintenance work is the more likely it will be done on a contract basis by outside staff. Complicated maintenance work that necessitates a highly specialized staff is likely to be done by a contract force.

It is a responsibility of the superintendent and the principal to formulate the kind of building operation and maintenance program that will extend the useful physical life of building and equipment. Davis indicated that the principal has primary responsibility for the utilization and care of the building. He outlined procedures for analyzing a variety of facility concerns including procedures for analyzing custodial problems.[33]

THE MANAGEMENT OF THE CLOSING AND DISPOSITION OF EDUCATIONAL FACILITIES

One new challenge for school management that appeared during the 1970s was when and how to close and/or to dispose of school attendance centers operating below the optimum capacity design levels. There were about 4625 fewer schools in operation in 1980–1981 compared with those at the beginning of the 1970s (90,821 in 1970–1971 compared with 86,198 in 1980–1981). There were more than 2500 fewer elementary schools, but actually an increase of more than 1000 secondary schools during that period.[34] The declines were largest among schools enrolling fewer than 100 and next largest for those with 1000 or more students; those with 250 to 499 students showed an increase of 16 percent. The closing of schools continued into the 1980s, for there were over 2200 fewer schools in 1982–1983 than there were in 1981–1982.

The management of retrenchment is sensitive and generates emotional stress among certain community groups, students, and educational personnel. The administrators may be caught between criticisms related to rising expenditures resulting in part from operating uneconomic school centers and those related to recommendations to close uneconomic attendance centers. The political and emotional factors should be considered by the administrator before submitting any rationally based recommendations to the school board on specific school closures. The primarily rational factors, rather than political and emotional, to be considered in arriving at a closing decision are:

1. *Location of Uneconomic Centers Within the System.* All other things being equal, facilities in the least appropriate locations and with declining school-age populations should be abandoned before others because the prognosis would be a continuing drop in operating efficiency. Some of the major indicators of problem sites are growing commercialization, major traffic arteries and traffic congestion, and in-migration of an older or very young resident to replace those who were parts of families with school-age children.

2. *Educational or Functional Quality of the Structure.* Facilities that are functionally obsolete (poorly designed to facilitate the new curriculum and instructional strategies of today) even though structurally sound deserve to be placed high on the list of those to be closed.

3. *Structural Quality.* Structural defects, whether obvious or not, inability to sustain earthquakes, fire dangers, and so on, rank high among the reasons for early abandonment and seldom generate much opposition to closure. Less obvious are defects in the quality of lighting (better called "visual environment"), heating, or air conditioning. These may be improved but often at a very high cost.

4. *Building Maintenance Costs.* Facilities that are more difficult and costly to maintain in a functional, safe, and attractive manner should be scheduled for abandonment when conditions warrant it.

5. *Site Inadequacies.* School sites that are too small for program operations or building capacity, that are noisy because of proximity to air traffic patterns or other reasons, that are poorly developed for educational use, and so on, deserve priority consideration for abandonment if there are other ways to serve the school-age population.

6. *Energy Utilization Factors.* Some structures have special design problems that preclude efficient use of energy and require higher building-operating costs. This can be a factor in closure decisions.

7. *Community Utilization.* Community needs that are served by the schoolhouse deserve special consideration in any planned abandonment decision.

8. *Ease of Conversion to Other Educational Use or for Sale.* Schools are usually in residential areas and their conversion to other uses may require some degree of rezoning. Those in commercial areas present less of a problem. Some closed schools have been sold and then converted to restaurants, town halls, museums, housing for the elderly, commercial office space, and other uses that are limited only by the imagination of the person and needs of the community. The cost of conversion and added traffic or social problems are also limitations. There is likely to be resistance from the community if the closed schoolhouse is to be converted to something that would change the character of the neighborhood, such as creating drug rehabilitation centers or special penal facilities.

There is no substitute for the exercise of administrator judgment in interpreting data gathered, weighting of all rational factors, as well as careful consideration of political, social, and political factors.

SUMMARY

The educational administrator must demonstrate leadership and management expertise in procuring and protecting educational resources as well as providing and propelling curriculum and instructional objectives and programs. Educational finance systems have been modified frequently to reflect emerging educational priorities and the ability to generate needed resources by the existing finance system. Nontax sources of school revenues were tried and when they failed to deliver the resources needed, local property taxes were authorized to support public education.

Resources allocated to public education doubled or almost tripled during each of the decades following World War II. Total educational expenditures include current expenses for recurring annual costs of salaries and materials, capital outlay costs for buildings and equipment, and debt service payments for bond interest. Current expenditures increased from less than $1 billion annually at the start of the twentieth century to an estimated $90 billion in 1980–1981; capital outlay climbed from less than $150 million to about $6.7 billion in 1980–1981; and debt service interest payments from less that $18 million to about $1.85 billion in 1980–1981. Total educational expenditures approached $100 billion in 1980–1981 and may be in the $200 billion to $250 billion range by the early 1990s. Much of the increase during the 1970s can be traced to inflation, for the unit costs increased 2.6 times when measured in unadjusted dollars but only 1.35 times when the 1980 dollars were adjusted for the impact of inflation.

During the early part of the twentieth century and before, 83 percent of all public school revenues came from local sources. The local share declined to only 44.5 percent by 1978–1979 to fall below the state's share of 45.7 percent for the first time in history; federal contributions were just below 10 percent and predicted to decline during the 1980s. The property tax has many shortcomings, is best suited for local taxing units, and may have reached its psychological limits for school support during the 1970s. State and federal tax resources are more varied, with the most prolific revenue raisers being such nonproperty taxes as the retail sales and income taxes.

Educational finance has a broad and a specific interpretation, with the more specific interpretation being only the generation and distribution of fiscal resources for public education. There are 50 different state-educational finance systems rather than a single national one. There is considerable variation in the magnitude of dollars generated for education in the states; in 1979–1980, 52 percent of the states recorded current expenditures of more than $1 billion annually. Inequality of local school-district property values and the failure of that tax to generate the revenues needed to keep pace with growth led to greater state contributions to the public educational finance system. The distribution of state monies to local systems started with crude flat grants and then moved to foundation program equalization and to "power equalization" of local school tax rates and more comprehensive educational programs.

The so-called voucher system of educational finance focuses on the distribution of state and federal educational dollars directly to parents of school-age children and has little to offer to the other dimensions of educational finance. It assumes that parents can influence the quality of education by moving students to specific types of schools, public or private, when armed with state-issued educational vouchers. Efforts to install this approach to state funds distribution have not met with success as yet.

There were near bankruptcies of school systems during the 1970s and other indications of fiscal crises. There were many court challenges of state-educational finance systems during the 1970s which focused not on forcing the state to generate more money for public education but upon the inequities (assumed to be violations of state and/or federal constitutions) in the distribution of property wealth among school districts. There was evidence of considerable effort to reform state educational finance systems.

The United States has the wealth to support public education, and such expenditures are considered an investment in the development of human resources. The quality and quantity of education influence the economic development of a nation, enhance the earning power of individuals, and reduce the incidence of social and welfare problems. Economic productivity is influenced by the quality of human capital as well as quantity of physical capital.

Fiscal and material resource management becomes important after funds have been received. The school board should delegate school business management to the superintendent of schools; any school business director or manager should be subordinate to the superintendent.

Effective fiscal administration rests upon budget making, accounting, auditing, and financial reporting.

The budget is the heart of financial management and is the fiscal translation of the educational program; the accounts reveal financial status, and the audit verifies its accuracy. All cost accounting depends on the accuracy of financial records. A well-designed and well-kept accounting system will facilitate the gathering of cost data, but cannot guarantee the correct interpretation of such information.

Facilities are financed largely by the issuance of bonds. Most schools issue serial bonds, for this provides a more systematic means of making principal payments. School property represents a tremendous investment and should be protected by a system of property accounting. Crimes against persons and vandalism of school property increased dramatically. Property accounting for schools lags far behind the recording of other financial transactions.

Insurance is protection against the likelihood of financial loss from various sources. There are a variety of school self-insurance plans, such as no-insurance, insurance reserve, and partial insurance.

There is a close relation between the school curriculum and the school plant. The school plant can be defined as the physical expression or space interpretation of the curriculum. The 1950s and 1960s were periods of great school-plant construction as well as of advances in design and architecture.

Major steps in school-plant construction include analysis of educational needs, development of a master building plan, procurement of the necessary site, preparation of educational specifications for each project, design of the building, securing bids and letting contracts to erect the building, and equipping and using the building.

School construction costs have increased, but not as much as the cost of other types of construction. Low initial cost of a building is not necessarily an indication of an economical structure.

The significant trends in school construction in the years following World War II are planning from the inside out, the team approach to planning, greater use of specialized resource persons, increase in size and specialization of instructional spaces, flexibility of design, concern for the shape and form of the building, use of larger school sites, expansion in complexity of a building, concern for lighting and for thermal environment, use of a variety of techniques and materials of construction, and concern for esthetics in building design.

The quality of custodial services is reflected in the condition of the building and its years of usefulness. The building custodian is responsible to the building principal.

NOTES

1. W. V. Grant and L. J. Eiden, *Digest of Education Statistics 1981*, National Center for Education Statistics, Washington, D.C.: GPO, 1981, p. 24.

2. N. B. Dearman and V. W. Plisko, eds., *The Condition of Education 1982 Edition*, Washington, D.C.: GPO, 1982, p. 41.

3. Ibid., p. 62.

4. S. J. Knezevich and John Guy Fowlkes, *Business Management of Local School Systems,* New York: Harper & Row, 1960, p. 47.

5. F. W. Swift, *Federal and State Policies in Public School Finance in the United States,* Boston: Ginn, 1931, p. 61.

6. R. L. Johns and E. L. Morphet, *The Economics and Financing of Education,* 3rd ed., Englewood Cliffs, N.J.: Prentice-Hall, 1975, p. 236.

7. See E. L. Lindman, "Dilemmas of School Finance," *ERS Monograph,* Arlington, Va.: Educational Research Service, 1975, 53 pp., for a concise review of this and other educational finance systems concepts.

8. Educational Research Service, "1980 Election Results: Initiatives, Propositions, and Constitutional Amendments," *ERS Research Digest,* Arlington, Va.: ERS, 1980, 4 pp.

9. See F. Harbison and C. A. Myers, *Education, Manpower, and Economic Growth,* New York: McGraw-Hill, 1964, p. 3.

10. Ibid., p. 13.

11. American Association of School Administrators, op. cit., p. 13.

12. Ibid., p. 34.

13. Ibid., p. 36.

14. H. B. Miller, *Rich Man, Poor Man,* New York: Cole, 1964, p. 145.

15. Christopher Johnson, "Our Investment in Public Education," *Today's Education,* Vol. 71, No. 1, pp. 15–17, February–March 1982.

16. See S. J. Knezevich, "Fiscal and Material Resource Management as an Aspect of Educational Logistics," in W. E. Gauerke and J. R. Childress, eds., *The Theory and Practice of School Finance,* Chicago: Rand McNally, 1967, chap. 7, where these ideas were developed originally.

17. Knezevich and Fowlkes, op. cit., chap. 3; see also B. K. Adams et al., *Principles of Public School Accounting,* OE-22025, Washington, D.C.: GPO, 1967, p. 260.

18. Knezevich and Fowlkes, op. cit.

19. C. T. Roberts and A. R. Lichtenberger, *Financial Accounting Classifications and Standard Terminology for Local and State School Systems,* Handbook II, rev. ed., DHEW Publication NO. (OE) 73-11800, Washington, D.C.: GPO, 1973, 194, pp.

20. Ibid.. p. 4.

21. Ibid., pp. 36–49.

22. John W. Maguire, "Political Techniques in School Bond and Millage Elections," *School and Society,* December 1971, pp. 514–515.

23. U.S. Office of Education, *Property Accounting Handbook,* Handbook NO. 3, Washington, D.C.: GPO, 1958.

24. W. W. Caudill, *Toward Better School Design,* New York: McGraw-Hill, 1954, chap. 1.

25. H. Fredrickson, "The Principal and School Plant Planning," *The Bulletin of the Wisconsin Secondary School Administrators Association,* Vol. 1, No. 3, Spring 1973, pp. 13, 16.

26. S. J. Knezevich, "Inadequate School Plant Facilities," *The American School Board Journal,* May 1954, p. 44.

27. Henry Barnard, *Principles of School Architecture,* Hartford, Conn.: Case, Tiffany, 1858, pp. 11–12.

28. Council of Educational Facilities Planners, *Thirteen Principles of Economy in School Plant Planning and Construction,* Columbus, Ohio: The Council, 1955.

29. William J. Zimmerman, *"The Relationship of Initial Cost and Maintenance Cost in Elementary School Buildings,"* doctoral thesis, Stanford, Calif.: Stanford University, 1959.

30. Educational Facilities Laboratories, op. cit., p. 74.

31. Council of Educational Facilities, op. cit.

32. American Association of School Administrators, *Schools for America,* Report of the AASA School Building Commission, Arlington, Va.: The Association, 1967, chap. 7.

33. Clark Davis, *The Principal's Guide to Educational Facilities,* Columbus, Ohio: Chas. Merrill, 1973, chap. 4.

34. N. B. Dearman and V. W. Plisko, op. cit., pp. 48 and 50.

CHAPTER REVIEW QUESTIONS

1. What factors stimulated the changing patterns of finance for schools during the nineteenth and twentieth centuries?

2. What evidence is there to support the contention that the United States has the financial capability to finance expanded educational programs?

3. Which taxes yield best for local governments? State governments? The federal government?

4. Does better education cost more? Justify your position.

5. What should be the fundamental purposes of school fiscal and material resource management?

6. What are the instruments necessary for efficient financial administration?
7. What is PPBS?
8. What changes in school accounting are necessary to develop a school program-budgeting system?
9. What is the relation between education and economic development of a nation?
10. What is a school building?

11. What have been the significant trends in school-plant construction?
12. What is the role of the school board in school-plant planning? Of the superintendent? Of specialists?
13. How can the educational usefulness of a school plant be extended?

SELECTED REFERENCES

Davis, J. Clark, and Loveless, E. E., *The Administrator and Educational Facilities,* Washington, D.C.: University Press of America, 1981, 258 pp.

Harbison, F., and Myers, C. A., *Education, Manpower, and Economic Growth,* New York: McGraw-Hill, 1964.

Johns, R. L., and Morphet, E. L., *The Economics and Financing of Education,* 3rd ed., Englewood Cliffs, N.J.: Prentice-Hall, 1975, 486 pp.

Johnson, C., "Our Investment in Public Education," *Today's Education,* Vol. 71, No. 1, pp. 15–17, February–March 1982.

Rakich, Ronald, "Risk Management," *The School Administrator,* November 1982, pp. 1, 10–11, 13.

24

PUBLIC RELATIONS, POLITICS, POLICIES, AND THEIR IMPACT ON EDUCATIONAL MANAGEMENT: GAINING COMMUNITY ACCEPTANCE AND UNDERSTANDING POWER STRUCTURES

Public schools were created by the people, represent one dimension of public policymaking, and must operate within a political environment. Politics, in its best interpretation, means being part of the political system or branch of government and subject to the influences of formal and informal coalitions of power in a community, state, and/or nation. There are political dimensions to the art of school administration. As Gregg put it, "politics . . . is public, not private, in the sense that its aim is the influencing of decisions relating to public issues within a political system."[1] In this sense the school is a political system within which power and influence swirl and is, as well, part of a broader political system for the state and nation. Education is the public's business. It is necessary for administrators to comprehend how public policy is shaped, that is, the nature of the political decision-making process of local school boards, state legislatures, and the federal Congress. The power structure at various levels is dynamic and the administrator must sense when a new power elite emerges. Maguire declared that school boards and adminis-

trators should be aware that the changing voter profile could have serious consequences in school elections.[2]

As one-teacher schools were replaced by many and large attendance centers, the distance between teachers and the people widened. The involvement of the citizenry through the town meeting was no longer feasible. Information-disbursing procedures effective in the small district failed in complex ones. The problem was intensified when professional administrators assumed executive responsibility for complex institutions.

The times demanded an executive organization, but the widening gap between school and community was an unwanted corollary. Nevertheless, public apathy could be tolerated as long as educational needs remained relatively unchanged, most needs were satisfied, and resource demands did not grow at unprecedented rates.

After World War II demands on public education increased at an unprecedented rate. What the public *did not know about school problems could hurt the system's development.* The basic notion that public education needs public sympathy and support for its continuance and expansion was rediscovered in the late 1940s. The continuing criticisms of public education following World War II further spotlighted the importance of effective relations between school, home, and community. Those responsible for the administration of public education started to redevelop the art of keeping people informed and interested in public education and of identifying and understanding the community power structure. Closer ties between the people and their schools were encouraged anew despite the ever-growing size and complexity of districts. Administrators became more sensitive to the need for a better understanding of the politics of school administration.

Public relations, politics, and policies are interrelated. Public relations, as its name implies, seeks to establish public understanding and community acceptance and support for public education as a whole and its operation within a specific district. Public information, communicated through whatever media or form, influences politics and the policy-forming process, and vice versa. Politics focuses on power distributions and utilization patterns in public agencies or government. It includes how individuals or groups gain access to or control over public decision-making power within governmental units. Lastly, policies are developed, adopted, and implemented to influence future courses of action; that is, there are ways to enhance consistency and fairness in government operations and in relationships with the public or special groups such as teachers and pupils.

PUBLIC CRITICISMS AND ATTITUDES TOWARD PUBLIC EDUCATION

Since the dawn of history social institutions responsible for education of children and youths have been prime targets of criticism, particularly during times of social unrest or upheaval such as an economic depression, loss of face from not being the first in something, embar-

rassment from a propaganda disadvantage, or internal civil rights or interracial conflicts. Criticisms of existing educational systems in all countries of the world have waxed and waned over past centuries. Their intensity can be predicted, for whenever a nation or culture is experiencing social or physical duress of any kind its social institutions will come under attack from its own people. Criticisms often have a strong emotional bias and, therefore, may continue long after charges that stimulated them were proved wrong. Emotions can overpower the rational, at least for a short time.

The United States was neither the first nor will it be the last to have its systems of public education suffer criticisms; our nation's schools are not the only ones to face such attacks at present. Criticisms of state systems of public education in the United States in the years following World War II reached a peak shortly before 1950, died down for a while, and then were triggered anew by the first Soviet success in orbiting a space satellite. The latter led to an attack on the quality of mathematics, science, and reading instruction in the public schools, which continued even after some spectacular space successes that clearly put the U.S. space program ahead of the Soviets. The public schools received no plaudits for the nation's successful space program. During the 1970s the more heated criticisms were directed at escalating school costs and lack of accountability. No issue facing public education is ever resolved with a degree of finality; even what many consider the basic traditions of public education are not immune to present or future challenges.

The school administrator must expect and accept criticisms as inevitable and part of the price for being involved in a socially sensitive institution. Public apathy is a far greater concern; criticism betrays a degree of interest and a point of departure for possible improved future relations. Positive criticisms honestly presented may be the stimulus for educational change. A defensive posture or propensity to dismiss abruptly all critics is not in the best interests of public education or educational administration. Conflict is a characteristic of our times and not always something that could have been avoided. Even the best led school districts will experience conflict. The behavior of the administrator under the stress and strain of continuing criticism is one measure of the quality of the professional.

During the 1970s and continuing in the 1980s the Kettering Foundation sponsored annual studies by the Gallup Poll Organization on public attitudes toward public education. Newspaper and news magazine headlines, more often than not, focused attention on what was negative; the perennial problem facing school public relations is the balanced portrayal of the public school story that goes beyond that which is likely to "grab the attention" of readers.

Data based on Gallup polls reveal that the percentage of parents rating schools "A" or "B" increased during the early 1970s to a peak of almost 50 percent in 1974. After that came a decline, to hit a low of about 34 percent in 1979; followed by small gains each year thereafter to reach 37 percent in 1982. Other surveys confirm this cycle of ratings but with different figures. The media interpretations up to 1979 were that there was a "loss of public confidence" in public education, which is valid within certain limits. A more precise interpretation is that the overwhelming majority of the public gave the schools a "passing" grade but not "high marks" or "failure." At no time did more than one in five of those surveyed give the public schools a "poor" or "failing" grade.

More detailed data analysis of the Gallup Poll and other opinion surveys indicate:

1. Although public confidence in educational leaders declined during the 1970s, the confidence rating was higher in each year than that recorded for leaders in Congress, major private business concerns, the federal executive branch, and the media or press. In short, during the 1970s *the public was very critical of most institutional leaders,* and did not single out educational leaders from others.
2. *Parents with children in public schools rate them substantially higher than those with children in parochial schools or with no school-age children.*

Thus, according to the 1979 Gallup report, with similar data indicated in other reports, public schools received an A or B rating from the majority, or 51 percent, of parents with children in public schools, but from only 23 percent of parents with children attending parochial schools. There are other data that support the generalization that those least involved in public education tend to give it the lowest marks and least support.

3. There were rating variations noted by regions and by racial backgrounds. Thus, blacks in the North are far more critical of public schools than are whites from the North or South. Nonetheless, less than 30 percent of all nonwhites "fail" public education with a rating of D or F.
4. Persons in communities of less than 50,000 rank their public schools substantially higher than those in larger population centers. The lowest rankings come from persons in central cities with populations of 500,000 or more. Public schools in the "Great Cities" enjoy less public confidence than elsewhere. The reverse is true for residents of small and rural communities who exhibit considerable faith and confidence in their public schools.
5. A resounding 60 percent of public school enrollees state they "enjoy very much" attending, whereas only 8 percent seem to "enjoy school very little." Almost 89 percent of the young persons sampled expressed positive feelings toward their public schools.

Public rating declines appeared to parallel the drop in school enrollments during the 1970s. Negative attitudes toward public education are influenced by such factors as escalating school costs and tax rates; social and/or economic conflicts within heterogeneous communities; loyalty to private or religious schools; integration conflicts and court orders that demand cross-district busing, and limited information about the quality of public school programs and opportunities.

Criticisms reach a crescendo followed by a substantial easing of negative attacks. Rational analysis of its substantive and emotional elements should lead the administrator to determine the source by specific individuals or groups, what triggered the attack, what can be done to correct the specific irritation, and how to minimize recurrence. One writer noted that perceptions of major school problems by professionals in education are not completely consistent with those of the public as a whole. Thus, polls and surveys of public opinions usually place lack of discipline, students' use of drugs, and poor curriculum/low standards, respectively, among the three top problems facing the public schools, whereas school officials did not perceive these as belonging in the top ten major problems and ranked them as 14, 15, and 16, respectively.[3] The top problem from the school officials' point of view was inflation/financial support, which was ranked fourth by the public in general (usually second in Gallup polls). Declining enrollment and governmental interference were rated the top second and third by school officials, but only in the middle of the second ten problems by the public. Lack of discipline was the number one complaint in 1982 and for more than two previous decades. Others move in and out of the top ten problems. Employing "good" teachers was one of the prime concerns until layoffs rather than teacher shortages began around the mid-1970s. Integration/desegregation through cross-district busing was the number 2 concern during the early 1970s, but dropped to about number 5 (number 7 in the 1982 Gallup poll) in the public's perception in 1981 and number 18 in the school official's perception. Rather unusual is the relatively low ranking given to crime and vandalism; in 1982 it ranked 13 in the Gallup Poll and 18 in the school officials' perception. If current publicity is a portent of things to come, crime and vandalism may emerge as one of the top five problems during the 1980s.

GROUPS ASSUMING PUBLIC LEADERSHIP ROLES IN SUPPORT OF PUBLIC EDUCATION

A number of community and national groups were formed at various points in history to rally to the support of public education during times of crises and/or severe criticism. The contributions of volunteers who promoted the cause of public education deserve special recognition.

PTA

The National Congress of Mothers was founded in 1897 for the promotion of education in motherhood, child health, child feeding, and morality through the development of a strong body and healthy mind. In 1908 it changed its name to the National Congress of Mothers and Parent-Teacher Association; shortened in 1924 to the National Congress of Parents and Teachers. It is referred to as the PTA.

The national organization represents the constituent state and local PTAs. Membership more than doubled in the two decades following the end of World War II, stabilized at a high level during the 1970s, and is presently an estimated 12 million members. Membership includes mostly teachers and parents of school-age children.

The PTA, the oldest of the formally organized public education support groups, is a general type of a citizens' organization concerned with the school as a whole and all its educational programs. There are, in addition, special-education interest groups such as the "parents of athletes" and "band mothers" whose focus on a single dimension of the school separate them from the PTA. PTA units that devote all or most of their time to purchase some special equipment or curtains for the school auditorium may neglect to focus on activities more crucial to the development of the education of the child and the promotion of public education in general.

The PTA faced intraorganizational conflicts during the past two decades. In some cases, special-interest groups attempted to take over the leadership and control to promote their single issue or limited purposes. Others with different agendas formed separate parent-teacher organizations unaffiliated with the national or state PTA. Some used the name which was very similar and was called the PTO (Parent-Teacher Organization).

The PTA is strongest at the elementary school level and weakest in secondary schools. It appears to have less impact and appeal in core cities where the largest number of disadvantaged pupils may be located. More militant groups from low socioeconomic areas have been critical of the PTA for being dominated by "middle-class values." Administrators of attendance centers (principals) tend to interact more frequently and directly with the PTA than do those at the central-office level.

The general objectives of the PTA are:

1. To promote the welfare of children and youths in the home, church, and community.
2. To raise standards of home life.
3. To secure adequate laws for care and protection of children and youth.
4. To bring closer relations between home and school so that parents and teachers may cooperate effectively in enhancing learning.
5. To develop between educators and the general public such united efforts as will secure for every child the highest advantages in physical, mental, social, and spiritual education.

The National Citizen's Commission

The National Citizen's Commission for the Public Schools (NCCPS) had a brief but significant history. It rekindled the American tradition of citizens banding together for the improvement and support of the public schools. It was organized in 1949 at a time when public schools faced growing criticisms. Many outstanding persons in business, labor, law, and publishing helped to found and to promote NCCPS being convinced that an informed citizenry was essential to the American democracy, and, that public schools were critically important to the nation. Roy E. Larson, then president of Time, Inc., was its first chairman and declared: "Problems of public education concern all of us and it is time for all of us to do something about it."

The NCCPS influenced public policymaking and decision making to promote the advancement of public education. The organization fought for the best education and made it available to every American child on equal terms. It sought to help Americans realize how important schools were to a dynamic democracy, and for that reason sought to arouse in each community the intelligence and will to improve public schools.

It was unique for containing built-in termination of the organization after six years. NCCPS was replaced by the National Citizen's Commission for Better Schools in January 1956; the latter terminated all formal activities at the end of 1959. The total life span of both was about ten years and during that time it contributed considerably.

The Advertising Council, a nonprofit organization, helped the NCCPS to arouse citizens and to stimulate communities to organize for school improvement. There was only a handful of citizen's committees during 1949, with less than 200 a year later, but many thousands by 1960 with estimates ranging from 7500 to 20,000. Only a fraction of the local and state education citizen's committees was in regular communication with NCCPS.

The NCCPS did much to counteract the unwarranted criticisms of public education and laid the foundation for improvement programs in public education as well as in the organization and involvement of lay advisory committees in a host of educational planning and operation activities.

The Roundtable of Public Schools

The Roundtable of Public Schools came into being in 1953. It was based on the idea that the most effective way to reach people and influence public opinion was through existing organizations—service clubs, business and industrial groups, farm and labor organizations, and so on—rather than to create new mechanisms. It was not an action body; it did not commit component organizations to anything. Its purpose was to improve the character and effectiveness of organizational efforts in behalf of public education.

Lay Advisory Committees

The political impact of lay advisory committees in education reached a high point during the 1950s. The NCCPS was instrumental in stimulating the great interest in forming and using lay advisory committees, and they served for a time as a national clearing house to enhance their productivity or more effective use. Lay advisory committees remain common today but as an ad hoc or special-purpose advisory group rather than as a continuing formal agency.

Such committees help to communicate information about schools to the community and funnel facts and feelings of the community to school officials. Their prime purpose is to minimize misinformation, misunderstandings, and mistrust.

Advisory committees include persons with a vital interest in public education, who are willing and able to devote time to study educational problems, and who can represent the various social groups or special interests in the community. The general principle of excluding persons who do not believe in public education should be interpreted carefully; it should not be assumed automatically that those who send their children to private schools are opposed to the principle of public education for all.

Responsibility for appointing or organizing a lay advisory committee should rest with an agency which has the confidence of the public. Many shy away from participation unless some sort of public recognition or status is granted to the lay advisory group. Furthermore, a self-appointed group that serves without public recognition is often a pressure group fighting for special favors or power rather than trying to solve a community problem. In communities where the board of education enjoys the respect of the citizenry, it usually takes the initiative and responsibility for appointment. If the local board is not held in good repute, some other public agency must assume this responsibility.

Activities of lay committees. Tenure of the committee is related to the number and intensity of problems that require attention. If there is a need for a special group, then concern about how to keep the committee busy is without foundation. The advisory committee should think of itself as a work group that gathers facts and information about the school and community. The airing of personal feelings during committee meetings has its advantages and disadvantages. If the lay committee becomes preoccupied with ventilation of personal prejudices, it may lose credibility with the public and professionals. The community treasures those things it helped to create.

The process of working out the answer to an educational problem is as significant as conclusions reached. Although professional educators can sometimes perform research on community educational problems in a shorter time, a lay group may be in a better position to communicate the special problems and answers to the community. In some instances, the lay group may be in a better position to obtain the information needed.

Relations with the school board. The relation between the lay advisory committee for education and the board of education often needs clear definition. A lay advisory group is not organized to take the place of the board.

The board of education cannot be forced to accept recommendations of a lay advisory group. It follows, however, that if the recommendations of such a group are repeatedly ignored or rejected, the morale and effectiveness of the group will be gravely impaired. The board of education has an obligation to inform the group when it disagrees with the advice offered.

The superintendent of schools is usually not a member of the lay advisory committee, but stands ready to serve in an advisory capacity if and when professional services are requested. The need for professional assistance from the superintendent or other members of staff will become apparent as the committee pursues its attack on educational problems.

Relations with the PTA. Does a lay advisory group duplicate the functions of the local PTAs? The NCCPS recognized the PTA as a lay group in education if actually functioning effectively within the community. If this is true, a need for another one may be questioned unless broader representation is sought. The citizen involvement movement stimulated membership in PTAs rather than decreased it. Special or ad hoc groups with broader representation should be able to work well and reinforce the contributions of the PTA.

Citizen Councils

Lay advisory groups grew out of local needs, were not mandated by any state or federal law, and were not provided financial support from state and/or federal legislation while deliberating upon education in general and district-wide policies. Closely related, but coming about a decade later, was another approach to lay participation in specific dimensions of education or in certain types of attendance centers. For want of a better title they are identified herein as "Citizen Councils" that took their rise during the late 1960s, flourished during the 1970s, and continued into the 1980s. These Councils did not grow out of the NCCPS thrusts and are unrelated in time and purposes with those groups that are concerned with the promotion of public education in general.

What makes the Councils unique and separate from earlier lay involvement in public education are at least the following: a Citizen Council (1) is encouraged if not mandated by a state or federal law and/or policy even though it functions at the local level; (2) tends to focus on a specific educational program such as the federal Title I program; (3) may demand and even obtain a court order for authority to monitor classroom activities on a regular basis; (4) may strongly influence administrative actions and decisions at attendance centers through pressures and authority rather than soundness of advice or arguments; and (5) may band with similar groups to form statewide coalitions of such Councils. It may not be appropriate to designate such groups as purely advisory or as deliberative bodies, for the monitoring and other authority go far beyond that of the typical ad hoc lay advisory groups.

The degree of involvement of Citizen Councils in the detailed and continuing operations of specific school buildings and programs is far greater than ever envisaged by other proponents of lay participation in promoting the cause of public education. Some have referred to what are called "Councils" herein as "citizen activist" groups and many have become controversial when they assumed more and more administrator prerogatives, that is, became lay administrators of particular dimensions of the school.

The federal education agency, usually some division of the U.S. Department of Education, stimulated the formation of what was called "parent advisory committees" (classified herein as Citizen Councils) for specific federally supported programs such as Title I of ESEA. As a condition for the award of federal funds for special programs for disadvantaged children and youths, such advisory groups were mandated and had to be given access to school documents and procedures plus the right to file grievances with a federal education agency if the local school resisted or refused access. This was a most unusual extension of lay group authority or political power into the administration of a public school.

The many advantages of parental involvement in the public schools should not obscure the problems inherent in the possible excesses in some situations. It is not unusual to find cliques that perpetuate power for themselves and special friends in leadership positions of some Citizen Councils to the exclusion of larger numbers and more representative points of view from other parents within the school community. Political problems of control by cliques with Councils may be exacerbated when appointed lay members receive a stipend for services, have access to travel expenses, or in other ways control the expenditure of public school funds without following election procedures for school board membership or qualifying as professionals with special preparation in educational administration. Terms of a specific length and strict limitations to no more than two concurrent appointments to a Council are desirable and help broaden the lay involvement base.

Interference by the Council, or any appointed leader therein, in the direct operation of a school or attempts to assume authority allocated to a professionally prepared and credentialed principal or project administrator represent an abuse of the lay participation concept which should be corrected. Likewise, persons seeking to promote a single issue, rather than educational objectives in general or specific educational program objectives, may use the Citizen Council as a platform to dramatize an unrelated cause at the expense of educational program objectives. Unfortunately, such abuses have generated conflicts in school systems. The roles, responsibilities, and limitations of Citizen Councils should be clarified and kept before such groups at all times.

Citizen involvement in public schools has been and can continue to be a positive force. It is essential for superintendents, principals, program managers, and so on, to develop the competencies required to work effectively with lay groups, to diagnose and correct special problems in lay committee operations, and to help fulfill the potential that resides within the concept and practice of lay involvement in education. One measure of administrative leadership is the existence of and effective operation of lay advisory groups in education.

POLITICS OF ADMINISTRATION: COMMUNITY DECISION MAKING

Interest in the politics of educational administration grew during the 1960s and the decades thereafter. It started with sociological analyses of the nature of the community, its power structure or manifestations of public leadership, and the process of public policy and decision making. The politics of education deals with the interaction between the school and the political system in which located.

Probing the social class and power structure in American communities started in the late 1920s and early 1930s with the work of the Lynds.[4] These were efforts outside the field of education. The Lynds were among the first to describe the power elite of a community and

the manner in which economic power was utilized in daily decision making in small American cities. Warner's group studied another locale identified as "Yankee City" in the 1930s.[5] They depicted the impact of shifting ownership and managership functions within the highly industrialized city from local people to others outside the community.

These studies supported the conclusion that people of high socioeconomic status are more likely to hold office in formal associations than people of lower socioeconomic status.

Hunter's studies of the community power structure in "Regional City" (Atlanta, Georgia)[6] suggested that a small homogeneous group of men formed a power elite and directed the affairs of this southern city.

Hunter's work opened a new dimension in community analysis and understanding of public decision making. Political scientists continued their interest in community decision making but preferred to call it "public leadership." Bell et al. classified various methods of studying community power structure or public leadership as one or a combination of the following five:[7]

1. Positional, or formal leadership, method. A public leader, or a member of the power elite, is identified by the organizational position held, which in the researcher's judgment is important, influential, or indicative of status. A person is identified as a public leader if: (a) an elected political leader, (b) a high civil servant or political appointee, (c) a major business executive, (d) a military officer of high rank, or (e) an officer holder in a voluntary or civic-minded association. Influence or power is related to the position held in private or public agencies.

The researcher is forced to select types of positions judged important in community decision making or public leadership. Disagreement among experts about power positions in a community is common.

2. Reputational, or nominal leadership, method. This method relies on opinions of other members of society whom the researcher thinks are qualified to identify members of the power structure. Emphasis is on the reputation a person enjoys, not the position held. The

method's validity depends upon the informant's knowledge of community affairs and sensitivity to power relations. Some researchers use a cross section of informants; others identify a limited number or a panel of experts judged by others to know the community well; and still others combine the two approaches by starting with a small number and then broadening the sample. Hunter utilized both positional and reputational methods. The definition or composition of the community's power elite varied with the method of selection employed. The reputational approach may also be referred to as the informal leadership pattern. Many significant decision makers at the local level are not in leadership positions in government, business, military, or civic associations. Those in the state and national power elite are more likely to occupy such posts.

3. Social participation method. Another assumption is that an individual's participation in a variety of activities is an index of social participation and, therefore, of access to the community's network of power and communications. Researchers do not use this method as frequently as the first two.

4. Influence, or opinion leadership, method. Opinion leaders or personal influentials in a community are not necessarily holders of formal positions of leadership. Whatever its validity, the method is based on asking individuals to whom they turn for advice and counsel on given matters. This approach rejects the concept of a generalized leadership type and suggests instead that each special area of decision making develops its own opinion leaders.

5. Decision-making, or event-analysis, method. This is an historical approach based on tracing the history of a particular decision or event and determining who was influential in making this come about. It works backward, but again depends upon opinions of others.

Another approach to community power-structure analysis involves identifying the number of times the person's name is mentioned in a local newspaper. This is of doubtful validity if top decision makers avoid publicity and contact with the mass media.

Bell et al. summarized a tremendous volume of research (over 570 items are listed in their bibliography) and reported major findings as:

1. Public leadership in the nation is a man's role.
2. The public leaders are most likely in the middle years of life; some elder members of society are powerful, but rarely are young adults described as leaders.
3. Leadership is not often in the hands of members of ethnic or religious minority groups. Where the concerns of the entire community or nation are involved, the vast majority of dominants are native-born white protestants, although exceptions are noted in some large urban areas.
4. Formal reputation and social participation types of leadership are displayed more often by people in the middle and upper social classes as well as by those with above-average formal education.[8]

Concern for identifying the power structure of the community and its impact on school decisions started in the late 1950s. Vidich and Bensman analyzed school politics in a small rural community called Springdale.[9] Goldhammer observed the effect of the formal and informal behavior of board members on community affairs in a small Oregon school district in the early 1950s.[10] Kimbrough reported on power structure in two Florida school districts.[11] Other studies were of school communities in Tennessee.

That there are individuals and groups within communities who exercise considerable influence on vital issues has been sensed intuitively by the more skillful practicing school administrators. Research on community power-structure analysis provided a theoretical framework for studying the interaction between the school and the political leadership in the community, state, and nation.

Research efforts on community power structure or public leadership are case studies confined to description, analysis, and interpretation of individual cities or rural communities. Generalizations from individual cases studies are fraught with danger. A description of a power elite in one community is not necessarily valid for another.

The methodology employed in determining the power elite influences the outcome of the study, as does the care the researcher uses in analyzing data. Personal prejudices or predispositions can affect interpretation of the facts.

Public leadership is not static. Shifts occur through time as well as because of new issues. Every administrator must be sensitive to the emergence of new groups which previously had no access to the community power elite. This is particularly true at present when the use of demonstrations amplified through the mass media, TV in particular, and coalitions can wrest control from what appear to be well-entrenched community power groups. Civil riots and other forms of unrest, as well as changing political climates, can significantly alter membership in the circle of community decision makers. Killian pointed out the sudden shift of the black community from accommodation to protest, from subservience to reaction.[12] He reported on the function of the black elite and the emergence of black leaders skilled in the techniques of bargaining.

When approval is needed for increasing taxes for school operations or financing a bond issue for new school facilities, the support of community decision makers is essential.

Every administrator needs sufficient staff to complete the study of social, political, and economic factors within the community; to determine the power elite on the variety of economic, social, and political issues within the community; and to recognize the emergence of new groups which may some day be a dominant force.

THE POLITICS OF EDUCATION

Determining what community voices carry the greatest weight or whose counsel is most often sought by those in formal decision-making positions is a beginning in developing a sensitivity to the politics of educational administration in particular and public education in general. The politics of education includes the study of the "power brokers," "political contacts," or "king-makers" who can influence the public decision-making process that affects the cause of public education in state capitals, in Washington, D.C., as well as within the local community.

Street demonstrations, media attention-getting activities, as well as the riots of past decades revealed that those considered at one time to be powerless and outside the power structure could employ the politics of discontent and take to the streets to communicate their messages, be heard by those at the helms of power, and stimulate change. Special-interest groups and single-issue organizations used demonstrations outside the board of education offices as media events to attract attention to their cause with "demands to be heard."

Power may be gained through the ballot box or through well-orchestrated demonstrations (peaceful or disruptive). Understanding who are the power seekers and the distribution of formal and informal power are far more difficult to obtain with precision in heterogeneous communities or in complex state and federal agencies than in fairly homogeneous centers and relatively simple governmental units. Complex coalition politics may be a way of life in heterogeneous and complex situations. Politics makes strange bedfellows, at least for short periods of time and until mutually desired objectives have been achieved. Politics is more an art than a science. The permutations and combinations possible for various coalitions of various political forces within a large urban center, a state, or a distant federal agency can stagger the imagination of even the mathematically oriented school administrator.

A substantial number of well-organized, well-financed single-issue factions emerged during the 1970s and many impacted upon education. Such groups sought to elect "their kind of person" to school boards or other positions to dominate educational policy development by refusing to allow other matters until their demands were satisfied.

The school administrator is often caught in the middle of school-community conflicts or where two or more single-issue proponents are dueling with each other. Some become casualties of intracommunity struggles. There have been massive power reorientations, unusually active coalition politics, and many confrontations with single-issue groups in the large urban school districts of the nation. Open and frequent school board meetings, special hearings and investigations, initiative elections, and other democratic procedures have not always succeeded in resolving highly emotional issues of which the public schools were only one small part.

In addition to the external or community political struggles and social and educational reforms, there are the internal district politics. Competition for power, promotion, and recognition within professional groups of the school system is part of internal politics. Campus or site, central-office, and system-wide political intrigues can be as fierce and debilitating as confrontations with external pressure groups. Professional personnel have been known to use friendships with community power brokers to nullify the authority of the chief school executive or principal.

Politics deals with decision-making power, its distribution and limitations, among persons who are part of the organization, community, state, region, and nation. Much of the literature on educational politics (as well as policy development reviewed later) that goes beyond local or community power analysis focuses on activities pursued prior to the passage of new legislation, procedures followed in the making of new laws, or the court's role in clarifying meanings or in interpreting laws. The political process begins with the activities of lobbyists, those employed or for other reasons dedicated to influencing legislators, or public policymakers, whose votes determine the fate of proposed legislation. The lobbyist has no formal legislative authority and must depend on human relations skills to influence outcomes, that is, on skills in understanding what motivates persons to vote or behave as they do. Education groups are comparative newcomers to the art of lobbying effectively at state and federal levels. Rational arguments, published data, and sympathy for the noble cause of education were the favorite tools of professional educators in years past.

These have merits but also limitations in influencing lawmakers.

Education groups did gain sophistication in the art of political action during the 1970s. Fragmentation of state and national education-oriented professional organizations is a problem, although coalitions were formed when mutual interests could be satisfied. This represents a significant departure from the historic posture of avoiding political entanglements. There is a greater willingness now on the part of various parts of the profession to be an integral part of the political process of formulating state and national policies with reference to education. The policymaking process is inseparable from state and national level politics, as will be reviewed more completely in the next section.

STATE AND NATIONAL POLICYMAKING IN EDUCATION

Policy and policymaking were defined in the local district context in an earlier chapter. A policy was interpreted to be a general declaration of intent to act in a specified manner when confronted with a specific situation or to achieve a stated result at some future point in time. Written policy statements, when implemented as time and situation allow, help insure consistency of decisions, actions, and treatments of persons without relying on the limitations of human memory. Locally developed policies contribute to the fairness and effectiveness of educational administration.

The scene shifted during the 1960s and 1970s as more publicity was given to the need for state and national educational policies. There were admonitions that the "federal government ought to have a policy on education"; there appeared to be agreement on that point without being sure what that meant or implied.

The waters were muddied somewhat when in recent years educational philosophers and historians began to exhibit a preference for the term *educational policy studies* as a more appealing descriptor for philosophical, sociological and historical foundations in education. Historical precedents and sensitivity to various philosophical positions can contribute useful insights, information, and concepts to the policymaking process. Educational policymaking at state and national levels, as defined herein, is oriented toward the resolution of more practical issues confronting local, state, and federal education agencies. This generally is outside the sphere of interest and expertise of the specialists in the educational foundations.

Public policymaking is better identified with the political arena and the administration of organizations in the public sector. A separation of administrative policymaking from public policymaking may help as well. The latter is broader and is not limited to the operational concerns of a specific organization as is the former. Policymaking is a special type of decision action. The more political, as opposed to the primarily operational or technical (such as those based on quantitative analysis, PERT, PPBS, etc.), dimensions of educational decision making can be said to be the primary domain of public policymaking.

One political scientist declared "according to the definition most commonly advanced, *policy* consists of several components: (1) goals; (2) a plan or strategy for achieving the goals, or rules or guides to action, or methods; and (3) action."[13] A public policy, therefore, is a statement of an identifiable and coherent behavior to be pursued and adopted by some public agency which is designed to clarify its goals, identify its strategies to facilitate goal attainment, and give consistency and/or relevance to subsequent decisions, expenditures, or other actions. The concept is complex and difficult because that is also the nature of the public or political process.

The cry for a coherent federal policy with reference to public education can be interpreted as a desire to clarify the national role in this field and also to give consistency and relevance to its myriad funding and other thrusts in public education that at times seem to contradict or cancel one another.

Court and legislative decisions at state and national levels may be viewed as "educational policy statements" expressed in the form of legal briefs, statutes (with supporting fiscal allocations and methods of distributions), or related state and national bureacratic regulations. Much literature on educational policy development and management focuses on how bills become law, how issue elections should be conducted and won, lobbying efforts of personnel and associations, ways of influencing state and/or national elected officials, U.S. or State Supreme Court decisions or interpretations of law, and so on. The variation in quality of publications ranges from some statements on how laws are made that do not go much beyond a junior high school civics text to sophisticated analyses of specific state or national policy statements, or a lack thereof.

The term *policy science* may be used to describe ways of improving the public policymaking process. It is the product or output of the policymaking process that is the best measure of its effectiveness. Policy statements should have substance, clarity, and relevance when it focuses on some dimension of public education such as educational finance, curriculum reform, or integration. Those without knowledge of the substance and technical dimensions of a given field face limitations in their contributions to the development of a coherent and relevant public policy. This suggests that policymakers in public education should have special knowledge and expertise, or at least access to persons who do, in some dimension of education as well as in its operation and administration. The other side of the coin is for leaders in education to develop expertise in the public policymaking process because their professional knowledge and experiences can help the quality and relevance of state- and national-educational policy statements.

PUBLIC RELATIONS IN EDUCATION

The purposes of public relations activities in education are to keep the public better informed about the schools, to earn community acceptance of the schools, and to reduce the incidence of uninformed criticisms. Formal or organized effort to these ends started soon after the turn of the century and came into its own shortly after World War I.[12] It has at times been almost indistinguishable from other vigorous movements, such as the community school, the citizens' advisory committee, politics of education, or the accountability movements. Much of the literature consists of rule-of-thumb techniques and common-sense observations, sometimes assembled by means of a canvass of experiences only.[15]

Bernays defined public relations as:

1. Information given to the public.
2. Persuasion directed at the public to modify attitudes and action.
3. Efforts to integrate attitudes and actions of an institution with its publics and of the publics with that institution.[16]

Public relations is concerned with personal and corporate behavior which has social and public significance. An individual responsible for the public relations of an institution is involved in directing, advising, and supervising those activities of the institution which affect or interest the public. Such an individual interprets the institution (or client) to the public and the public to the institution. The purpose of all such activities is to promote harmony and understanding between the group and the public it serves and upon whose good will it depends.[17] One may rightfully question the broadness of activities defined as public relations, because they appear to encompass almost the entire range of public school activities.

As applied to school personnel, "good public relations" may mean:

1. A good public opinion (which unfortunately is not described in any further detail).
2. The absence of political crisis in the community with respect to the school or a minimum of potentially disruptive criticism of the school.
3. The involvement of the citizens in formulating school policies (it is not always clear whether this is regarded as a means or an end in itself).

4. The attainment of a favorable vote on a bond or a tax referendum.[18]

Considering public relations as information, persuasion, and integration between the institution and the public helps to avoid some of the confusion. It is a way of influencing public policy or decision making and hence may be seen as a part of the politics of education.

In its broad sense, school public relations involves all contacts through which an impression or image about the public schools is established in the minds of various groups of people. There is little empirical evidence, however, to determine the effectiveness of various devices for evaluating public-relations programs and activities. Most "research" in public relations is little more than a collection of judgments of panels of educators regarding the suitability, effectiveness, and success of practices employed. This leaves unresolved the question of the criteria utilized by panel members "judging" the "public-relations practices."

PURPOSES OF SCHOOL PUBLIC RELATIONS

School public relations may create a more desirable image of the educational institution. Other purposes are:

1. To inform the public about the schools.
2. To establish confidence in the schools.
3. To rally support for proper maintenance of the educational program.
4. To develop an awareness of the importance of education in a democracy.
5. To improve the partnership concept by uniting parents and teachers in meeting the educational needs of children.
6. To integrate the home, school, and community in improving educational opportunities for all children.
7. To evaluate the offerings of the schools and the needs of the children of the community.
8. To correct misunderstanding about the aims and objectives of the school.[19]

HUMAN RELATIONS AND PUBLIC RELATIONS

What is known as public relations might better be called human relations. This shifts the emphasis from gimmicks and journalistic talent alone to an understanding of social psychology of groups and individual human behavior under various conditions of stress.

The right words are those that succeed in conveying feelings and ideas. What influences other groups is a problem of social psychology, not a question of knowing how to formulate and time press releases. Human relations skill is the capacity of people to communicate feelings and ideas to others, to receive such communications from others, and to respond to their feelings and ideas in such a fashion as to promote congenial participation in a common task.[20]

The more defensible conclusions are that "some kinds of communications on some kinds of issues, brought to the attention of some kinds of people under some kinds of conditions, have some kinds of effects." The complexity of the "effect" problem has defied the superficial analysis of the proponents of the school public-relations movement.[21]

The communications challenge increases in significance when the primary role of the administrator becomes that of mediator among groups contesting for power or attempting to influence public decision making.

THE SCHOOL PUBLIC-RELATIONS PLAN

The usual admonition that the school administrator has a responsibility to communicate the school story to the people does not answer the question "what story?" Although it is encouraging that all media—newspapers, radio, and television—exhibit a growing interest in the school story, their avidity puts even greater pressure on school officials. It is not possible to "manage" school news, but the most likely impact of each story should be assessed beforehand.

The first step is the generation of a model public-relations program in terms of the missions of the school to be projected. Model creation is a responsibility of the total staff, not simply the public-relations department. It is a top-echelon function that requires creativity, understanding of the totality of educational operations, and knowledge of the technical aspects of public-relations operations. The model provides the framework for action. It is useful in deciding the priority of various school stories and what aspect of each story deserves prominence. The model is based on the identification and ranking of significant factors that help the various publics comprehend the missions of the school and judge its contributions and activities. It is a representation of the reality that confronts the educational institution, but it includes only those elements essential to describing the missions, sensing who is to be reached, knowing what kinds of information in what format reaches the various publics, and developing an organization to execute the operation of a public-relations subsystem.

The public-relations model defines what is to be achieved before it specifies how it is to be achieved. Day-by-day school activities, future educational plans, and communication with external and internal environments are some of the subsystems in the model. What stories should be written (and how released, how slanted, and how timed) about any of the school subsystems can be answered through a public-relations model.

Image (or posture) is defined as the total impression people, usually outside the school environment, have of the educational system—its staff, its clientele, and its activities. Again, to suggest that the public-relations plan starts with a definition of the missions (or image or posture) of the educational institution that are to be crystallized in the minds of people is not to infer management of school news. On the contrary, the release of distorted or unsupported information on school activities will surely backfire and place the school and its administration in an embarrassing position.

Various releases can help to project the special skills, preparation, and insights of the teaching staff; how well various types of pupils are learning; how efficiently school funds are expended and protected. Communication is an art, which, when done well, presents not a sales pitch, but accurate and objective information on school operations.

Knowing what to say is the beginning. The public-relations model must also recognize the various avenues of dissemination and the audience each will reach. Publics can be classified by religious inclination, socioeconomic status, race, national background, economic orientation (industrial or agricultural, union or management), political belief (conservative or liberal), age grouping (senior citizens, young adults, or mature citizens), and civic affiliation. Publics can also be classified by school orientation—PTA members, childless couples, singles, parents of children attending private schools, and parents of children attending public schools. One individual can play a role in many different publics.

Once policies have been outlined, an organization to execute them can be fashioned. The continuing involvement of many people is desirable, but a specially skilled public-relations team should be in charge.

There must be continuous evaluation to determine how well the public-relations model corresponds with reality and whether the desired image of the school has been in fact projected.

The development and execution of a public-relations plan can be summarized as follows:

1. Define the missions (or image or posture) of the educational system to be projected.
2. Determine whether the specific purpose is for straight information giving or for influencing public decision making in a given way.
3. Determine what kinds of communications will help or hinder the redevelopment of the posture desired, recognizing that distortion of the truth or news management must be avoided.
4. Identify the optimum avenues for projecting the missions of the school (based on an understanding of the appropriate media, fre-

quency of communication, and the tone of the message).
5. Know the variety of publics to be reached (classified by religion, socioeconomic status, nationality grouping, political belief, age level, educational orientation).
6. Develop an organization unit or division to operate the plan that involves many people but recognizes that a team of specialists is needed.
7. Allocate the resources to accomplish the public-relations program.
8. Execute the program.
9. Evaluate its effectiveness on a continuing basis.

Public relations is more than telling and selling; it is a sensitivity to community interests and desires. What the people want to know about schools is not always the same. Certain insights and attitudes can be gained best by participation in citizen committees. Involving people in school activities and designing ways to help them participate in arriving at significant educational decisions are as much a part of public relations as writing a story for release to the press. Community involvement in education is a characteristic of a dynamic and effective school public-relations program.

TECHNIQUES OF SCHOOL PUBLIC RELATIONS

There is no dearth of suggestions about who should be involved and what approaches are most effective in establishing the desirable image of the school. No amount of press, radio, or TV releases will overcome dissatisfaction by the child and parent about what is being accomplished in the classroom. Thus, the classroom teacher plays the paramount role in fostering desirable school-community relations. The teacher's deep concern in meeting the educational and other needs of the child and in working in close and harmonious relation with parents and other interested adults is a keystone in effective school-community relations.

The profession took hold in the 1920s and

came of age at approximately the end of 1941.[22] It served to fill the gap caused by the lack of organization and information within the school system about how to gather data and release stories about educational activities to the various mass media of communication or to individuals and groups.

The responsibilities of the school public-relations division include organizing and releasing school publicity to news outlets, maintaining a calendar of school publicity, searching out news and information in the system, and maintaining a file of stories released.

Determining what makes a good news story; developing steps in preparing a news story; using newspapers, radio, and television effectively; preparing graphic and pictorial materials; creating a letter or other ways of sending messages to parents; utilizing school-oriented or school-operated publications; and creating special reports to the public are some of the more technical aspects of school public-relations procedures.[23]

SCHOOL REPORTING AND REPORTERS

Interest in school news is a relatively recent development that resulted in considerable and detailed newspaper and magazine coverage of school events. Major newspapers may have several full-time education reporters whose stories may appear on the first page, right-hand column. People have demonstrated sincere interest in what is happening in public schools, the media has responded with print and video coverage, and, in general, the schools have benefited from improved coverage from the media.

Dapper observed that good public relations begins with a good product and continues with skillful use of every device available to inform people about it.[24] Writing from the point of view of the reporter, she said that a school public-relations officer "can be a blessing or a curse."

Mistrust and misinterpretation can arise on both sides. Education reporters complain about the school's fear of the press, failure to recognize deadlines, and inability to understand that the editor, not the reporter, determines headlines and the position in the paper of the school news item, and that the reporter is rarely consulted about what appears on the editorial page.

Administrators have a responsibility to keep the newspaper informed, to work with reporters, and to supply effective photographs and stories. Most administrators lack journalistic talents, and hence those who have such gifts as well as the ability to get along with representatives of the mass media must become an important part of the administrative team.

SUMMARY

The term *politics of education* has changed from implying partisanship to connote the understanding of power structures and the influencing of public decision or policymaking. Schools serve the educational needs of the community and, in turn, draw support and strength from the community.

Public relations, politics, and policies are unique but interrelated concepts. Criticisms of educational systems, past and present, in the United States and those in other nations have waxed and waned. They often have a strong emotional bias and may continue long after conditions which triggered them have disappeared. Administrators must expect school criticisms and avoid a defensive posture or dismissal of all critics.

Polls reveal that the percentage of parents giving public schools high marks declined during the 1970, but there were small gains again during the early 1980s. Those involved in public schools rank them higher than persons without school-age children or whose offsprings attend private schools. Although public confidence in educational leaders declined during the 1970s, such confidence remained higher than that for leaders in business and government. The perceptions of major school problems by school officials are not consistent with those of the public as a whole who viewed lack of discipline, student use of drugs, and poor curriculum/low standards as the three most serious, whereas school officials ranked these much lower.

The PTA is the oldest of the formally organized public education support groups. The NCCPS had a brief but significant impact on the stimulation of lay advisory groups in education which flourished during the 1950s and 1960s. Lay advisory committees were deliberative and consultative bodies appointed by some recognized public body as the school board. They grew out of local voluntary desires to involve citizens in supporting and promoting the cause of public education. Citizen Councils are a more controversial type of lay advisory group often mandated by state or federal law and with a greater propensity to become involved in monitoring operations of specific programs in an attendance center. Citizen involvement in the public schools has been and can continue to be a positive force, and administrators need special competencies to work with them. There are many approaches to identifying people who occupy positions of public leadership. The formal-leadership method identifies the power elite on the basis of formal positions of authority. The reputational approach relies more on reputation than position held. Another method relies on activity in civic or voluntary community organizations.

One danger in analysis of community power structure is generalizing from a few case studies. Another is assuming that communities are static and that social changes do not alter the power structure. Subtle shifts can catapult new groups into positions of dominance. Every school administrator needs sufficient staff to study the nature of and modifications in the social, political, and economic factors within the community.

The politics of education includes the understanding of formal and informal decision makers at the state and federal levels as well as the community power structures. Education groups gained sophistication in the art of political action during the 1970s; this is a departure from the historic posture of avoiding political entanglements. Public policymaking that goes beyond the local district is related closely to politics. Specific knowledge of the dimension of education to be covered in a policy statement is as essential as knowledge of policy science.

School public relations is concerned with giving information to the public and modifying and integrating attitudes and actions of the institution with its publics and of the publics with the institution through persuasive efforts. It focuses on developing a desirable image of the institution.

Human relations can change the emphasis from techniques and procedures to understanding the social psychology of human behavior in groups and a means of influencing it. To the extent it attempts to influence public decision making, it merges with the politics of education.

The development of a public-relations model helps determine what story to use, how to slant it, what kind of communication will help or hinder the development of a given posture, what avenues of dissemination are best, what specific publics are to be reached, and what the requirements are for a public relations organization; it also serves as the basis for subsequent evaluation.

Educational reporting has improved. The interest of the people in the schools is evidenced by the frequency with which school news appears on the front page. Misunderstanding occurs between education reporter and school when either side is insensitive to problems and limitations of each.

NOTES

1. Russell T. Gregg, "Political Dimensions of Educational Administration," *Teachers College Record,* LXVII, November 1965, pp. 118–128.

2. John W. Maguire, "Changing Voter Profiles and School Elections," *Intellect,* Vol. 101, No. 2344, November 1972, p. 110.

3. Jerry Duea, "School Officials and the Public Hold Disparate Views on Education," *Phi Delta Kappan,* March 1982, pp. 477–479.

4. R. S. Lynd and H. M. Lynd, *Middletown,* New York: Harcourt Brace Jovanovich, 1929; and *Middletown in Transition,* New York: Harcourt Brace Jovanovich, 1937.

5. There are many volumes published by the Warner group, one of which is W. L. Warner and T. S. Lunt, *The Social Life of a Modern Community,* New Haven, Conn.: Yale, 1941.

6. Floyd Hunter, *Community Power Structure,* Chapel Hill, N.C.: University of North Carolina Press, 1953.

7. S. Bell, R. J. Hill, and C. R. Wright, *Public Leadership,* San Francisco: Chandler, 1961, chap. 2.

8. Ibid., chap. 9.

9. A. J. Vidich and Joseph Bensman, *Small Town and Mass Society,* Garden City, N.Y.: Doubleday, 1958.

10. Keith Goldhammer, "Community Power Structure and School Board Membership," *American School Board Journal,* Vol. 130, March 1950, pp. 23–25.

11. R. B. Kimbrough, *Community Power Structure and Analysis,* Englewood Cliffs, N.J.: Prentice-Hall, 1964.

12. J. M. Killian, "Community Structure and Role of Negro Leader Agent," *Sociological Inquiry,* Vol. 35, Winter 1965, pp. 69–79.

13. Vernon Van Dyke, "Process and Policy as Focal Concepts in Political Research," in *Political Science and Public Policy,* Austin Ranney, ed., Chicago: Markham, 1968, p. 27.

14. W. W. Charters, Jr., "Public Relations," in Chester W. Harris, ed., *Encyclopedia of Educational Research,* 3rd ed., New York: Macmillan, 1960, pp. 1075–1081.

15. Ibid.

16. Edward L. Bernays, *Public Relations,* Norman, Okla.: University of Oklahoma Press, 1952, p. 3.

17. American Association of School Administrators, *Public Relations for America's Schools,* 28th Yearbook, Arlington, Va.: The Association, 1950, p. 12.

18. Charters, op. cit., p. 1076.

19. American Association of School Administrators, op. cit., p. 14.

20. F. J. Roethlisberger, *Training for Human Relations,* Boston: Division of Research, Harvard, 1954, p. 172.

21. Charters, op. cit., p. 1078.

22. Bernays, op. cit., chaps. 9 and 10.

23. American Association of School Administrators, op. cit., chap. 12.

24. Gloria Dapper, *Public Relations for Educators,* New York: Macmillan, 1964, p. 5.

CHAPTER REVIEW QUESTIONS

1. What are the similarities and differences between public relations, politics, and public policymaking?

2. Why are social institutions such as public education subjected to periodic and often severe criticisms from the public?

3. What should be the response of the school administrator in the face of criticisms of the schools or educational leadership?

4. Why do the perceptions of major school problems by the public differ from those of school officials?

5. What are the contributions and possible problems in the appointment and operation of various types of lay advisory groups in education?

6. How do the so-called Citizen Councils differ from other advisory groups?

7. What are the major methods of identifying members and analyzing the operations of a community power structure?

8. What is policy science?

9. Why have various education groups become more active in what is called the politics of education?

10. What are the essential elements of a public-relations model or plan?

SELECTED REFERENCES

Bell, W., Hill, R. J., and Wright, C. R., *Public Leadership,* San Francisco: Chandler, 1961.

Dapper, Gloria, *Public Relations for Educators,* New York: Macmillan, 1964.

Duea, Jerry, "School Officials and the Public Hold Disparate Views on Education," *Phi Delta Kappan,* March 1982, pp. 477–479.

Holliday, Albert E. ed., *The Public Relations Almanac for Educators, Volumes I and II,* Camp Hill, Pa.: Education Communication Center, 1982.

Institute for Responsive Education, *Citizen Participation in Education: Annotated Bibliography,* Boston: IRE, 1978.

Kirst, Michael W., *Politics of Education,* Berkeley, Cal.: McCutchan, 1970.

Maguire, John W., "Changing Voter Profiles and School Elections," *Intellect,* Vol. 101, No. 2344, November 1972.

Sumption, M. R., and Engstrom, Y., *School-Community Relations,* New York: McGraw-Hill, 1966.

Wayne, Edward, *The Politics of School Accountability,* Berkeley, Cal.: McCutchan, 1972.

25

ACCOUNTABILITY, APPRAISAL, AND PAST AND PRESENT CHALLENGES OF EDUCATIONAL ADMINISTRATORS

"Administrators should be held accountable for what happens in the public schools" was declared with great vigor during the early 1970s, then died down, but did not disappear completely during the 1980s. Accountability fires the imagination of many, but is subject to vague or conflicting interpretations.

Appraisal was related in part to accountability. Few school districts had formal administrator appraisal systems prior to 1960. The pressures to establish administrator evaluation systems intensified thereafter; it will be the unusual system that does not have administrator appraisal on an annual and continuing basis by the end of the 1980s.

The final section of this chapter reviews the many challenges that faced administrators in years past in order to place present ones in proper perspective.

EDUCATIONAL ACCOUNTABILITY

About 31 states passed some kind of accountability legislation or joint resolution by the fall of 1973. The substance of the idea can be traced to the Biblical idea of an impending Judgment Day when all will be accountable to the Creator. The concept was not strange to secular literature nor did administrators of secular institutions overlook the fact of an eventual day of reckoning for decisions and actions. Over 50 years ago educational administrators confronted with financial accountability pressures designed systems of financial accounting, budgeting, fiscal auditing and reporting to satisfy the then existing demands for better accountability in education.

Lessinger, one of the early writers in educational accountability, emphasized that it is not traditional perceptions that makes accountability so popular or that will make it endure.[1] He recognized "three distinct, but interactive types," namely, performance accountability, professional accountability, and system accountability. He cited "exponential cost increases," public dissatisfaction with educational outcomes, and public interests in adapting "modern management procedures" to educational institutions as reasons for the "rediscovery of and widespread demands for accountable education."[2]

Accountability today is a more comprehensive concept that embraces all of education and not simply safeguarding inputs to assigned uses. Current interpretations of accountability stress relevance of educational goals, effectiveness of instructional and administrative strategies at all levels, and assessment of educational outcomes achieved.

In an operational accountability system *every person (or group) in the organization is answerable (or responsible), to some degree, to another person (or position) for something (or objectives) expressed in terms of performance levels (or results or achievements) to be realized within certain constraints* (such as a specific time period or within stated financial limits).[3]

Accountability is a goal-referenced term; its primary focus is upon outcomes or results achieved rather than activities pursued or completed. It is easily misconstrued; some misinterpret its meaning by assuming that the root word *account* gives it a business and profit orientation. The primary focus of educational accountability is learning outcomes, not school business management.

A more precise type of an accountability system may be designed where single or limited objectives are pursued, and when results can be measured with a high degree of accuracy. Accountability is far more difficult to establish and to measure in multipurpose educational institutions where the end products are difficult to define and even more perplexing to measure with precision.

Through accountability a clearer definition of where the institution is going, more prudent resource allocations, improved resource utilization patterns, and better information on the performance qualities of personnel and teachers as they relate to organizational objectives become possible. An accountability system gives administrators and other policymakers an important new capability by providing them with data necessary to make more definitive judgments on how well (or poorly) the organization's resources have been used to achieve stated purposes. For that reason policymakers and administrators alike should welcome rather than resist the design and implementation of an educational accountability system at local and state levels.

At present, teachers are held accountable for implementation of instructional activities with pupils. Administrative procedures require that teachers be present in classrooms by a given time and leave no earlier than a stated time. This is accountability for the performance of a service, not learning outcomes. The traditional teaching contract is a "performance" contract only in the sense of performing a set of activities within a school classroom.

Teachers may be held accountable for results, that is, for pupil learning up to a previously specified level. Accountability for a product or outcome is far more demanding, if not frightening, for those who may feel that there are too many variables related to the complex learning process that are not susceptible to control by the teacher. The "performance contract" talked about during the past two decades was not performance of a set of services but rather variable payments contract based on the degree to which various instructional outcomes were realized by teachers. This switches the focus from accountability for instructional inputs and processes to accountability for results or instructional outcomes.

The outcomes-oriented conceptualization of accountability presented herein bears a close relationship to the management-by-objectives (MBO) system described more fully in Chapter 6. Operation in the MBO mode is part of an overall accountability strategy. The success of the system depends in part upon mutual acceptance as well as mutual understanding of educational goals; it will not work if administrators have one set of objectives and teachers another.

Conflicting Conceptualizations of Educational Accountability

Not everyone talking about accountability has the same set of concepts in mind; it has been appropriated as a subterfuge or cover to promote special interests. This may help to explain why teacher organizations raise questions about accountability; particularly when it may appear as the new disguise for establishing a merit pay system, which has been resisted by teachers' associations and unions.

Others may try to use accountability as a means of justifying tax support of private schools. The voucher system of distributing state and federal contributions for education directly to parents, described more fully in Chapter 23, makes the bold assumption that there can be no truly operational accountability system in education unless parents have a choice in determining which particular school attendance center and which system of education (public or private) shall receive the educational-voucher payment for education of the pupil. This is quite different from the concept of accountability reviewed earlier, namely, the optimum resource utilization or management-by-objectives approaches within existing publicly supported educational systems. The competitive conceptualization of accountability proposed by voucher advocates is neither consistent with nor crucial to the optimum resource utilization of outcomes-oriented conceptualization of accountability.

ACCOUNTABILITY STRATEGIES

The school executive's accountability strategy would include establishment of accountability centers through the system—at the classroom, building, and/or district level. In the internally directed comprehensive educational accountability plan, at least the following practices or techniques should be in operation:

1. *Identification and clarification of significant objectives* to understand their operational implications and to determine whether attainment of any or all is realistic in view of the constraints under which the institution functions. There is little hope for the installation of an operational accountability system unless the administrator demonstrates skill in preparing quality performance objectives.

2. *Creation of an accountability team for the school system.* It is not a burden carried by the superintendent alone whose first responsibility is to create a team with each member accepting a definite assignment or set of responsibilities that is part of the total plan. Accountability is off to a promising start when all personnel know and accept the missions they are expected to fulfill and the degree of responsibility each has (as a person or as a member of the team).

3. *Development of an accountability chart* indicating who is to be responsible for what. Such a chart is drawn from data obtained after fulfillment of points 1 and 2 mentioned in the previous paragraphs.

A related question is whether the individual alone, the group within a building, or those employed within the total system should be held responsible for realization of particular goals. This is part of the debate on individual versus joint accountability. Joint accountability is the more rational basis when learning specialists have collective responsibility for a certain impact on the lives of the learners. This avoids the difficult operational problem of disentangling the contributions of many who influence learner's progress.

4. *Continuation of the search for alternative approaches to educational objectives.*

5. *Development and implementation of output-oriented management systems, such as the planning-programming-budgeting system (PPBS) and management-by-objectives (MBO).*

6. *Development and utilization of computer-based information systems* capable of providing the data needed to fulfill the demands of educational accountability. Accountability calls for a variety of and frequent reports and analyses of data. No administrator can hope to install an operational accountability system without a solid information base.

7. *Creation of a system for education auditing* to verify the quality of reports and activities. An audit substantiates progress (or lack of it) toward achieving goals and verifies other data available; it is one of the culminating steps in the control and feedback process. Through the independent audit—carried out by both internal and external agencies or personnel, independent of the person completing the task—the accuracy, integrity, and authenticity of previous reports and documents can be ascer-

tained. Independent external audits occur less frequently than in-house audits by someone on the superintendent's staff.

8. *Design and operation of a total staff appraisal system* that would include specification of effectiveness models, performance indicators, ways of measuring performance (instruments used), and decision points for the interpretation of evaluative data. By the same token, those evaluated have a right to know how their performances will be monitored, what standards will be applied, when periodic evaluations will occur, what rewards or penalties are in store, and what feedback they can expect on their performance appraisals.

9. *Dedication of ample resources to make the accountability system work.* The amount will vary with the comprehensiveness and complexity of demands placed on the institution.

10. *Recognition of educational accountability as being as much an attitude as a set of techniques.* There is limited agreement among the states that passed some form of accountability legislation. In 11 states accountability was equated with PPBS, in 2 a management information system, and in 5 a uniform accounting system. Twenty-two such states view it as a state testing or assessment program. In 10 states accountability demanded evaluation of professional employees.

The national assessment of educational progress that had its origins in the 1960s was an expression of instructional accountability. A few states passed laws mandating program budgeting in the hope that this would hold schools accountable for escalating expenditures and also to establish a better relationship between objectives and expenditures. The minimum competency-testing laws approved by a majority of the states during the 1970s can be classified among more recent efforts to hold public schools accountable for student-learning results.

ADMINISTRATOR APPRAISAL

During the early 1960s only a minority of districts appraised school executives; the few who did so employed informal and simplistic approaches. Some express concern that such appraisal will weaken the leadership or authority of educational administrators. The present focus, however, is upon how to insure objectivity, fairness, and accuracy of interpretation and utilization of the results of administrator appraisal systems. Appraisal is a means to an end: It can serve as the basis for the design of professional improvement programs and for more effective administrator performance.

The formal approaches began, by and large, with evaluation of principals and then later included other types of administrators. The traditional approach is that the immediate superior evaluates subordinate administrators. At the superintendency level the formal appraisal was performed by the board of education. Some used the client-centered approach where evaluatees participate in the appraisal of evaluators. In a few school districts the evaluation of principals by teachers was a part of the negotiated work contract. This is open to serious question even though it may be desirable to include the perceptions of teachers as part of the overall appraisal system for administrators.

The many factors and pressures that stimulated the development of administrator appraisal systems would include at least the following: the social ferment of the times that seems to stimulate people to question and seek appraisal of all facets of organizations; escalating costs of schools with administrator salaries appearing as the largest; accountability thrusts described earlier; teacher appraisal pressures leading teachers to clamor for administrator evaluation as well; growing concerns for administrative obsolescence and the need to develop approaches for early detection of such problems; efforts to identify the right principal for the right school situation imply some type of measure of administrator effectiveness; and the growing feelings among school boards that administrator appraisal is one of their important responsibilities.

An objective, fair, and relevant personnel evaluation system should incorporate at least the following: agreement on the theory or conceptual framework which shall undergird the appraisal efforts; specification of objectives of the evaluation system; design and adoption of an administrator effectiveness model; creation of an evaluation-monitoring subsystem to prepare data-gathering instruments, provide special training for the evaluative data gatherers, and define any other evaluation procedures; collection of relevant evaluative data; determination of who shall interpret the evaluative data collected on one or more persons; and finally, specification of what is to be done with the evaluative data and decisions as well as alternative courses of action that should follow from appraisal data interpretations.

There is more to an evaluation system than simply labeling a person good, bad, or indifferent. Providing the basic data essential to the orderly dismissal of incompetents is an extremely limited use of the potential inherent in appraisal data; less than 1 percent of personnel face such action annually where quality selection procedures are operative.

The purposes of administrator appraisal may include identifying those worthy of promotion from probationary status, determining regular and merit compensation, providing documentation for orderly dismissal of incompetents, satisfying state legislature or local school board demands for appraisal, and/or collecting data important to the design of professional development programs.

Appraisal assumes that there exists some model of an effective administrator. The data collected about a given individual are compared with the effectiveness model and a judgment is made as to how closely the real person matches the ideal of effectiveness. The many alternative models are summarized in Table 25.1. In most cases the effectiveness model has to be assumed from the kinds of data being collected. Research and the existing literature have little to offer and most conclude that we know little about managerial effectiveness.

The data-gathering instrument helps focus attention of the data gatherer on important elements. The instrument designed should help provide data on how well the administrator is:

1. Fulfilling legal responsibilities of the position. (This includes satisfying state and federal education reporting and other demands in a timely fashion.)

2. Fulfilling position description or responsibilities. (This includes the general and specific management functions such as coordinating administrators and supervisors, preparing budgets, employing personnel, and so on.)
3. Satisfying change-agent demands. (This would be introduction of new and effective personnel, programs, and operations.)
4. Completing decision-making demands of the position.
5. Executing the educational planning needs for the district.
6. Satisfying leadership roles and team demands. (This includes professional staff-superintendent and also student-superintendent relations.)
7. Fulfilling the instructional and other educational service functions of the office. (This includes levels and trends in student learning outcomes as well as the quality of educational services available.)
8. Maintaining effective school board-superintendent and community-superintendent relations.
9. Managing the pressures and/or conflicts inherent in the position.
10. Meeting the necessary personal behavior, growth, and productivity demands.

There are issues related to actual implementation or procedures to be followed in an administrator appraisal system such as:

1. Where does one gather evaluative data on the administrator?
2. Who should evaluate the administrator?
   a. Should teachers, superiors, board members, community leaders, students, custodians, or others be involved and to what degree?
   b. Should cooperative appraisal be encouraged (where evaluatee and evaluator negotiate and agree on job targets and procedures to be used in the appraisal process)?
   c. Should administrative peers be involved in the evaluation (should a team of administrators in similar positions be asked to submit professional judgments)?

3. How frequently should an administrator be appraised? Annually, more frequently, or at contract renewal time only?
4. What kind of instrument should be used?
5. Should the emphasis be on MBO or the results-oriented appraisal approach?
6. How much time and what magnitude of resources should be allocated for such purposes?
7. What are the legal ramifications of such procedures?
8. Should compensation charges be tied to administrator appraisal findings?

The results-oriented emphasis identified with MBO/R has much to offer in the design of administrator evaluation. The same can be said for competency-based evaluation (CBE).

A competency may be defined as the skill or capability to achieve an objective or demand of a position within a predetermined level of quality. Competency-based evaluation (CBE) is consistent with the spirit of the systems approach to performance appraisal and is an extension of the results-oriented appraisals approach in MBO/R. It can be outlined as:

TABLE 25.1

ALTERNATIVE MODELS OF ADMINISTRATOR EFFECTIVENESS

Type A: Input models

Effectiveness is:

1. A constellation of administrator traits or personality (such as honesty, dependability, and industriousness). Some call this charisma determination. It is the most common model assumed in the traditional approaches to evaluation.

Type B: Process or behavior models

Effectiveness is:

2. A series of administrator behaviors or role-performances (such as diagnosing problems, managing operations, and introducing change).
3. A series of teacher and/or pupil activities within the system (This is the "reflection theory," that is, effectiveness is reflected in what others are doing who are influenced by the administrator).
4. A set of interactions between the administrators and others (teachers, pupils, lay persons, supervisors, etc.).
5. A set of skills in utilizing technology or media (such as knowing how to use a computer in administration).
6. Competency in management of the technical dimensions of administration.

Type C: Outcome models

Effectiveness is:

7. A set of teacher and/or pupil performance levels.
8. A given standard of building appearance, safety, and security.
9. A specified level of pupil, teacher, and/or community control or influence.
10. A consensus of teacher, pupil, parental, or community reactions to the principal.
11. A set of decisions rendered by the administrator—the ultimate impact of these on the organization.
12. A cluster of problems resolved by the administrator.
13. What the evaluator says is effectiveness.
14. Attainment of any set of predetermined objectives or growth levels (management-by-objectives).

Type D: Eclectic models

Effectiveness is:

15. Any combination of two or more models of types A, B, and C.

Step 1. Specification of objectives or results to be achieved by a person in a given position.

The first step specifies determination of "competency for what?"

Step 2. Identification of professional competencies needed to satisfy predetermined objectives. Sometimes competencies may be related to roles to be played.

Step 3. Conversion of competencies into performance or observed behaviors that can be measured. Indicators and measures must be specified for each competency.

Step 4. Design of an assessment system to measure competencies from at least two vantage points, namely, were objectives achieved and did the person have the skills necessary to meet the situation? Effectiveness is a matter of degree and not an all-or-none proposition.

Step 5. Determination of which competencies are lacking in order to improve performance by coaching.

Step 6. Operation of in-service or "coaching" clinics to improve effectiveness of personnal.

The flow of ideas may be summarized as: objectives → competencies → performance objectives → appraisal → coaching → effectiveness.

The emphases of conventional appraisal and CBE may be contrasted as follows:

Conventional	CBE
Do things *right* →	Do *right* things
Emphasize inputs →	Specify outputs
Identify traits →	Measure competencies
Discharge duties →	Obtain results
Solve problems →	Produce creative alternatives
Safeguard resources →	Optimize resources
Performing functions →	Satisfying objectives

There were indications in the 1982 AASA study of the superintendency that appraisal of the chief executive was being granted a higher priority, formal evaluation procedures were no longer unusual, and more effective procedures were being developed.[4] This same source reported that the major reasons for school board evaluation of superintendents were to: "provide periodic and systematic accountability," "help you establish relevant performance goals," "identify areas needing improvement," "assess present performance in accordance to prescribed standards," "determine salary for the following year," and "comply with board policy."[5]

The evaluative methods most frequently used as seen by superintendents were: discussion at board-superintendent meetings, discussion at executive sessions with only board members present, ratings forms, "observation and association of board and superintendent at meetings, other times," appraisal based on goals and objectives satisfied during the previous year, and "criteria previously agreed to by the board and the superintendent."[6]

In 1982 about 77 percent of the superintendents were appraised at least once a year, about 11 percent at contract renewal time, and only 5 percent "never." (The other indications were of the "don't know" or "other" times.)

REVIEW OF SOME PAST AND PRESENT ADMINISTRATIVE CHALLENGES

The administrator is a creature of the times and specific environments that often influence professional and personal behavior. The simple pioneer culture of the early nineteenth century generated one set of demands upon administrative positions that helped define standards for measuring effectiveness of performance in the position. About a century later the school superintendents of the Great Depression decade fashioned new approaches and developed new sets of skills to cope with the pressures and challenges of that period. Each period in educational history made special demands upon school administrators; thus it would not be surprising that what will be in store for them some

15 to 25 years hence will not be the same as that likely to be experienced during the 1980s.

Each time new challenges confront education there is talk about the superintendency, principalship, and so on, being impossible positions. This may be true if competencies possessed and approaches used at one time are unchanged in the face of technological, educational, and social revolutions. A world in ferment is a world unsafe for public schools guided by administrative techniques designed and developed to meet the demands of organizations of a previous era.

People with special skills and talents are the most important resource in the educational process and systems. Destruction of school plants, books, equipment, computers, and supplies could reduce the quality of education, but would not bring it to an end. The loss of all professionally prepared teachers, administrators, and support personnel would do far greater damage and come closer to bringing public education to a complete halt. Witness the devastation to the economic, social, and educational institutions in Germany and Japan at the end of World War II. Both countries were able to come back quickly and with unexpected vigor because there were the professional talents to lead the way to repair physical structures and replace equipment and supplies.

The tempered optimism for the future of public education in general and educational administration in particular is based upon prior records of rising to the challenge and resolving almost impossible problems. The hope lies in the desires of the nation for quality education and the availability of professional talents to cope with adversity. What follows is an outline of some very specific challenges to public education that seemed to many to be impossible and the consequent deterioration if not destruction of public education that appeared to be near at hand.

Fifty years ago the nation was in the midst of one of its most severe and extended economic depressions. School administrators fought hard along with some public and professional leaders to identify new sources of funds to keep schoolhouse doors open and to insure the survival of public education pro-

grams for learners of all ages. Operation in the retrenchment mode at that time was essential to survival as school terms were shortened, programs slashed, and teachers and other personnel paid in "script"—a form of an IOU to pay salaries when money becomes available in the district's treasury. The Great Depression experience influenced administrator decision making, making it more conservative and cost conscious, for many decades to come. The very severe educational fiscal crisis was only one of many that characterized professional life during the 1930s; other important ones were:

1. An oversupply of teachers, considerable unemployment among educators, and very low salaries prevailed. (A milder repetition of this was to recur some 40 years later.)
2. The high point in local control and support of public education during the twentieth century was reached, followed by a decline in local influence that would continue for another 50 years and probably until the end of this century. State education officials were tolerated during the 1930s by local school boards and school administrators; federal education agencies were a long distance from daily educational operations, had even more limited roles to play, and placed primary emphasis on gathering national data on elementary and secondary education.
3. The fertility rate during the Depression years of the 1930s was the lowest in the nation's history up to that point, and remained that way until new lows were recorded during the 1970s. The birthrate, which has a significant impact on school enrollments in subsequent years, during the 1930s was very low—less than 20 per 1000.
4. The prestige and image of educational excellence in the so-called Great Cities or very large urban school districts peaked out during the 1930s; it would be downhill for the next 50 years.
5. It was a time of continuing dominance of the public school system by a single and strong administrative personality; most school systems operated a one-person-office-of-school-superintendent.

6. Administrators were forced to develop a high level of competencies in educational finance to insure survival of district operations; most remained committed, nonetheless, to considerable involvement in promoting instructional and educational program excellence.

7. The typical educational administrator of the decade held a bachelor's degree, attainment of a master's degree was relatively unusual, and an earned doctorate was a rarity.

There were two very different halves during the next decade. The first half of the 1940s was dominated by World War II. The conservative and retrenchment attitudes of the previous decade prevailed with little thought of what was to happen after the war. The last half saw the beginning of a spectacular turnaround—the start of 25 years of continuous school enrollment growth. Other important factors that characterized education during the 1940s were:

1. The teacher shortage began to be felt during the last half of the decade, thus reversing the condition of surplus that characterized the previous 15 years. This shortage was to continue in most areas of instructional specialization for over 25 years.

2. The basic teacher salary levels stipulated in formal salary schedules remained virtually unchanged, but the introduction of a special device called "cost of living bonus" increased the amount actually paid teachers. In some cases the "bonus" exceeded the amount called for in the formal schedule. It was related in part to the continuing influence of the depression psychology which led boards and administrators to believe that the "extra high" remuneration levels were temporary and there would be a return to the "sound levels" set in the formal teacher salary schedule. It was not until the next decade that this was recognized as a false hope.

3. Orientation programs for new teachers hired to meet the expanding enrollments during the last half of the 1940s were among the major challenges facing school personnel administration.

4. Creation of new and rapidly growing school districts surrounding large urban and suburban centers occurred at about the same time a reduction in rural school districts began in earnest. School district reorganization was one of the major challenges that emerged and was destined to continue for at least another 20 years. Reorganization was a very emotional and traumatic experience for people in rural and small communities as well as its school administrators.

5. There were increases in the number and different types of administrative positions during the last half of the 1940s.

6. Criticisms of public schools reached a new high by the end of the decade with accusations of "being soft on Reds" that were used more commonly against other institutions and persons at the time.

7. There were relatively few indications of interest in applying new technology and the systems approach to educational administration.

8. Great difficulty was experienced in procuring additional funds for current expenses and capital outlays to teach and house the greatly increased numbers being enrolled in the public schools.

9. Peaceful and professional relations prevailed between all school personnel with few signs of militant behavior among professionals.

The new era in public education emerged during the 1950s; the previous decade ended with hints of what was to come. The depression psychology, conservative approaches to management, and the retrenchment fears that dominated the thought and actions of most educational administrators came to an end. It became apparent that the "old days" of the 1930s were not likely to return nor should they be considered the norm for administrative behavior. By the end of the 1950s there was a 180-degree shift in educational planning away from concern for overbuilding and maintenance of static operations to planning for growth in students and expansions into new and different programs. It was one of the two most dynamic decades in the history of public education with most looking for bigger things and with a commitment to change. Among the more important developments in education during the 1950s were:

1. There was a very acute shortage of teachers and other educational personnel that had serious implications for program operations. School personnel administrators were hard put to find substitutes or temporary personnel.
2. The peak of the "baby boom" came in 1957 when 4.3 million were born; 4 million or more were born each year from 1954 to 1964. Enrollments increased each year and there was a feeling this would continue indefinitely.
3. This decade was the beginning of the "golden age" for educational facilities planning and construction in spite of the great difficulty of obtaining approval for massive school bond issues and finding personnel with the expertise to design functional school plants.
4. The one-person-office-of-school-superintendent encountered some overload problems; the need for central-office staff expansion ran into resistance, but the seeds of the administrative team concept were planted by some professional pioneers.
5. Television and computer technology began to spread and develop rapidly outside education. The computer was still too costly and applications to education lagged behind other fields; audiovisual aids found expanded use in the classroom and TV was just beginning to be used.
6. Growth in faculty, facilities, and programs strained school budgets and generated a financial crisis of far greater magnitude than that noted in the previous two decades.
7. Criticisms found during the 1940s waned, new ones emerged, and the new complaints focused upon overcrowded schools, double sessions, discipline problems, and quality of mathematics and science instruction.
8. Curriculum innovations appeared and received greater acceptance.

9. Schools in the Great Cities started to lose their luster as criticisms of their program quality mounted.
10. The historic *Brown* v. *Board of Education* decision overturned the *Plessy* doctrine; elimination of the dual education systems of the South and other civil rights disputes began in public education.
11. Teacher salaries continued to escalate, the massive "cost of living bonuses" came to an end, and frequent and substantial upward revisions of teacher salary schedules were made.
12. The U.S. Office of Education expanded with the advent of more special federal education programs that overshadowed the historic statistics-reporting functions. Federal contributions to and involvement in education set new high levels during each year of the decade.
13. Theory as applied to educational administration started to receive serious attention in administrator preparation programs.

The great growth psychology started a decade earlier continued, but by the end of the 1960s there began to be serious doubts about its extension into the 1970s. The 1960s could be looked upon as the decade of revolutions in education whose seeds were planted a decade earlier and would not be completed for at least another decade. Some of the most significant events in the history of public education took place during the 1960s. Among these and lesser events were:

1. The civil rights revolution in education reached full force, touched all parts of the nation (not just the South), and impacted most heavily upon the "Great Cities" and environs where most minorities migrated. There were a large number of court actions and community disruptions around the various issues related to integration/desegregation. Administrators were caught in the middle, were frequent targets of the critics, and made increased numbers of court appearances. The social revolution was felt in all parts of the school district.

2. The "Great Society" programs stimulated during the Kennedy/L. B. Johnson presiden-

cies began yet another substantial increase in federal expenditures for public education, but the funds were targeted for specific populations such as the "educationally disadvantaged." Schools were tied more closely than ever before in history to the resolution of the problems facing society such as ending the harsh cycle of poverty, promoting racial integration, and equal employment opportunity.

3. Teacher shortages eased and were only spotty or limited to selected fields by the end of the 1960s.

4. The school personnel revolution began in earnest with militant teacher behavior; teacher organizations granted highest priority to the pursuit of economic gains and improvement in working conditions for teachers; teacher strikes escalated from a mere handful each year to a hundred or more annually; and serious rifts developed between teachers and administrators. New competencies were demanded from those who would be personnel administrators or superintendents.

5. Technology granted more serious attention and computers began to gain a foothold in public schools. The progress was slow, costly, and very frustrating for the pioneers. Experiments in computer-managed and computer-assisted instruction were given high visibility implementations in the schools.

6. Enrollment expansion continued with new record levels set each year.

7. It was the beginning of the end for the "baby boom" and the start of the "baby bust." Birthrate and numbers started what proved to be an extended decline; the last 4-million-births year was 1964. The sharp drop in numbers of live births in the year that followed was the portent of drops that would continue for ten years to hit a low of 3.14 million live births in 1974–1975.

8. Feverish pace of school-plant construction continued unabated.

9. More very large enrollment school districts were noted.

10. The financing of growth continued as the unresolved problem that perplexed state and local educational administrators.

11. The fiscal, social, and personnel prob-

lems of public education in the large city schools became more severe and were exacerbated by considerable media attention.

12. "White flight" from the big city school systems became more pronounced. Over half these systems found that the students from minority backgrounds constituted the majority of those enrolled.

13. Student activism, crime, and vandalism on school premises appeared as serious educational problems for the first time in many school districts.

14. Illicit drug use in society spilled over into schools with increased use by students and on school campuses.

15. New administrative technologies such as PERT, PPBS, and systems management began to receive serious attention with some attempts to implement such practices in educational systems.

16. Criticisms of school administrators for the problems facing public education increased. Turnover in administrative positions escalated as well.

The great growth psychology experienced in education over a period of about 25 years was reversed during the 1970s. The civil rights and school personnel revolutions continued right through the decade. But many other trends were reversed to characterize the 1970s as the "reversal decade." Some of the significant events of the prior decade would be at least the following:

1. Enrollments peaked out and a decline started early in the 1970s. The elementary schools were the hardest hit; growth continued at the secondary school level until the end of the 1970s.

2. The birthrate dropped to its lowest levels in the history of the nation, but the number of live births held fairly steady at just under 3.2 million each year up to 1975. The last half of the decade saw the live birth numbers move above that figure. The large number of women in the "child-bearing age" group prevented the number of live births from being even lower, given the record low birth rates.

3. "White flight" from the large city school systems continued; percent of minority student

enrollments in large cities escalated from 48.8 percent in 1970 to 67.1 percent by 1974.

4. Painful retrenchment in number of schools operated and a reduction in size of the professional work force in educational systems were implemented for the first time in about 40 years. The schoolhouse construction boom eased considerably and could be said to have ended for all practical purposes.

5. Two serious energy crises hit the schools, with rapidly rising energy costs further compounding the educational financing problems.

6. It was the decade of the worst and longest sustained inflation in the history of the nation. Inflation was partially responsible for escalating budgets in an era of declining enrollments.

7. The property tax, long the backbone of local district revenues, took the brunt of taxpayers' ire over higher taxes. Severe limits were placed on the property tax rate in some states. This forced many states to greatly increase contributions for the financing of public education. The limitations also added to the fiscal crisis facing public education.

8. The bankruptcy of several large city school districts almost became a reality during the late 1970s. This was the most serious manifestation of the fiscal crisis facing all of public education resulting from the combined impact of at least the following: inflation; magnitude of salary increases for all personnel to keep up with inflation or for other reasons; federal stimulation grants for programs that later had to be supported from local and state funds when the stimulation grant was withdrawn; taxpayer resistance to increases in the local property tax; crosstown busing costs; and the demands to teach all or provide special programs to all that needed them without regard to their fiscal implications.

9. School desegregation continued with school busing becoming the primary strategy for its realization. This and the threat of creating metropolitan school districts increased the emotions and conflict surrounding such issues.

10. The numbers of teacher strikes each year exceeded 100 each year and hit a new peak of more than 200 in one year. NEA was recog-

nized by an official federal agency as a labor union.

11. Crime, violence, vandalism, and illicit drug abuse became worse and necessitated the formation of special and sizable school security forces to cope with the situation.

12. Courts began to assume a measure of control over and monitor closely the operations of several school systems as the result of desegregation conflicts.

13. The legal departments of large school systems and the funds allocated for legal defense from other lawyers increased tremendously in response to the volume of litigation involving the public schools.

14. Education became more heavily involved in politics and there was increased politicization of education in local communities.

15. Technology was put to greater use in public education, with the computer being commonplace in most large systems and easy access to computer services for all others. Microcomputers were adopted in greater numbers for instructional purposes by the end of the 1970s.

16. MBO stirred interest early in the decade which lessened considerably thereafter. PPBS all but disappeared from the literature by the end of the 1970s.

17. Administrator organizations cut all ties with the National Education Association; those formerly housed in the NEA building moved out.

18. Single-issue pressure groups confronted public schools in greater numbers than ever.

19. State administrator organizations gained substantial new strength with national organizations faring less well.

20. Conflict within school systems increased.

21. Boards of education became more involved in the operational details of school systems, more frequent references were made to the school superintendency as an "impossible position," and substantial increases in administrator turnover (or briefer tenure in office) characterized this decade.

22. Minimum competency testing reached its zenith with a majority of states approving its supporting legislation.

23. Accountability demands increased and assumed many different forms during the decade.

24. Confidence in educational leadership declined in public polls, which paralleled the falling enrollments and escalating taxes for schools.

25. Criticisms of public education took such forms as the demand to return to the "basics"; institution of the voucher system for distributing state funds to schools; creation of more alternative schools, and what is called "improved education."

26. Around the end of the decade the U.S. Department of Education won congressional approval to replace the Office of Education. It became an operational reality by the end of the 1970s and became almost immediately embroiled in partisan politics which threatened its longevity.

The above rather broad outlines of some major characteristics is not an exhaustive accounting of problems, concerns, or crises that faced education during each of the five previous decades. The points being made are that each decade had its challenges, school administrators faced serious conflicts during each decade, and there never was a time during the last 50 years when there were no crises or "revolutions." To illustrate, there never was a decade when educational finance was not at least a serious concern. Most of the prior challenges were met, adjustments were made, and a price was paid.

Reflections on the past may help to project what may occur in the short- and long-range future. It is not difficult to predict that the 1980s will be as turbulent as the two previous decades. To illustrate, it is rational to expect a continuation of conflicts which had their roots in previous times such as the ongoing social reform in race relations; substantial revision in the systems used to generate revenues for the support of public education; continuing accommodations to the new pattern of teacher-administrator or teacher-community relations; finding ways to cope with the incidence of crime and violence on school premises; more exciting adaptations of minicomputers to instructional and school management concerns, and so on.

Educational administrators will not disappear or be replaced by another management mechanism or managers from other fields. Crises and conflicts heighten the need for more effective leadership and management competencies rather than vice versa. School administrators must continue to grow professionally, must acquire quickly whatever new competencies are demanded, and must be able to work in a highly stressful environment. Future challenges in public education will be satisfied by all levels of government working together, community leaders supporting local schools, and all professional educators joining together to resolve the problems of delivering quality educational service, serious constraints in resources notwithstanding.

SUMMARY

Accountability is an old concept expanded and refined to apply to all dimensions of educational institutions. It is presently a more comprehensive concept that includes performance, professional, and system accountability.

Accountability as a system of operation is based on specification of desirable and measurable outcomes, the assignment of responsibilities for the achievement of objectives, and subsequent assessment. Within an operational system every person is answerable to another for something expressed in performance terms and realized under certain constraints.

Accountability is less precise and more difficult to achieve in education than in other endeavors. Educational institutions have multiple objectives and end products are more difficult to measure. It is a means to an end whose fundamental purpose is to optimize relationships between resources and results.

There can be accountability for services as well as for achievement of a product related to a goal. The traditional teaching contract is a "performance" contract with emphasis on services performed rather than outcomes achieved. The so-called accountability movement seeks to switch the focus from accountability for inputs to instructional outcomes. It is closely related to the MBO concept.

There are other and conflicting interpretations of accountability. Some individuals use the concept to justify tax support of private schools. These are the competitive conceptualizations of accountability which are different from the optimum resource utilization to achieve desired goals.

The design of an educational accountability strategy would include definition of objectives, creation of an accountability team, development of an accountability chart, searching for alternatives, implementation of output-oriented management systems, utilization of computer-based information systems, creation of educational auditing approaches, design of staff appraisal systems, allocating resources for accountability, and viewing accountability as a frame of mind as well as a set of techniques.

Appraisal and accountability are complementary concepts. The development of a total evaluation system calls for more than a new rating scale. Its rationale should be based on more than the orderly discharge of incompetents. The emphasis belongs on analysis of administrator performance leading to in-service activities contributing to the attainment of greater effectiveness.

Appraisal, by implication or explicit statements, rests on a model of administrator effectiveness. The evaluative data collected are then compared to such a model. There are a number of input, process, output, and eclectic models. The trait or personality model is the most common one and undergirds the historic and traditional approaches to appraisal.

There are many perplexing and unresolved issues in instrument construction as well as in other general dimensions of administrator appraisal.

There never was a time when public education was not confronted with crises and conflicts or when school administrators were not forced to acquire new competencies. Each decade presented a set of new challenges and had some unique characteristics: The 1930s was the Great Depression decade; the 1940s the split and transition decade; the 1950s the great growth decade; the 1960s the civil rights and personnel relations "revolutions" decade; and the 1970s the "reversal" decade. The 1980s are not expected to be any less turbulent; many problems whose roots may be traced to earlier times will continue to at least the end of the present century. The revision or reform of educational finance is the perennial challenge. Crises and conflicts heighten the need for effective leadership and efficient management. Effective school administrators will continue to be in demand and will not be replaced with managers from other fields or by other mechanisms.

NOTES

1. Leon M. Lessinger, "Accountability: Present Forces and Future Concerns," *New Directions for Education,* Vol. 1, No. 1, Spring 1973, pp. 1–9.
2. Ibid.
3. The ideas that follow were published originally in S. J. Knezevich, "Implementing Accountability Systems," *New Directions for Education,* Vol. 1, No. 1, Spring 1973, pp. 11–20.
4. L. L. Cunningham and J. T. Hentges, *The American School Superintendency 1982: A Summary Report,* Arlington, Va.: American Association of School Administrators, 1982, pp. 33–35.
5. Ibid., pp. 33–34.
6. Ibid., pp. 34–35.

CHAPTER REVIEW QUESTIONS

1. In what ways are accountability and appraisal similar? Dissimilar?
2. Why is the pressure for greater accountability likely to intensify rather than decrease during the 1980s?
3. Who should be on the accountability team?

4. Why is accountability more difficult to implement in educational institutions?
5. What are the essential elements of an educational accountability strategy?
6. Which of the many models of administrator effectiveness do you feel hold the most promise? Justify your stand.
7. What are the major issues in administrator appraisal?

8. Who should assume primary responsibility for the design of an administrator appraisal system?
9. Why is administrator appraisal more than a matter of designing a new rating scale or other type of evaluative instrument?
10. How does the competency-based evaluation approach differ from the traditional?

SELECTED REFERENCES

Browder, L. H., Jr., ed., *Emerging Patterns of Administrative Accountability,* Berkeley, Calif.: McCutchan, 1971

Browder, L. H., Jr., and Atkins, W. A., Jr., and Kaya, Esin, *Developing an Educationally Accountable Program,* Berkeley, Calif.: McCutchan, 1973.

Cunningham, Luvern L., and Hentges, Joseph T., *The American School Superintendency 1982 A Summary Report,* Arlington, Va.: American Association of School Administrators, 1982.

House, Ernest R., *School Evaluation, the Politics and Process,* Berkeley, Calif.: McCutchan, 1973,

Knezevich, Stephen J., ed., "Creating Appraisal and Accountability Systems," *New Directions for Education,* Vol. 1, No. 1, Spring 1973.

Lessinger, L. M., *Every Kid a Winner: Accountability in Education,* Palo Alto, Calif.: Science Research Associates, 1970.

NAME INDEX

SUBJECT INDEX